Varieties of Attention

This is a volume in
ACADEMIC PRESS
SERIES IN COGNITION AND PERCEPTION

A Series of Monographs and Treatises

A complete list of titles in this series appears at the end of this volume.

Varieties of Attention

Edited by

RAJA PARASURAMAN

Department of Psychology
The Catholic University of America
Washington, D.C.

D. R. DAVIES

Department of Applied Psychology
University of Aston
Birmingham, England

1984

ACADEMIC PRESS, INC.

Harcourt Brace Jovanovich, Publishers

Orlando   San Diego   New York
Austin   London   Montreal   Sydney
Tokyo   Toronto

ACADEMIC PRESS, INC.
Orlando, Florida 32887

United Kingdom Edition published by
ACADEMIC PRESS, INC. (LONDON) LTD.
24/28 Oval Road, London NW1 7DX

Library of Congress Cataloging in Publication Data

Main entry under title:

Varieties of attention.

    (Academic Press series in cognition and perception)
    Includes bibliographies and index.
    1. Attention. I. Parasuraman, R. II. Davies,
D. R. (David Roy) III. Series.
BF321.V28 1983   153.7'33   83-8765
ISBN 0-12-544970-4

PRINTED IN THE UNITED STATES OF AMERICA

85 86 87 88   9 8 7 6 5 4 3 2

Contents

4. A Unified Theory of Attention and Signal Detection
George Sperling

5. Mathematical Models of Attention
John A. Swets

6. Sustained Attention in Detection and Discrimination
Raja Parasuraman

7. The Control of Attention in Visual Search
Patrick Rabbitt

8. Brain Mechanisms of Visual Selective Attention
M. Russell Harter and Cheryl J. Aine

9. The Orienting Reflex: Performance and Central Nervous System Manifestations
John W. Rohrbaugh

10. Spatial Orientation following Commissural Section
Jeffrey D. Holtzman, Bruce T. Volpe, and Michael S. Gazzaniga

Contributors

Numbers in parentheses indicate the pages on which the authors' contributions begin.

CHERYL J. AINE (293), Department of Psychology, University of North Carolina, Greensboro, North Carolina 27412

D. R. DAVIES (395), Department of Applied Psychology, University of Aston, Birmingham B4 7ET, England

SUSAN T. DUMAIS (1), Bell Laboratories, Murray Hill, New Jersey 07974

MICHAEL S. GAZZANIGA (375), Department of Neurology, Division of Cognitive Neuroscience, Cornell University Medical College, New York, New York 10021

M. RUSSELL HARTER (293), Department of Psychology, University of North Carolina, Greensboro, North Carolina 27412

ROBERT HOCKEY (449), Department of Psychology, University of Durham, Durham DH1 3LE, England

JEFFREY D. HOLTZMAN (375), Department of Neurology, Cornell New York Hospital, New York, New York 10021

D. M. JONES (395), Department of Applied Psychology, University of Wales, Institute of Science and Technology, Cardiff CF3 70X, Wales

DANIEL KAHNEMAN (29), Department of Psychology, University of British Columbia, Vancouver, British Columbia V6T 1W5, Canada

NEVILLE MORAY (485), Department of Industrial Engineering, University of Toronto, Toronto, Ontario M5S 1A4, Canada

RAJA PARASURAMAN (243), Department of Psychology, The Catholic University of America, Washington D.C. 20064

PATRICK RABBITT (273), Department of Psychology, University of Durham, Durham DH1 3LE, England

JAMES REASON (515), Department of Psychology, University of Manchester, Manchester M13 9PL, England

JOHN W. ROHRBAUGH[1] (323), Nebraska Psychiatric Institute, University of Nebraska Medical Center, Omaha, Nebraska 68106

WALTER SCHNEIDER (1), Department of Psychology, University of Illinois at Urbana-Champaign, Champaign, Illinois 61820

RICHARD M. SHIFFRIN (1), Department of Psychology, Indiana University, Bloomington, Indiana 47401

GEORGE SPERLING (103), Department of Psychology, New York University, New York, New York 10003

JOHN A. SWETS (183), Bolt Beranek and Newman Inc., Cambridge, Massachusetts 02238

ANN TAYLOR (395), Department of Psychology, University of Leicester, Leicester, England

ANNE TREISMAN (29), Department of Psychology, University of British Columbia, Vancouver, British Columbia V6T 1W5, Canada

BRUCE T. VOLPE (375), Department of Neurology, Cornell New York Hospital, New York, New York 10021

CHRISTOPHER D. WICKENS (63), Department of Psychology, University of Illinois at Urbana-Champaign, Champaign, Illinois 61820

[1]Present address: Section on Clinical Research, Laboratory of Clinical Studies, National Institute on Alcohol Abuse and Alcoholism, Bethesda, Maryland 20205

Preface

The title of this book was used by William James as a section heading in the chapter on attention in his *Principles of Psychology,* published in 1890. James linked attention to interest and emphasized its active role in shaping conscious experience. He distinguished between sensorial and intellectual attention, which could be immediate (intrinsically interesting) or derived, as well as active (voluntary or effortful) or passive (nonvoluntary or effortless). James argued that voluntary attention is always derived; that is, the topic or stimulus to which attention is directed "owes its interest to association with some other immediately interesting thing" (p. 416). According to James, the immediate effects of attention "are to make us: (a) perceive, (b) conceive, (c) distinguish, (d) remember better than otherwise we could" (p. 424).

Other leading figures in the early history of experimental psychology, notably Pillsbury, Titchener, and Wundt, shared James's belief that the problem of attention was of prime psychological importance. Titchener, for example, regarded the "discovery" of attention as one of three major achievements of the application of the experimental method to psychology. As he points out in his celebrated *Lectures on the Elementary Psychology of Feeling and Attention,* published in 1908, by the *discovery* of attention Titchener meant the "explicit formulation of the problem; the recognition of its separate status and fundamental importance; the realisation that the doctrine of attention is the nerve of the whole psychological system, and that as men judge it, so shall they be judged before the general tribunal of psychology" (p. 172). For Titchener, attention not only determined the contents of consciousness but influenced the quality of conscious experience, and this belief prompted a search for conditions under which a sensation appeared "with maximal clearness in consciousness."

The study of attention is often regarded as having undergone a severe and prolonged decline with the advent of behaviorism at the beginning of World War I. In the late 1940s this decline was arrested, and indeed reversed, by psychologists and engineers concerned with issues in human–machine interaction, particularly in military systems. As Broadbent (1980) has pointed out, "It was only when applied psychologists were summoned to look at modern communication centres, and realized that there was nothing in the academic theory of the time to handle these problems, that attention had to be brought back into respectability" (p. 118). An instance of such an applied problem is that of sustained attention, highlighted by the difficulty of maintaining vigilance experienced by ship's lookouts and airborne radar operators during World War II. But while it is clear that research on attention decisively changed direction after World War II as part of the general shift from stimulation to information inspired by developments in communications engineering and computer science, interest in attention nevertheless remained at a high level through World War I and during the 1920s and 1930s, as the periodic reviews of the attention literature in the *Psychological Bulletin* by Pillsbury and later by Dallenbach attest. In his review for the period 1925–1928, Dallenbach recorded that "more studies and researches have been reported during the past three years upon the general topic of attention than in any similar period of the history of the subject" (p. 493). The section headings of Woodworth's chapter on attention in his textbook of experimental psychology, published in 1938, also indicate the range of topics under investigation during this period: "The span of apprehension"; "Shifts and fluctuations of attention"; "Distraction"; and "Doing two things at once." To this list may be added studies of automatic reactions and attention-automatization conducted by Solomons in the 1890s and Ford in the 1920s, and studies of blocking and interference by Bills and by Stroop in the 1930s.

As this brief historical overview suggests, many fundamental concepts in attention were proposed several decades ago. Modern research on attention uses many of the same concepts, but does so in a framework composed of different processes, newer tasks, methods, and measures, and evolving theories. Furthermore, the central importance of attention is no longer in question. Attention is now seen as lying "at the very core of cognitive psychology" (Keele & Neill, 1978), and as playing a significant part in several other areas of inquiry, including neuropsychology, developmental psychology, and psychopathology. Yet as Posner (1975) has remarked, "attention is not a single concept, but the name of a complex field of study" (p. 441). In this book we cover the major topics in this field of study. The range of topics can be guided by a rough division of the field into four categories: processes, tasks, methods and measures, and theories.

First, attention involves a variety of processes: (1) a selective process, whereby some information coming from the internal or external environment is analyzed and perceived, while other information is ignored; (2) an intensive process, whereby the amount of attention devoted to a particular information source can be varied, so that people sometimes feel that they are concentrating so hard on a particular task or activity that they are oblivious to their surroundings, while at other times they are easily distracted by whatever is going on around them; and (3) an alerting and sustaining process, whereby receptivity to input information can be heightened over the short term—for instance, when the arrival of a signal requiring action is imminent—or maintained over the long term—as when a task requiring vigilance or sustained attention is being performed. Second, a variety of tasks have been used to examine these putative processes. For example, tasks used in the investigation of selective processes can be classified either as focused-attention or divided-attention tasks, and within each of these categories a further classification can be made based on the nature of the selection involved, whether among sensory inputs, stimulus dimensions, or sets of critical features. Third, a variety of methods and a number of measures have been used in attention research, from relatively simple speed and accuracy scores to sophisticated mathematical measures and physiological indexes of central and autonomic nervous-system function. Fourth, a variety of theories of attention have been advanced that, although sharing a number of assumptions, take different views of the nature of attention. Some theories view attention as a mechanism for separating wanted from unwanted information and seek to specify the number of such mechanisms and their location in the information-processing sequence. Others view attention as a "processing resource," which can be variably allocated in accord with prevailing information-processing demands. Still others focus on types of information processing and explore the question of whether some kinds of processing can occur with minimal attentional involvement or without drawing upon attentional resources at all.

Many of these themes are examined by the contributors to this book, some of whom present accounts of original research designed to clarify specific issues, while others provide general reviews of particular areas. As is usual in joint ventures of this kind, some issues have received greater emphasis than others in this book, whereas certain topics that one might wish to cover could not be because of space or other reasons. Our intention was not to be comprehensive, but to combine major topics in mainstream attention research with topics of unusual interest or with viewpoints that might not be covered in a standard review. As suggested by its title, this book brings together several different attributes and conceptualizations of attention into a single volume. We have tried to balance theory with practice, cognitive with biological approaches, and qualitative with quantitative models. Thus, this book differs from other books on attention in its scope and in its aim of providing an integrative treatment of attention processes.

The first two chapters of *Varieties of Attention* examine an old and fundamental issue: the "automatization" of attention with practice and skill, first considered by Solomons and by James in the 1890s. In Chapter 1, Schneider, Dumais, and Shiffrin review findings on focused and divided attention. They propose that an analysis of attentional performance requires a distinction between two qualitatively different processes, automatic and control processing. *Control* processing is effortful (requires attention) and under voluntary control; *automatic* processing does not require attention. Schneider *et al.* suggest that deficits in divided attention, and performance changes with practice, are determined by the development and interaction of automatic and control processes. In Chapter 2, Kahneman and Treisman also discuss automaticity and its relation to "early-" and "late-selection" models of attention. However, they stress the necessity for the concept of filtering (early selection) and present findings suggesting that some "automatic" processes in fact require attention. According to a late-selection model, and in theories of attention that emphasize automaticity, perceptual processing occurs more or less independently of attention. Kahneman and Treisman suggest, on the other hand, that attention plays a crucial role in perception. They propose an alternative framework for the study of attention, based on an organizational metaphor for mind, that suggests an accommodation between early-selection and late-selection models of attention.

The early- and late-selection models have been described as *structural* models of attention. These models are concerned with the structure of stages of human information-processing, and with possible bottlenecks that limit attentional performance at different stages. Capacity or resource models, examined in Chapters 3 and 4, take a somewhat different (though not necessarily opposing) approach. Here the concern is not with structural limitations on attention, but with the demands of different stages and tasks on a hypothetical central pool of attentional capacity. In Chapter 3, Wickens reviews the development of resource theory, with special reference to performance on time-shared tasks. He proposes the need for multiple pools of resources for describing time-sharing performance and outlines a hierarchical model for processing resources. Wickens also discusses the application of multiple-resource theory to the measurement of operator mental workload in human–machine systems. In Chapter 4, Sperling describes a new theory of attention based on the optimization of processing resources. The theory is illustrated for a variety of attentional tasks and is also shown to be applicable to the analysis of behavior in other areas of psychology and the social sciences (e.g., economics) where the optimum allocation of limited resources is important.

Chapters 5 and 6 examine attentional processes in detection and discrimination tasks. In Chapter 5, Swets reviews quantitative models of attention in auditory signal detection, visual form detection, and vigilance. In Chapter 6, Parasuraman reviews studies of detection and discrimination performance on sustained attention or vigilance tasks. He distinguishes between the overall level of vigilance, criterion shifts, and sensitivity decrement and discusses some of the processes underlying these different aspects of vigilance.

Chapters 7 through 10 are concerned with a number of different aspects of visual selective attention and with the orientation of attention to visual space. In Chapter 7, Rabbitt reviews visual search studies investigating the mechanisms involved in knowing where to look for targets on a visual display and in their categorization and identification. Rabbitt's chapter is followed by three chapters that take a psychobiological approach to visual attention. In Chapter 8, Harter and Aine discuss the use of event-related potentials (ERPs) to disclose neurophysiological mechanisms of visual selective attention. They present evidence for the existence of multiple selective mechanisms that are associated with different projection pathways at different levels of the nervous system. In Chapter 9, Rohrbaugh reviews the use of ERPs and other measures in the analysis of the orienting of attention. He discusses the concept of the orienting reflex and its functional significance for sensory and cognitive processes. In Chapter 10, Holtzman, Volpe, and Gazzaniga examine the orienting of attention to visual space in commissurotomy patients. They provide evidence that visual information used for orienting is distinguishable from that used for stimulus identification, and that commissurotomy does not lead to dual spatial-attention systems.

Chapters 11 and 12 discuss individual and environmental determinants of attentional performance. In Chapter 11, Davies, Jones, and Taylor review individual and group differences in the performance of selective attention tasks such as dichotic listening, central–incidental learning, and the Stroop test, and in sustained attention tasks such as vigilance. In Chapter 12, Hockey examines the effects of environmental stressors on the allocation of attention. Research by Hockey and others has shown that states of high and low arousal affect attention allocation in different ways. Noting the limited applicability of general arousal theory, Hockey outlines an alternative approach based on the mapping of qualitative patterns of performance changes in response to environmental stressors.

The final two chapters are concerned with the analysis of attention in real settings. In Chapter 13, Moray discusses a number of quantitative, analytical models of visual attention to dynamic visual displays of the type prevalent in human–machine systems such as process control and radar. In Chapter 14, Reason describes his pioneering work on slips of action in everyday life. Taking as his text William James's statement that ''habit diminishes the conscious attention with which our acts are performed'' (p. 114), Reason explores the relationship between attention and skilled performance and provides a taxonomy of the varieties of cognitive failure in which attention is implicated.

This book was made possible through the assistance and cooperation of a number of persons. First, we thank the authors of individual chapters for their contributions. We are particularly grateful to Russell Harter and Cheryl Aine, who contributed an excellent chapter at very short notice. Jackson Beatty and Anthony Watkinson helped in initiating this project. James Hoffman, David Laberge, Donald Lindsley, Keith Nuechterlein, and Thomas Sanquist made a number of useful comments and suggestions. James H. Howard, Jr., generously provided access to word-processing facilities. Finally, special thanks are due Maria Garcia, Beryl Herbert, Nance Humphreys, Janet McLeod, and Anne van der Salm for secretarial assistance.

References

Broadbent, D. E. The minimization of models. In A. J. Chapman & D. M. Jones (Eds.), *Models of man*. Leicester: British Psychological Society, 1980, pp. 113–128.

Dallenbach, K. M. Attention. *Psychological Bulletin,* 1928, *25,* 493–511.

James, W. *The principles of psychology* (2 vols.). New York: Holt, 1890. Reprinted by Dover, 1950.

Keele, S. W., & Neill, W. T. Mechanisms of attention. In E. C. Carterette & M. P. Friedman (Eds.), *Handbook of perception* (Vol. 9). New York: Academic Press, 1978.

Posner, M. Psychobiology of attention. In M. Gazzaniga & C. Blakemore (Eds.), *Handbook of psychobiology*. New York: Academic Press, 1975.

Titchener, E. B. *Lectures on the elementary psychology of feeling and attention*. New York: Macmillan, 1908.

Woodworth, R. S. *Experimental psychology*. New York: Holt, 1938.

Varieties of Attention

1

Automatic and Control Processing and Attention[1]

Walter Schneider, Susan T. Dumais, and Richard M. Shiffrin

Introduction

Human performance in almost any cognitive or motor skill shows profound changes with practice. Consider the changes that occur while learning to type, play a musical instrument, read, or play tennis. At first, effort and attention must be devoted to each movement or minor decision, and performance is slow and error prone. Eventually, long sequences of movements or cognitive acts are carried out with little attention, and performance is quite rapid and accurate. For example, the beginning reader may need a few seconds to encode each new letter and be error prone, whereas the expert can accurately encode 25 letters per second and still have sufficient capacity available to encode the material semantically. The striking changes that occur with practice have led many researchers to propose that qualitative changes occur in the processing (James, 1890; La-Berge, 1975; Posner & Snyder, 1975; Shiffrin & Schneider, 1977).

The present chapter reviews evidence that human performance is the result of two qualitatively different processes referred to as automatic and control processing and describes many of the attentional phenomena in terms of this distinction. *Automatic processing* is a fast, parallel, fairly effortless process that is not limited by short-term memory (STM) capacity, is not under direct subject control, and is responsible for the performance of well-developed skilled behaviors. Automatic processing typically develops when subjects process stimuli consistently over many trials. For example, practice at dialing a specific phone number several hundred times will develop automatic processes to produce that phone number. Dialing that number becomes fast and fairly effortless, can be done while engaged in other activities, and can even occur unintentionally (e.g.,

[1]This research was supported by National Institutes of Mental Health Grant No. 5 R01MH 31425 and Office of Naval Research Contract No. N000014-78-C-0012 by the first author and by Public Health Service Grant No. 12717 by the second author.

dialing one's home number while attempting to dial another number with the same starting sequence). *Control processing* is characterized as a slow, generally serial, effortful, capacity-limited, subject-regulated processing mode that must be used to deal with novel or inconsistent information. Control processing is expected when the subject's response to the stimulus varies from trial to trial. For example, practice at dialing a varied set of phone numbers will result in little if any improved ability to dial new numbers. Dialing each new number is slow, effortful, and must be done without thinking about any other tasks. From the automatic–control processing perspective, skill does not develop from practicing the skill per se, but rather from practicing consistent components of the skill. Consistent practice develops automatic component processes that exhibit fast, accurate, parallel processing.

The automatic–control processing approach suggests several generalizations about the attentional literature. First, performance in a given paradigm can be very different depending on whether a preponderance of control or automatic processing is involved. Second, performance should change due to the development of automatic processes when subjects are given extensive, consistent practice. Consistent practice is assumed to occur when the stimuli and responses are *consistently mapped* (CM)—that is, across training trials the subject makes the same overt or covert response each time the stimulus occurs. If the stimuli and responses are *variably mapped* (VM) across trials—that is, the responses change across trials—no automatic processing should develop and performance should change little with practice. Such results were demonstrated by Schneider and Shiffrin (1977b) and Shiffrin and Schneider (1977). Third, as performance becomes more automatic, subjects should have more difficulty controlling and modifying their ongoing processing. Fourth, because control processes are capacity limited, reductions in capacity (e.g., through drugs, fatigue, motivation, load) should much more severely harm control processes than automatic processes. Fifth, certain types of memory modification may be largely a control-processing function. Automatic processing may not produce evidence that memory for its occurrence has been stored and/or retrieved.

This chapter briefly reviews pertinent research in divided attention, focused attention, attentional capacity, and learning paradigms. These paradigms are dealt with from a variety of viewpoints throughout this book and have been extensively reviewed elsewhere (Broadbent, 1958, 1971; Kahneman, 1973; Moray, 1969a, 1969b).

Even brief consideration of any complex task, such as tennis playing, makes it clear that such tasks are carried out with a mixture of automatic and control processes, possibly organized in a systematic network or hierarchy, with many of the automatic processes operating in parallel. It is our belief that this state of affairs holds true for far simpler tasks as well. In fact, it would be hard to find any task that is not accomplished through the use of both automatic and control processes. Because most selective attention paradigms involve very simple tasks, relatively few processes may be invoked; and it may be that most of the observed performance is due to one process, either automatic or controlled. Therefore, we may occasionally refer to the processes involved in carrying out a task as if they were wholly automatic or controlled. In all such cases, the reader should understand that these statements are designed to simplify the discussion; the intended referent is always a major component process. We assume as a working hypothesis that all tasks are accomplished with a mixture of both types of processes.

Attentional Paradigms

Selective Attention

The process of *selective attention* is one in which "the organism *selectively attends* to some stimuli, or aspects of stimuli, in preference to others" (Kahneman, 1973, p. 3). This concept presupposes that there is some bottleneck, or capacity limitation, in the processing system and that subjects have the ability to give preference to certain stimuli so that they pass through this bottleneck easily and at the expense of other stimuli.

Divided Attention

Many studies show that subjects exhibit reduced performance when they try to accomplish simultaneously an increased number of tasks or to attend simultaneously to an increased number of stimuli. These are studies of divided attention deficits and are discussed at length in the literature (e.g., Kahneman, 1973). From a theoretical point of view, it is desirable to ascertain the locus of such deficits, their cause, and the conditions that allow these deficits to be bypassed. In this section, we show that the automatic–control distinction goes a long way toward predicting the answers.

The simultaneous–successive paradigm provides a straightforward test of the ability of subjects to give preference to perceptual processing of simple stimuli presented at threshold. Subjects are presented a number of stimuli on independent channels (e.g., retinal locations). In the *successive* condition, information is presented on only one channel at a time such that subjects may give preference to each channel (stimulus) individually. In the *simultaneous* condition, information is presented on all channels simultaneously. In either condition, the subject must identify the target, the presence of the target, or its position. If a single channel can be given preference, then subjects should be far superior when they need process only one channel at a time than when they must deal with many channels at once.

Eriksen and Spencer (1969) presented nine stimuli, with the interstimulus interval (ISI) ranging from 5 msec (effectively simultaneous) to several seconds and with the order of the stimuli not known to the subject. They found no benefit for the successive condition. Shiffrin and his colleagues have demonstrated equal simultaneous and successive performance even when the order of the presentation of the successive stimuli is known to the subject. They showed this for visual stimuli (Shiffrin & Gardner, 1972; Shiffrin, Gardner, & Allmeyer, 1973; Shiffrin, McKay, & Shaffer, 1976), for auditory speech stimuli (Shiffrin, Pisoni, & Casteneda–Mendez, 1974), for tactile stimuli (Shiffrin, Craig, & Cohen, 1973), and across modalities (Shiffrin & Grantham, 1974). In all cases, there was no benefit for processing the channels successively. These results indicate that processing is parallel and not capacity limited (at least within the ranges tested).

Because a long history of research results indicates the existence of selective attention bottlenecks, the results of the simultaneous–successive studies are somewhat puzzling. Many attention experiments show a decline in performance as simultaneous processing load increases (see Kahneman, 1973). The solution to this puzzle depends on the fact that the simultaneous–successive studies have all used CM stimuli; that is, the target stimuli have remained fixed over trials, as have the distractor stimuli. Under these circumstances, the subject may learn to attend automatically to a target whenever it appears. As a result, target position is attended first even in the stimultaneous conditions, thereby producing equal performance.

This situation and the argument are best demonstrated through an example. Let us suppose that a simultaneous display consists of four alphabetic characters arranged in a square. Three positions are occupied by distractors (e.g., the letter L). The other position is either the letter T or F, and the subject's task is to say which occurs on a given trial. The target position and identity vary randomly from trial to trial, but the set of target characters (T, F) and the distractor characters (L) do not change over trials. Masking displays precede and follow each character, and the character presentation time (t) is adjusted until performance is at threshold (e.g., .75 correct choice).

The successive condition is similar except that a trial consists of successive presentation of the stimuli, each stimulus preceded and followed by masks and presented for t msec. In a typical paradigm, two stimuli along a display diagonal are presented together for t msec and followed 500 msec later by the two stimuli on the other diagonal.

We argue that the consistent training over trials leads the targets (e.g., T and F) to attract attention automatically. The targets become figures that appear to pop out from the background distractors (for models, see Hoffman, 1979;

Shiffrin & Giesler, 1973). Because performance is equivalent in the simultaneous and successive conditions, we conclude that the information extraction that leads to the automatic allocation of attention is minimally affected by the number of stimuli processed simultaneously (except when lateral masking is allowed to vary between conditions). If automatic processing directs limited control processing to the channel with the target, only one STM comparison will be required for the subject to respond to the presence of a target. Therefore processing should be independent of the number of simultaneous channels. This argument is bolstered by a study by Foyle and Shiffrin (Note 1). In the consistent training paradigm described above, successive and simultaneous performances were equal. However, when the targets and distractors changed roles from trial to trial, then successive presentation was superior to the simultaneous presentation. Foyle and Shiffrin argued that information extraction for each display position in the VM condition is unaffected, but that attention is not drawn automatically to the target position. Thus the decision process must consider each position in turn. Because memory decays as the decision process proceeds, there is a deficit in the processing of simultaneous displays. Foyle and Shiffrin also found that there were strict limits on the conditions that produce simultaneous–sequential equality. When the stimuli became confusable, and when the display size increased; a sequential advantage appeared. The ability to utilize automatic processing apparently decreases under these conditions. This is understandable when one realizes that the stimuli are presented under threshold conditions. Each stimulus may be perceived incompletely and inaccurately. Under such conditions, the consistency necessary for automatic processing to develop goes away as confusability and display size increase.

In summary, we suggest that benefits and costs of selective attention are seen when control processing is used (as induced by VM conditions). On the other hand, automatic processing in the right situations can sometimes bypass the selective-attention bottleneck. Finally, note that our suggested basis for the effects seen in these studies is a training of attention itself. Thus attention may be thought of as a trainable response in its own right. We return to this point later.

A major research paradigm used to examine limitations in information processing is *dichotic listening,* in which subjects are presented different streams of auditory stimuli in each ear; the subject is told either to attend to one ear, or to attend to both. For the unpracticed subject, target detection performance drops substantially when subjects shift from attending to a single ear to attending to both ears (Treisman, 1960). However, after extended (4–10 hours) CM training at detecting a specific target, performance is equivalent whether subjects are attending to one or both ears as long as both channels do not simultaneously contain targets (Duncan, 1980; Moray, 1975).

In *auditory shadowing* paradigms, subjects are required to repeat orally a stream of speech presented in one ear while also trying to process information presented in the other ear (see Cherry, 1953; Moray, 1959; Treisman, 1960, 1969). Treisman (1960) found that target detection in the shadowed ear was far superior to that in the unshadowed ear except when the targets differed from the shadowed message on some simple acoustic feature (e.g., targets were tones). Moray (1959) showed that the information in the nonshadowed ear could not be recalled, recognized, or relearned more easily. These experiments suggest that information in the nonshadowed ear is either not processed or not remembered. The results from the simultaneous–successive paradigm suggest that the loss might be due to memory decay rather than the absence of processing. Such shadowing experiments generally give subjects little practice and, hence, a selective attention benefit due to control processing is expected. However, if subjects are given CM training on detecting a target; automatic processing should develop, and the nonshadowed information should also elicit response. Moray (1959) found that subjects did detect their own name when it was presented in the nonshadowed ear, suggesting that the extralaboratory CM training of responding to one's own name results in an ability to detect it on an unattended channel.

In a *multiple-frame visual-search* paradigm, subjects are presented a series of frames in immediate succession, each of which is presented for a brief period of time (referred to as the *frame time*) (Schneider & Shiffrin, 1977b). In advance of each trial, the subject is presented with several characters referred to as the *memory set* and is then required to detect any memory-set items that appear in subsequent frames. In experiments by Schneider and Shiffrin (1977b), the elements presented on each frame were characters or random dot masks. The frame time was kept constant across the 20 frames of each trial, and the basic dependent variable was the psychometric function relating accuracy to frame time in each condition. The independent variables were the *frame size* (number of characters per frame), memory-set size, frame time, and the type of mapping (CM or VM). In one CM condition, subjects consistently searched for digits among letters. In a comparable VM condition subjects searched for a random subset of target letters on each trial. The results (Figure 1.1B) showed that performance (accuracy) in the VM conditions was strongly affected by increases in memory-set size and frame size. Performance in the CM conditions (Figure 1.1A) was virtually unaffected by frame and memory-set size. In fact, all the CM conditions were superior to even the easiest VM condition. Performance in the CM condition was qualitatively different from that in the VM condition; with the CM condition showing superior performance, minor effects of load, and performance limited by perceptual factors (see Schneider & Shiffrin, 1977b). Similar CM and VM differences have been found in an auditory version of the multiple-frame task (Poltrock, Lansman, & Hunt, 1982).

A *single-frame search* paradigm is similar to the multiple-frame paradigm except subjects are presented only one frame and the primary dependent variable is reaction time. Subjects are presented a memory set of one or more items and

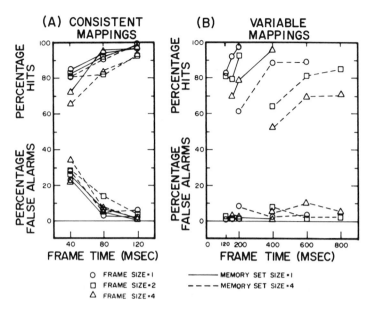

Figure 1.1 Hits and false alarms as a function of frame times for each of 12 conditions. (From Schneider & Shiffrin, 1977b.)

are required to detect the presence of any of the items in a single display containing at most one target and possibly multiple distractors. *Visual-search experiments* measure the length of time necessary to detect a given number of the memory set in a single display containing a large number of distractors (Neisser, 1963). *Memory-search experiments* typically measure the time necessary to compare a single display item to a series of items in memory (Sternberg, 1966, 1969a, 1969b, 1975). Both VM and CM conditions have shown substantially different results in either type of single-frame experiment (for a review, see Schneider & Shiffrin, 1977b).

The Schneider and Shiffrin (1977b) studies varied both frame size and memory-set size within subjects. In the VM condition, reaction time increased linearly with memory-set size and frame size, and the slope of negative reaction times was twice that of positive. For the CM conditions, there was little effect of memory-set size, no effect of frame size, and positive and negative slopes were about equal. Similar effects were found for the reaction-time variances.

Fisk and Schneider (1983) have examined CM and VM single-frame search with words and categories. In the category condition, subjects were presented one to four category names and then two words. If either of the two words was a member of any of the presented categories, subjects pressed the target-present button; otherwise they pushed the target-absent button. The results for the VM

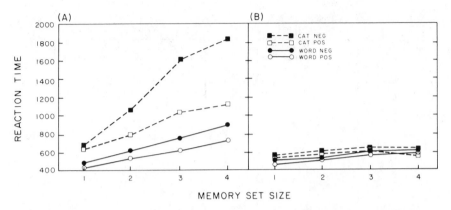

Figure 1.2 Category and word search reaction time as a function of the number of items in memory: (A) VM search; (B) CM search. The probe display always contained two words. Both A and B represent performance after extensive training (over 2880 trials per subject per condition). (From Fisk & Schneider, 1983.)

conditions are presented in Figure 1.2A. In the category VM search, the memory comparison time was 92 msec for positive responses and 202 msec for negative. For the VM word search, the slopes were 47 and 68 msec, respectively. In contrast, in the CM conditions (Figure 1.2B), the category slope was 2 msec for positives and 10 msec for negatives. In the CM word search, the slope was 19 msec in both conditions. The contrast between Figures 1.2A and 1.2B illustrates the large differences between VM and CM searches. In the category-search condition, the CM slope was 98% less than the VM slope. The similarity of character-, word-, and category-search results indicates that the characteristics of automatic and control processing generalize to various levels of stimulus processing complexity.

Single-frame search experiments have demonstrated that extended training reduces the slope of the search function (i.e., the comparison time per character) only in CM conditions. In CM conditions, performance improves substantially with training; for example, the memory-comparison slope decreased from 28 msec/item to 19 msec/item over 30 days of practice (Kristofferson, 1972b). In the category-search condition (Fisk & Schneider, 1983) the slope dropped from 92 to 2 msec. Generally, performance on the first block of CM training is equivalent to VM performance; but with training, CM performance improves.

In contrast, Kristofferson (1972a) found that the memory search slope in VM conditions was 36.8 msec on Days 1–5 and 36.0 msec on Days 26–30. Thus single-frame VM search rate does not change with practice. Similarly, Shiffrin and Schneider (1977, Experiment 2) found no differences in slope between the second week and the twentieth week of training. (In both Kristofferson's and Shiffrin & Schneider's studies, the base reaction-time level continues to decrease with practice. Presumably, the base reaction-time represents consistent aspects of the task that are becoming increasingly automatized with practice.) In a word-search experiment, Fisk and Schneider (1983) found no improvement with VM practice. In a category-search condition, they found a 23% reduction in slope early in practice, and a stable slope thereafter.

In summary, these results from the selective-attention paradigm illustrate two generalizations. First, performance in the same paradigm can be quite different depending on the degree to which automatic and control processing take place, with severe bottlenecks appearing when control processing is utilized. Second, performance changes dramatically as subjects are provided CM training but not when they are provided VM training. For a more detailed review of the selective-attention literature bearing on these matters, see Schneider and Shiffrin (1977b) and Shiffrin and Schneider (1977).

Focused Attention

Focused attention studies examine the ability of subjects to reject irrelevant messages. A classic example involving the need to ignore irrelevant inputs is a cocktail party situation in which a guest tries to listen to one conversation and ignore all others. An understanding of automatic and control processes helps explain why focusing succeeds or fails.

Eriksen and Eriksen (1974) demonstrated an inability of subjects to ignore irrelevant inputs in a choice reaction-time task. One of four letters was presented just above a fixation point. If the letter was H or K, subjects pushed one button, if it was S or C, they pushed a different button. The target letter was flanked on each side by three letters. The flanking conditions of present interest were (1) no letters, (2) the same letters, (3) different letters with the same response, (4) different letters similar in shape to a letter with the same response, (5) different letters similar in shape to a letter with a different response, or (6) a letter with the opposite response. Response latencies at the closest letter spacing were 430, 455, 460, 495, 515, and 555 msec, respectively. The presence of neighboring letters slowed reaction times. The more similar the neighboring letters were to letters with an incompatible response, the slower was the response. The differences among conditions decreased as flanking letters were moved further from the target letter. If subjects could focus only on the target letter, flanker letters would have been irrelevant; but clearly they could not. These effects were not due simply to lateral masking because the interference effect was clearly dependent on the response mapping of the stimulus. Note that subjects received extensive CM training in responding to the target letters only. Thus this training on a relevant location was not sufficient to block automatic processing of neighboring letters. Neither was any control process invokable by the subject capable of blocking the distraction by the flanking letters. The names of the flanking letters are apparently processed automatically, causing interference that could not be completely suppressed.

Shiffrin and Schneider (1977, Experiment 4a) found subjects can focus attention in VM search conditions (in which controlled search is used). Utilizing a multiple-frame procedure, they required subjects to search with frame size (F) of 2, 4, and 4/diagonal. In the $F = 4$/diagonal condition, each frame contained four letters, but only letters along one diagonal were relevant. In the $F = 2$ condition, two positions contained targets, and two contained random dot masks. In the $F = 4$ condition, each of the four positions contained a letter that could be a target. Estimated detection probabilities were $F = 2$, .80; $F = 4$/diagonal, .80; and $F = 4$, .63. The equivalence of the $F = 2$ and $F = 4$/diagonal conditions shows subjects were clearly able to ignore the irrelevant letters. We suggest that the names of all letters were processed in all conditions; but the order of the comparison process, and the speed, were not affected by this processing. In the $F = 4$/diagonal condition subjects compared the two positions on the diagonal without wasting comparison time on the items that were not on the diagonal.

Shiffrin and Schneider (1977, Experiment 4d) found subjects could not focus attention sufficiently to ignore stimuli that were previously CM targets. In the experiment, subjects carried out a VM search along one diagonal in a multiple-frame task. Previously valid CM targets (referred to as *foils*) occasionally appeared on the diagonal that was to be ignored. Hit rate for the no-foil condition was 84%. If the foil occurred during the same frame as the VM target, the hit rate was 62%; and if the foil followed the target by 200 msec, the hit rate was 77%. The CM foil interfered with VM processing not only when the foil occurred simultaneously with the VM target, but also even when the foil appeared 200 msec later. These results demonstrate that CM processing is not under direct subject control. CM targets can not be ignored even when they are known to be irrelevant, when they occur in consistently invalid display locations, or when subjects are instructed to ignore them.

The classic example of the inability of subjects to exclude irrelevant information is the Stroop (1935) Color–Word Interference Test. This task requires that subjects vocalize the color of ink in which incompatible color names are printed (e.g., to say "green" when presented with the word *red* printed in green ink). Subjects have a great deal of difficulty ignoring the incompatible printed word when trying to vocalize the color of the ink. The vocal reaction time is much slower when the printed name is incompatible with the ink color than when the printed name is compatible or neutral (Dyer, 1973). Because subjects have consistently responded to the word *red* by vocalizing "red," this automatic process should interfere with orally identifying a different color of ink. A poor reader who has not yet developed automatic word encoding of the color names should not, and does not (Gibson, 1971) show Stroop interference effects as strongly as expert readers.

The difficulty of blocking automatic processes can result in negative transfer effects when subjects are asked to perform tasks incompatible with previously learned automatic processes. Utilizing a multiple-frame paradigm, Shiffrin and Schneider (1977, Experiment 1) consistently trained subjects to search for targets from the first half of the alphabet in frames with distractors from the second half. After extensive training the target and distractor sets were reversed; that is, subjects had to search for targets from the second half of the alphabet in frames with distractors from the first. The results were quite dramatic. The hit rate just after reversal dropped well below that seen at the start of training when subjects were completely unpracticed. Very gradually thereafter, the hit rate recovered so that after 2400 trials of reversal training, subjects reached the level of 900 trials of original training.

Note that these negative transfer results and the Stroop results do not show that subjects cannot counteract automatic processes, but rather show that such counteracting is difficult and consumes resources. Subjects can respond correctly even when there are strong competing automatic processes. Logan (1980) has demonstrated that attentional processing can reduce Stroop interference. Posner and Snyder (1975) have reviewed evidence that effortful control processing is necessary to block automatic activation of priming words (see also Logan, 1980).

The ability of subjects to counter competing automatic processes via effortful use of focal attention is shown in probe-indicator paradigms. Eriksen and his colleagues have used a probe-indicator technique in which a bar appears before a display of nine letters in a circle (Colegate, Hoffman, & Eriksen, 1973; Eriksen & Collins, 1969; Eriksen & Hoffman, 1972, 1973; Eriksen & Schultz, 1979). The subject's task is to make a response appropriate to the probed letter. The earlier the probe indicator is available the less affected is the response mapping of the neighboring letters (Eriksen & Hoffman, 1973).

These results support the generalization that subjects have difficulty controlling automatic processes but that some control is possible. Control processing may be providing some stimulus components necessary for automatic processing to take place. Once the appropriate enabling stimuli occur (both external and internal), the automatic process may take place without additional control or effort by the subject. Subjects have difficulty ignoring or excluding automatic processes if the appropriate internal conditions are met and stimuli elicit competing automatic responses. Subjects appear to have little difficulty focusing attention when only control processing (e.g., VM search) is involved.

Attentional Capacity and Effort

Much research in attention assumes that there is a limited pool of attentional resources, or capacity, that can be distributed across tasks (e.g., Kahneman,

1973). Capacity experiments typically examine how subjects' performance trades off between two tasks as task demands and subject effort change (Navon & Gopher, 1979). For example, according to simple capacity models if the subject has 100 units of capacity and is required to perform 2 tasks each requiring 75 units, performance should decline when shifting from performing the tasks individually to performing them simultaneously.

Automatic–control processing theory assumes attentional capacity limitations are the result of competition between control processes. Hence combining tasks in which control capacity is exceeded should result in reduced performance. Control-processing resources are assumed to be severely limited and may be somewhat differentiated (Wickens, 1980; and Swets, Chapter 5, this volume). On the other hand, combination of automatic processes can occur in parallel without reductions in performance and not be limited by control-processing resources. Thus, combining tasks can have quite different consequences, depending on whether they are carried out primarily with automatic or control processes. Schneider and Fisk (1982a) have examined subjects' ability to perform automatic and control processing simultaneously. The experiment required subjects to perform a VM search (digit among digits) on one diagonal and a CM search (letter among digits) on the other diagonal. Subjects pushed a button at the end of 12 frames indicating whether they saw a target. In the dual-task conditions, subjects searched on the CM diagonal for any letter and on the VM diagonal for a specific digit. In the single-task conditions subjects searched for a target on one diagonal only. The results are presented in Figure 1.3A. The measures on the axes are A's, A' being a nonparametric analog of d' (Craig, 1979; Norman, 1964) that has a range of .5 for chance performance to 1.0 for perfect detection.[2]

Performance in the single-task conditions that required automatic detection only (CM) is shown on the horizontal axis in Figure 1.3A. Performance in the single-task conditions that required controlled search only (VM) is shown on the vertical axis in Figure 1.3A. Joint performance levels in which both tasks had to be performed simultaneously are plotted in the interior of the graph. The different curves correspond to different frame times; the frame time determines the level of difficulty. The rectangular shape of these POC curves indicated that both tasks could be carried out together without noticeable loss (see Norman & Bobrow, 1976). As a measure of the dual-task trade-off, we can compare the area of the obtained POC to the area of the rectangle projected from the single-task performance levels. For joint CM and VM search (Figure 1.3A) this ac-

[2]The A' measure is used here because a considerable bias shift occurred for the CM task in the dual condition. That is, subjects in the dual-task condition were much less likely to emit a CM response than in the CM single-task condition. This conservatism reduced "hits" when targets were present, but also dropped "false alarms" when targets were absent, so that sensitivity for CM items remained unchanged.

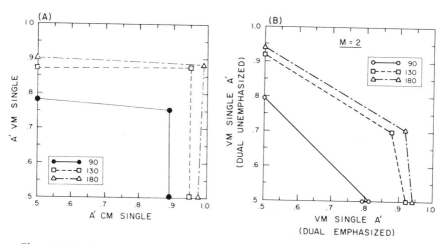

Figure 1.3 Dual task POCs for (A) a CM and VM letter search task, and (B) two VM letter search tasks. (From Schneider & Fisk, 1982a.)

counts for 98.1% of the area of the projected no-trade-off POC. This suggests that the CM and VM comparison processes do not compete very much for resources.

In a second experiment, subjects attempted to perform control processing on both diagonals simultaneously. In this experiment, A' dropped 10–15% on each diagonal below the single-task controls (Figure 1.3B). In this case, the dual-task POC area accounted for only 68.7% of the projected single-task area (note, 50% would represent a direct trade-off between resources). Even with extended training, subjects could not perform both VM tasks without deficit.

Fisk and Schneider (1983) had subjects perform an automatic search for members of a category while simultaneously performing a digit-recall task. Subjects could carry on a digit-span task and simultaneously determine whether each of 16 words were members of the categories four-footed animals, human body parts, fruits, or furniture without measurable (less than 2%) deficit in either the digit-span or detection tasks.

Practice can greatly reduce resource requirements in an automatic-processing search but not in a controlled search. Fisk and Schneider (in press) had subjects perform a dual-task VM digit search and semantic search (e.g., respond to every animal word). Figure 1.4 shows the results. On the first replication adding the digit-search task resulted in a substantial performance decrement for both CM semantic search (45%) and VM search (49%). After eight 45-minute sessions, the CM decrement had reduced to 1%, whereas the VM decrement was 61%.

It should be noted that this dual task is extremely difficult. Subjects initially felt the dual task was impossible; but with training, subjects could perform both the digit search and the CM semantic search without deficit. In contrast, subjects

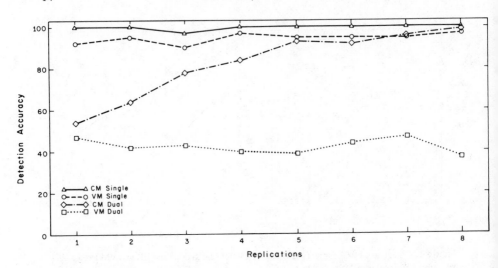

Figure 1.4 Single and dual task CM and VM semantic category search over 8 hours of training. In dual task conditions subjects performed a simultaneous digit search task. (From Schneider & Fisk, in press.)

could not perform the digit search in combination with a VM category-search task without deficit.

These results indicate that some automatic processes do not require control-processing resources.[3] This fact has several implications. First, whether or not one can perform multiple tasks without deficit depends critically on whether the additional tasks depend primarily on automatic or control processing. Second, automatic processing can allow subjects to perform very complex tasks because the automatic components can be effectively cost free. The evidence that semantic categorization can be effectively cost free (Fisk & Schneider, 1983) indicates that processing stimuli at the feature, word, and semantic meaning levels can be done without reducing resources available for other tasks. This suggests that there is no inherent limit to complexity of an automatic process (Fisk & Schneider, 1983; Schneider, Note 2).

After a great deal of consistent practice, subjects in a number of studies have been able to perform complex dual tasks with little or no dual-process perfor-

---

[3]Actually, because two targets never occurred simultaneously, it would be more accurate to say that the requirement to monitor the stimuli for the possible presence of CM targets does not require resources (Dumais, 1979; Duncan, 1980). Nevertheless, the distractor stimuli are processed and even may affect attentional responses. For example, Dumais (1979) showed that distractors trained in CM tasks could lead to almost complete positive transfer if retained in a new CM task using new targets (or old VM targets). Apparently, the CM training caused the distractors to attract attention to a lesser degree than even new or untrained stimuli.

mance decrement. For example, subjects have been able to read while writing (Downey & Anderson, 1915), type while shadowing prose (Shaffer, 1975), read one passage while transcribing dictation (Hirst, Spelke, Reaves, Caharack, & Neisser, 1980; Spelke, Hirst, & Neisser, 1976), shadow verbal messages while playing a piano (Allport, Antonis, & Reynolds, 1972), and fly complex aircraft formation maneuvers while digit canceling (Colle & De Maio, Note 3). In each case it seems that at least one of the simultaneous tasks is carried out largely by automatic processes that do not require substantial resources.

The automatic–control processing framework contrasts with the "attention-is-a-skill" hypothesis (Hirst *et al.*, 1980; Spelke *et al.*, 1976), which proposes that extended time-sharing training is sufficient to eliminate dual-task interference. We have found that extended training is *not* sufficient to eliminate dual-task trade-offs. For situations in which stimuli and responses are VM, dual-task trade-offs occur even after extended training (as discussed above and shown in Figure 1.4; see also, Logan, 1979; Fisk & Schneider, in press; Fisk & Schneider, 1983; Shiffrin & Schneider, 1977). The reasoning behind the "attention-is-a-skill" hypothesis seems to be that only "simple" tasks and processes can be auto-matized (Hirst *et al.*, 1980, p. 116). However, we argue that automatic processes can be very complex.

Any physiological or psychological effects that reduce capacity should primarily affect the performance of control processes and have only a minor effect on automatic processing. Research on "vigilance" provides an illustration. A *vigilance decrement* is a decrement in performance that occurs during the course of continuing performance on some task (see Parasuraman, Chapter 6, this volume). One interpretation of this decrement is that it results from an inability of subjects to maintain proper allocation of control processes for extended periods of time (Fisk & Schneider, 1981). Such an argument leads to the prediction that VM search would show vigilance decrements, but CM search would not. In a continuous multiple-frame experiment of 50 minutes duration, Fisk and Schneider (1981) showed that detection sensitivity dropped considerably in the VM condition (from .91 to .81 A' units) but dropped in the CM condition only slightly (from .88 to .84 A' units). The VM decrement over time was highly significant, whereas the CM drop was not. The experiments indicate that subjects find continual control processing very effortful, and reductions in effort result in performance decrements.

Alcohol ingestion can also reduce capacity. A review of the alcohol literature reveals alcohol tends to affect effortful processing to the degree that limits are placed on STM, the task situation is relatively novel, stimuli are at perceptual threshold, and the subject's responding and/or attending is inconsistent. Generally, alcohol causes a slowing of reaction time in choice reaction-time tasks. However, there are exceptions that show little or no effect of alcohol on reaction time with tasks of high stimulus–response (S–R) compatibility (for example,

Carpenter, 1962; Huntley, 1972; Moskowitz, 1973). Well-practiced "real-world" skills, which may be considered largely automatic, seem to show a resistance to the normal effects of alcohol. For example, a string of well-learned words (e.g., months of the year) is readily recallable when the subject is under the influence of alcohol (Birnhaum & Parker, 1977, p. 101). Forney, Hughes, Hulpiew, and Davis (reported in Huntley, 1973, p. 153) found that low levels of alcohol had little effect on driving ability in skilled driving competition when the subject was driving forward. However, it was found that alcohol significantly reduced performance when driving in reverse (a skill that presumably is unfamiliar and requires control processing).

Fisk and Schneider (1982) have examined the effects of alcohol on automatic- and control-processing performance. Subjects were tested in a sober and an alcoholic state (.1% blood-alcohol level). In a CM search task, alcohol resulted in a 2.2% drop in detection performance. In VM search, the drop was 9.6%. In a VM search task in which subjects also had to maintain an inconsistent response mapping, performance dropped 28.3% (CM search in this condition reduced by only .16%). The data suggest that alcohol reduces the ability to perform control processing, particularly if control processing must be divided in two regions (e.g., dealing with a variable mapping both at the comparison and response stage).

In summary, whether two tasks can be performed without deficit depends on whether the resource demands of both tasks exceed control-processing capacity. If subjects are consistently trained, and performance on one task is largely automatic; that task should not reduce control-processing resources. Because control processing is effortful and resource limited, manipulations that make the task more arduous or decrease capacity should reduce performance in control-processing tasks.

There are three important qualifications to make before closing this discussion of capacity limitations. Our summary conclusions concerning capacity limitations (and attention as well) are true only to the extent that the attention process itself is not placed in an automatic mode of action. In several studies, we have shown that attention can be automatized. For example, stimuli can be trained to attract attention automatically. In such cases, whenever the instigating stimulus invokes the automatic call for attention, the system's control processing is disrupted (at least briefly). In these instances, the effects of automatic processing are difficult to distinguish from those of control processing (because, in effect, the automatic process "controls" the control-processing system). Thus, for example, in the Schneider and Fisk (1982a) search studies, the requirement to look for a single target did not hinder a simultaneous controlled search because two targets did not occur simultaneously. However, the presence of an actual automatic target on a trial can be quite harmful to simultaneous controlled search (Duncan, 1980; Shiffrin & Schneider, 1977, Experiment 4d). The automatic processing, until the call of attention, can be accomplished without reducing control process resources. The generalizations we have been drawing here do not necessarily apply during those intervals in which automatic processes direct control processes.

Some initial evidence suggests that the consumption of control-processing resources caused by automatic processing of targets can be reduced by proper training. Schneider and Fisk (Note 4) trained two subjects to perform a joint CM category–word search and a VM digit search concurrently. After over 8 hours of dual-task training (some 1500 trials), subjects could perform both tasks together without deficit, given the targets did not occur simultaneously. Performance was then tested for both simultaneous targets and nonsimultaneous targets. Initially, the deficit for simultaneous targets relative to nonsimultaneous targets (with at least a 4-second delay between targets) was 46% for word targets and 34% for digit targets. However with 1008 additional dual-task training trials in which most of the trials contained simultaneous or nearly simultaneous targets, the deficit for simultaneous targets was reduced to 18% for words and 14% for the digits. Schneider and Shiffrin (1977b, Experiments 3a, 3b, 3c) found no differences in detection of CM targets, simultaneous targets, or temporally displaced targets as long as the targets were different. The data suggest that extended training can greatly reduce the deficit caused by simultaneous CM targets. Hence, automatic processing of both targets and distractors can become effectively resource free.

The second qualification is that the proposal that automatic processes are not limited by control processing resources does not imply that there are no limits to automatic processing capacity (for a detailed discussion of this issue, see Schneider, Note 2). As the number of stimuli processed through a modality increase, the stimuli cause interference (e.g., lateral inhibition) and result in degradations in processing. Most of the research showing no performance reduction with increasing numbers of channels have tested in the range of 1 to 9 simultaneous inputs (although there is 1 study that examined 49 inputs; Shiffrin et al., 1976). We know that as the amount of consistent training increases so does the number of stimuli that can be processed simultaneously without interference. Greatly reducing attentional resources via the use of secondary tasks does not reduce automatic processing accuracy in either simple or complex search tasks (see above). Future research will have to determine how the capacity of automatic processing changes as a function of the number of stimuli, interitem confusability, and practice levels.

The third qualification concerns the prediction that automatic processing does not consume limited control-processing resources. This principle does not imply that performance of an automatic process can not benefit from the allocation of control processing resources (Schneider, Note 2). Consider a simple case in which a response could be made either on the basis of a controlled or automatic process, whichever was finished first. If automatic and control processing are parallel and independent, and there is some overlap in the distribution of the completion times of the two processes; using both processes will improve performance.

If automatic processing can be performed without reducing available control processing resources, then automatic component processes can be cascaded to perform complex processing tasks. In reading, for example, word encoding can be performed fairly accurately with minimal resources (judging from the high correlation between verbal and reading comprehension in good readers). The possibility that word encoding might be improved if attentional resources are allocated to the encoding task does not reduce the importance of developing automatic component skills. It is through the use of automatic components that word encoding can occur with substantial accuracy while almost all control-processing resources are allocated to the semantic integration aspect of reading.

Automatization of Attention

In this section, we discuss the automatization of attention. Although the search paradigms discussed here ensure that attention is one of the processes being automatized, we think it likely that the conclusions should generalize to the automatization of other processes as well.

Consistency

In nonlaboratory situations, training is unlikely to be perfectly consistent; yet automatic responses develop. Schneider and Fisk (1982b) examined the automatization of attention when the degree of consistency during training was experimentally varied. They manipulated consistency by holding constant the number of times various items appeared as targets and varying the number of times these items appeared as distractors. The target and distractor sets were selected from a set of nine consonants. Five consistency conditions were used; a given item could be (1) always a target and never a distractor (CM control); (2) a target twice as often as a distractor; (3) a target and a distractor equally often; (4) a target half as often as a distractor; and (5) a target approximately one-seventh as often as a distractor. This fifth condition is a VM control because the ratio is typical of those holding in previous VM conditions (e.g., Schneider & Shiffrin, 1977b). After an average of 670 such training trials per CM letter, Schneider and Fisk found that detection accuracies across conditions were 83%, 74%, 68%, 58%, and 54%, respectively. The fourth and fifth conditions did not differ significantly either from each other or from initial performance. Thus in the case in which a letter appeared as a distractor twice as often as it was a target (33% consistency), 670 training trials resulted in no improvement in performance. The results indicate that automatic processes develop as a multiplicative function of the number of trials and degree of consistency. Practice alone does not produce automatization, fairly consistent practice is needed. Consistency has also been shown to be critical in sequential motor-response procedures (Schneider & Fisk, 1983). In consistent responding paradigms, pauses between responses reduced and became less variable with practice. However, if the button sequence was varied from trial to trial, there was no benefit of practice.

Automatization of a Consistent Component Process

Performance improvements associated with automatic processing occur in consistent processing stages even when the total task is not consistent from stimulus to response. Fisk and Schneider (Note 5) tested subjects in conditions in which the subjects attended consistently to a given letter but responded in different ways on different trials (i.e., on half the trials, they responded with the position of the target; and on half the trials, they responded with the position opposite the target). There were no differences in asymptotic detection performance between the consistent-attending–consistent-responding group and the consistent-attending–inconsistent-responding group although the latter group did not perform as well during training. The data indicate that automatic processing develops when the processing for one component of a task is consistent, even if the entire task from stimulus to response is not consistent.

Searching versus Detecting

During consistent training, subjects in search tasks both search for and detect targets with a fixed ratio of the two frequencies. Schneider and Fisk (Note 6) removed this confounding procedure. Subjects searched for a target in a 12-frame multiple-frame procedure. When a given stimulus was sought 6 times per block, CM hit rate improved from 64 to 71% as the number of target presentations increased from 2 to 4. When the number of "target-present searches" was constant (at 4), increasing the number of target absent searches from 2 to 16 resulted in a *decrease* in detection accuracy from 71 to 57%. All search conditions were significantly better than a VM search condition (45%). These results suggest that automatic attending develops as a consequence of consistent repetition of the appropriate S–R mapping (detection), not from simply the attempt to execute it (searching).

Transfer of Automatic Processes

Automatic processes show high transfer to processing stimuli in the same class as the trained stimuli. Schneider and Fisk (in press) trained subjects to detect CM words from a category (e.g., colors). After extensive training, subjects were presented new words from the categories they had been trained to detect. Performance on the new words from the trained category was compared to performance on the words used in training and new words from a new category. Using a reaction-time measure, there was a 92% positive transfer to new words from the trained category. Using a detection measure under high work load, the transfer was 72%. The demonstration that automatic processes show high positive transfer is particularly critical when considering "real-world" learning. There are few individual stimuli that are normally processed for the number of trials required to show substantial automatic processing. However, there are many classes of stimuli that are consistently processed (e.g., learning to catch flying objects, rather than a specific object).

Other Factors Affecting Automatization

Although we cannot describe the results in any detail (Schneider, Note 7), it is useful to list several other factors affecting the rate of automatization: (1) similarity or feature overlap between target and distractor set—learning is faster with greater dissimilarity; (2) history of training—prior antagonistic CM training hinders automatization (in addition, prior VM training appears to slow automatization compared to no prior training); and (3) type of task—multiple-frame tasks requiring accuracy appear to lead to faster automatization than do single-frame tasks requiring rapid responding. Automatic processing still improves after years of training. Crossman (1959) found that cigar rolling was still improving after 2 years of practice and digit addition after 10,000 trials.

The Role of Attention in Distinguishing Automatic and Control Processes

Table 1.1 provides a partial listing of the characteristics that have been proposed to distinguish automatic and control processing. None of these characteristics provides a necessary and sufficient basis for distinguishing the two types of processes. Perhaps the best properties for distinguishing the two processing types are those involving attentional control and resource demands. The problem in stating any general rule, however, lies in the fact that attention itself can be

TABLE 1.1

Some Characteristics of Automatic and Control Processes

Characteristic	Automatic processes	Control processes
Central capacity	Not required	Required
Control	Not complete	Complete
Indivisability	Wholistic	Fragmentized
Practice	Results in gradual improvement	Has little effect
Modification	Difficult	Easy
Serial–parallel dependence	Parallel Independent	Serial Dependent
Storage in LTM	Little or none	Large amounts
Performance level	High	Low, except when task is simple
Simplicity	Irrelevant	Irrelevant
Awareness	Low	High
Attention	Not required but may be called	Required
Effort	Little if any	Much

automatized (orienting response). Thus an automatic process can call attention and thereby cause a demand on resources (indirectly).

We suggest a two-part definition that is sufficient to establish the presence of a large class of automatic and control processes. It may be stated as follows:

1. Any process that does not use general, nonspecific processing resources and does not decrease the general, nonspecific processing capacity available for other processes is automatic.

2. Any process that demands resources in response to external stimulus inputs, regardless of subjects' attempts to ignore the distraction, is automatic.

These criteria provide a working definition for asymptotic automatic processing (see Shiffrin, Dumais, & Schneider, 1981 for more details). In processes that are poorly developed, automatic processing might somewhat decrease general processing capacity.

Functions and Limitations of Automatic and Control Processing

It is important to consider the potential functions of automatic and control processes. We suggest that control processing performs at least the following functions: First, control processes should be instrumental in the development of new automatic processes. For example, storage in long-term memory (LTM) seems to occur primarily when control processing occurs (Underwood, 1976, Chap. 4; Fisk & Schneider, in press). Second, control processing is used to deal with tasks that cannot be carried out by automatic processing. These tasks include novel tasks, and tasks for which requirements are inconsistent (i.e., they change over time). Such tasks might include those of threshold detection (for which the stimuli are sometimes ambiguous) and those of fine motor control in the early stages of practice. Third, control processing is used to maintain the activity of nodes in memory. An unattended automatic process input decays rapidly. For example, digits presented in an unattended ear automatically activate their nodes, but the nodes decay to chance in no more than 3 seconds (Glucksberg & Cowen, 1970). Hence, if an automatic process is to maintain performance for greater than 3 seconds, the top node must be activated either by control processing or by continuous stimulation from external stimuli (e.g., external context). Fourth, control processing is used to activate nodes in order to enable automatic processes to occur. In effect, this allows indirect control of automatic processing. Fifth, control processing may be able to block and modify existing automatic processes. An illustration of this is that one normally brakes for a red light but may run the light without braking in special circumstances. It may be in this way that old automatic processes are modified. Note, however, that control of automatic processing can be quite difficult (e.g., consider a Stroop task).

Functions of automatic processing include the following: First, they are used to perform habitual behaviors. Second, they may be used to interrupt ongoing control processing and forcefully reallocate attention and resources (see Rabbitt, 1978; Shiffrin & Schneider, 1977, p. 153). Third, they may be used to bias or prime memory in preparation for later inputs (Logan, 1980; Neely, 1977; Posner & Snyder, 1975).

There is rarely any task in which processing is purely controlled or purely automatic (Schneider & Fisk, 1983). In general, the two processes share the same memory structure and continuously interact. Automatic processing may initiate control processing by causing an orienting or attentional response, and controlled processing may activate an automatic process. For example, in playing tennis, an expert player may adopt a strategy to place the ball in the right far corner. Automatic processes are used in executing this strategy. In this example, control processing is used to set and maintain the top level of a behavior hierarchy, and automatic processes execute the appropriate movements.

The continual interaction of automatic and control processing complicates any attempt to provide an operational definition of automatic processing. Just as we think all memory is a joint product of retrieval from STM and LTM systems, we also believe all behaviors are the joint result of automatic and control processing.

The complementary interaction of automatic and control processing enables a system with a stringent capacity limitation to perform complex processing. Those aspects of behavior that can be processed consistently are automatically processed and do not use up resources. However, because nodes activated by automatic processing decay rapidly, control processing can be used to maintain a few critical nodes in memory.

The interaction of automatic and control processes allows a limited capacity processor to accomplish very complex tasks (Schneider & Fisk, 1983). We assumed that control processing modifies memory and leads to the development of automatic processing. In this sense, the limited control-processing system lays down "stepping stones" of automatic processing (Schneider & Shiffrin, 1977a). As long as the stimuli can consistently evoke a given response, no limited control-processing resources need be expended. Thus automatic processes can be cascaded, enabling complex processing to be carried out. Fisk and Schneider (1983) have shown that subjects can categorize words into superordinate categories without reducing STM capacity, suggesting that feature extraction, word encoding, and semantic categorization can all be done with no cost in control-processing resources.

Control processing may be able to provide flexible control of normally inflexible automatic behavior. In many activities there is a need to produce unexpected or novel action patterns. The tennis player who changes strategy does not modify his or her overlearned patterns of meeting the ball, but rather chooses among many possible sets of automatic responses. The choice may be made by changing an internal stimulus that acts as a trigger for the automatic behavior (in combination with the external stimuli). In this way, classes of automatic processes can be switched quickly, although the automatic behaviors are not individually changed.

Conclusions

We have very selectively reviewed certain findings concerning divided attention, focused attention, and attentional capacity. The results suggest (1) performance differs to the degree that automatic or control processing determines performance, (2) performance improves with extensive CM training, (3) automatic processes are difficult to control, and (4) capacity reductions primarily harm control processing. The development of automatic processes were examined, and performance was seen to improve as a function of consistent executions. We have discussed the functions, limitations, and interactions of automatic and control processing and have suggested that automatic processing can be defined in terms of capacity limitations and control. Although the automatic–control processing framework can be used to organize much of the attention literature, at present it raises more questions than it answers. Future research must unravel the complex interactions of these different but complementary processes.

Reference Notes

1. Foyle, D., & Shiffrin, R. M. *Automatic processing of threshold stimuli in selective attention.* Manuscript submitted for publication, 1982.
2. Schneider, W. *Automatic/control processing the limits and potential.* Paper presented at the meeting of the American Psychological Association, Washington, D.C., August 1982.
3. Colle, H. A., & De Maio, J. *Measurement of attentional capacity load using dual-task performance operating curves.* (Interim Report AFHRL-TR-78-5). Brooks Air Force Base, Texas: Air Force Systems Command, April 1978.
4. Schneider, W., & Fisk, A. D. Unpublished research, 1982.
5. Fisk, A. D., & Schneider, W. *Task versus component consistency in the development of automatic processes: Consistent attending versus consistent responding.* Manuscript submitted for publication, 1982.
6. Schneider, W., & Fisk, A. D. *Visual search improves with detection searches, declines with nondetection search* (Tech. Rep. 8004). Champaign, Ill.: University of Illinois, Human Attention Research Laboratory, February 1980.
7. Schneider, W. Unpublished research, 1982.

References

Allport, D. A., Antonis, B., & Reynolds, P. On the division of attention: A disproof of the single channel hypothesis. *Quarterly Journal of Experimental Psychology*, 1972, *24*, 225–235.

Birnbaum, I. M., & Parker, E. J. Acute effects of alcohol on storage and retrieval. In I. M. Birnbaum & E. S. Parker (Eds.), *Alcohol and human memory*. Hillsdale, N.J.: Erlbaum, 1977.

Broadbent, D. E. *Perception and communication*. London: Pergamon, 1958.

Broadbent, D. E. *Decision and stress*. London: Academic Press, 1971.

Carpenter, J. A. Effects of alcohol on some psychological processes: A critical review. *Quarterly Journal of Studies on Alcohol*, 1962, *23*, 274–314.

Cherry, C. Some experiments on the reception of speech with one and with two ears. *Journal of the Acoustical Society of America*, 1953, *25*, 975–979.

Colegate, R. L., Hoffman, J. E., & Eriksen, C. W. Selective encoding from multi-element visual displays. *Perception & Psychophysics*, 1973, *14*, 217–224.

Craig, A. Nonparametric measures of sensory efficiency for sustained monitoring tasks. *Human Factors*, 1979, *21*, 69–78.

Crossman, E. R. F. W. A theory of the acquisition of speed-skill. *Ergonomics*, 1959, *2*, 153–166.

Downey, J. E., & Anderson, J. E. Automatic writing. *American Journal of Psychology*, 1915, *26*, 161–195.

Dumais, S.T. *Perceptual learning in automatic detection: Processes and mechanism*. Unpublished doctoral dissertation, Indiana University, Bloomington, IN: 1979.

Duncan, J. The locus of interference in the perception of simultaneous stimuli. *Psychological Review*, 1980, *87*, 272–300.

Dyer, F. N. The Stroop phenomenon and its use in the study of perceptual, cognitive, and response processes. *Memory and Cognition*, 1973, *1*, 106–210.

Eriksen, B. A., & Eriksen, C. W. Effects of noise letters upon the identification of a target letter in a nonsearch task. *Perception & Psychophysics*, 1974, *16*, 143–149.

Eriksen, C. W., & Collins, J. F. Temporal course of selective attention. *Journal of Experimental Psychology*, 1969, *80*, 254–261.

Eriksen, C. W., & Hoffman, J. E. Temporal and spatial characteristics of selective encoding from visual displays. *Perception & Psychophysics*, 1972, *12*, 201–204.

Eriksen, C. W., & Hoffman, J. E. The extent of processing of noise elements during selective encoding from visual displays. *Perception & Psychophysics*, 1973, *14*, 155–160.

Eriksen, C. W., & Schultz, D. W. Information processing in visual search: A continuous flow conception and experimental results. *Perception & Psychophysics*, 1979, *25*, 249–263.

Eriksen, C. W., & Spencer, T. Rate of information processing in visual perception: Some results and methodological considerations. *Journal of Experimental Psychology Monographs*, 1969, *79*(2).

Fisk, A. D., & Schneider, W. Control and automatic processing during tasks requiring sustained attention: A new approach to vigilance. *Human Factors*, 1981, *23*, 737–750.

Fisk, A. D., & Schneider, W. Type of task practice and time-sharing activities predict performance deficits due to alcohol ingestion. *Proceedings of the Human Factors Society*. Santa Monica, Calif.: Human Factors Society, 1982.

Fisk, A. D., & Schneider, W. Category and word search: Generalizing search principles to complex processing. *Journal of Experimental Psychology: Learning, Memory, and Cognition*, 1983, *9*, 177–195.

Fisk, A. D., & Schneider, W. Memory as a function of attention, level of processing, and automatization. *Journal of Experimental Psychology: Learning, Memory, and Cognition*, in press.

Gibson, E. J. Perceptual learning and the theory of word perception. *Cognitive Psychology*, 1971, *2*, 351–358.

Glucksberg, S., & Cowen, G. N. Memory for nonattended auditory material. *Cognitive Psychology*, 1970, *1*, 149–156.

Hirst, W., Spelke, E. S., Reaves, C. C., Caharack, G., & Neisser, U. Dividing attention without alternation or automaticity. *Journal of Experimental Psychology: General*, 1980, *109*, 98–117.

Hoffman, J. E. A two-stage model of visual search. *Perception & Psychophysics*, 1979, *25*, 319–327.

Huntley, M. S. Influences of alcohol and S–R uncertainty upon spatial localization time. *Psychopharmacologia*, 1972, *27*, 131–140.

Huntley, M. S. Alcohol influences upon closed-course driving performance. *Journal of Safety Research*, 1973, *5*, 149–164.

James, W. *Principles of psychology* (Vol. 1). New York: Holt, 1890.

Kahneman, D. *Attention and effort*. Englewood Cliffs, N.J.: Prentice-Hall, 1973.

Kristofferson, M. W. Effects of practice on character classification performance. *Canadian Journal of Psychology*, 1972, *26*, 54–60. (a)

Kristofferson, M. W. When an item recognition and visual search functions are similar. *Perception & Psychophysics*, 1972, *12*, 378–384. (b)

LaBerge, D. Acquisition of automatic processing in perceptual and associative learning. In P. M. A. Rabbitt & S. Dornic (Eds.), *Attention and performance V*. New York: Academic Press, 1975.

Logan, G. D. On the use of a concurrent memory load to measure attention and automaticity. *Journal of Experimental Psychology: Human Perception and Performance*, 1979, *5*, 189–207.

Logan, G. D. Attention and automaticity in Stroop and priming tasks: Theory and data. *Cognitive Psychology*, 1980, *12*, 523–553.

Moray, N. Attention in dichotic listening. Affective cues and the influence of instructions. *Quarterly Journal of Experimental Psychology*, 1959, *11*, 56–60.

Moray, N. *Attention: Selective processes in vision and hearing*. New York: Academic Press, 1969. (a)

Moray, N. *Listening and attention*. Harmondsworth, Middlesex, Eng.: Penguin, 1969. (b)

Moray, N. A data base for theories of selective listening. In P. M. A. Rabbitt & S. Dornic (Eds.), *Attention and performance V*. New York: Academic Press, 1975.

Moskowitz, H. Laboratory studies of the effects of alcohol on some variables related to driving. *Journal of Safety Research*, 1973, *5*, 185–199.

Navon, D., & Gopher, D. On the economy of the human-processing system. *Psychological Review*, 1979, *86*, 214–255.

Neely, J. H. Semantic priming and retrieval from lexical memory: Roles of inhibitionless spreading activation and limited-capacity attention. *Journal of Experimental Psychology: General*, 1977, *106*, 226–254.

Neisser, U. Decision time without reaction time: Experiments in visual scanning. *American Journal of Psychology*, 1963, 376–385.

Norman, D. A. A comparison of data obtained with different false alarm rates. *Psychological Review*, 1964, *71*, 243–246.

Norman, D. A., & Bobrow, D. J. On the analysis of performance operating characteristics. *Psychological Review*, 1976, *83*, 508–519.

Poltrock, S. E., Lansman, M., & Hunt, E. Automatic and controlled attention processes in auditory target detection. *Journal of Experimental Psychology: Human Perception and Performance*, 1982, *8*, 37–45.

Posner, M. I., & Snyder, C. R. R. Attention and cognitive control. In R. L. Solso (Ed.), *Information processing and cognition: The Loyola Symposium*. Hillsdale, N.J.: Erlbaum, 1975.

Rabbitt, P. Sorting, categorization, and visual search. In E. C. Carterette & M. P. Friedman (Eds.), *Handbook of perception*. New York: Academic Press, 1978.

Schneider, W., & Fisk, A. D. Concurrent automatic and controlled visual search: Can processing occur without resource cost? *Journal of Experimental Psychology: Learning, Memory, and Cognition*, 1982, *8*, 261–278. (a)

Schneider, W., & Fisk, A. D. Degree of consistent training: Improvements in search performance and automatic process development. *Perception & Psychophysics*, 1982, *31*, 160–168. (b)

Schneider, W., & Fisk, A. D. Attention theory and mechanisms for skilled performance. In R. Magill (Ed.), *Memory and control of action*. New York: North-Holland, 1983.

Schneider, W., & Fisk, A. D. Automatic category search and its transfer. *Journal of Experimental Psychology: Learning, Memory, and Cognition*, in press.

Schneider, W., & Shiffrin, R. M. Automatic and controlled information processing in vision. In D. LaBerge & S. J. Samuels (Eds.), *Basic processes in reading: Perception and comprehension*. Hillsdale, N.J.: Erlbaum, 1977. (a)

Schneider, W., & Shiffrin, R. M. Controlled and automatic human information processing: I. Detection, search, and attention. *Psychological Review*, 1977, *84*, 1–66. (b)

Shaffer, L. H. Multiple attention in continuous verbal tasks. In P. M. A. Rabbitt & S. Dornic (Eds.), *Attention and performance V*. New York: Academic Press, 1975.

Shiffrin, R. M., Craig, J. C., & Cohen, U. On the degree of attention and capacity limitations in tactile processing. *Perception & Psychophysics*, 1973, *13*, 328–336.

Shiffrin, R. M., Dumais, S. T., & Schneider, W. Characteristics of automatism. In J. B. Long & A. D. Baddeley (Eds.), *Attention and performance IX*. Hillsdale, N.J.: Erlbaum, 1981.

Shiffrin, R. M., & Gardner, G. T. Visual processing capacity and attentional control. *Journal of Experimental Psychology*, 1972, *93*, 72–82.

Shiffrin, R. M., Gardner, G. T., & Allmeyer, D. H. On the degree of attention and capacity limitations in visual processing. *Perception & Psychophysics*, 1973, *14*, 231–236.

Shiffrin, R. M., & Geisler, W. S. Visual recognition in a theory of information processing. In R. L. Solso (Ed.), *Contemporary issues in cognitive psychology: The Loyola Symposium*. New York: Holt, 1973.

Shiffrin, R. M., & Grantham, D. W. Can attention be allocated to sensory modalities? *Perception & Psychophysics*, 1974, *15*, 460–474.

Shiffrin, R. M., McKay, D. P., & Shaffer, W. O. Attending to forty-nine spatial positions at once. *Journal of Experimental Psychology: Human Perception and Performance*, 1976, *2*, 14–22.

Shiffrin, R. M., Pisoni, D. B., & Casteneda-Mendez, K. Is attention shared between the ears? *Cognitive Psychology,* 1974, *6,* 190–215.

Shiffrin, R. M., & Schneider, W. Controlled and automatic human information processing: II. Perceptual learning, automatic attending, and a general theory. *Psychological Review,* 1977, *84,* 127–190.

Spelke, E., Hirst, W., & Neisser, U. Skills of divided attention. *Cognition,* 1976, *4,* 215–230.

Sternberg, S. High speed scanning in human memory. *Science,* 1966, *153,* 652–654.

Sternberg, S. The discovery of processing stages: Extensions of Donder's method. In W. G. Koster (Ed.), *Attention and performance II.* Amsterdam: North-Holland, 1969. (a)

Sternberg, S. Memory scanning: Mental processes revealed by reaction time experiments. *American Scientist,* 1969, *57,* 421–457. (b)

Sternberg, S. Memory scanning: New findings and current controversies. *Quarterly Journal of Experimental Psychology,* 1975, *27,* 1–42.

Stroop, J. R. Studies of interference in serial verbal reactions. *Journal of Experimental Psychology,* 1935, *18,* 643–662.

Treisman, A. M. Contextual cues in selective listening. *Quarterly Journal of Experimental Psychology,* 1960, *12,* 242–248.

Treisman, A. M. Strategies and models of selective attention. *Psychological Review,* 1969, *76,* 282–299.

Underwood, G. *Attention and memory.* New York: Pergamon, 1976.

Wickens, C. D. The structure of attentional resources. In R. Nickerson and R. Pew (Eds.), *Attention and performance VIII.* Hillsdale, N.J.: Erlbaum, 1980.

Changing Views of Attention and Automaticity

Daniel Kahneman and Anne Treisman

Introduction

There are two main interpretations of the adaptive function of selective attention, corresponding to two problems that an organism must solve. One view emphasizes the richness and complexity of the information that is presented to the senses at any one time and the consequent risk of confusion and overload (Broadbent, 1958). The other view emphasizes the diverse and incompatible response tendencies that may be instigated at any one time and the consequent risks of paralysis and incoherence (Posner, 1978; Shallice, 1972). The function of attention in the first view is to ensure adequate perceptual processing of the currently important sensory messages; in the second view, it is to ensure adequate execution of the currently most important action. The main mechanism of attention in the first view is selective processing; in the second, it is the adoption of an appropriate set.

It is of course quite possible—indeed likely—that organisms are threatened both by perceptual overload and by response incoherence, and that different selective processes must be employed to control the two threats. However, the emphasis on each of these problems tends to suggest a different approach to the study of attention. The revival of interest in attention in the 1950s was motivated at least in part by the discovery of surprising limitations in the handling of simultaneous messages by air-traffic controllers and by subjects in dichotic listening tasks. Perceptual overload seemed to be the problem, and the experimental situations of the time were designed to induce overload in order to explore the efficacy with which limited resources could be directed to the most relevant information. However, subsequent studies raised doubts about the existence of perceptual limits because subjects were sometimes able to monitor several input channels at once with little or no impairment (e.g., Shiffrin, 1975; Shiffrin & Grantham, 1974). In the simpler experimental situations that were widely adopted for the study of attention, perceptual processing often appeared to be independent of attention, and the two major treatments of attention in the late 1970s both emphasized automaticity in information processing (Posner, 1978; Shiffrin & Schneider, 1977).

Indeed, the study of attention underwent a significant paradigm shift during

29

the decade of the 1970s, almost a reversal of figure and ground: the null hypothesis for research was inverted as the focus of interest moved from the nature of attention limits to the exploration of automatic processing. Thus, several studies in the early 1970s tested and rejected the claim that stimuli presented to an unattended channel receive no semantic processing at all (Corteen & Wood, 1972; Lewis, 1970; MacKay, 1973; von Wright, Anderson, & Stenman, 1975). A few years later, the reversal of figure and ground was evident in a spate of reports describing effects of attention on operations that had previously been thought automatic (Francolini & Egeth, 1980; Hoffman, Nelson, & Houck, 1983; Johnston & Dark, 1982; Kahneman & Henik, 1981; Paap & Ogden, 1981). The belief in automaticity and late selection had become general enough to be worth testing and challenging. Consider an illustrative case history: in 1960, it was shown that on 6% of trials, subjects reported a word presented to the unattended ear if that word was highly probable in the attended message (Treisman, 1960). This finding was important in 1960 as a challenge to an early-selection theory. It was subsequently cited by several authors without mention of the rarity of intrusions from the rejected ear, in statements that began with "Subjects . . ." or even "Subjects frequently . . .". If the same paper were to be rewritten now, it would have to stress the newly surprising fact that on 94% of trials, the highly probable word was not reported.

We begin this chapter by a brief review of the abrupt change in the dominant theory of attention. We make no attempt to be comprehensive in our treatment; our aim is simply to sketch with broad strokes a view of some of the main trends in attention research since 1950, giving examples of experiments rather than listing all the relevant papers. For comprehensive reviews of the field, see Broadbent (1982) and Keele and Neill (1979). We argue that changes occurring in the late 1970s and early 1980s resulted in part from the adoption of new experimental paradigms to study attention, which, in turn, were anchored in a new view of the relation between perception and long-term memory (LTM). We also describe several series of experiments in which we tested null hypotheses derived from the notion of automatic semantic processing. Our results indicate a substantial susceptibility of "automatic" processes to attention effects. Finally, we sketch a framework for the study of attention that may accommodate the different lines of evidence from which "early-selection" and "late-selection" models of attention have drawn support.

The Disputed Nature of Attention

Research Paradigms in Attention: Trends and Consequences

Studies of attention fall into two broad classes, which are concerned respectively with divided and with focused (or selective) attention. Divided attention tasks are used to establish limits to performance and to measure which different tasks can be combined without loss. They are analyze the causes of dual-task decrements and to locate the stages of proc~~~. that limit performance. Tasks of selective or focused attention are used to study resistance to distraction and to establish the locus beyond which relevant and irrelevant stimuli are treated differentially (see also Davies, Jones, & Taylor, Chapter 11, this volume).

Early studies of attention (reviewed by Broadbent, 1958) typically involved complex competing messages, often speech, which constituted a high perceptual load. People appeared to do quite poorly in dividing attention between such messages, but they were very successful in focusing attention at will on one of them. Attention was viewed as selecting messages arriving on a "channel." The main experimental problems were the effectiveness of selective attention in protecting the relevant messages and the quality of processing of the information presented to rejected channels. Table 2.1 lists some characteristics of the filtering paradigm which was developed to study these problems. This paradigm is com- pared to the research methods that became popular in the 1970s and that we label the "*selective-set*" paradigm. (Note that there were also studies of "selective set" in the 1960s and earlier and that studies of "filtering" still continue to appear. We summarize what seems to us to be a statistical shift in the dominant approach.)

We define the *filtering paradigm* by three features: (1) the subject is exposed simultaneously to relevant and irrelevant stimuli, (2) the relevant stimuli control a relatively complex process of response selection and execution, and (3) the property that distinguishes the relevant from the irrelevant stimuli is usually a simple physical feature and is different from the property that determines the appropriate response. Thus a filtering task comprises two distinct functions that are controlled by different aspects of the information presented to subjects: *stimulus choice,* the segregation of relevant items from irrelevant ones, must be guided by some identifying property such as the color of a row of letters or the location of an auditory source; *response choice,* for example in reading or shad- owing the relevant message, is controlled by other properties of the relevant items, such as their shape or sound. The two classic examples of the filtering paradigm are the selective shadowing task, which Cherry (1953) invented in his pioneering studies of the cocktail-party effect, and the partial-report technique introduced by Sperling (1960) to study short-term visual storage.

In the *selective-set paradigm,* the subject is prepared for particular stimuli and is instructed to indicate by a speeded response the detection or recognition of those stimuli. Thus, the subject chooses which of several *possible* stimuli to expect or search for rather than which of several *actual* stimuli to analyze. The main variants of the set paradigm are studies of search (e.g., Schneider, Dumais, & Shiffrin, Chapter 1, this volume) and studies of the costs and benefits of

TABLE 2.1

Differences between the Filtering and Selective-Set Paradigms

Characteristic	Filtering paradigm	Selective-set paradigm
Designs	Selective listening	Search
	Partial report	Priming
Modality	Auditory or visual	Visual
Vocabulary of stimuli	Large	Small
Response choice	Large	Small
Memory load	High	Low
Measure	Accuracy	Reaction time
Items selected	Subset of presented stimuli	Subset of possible stimuli
Null hypothesis	Perfect early selectivity	Full automaticity
Standard interpretation	Selective attention prevents or reduces perceptual processing of unattended stimuli	Selective attention selects and speeds responses to expected targets

expectations (Posner, 1978). In both variants, attention is set, either by intention or by spreading excitation, to detect one or more potential targets.

Filtering and set differ sharply in the simplicity of the experimental situation and of the subject's task. The response vocabulary is minimal in studies of set, often comprising only ''yes'' and ''no'' key presses and sometimes only a ''yes'' response. Furthermore, a single response is usually obtained on each trial, in contrast to the continuous shadowing or complex reports often used in earlier filtering tasks. The transition from filtering to set was motivated largely by the wish to study selective attention with a minimal involvement of memory and response load. A cascade of technical improvements led investigators from selective shadowing to auditory monitoring (Moray & O'Brien, 1967), and eventually to visual search (usually for letters or digits) as modal designs for the study of selective attention. There is no assurance, of course, that the same mechanisms of selection and the same limits to performance are relevant in visual search for single letters and in selective shadowing of continuous speech.

The model situations investigated by Posner and his associates (Posner, 1978, 1982) are especially austere. Posner has generally studied attention in displays that include a single stimulus, in contrast to the multielement displays used in search and filtering studies. The experimental manipulations control the subject's readiness for the imperative stimulus by providing advance cues of variable validity. This design involves selection only in the sense that the subject is selectively prepared for some events rather than for others. Here again it appears plausible that the processes and mechanisms involved in these simple tasks may be different from those involved in the more complex filtering tasks.

Results and Conclusions of Filtering Experiments

The standard experimental results in the filtering paradigm and in the selective set paradigm suggest different views of the mind. Subjects in a filtering study appear to focus attention efficiently on the relevant stimuli and to perceive little of the unattended stimuli (Cherry, 1953; Moray, 1959; Neisser & Becklen, 1975). The successes of focused attention are matched by dramatic failures in some attempts to divide attention between two tasks, channels, or messages although the extent of the decrement varies in different studies. These observations suggested an early-selection model of attention. In his original statement of filter theory, Broadbent (1958) assumed that stimuli are briefly stored and analyzed in parallel for elementary characteristics at the preattentive level, or S-system, with only a selected subset allowed by the filter into the higher level processing offered by the P-system.

The first version of filter theory was quickly amended when it was shown that people (sometimes) respond to their name on a rejected channel (Moray, 1959) and (occasionally) respond to the meaning of items on that channel (Treisman, 1960). The modified filter-attenuation version assumed that the filter only reduces the information available on a rejected channel and that this reduced information is sometimes sufficient to activate highly primed entries in the mental dictionary (Treisman, 1960). The operation of priming was assumed to be involuntary and unconscious, features later stressed in theories of selective-set (Posner, 1978).

Subsequent demonstrations that divided attention is possible and that interference is reduced or eliminated when concurrent tasks differ sufficiently from one another provided evidence against the idea of a single central bottleneck (Allport, Antonis, & Reynolds, 1972; Kleiman, 1975; Rollins & Hendricks, 1980; Shaffer, 1975; Treisman & Davies, 1973). Thus speech and music, or auditory and visual words, can more easily be processed in parallel than two auditory or two visual messages of the same type. These observations suggest that the brain is organized as a modular system (Allport, 1980; Allport et al., 1972; Navon & Gopher, 1979; Treisman, 1969; see also Wickens, Chapter 3, this volume) and that interference arises chiefly within rather than between the separate, semi-independent subsystems. If this is the case, then the need for early selection should also arise only when concurrent activities engage the same processing mechanisms or resources. Whether there is in addition some central shared resource or limit (Kahneman, 1973) remains an open question. In this chapter, we discuss only tasks that would be expected to share the same subsystems, and do not distinguish general from specific capacity.

Results and Conclusions of Selective-Set Experiments

In marked contrast to the filtering paradigms, results in the selective-set paradigm often reveal a rather impressive ability to process multiple stimuli, even in the same modality and of the same type. In many search tasks, for example, the target appears to "pop out" of the field of distractors regardless of their number (Egeth, Jonides, & Wall, 1972; Schneider & Shiffrin, 1977). This finding suggests that the processing of distractors is performed in parallel over the entire array and is not subject to attention limits. Observations of slow or serial search in some conditions can often be attributed to a combination of local feature interactions among similar stimuli (Bjork & Murray, 1977; Estes, 1972, 1975) and overloading of a decision mechanism (Estes, 1972, 1975; Hoffman, 1978, 1979).

Some results in both priming and search also contrast with the successful resistance to distraction observed in filtering. Involuntary processing of priming stimuli may disrupt the subject's intended response to targets (Neely, 1977; Warren, 1974). Involuntary processing can also be demonstrated in search, after prolonged practice with particular targets. The set to attend to these targets eventually becomes automatized and voluntary control over attention is lost (Schneider & Shiffrin, 1977). It seems fair to conclude that the subjects in set paradigms resemble automatic processors more than do the subjects in standard filtering studies.

The evidence for automatic processing in studies of set has often been interpreted as supporting the late-selection model of attention, first proposed by Deutsch and Deutsch (1963), in which perceptual processing to the semantic level is automatic and entirely independent of attention, and where attention merely controls the choice of stimuli that will be remembered and acted on (Duncan, 1980). However, we see some reasons to doubt inferences from automaticity in studies of set to the locus of selection in filtering.

First, the marked differences between the paradigms make it unlikely that the same type of perceptual processing is required. In many search studies, the target is defined by a simple feature; once this has been detected, the response is immediately determined. Such studies effectively curtail the required perceptual processing to a stage that filter theory considers preattentive. Selection seems to occur late, since all relevant perceptual activity precedes it, and the processing of rejected distractors is accepted as a model of perceptual analysis in general. In the more complex filtering design, however, further processing of relevant stimuli is required before a response can be chosen. It is natural in this context to describe selection as occurring "early" because most of the significant perceptual processing follows attentional selection.

The dependent variables typically differ too: priming and search studies commonly measure the speed of response to primed targets and the delays caused by distractors or by the presentation of unexpected targets; filtering studies measure the accuracy of continuous responses to selected incoming stimuli and the occurrence or nonoccurrence of responses to unattended stimuli. An increase in response latency can readily be attributed to a late stage of decision or of response selection; a failure to "see" or to "hear" an unattended item more strongly suggests a perceptual loss (although work on subliminal perception, which is discussed in a subsequent section of this chapter, has questioned this assumption).

Finally, the focus of attention is differently directed in the filtering and in the set paradigms. In filtering studies, subjects select a subset of presented stimuli for further processing; in search and priming studies, a subset of possible targets is primed or expected. It is logically quite possible that the concurrent processing of multiple incoming stimuli and the concurrent priming or preactivation of multiple nodes or logogens are subject to quite different limitations.

Automaticity of Semantic Processing: Some Evidence

We have argued in the preceding sections that some standard observations in the selective set paradigm suggest a different view of the mind from that suggested in filter theory, but that neither parallel search nor passive priming provide substantive evidence against the possibility that attention affects perception in the filtering paradigm. We now discuss in greater detail three major findings that have contributed substantially to the growing popularity of generalized late-selection models: semantic processing of unattended material, the category effect, and subliminal perception. None of the three, we believe, provides compelling support for the view that perceptual processing is completely automatic.

Semantic Processing of Unattended Material

The first line of evidence comprises demonstrations of semantic processing of material presented on unattended channels. Many such demonstrations have been reported. Some of the best known are by Corteen and Wood (1972), Corteen and Dunn (1974), Lewis (1970), MacKay (1973), and von Wright et al. (1975). The study by Corteen and Dunn (1974), in particular, suggested an important dissociation between the significant effects of unattended shock-associated words on skin conductance and the nearly total lack of effect of these words in controlling instrumental responses. Although some doubts have been raised (Dawson & Schell, 1982; Treisman, Squire, & Green, 1974; Wardlaw & Kroll, 1976), the basic facts are reasonably well established. What is not clear is how far the new results go beyond the early observations of semantic processing of unattended items that led to the formulation of the attenuation version of filter theory (Treisman, 1960, 1964a).

The effect is typically a small one: in 12 papers (4 measuring galvanic skin responses, 4 measuring target detection, and 4 measuring biased interpretation of a concurrent attended homonym) reasonable estimates of the proportion of trials showing semantic processing of unattended words ranged from about 2% to about 38% and averaged 16% (Bookbinder & Osman, 1979; Corteen & Dunn,

1974; Corteen & Wood, 1972; Dawson & Schell, 1982; Johnston & Wilson, 1980; Lackner & Garrett, 1972; MacKay, 1973; Moray & O'Brien, 1967; Newstead & Dennis, 1979; Treisman & Geffen, 1967; Treisman & Riley, 1969; Wardlaw & Kroll, 1976). The evidence suffices to reject the null hypothesis that stimuli on an unattended channel are never processed semantically. It appears quite insufficient to justify the acceptance of the converse null hypothesis, that attention does not affect perception.

The same conclusion applies to other demonstrated failures of selective attention, including the elicitation of Stroop-like effects by stimuli at some distance from the focus of attention (Gatti & Egeth, 1978; Eriksen & Eriksen, 1974; Eriksen & Hoffman, 1973; Eriksen & Schultz, 1979). Here again, one may choose to be impressed either by the fact that irrelevant stimuli are processed, sometimes and to some degree, or by the remarkable ability to focus visual attention without moving the eyes. Indeed, the fact that the effectiveness of irrelevant stimuli often varies with their distance from the relevant stimuli appears to support some form of early selection, although the observed interference has been cited as evidence for automatic processing.

On the other hand, there is evidence that appears inconsistent with complete semantic processing on every trial. Treisman and Riley (1969) compared the detection of a target defined by a physical property (voice quality) and by a semantic category (digit rather than letter). The physically defined targets were always detected, even when they appeared on a rejected channel; but the direction of attention had a very large effect on the detection of semantically defined targets. Johnston and Dark (1982) showed a clear difference between attended and unattended auditory words in the degree to which they primed one meaning of occasional visually presented homonyms. Perhaps the most dramatic contrast is one of the first reported (Cherry, 1953), that between detection of a change of voice in the unattended message (almost inevitable) and detection of a change of language (almost impossible). The effects of attention on semantic processing in these studies cannot easily be attributed to factors of response or memory.

The Category Effect

The second line of evidence for late selection is known as the category effect. This effect was initially observed by Brand (1971) and then extended and analyzed in an impressive series of studies (Egeth *et al.*, 1972; Gleitman & Jonides, 1976, 1978; Jonides & Gleitman, 1972, 1976; Taylor, 1978). The essential result is that it is much easier to find any letter among digits, or any digit among letters than it is to find either a specified digit or a specified letter among items of the same category. In some studies, although not in others (Francolini & Egeth, 1979), the target item "pops out" of an array of distractors of a different category and the display size function is flat. The category effect has often been taken to imply that the category label (digit or letter) is produced automatically and in parallel for all items in the search display. An item of the target category could then be distinguished from its background by a category code, just as a red target can be segregated by its color from a field of blue distractors.

It appears possible to account for the category effect without invoking the radical assumption that all items in a display are automatically encoded to a semantic level. Assume instead that a highly familiar and perceptually unitized item that has been adopted as a target has a high probability of attracting attention in a field of distractors—much as a red item does in a field of other colors— provided that the distractors are not confusable with the target and that they do not compete with it in attracting attention. In this view, "pop out" or very rapid search is the normal state of affairs with targets that are simple, familiar, and adequately distinguishable from the background items. Another condition for rapid search is that the distractors should also be familiar, perhaps because unfamiliar characters attract attention (Richards & Reicher, 1978; Reicher, Snyder, & Richards, 1976). What requires explanation, then, is not why a target digit is found quickly in a field of letters, but why it is so hard to find in a field of digits, assuming that discriminability of these simple shapes is approximately equal within and between categories.

A possible explanation was suggested by Deutsch (1977), who pointed out that the categories of digits and letters are small, and that the associative connections among their members are exceptionally strong. Because of these internal associations, the designation of any digit or letter as a target is likely to prime all members of its category (Taylor, 1978). As a consequence, items other than the target will tend to attract and to hold attention, almost as if they were also targets. We assume that a distractor that has attracted attention will only be rejected by time-consuming further analysis, thus slowing down the search. A target digit is hard to find among other digits because they compete with it for attention. The search for a digit among letters is fast because the letters have not been primed, not because they are all simultaneously coded as letters. As Deutsch (1977) noted, the involuntary spread of priming from the target to other members of its category could explain the well-known "oh–zero" effect. A target that has been designated as "zero" is harder to find among digits than among letters and the same target when designated as "oh" is harder to find among letters than among digits (Jonides & Gleitman, 1972). This observation is easily explained as a consequence of the spread of priming from a designated target to other members of its category.

A crucial prediction of this analysis has been tested and confirmed. When the subject is searching for target digits among digits, an isolated trial on which the background items are letters yields a "pop-out" effect (Gleitman & Jonides, 1978). However, this effect is abolished when the subject is assigned a dual-search set, for example, "Search for *D* or *7*." In that case, an isolated trial in which the target digit appears on a background of letters does not yield unusually fast detection. The elimination of "pop out" is expected because the dual set primes items in both categories.

There is much evidence for the key assumption that the designation of a target primes its associates, and that rejection of primed distractors is slower than rejection of unprimed ones. For example, Bruce (1979) has shown that subjects instructed to look for a picture of one politician are relatively slow to reject pictures of other well-known political figures. A similar analysis can be applied to other studies that have demonstrated facilitatory or disruptive effects of semantic categories in search (Henderson & Chard, 1978; Karlin & Bower, 1976), or "automatic" encoding of irrelevant words in categorization (Shaffer & La-Berge, 1979). The only mechanism that is required to explain these observations is the automatic priming of words that are associated with the target of search. Primed items, we suppose, are recognized faster and are more likely to attract and hold attention than unprimed ones. An alternative view, compatible with Eriksen and Schultz's (1979) analysis of search tasks, is that members of the target category elicit response tendencies that must be suppressed. (Other studies that make similar points are reviewed by Rabbitt, Chapter 7, this volume). Semantic effects in search could perhaps be used to probe the organization of LTM, much as the release from proactive inhibition has been used for the same purpose (Wickens, 1970). We conclude, contrary to many discussions in the literature, that the category effect does not provide compelling proof that category labels are produced automatically and in parallel for all items in an array.

Subliminal Perception

The third source of support for the notion of automatic semantic encoding, the demonstration of semantic encoding of material that is presented subliminally, is only indirectly related to the issue of selective attention, but is nevertheless quite suggestive. The revival of interest in subliminal perception is due in large part to some widely discussed experiments by Allport (1977) and Marcel (1983; Marcel & Patterson, 1978), in which stimuli that the subject does not consciously "see" as distinct objects, let alone recognize, nevertheless prime semantic associates. Priming by subliminal words has been shown to affect the speed of lexical decisions (Balota, 1983, Fowler, Wolford, Slade, & Tassinary, 1981; Marcel, 1983), Stroop performance (Marcel, 1983), and picture naming (McCauley, Parmelee, Sperber, & Carr, 1980). A new "New Look" is arising (Dixon, 1981) 30 years after the first flurry of excitement about subliminal perception in the 1950s.

The history of the first "New Look" suggests that the provocative observations of semantic processing of subliminal stimuli will be subjected to searching, often hostile scrutiny (e.g., Merikle, 1982). We are not here concerned with the validity of the positive results. Our concern is with the significance of these results, if they are valid, with respect to the issues of automaticity and attention. Would they demonstrate complete automaticity of perceptual analysis and support late selection? We are not sure. The reason for doubt is simply that demonstrated subliminal effects indicate a dissociation between perception and consciousness that is not necessarily equivalent to a dissociation between perception and attention. In the wave of studies published since 1975, the relevant stimuli have been rendered subliminal by a pattern mask, often presented dichoptically. To establish that the presentation is subliminal, the experimenter ensures that the subjective experience of a display that includes a word cannot be discriminated from the experience produced by the mask on its own. The mask, however, is focally attended. Any demonstration that an undetected aspect of an attended stimulus can be semantically encoded is theoretically important, but a proof of complete automaticity would require more. Specifically, the priming effects of a masked stimulus should be the same regardless of whether or not that stimulus is attended, and regardless of the number of stimuli simultaneously presented. These predictions have yet to be tested. Until they are confirmed, observations of subliminal effects will bear on the relation of perception and attention to consciousness, but not necessarily on the relation of perception to attention.

The Display-Board Model of the Mind and the Explanation of Filtering

What is the outcome of perceptual processing? And what is selected by selective attention? For filter theory, perceptual processing consists of tests and measurements on messages that originate in events or objects in the environment. Attention selects for detailed processing one of these messages, which is identified by the "channel" on which it is delivered. The view that selective attention is concerned with messages (Broadbent, 1958), inputs (Treisman, 1969), or perceptual objects (Kahneman, 1973) is consistent with naive phenomenology. In terms of everyday language, the perceiver "listens to that voice" or "looks at that spot."

Other analyses of information processing on the other hand, have emphasized identification and labeling, at the expense of any contact with the phenomenology of object perception. As we shall see, the emphasis on identification has important implications for models of attention. Identification requires structures that are tuned for the detection of specific events. In the standard models of identification, properties and familiar objects or events (recurrent clusters of properties) are all represented by connected nodes in LTM. These nodes are assumed to be activated by the presence of an appropriate stimulus or by excitation derived from other nodes, and mental life consists of the succession of patterns of activation in LTM. This view has perhaps been articulated most clearly by Shiffrin and Schneider (1977) and by Johnston and Dark (1982), but it is implicitly accepted in many discussions of cognitive processes. We call it the *display-board model of the mind*. Imagine a board with numerous bulbs that can be individually turned on, perhaps at different brightness levels. The presentation of an object will turn on the lights that designate its various properties, the light that designates its name, and perhaps also the lights that encode associated events, intentions, and responses. In the version of the model that Shiffrin and Schneider (1977) have developed, the activity that is automatically produced by a stimulus is very short-lived unless it is supported by internal sources of excitation, such as intentions or expectations.

The display-board model provides an elegantly simple representation of the hierarchical encoding of stimuli, of the spreading of activation through the associative network, and of the permanently or temporarily lowered activation thresholds of selected nodes. It provides a useful model for the mechanisms of selective set: expectancies and late selection. Expectancies facilitate the activation of particular psychological pathways (Posner, 1978) or alter the activation thresholds of nodes in LTM (LaBerge, 1975; Shiffrin & Schneider, 1977). Other selective effects occur at a later stage of controlled retrieval, comparison and decision, which is concerned with the production of responses appropriate to the subject's intentions and circumstances.

The existence of expectancies and response selection is not controversial. Indeed, the notion of a dictionary with units that have variable thresholds had been used earlier to explain apparent failures of perfect filtering within the general context of a filter theory (Broadbent, 1971; Treisman, 1960, 1964b). However, filter theory also included a selective device that could be controlled by the elementary physical properties detected in an early, parallel, and automatic stage of processing. What devices in the new display-board models perform the function of a filter in a filter theory? There appear to have been two answers to this question, which put the burden respectively on the expectancy mechanism and on the late-selection device.

LaBerge (1976) proposed that attention can be directed to a particular node in the information-processing sequence, with the effect that the activation of that node by appropriate signals is facilitated. It is easily seen that such a mechanism could explain, for example, the speedy detection of the word HOUSE. LaBerge also proposed that attention to the node that represents the feature *red* could allow the subject to select the red letters in a display. Our impression is, however, that in this system attending to the *red* node can facilitate only the perception that there is red in the display, but not the processing of other properties of the red items, for example, the reading of the word HOUSE if it is printed in red. An expectancy device can search, but it cannot filter.

For a further demonstration of the independence of filtering and expectancies, consider the ancient studies of selective listening in which the subject was instructed to shadow a message presented to the right ear and to ignore a message simultaneously presented to the left ear. This task is easy even when the messages consist of randomly selected words so that the listener cannot predict the words that will be included in the relevant message. Effective filtering clearly does not require the support of expectancies.

An alternative approach attributes filtering to a late-selection device (Duncan, 1980; Shiffrin & Schneider, 1977). According to such models, the same device functions in both the following tasks: (1) "Shadow all you hear in your left ear, animal names as well as furniture items." (2) "Shadow all the animal names, regardless of which ear you hear them in." Performance would be mediated in both tasks by late selection, perhaps aided in the second task by priming of the animal names. This analysis suggests that performance with semantic selection should be better than in filtering by ear, but in fact selection by ear is very much easier. It is a major advantage of filter theory that it can explain this fact, by the assumption that the control of selection by a physical attribute is assigned to a preattentive system, whereas selection by semantic category requires attentive processing. The rule that selection by stimulus set is easier than by response set (Broadbent, 1970) is surely one of the most salient and robust observations of the filtering paradigm (Johnston & Heinz, 1978, 1979; Keren, 1976; Treisman & Riley, 1969). There is also a clear difference in the latency and origin of the components of the evoked response that are affected by stimulus set and by response set (Hink, Hillyard, & Benson, 1978; see also Harter and Aine, Chapter 8, this volume). Late-selection models provide no explanation beyond an attempt to dismiss observed differences in selective efficacy as a "purely empirical matter" (Duncan, 1981, p. 92).

There are two related problems for the current theories of attention that take the display board as their dominant model and selective set as their dominant paradigm. First, the great simplification of experimental designs has lent credence to theories that do not adequately explain the basic observations of the more complex filtering paradigm. Second, it appears difficult to represent *all* of perception by the selective activation of semipermanent structures in LTM. Objects can be perceived without being identified, and the various properties of a perceived object are bound together by more than mere temporal synchrony. The display-board model provides no simple way of representing the perceptual unity of objects and events, and we therefore suspect that it is not an adequate model for either perception or attention.

New Experimental Tests of Automaticity

The previous sections outlined and assessed the evidence that led to the hypothesis of complete automaticity of perceptual analysis. In the second part of the present chapter we describe some specific tests of this hypothesis. We begin with a discussion of some conceptual issues that arise in devising such tests.

Criteria of Automaticity

There is general agreement on the criteria by which a mental operation can be recognized as automatic (Hasher & Zacks, 1979; Logan, 1980; Posner, 1978; Regan, 1981; see also Schneider et al., Chapter 1, this volume). An *automatic process* is involuntary; that is, it can be triggered without a supporting intention and, once started, cannot be stopped intentionally. An automatic process does not draw on general resources, is not subject to interference from attended activities, and does not interfere with such activities. In addition, automatic processes do not interfere with one another, and several such processes can operate in parallel without capacity limits. Finally, some authors note that automatic processes are often unconscious. The criteria probably covary in most situations, but they may be separable. Regan (1981) has noted a particularly important distinction between two senses of "automatic": involuntary and effortless. These need not coincide: an effortful activity can be elicited without voluntary control (Paap & Ogden, 1981).

Three levels of automaticity can be distinguished in perception: (1) An act of perceptual processing is *strongly automatic* if it is neither facilitated by focusing attention on a stimulus, nor impaired by diverting attention from it (Shiffrin, 1975; Shiffrin & Grantham, 1974). (2) It is *partially automatic* if it is normally completed even when attention is diverted from the stimulus, but can be speeded or facilitated by attention (LaBerge, 1973, 1975). (3) A perceptual process is *occasionally automatic* if it generally requires attention but can sometimes be completed without it.

Strong and partial automaticity have not been sharply distinguished by proponents of automatic perceptual processing; statements that appear to imply a belief in the stronger claim are often found in close proximity to statements that allow for some beneficial effects of attention (Duncan, 1980; Posner, 1978; Shiffrin, 1976, 1977; Shiffrin & Schneider, 1977). Unfortunately, partial automaticity is quite difficult to prove or reject. It differs only in degree from the occasional automaticity allowed by believers in early selection (Johnston & Heinz, 1978; Treisman, 1960, 1964a; Kahneman, 1973). The claim that *all* presented items automatically activate nodes representing their identity (Posner, 1978; Shiffrin & Schneider, 1977) is difficult to distinguish experimentally from the possibility that only some do so, particularly when the speed of identification is allowed to vary with attention. What remains of the theoretical debate is a significant difference in emphasis. Early-selection theories emphasize contrasts in the depth of processing of attended and unattended stimuli, whereas proponents of partial automaticity stress the possibility of deep and extensive analysis without conscious attention. It is easier for theorists on each side to embarass one another than to prove one another wrong, and even the embarrassment is fairly mild because the contrasting positions are not held dogmatically (Shiffrin, 1977). The experiments we report in this section certainly conflict with claims of strong automaticity; we believe that the consistent attention effects that we obtain in a variety of paradigms impose restrictions even on milder claims concerning the automaticity of perceptual processing.

Filtering in the Stroop Design

Reading familiar words is often invoked as the prototype of a highly automatized skill, and the Stroop task is often cited to illustrate the automaticity of reading. The subject tries to identify the color of the ink in which a word is printed, but the shape of the word quickly and automatically activates its node or logogen, thus causing interference (Morton, 1969; Posner & Snyder, 1975). Stroop interference demonstrates the automaticity of reading because subjects appear to read uncontrollably even when it is in their best interest not to do so. That reading the color words in the Stroop task is involuntary we can surely grant. However, we question the far-reaching implications that are drawn for the automaticity of semantic processing. In this section, we show that an attended stimulus produces much more Stroop interference than an unattended one. In the next section, we demonstrate that potential sources of Stroop effects are subject to mutual interference.

Imagine a display that is tachistoscopically presented. The display consists of a square and a circle that appear unpredictably on either side of the fixation point. The words RED and GREEN are printed, respectively, in the circle and in the square. The word RED is printed in green ink, and the word GREEN is printed in red ink. Now imagine a display that is similar in all respects to the one just described, except that the words RED and GREEN exchange places, so that the color in which each word is printed corresponds to the meaning of that word. Consider a subject who is assigned the task of naming, as quickly as possible, the color of the ink in the circle. The correct response is *red* in both cases. Will the response be made more easily and quickly to one of these displays than to the other?

The answer people give to this question varies strongly with psychological sophistication. The lay person merely smiles because the result is intuitively obvious. Not so most attention theorists. Indeed, it is not at all obvious how a theory that contains the strong version of automaticity can explain a difference between the two conditions. Note that the subject is assumed to be fixating at the center, so that the quality of the sensory inputs is the same for both cards. If reading is automatic, then the logogens for *red* and *green* must both be activated

TABLE 2.2

Mean Correct Reaction Time and Percentage Errors for Different
Conditions of Color-Word Naming in the Stroop Task[a]

Conditions[b]	Mean reaction time (msec)	Errors (%)
Neutral–neutral	906	3
Neutral–compatible	944	4
Neutral–conflicting	956	2
Compatible–neutral	858	1
Conflicting–neutral	1108	15

[a]From Kahneman and Henik (1981).
[b]The first word in each pair controlled the color-naming response.

by the printed words, equally on the two trials. Any facilitation or interference
that is produced by such automatic activation should also be the same.

Several versions of this experiment have been run (Kahneman & Henik,
1981). The results clearly favor the common-sense answer. In one of the experiments, the words in the display could be neutral, compatible with the correct
response, or conflicting. The results are given in Table 2.2. They show significant interference by a color word (even a compatible one, in this case) that is
distant from the area to which attention is directed. However, this effect is quite
small in comparison to the effect of an incompatible word that is physically
conjoined with the relevant color.

These results lend themselves readily to interpretation as an example of filtering in a discrete task. As in any instance of filtering, several stages of processing
are involved. The relevant circle is found at an early stage. Attention is paid to it.
The allocation of attention to the circle facilitates the processing of all aspects of
that object and their associated responses. In particular, attention facilitates the
responses that belong to the set of color names because these responses have also
been primed by the color-naming instruction. Thus, there appears to be no
specific control over the reading of the attended word, which is in that sense
automatic. This automatic process, however, is shown to depend on the allocation of attention by the finding that a conflicting word in the unattended square
produces much less interference than the same word in the attended circle. It
seems appropriate to ask how automatic an automatic process is, if it depends on
attention. These results are obviously incompatible with the claim that the reading of words in the Stroop task is strongly automatic. A similar conclusion has
been reached by Francolini and Egeth (1980) on the basis of rather similar
experiments.

The interpretation that we suggest assumes that visual attention is especially
effective when it selects an input (Treisman, 1969) or an object (Kahneman,

1973). After an object has been selected, an additional selective operation must be invoked to determine which of its properties will be allowed to control responses. In general, the priming of a response category is enough to do most of the work of selection because different properties of an object are rarely linked to different members of the same class of responses. Thus, the tendency to read a neutral word is relatively weak in the Stroop situation because the subject is set to say color words. Color names are much more likely to be read than other words, because they are primed by the task. In general, interference is expected to occur when an irrelevant property of the selected object evokes a strongly primed response. A similar argument can be applied to parts of objects as well as to their properties. Attention to irrelevant parts of relevant objects is obligatory. The visual suffix effect, and perhaps the auditory suffix effect as well, could be interpreted in the same vein: If an irrelevant member of a relevant group of items is not perceptually separated from its relevant neighbors, it is processed as if it were relevant (Kahneman, 1973; Kahneman & Henik, 1977, 1981).

Visual filtering is a robust effect, which we have demonstrated in several experiments. In one of the studies in this series we presented two words on either side of the fixation point. One of the words was always printed entirely in black. The other word was printed in colored ink, and the subject's task was to report that color. Here again, Stroop interference was much more pronounced when the colored ink and an incompatible color name were conjoined than when they were spatially separated (Kahneman & Henik, 1981).

The results of these experiments illustrate the concept of filtering in visual presentation. They present some difficulties both for the claim that reading is strongly automatic and for the interpretation of Stroop interferences as evidence of such automaticity. The major conclusion is that it is essential to distinguish selection of inputs, or objects, from selection of properties. As we have seen, observers are capable of efficient rejection of irrelevant objects, but the irrelevant properties (and perhaps parts) of an attended object cannot be prevented from contacting their nodes and from activating irrelevant responses. The distinction between selection of objects (or inputs) and selection of properties (or analyzers; Treisman, 1969) seems salient and fundamental; yet it is often ignored in psychological research and theory.

The difference between objects and properties was lost to psychology with the adoption of the ambiguous term "stimulus": both an object (for example, a red O) and a property (redness or circularity) can be called a stimulus. In the behaviorist tradition, the term was applied to "whatever controls a response." Because discriminative responses are controlled by properties ("Peck the key if the cage is illuminated, not if it is dark"), it is most natural in that tradition to think of stimuli primarily in terms of properties and to ignore the notion of objects altogether. This legacy has influenced the study of information processing. It is illustrated by treatments that interpret Stroop interference as a failure of selective attention and as evidence of the automaticity of processing. In fact, the Stroop effect only demonstrates that people do not easily ignore irrelevant *properties* of an attended object. On the other hand, our results further support the conclusion of other studies of filtering that irrelevant *objects* can be rejected quite effectively.

The Dilution Effect

The series of experiments discussed in the preceding section tested whether automatic reading is affected by the voluntary direction of attention. We now turn to another way of testing the notion of automatic activation, which we label *the dilution effect*. The experiments discussed in this section test whether automatic reading is affected by the mere presence of other stimuli. According to the strong version of automaticity, the activation of a node by a familiar stimulus does not compete with the concurrent processing of other objects in the field. It is therefore of interest to ask whether the reading of color words in the Stroop situation is impaired by the presence of other irrelevant stimuli. The strong claim of automaticity allows no mechanism, other than sensory interference, that could produce such an effect.

This question has been studied in a series of experiments (Kahneman & Chajczyk, 1983). In a typical study the subjects are shown for 200 msec a colored bar centered on the fixation point and are asked to name its color. A single word is presented on some trials above or below the bar. The word is sometimes unrelated to the color-naming task, sometimes congruent with the correct response for that trial, and sometimes it is the name of another color. As has been previously reported (Dyer, 1973; Gatti & Egeth, 1978), the presentation of a color name affects the speed at which the color of the bar is named. Interference and facilitation are both obtained, although the magnitude of the effects is smaller than when the subjects are asked to name the ink in which a color word is printed.

The occurrence of Stroop interference in this situation represents at least a partial failure of selective attention to objects. The relevant color bar is presented at the fixation point and the subject is encouraged to focus attention on that area; the word is irrelevant to the task and its reading is presumably involuntary and is automatic in that sense. To determine whether this reading is also automatic in another sense, we used a minimal variation of display size: In several *dual* conditions, a neutral word was added to the display on the other side of the relevant color bar. Our question was whether the presentation of the added neutral word would affect the amount of interference or facilitation produced by the color word.

The basic outcome of this series of studies is illustrated in Table 2.3. The 12 subjects in this particular experiment had 48 trials in each of the six conditions.

TABLE 2.3

Mean Color-Naming Times for Each of Six Conditions of a Stroop Interference Task[a]

Condition	Mean reaction time (msec)	Color-word effect	Dilution
Single conflicting	682	72	—
Conflicting–neutral	650[b]	36	36
Single neutral	610	—	—
Dual neutral	614[c]	—	—
Single congruent	561	49	—
Congruent–neutral	585[d]	29	20

[a]From Kahneman and Chajczyk (1983, Experiment 1).
[b]$t = 3.11, p < .01$.
[c]ns.
[d]$t = 3.01, p < .01$.

As can be seen by comparing the conflicting and congruent conditions to the neutral condition, the color words have a substantial effect on the speed with which the color of the bar is named. We use the term *color-word impact* for the difference in color-naming time between conflicting and congruent conditions. The impact of a single word is 121 msec; it is reduced to 65 msec by the concurrent presentation of a neutral word on the opposite side of the bar. This pattern of results defines the dilution effect: the neutral word dilutes both the interference and the facilitation produced by color names.

Another experiment in this series established that the dilution effect is not eliminated when the words are presented quite far from the fovea. Only conflicting color names were used in this experiment, to ensure the subjects' incentive to avoid attending to the color word. Stroop interference was 74 msec for a word shown 2° above or below the bar; the diluted interference at that distance was 27 msec. The corresponding values at 4° eccentricity were 40 and 19 msec. The larger distance was associated with less interference but the proportional dilution did not change significantly. The dilution effect is thus unlikely to arise from peripheral interactions between the words. A central effect is involved.

Some words cause greater dilution than others, but we do not yet have an explanation of this variation, which was discovered accidentally. Most of our experiments used a small set of colors (red, green, blue, and brown) and of neutral words (cute, most, long, and shoe). We accidentally discovered a much smaller effect with another set of words (shy, few, time, angle, and brave). An experiment was then run to establish whether the dilution effect is the rule or the exception when a representative pool of words is used. Sixty high-frequency words were selected from the Kučera–Francis norms (40 four-letter and 20 five-letter words). In this experiment the displays were presented on a color terminal

(Intecolor 8001) controlled by a computer that randomly assigned words to experimental conditions. The dilution effect was replicated: Adding a neutral word slowed color naming in the congruent condition (from 588 to 607 msec) and speeded color naming in the conflicting condition (from 706 to 669 msec). Both results were highly significant.

A dilution effect can be obtained even when the diluting stimuli are not words at all. We found substantial dilution by a row of Xs, although less than by a neutral word. The demonstration of dilution with unreadable stimuli eliminates conflict or coactivation in the reading system (Miller, 1982) as an interpretation of dilution. The pattern of results looks much like distraction; the diluting stimulus distracts the subject from the color word, and a neutral word is a more effective distractor than is a row of Xs. This distraction effect is paradoxical, however, because it occurs entirely outside the focus of attention. Clearly, the dilution effect is not compatible with the idea that the reading of peripherally presented words is automatic and free of capacity limits.

Intentional Reading and an Early-Interference Effect

It seems from the Stroop studies that words presented outside the focus of attention do not automatically achieve their full potential to affect behavior. The impact of an irrelevant word, whether for good or for bad, is reduced by the presence of other objects in the field. We now ask what happens when reading is the primary task. Is intentional reading also subject to interference from the mere presence of other stimuli? If so, what variables determine the interference?

In the following series of experiments, we show that intentional reading of a single word is impaired by the presence of any other object in the field whenever there is prior uncertainty about their locations. Interference occurs even when the competing object is so different from the word that selection should be no problem. Thus we further limit the concept of automatic reading: The response to a word is affected by the presence of other visual objects in a manner that makes it unlikely that the printed word automatically activates its perceptual and motor representation in LTM.

Filtering Cost in Reading

In several experiments (Kahneman, Treisman, & Burkell, 1983), our subjects' task was simply to read as quickly as possible a word that appeared unpredictably above or below the fixation point. On half the trials, another object was presented on the opposite side of fixation; the resulting delay in reading time was measured. We label this delay a filtering cost because it appears when attention must be narrowed down onto one of the stimuli presented to permit a specific response.

In one version of the experiment, two words were presented and subjects were told to read whichever word they wished. If reading is entirely automatic, the response to these dual displays could only be faster than the reading of a single word because the more rapidly processed member of the pair should be read. In fact, the presentation of two words caused a slight, but highly consistent slowing of the reading time: from 570 to 595 msec. The distance of the words from the fixation point was not critical. An interference effect of 18 msec was still found when the nearest contours of the interacting words were 3.6° apart across the fovea.

Does the interference arise between competing nodes within the lexicon or display board, or does it depend simply on the presence of another object in the field? In another condition we used a stimulus that in its visual features seemed as different as possible from a word and could not conceivably draw on lexical resources or compete, either phonologically or semantically, with reading the word: a word-sized patch of randomly placed black dots. Again we presented a word above or below fixation, with dots in the other location on half the trials. Again we found a delay of the same extent: 34 msec. A similar result was obtained with a variety of colored shapes as interfering stimuli.

The effect seemed sufficiently surprising to warrant further investigation. We ran a number of variants of the experiment to narrow down the possible interpretations. When the dots were always shown at the fovea with the word above or below them, the delay of reading was much less than in the earlier experiment (only 10 msec), despite the fact that the interfering stimulus was now spatially closer to the word. This result makes peripheral interaction an unlikely explanation. When the word was consistently at the fovea, there was no interference from dots above or below it. When there was spatial uncertainty, however, interference was inversely related to the distance separating the word from the dots but independent of the size of the patch of dots. The importance of spatial uncertainty implicates a central attentional factor, and the interfering effect of unreadable objects eliminates conflict between reading responses as an explanation. Neither peripheral interference nor interference between central nodes in the lexical display board seem apt accounts of the 30-msec delay.

Reading, Attention, and Search

If the interference is indeed attentional, precuing the location of the word should eliminate it. The following experiment tested this prediction. We also changed the nature of the irrelevant stimuli to test the generality of the phenomenon. Finally, we varied the number of distractors to determine whether the delay increases with display size. A color terminal was used to show displays comprising one 3-letter word in white uppercase letters and a variable number of shapes, each in a different color and each subtending about the same visual angle as a word. These stimuli were randomly located in any of six possible positions arranged in a clock face around the fixation point. Two conditions were compared: (1) In the precued condition, the critical display was preceded 100 msec earlier by three white dots in the position that the word would occupy; (2) in the control condition, one dot appeared in each of the six possible stimulus locations, giving the same temporal warning but no information about the location of the word. We found that (1) in the control condition, the colored shapes produced the expected delay in reading the word; (2) moreover, the delay increased with the number of irrelevant objects, averaging 14 msec per extra object; and (3) the delay was completely eliminated when a precue informed the subject where the word would appear. This clearly ties the interference to attention because the precue could have no effect on peripheral sensory interaction between the word and the colored objects. There was no time for eye movements to occur because the critical displays were masked after 150 msec (i.e., 250 msec after onset of the cue).

The findings are surprising because search for a target defined by a simple feature normally shows no effect of display size (Treisman & Gelade, 1980). In all the experiments described so far, the word differed from the irrelevant stimuli in several obvious features. Why then did we obtain an effect of display size on reading time? The paradox may be resolved by noting that the reading task involves filtering. We pointed out earlier that filtering tasks require further analysis of attended stimuli beyond their detection in order to determine the appropriate response. In search tasks, on the other hand, the detection of the target suffices to trigger a response without further analysis.

Another experiment was designed to compare filtering and search tasks in the same displays. The displays were similar to those of the uncued condition in the previous experiment, but four-letter words were used, and there was no masking. In the reading condition, subjects read the word as before. The results replicated previous studies of the filtering cost, with substantial delays of reading, increasing with the number of irrelevant colored shapes. There was also a detection condition, in which the word was replaced by a colored shape on half the trials; the subjects indicated the presence of a word by pressing a key. The number of colored shapes had very little effect on the speed of positive detection responses. The qualitative difference between filtering and search suggests that detection may require much less processing than reading. We can detect a target without attending to it and perhaps even without locating it in the display (Treisman & Gelade, 1980). Reading, on the other hand, appears to require both that the word be found and that attention be directed to its location. These extra operations take longer when additional distractors are present. The difference between reading and detection is clearly established when the vocabulary of stimuli and responses is large. Whether the same rules apply to constrained vocabularies (digits or letters) is a matter for further research.

Attention and Object Integrality

We have argued that attention selects *objects* in their spatial locations, not properties or internal nodes. Thus response conflict in the Stroop task is greater when the irrelevant stimulus evoking the competing response is perceived as part of the attended object (Kahneman & Henik, 1981). Filtering costs, on the other hand, should be reduced when the relevant and irrelevant stimuli are perceived as belonging to the same object, if we are correct in attributing the cost to competition for attention and not to competition for response. The next experiments (Treisman, Kahneman, & Burkell, 1983) used an interfering object in the shape of a colored frame. The frame could appear either around the word that was to be read or on the opposite side of fixation. Peripheral sensory interactions could only be greater when the frame was close to the word, but the reading delay was 42 msec when the frame was separated from the word and 21 msec when it surrounded the word. The result confirms the conclusion that the delay arises from competition between objects for the control of attention.

We have seen that a separated frame delayed reading more than did a frame that surrounded the word. Did the separate frame attract processing resources from the word? On such a hypothesis one would also expect the frame to be better perceived in the separate than in the combined display. In contrast, our analysis suggests that competition between the word and the frame should be less severe in the combined display. Competition is between objects; there is less of it between different parts of an object and perhaps none between its different features (Kahneman, 1973; Treisman, 1969). Consequently, the frame should be perceived more easily when it surrounds the attended word than when it is separate.

A dual-task experiment was designed to test the alternative hypotheses. The subjects were required on each trial to read the word as quickly as they could; this was the primary task. The frame was positioned either just above or just below fixation, so that one of its horizontal edges passed through the fixation point. A small gap was made in the fixated edge, to the left or to the right of fixation. The subjects' secondary task was to report the position of that gap. The exposure was followed by a field that included a thin masking stripe of random black and white squares that covered the central edge and made the gap less detectable without masking the word. The duration of exposure of the word and frame was varied continuously by a staircase method to maintain the error rate in gap location at 25%.

As before, the reading delay was greater by 17 msec when frame and word were separate than when they were together. The interesting finding was that subjects also made significantly more errors in locating the gap when the frame was separate (27%) than when it was around the attended word (16%). Thus, the frame and the word were both better perceived when they were combined in one perceptual object than when they formed two separate objects. Hoffman, Nelson, and Houck (1983) report a related finding, that it is easier to divide attention between two stimuli when they are spatially close together than when they are distant. In the present experiment, the distance between the gap and the word was constant, and we varied the belongingness or integrality of the two stimuli. Any account of filtering costs must incorporate the notion of unitary versus separate objects.

Selective Attention under Masking

In a final series of experiments, we looked at the accuracy of reading the relevant word when it was followed by a mask as a function of whether the word was presented alone or with another stimulus. If the filtering costs in the experiments so far described reflect an early perceptual interference, we should expect the presence of an irrelevant stimulus also to reduce accuracy under masking. If, on the other hand, the interference was due to some form of competition to initiate and to control responses, interference could vanish in a situation in which accuracy was stressed rather than speed.

Stimuli for this experiment were presented on a graphics display, permitting accurate control of exposure duration, and were immediately followed by a pattern mask. The subject was instructed to read an uppercase word from a display that could contain a single word, two different words, or an uppercase word and a distractor, which could be a scrambled word, a row of X's or a word in lower case. The items could appear in two positions, above and below fixation. The duration of exposure was varied for each subject, so as to maintain average accuracy (over all conditions) at 50%. The percentage of correct responses in the different conditions is shown in Table 2.4. The decrement of 10% caused by the row of Xs was highly significant; performance in the two other distractor conditions was almost halved. In particular, selection between a word and a nonword, both in uppercase, was nearly impossible under conditions of pattern masking. To a first approximation, it appears that subjects were only able to process a single item, and that they could attempt to choose the appropriate location only when the distractor was marked by salient physical characteristics (the repeated shapes of the row of Xs).

The results are difficult to reconcile with the ideas that lexical access is automatic and that limits to concurrent perceptual processing only concern the number of active nodes that can be checked or retrieved within the lexical memory (Shiffrin & Schneider, 1977). In particular, scrambled letters do not access a lexical node because they do not form a word. Selection should therefore be easy because only the node corresponding to the relevant word is active. Although these conditions appear optimal for late selection to operate, selective reading was apparently almost impossible. We know of few other results that provide such strong indications of the limitations of late selection.

TABLE 2.4

Percentage of Correct Responses for Each
Condition in Reading One Word Followed
by a Mask

No distractor	
Single word	63
Two words	62
Distractor present	
Lowercase word	38
Scrambled uppercase word	35
Row of Xs	53

Two additional experiments were run to test the possibility of semantic selection (Allport, 1977; Marcel, 1983). Subjects were asked to indicate whether or not a display contained an animal name. Reaction time was used as the measure in one of the experiments, and accuracy (with a pattern mask) in the other. The mean positive reaction time and percentage correct (adjusted for chance success) in the various conditions of the two experiments were as follows: When no distractor was shown, accuracy was 64% and reaction time 826 msec for a single word; when a distractor was shown, these values were 34% and 1098 msec for a word and 49% and 929 msec for a row of Xs.

The conclusions of the previous experiment are confirmed. If two words can automatically register their identity or their meaning, it is hard to explain the marked interference that is observed in these studies.

Discussion and Conclusions

We have reported the following main results: (1) The impact of color words in the Stroop situation varies with the spatial allocation of attention; a color word in a rejected location has little effect on color naming. (2) The impact of a color word on color naming is reduced by the presence of words or other shapes in the field. Thus, an effect that resembles attentional competition can be observed outside the intended focus of attention. (3) The intentional reading of a word is also retarded (30 msec, approximately) by the presence of other objects in the field. This interference occurs even when the target word and the interfering objects are highly discriminable. It is an attentional effect that is completely eliminated by precuing the relevant location and is reduced when the potentially interfering stimluus and the word can be attended as a unit. (4) The ability to report a word that is followed by a pattern mask is severely impaired by the concurrent presentation of a random string of letters in another position; the results indicate that subjects attend to an object in a particular spatial position, not to a lexical entry activated by the word.

All these results are surprising within a framework that describes information processing in terms of automatic access to nodes in LTM. We repeatedly found that the impact of an item was affected by the intentional direction of attention or even by the mere presence of other objects in the field. Processing that might be expected to be automatic was thus shown to depend on attention. Another recurrent theme in these studies, which does not fit with a display-board model, is the obvious importance of spatial factors. Attention is assigned to objects, or to the locations that objects occupy, rather than to nodes in LTM.

We now sketch an alternative to the display-board metaphor, which is designed to cope with the evidence for filtering and for the role of objects in the control of attention. As will become clear, the proposed metaphor suggests a possible resolution for the old debate between proponents of early and of late selection.

Perceptual processing is equated in the display-board analogy with the temporary activation of nodes in long-term conceptual memory. Instead, we suggest that perception is mediated by the creation of new, temporary representations of objects and events, a perceptual analogue of *episodic* memory (Kahneman & Henik, 1981; Treisman & Schmidt, 1982). The analogy we propose is the information room of a police station. Messages constantly arrive, reporting incidents in the world outside. Some of these messages indicate the beginning of a new incident. Others provide updated information about an incident previously reported, such as the current location of a fleeing burglar, or his name if he has been identified. The information is used accordingly, to open a new file or to update an existing one. We think of the perceptual system as opening an object file when an object or event is first sensed. The initial entry and the identifying label for the file simply state the location and time. As information about the features of the object is received, it is entered in appropriate slots in the file. Color, size, shape, brightness, and direction of movement are specified early, but can be updated if and when they change. At some stage, the object may be identified by matching it to specifications in long-term perceptual memory. This allows retrieval and storage in the file of a name or category and of previously learned facts relating to the object and may also guide the accumulation of further sensory information.

We propose the notion of an object file as the representation that maintains the identity and continuity of an object perceived in a particular episode. The identity of the object is carried by the fact that information is entered on a particular file, rather than by a name or a particular enduring set of features. The object-file analogy resembles the notions of message center or blackboard proposed by other authors (Lindsay & Norman, 1972; Reddy, Erman, Fennell, & Neely, 1973; Rumelhart, 1976) as a device to combine information from different sources (context, sensory data, rules of syntax, etc.) in the perception of spoken or written words. In addition, however, it explicitly accounts for the segregation of the information pertaining to different objects. Marr (1976) and Fox (1977) introduced the related idea of "place tokens" or "object tokens" as a means of referencing particular local aggregates of features that were likely to be the precursors of perceived objects. Such a notion appears necessary to accommodate the phenomenological experience of a world comprised of coherent objects and events. It also has several advantages in dealing with the phenomena of attention:

1. The distinction between episodic tokens and semantic types may help to explain filtering. Within the present framework, it is natural to think of the object file as defined by salient physical properties of the object, including in particular the time and location of its initial appearance. The semantic knowledge associated with the object may become available in the file much later, and may not be the feature by which the content of the file is most easily accessed. The intention to select for special processing any object that possesses certain physical properties could become effective more quickly, and could be easier to follow, than an instruction to select objects that belong to a particular semantic category. This difference could account for the major line of evidence that favors early selection over late selection in attention: that selection by stimulus set is generally much easier and more effective than selection by response set.

2. The analogy helps explain why it is difficult to direct attention to a specific feature of an object. Our assumption is that attention affects the object file as a unit, whether by controlling the entry of information into it or by controlling the outflow of information from it. As a result, Stroop interference is especially severe when the color and the word belong to the same object because it appears impossible to attend to the color without simultaneously facilitating the response to the word. It also appears relatively easy to divide attention between different properties or parts of the same object, as illustrated by our combination of a reading task with the detection of a gap in a frame surrounding the word.

3. The analogy is compatible with research suggesting a crucial role for attention in the perception of objects (Treisman & Gelade, 1980). Whenever a task requires an object to be identified by a *conjunction* of properties, attention must be focused on each object in turn: search is serial, and each object is correctly identified only if it has been accurately localized. When attention is diverted or overloaded, illusory conjunctions may be formed that recombine the features of different physical objects (for example, an illusory yellow shirt generated from a yellow chair and a red shirt; Treisman & Schmidt, 1982). These mistakes could reflect confusions in keeping track of which features should be entered in each of several concurrently active object files.

4. The notion of object files suggests a possible compromise between early and late selection. The classic question of attention theory has always been whether attention controls the buildup of perceptual information, or merely selects among the responses associated with currently active percepts. In the terms of our analogy, the question is whether focusing attention on an object file facilitates the accumulation of information *in* it, the dissemination of information *from* it, or perhaps both. A possible alternative to the early-selection hypothesis is that attention (1) has no effect on the buildup of information in the object file, (2) affects only the output of object files, and (3) can be directed to an object file only by physical characteristics. Such a mechanism would be an early-selection device in the sense that its selective functions are controlled by elementary features. However, the effect of attention, as in late-selection theories, would be to control access to the executive devices that produce responses. A rather similar idea has been advanced by Eriksen and Schultz (1979) and by Posner, Davidson, and Snyder (1980) who suggested that one of the effects of attending to a location is to enhance the readiness to respond to any event in that location.

5. The suggestion that attention controls the dissemination of information from object files could be elaborated in several different ways. The simplest possibility is that the information is made

available (or conscious) on an all-or-none basis. A more complex arrangement would assign different levels of urgency or priority to the information sent from a particular object file; an attended object could be assigned high priority in this fashion. The most intriguing possibility is that the information in the object file (or different parts of that information) could be made selectively available to some agencies of the mind but not to others. The well-known study by Corteen and Dunn (1974), for example, suggested that shock-related words presented on the unattended ear in a dichotic shadowing situation can cause electrodermal responses although they have no access to the control of instrumental responses. The revival of interest in subliminal perception is also focused on a notion of dissociation (Allport, 1979; Dixon, 1981; but see also Merikle, 1982).

Dissociation phenomena are troubling because they raise doubts about the validity of our sense of personal identity. If my skin responds to the emotional significance of words that I have not seen, do *I* know the meaning of these words? There seems to be no good answer to this question. The solution to the dilemma may be to revise our criteria for the use of epistemic words such as *know, see,* or *understand.* In particular, the suggestion has been made by authors in the traditions of artificial intelligence (Hinton & Anderson, 1981; Minsky, 1980), philosophy (Dennett, 1978), and experimental psychology (Allport, 1980) that we should treat the mind as a collectivity of semi-independent entities, rather than as a single entity.

Perhaps we should take as our model of the mind a large organization, such as General Motors or the Central Intelligence Agency. Under what conditions can such an organization be said to know something? Certainly, the organization "knows" a fact if all its significant members act coherently on it. But there are many borderline cases. Does the CIA know a fact if one functionary in that organization knows it but has told nobody else or is believed by no one? Does an organization know a fact if the lower echelons act on it but without informing higher echelons that they do so? The evidence of dissociation phenomena suggests that it may at times be as difficult to assign epistemic states to individuals as it is to assign such states to organizations.

It now appears at least conceivable that future discussions of attention will be conducted within the framework of an organizational metaphor for the mind. The notion of modularity was introduced earlier in attention research (and in this chapter) to account for the surprising efficiency of performance in combining concurrent tasks that engage very different processors or resources. It may be equally helpful or necessary in accounting for dissociations in the availability of information. It is disconcerting, but perhaps also encouraging, that many of the questions with which we have been concerned for years—including the question of automaticity that is the focus of this chapter—will turn out, in such a framework, to be slightly out of focus. Some "attentional" limits may turn out to be failures in the dissemination of information rather than in its processing. Certain systems (e.g., autonomic control centers) may have access to detailed representations of states of affairs of which other systems (e.g., those controlling voluntary instrumental responses and/or conscious awareness) remain ignorant.

The participants in the debate about the automaticity of semantic processing and early selection have shared many presuppositions. In particular, they have shared the notion of a standard path of information processing and the idea that attention operates at one or more bottlenecks (or roadblocks) along that path to select the messages that should be processed further, or perhaps to attach to each message a single value of relevance. While we continue the debate within the old framework, we should remain alert to the possibility that it could soon become obsolete.

References

Allport, D. A. On knowing the meaning of words we are unable to report: The effects of visual masking. In S. Dornic (Ed.), *Attention and performance, VI*. Hillsdale, N.J.: Erlbaum, 1977.

Allport, D. A. Conscious and unconscious cognition: A computational metaphor for the mechanism of attention and integration. In L. G. Nilsson (Ed.), *Perspectives on memory research*. Hillsdale, N.J.: Erlbaum, 1979.

Allport, D. A. Patterns and actions. In G. L. Claxton (Ed.), *New directions in cognitive psychology*. London: Routledge & Kegan Paul, 1980.

Allport, D. A., Antonis, B., & Reynolds, P. On the division of attention: A disproof of the single channel hypothesis. *Quarterly Journal of Experimental Psychology*, 1972, *24*, 225–235.

Balota, D. A. Automatic semantic activation and episodic memory encoding. *Journal of Verbal Learning and Verbal Behavior*, 1983, *22*, 88–104.

Bjork, E. L. & Murray, J. T. On the nature of input channels in visual processing. *Psychological Review*, 1977, *84*, 472–484.

Bookbinder, J. & Osman, E. Attentional strategies in dichotic listening. *Memory and Cognition*, 1979, *7*, 511–520.

Brand, J. Classification without identification in visual search. *Quarterly Journal of Experimental Psychology*, 1971, *23*, 178–186.

Broadbent, D. E. *Perception and communication*. London: Pergamon, 1958.

Broadbent, D. E. Stimulus set and response set: Two kinds of selective attention. In D. I. Mostofsky (Ed.), *Attention: Contemporary theories and analysis*. New York: Appleton-Century-Crofts, 1970.

Broadbent, D. E. *Decision and stress*. London: Academic Press, 1971.

Broadbent, D. E. Task combination and selective intake of information. *Acta Psychologica*, 1982, *50*, 253–290.

Bruce, V. Searching for politicians: An information processing approach to face recognition. *Quarterly Journal of Experimental Psychology*, 1979, *31*, 373–395.

Cherry, E. C. Some experiments on the recognition of speech with one and with two ears. *Journal of the Acoustical Society of America*, 1953, *25*, 975–979.

Corteen, R. S., & Dunn, D. Shock-associated words in a nonattended message: A test for momentary awareness. *Journal of Experimental Psychology*, 1974, *102*, 1143–1144.

Corteen, R. S., & Wood, B. Autonomic responses for shock-associated words in an unattended channel. *Journal of Experimental Psychology*, 1972, *94*, 308–313.

Dawson, M. E., & Schell, A. M. Electrodermal responses to attended and nonattended significant stimuli during dichotic listening. *Journal of Experimental Psychology: Human Perception and Performance*, 1982, *8*, 315–324.

Dennett, D. C. *Brainstorms*. Cambridge, Mass.: Bradford Books, 1978.
Deutsch, J. A. On the category effect in visual search. *Perception & Psychophysics*, 1977, *21*, 590–592.
Deutsch, J. A. & Deutsch, D. Attention: Some theoretical considerations. *Psychological Review*, 1963, *70*, 80–90.
Dixon, N. *Preconscious processing*. New York: Wiley, 1981.
Duncan, J. The locus of interference in the perception of simultaneous stimuli. *Psychological Review*, 1980, *87*, 272–300.
Duncan, J. Directing attention in the visual field. *Perception & Psychophysics*, 1981, *30*,90–93.
Dyer, F. N. The Stroop phenomenon and its use in the study of perceptual, cognitive, and response processes. *Memory & Cognition*, 1973, *1*, 106–120.
Egeth, H., Jonides, J., & Wall, S. Parallel processing of multielement displays. *Cognitive Psychology*, 1972, *3*, 674–698.
Eriksen, B., & Eriksen, C. W. Effects of noise letters upon the identification of a target letter in a nonsearch task. *Perception & Psychophysics*, 1974, *12*, 201–204.
Eriksen, C. W., & Hoffman, J. E. The extent of processing of noise elements during selective encoding from visual displays. *Perception & Psychophysics*, 1973, *14*, 155–160.
Eriksen, C. W., & Schultz, D. W. Information processing in visual search: A continuous flow model and experimental results. *Perception & Psychophysics*, 1979, *25*, 249–263.
Estes, W. K. Interaction of signal and background variables in visual processing. *Perception & Psychophysics*, 1972, *12*, 278–286.
Estes, W. K. The locus of inferential and perceptual processes in letter identification. *Journal of Experimental Psychology: General*, 1975, *104*, 122–145.
Fowler, C. A., Wolford, G., Slade, R., & Tassinary, L. Lexical access with and without awareness. *Journal of Experimental Psychology: General*, 1981, *110*, 341–362.
Fox, J. Continuity, concealment and visual attention. In G. Underwood (Ed.), *Strategies of information-processing*. New York: Academic Press, 1977.
Francolini, C. M., & Egeth, H. E. Perceptual selectivity is task-dependent: The pop-out effect poops out. *Perception & Psychophysics*, 1979, *25*, 99–110.
Francolini, C. M., & Egeth, H. E. On the non-automaticity of "automatic" activation: Evidence of selective seeing. *Perception & Psychophysics*, 1980, *27*, 331–342.
Gatti, S. W., & Egeth, H. E. Failure of spatial selectivity in vision. *Bulletin of the Psychonomic Society*, 1978, *11*, 181–184.
Gleitman, H., & Jonides, J. The cost of categorization in visual search: Incomplete processing of target and field items. *Perception & Psychophysics*, 1976, *20*, 281–288.
Gleitman, H., & Jonides, J. The effect of set on categorization in visual search. *Perception & Psychophysics*, 1978, *24*, 361–368.
Hasher, L., & Zacks, R. T. Automatic and effortful processes in memory. *Journal of Experimental Psycholgoy: General*, 1979, *108*, 356–388.
Henderson, L., & Chard, J. Semantic effects in visual word detection with visual similarity controlled. *Perception & Psychophysics*, 1978, *23*, 290–298.
Hink, R. F., Hillyard, S. A., & Benson, P. J. Event-related brain potentials and selective attention to acoustic and phonetic cues. *Biological Psychology*, 1978, *6*, 1–16.
Hinton, G. F., & Anderson, J. A. (Eds.), *Parallel models of associative memory*. Hillsdale, N.J.: Erlbaum, 1981.
Hoffman, J. E. Search through a sequentially presented display. *Perception & Psychophysics*, 1978, *23*, 1–11.
Hoffman, J. E. A two-stage model of visual search. *Perception & Psychophysics*, 1979, *25*, 319–327.
Hoffman, J. E., Nelson, B., & Houck, M. R. The role of attentional resources in automatic detection. *Cognitive Psychology*, 1983, *51*, 379–410.

Johnston, W. A. & Dark, V. J. In defence of intraperceptual theories of attention. *Journal of Experimental Psychology: Human Perception and Performance*, 1982, *8*, 407–421.

Johnston, W. A., & Heinz, S. P. Flexibility and capacity demands of attention. *Journal of Experimental Psychology: General*, 1978, *107*, 420–435.

Johnston, W. A., & Heinz, S. P. Depth of nontarget processing in an attention task. *Journal of Experimental Psychology: Human Perception and Performance*, 1979, *5*, 168–175.

Johnston, W. A., & Wilson, J. Perceptual processing of nontargets in an attention task. *Memory & Cognition*, 1980, *8*, 372–377.

Jonides, J., & Gleitman, H. A conceptual category effect in visual search: "O" as letter or digit. *Perception & Psychophysics*, 1972, *10*, 457–460.

Jonides, J., & Gleitman, H. The benefit of categorization in visual search: Target location without identification. *Perception & Psychophysics*, 1976, *20*, 289–298.

Kahneman, D. *Attention and effort*. Englewood Cliffs, N.J.: Prentice-Hall, 1973.

Kahneman, D., & Chajczyk, D. Tests of the automaticity of reading: Dilution of Stroop effects by color-irrelevant stimuli. *Journal of Experimental Psychology: Human Perception and Performance*, 1983, *9*, 497–509.

Kahneman, D., & Henik, A. Effects of visual grouping on immediate recall and selective attention. In S. Dornic (Ed.), *Attention and performance, VI*. Hillsdale, N.J.: Erlbaum, 1977.

Kahneman, D., & Henik, A. Perceptual organization and attention. In M. Kubovy and J. R. Pomerantz (Eds.), *Perceptual organization*. Hillsdale, N.J.: Erlbaum, 1981.

Kahneman, D., Treisman, A., & Burkell, J. The cost of visual filtering. *Journal of Experimental Psychology: Human Perception and Performance*, 1983, *9*, 510–522.

Karlin, M. B., & Bower, G. H. Semantic category effects in visual search. *Perception & Psychophysics*, 1976, *19*, 417–424.

Keele, S. W., & Neill, W. T. Mechanisms of attention. In E. C. Carterette & M. P. Friedman (Eds.), *Handbook of perception* (Vol. 9). New York: Academic Press, 1979.

Keren, G. Some considerations of two alleged kinds of selective attention. *Journal of Experimental Psychology: General*, 1976, *105*, 349–374.

Kleiman, G. M. Speech recoding in reading. *Journal of Verbal Learning and Verbal Behavior*, 1975, *14*, 323–389.

LaBerge, D. Attention and the measurement of perceptual learning. *Memory & Cognition*, 1973, *1*, 268–276.

LaBerge, D. Acquisition of automatic processing in perceptual and associative learning. In P. M. A. Rabbit & S. Dornic (Eds.), *Attention and performance V*. New York: Academic Press, 1975.

LaBerge, D. Perceptual learning and attention. In W. K. Estes (Ed.), *Handbook of Learning and Cognitive Processes* (Vol. 4). Hillsdale, N.J.: Erlbaum, 1976.

Lackner, J. R., & Garrett, M. F. Resolving ambiguity: Effects of biasing context in the unattended ear. *Cognition*, 1972, *1*, 359–372.

Lewis, J. Semantic processing of unattended mirages using dichotic listening. *Journal of Experiment Psychology*, 1970, *85*, 225–228.

Lindsay, P. H., & Norman, D. A. *Human information processing*. New York: Academic Press, 1972.

Logan, G. D. Attention and automaticity in Stroop and priming tasks: Theory and data. *Cognitive Psychology*, 1980, *12*, 523–553.

MacKay, D. Aspects of the theory of comprehension, memory and attention. *Quarterly Journal of Experimental Psychology*, 1973, *25*, 22–40.

Marcel, A. Conscious and unconscious perception: Experiments on visual masking and word recognition. *Cognitive Psychology*, 1983, *15*, 197–237.

Marcel, A., & Patterson, K. Word recognition and production: Reciprocity in clinical and normal studies. In J. Requin (Ed.), *Attention and performance VII*. Hillsdale, N.J.: Erlbaum, 1978.

Marr, D. Early processing of visual information. *Philosophical Transactions of the Royal Society, London, B,* 1976, *275,* 483–524.

McCauley, C., Parmelee, C. M., Sperber, R. D., & Carr, T. H. Early extraction of meaning from pictures and its relation to conscious identification. *Journal of Experimental Psychology,* 1980, *6,* 265–276.

Merikle, P. M. Unconscious perception revisited. *Perception & Psychophysics,* 1982, *31,* 298–301.

Miller, J. Divided attention: Evidence for coactivation with redundant signals. *Cognitive Psychology,* 1982, *14,* 247–279.

Minsky, M. K-lines: A theory of memory. *Cognitive Science,* 1980, *4,* 117–133.

Moray, N. P. Attention in dichotic listening: Affective cues and the influence of instructions. *Quarterly Journal of Experimental Psychology,* 1959, *11,* 56–60.

Moray, N. P., & O'Brien, T. Signal detection theory applied to selective listening. *Journal of the Acoustical Society of America,* 1967, *42,* 765–772.

Morton, J. Interaction of information in word recognition. *Psychological Reveiw,* 1969, *76,* 165–178.

Navon, D., & Gopher, D. On the economy of the human processing system. *Psychological Review,* 1979, *86,* 214–255.

Neely, J. M. Semantic priming and retrieval from lexical memory: Roles of inhibitionless spreading activation and limited capacity attention. *Journal of Experimental Psychology: General,* 1977, *106,* 226–254.

Neisser, U., & Becklen, R. Selective looking: Attending to visually specified events. *Cognitive Psychology,* 1975, *7,* 480–494.

Newstead, S. E., & Dennis, I. Lexical and grammatical processing of unshadowed messages: A re-examination of the MacKay effect. *Quarterly Journal of Experimental Psychology,* 1979, *31,* 477–488.

Paap, K. R., & Ogden, W. G. Letter encoding is an obligatory but capacity-demanding operation. *Journal of Experimental Psychology: Human Perception and Performance,* 1981, *7,* 518–528.

Posner, M. I. *Chronometric explorations of mind.* Hillsdale, N.J.: Erlbaum, 1978.

Posner, M. I. Cumulative development of attentional theory. *American Psychologist,* 1982, *37,* 168–179.

Posner, M. I., Davidson, B. J., & Snyder, C. R. R. Attention and the detection of signals. *Journal of Experimental Psychology: General,* 1980, *109,* 160–174.

Posner, M. I., & Snyder, C. R. R. Facilitation and inhibition in the processing of signals. In P. M. A. Rabbitt & S. Dornic (Eds.) *Attention and performance V.* London: Academic Press, 1975.

Reddy, D. R., Erman, L. D., Fennell, R. D., & Neely, R. B. The HEARSAY speech understanding system: An example of the recognition process. *Proceedings of the Third International Joint Conference on Artificial Intelligence,* 1973, Stanford, California.

Regan, J. Automaticity and learning: Effects of familiarity on naming letters. *Journal of Experimental Psychology: Human Perception and Performance,* 1981, *7,* 180–195.

Reicher, G. M., Snyder, C. R. R., & Richards, J. T. Familiarity of background characters in visual scanning. *Journal of Experimental Psychology,* 1976, *2,* 522–530.

Richards, J. T., & Reicher, G. M. The effect of background familiarity in visual search: An analysis of underlying factors. *Perception & Psychophysics,* 1978, *23,* 499–505.

Rollins, H. A., Jr., & Hendricks, R. Processing of words presented simultaneously to eye and ear. *Journal of Experimental Psychology: Human Perception and Performance,* 1980, *6,* 99–109.

Rumelhart, D. G. Toward an interactive model of reading. In S. Dornic (Ed.), *Attention and performance VI.* London: Academic Press, 1976.

Schneider, W., & Shiffrin, R. M. Controlled and automatic human information processing: I. Detection, search and attention. *Psychological Review,* 1977, *84,* 1–66.

Shaffer, L. H. Multiple attention in continuous verbal tasks. In P. M. A. Rabbitt & S. Dornic (Eds.), *Attention and Performance V.* New York: Academic Press, 1975.

Shaffer, W. O., & LaBerge, D. Automatic semantic processing of unattended words. *Journal of Verbal Learning and Verbal Behavior*, 1979, *18*, 413–426.

Shallice, T. Dual functions of consciousness. *Psychological Review*, 1972, *79*, 383–393.

Shiffrin, R. M. The locus and role of attention in memory systems. In P. M. A. Rabbitt & S. Dornic (Eds.), *Attention and performance V*. London: Academic Press, 1975.

Shiffrin, R. M. Capacity limitations in information processing, attention, and memory. In W. K. Estes (Ed.), *Handbook of learning and cognitive processes* (Vol. 4). Hillsdale, N.J.: Erlbaum, 1976.

Shiffrin, R. M. Attentional control. *Perception & Psychophysics*, 1977, *21*, 93–96.

Shiffrin, R. M., & Grantham, D. W. Can attention be allocated to sensory modalities? *Perception & Psychophysics*, 1974, *15*, 460–474.

Shiffrin, R. M., & Schneider, W. Controlled and automatic human information processing: II. Perceptual learning, automatic attending and a general theory. *Psychological Review*, 1977, *84*, 127–190.

Sperling, G. The information available in brief visual presentations. *Psychological Monographs*, 1960, *74*(11, Whole No. 498).

Taylor, D. A. Identification and categorization of letters and digits. *Journal of Experimental Psychology: Human Perception and Performance*, 1978, *4*, 423–439.

Treisman, A. M. Contextual cues in selective listening. *Quarterly Journal of Experimental Psychology*, 1960, *12*, 242–248.

Treisman, A. M. Selective attention in man. *British Medical Bulletin*, 1964, *20*, 12–16. (a)

Treisman, A. M. Verbal cues, language and meaning in selective attention. *American Journal of Psychology*, 1964, *77*, 206–219. (b)

Treisman, A. M. Strategies and models of selective attention. *Psychological Review*, 1969, *76*, 282–299.

Treisman, A. M., & Davies, A. Divided attention to ear and eye. In S. Kornblum (Ed.), *Attention and performance IV*. New York: Academic Press, 1973.

Treisman, A. M., & Geffen, G. Selective attention: Perception or response? *Quarterly Journal of Experimental Psychology*, 1967, *19*, 1–18.

Treisman, A. M., & Gelade, G. A feature integration theory of attention. *Cognitive Psychology*, 1980, *12*, 97–136.

Treisman, A. M., Kahneman, D., & Burkell, J. Perceptual objects and the cost of filtering. *Perception & Psychophysics*, 1983, in press.

Treisman, A. M., & Riley, J. Is selective attention selective perception or selective response? A further test. *Journal of Experimental Psychology*, 1969, *79*, 27–34.

Treisman, A. M., & Schmidt, H. Illusory conjunctions in the perception of objects. *Cognitive Psychology*, 1982, *14*, 107–141.

Treisman, A. M., Squire, R., & Green, J. Semantic processing in dichotic listening? A replication. *Memory & Cognition*, 1974, *2*, 641–646.

von Wright, J. M., Anderson, K., & Stenman, U. Generalization of conditioned GSRs in dichotic listening. In P. M. A. Rabbitt & S. Dornic (Eds.), *Attention and performance V*. London: Academic Press, 1975.

Wardlaw, K. A., & Kroll, N. E. A. Autonomic responses to shock-associated words in a non-attended message: A failure to replicate. *Journal of Experimental Psychology: Human Perception and Performance*, 1976, *3*, 357–360.

Warren, R. E. Association, directionality and semantic encoding. *Journal of Experimental Psychology*, 1974, *102*, 151–158.

Wickens, C. D. Encoding categories of words: An empirical approach to meaning. *Psychological Review*, 1970, *77*, 1–15.

3

Processing Resources in Attention[1]

Christopher D. Wickens

Introduction

Examples abound of time-sharing that is effective (e.g., walking while talking, reading while listening to music) and of time-sharing that is inefficient (e.g., talking while reading, problem solving while listening). The concept of processing resources is proposed as a hypothetical intervening variable to account for variations in the efficiency with which time-sharing can be carried out; that is, the degree to which two tasks can be performed concurrently as well as each can be performed in isolation. Tasks are assumed to demand resources for their performance, and these resources are limited in their availability. Therefore, when the joint resource demand of two tasks exceeds the available supply, time-sharing efficiency drops and will be more likely to do so as the difficulty of either component task increases. For example, conversation with one's passenger in a car will normally be disrupted if the demands of the concurrent driving task are increased by poor visibility or heavy traffic. Alternatively, driving performance may degrade as the conversation becomes extremely interesting.

A second intervening variable proposed to explain variance in time-sharing efficiency is the concept of structure. According to a structural view, two tasks will interfere because they compete for common processing mechanisms or structures (e.g., stages of processing, modalities of input, requirements for manual response). For example, listening to music will be more disrupted by the simultaneous requirement to understand a conversation (which also demands the auditory channel) than by reading a paper (which involves visual input).

Perhaps Paulhan (1887) first called attention to the importance of these two variables in dual-task performance by stating, "The most favorable condition for doubling the mind [is] its simultaneous application of two *easy* and *heterogenious* operations" (p. 684; emphasis added). These two sources of variance in

[1] A major portion of this chapter was written while the author was supported by a research contract (Number N-000-14-79-C-0658) from the Office of the Naval Research Engineering Psychology Program. Gerald Malecki was the technical monitor. The author wishes to acknowledge the helpful comments of William Derrick, David Navon, and Walter Schneider in the preparation of this chapter.

time-sharing performance have been associated more recently with two classes of theories of attention: capacity theories (e.g., Kahneman, 1973; Knowles, 1963; Moray, 1967) and structural theories (Broadbent, 1958; Keele, 1973; Welford, 1967). Both theoretical developments have taken place somewhat independently since the 1950s, and each traces its origins to somewhat different historical roots.

Historical Overview

Structural Theories

Experimental investigations of dichotic listening of verbal material in the 1950s and 1960s (e.g., Broadbent, 1958; Cherry, 1953; Moray, 1959; Treisman, 1964), revealed that attention was severely limited when divided between two independent channels of auditory verbal input. These, and a host of other studies, generated classes of theories concerned with locating the "bottleneck" in human information processing. At what stage of processing does a parallel system, capable of processing separate channels concurrently, "narrow" to a serial system that must handle only one channel at a time? A major dichotomy emerged between early-selection theories (e.g., Broadbent, 1958; Treisman, 1969) that considered the bottleneck to occur at perception, and late-selection theories (e.g., Deutsch & Deutsch, 1963; Keele, 1973; Norman, 1968) that localized the serial limitation in the processing sequence at the point at which decisions were made to initiate a response (either an overt motor response or a covert response, such as storing material in long-term memory [LTM], or rehearsing it).

In parallel with dichotic-listening research, a related series of investigations were performed that investigated structural limitations from a different perspective. Typical were those of Bertelson (1967) and Welford (1967), employing the *double-stimulation,* or *psychological refractory-period,* paradigm in which the subject must perform two independent reaction-time tasks in close temporal proximity (Kantowitz, 1974); and those of Noble and Trumbo and their colleagues (Noble, Trumbo, & Fowler, 1967; Trumbo & Milone, 1971; Trumbo, Noble, & Swink, 1967), using a dual-task paradigm. These researchers drew conclusions similar to those drawn by the late-selection theorists that the major limiting bottleneck in the information-processing sequence lies at the stage of response initiation. (But see Briggs, Peters, & Fisher, 1972, for time-sharing data in support of an early-selection bottleneck.)

According to the view put forth by late-selection theories then, attention in task performance becomes nearly synonymous with the availability of a dedicated decision-making–response-selection mechanism. A subsequent modification of the bottleneck models postulated that there is not a single stage or mental operation that acts as the source of interference, but instead a single limited-capacity central processor (LCCP) (Kerr, 1973). Like a single-server queue, this processor must be engaged to complete certain mental operations, such as selecting a response, performing a mental transformation, or rehearsing material. According to this view, when the LCCP is in the service of an operation for one task; it is unavailable to a concurrent task that also might require that service, and the performance of the second task will deteriorate accordingly. By postulating a number of mental operations that require the LCCP in order to proceed, such a view permits there to be more than a single "bottleneck" within the processing system.

The intent of this section is not to review the vast body of experimental data generated in an effort to choose between early-selection and late-selection theories or to support theories such as the LCCP that amalgamate both positions. Rather, the intent is to emphasize that the focus of these investigations and subsequent theories has been on differences in task *structure* (primarily related to stages of processing) that impact on dual-task performance efficiency. It should be noted that many structural theories in fact acknowledge the role of task difficulty (a capacity concept) in generating interference by assuming that more difficult tasks occupy the bottleneck or the LCCP for a relatively longer duration. Yet the emphasis of these theories remains on structure, and the bottleneck or LCCP is conventionally assumed to service only one process or task at a time.

Capacity Theories

An important historical root of capacity theory lies in the human-factors concern with the measurement of human operator workload. Knowles (1963) presented a conceptual model of the human operator as possessing a "pool" of limited-capacity resources. As a primary task demands more of these resources (becomes more difficult); fewer are available for a concurrent "secondary" task, and the latter deteriorates. In this manner, primary-task workload is inversely reflected in secondary-task performance. An implicit characteristic of capacity, in Knowles' paper as well as in later conceptions, concerns its divisibility and allocation properties. Whereas structures in the structural theories were assumed to be dedicated to one task at a time, the contrasting view holds that capacity can be allocated in graded quantity between separate activities.

In 1967, two important papers both contributed to the refinement of capacity theory (Moray, 1967; Taylor, Lindsay & Forbes, 1967). Moray emphasized the contrast that the capacity view posed to the ongoing debate over early- and late-selection theories by drawing the analogy between human processing resources and the limited capacity of a time-shared computer. In either the computer or the human information processor, resources can be allocated to any activity, or stage of processing, as dictated by a higher level executive program. With this flexibility available, Moray argued there was no need to assume a given locus of task interference (or bottleneck of attention). The source of interference would depend merely on the capacity demands at any particular stage of processing. In the same volume, Taylor, *et al.* (1967) outlined a quantitative theory of the sharing of capacity between channels of perceptual input, thereby highlighting the sharability—as opposed to the dedicated nature—of attention.

Whereas Moray and Taylor *et al.* were concerned with the allocation of capacity, the aspect of capacity theory that emphasizes the difficulty or intensive aspects of attention has been heavily invoked in two somewhat different domains. Following Knowles's (1963) original paper, many engineering psychologists—concerned with the measurement of human operator workload in applied settings such as the aircraft cockpit or the process-control monitoring station—adopted a conceptual model asserting that workload is proportional to the demands imposed by tasks on the operator's limited capacity (Rolfe, 1971). Thus, great interest has been focussed since the late 1970s in applied research on the representation and measurement of available and used capacity and on the relation between capacity-based workload measures and alternative indices relating to subjective scales or physiological parameters (Moray, 1982; Moray, Johanssen, Pew, Rasmussen, Sanders, & Wickens, 1979).

At a more theoretical level, investigators of automatization in perceptual or motor learning have invoked the concept of capacity as a commodity in which utilization is reduced as learning proceeds (LaBerge, 1973; Logan, 1979; Schneider & Fisk, 1982). In a similar vein, the concept of "levels of processing" in encoding and memory (Craik & Lockhart, 1972) employs the capacity metaphor when describing the amount of processing invested in the encoding process. In either case, investigators often converge on assumptions of capacity usage in performing a primary task (to be learned or remembered) by inferring residual capacity from secondary-task "probes" (e.g., Eysenck & Eysenck, 1979; Posner & Keele, 1969; Tyler, Hertal, McCalum, & Ellis, 1979; Underwood, 1976). For example, longer reaction times to probe stimuli are presumed to reflect greater capacity demands (less automation, deeper processing) of the primary task.

During the 1970s, theoretical treatments by Kahneman (1973), Norman and Bobrow (1975), and Navon and Gopher (1979) have made invaluable contributions to the development of the concept of capacity or resources as an intervening variable in dual-task performance. These papers have facilitated the evolution of the resource metaphor from a loose concept to a quantitative theory with testable predictions and important implications for the use of capacity assumptions in workload measurement and learning and memory research. The discussion of resource theory that follows, borrows equally from Kahneman's initial formulation and the subsequent modifications and elaborations proposed by Norman and Bobrow and by Navon and Gopher.

Resource Theory

Defining Elements

The terms *capacity, attention, effort,* and *resources* have all been used synonymously to refer to the inferred underlying commodity, of limited availability, that enables performance of a task. The term *resources* is preferred here over the other three because *capacity* suggests a maximum limit itself rather than a variable commodity, *attention* (as various chapters in this volume attest) possesses a variety of ambiguous meanings, and *effort* suggests a motivational variable that may (but does not necessarily have to) correlate with the commodity enabling performance. Resource theory, as it is loosely conceived, may be described by three basic elements, each of which are described in the following.

The Performance–Resource Function

The quality of performance is a monotonically nondecreasing function of the hypothetical resources invested in a task. This proposition is manifest in two forms. Under single-task conditions, if one "tries harder" on a task (invests more effort), performance at least will not deteriorate and probably will improve. Although this assumption is intuitively appealing, it has received little direct experimental confirmation because practically all investigations assume that subject effort is at maximum from the outset. Experimental investigations by Hafter and Kaplan (Note 1) and by Watson and Clopton (1969) in which effort was modulated by payoff and instruction, however, seemingly confirm the validity of this assumption.[2]

Under dual-task conditions, the relation between performance and resources is more easily measurable, but requires greater assumptions concerning the underlying processes. When a subject performs two tasks concurrently, and is requested to allocate attention disproportionally in favor of one task or the other (either explicitly, or implicitly by differential payoff schedules), performance is observed consistently to vary as a function of these instructions (e.g., Gopher, 1980; Gopher & North, 1977, Navon & Gopher, 1980; Friedman, Polson, Gaskill, & Dafano, 1982; Sperling & Melchner, 1978; Vidulich & Wickens, 1981; Wickens & Gopher, 1977). Under these circumstances, resource theory infers that the subject is modulating the supply of resources between the tasks in order to obtain the desired levels of differential performance.

A major contribution of Norman and Bobrow's (1975) paper was the introduc-

---

[2]It may be noted that the Yerkes–Dodson law—the inverted U-shaped function relating performance to arousal (Easterbrook, 1959)—predicts that the relation between effort and performance will not be monotonic if increased effort induces increased arousal; trying too hard at a task may induce a deterioration in performance, particularly if the task is complex.

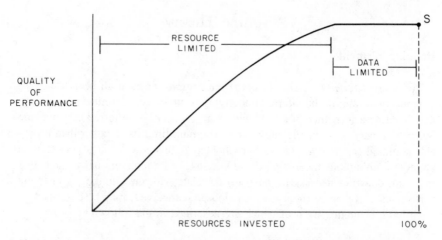

Figure 3.1 Hypothetical performance–resource function. Single-task performance is at point *S*.

tion of the hypothetical construct of the *performance–resource function* (PRF).
If two tasks do in fact interfere with each other (are performed less well) because
they are sharing resources to which each previously had exclusive access, then
there must be some underlying hypothetical function that relates the quality of
performance to the quantity of resources invested in a task. This function is the
PRF, an example of which is shown in Figure 3.1. Maximum single-task performance occurs when all resources are invested in the task (point *S*). Partial
diversion of resources ot a concurrent task will depress performance accordingly.
As more resources are invested, performance will improve up to the point at
which no further increase in performance is possible. At this point, the task is
said to be *data limited* (limited by the quality of data, not by the resources
invested). A task might be data limited either because the measurement scale can
go higher (100% correct on an easy test is achieved with little effort) or because
the quality of the data (either perceptual data or data in memory) is poor (e.g.,
one cannot understand a faint conversation no matter how hard one "strains
one's ears"). When performance changes with added or depleted resources, the
task is *resource limited*.

It is tempting to assume that the actual form of the PRF can be constructed
from a dual-task experiment in which conditions of variable resource allocation
are imposed. An example is the investigation by Wickens & Gopher (1977) in
which three different priority manipulations called for the subjects to distribute
fixed percentages of resources between a tracking and a reaction-time task.
Hypothetical performance on two tasks under such a set of allocation policies is
depicted in the two PRFs shown in Figure 3.2a. It should be noted that this
representation assumes that (1) subjects actually allocate resources as com-
manded, (2) resources deployed in performance of the two different tasks are

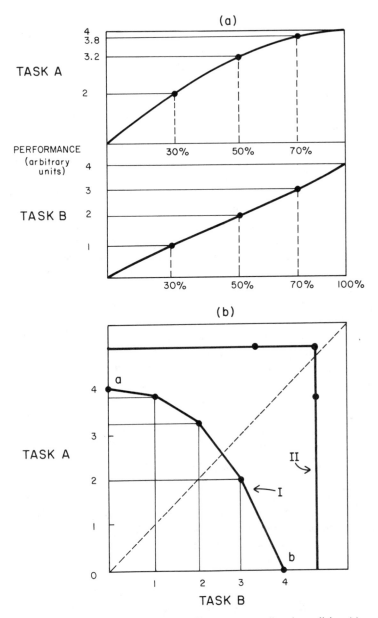

Figure 3.2 Performance of two tasks under different resource allocation policies, (a) as represented on two PRFs, and (b) the same points represented in The Performance Operating Characteristic (POC; Curve I). The performance measures 1–4 in arbitrary units are those derived from the PRFs in (a). Single-task performance indicated by points a and b. Curve II is a boxlike POC, whose implications are discussed in the text.

functionally equivalent and maximally effective for each task. The second assumption may not always be valid however, as is shown in the following.

In theory, it is of course possible to construct a PRF using single-task performance data only. A subject performs the task at varying levels of effort, and reports the subjective effort invested in performance at each level. The difficulty here is with the psychological meaning of "effort" and the psychophysical scale relating effort to the subject's numerical setting. A study conducted with Mike Vidulich in our laboratory suggests that subjects do appear to be able to allocate partial resources to a single task and to do so in a graded quantity in a reliable, repeatable manner. We asked subjects to perform a wide variety of tracking tasks with different difficulty characteristics, at each of three different levels of effort: 100, 70, and 30%. We observed that performance, measured in terms of the percentage of increase from a minimum root mean squared (RMS) tracking error, was a linear function of the percentage of resource investment. Furthermore, there was no evidence for any difference between the various levels of task difficulty in the slope of the regression line relating effort to performance. This constancy provides further evidence for the concept of an underlying resource that governs performance.

However, we also compared the absolute level of tracking performance at 70 and 30% resource investment, with the level at equivalent investment percentages when resources were divided between tracking and a reaction-time task. Performance with both 30 and 70% resources allocated to tracking was far better in the dual-task than in the single-task situation. This finding indicated that the inferred PRF from dual-task trials will not necessarily reflect the actual PRF if the two tasks are substantially different. It is in fact a finding supportive of the view that there is more than one sort of resource in the processing system. This point receives further discussion later in the chapter.

The Performance Operating Characteristic

When the two tasks are time-shared, and resources are allocated differentially between them, the joint performance of both may be depicted as two separate PRFs, as shown in Figure 3.2a. Alternatively, these data may be captured by plotting a single point for each condition in a *Performance Operating Characteristic*, (POC), in which the performance on each task is represented on the two axes (Figure 3.2b). Such a representation is quite analogous to the cross-plot of hit and false-alarm rate as response bias is varied in the receiver operating characteristic (ROC) curve of signal detection theory (Green & Swets, 1966) or to the cross-plot of reaction time and error rate in the speed–accuracy operating characteristics (SATOs; Pew, 1969). In evaluating the POC depicted in Figure 3.2b, or any other POC, it is important to note the following five particular "landmarks" or characteristics.

Single-Task Performance This characteristic is shown by the point of intersection of the POC with the two axes (points a and b in Figure 3.2b). These points may not be continuous with the projection of the function into the axes as shown in Figure 3.2b. If the single-task points are higher (better performance), then there is—in the words of Navon and Gopher (1979)—a *cost of concurrence*. The act of time-sharing itself may pull resources away from both tasks above and beyond what each task demands by itself. This discrepancy might result from the resource demands of an "executive time-sharer" (Hunt & Lansman, 1981; Moray, 1967; McLeod, 1977; Taylor, Lindsay, & Forbes, 1967), which is utliized only in dual-task situations. The resource demands of this executive (and consequent effects on performance) are not manifest, then, in single-task performance.

An alternative source of the cost of concurrence results if the requirement to time-share induces a degree of peripheral interference. For example, time-sharing two visual tasks separately displayed in the visual field may prevent both from achieving simultaneous access to foveal vision. The requirement to perceive through peripheral vision (or to engage in a time-consuming scan pattern) will lower the level of dual-task performance on one or both tasks. The term *peripheral interference* is defined here to refer to situations in which dual-task performance deteriorates as a result of physical constraints on the processing system. Thus, the eye cannot view two separated locations at once, nor can a given finger simultaneously depress two keys, or the mouth utter two words at once. Physical characteristics of the basilar membrane may cause the masking of acoustic stimuli associated with one task by stimuli associated with another. Peripheral interference here is distinct from the concept of *structural interference* that has been invoked to account for such instances as the difficulty in simultaneously performing two independent motor acts (e.g., rubbing the head and patting the stomach). Although also related to the similarity of demands on the motor system, peripheral interference is not due to the physical constraints of the limbs and therefore may be overcome with practice. As is described in the following, structural interference is compatible with concepts of resource theory; peripheral interference is not.

Time-sharing Efficiency This characteristic of the two tasks is indicated by the average distance of the curve from the origin, (0) in Figure 3.2b. Obviously, the farther from the origin the curve is, the closer dual-task performance will be to single-task performance (efficient time-sharing). Thus, the projection of any point in the POC space onto the dashed line in Figure 3.2b reflects the level of time-sharing efficiency.

Degree of a Linear Exchange This relationship between the two variables in the POC function indicates the extent to which resources are shared or exchangeable between the tasks. A POC such as Curve I shown in Figure 3.2b indicates that a given number of units of resources removed from Task A (thereby decreasing its performance) can be transferred to and utilized by Task B (improving its performance). A discontinuous or rectangular POC (Curve II) suggests that one of two situations exists: either (1) one of the tasks is in a data-limited region for the range of the POC in question—in this case, withdrawing resources from Task A (the data-limited task) will not deteriorate its performance but can improve task B's performance; or (2) the resources are not interchangeable between tasks so that resources withdrawn from Task A (thereby decreasing Task A's performance) cannot be used to benefit performance on Task B. (This latter case is discussed in detail later in the chapter.) In either case, performance change in one task will not occur concurrently with a change in the other, and so the POC will be parallel to one of the axes.

Allocation Bias Bearing in mind that the POC is actually a series of points, each one collected in a different time-sharing trial, then allocation bias is indicated by the proximity of a given point on the POC to one axis over the other: Movement along a POC indicates a shift in resource allocation. Points on the positive diagonal, however, can only be assumed to reflect a 50% allocation between tasks to the extent that the PRFs for the two tasks are equivalent. If they are not, as in the case in figure 3.2a, then the 50% point may be shifted to one side or another. However, because the PRF is normally derived from the POC, one must often assume that performance on a condition in which equal allocation instructions are given defines the negative diagonal.

Efficiency and Allocation in Combination A problem of considerable theoretical complexity is encountered whenever differences between points in the POC space that differ in both efficiency and allocation and do not lie along, or close to, the positive diagonal are compared. An analogous problem is, of course, encountered in signal detection theory when differences in sensitivity are assessed between conditions that also differ in terms of response bias. Fortunately, in this case, the normative model of signal detection theory allows equivalence in sensitivity to be assumed across different levels of bias. In fact, transforming the hit and false-alarm axes to probability scales allows equal Euclidian distances to represent equal sensitivity changes at all levels of bias and sensitivity.

Unfortunately, the lack of an underlying model of how resource allocation generates performance makes such comparisons considerably more difficult in the POC space. Two problems in particular are encountered: (1) Unlike hit and false-alarm rate in signal detection, the performance measures on the two tasks may be expressed in totally different units. (2) Unless an explicit assumption is made about the invariant form of all PRFs, there is no scale that can readily map a unit change in performance to a unit change in resource allocation.

In dealing with the first of these issues, I have assumed (Wickens, 1980; Wickens, Mountford, & Schreiner, 1981; Wickens et al., 1983) that equal changes in resource allocation across different tasks are equivalent to equal units of variability within those tasks. This assumption, analogous to assumptions made by Fechner (1860) in psychophysical scaling dictates that the axes of the POC space be normalized by an assessment of within-subject, trial-to-trial variability. When this is done, then differences in the POC space between conditions may be more readily compared. The second problem, related to differences across levels of performance, is also complex. In this case, the assumption of the form of the PRF has some critical statistical implications. If a logarithmic PRF is assumed, then equal variation in resources allocation will produce smaller variation in performance at high levels of performance than at low levels. If on the other hand a linear PRF is assumed (Sperling & Melchner, 1978), then statistical differences will be roughly equivalent across all levels of allocation.

Automation and Task Difficulty

An important characteristic of resource theory is its ability to treat the effects of practice and task difficulty as different manifestations of the same underlying construct—the marginal efficiency of resource investment, or the gain in performance achieved per invested unit of resources (Navon & Gopher, 1979).

Figure 3.3 shows the PRFs underlying three tasks, A, B, and C. The only difference between Task C and Task B lies in the assymptote of the data limit. Thus, although Task B is more difficult than Task C, under single-task conditions, the subject could not regain performance on Task B by investing more resources. Task B demands fewer resources to reach equivalent performance levels to that achieved in Task A, and, in fact, Task B contains a greater "data-limited" region. Task B then differs from Task A by being of lesser difficulty and/or having received more practice (is more automated). Note that Task B may

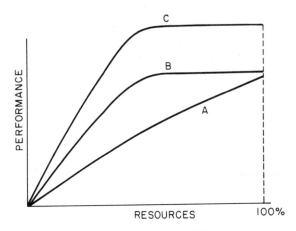

Figure 3.3 Performance–resource functions for tasks differing in practice or difficulty. A = difficult; B = easier, or practiced; C = higher data-limited asymptote.

not necessarily be performed better than Task A (at 100% resource investment in Task A), but can simply be performed at that maximum level with more "spare capacity." According to these representations, characteristics such as the "automaticity" of perception of words or letters need not be viewed as qualitatively different from attention-demanding perceptual activities (e.g., Kerr, 1973) but merely as resulting from a quantitative change in the PRF. In this manner, the distinction made by Schneider and Shiffrin (1977) between automatic and control processes (see also Schneider, Dumais, & Shiffrin, Chapter 1, this volume) assumes a difference in the data-limited region of the underlying PRF (Schneider & Fisk, 1982).

In terms of a POC representation, the easier or more practiced version of a task generates a POC that is farther from the origin than is the POC of the more difficult task. The degree to which the two POC curves are parallel, diverge, or converge as allocation is varied depends, of course, on the form of separation of the two PRFs (Figure 3.3). Figure 3.4 presents two POCs for versions of Task A that have different levels of difficulty and are time-shared with Task B, and shows a POC in which there is some divergence. Conversely, the form of the empirical POCs provides some insight as to the nature of the underlying PRFs. In general we expect some divergence between the curves as emphasis is shifted toward the task in which difficulty is varied—as is shown in Figure 3.4, which might represent the performance of Tasks B and C, whose PRFs are shown in Figure 3.3. The extent to which the POCs will reconverge as emphasis is shifted further, toward the vertical axis of Figure 3.4, depends on the extent to which the easier task has a higher data limited asymptote than the difficult task. In Figure 3.3, the PRFs indicate that the easier task (B) possesses a greater data-limited region than does the more difficult task (A). Therefore, considerable convergence would be found in the POC for Tasks B and A.

The representation shown in Figure 3.4 makes an important point relevant to investigators who use performance on a secondary task to infer the resource demands of the primary task. Suppose two versions of a primary task (A_1 and A_2) are time-shared with a secondary task (B). If Task B time-shared with A_2 (B_2), yields better performance than B time-shared with A_1 (B_1), as shown on the abscissa of Figure 3.4, then the investigator might conclude that A_2 is the easier version of the primary task. Yet from the shape of the underlying POC in Figure 3.4, it is apparent that this is not the case. It is only because the subjects allocated resources in favor of Task B when paired with A_2 to a greater extent than when paired with A_1 that this spurious result was obtained. It is important then to represent dual-task results in a POC space (even if only one allocation policy is used), rather than reporting only secondary-task performance decrements. In this way, the investigator can present a more informative picture of how the subject is allocating resources in different conditions.

Here again, the analogy with signal detection theory is direct. In signal detec-

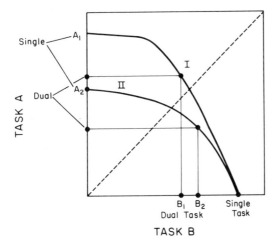

Figure 3.4 Two POCs between Task A and Task B in which Task A differs in difficulty (I = easy, II = difficult). Single task levels of Task A are shown at A_1 (easy) and A_2 (difficult). Dual task performances of Task B are shown when B is time shared with the easy version of A (Point B_1), and with the difficult version (Point B_2). The figure shows the trade-off between the decrements of the two tasks.

tion, the investigator reports both hits and false alarms, and interprets these in terms of an efficiency index (d') and a cognitive bias (β). In dual-task performance, both primary- and secondary-task decrements are reported and interpreted analogously in terms of an efficiency index (the distance from the origin of the POC) and of an allocation bias (the distance from the positive diagonal). However, as we noted above, the theoretical models underlying these distance measures are far more primitive in the case of the POC.

Limitations of Single-Resource Theory

In the preceding presentation of resource theory, it has been assumed that only a single reservoir of undifferentiated resources, which is equally available to all stages of processing or mental operations, exists within the human processing system. It is important to contrast this conception of the mechanism underlying time-sharing phenomena with alternative conceptual viewpoints. As is seen below, capacity theory has been expanded in two directions in an effort to account for four basic experimental phenomena in dual-task research, each of which presents some difficulties for a single-resource model. These four phenomena— difficulty insensitivity, perfect time-sharing, structural alteration effects, and difficulty–structure uncoupling—each relate to the structural aspects of the tasks.

Difficulty Insensitivity

Several examples may be cited in which increases in the difficulty or demand of a primary task, presumably consuming more resources (as allocation is held constant), fail to influence the performance of a secondary task. It is necessary here to insure that the decrement in the primary task caused by performance of the secondary, does not increase across levels of primary-task difficulty. In a study by North (1977), subjects time-shared a tracking task with a discrete digit-processing task. The discrete task required subjects to perform mental operations of varying complexity on visually displayed digits, and to indicate their response with a manual key press. In the simplest condition, subjects merely pressed the key corresponding to the displayed digit. A condition of intermediate demand required the subject to indicate the digit immediately preceding the displayed digit in time—a running memory task. In the most demanding condition, subjects were required to perform a classification operation on a pair of displayed digits. These three operations apparently imposed different resource demands, as indicated by their single-task performance level and their interference with simple digit canceling. However, when the digit tasks were performed concurrently with the tracking task, all three had equivalent disruptive effects on tracking performance. Analogous examples of difficulty insensitivity may be found in investigations by Isreal, Chesney, Wickens, and Donchin (1980), Kantowitz and Knight (1976), and Wickens and Kessel (1979). (See Wickens, 1980 for a summary of such studies.)

Perfect Time-sharing

An example of perfect time-sharing is provided by Allport, Antonis, and Reynolds (1972), who demonstrated that subjects could sight-read music and engage in an auditory shadowing task concurrently as well as they could perform either task by itself. Wickens (1976) observed a similar finding when an auditory signal detection task was time-shared with a response-based force-generation task. Shaffer (1975) has noted a high degree of efficiency with which a skilled typist could time-share typing with auditory shadowing.

It is possible that both difficulty insensitivity and perfect time-sharing could be accounted for within the framework of undifferentiated capacity theory if it is assumed that one or both tasks in either case possess large data-limited regions. In the case of difficulty insensitivity, this would allow the added resource demands of the more difficult version of a task to be met by diverting resources from the concurrent task without sacrificing the latter's performance. In the case of perfect time-sharing, both tasks must have considerable data-limited regions so that an appropriate allocation policy can be chosen to produce perfect performance for both tasks while sharing resources.

Although a data-limited explanation can, in theory, account for difficulty insensitivity and perfect time-sharing, it appears doubtful that the examples just described involved heavily data-limited tasks. Neither North's (1977) tasks nor those of Allport *et al.* (1972) were predictable or repetitive in a manner that might easily give rise to automation. All tasks, furthermore, appeared to involve a relatively heavy time pressure, either through forced pacing or through a self-paced schedule in which performance was measured in terms of the number of responses made per unit time (North's tasks).

Structural Alteration Effects

Structural alteration effects refer to instances in which the change in a processing structure (modality of display, memory code, modality of response) brings about a change in interference with a concurrent task, even when the difficulty (demand for resources) of the changed task has not been altered. Such examples have been observed with regard to input modality (e.g., Isreal, 1980; Martin, 1980; Rollins & Hendricks, 1980; Treisman & Davies, 1973; Vidulich & Wickens, 1981; Wickens *et al.*, 1983), response modality (e.g., Harris, Owens, & North, 1978, McLeod, 1977; Wickens, 1980, Wickens *et al.*, 1983), and codes of central processing (verbal versus spatial; Friedman, Polson, Dafoe, & Gaskill, 1982; McFarland & Ashton, 1978; Wickens & Sandry, 1982; Wickens *et al.*, 1983). If the difficulty of the altered task truly remains unchanged (and performance or subjective ratings of single-task controls must guarantee this), then the resource demands should be very similar or identical across tasks. No change in interference with the concurrent task, therefore, should be predicted under the assumption of undifferentiated resources. (When input or output structures are altered, it is important also that the investigator guard against interference changes due to peripheral interference. Considerable care was taken in this regard in most of the investigations cited in the preceding.) It should be noted that in many of these investigations, the magnitude of the change in interference is sometimes small, relative to the absolute size of the time-sharing decrements.

Uncoupling of Difficulty and Structure

The *uncoupling of difficulty* refers to instances in which the more difficult of two tasks when paired with a third task actually interferes less with the third task than does the easier of the two tasks when it is paired with the third task. This effect was noted by Wickens (1976) in a study in which tracking was paired with an auditory signal detection task and an open-loop force-generation task. The signal detection task was assessed by subjects to be the more difficult, and therefore, presumably, it demanded more resources. Yet signal detection interfered less with tracking than did the force task.

Multiple-Resource Theory

It is evident from the last two examples that some restructuring of the un-differentiated-resource view is required. This has proceeded in two directions. Kahneman (1973), in modifying undifferentiated capacity theory as presented in the early chapters of his book, acknowledges the potential role of structural factors in contributing to interference between tasks. The model that emerges is one in which competition between tasks for the general pool of resources proceeds in conjunction with competition for more or less dedicated satellite structures (e.g., modalities of encoding and response). An alternative modification—which is in many ways quite similar to Kahneman's proposal, yet entails a few fundamentally different assumptions—postulates the existence of multiple resources (Friedman *et al.*, 1982; Isreal, Chesney, Wickens, & Donchin, 1980; Kantowitz & Knight, 1976; Navon & Gopher, 1979; Sanders, 1979; Wickens, 1980; Wickens & Kessel, 1980). According to the multiple-resource view, there is more than one commodity within the human processing system that may be assigned resourcelike properties (allocation, flexibility, sharing).

The implications of this view for time-sharing are fourfold:

1. To the extent that two tasks demand separate rather than common resources, they will be time-shared efficiently; therefore, structural alteration effects occur when the change in task structure brings about less overlap in resource demands.

2. To the extent that tasks share common resources, a relatively smooth POC can be generated between them; (Figure 3.2b Curve I). If not, the POC will be "boxlike" (Figure 3.2b Curve II). This is because if resources are disjoint between tasks, those resources freed from one task cannot be used to improve performance on the other. Perfect time-sharing results when the two tasks demand entirely nonoverlapping sets of resources. Difficulty–structure uncoupling will result when two tasks that place heavy resource demands on separate resources are compared with two tasks of lesser demands, but imposed on a common resource.

3. A change in the difficulty of a task is defined as increasing the demand for one or more of the resources on which its performance depends. If part of those resources are also required for performance of a concurrent task, the concurrent task will be affected. If, on the other hand, the resources affected by the difficulty manipulation are not used in performing the concurrent task, the latter will remain unaffected. These two relations are shown in Figure 3.5A and B, respectively. According to the multiple-resources conception, difficulty insensitivity arises in the case shown in Figure 3.5B. Here, additional resources cannot be transferred from the concurrent task to compensate for the added demand imposed on the manipulated task (or if resources are transferred, performance of the manipulated task cannot benefit from their increased availability).

4. If a task is made more difficult, in a manner that demands more resources shared with a concurrent task, performance will thus be more dependent on the shared resource. As a consequence there will be a greater effect of priorities, or resource allocation, on that task's performance. Stated in other terms, the effect of difficulty should interact with priorities if difficulty manipulates the demand for shared resources. The extent to which tasks share a common resource and therefore generate an exchanging POC dictates the degree to which performance on a "primary" task for which the difficulty is varied can be preserved through resource reallocation by sacrificing a secondary task. In Figure 3.6A, a case in which this is possible is illustrated, and in Figure 3.6B, a case in which this is not possible is demonstrated.

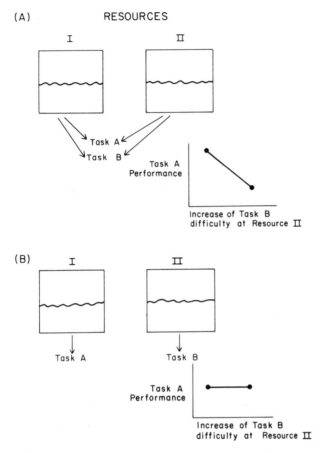

Figure 3.5 Difficulty performance trade-offs, when Task B is manipulated at Resource II: (a) Tasks A and B share resources I and II; (b) Tasks A and B demand exclusively resources I and II. Difficulty insensitivity results.

If resources do in fact, reside in separate reservoirs,[3] then it is important to identify the functional composition of these reservoirs. Examining a large number of dual-task studies that produced structural alteration effects and difficulty insensitivity, Wickens (1980), has argued that resources may be defined by a three-dimensional metric consisting of stages of processing (perceptual–central versus response), codes of perceptual and central processing (verbal versus spatial), and modalities of input (visual versus auditory) and response (manual versus vocal). It is possible that the response modality dimension is similar to the

---

[3]The reader should be cautioned from interpreting the hydraulic metaphor too literally.

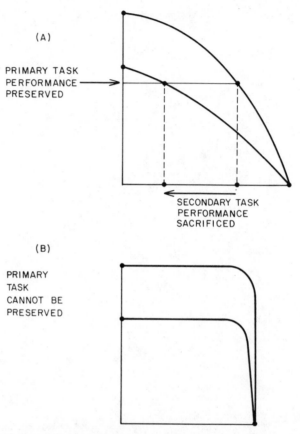

Figure 3.6 Performance Operating Characteristic representation of (A) a case in which resources from a secondary task on the abscissa can compensate for difficulty changes in primary task on the ordinate; and (B) a case in which this reallocation is not possible.

central-processing code dimension, assuming that manual responses generally tend to be those that are spatially guided and vocal productions are, by and large, verbal. If this is the case, then the "structure" of resources may be conceptually depicted in the heuristic representation of Figure 3.7. The dimensions underlying this structure are now briefly summarized.

Stages of Processing

The argument that stages define resource pools posits that perceptual and central processing rely upon common resources and these in turn are functionally separate from those resources underlying response processes. Supportive evidence is provided when the difficulty of responding in a task is manipulated and

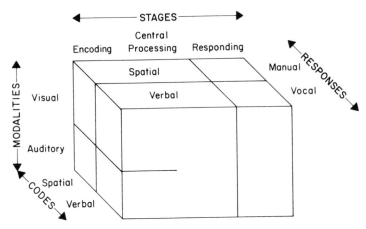

Figure 3.7 A proposed dimensional structure of human processing resources. The absence of a complete separation of auditory and visual resources through the perceptual–central processing stages indicates uncertainty as to whether the benefit of cross-modality presentation is preserved in central processing.

this manipulation does not affect performance of a concurrent task for which the demands are more cognitive or perceptual in nature (or alternatively when manipulation of the perceptual–cognitive difficulty of a task does not influence performance of a response-demanding task). Such evidence has been provided by the difficulty insensitivity demonstrated in experiments by Isreal, Chesney, Wickens, and Donchin (1980) and Isreal, Wickens, Chesney, and Donchin (1980). In these experiments, subjects performed a task in which they had to discriminate between two pitches of auditory stimuli presented in a Bernoulli sequence and maintain a mental count of the number of occurrences of stimuli of one pitch. Event-related brain potentials (ERPs) elicited by the stimuli were recorded; and the amplitude of the late positive, or P300 component, of the ERP was inferred to reflect processing of the discrimination task. The P300 amplitude, assumed to depend on perceptual and central processing resources, was influenced by manipulations of display load of a concurrent task (Isreal, Wickens, Chesney, & Donchin, 1980) but was unaltered by the requirement to generate manual responses or by manipulations of the frequency of responding in a concurrent tracking task (Isreal, Chesney, Wickens, & Donchin, 1980). Presumably, the latter manipulation influenced the difficulty of selecting and executing responses.

The demonstration by Wickens (1976) of difficulty–structure uncoupling when the signal detection and force-generation tasks are time-shared with tracking also provides evidence for stage-defined resources. The more demanding signal detection task requires perceptual resources different from the response-related resources entailed in tracking and force generation. Other evidence for stage-related resources is provided by difficulty insensitivity findings of Kantowitz and Knight (1976) and Wickens and Kessel (1980). Furthermore, Shaffer (1971, 1975) has argued from a close analysis of transcription skills such as typing that perceptual, translational, and response processes can all proceed effectively in parallel. Finally, a number of experiments in our laboratory seem to indicate that the effect of manipulating resource competition between tasks at encoding is relatively independent of the effect of manipulating competition at response (Vidulich & Wickens, 1981; Wickens, 1980; Wickens *et al.*, 1983). An independence of the effects of encoding and response manipulations of this sort would seemingly indicate a corresponding independence of resources.

Codes of Perceptual and Central Processing

The notion that spatial and verbal processes may each draw on functionally separate resources, and that these may be anatomically related (in most subjects) to the right and left cerebral hemispheres, respectively, is supported by the research and theory of Kinsbourne and his colleagues summarized by Kinsbourne & Hicks (1978). In a prototypical experiment, they observed that there is greater interference of a verbal task with dowel balancing when the latter was performed with the right hand (controlled by the hemisphere engaged in verbal processing) than with the left (controlled by the unused "spatial" hemisphere). McFarland and Ashton (1978) report that this handedness asymmetry of interference was reversed when a spatial memory task was substituted for the verbal task. Brooks (1968) has obtained evidence that imaging tasks that require spatial working memory are performed more efficiently if their response is verbal and vocal than if it is manual, whereas verbal imaging tasks are performed better with a spatially guided manual response than with a verbal response. These are presumably conditions in which processing and response functions are under the control of separate, rather than common, hemispheres. Similar demonstrations of "code-specific" interference are provided in the experiments of Baddeley and his colleagues (Baddeley, Grant, Wight, & Thompson, 1975; Baddeley & Lieberman, 1980).

In the perceptual domain, Moscovitch and Klein (1980) observed that recognition performance was more impaired when two spatial targets were presented simultaneously (a face and a random polygon), rather than when a spatial and a verbal target were presented simultaneously. Finally, conclusions of hemispherically defined resources have been drawn from reaction-time tasks. Here response latencies are lengthened when the hemisphere of stimulus processing is the same as that controlling the response (e.g., Allwitt, 1981; Dimond & Beaumont, 1972; Green & Well, Note 2; Wickens & Sandry, 1982).

An assertion that separate resources underlie verbal and spatial central processing (as well as encoding and response) could plausibly account for the results of Allport *et al.* (1972) in which perfect time-sharing was observed between two information-processing tasks involving all stages of processing (music sight-reading and verbal shadowing). This explanation assumes that music sight-reading involves some degree of right hemispheric processing coupled with visual input and manual output (Nebes, 1977), whereas the verbal shadowing is assumed to require left hemispheric processing coupled with auditory input and vocal output.

Modalities of Input and Response

It seems apparent that we can sometimes divide attention between the eye and ear, better than between two eyes or two ears. This observation is clearly true (and of trivial theoretical interest) if peripheral interference is allowed to dominate in the intramodality conditions. Most studies have not carefully controlled for this factor, but four that have (Isreal, 1980; Martin, 1980; Rollins & Hendricks, 1980; Treisman & Davies, 1973) suggest that there is indeed still an advantage to cross-modal presentation. Treisman and Davies observed more efficient detection of both spatial–temporal patterns and semantic targets in a cross-modal than in an intramodal presentation. Rollins and Hendricks (1980) and Martin (1980) replicated this result even when the depth of semantic processing of the auditory stimuli was systematically varied. Isreal replicated the greater effect of intra- versus cross-modality interference between tracking and reaction time when the modality of both tasks was manipulated orthogonally by using auditory or visual reaction-time stimuli coupled with an auditory or visual tracking display. Considering response modalities, investigations by Harris *et al.* (1978), McLeod (1977), Vidulich and Wickens (1981), Wickens (1980) and Wickens *et al.,* (1983), have all shown the greater time-sharing efficiency of tracking with a discrete task that used vocal as opposed to manual responses.

Contrast between Models of Time-sharing

Multiple versus Single Resources: The Influence of Priorities

Careful scrutiny reveals that there really are not major differences between the multiple-resource model and Kahneman's model, which assumes an undifferentiated resource with competition for satellite structures. Both predict that time-sharing will be less efficient if two tasks share common structures. According to Kahneman's conception, this results from direct competition for the structures. According to a multiple-resources conception, it results from competition for the resources that enable the structures to function. Like multiple-resource theory, an undifferentiated-resource view can also account for difficulty insensitivity, as long as the concept of data limits is invoked. However, the undifferentiated-resource view really cannot easily accommodate the examples of perfect time-sharing of two resource-demanding tasks, such as Allport et al.'s (1972) demonstration with individuals who could concurrently sight-read music and engage in an auditory shadowing task. It is possible in this model to assume that two such tasks can be efficiently (but not perfectly) time-shared if their input and output structures (encoding and response) are separate. But if both tasks demand some degree of central processing from a single resource (decision making, memory, or translatory operations), interference *must* occur unless the tasks are heavily data limited. If they are not, then it appears necessary to assume that there are separate resources at a central level in order to explain perfect time-sharing.

Broadbent (1982) has argued that the sight reading task investigated by Allport et al. allows the use of preview of the stimulus sequence, so that efficient stimulus-sampling strategies employed by the subjects, coupled with insufficiently sensitive performance measures obscure a dual task performance decrement. Although these arguments may be valid, the important point is not so much whether time sharing is absolutely perfect or not, but that the decrement is as small as it is.

Perhaps the clearest difference between the two models relates to the fact that the undifferentiated-capacity model postulates only a single commodity with resourcelike properties (sharability and flexibility under different allocation policies), whereas the multiple-resource view postulates more than one such commodity. To establish the latter assertion empirically, one of two experimental techniques are required. These relate to changes in the POC with changes in resource overlap and to the effect of difficulty manipulations on the POC. Each of these are now described in turn.

Performance Operating Characteristic and Resource Overlap Changes

It is necessary not only to identify a smooth exchanging POC between two tasks, both of which impose a major demand on the potential resource in question; but also to show that the POC becomes discontinuous when the resource is not shared. As an example, Sperling and Melchner (1978) observed that continuous POCs could be generated between detection of the outer and inner rings of a display of letters and digits, even as these were presented tachistoscopically so that no differential fixation could be utilized. Because the major demands of this task are visual, it might be assumed that the process of visual encoding possesses resourcelike properties. However, in order to establish firmly that the identified resource is indeed visual, and not of a general perceptual nature, it would be necessary to establish that a less continuous POC was manifest in a cross-modal condition (e.g., between visual and auditory detection). In order to demonstrate that the resource was not of an undifferentiated nature, it would also be necessary to demonstrate that a smooth POC *could not* be generated if a response-loading task is substituted for one of the detection tasks.

Vidulich and Wickens (1981) compared intra- with cross-model resource allocation at both the encoding and response stages. Their subjects time-shared a Sternberg memory-search task (Sternberg, 1969) with tracking. The former task could be presented in either the auditory or visual modality and subjects responded either manually or vocally. Two different priority instructions emphasized each task in different conditions. As predicted either by an undifferentiated-capacity-with-structure theory or by multiple-resource theory, the time-sharing efficiency was an inverse function of the amount of resource overlap between the visual–manual tracking task and the input–output modalities of the memory-search task. However, two characteristics appeared to be directly compatible with a multiple-resource view: (a) In the auditory–vocal condition, time-sharing was nearly perfect. This is similar to the findings of Allport *et al*.'s (1971) experiment in which an auditory–verbal–vocal task is shared with a visual–spatial–manual one. Separate resources lead to high time-sharing efficiency. (b) The effect of the priority manipulation—the separation of points in the POC space—was a monotonically increasing function of the degree of overlap between input–output modalities of the two tasks. These results confirm that as more structures are shared between tasks there exists a greater degree of the exchangeable allocatable commodity, operationally defined to be resources that can modulate performance according to task priorities.

An investigation by Friedman *et al*. (1982) drew similar conclusions with regard to the resource properties of cerebral hemispheres. They required subjects to time-share a memory and detection task with different allocation priorities between the two tasks. By manipulating the hemisphere engaged in perception via lateral visual field presentation and the code of analysis of the perceptual task (spatial–verbal), they observed that when a single hemisphere was engaged in the two tasks, large interference was produced, and the manipulation of priorities exerted a major affect on performance. The use of different hemispheres greatly improved time-sharing and attenuated the effect of priority manipulation.

Effect of Difficulty Manipulations on the Performance
Operating Characteristic

Navon and Gopher (1979) have argued that support for a multiple-resources conception is provided by an interaction between task difficulty and priorities. As described earlier, this interaction takes the form that priorities exert a greater influence on performance when the demand for a common resource is high (difficulty is increased) than when it is low. Two investigations provide support for such a position. Gopher, Brickner, and Navon (1982) required subjects to time-share tracking with a digit-classification task at three different levels of priority emphasis. The digit task could be made more difficult in either of two dimensions. One varied its cognitive–verbal demands, the other the complexity of its motor responses. Only with the latter manipulation was the effect of priorities enhanced. Gopher et al. assumed that the increased demand for spatial–motor responses associated with the increased response complexity created a greater demand for the shared spatial and motor responses of tracking. Therefore, priority effects were enhanced. The increased demand for verbal–cognitive resources of the digit task imposed no demand on tracking resources. Therefore, the priority effect was uninfluenced.

In the study by Vidulich and Wickens (1981) described in the preceding, subjects time-shared the tracking and memory-search tasks at two different levels of tracking difficulty, determined by the *order* of the tracking control dynamics. Wickens and Vidulich found that the cost of manual responses for the memory-search task was greater in second- than in first-order control, suggesting that the locus of higher order control in their experiment was on response-related resources. This finding would predict that priorities would interact with control order when there was competition for shared outputs (the memory task required a manual response) to a greater extent than when there was not. This was exactly the result obtained by Vidulich and Wickens.

In summary, although the data are still scant, because few investigators manipulate priorities within their dual-task conditions, the existing evidence is certainly consistent with the notion that more than one entity within the human processing system possesses resourcelike properties.

Resources versus the Dedicated Central Processor

As noted previously, an important defining property of resources concerns the sharable characteristics of their allocation. Through careful modeling and experimental design, Long (1976) and Tulving and Lindsay (1967) have concluded that in detection and recognition tasks processing truly is shared simultaneously between auditory and visual signals rather than switched discretely. This demonstration of "shared capacity" relates closely to the issue of parallel versus serial processing (e.g., Taylor, 1976; Townsend, 1974); and as such, provides a point of convergence between the limited-capacity central processor view and the resource view (whether undifferentiated or multiple). Clearly, the dedicated processor of a bottleneck or LCCP model can be made to mimic the sharable qualities of a resource if a) the processor can switch with sufficient rapidity between tasks or channels of information, and b) the processor is capable of adjusting the "dwell time" proportionately according to operator strategies and task priorities. At lower frequencies of sampling—such as those involved in visual fixation strategies—the latter is clearly an available strategy and, further-more, can be easily validated by objective measurement (e.g., Senders, 1964; Swets, Chapter 5, this volume).

If a higher frequency switching is postulated however, it appears nearly im-possible to distinguish whether processing resources or structures are truly shared between tasks or are modulated by rapid switching. Indeed, it does appear that at some levels of processing, discrete attention switching is clearly an identifiable phenomenon (LaBerge, Van Gilder, & Yellott, 1971; Kristofferson, 1967). The position argued here is that the critical frequency, above which discrete switch-ing is referred to as shared resources, is somewhat arbitrary. Very rapid intertask (or interchannel) switching may, for all intents and purposes, be labeled as shared resources.

A Hierarchical Structure of Resources

The structure of multiple resources presented in Figure 3.7 suggests a set of independent, nonoverlapping reservoirs each defined by a combination of levels on the three dichotomous dimensions. If taken literally, the implications of this representation are (1) tasks demanding completely nonoverlapping resources will always be perfectly time-shared; and (2) if two tasks utilize partially separate resources, their degree of interference (or time-sharing efficiency) will be un-affected by the "functional distance" (within the matrix of Figure 3.7) between the nonoverlapping component of these resources. As an explicit example of these implications, consider the resource composition of two perceptual encod-ing tasks, represented in the encoding stage of Figure 3.7—a 2 × 2 matrix of resources defined by modality (auditory–visual) and code (spatial–verbal). Sev-eral investigators (e.g., Treisman & Davies, 1973) have shown that two tasks within a single cell (e.g., two auditory–verbal tasks) will interfere to a greater extent than two tasks in adjacent cells (e.g., auditory–verbal and visual–verbal, or auditory–verbal and auditory–spatial). The data do not support the assertion, however, that two tasks demanding adjacent cells will be perfectly time-shared. Indeed, in Treisman & Davies's experiment, the authors observed that the cross-modal (auditory–visual) conditions demonstrated considerable interference. Cor-respondingly, a visual detection task demanding both spatial and verbal process-ing may be expected to show some degree of interference, albeit less than the degree shown with two verbal or two spatial tasks (Moscovitch & Klein, 1980).

These considerations suggest that human processing resources may be defined hierarchically. One example of such a scheme proposes the existence of auditory and visual resources that are separate to some degree, each one exclusive to the specific modality. These cannot be transferred to the other modality to facilitate performance but can be shared by two tasks within the modality. In addition, there exist pools or more general verbal–perceptual resources and spatial–perceptual resources. Each of these are sharable between modalities, but not between codes. Above this level in the hierarchy exists a pool of general perceptual–central processing resources, available to both spatial and verbal processing of either auditory or visual information, but not available to response processes. Finally at a most general level, there might indeed exist a pool of "undifferentiated resources" that is available to and demanded by all tasks, modalities, codes, and stages as required. These general resources may be assumed to represent that which is conventionally labeled attention, consciousness, the bottleneck, or the LCCP of the structural theories. Acknowledging the existence of general resources does not, however, in any way obviate the explanatory value of the multiple-resource concept.

The hierarchical representation just described, although accounting for increasing interference as a function of the increasing proximity of tasks within the resource space, is not entirely adequate. The problem is that this hierarchy explicitly proposes a dominance ordering of dimensions that places modalities below codes and codes below stages. According to this representation, a given structural alteration effect will only be observed within the level of a shared structure above it in the hierarchy. More specifically, this scheme predicts that the effect of shared versus separate modalities in time-sharing will only be observed if both tasks share a common code of processing (e.g., both are spatial). Data collected by Vidulich and Wickens (1981) clearly suggest that this is not the case. Likewise, the hierarchical model described predicts that the effect of shared versus separate codes will only be observed if a common stage of processing is employed. Brooks's (1968) demonstration of the interaction between spatial and verbal working-memory tasks and response modalities provides evidence against this interpretation.

Although some degree of dominance ordering between dimensions may in fact exist (e.g., it may make more of a difference in time-sharing efficiency to employ separate stages than to employ separate codes), it is unlikely that this ordering is unidirectional. That is, it is probable that separate codes will improve time-sharing efficiency over shared codes even if separate stages are also used. It is probable, therefore, that some aspect of a "shared-features" model must be employed to predict interference, a *feature* being defined as a level along each of the these dichotomous dimensions of the resource space. Indeed, Derrick (1981) obtained a high correlation ($r = +.76$) between the predicted interference according to a shared-features model, and the actual interference observed across 10 conditions created by 4 tasks shared in all pairwise combinations.

On the Relation between Resources and Strategies

The relation between resources and the strategies adopted by subjects in dual-task performance may be articulated at levels both within and between tasks. At a within-task level, it is clear that different performance strategies can be employed that may increase or decrease the resource demands of component tasks. Shifts in the SATO of reaction time in control and response timing in tracking, or in rehearsal strategies in memory tasks, can easily have an impact on the the total resources demanded by a task as well as on the locus of task-resource demands. Two specific examples may be cited: First, encoding or rehearsal of verbal material may differ in the "depth of processing" (Craik & Lockhart, 1972), and this would presumably alter the emphasis on phonetic as opposed to semantic codes (Posner, 1978). Such a shift, in turn, would vary the relative interference with tasks that differed in their dependence on verbal as opposed to auditory resources (Martin, 1980). Second, tracking a system with sluggish dynamics may be accomplished either by a perceptual strategy that focuses on extracting the higher derivatives of the error signal as a means of prediction and anticipation, or by a strategy in which impulse control is delivered to correct a deviation in error position (Wickens, Gill, Kramer, Ross, & Donchin, 1981). In an experiment conducted in our laboratory with Barry Goettle, we have found that subjects can be trained to adopt one strategy or the other to obtain equivalent tracking error. Yet the consequences to performance on a concurrent memory-search RT task are quite different. Latency is prolonged when the perceptual strategy is employed, whereas the proportion of "fast guess" RT errors increases when the response strategy is adopted.

At a between-task level, strategies may be employed in adopting a particular allocation policy between tasks. As an example, if one of two time-shared tasks had a large data-limited region—such that perfect performance could be achieved at only 30% resource investment, and the other task was resource limited across the entire range of performance, a 50–50 allocation policy would clearly be nonoptimal. Instead, a strategy of investing 30% resources in the data-limited task would generate a higher level of combined performance. Correspondingly, the slope of the two PRFs dictates the particular operating point that will generate maximum dual-task performance efficiency. As an example, Schneider and Fisk (1982) demonstrated that the efficiency of time-sharing two detection tasks—one a highly automated task of detecting "consistently mapped (CM) targets" (Schneider & Shiffrin, 1977; Schneider et al., Chapter 1, this volume) and the other a resource-limited task of detecting variable mapped (VM) targets—was influenced by the strategy of resource allocation adopted by the subject. Only when the subject was instructed to emphasize the resource-limited task did the time-sharing efficiency of the two tasks approach maximum.

Another demonstration of the importance of allocation strategy in dual-task performance was provided by Brickner in a study reported by Gopher (1980). Two groups of subjects practiced in a dual-task paradigm either under fixed conditions or variable priority allocation conditions. When both groups were transferred to a different time-sharing paradigm in which tasks of various difficulty levels were shared, the variable training group performed better. Presumably the skills in differential resource allocation that they had acquired in training proved useful in optimally adjusting the resource supply to tasks that varied in their resource demand.

In a related study Tsang (1983) has demonstrated the importance of instructing subjects to allocate resources appropriately between two tasks in a dynamic environment in which the difficulty (resource demands) of the primary task is continuously fluctuating. Under normal circumstances, subjects have a great deal of difficulty maintaining performance of the emphasized task at the optimum level by borrowing and returning resources from the secondary task as needed (Wickens, Tsang, & Benel, 1979). However, when explicit attention is directed toward optimum allocation strategies, Tsang found that performance improved.

What Are Resources?

In the preceding discussion, the concept of resources has been invoked as an inferred quantity or hypothetical intervening variable to account for differences in time-sharing efficiency. Does this variable possess a physically identifiable counterpart? Various candidates appear plausible. Beatty (1982) has marshaled convincing evidence that pupil dilations mimic very closely changes in processing that correspond to increased resource mobilization (e.g., increase in task difficulty). His arguments that pupil dilation represents a direct manifestation of reticular activation system activity suggest that this activity may, indeed, be termed a resource. Other intriguing evidence has correlated performance changes with changes in blood flow to various areas of the brain (Gur & Reivich, 1980) or with the brain's metabolism of glucoproteins (Sokoloff 1977). However, the response time of both of these measures appear to be somewhat slow when compared with the bandwidth of performance change under resource mobilization (Wickens *et al.* 1979; Tsang, 1983).

Although these candidates suggest that resources are a generalized commodity, an alternative conception presented by Kinsbourne and Hicks (1978)—more compatible with the multiple-resource model presented here—considers resources to reflect the actual competition for a functional cerebral "space." Two tasks with demands in close proximity within this functional space share resources—neural processing mechanisms—and will interfere with each's performance. Where this space contains discontinuities (as between cerebral hemispheres or processing modalities), adoption of a multiple-resources conception becomes quite plausible. The concept of functional cerebral space is, of course, compatible with the concept of resources as a more generalized commodity. Within the hierarchical model described in the preceding section, the generalized commodity describes resources at the highest level; the functional cerebral space describes them at lower levels.

A final caution is in order. The concept of multiple resources has been invoked as a means of accounting for empirical phenomena in dual-task performance. In the representation presented here, the resource dichotomies are defined across boundaries (stages, codes, and modalities) for which independent evidence derived from anatomical or clinical data or other experimental paradigms suggests that there is a major dicontinuity in processing. I do not intend to argue that there are not other discontinuities that define resource pools. For example, Navon and Gopher (1980) have argued that tracking in horizontal versus vertical axes is enabled by separate computational–perceptual resources. Nor do I argue that proximity along other dimensions of processing (e.g., perceptual-feature similarity or proximity of responding fingers) will not also influence the degree of interference between tasks. I propose, however, as a note of caution that the explanatory and predictive power of the multiple-resources concept may be greatly diminished as the number of dimensions of separate resources proliferate (see Navon & Gopher, 1979, p. 249, for compatible views). Future research will, it is hoped, identify those categorical distinctions that account for the greatest variance in time-sharing efficiency, designate these as resources, and acknowledge that further variance in time-sharing efficiency can be accounted for by other aspects of task similarity (e.g., perceptual features, response fingers). It is with this parsimony in mind that the structural configuration in this chapter has been presented.

Applications of Multiple-Resource Theory

Although the increased sophistication and power of computer technology has produced a trend toward automating many functions in many aviation-, computer-, and process-control environments, this trend has not necessarily unburdened the human operator–supervisor, but has often merely shifted the qualitative nature of processing load from output to perception and understanding (Danaher, 1980; Wickens & Kessel, 1979). The tremendous load imposed on the human operator in many of these sytems is relevant to our preceding theoretical discussions of attention and multiple resources in two contexts: (1) exploitation of multiple resources in the configuration of task integration in order to increase the potential information-processing capabilities of the human operator, and (2) measurement of operator workload.

Task Configuration

The representation in Figure 3.7 suggests that the processing capacity of the human operator may be greatly influenced by the resource composition of tasks imposed on an operator in dual-task situations. Indeed Allport *et al.*'s (1972) demonstration of "perfect time-sharing" provided such an example. Often system requirements leave the designer little choice as to what resource demands a task will impose. For example, the aircraft pilot must navigate the plane through space. This is inherently a spatial task, just as storage of information concerning the call numbers of other aircraft seems to be inherently verbal. Yet in other circumstances, considerable flexibility is available. With increasing computer technology available in the areas of voice recognition and synthesis, choices may be made about whether to "display" instrument information visually or auditorily, or about whether to accept commands by discrete manual action or by the operator's voice. In the input mode, options often exist to display information verbally (e.g., digital meters) or spatially (analog symbology). At a central processing level, some potential seemingly exists for training subjects to utilize either a spatial or verbal code for certain computational and problem-solving operations.

There are a number of human engineering factors that ideally should contribute to the system designer's decision as to which of these flexible options are selected and implemented in a particular system (Wickens *et al.*, 1983). It is important, for example, that the compatibility of a particular form of information to be relayed through visual versus auditory channels be considered, given the parallel and serial aspects of the two modalities, respectively (Vidulich & Wickens, 1982). However, in light of the previous data, a design criterion that seeks to minimize the overlap of demands on common resources for tasks that will, or should be performed simultaneously should be of critical importance. It is dubious that "perfect" time-sharing will ever be achieved (or objectively measurable) outside of the idealized laboratory conditions, but it is possible that judicious selection of input and output and codes, so as to distribute demands across resources, can reduce the critical probability of human error.

Workload Assessment

We noted at the outset of this chapter that the measurement of human operator workload represented a strong impetus for the development of the concept of resources. In early treatments (Knowles, 1963; Rolfe, 1971), the workload of a task was conceived as inversely related to the percentage of "residual capacity" not allocated to a primary task. Since the mid-1970s, the concept of human operator workload has benefitted from a resurgence of both theoretical and applied interest, as witnessed by the growing number of volumes and conferences addressing the subject (*Ergonomics Journal*, 1978; Moray, 1979; Ogden, Levine, & Eisner, 1979; Roscoe, 1978; Shingledecker, 1981; Wierwille & Williges, 1978, 1980; Wierwille, Williges, & Schillett, 1979; Williges & Wierwille, 1979). Although the number of proposed measures of operator workload has proliferated (Wierwille and Williges (1978) have enumerated some 28 different techniques), there is still a lack of any clear consensus of just what workload is and whether the various measures are tapping the same, or different, constructs. Probably the only statement that can be made for which there is universal consensus is that workload is multidimensional (Hartman, 1980; Moray *et al.*, 1979; Wickens, 1979). In the following pages, the implications of the multiple-resources concept to four major classes of workload measures—primary-task parameters, secondary-task performance, physiological measures, and subjective ratings—are considered.

Primary-Task Parameters

A major goal of workload research is to enable the system designer to predict what effect a particular design innovation (conceptually, a change in a parameter of a primary task) will have on the workload experienced by the operator when performing the task. Will the innovation increase or decrease resource demands? If either, then by how much? This consideration makes pertinent an important distinction between task workload, task-difficulty manipulations, and task performance. A laboratory investigator may manipulate a particular task parameter under the assumption that workload is being increased, for example in a detection task by degrading a target or placing more targets on a screen or in a tracking task by increasing the frequency of required corrections. Yet, whether or not (or by how much) workload actually is increased is critically dependent on the operator's response to the manipulation. If he or she continues to respond identically as before, that is, ignoring the added information imposed by the manipulation (e.g., added display elements or increased tracking frequency), it is doubtful that the experienced (or measured) workload will have increased. The parameter change will be manifest as a greater decrement between obtained and desired (i.e., perfect) performance, but the investigator should neither expect any concurrent workload measures to reflect this manipulation nor fault the measures if they do not so respond. Correspondingly, if the manipulation shifts the asymptote of a data limit downward but does not change the point at which resource limits change to data limits (compare Curves B and C in Figure 3.3), no increase in resource damand is imposed. In order to specify accurately workload effects from primary-task manipulations, it is necessary to include a description both of the nature and magnitude of a manipulation of primary-task difficulty, and of the change (or lack of change) in primary-task performance.

Within the context of multiple-resources theory, primary-task performance constitutes one of two examples of vector measures. An accurate specification of the workload imposed by a task or a task manipulation must account for the dimensions of resources outlined in Figure 6.7 (or for the dimensions of whatever other multiple-resource model might be proposed). At least, the measure should reflect resources imposed by task performance both on encoding and central processing and on responses of a verbal and spatial nature.

When assessing the absolute workload imposed by a task, in contrast to the workload *change* induced by a task manipulation, a useful primary-task measure is the *primary-task workload margin*. In deriving the workload margin, a criterion level at which a task is to be performed must be specified. In applied contexts, this criterion is often supplied by a systems engineer—for example, the maximum allowable deviation from a glide slope in an approach to landing an aircraft or the allowable error rate and typing speed for a clerk typist. A primary-task parameter is then chosen that will deplete resources of a particular nature, and this parameter is manipulated until it reaches a level such that performance falls below the criterion. For example in the aviation-control situation, a small dynamic instability in the actual flight control surface could be gradually increased until performance error is sufficiently deviant (Jex & Allen, 1979). This level (the magnitude of the parameter manipulation) is the *workload margin* because it provides an index of how much additional demand from the initial task conditions the resource in question can bear before performance becomes unsatisfactory. The workload margin is a vector measure because one such dimension should ideally be supplied for each postulated resource.

The Secondary-Task Technique

Imposing a secondary task as a measure of residual resources not utilized in the primary task is an often-employed technique closely related to the primary-task workload margin (Ogden *et al.*, 1979; Rolfe, 1971). Rather than "absorbing" the capacity by increasing the difficulty of the original activity, resources are absorbed by a new activity, the secondary task. Secondary-task performance is thus, ideally, inversely proportional to the primary-task resource demands. Like the workload margin, as a vector quantity the secondary-task technique must also account for the dimensionality of resources. Workload differences attributable to a manipulation of a primary-task variable can be greatly underestimated if there is a mismatch between the resource demands of the primary-task manipulation and those of prominent importance in the secondary task. An example of such a mismatch might be provided by the use as a secondary task of an auditory word-comprehension or mental arithmetic task (auditory, verbal, perceptual–central) to assess the workload attributable to manipulations of tracking-response load (visual, spatial, response). Although some competition will be expected for any "general" resources within the system, the structure-specific contributions to resource demands will be underestimated.

A problem encountered with the secondary-task technique is the interference and disruption that it often causes with the primary task. It is interesting that one of the solutions offered to this problem is to choose secondary tasks that are dissimilar from the primary task so that "structural interference" is avoided (Ogden *et al.*, 1979). The preceding discussion suggests that this remedy may be employed only with a potential cost—a reduced sensitivity to resource-specific attributes of primary-task workload. The ideal secondary-task technique, then, would logically be one that employs a battery of secondary-task measures, a suggestion offered by Kahneman (1973). For cases in which one level of a dimension can be easily discounted as not contributing to primary-task performance, the dimensionality of the battery may be reduced accordingly. For example, a verbal processing task with no spatial components need not be assessed with a spatial secondary task. However, in cases in which an activity is performed that potentially engages all "cells" of the structure illustrated in Figure 3.7, a secure workload measure should involve a battery that also incorporates those cells.

Primary- versus Secondary-Task Measures

In spite of its shortcomings, use of the secondary task as a workload measure possesses one major advantage over such use of the primary task. So long as structure, or resource overlap, is held constant, then changes in performance of the former clearly reflect changes in the resource demand of the latter. As has been shown here, this is not the case with primary-task performance measures because a change in the primary task may reflect changes in the data-limited assymptote that are, therefore, unrelated to resource demand (compare Curves B and C in Figure 3.3). It would seem desirable, therefore, to have a direct measure of the resources invested in the primary task that is not manifested as primary-task performance. An experiment by Wickens, Kramer, Vanasse, and Donchin (1983) seems to have demonstrated that such a measure can be provided by the event-related brain potential (ERP). They found that changes in ERP amplitude elicited by primary-task stimuli in a step-tracking task were directly proportional to manipulations of primary-task difficulty. This conclusion was further validated by measuring subjective difficulty and by observing the reciprocity of primary-task ERPs and ERPs elicited by a secondary task as difficulty was varied. A related line of evidence for reciprocity of the primary- and secondary-task resources has been provided by a study of individual differences in time-sharing by Hunt and Lansman (1981).

Physiological Measures

From the standpoint of multiple-resource theory, physiological indices of workload, along with subjective ratings, represent a class of scalar measures. The term *scalar* is adopted because for any given physiological index (e.g., heart rate, electroencephalogram (EEG), pupil diameter, galvanic skin response

(GSR); see Williges and Wierwille, 1979, for a comprehensive summary), there is probably a many-to-one mapping from the demands imposed on the separate resources to variance in the particular measure in question. The challenge to the investigator of these measures must be to establish the nature of this mapping. Does a given measure reflect variation on only certain dimensions, in which case the measure is somewhat *diagnostic* and adopts the more vector properties of a secondary task? Does it reflect variation in only the most demanded resource from any pool? Or does it reflect the aggregate demands imposed on all resources, in which case its diagnosticity is sacrificed for greater total *sensitivity?* The trade-off between diagnosticity and sensitivity of measures is important. There is some evidence in this regard that pupil diameter may be equally responsive to manipulations of response load (e.g., the frequency of response corrections in tracking; Qiyuan, Parasuraman, & Beatty, 1981) as well as to encoding and central processing load (Beatty & Kahneman, 1966). A similar status is suggested by heart rate variability measures (Mulder & Mulder, 1981; Derrick, 1981). These measures are highly sensitive and reflect the total resource demands imposed on the system but are undiagnostic with regard to the locus of demand. On the other hand, use of the ERP as a measure (Isreal, Chesney, Wickens, & Donchin, 1980; Isreal, Wickens, Chesney, & Donchin, 1980; Wickens, Kramer, Vanasse, & Donchin, 1983) sacrifices this global sensitivity for greater diagnosticity of the earlier processing stages. Absolute heart rate (as opposed to its variability) seems to show diagnosticity at later stages.

Subjective Measures

   Subjective ratings of task difficulty represent perhaps the most acceptable measure of workload from the standpoint of the actual system user who feels quite comfortable in simply stating, or ranking, the subjective feelings of "effort" or attention demands encountered in performing a given task or set of tasks. Some have argued (Sheridan, 1980) that these measures come nearest to tapping the essence of mental workload. Yet at the present time, subjective ratings must accept the same status as scalar measures (as do physiological indexes) because of the difficulty that is encountered in introspectively diagnosing the source of resource demands within a dimensional framework (Nisbett & Wilson, 1971). When asked to rate "response load" for example, people will encounter difficulty in separating the mental workload of response selection and programming from the physical muscular workload of execution (Moray, 1982). In addition to the common psychophysical problems associated with subjective scaling and response biases, there are still too little data available to make strong assertions concerning the degree of sensitivity of subjective effort to the different dimensions of resource demand. Moray (1982) has provided a comprehensive review of the existing work in the area but concludes that far more research must be undertaken before the meaning, sensitivity, and diagnosticity of subjective measures can be well established.

Concluding Remarks

If all measures of workload demonstrated high correlation with each other, and residual variance was due to random error, there would exist little need for further validation research in the area; the practitioner could adopt whichever technique is methodologically simplest and most reliable for the workload measurement problem at hand. However, such an ideal is not the case, and systematic instances of lack of correspondence between measures are readiy available. For example, Derrick (1981), and Wickens and Yeh (1983) obtained data suggesting that subjective measures were relatively more sensitive to the number of competing activities, whereas primary-task performance reflected to a greater extent the difficulty of a given single-task activity. Wickens and Yeh (1983) also found that performance was relatively more sensitive to the competition between tasks for shared resources, and subjective measures to the demand for separate resources.

When such dissociation of measures appears, the question of which is the "best" measure clearly depends on the use to be derived from that information. If workload is to predict performance margins or the "residual attention" that an operator has to cope with failures in critical operational environments, it seems wiser to adopt a system that manifests greater residual attention by primary- or secondary-task measures despite the fact that it may demonstrate higher subjective ratings of difficulty (Herron, 1980). If, on the other hand, the issue is one of consumer usability, of setting work–rest schedules, or of job satisfaction, and variations in performance are relatively less critical, then greater weight should be provided to the subjective measure. That such dissociations between measures occur should not be viewed as a source of discouragement, but rather as one more testimony as to the complexity of human attentional mechanisms. This complexity should instigate more fundamental research into the relations between the subjective, objective, and physiological realms of human performance, and their relation to the underlying structure of processing resources.

Reference Notes

1. Hafter, I., and Kaplan, R. A. *The interaction between motivation and uncertainty as a factor in detection.* Unpublished manuscript, 1977.
2. Green, J., and Well, A. D. *Interference between processing demands within a cerebral hemisphere.* Paper presented at the meeting of the Psychonomic Society, Washington, D.C., November, 1977.

References

Allport, D. A., Antonis, B., & Reynolds, P. On the division of attention: A disproof of the single channel hypothesis. *Quarterly Journal of Experimental Psychology, 1972, 24,* 225–235.

Allwitt, L. F. Two neural mechanisms related to modes of selective attention. *Journal of Experimental Psychology: Human Perception and Performance, 1981, 7,* 324–332.

Baddeley, A. D,, Grant, S., Wright, E., & Thomson, N. Imagery and visual working memory. In P. M. A. Rabbitt & S. Dornic (Eds.), *Attention and performance V.* New York: Academic Press, 1975.

Baddeley, A. D., & Lieberman, K. Spatial working memory and imagery mnemonics. In R. Nickerson (Ed.), *Attention and performance VIII.* Englewood Cliffs, N.J.: Erlbaum, 1980.

Beatty, J. Task evoked pupillary responses, processing load, and the structure of processing resources. *Psychological Bulletin, 1982, 91,* 276–292.

Beatty, J., & Kahneman, D. Pupillary changes in two memory tasks. *Psychonomic Science, 1966, 5,* 371–372.

Bertelson, P. The psychological refractory period of choice reaction times with regular and irregular ISI's. *Acta Psychologica, 1967, 27,* 45–56.

Briggs, G., Peters, G. C., & Fisher, R. P. On the locus of the divided attention effect. *Perception & Psychophysics, 1972, 11,* 315–320.

Broadbent, D. *Perception and communication.* Oxford: Permagon, 1958.

Broadbent, D. Task combination and the selective intake of information. *Acta Psychologica, 1982, 50,* 253–290.

Brooks, L. R. Spatial and verbal components of the act of recall. *Canadian Journal of Psychology, 1968, 22,* 349–368.

Cherry, C. Some experiments on the recognition of speech with one and two ears. *Journal of the Acoustical Society of America, 1953, 23,* 915–919.

Craik, F. I. M., & Lockhart, F. S. Levels of processing: A framework for memory research. *Journal of Verbal Learning & Verbal Behavior, 1972, 11,* 671–684.

Danaher, J. W. Human error in ATC system operations. *Human Factors, 1980, 22,* 535–545.

Derrick, W. D. The relation of multiple resource theory to performance, heart rate variability, and subjective measures of mental workload. In A. Sugarman (Ed.), *Proceedings of the 25th Meeting of the Human Factors Society,* Santa Monica, Calif.: Human Factors Press, 1981.

Deutsch, J. A., & Deutsch, D. Attention: Some theoretical considerations. *Psychological Review, 1963, 70,* 80–90.

Dimond, S. J., & Beaumont, J. G. Processing in perceptual integration between and within the cerebral hemispheres. *British Journal of Psychology, 1972, 63,* 509–514.

Easterbrook, J. A. The effect of emotion on cue utilization and the organization of behavior. *Psychological Review, 1959, 66,* 183–201.

Ergonomics Journal (entire issue), 1978, *21,* No. 3.

Eysenck, M. W., & Eysenck, M. C. Processing depth, elaboration of encoding, memory stores, and expended processing capacity. *Journal of Experimental Psychology: Human Learning & Memory, 1979, 5,* 422–484.

Fechner, G. T. *Element der Psychophysik.* Leipzig: Breitkopf and Harterl, 1860. English translation of Vol. 1 by H. E. Adler (D. H. Howes and E. G. Boring, Eds.). New York: Holt, Rinehart, & Winston, 1966.

Friedman, A., Polson, M. C., Gaskill, S. J., & Dafoe, C. G. Competition for left hemisphere resources: Right hemisphere superiority at abstract verbal information processing. *Journal of Experimental Psychology: Human Perception Performance, 7,* 1031–1051.

Gopher, D. On the training of time-sharing skills: An attention viewpoint. In G. Corrick, M.

Hazeltine, & R. Durst (Eds.). *Proceedings of the 24th Annual Meeting of the Human Factors Society*. Santa Monica, Calif.: Human Factors Press, 1980.

Gopher, D., Brickner, M., & Navon, D. Different difficulty manipulations interact differently with task emphasis: Evidence for multiple resources. *Journal of Experimental Psychology: Human Perception & Performance*, 1982, *8*, 146–157.

Gopher, D., & North, R. A. Manipulating the conditions of training in time-sharing. *Human Factors*, 1977, *19*, 583–593.

Green, D., & Swets, J. *Signal detection theory and psychophysics*. New York: Wiley, 1966.

Gur, R. C., & Reivich, M., Cognitive task effects on hemispheric blood flow in humans. *Brain & Language*, 1980, *9*, 78–92.

Harris, S., Owens, J., & North, R. A. A system for the assessment of human performance in concurrent verbal and manual control tasks. *Behavior Research Methods & Instrumentation*, 1978, *10*, 329–333.

Hartman, B. O. *Evaluation of methods to assess workload*. (AGARD Advisory Report No. 139). London: Hartford House, 1980.

Herron, S. A case for early objective evaluation of candidate display formats. In G. Corrick, M. Haseltine, & R. Durst (Eds.), *Proceedings of the 24th Annual Meeting of the Human Factors Society*. Santa Monica, Calif.: Human Factors Press, 1980.

Hunt, E., and Lansman, M. Individual differences in attention. In R. Sternberg (Ed.) *Advances in the psychology of intelligence* (Vol. *1*). Hillsdale, N.J.: Erlbaum, 1981.

Isreal, J. B. *Structural interference in dual task performance: Behavioral and electrophysiological data*. Unpublished doctoral dissertation, University of Illinois, 1980.

Isreal, J. B., Chesney, G. L., Wickens, C. D., & Donchin, E. P300 and tracking difficulty: Evidence for multiple resources in dual-task performance. *Psychophysiology*, 1980, *17*, 259–273.

Isreal, J. B., Wickens, C. D., Chesney, G. L., & Donchin, E. The event-related brain potential as an index of display-monitoring workload. *Human Factors*, 1980, *22*, 211–224.

Jex, H. R., & Allen, W. A proposed set of standardized sub-critical tasks for tracking workload calibration. In N. Moray (Ed.), *Mental workload: Its theory and measurement*. New York: Plenum Press, 1979.

Kahneman, D. *Attention and effort*. Englewood Cliffs, N.J.: Prentice-Hall, 1973.

Kantowitz, B. H. Double stimulation. In B. H. Kantowitz (Ed.), *Human information processing*. Hillsdale, N.J.: Erlbaum, 1974.

Kantowitz, B. H., & Knight, J. L. Testing tapping time-sharing (Pt. 2): Auditory secondary task. *Acta Psychologica*, 1976, *40*, 343–362.

Keele, S. W. *Attention and human performance*. Pacific Palisades, Calif.: Goodyear, 1973.

Kerr, B. Processing demands during mental operations. *Memory and Cognition*, 1973, *1*, 401–412.

Kinsbourne, M., & Hicks, R. Functional cerebral space. In J. Requin (Ed.), *Attention and performance VII*. Hillsdale, N.J.: Erlbaum, 1978.

Knowles, W. B. Operator loading tasks. *Human Factors*, 1963, *5*, 151–161.

Kristofferson, A. Attention and psychological time. *Acta Psychologica*, 1967, *27*, 93–101.

LaBerg, D. Attention and the measurement of perceptual learning. *Memory & Cognition*, 1973, *1*, 268–276.

LaBerge, D., Van Gilder, P., & Yellott, S. A cueing technique in choice reaction time. *Journal of Experimental Psycholgoy*, 1971, *87*, 225–228.

Logan, C. D. On the use of a concurrent memory load to measure attention and automaticity. *Journal of Experimental Psychology: Human Perception & Performance*, 1979, *5*, 189–207.

Long, J. Division of attention between non-verbal signals: All or none or shared processing. *Quarterly Journal of Experimental Psychology*, 1976, *28*, 47–69.

McFarland, K., & Ashton, R. The influence of concurrent task difficulty on manual performance. *Neurophysiologica*, 1978, *16*, 735–741.

McLeod, P. A dual task response modality effect: Support for multi-processor models of attention. *Quarterly Journal of Experimental Psychology*, 1977, *29*, 651–667.

Martin, M. Attention to words in different modalities: Four channel presentation with physical and semantic selection. *Acta Psychologica*, 1980, *44*, 99–115.

Moray, N. Attention in dichotic listening. *Quarterly Journal of Experimental Psychology*, 1959, *11*, 56–60.

Moray, N. Where is attention limited. A survey and a model. *Acta Psychologica*, 1967, *27*, 84–92.

Moray, N. Models and measures of mental workload. In N. Moray (Ed.), *Mental workload: Its theory and measurement*. New York: Plenum Press, 1979, 13–21.

Moray, N. Subjective mental load. *Human Factors*, 1982, *23*, 25–40.

Moray, N., Johannsen, G., Pew, R. W., Rasmussen, J., Sanders, A. F., & Wickens, C. D. Report of the experimental psychology group. In N. Moray (Ed.), *Mental workload: Its theory and measurement*. New York: Plenum, 1979.

Moscovitch, M., & Klein, D. Material-specific perception for visual words and faces. *Journal of Experimental Psychology: Human Perception and Performance*, 1980, *6*, 590–603.

Mulder, G., & Mulder, L. J. M. Information processing & cardiovascular control. *Psychophysiology*, 1981, *18*, 392–402.

Navon, D., & Gopher, D. On the economy of the human processing system. *Psychological Review*, 1979, *86*, 214–255.

Navon, D., & Gopher, D. Interpretations of task difficulty. In R. Nickerson (Ed.), *Attention and Performance VIII*. Hillsdale, N.J.: Erlbaum, 1980.

Nebes, R. D. Man's so-called minor hemisphere. In M. C. Wittrock (Ed.), *The human brain*. Englewood Cliffs, N.J.: Prentice-Hall, 1977.

Nesbit, P. E., & Wilson, T. D. Telling more than we know: Verbal reports on mental processes. *Psychological Review*, 1971, *84*, 231–259.

Noble, M., Trumbo, D., & Fowler, F. Further evidence on secondary task interference in tracking. *Journal of Experimental Psychology*, 1967, *73*, 146–419.

Norman, D. Toward a theory of memory and attention. *Psychological Review*, 1968, *75*, 522–536.

Norman, D., & Bobrow, D. On data limited and resource limited processing. *Journal of Cognitive Psychology*, 1975, *7*, 44–60.

North, R. A. *Task components and demands as factors in dual-task performance* (Report No. ARL-77-2/AFOSE-77-2). Urbana, Ill.: University of Illinois at Urbana–Champaign, Aviation Research Laboratory, January, 1977.

Ogden, G. D., Levine, J. M., and Eisner, E. J. Measurement of workload by secondary tasks. *Human Factors*, 1979, *21*, 529–548.

Paulhan, M. *Revue Scientifique*, 1887, *39*, 684.

Pew, R. W. The speed–accuracy operating characteristic. *Acta Psychologica*, 1969, *30*, 16–26.

Posner, M. I. *Chronometric explorations of the mind*. Hillsdale, N.J.: Erlbaum, 1978.

Qiyuan, J., Parasuraman, R., and Beatty, J. Physiological assessment of operator workload during manual tracking (Pt. 1): Pupillary responses. *Proceedings of the 17th Annual Conference on Manual Control*. Jet Propulsion Lab JPL-81-3. Pasadena, Calif.: 1981.

Rolfe, J. M. The secondary task as a measure of mental load. In W. T. Singleton, J. G. Fox, & D. Whitfield (Eds.), *Measurement of man at work*. London: Taylor and Francis, 1971.

Roscoe, A. H., (Ed.) *Assessing pilot workload* (AGARD-AG-233). London: Hartford House, February, 1978. (AD A051 587)

Sanders, A. F. Some remarks on mental load. In N. Moray (Ed.), *Mental workload: Its theory and measurement*. New York: Plenum Press, 1979.

Schneider, W., & Fisk, A. D. Concurrent automatic and controlled visual search: Can processing occur without resource cost. *Journal of Experimental Psychology: Learning, Memory & Cognition*, 1982, *8*, 261–278.

Schneider, W., & Shiffrin, R. M. Controlled and automatic human information processing (Pt. 1): Detection, search, and attention. *Psychological Review*, 1977, *84*, 1–66.

Senders, J. W. The operator as a monitor and controller of multidegree of freedom systems. *IEEE Transactions on Human Factors in Electronics*, 1964, *HFE-5*, 2–5.

Shaffer, H. L. Multiple attention in continuous verbal tasks. *In P. M. A. Rabbitt & S. Dornic (Eds.), Attention and performance V*, London, Academic Press, 1975.

Shaffer, H. L. Attention in transcription skill. *Quarterly Journal of Experimental Psychology*, 1971, *23*, 107–112.

Sheridan, T. Mental workload: What is it? Why bother with it? *Human Factors Society Bulletin*, 1980, *23*, 1–2.

Shingledecker, C. A. *Register of research in progress on mental workload*. Aerospace Medical Research Laboratory, Wright–Patterson AFB, Ohio. January, 1981.

Sperling, G., & Melchner, M. Visual search, visual attention and the attention operating characteristic. In J. Requin (Ed.), *Attention and performance VIII*. Hillsdale, N.J.: Erlbaum, 1978.

Sokoloff, L. The (^{14}C)-deoxyglucose method for the measurement of local cerebral glucose utilization. *Journal of Neurochemistry*, 1977, *28*, 897–916.

Sternberg, S. The discovery of processing stages: Extensions of Donders' method. *Acta Psychologica*, 1969, *30*, 276–315.

Taylor, D. A. Stage analysis of reaction time. *Psychological Bulletin*, 1976, *83*, 161–191.

Taylor, M. M., Lindsay, P. M., & Forbes, S. M. Quantification of shared capacity processing in auditory and visual discrimination. *Acta Psychologica*, 1967, *27*, 223–229.

Townsend, J. T. Issues and models concerning the processing of a finite number of inputs. In B. H. Kantowitz (Ed.), *Human information processing: Tutorials in performance and cognition*. Potomac, Md.: Erlbaum, 1974.

Treisman, A. M. Selective attention in man. *British Medical Bulletin*, 1964, *20*, 12–16.

Treisman, A. M. Strategies and models of selective attention. *Psychological Review*, 1969, *76*, 282–292.

Treisman, A. M., & Davies, A. Divided attention to ear and eye. In S. Kornblum (Ed.), *Attention and performance* (Vol. 4). New York: Academic Press, 1973.

Treisman, A. M., & Riley, J. G. Is selective attention selective perception or selective response? A further test. *Journal of Experimental Psychology*, 1969, *79*, 27–34.

Trumbo, D., & Milone, F. Primary task performance as a function of encoding, retention, and recall in a secondary task. *Journal of Experimental Psychology*, 1971, *91*, 273–279.

Trumbo, D., Noble, M., & Swink, J. Secondary task interference in the performance of tracking tasks. *Journal of Experimental Psychology*, 1967, *73*, 232–240.

Tsang, P. *The structural constraints and the strategic control of attention allocation*. Unpublished Ph.D. dissertation. University of Illinois at Champaign, 1983.

Tulving, E., & Lindsay, P. H. Identification of simultaneously presented simple visual and auditory stimuli. *Acta Psychologica*, 1967, *27*, 101–109.

Tyler, S., Hertal, P., McCalum, M., & Ellis, H. Cognitive effort & memory. *Journal of Experimental Psychology: Human Learning & Memory*, 1979, *5*, 607–617.

Underwood, G. *Attention and memory*. Oxford, England: Permagon, 1976.

Vidulich, M., & Wickens, C. D. *Time-sharing manual control and memory search: The joint effects of input and output modality competition, priorities and control order* (University of Illinois Engineering–Psychology Laboratory Technical Report EPL-81-4/ONR-81-4). December, 1981.

Vidulich, M. & Wickens, C. D. The influence of S–C–R compatibility and resource competition on performance of threat evaluation and fault diagnosis. In R. E. Edwards (Ed.) *Proceedings of the 26th Annual Meeting of the Human Factors Society*. Santa Monica, Calif.: Human Factors Press, 1982.

Watson, C. S., & Clopton, B. M. Motivated changes of auditory sensitivity in a simple detection task. *Perception and Psychophysics,* 1969, *5,* 281–287.

Welford, A. T. Single channel operations in the brain. *Acta Psychologica,.* 1967, *27,* 5–22.

Wickens, C. D. The effects of divided attention on information processing in tracking. *Journal of Experimental Psychology: Human Perception and Performance,* 1976, *1,* 1–13.

Wickens, C. D. Measures of workload, stress and secondary tasks. In N. Moray (Ed.), *Mental workload: its theory and measurement.* New York: Plenum, 1979, 79–99.

Wickens, C. D. The structure of attentional resources. In R. Nickerson (Ed.), *Attention and performance VIII.* Hillsdale, N.J.: Erlbaum, 1980.

Wickens, C. D., Gill, R., Kramer, A., Ross, W., & Donchin, E. The processing demands of higher order manual control. In J. Lyman & A. Besczy (Eds.) *17th Annual Conference on Manual Control.* JPL 81-3, Pasadena, Calif.: Jet Propulsion Lab., October, 1981.

Wickens, C. D., & Gopher, D. Control theory measures of tracking as indices of attention allocation strategies. *Human Factors,* 1977, *19,* 349–365.

Wickens, C. D., & Kessel, C. The effect of participatory mode and task workload on the detection of dynamic system failures. *IEEE Transactions on Systems Man & Cybernetics,* 1979, *13,* 21–31.

Wickens, C. D., & Kessel, C. The processing resource demands of failure detection in dynamic systems. *Journal of Experimental Psychology: Human Perception and Performance,* 1980, *6,* 564–577.

Wickens, C. D., Kramer, A., Vanasse, L. & Donchin, E. The performance of concurrent tasks: A psychophysiological analysis of the reciprocity of information processing resources. *Science,* 1983, *221,* 1080–1082.

Wickens, C. D., Mountford, S. J., & Schreiner, W. Time-sharing efficiency: Evidence for multiple resource, task-hemispheric integrity and against a general ability. *Human Factors,* 1981, *23,* 211–229.

Wickens, C. D., & Sandry, D. L., Task hemispheric integrity in dual task performance. *Acta Psychologica,* 1982, *52,* 227–248.

Wickens, C. D., Sandry, D. L., & Vidulich, M. Compatibility & resource competition between modalities of input, control processing and output: Testing a model of complex performance. *Human Factors,* 1983, *25,* 227–248.

Wickens, C. D., Tsang, P., & Benel, R. The dynamics of resource allocation. *Proceedings of the 23rd Annual Meeting of the Human Factors Society,* Santa Monica, Calif.: Human Factors Press, 1979.

Wickens, C. D. & Yeh, Y. Y. The dissociation between subjective workload and performance: A multiple resources approach. In L. Haugh & A. Pope (Eds.). *Proceedings of the 27th Annual Meeting of the Human Factors Society.* Santa Monica, Calif.: Human Factors Press, 1983.

Wierwille, W. W., & Williges, R. C. *Survey and analysis of operator workload assessment techniques* (Report No. S-78-101). Blacksburg, Va.: Systemetrics, September, 1978.

Wierwille, W. W., and Williges, B. H. *An annotated bibliography on operator mental workload assessment.* Patuxent River, Md.: (Report SY-27R-80). Naval Air Test Center, March, 1980.

Wierwille, W. W., Williges, R. C., and Schiflett, S. G. Aircrew workload assessment techniques. In B. O. Hartman and R. E. McKenzie (Eds.), *Survey of methods to assess workload* (AGARD-AG-246). London: Hartford House, August, 1979, 19–53.

Williges, R. C., & Wierwille, W. W. Behavioral measures of aircrew mental workload. *Human Factors,* 1979, *21*(5), 549–574.

4

A Unified Theory of Attention and Signal Detection[1]

George Sperling

Introduction

The plan of this chapter is to review some experiments on attention, mostly from my laboratory, and to show how all these experiments and experiments on signal detection are subsumed under the same theoretical description.[2] The kind of attention tasks under consideration are exemplified by the concurrent tasks of driving an automobile while listening to a news broadcast on the radio. Can a driver do both tasks simultaneously without loss? Or does driving suffer when too much attention is paid to the news? Or is memory for some news events lost because of momentary concentration on a traffic obstacle?

The concurrent tasks of driving and listening are prototypical of the ones under consideration here. But driving–listening is complicated because the difficulty of each task varies from moment to moment and because difficulty depends not only on the present stimuli but also on previous stimuli and on previous responses to previous stimuli. Before a good understanding of such a complex situation is possible, it is necessary to understand some simpler ones. Considered first are some simpler (but not simple!) visual concurrent tasks in which both tasks involve visual stimuli and in which the relevant stimuli are condensed into essentially an instantaneous flash. The interest here is in examining how visual attention is distributed over the visual field in a single instant of time and in how long it takes to shift attention within the visual field. In the course of this examination, it will become useful to discard ''attention'' as an explanatory concept (while retaining it as a description of the situation) and to replace it with ''processing resource.'' A calculus for processing resources is developed.

[1]Preparation of this article was made possible by United States Air Force, Life Sciences Directorate, Grant AFOSR 80–0279.

[2]The theory of attention (concurrent–compound tasks, operating characteristics, optimization) was first published in Sperling and Melchner (1976a, 1978b) and elaborated in two hitherto unpublished talks (Sperling, Note 1, Note 2).

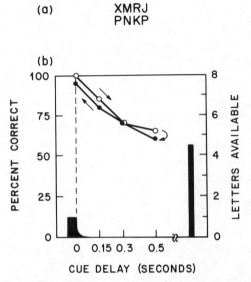

Figure 4.1 (a) Stimulus configuration for a two-alternative partial-report procedure, and (b) partial-report accuracy as a function of cue delay. The right-hand ordinate, letters available, is the mean fraction of letters correct times the number of letters in the stimulus. The mean number of letters in a whole report is shown in the bar on the right. The stimulus is indicated on the abscissa, beginning at cue delay −0.05 seconds and ending, except for a very brief decay, at 0.0 seconds. Arrows indicate the sequence in which blocks of trials were conducted. Data are shown for one subject, ROR. (From Sperling, 1960.)

Experiments

Three Experiments in Visual Attention

Partial-Report Procedure

Estimating the Capacity of Visual Information Storage (VIS) The partial-report task was originally used by Sperling (1959, 1960) to demonstrate and measure the duration of short-term visual information storage—subsequently called *iconic memory* by Neisser (1966). A subject views an array, for example, two rows of four letters, exposed very briefly so that he or she cannot make an eye movement during the exposure. After the exposure, a cue (for example, a high- or low-pitched tone) directs the subject to report the letters of either the upper or the lower row (partial report). In control conditions, all letters of both rows must be reported (whole report).

In the whole-report condition, subjects typically report less than 5 letters correctly. In the partial-report condition, they can report about 3.5 of the 4 letters in the cued row, provided that the tonal cue follows the exposure within a few tenths of a second (Figure 4.1). Because the choice of tonal cue is random from trial to trial and unknown to the subject, we infer that the subject must have available 7 of the 8 stimulus letters at the time of the cue in order to maintain such a high accuracy of partial report. These available letters constitute visual information storage (VIS). In similar experiments involving larger arrays with more letters (and more tonal signals), estimates of the capacity of VIS have been as high as 17 (of 18) letters (Sperling, 1963). Estimates of VIS could be made even higher if there were some reason to construct still larger stimulus arrays and corresponding sets of cue signals. Typically, VIS decays within a few tenths of a second, but may not do so for seconds under conditions that produce long-lasting afterimages.

The Role of Attention in Partial Report Procedures In traditional terms, the cue directs the subject to attend to a particular row and to memorize the letters of just that row for later recall. A subject cannot memorize more than four or five letters from a brief exposure, but as long as VIS exceeds the subject's short-term memory (STM) capacity, the subject has a choice of what to memorize; attention determines that choice.

In contemporary terms, it might be said that the subject has several *information processing resources*[3] available: VIS, STM, and a transfer process from VIS to STM. The transfer process is under voluntary control—the cue to attend to (and to report) a particular row being translated into control instructions for the transfer process. The *limiting resource* is the limited five-item capacity of STM. At this point, I have simply introduced novel words for familiar processes. But there is a lot more to the analysis of the partial report-procedure, and this example is considered again later.

Visual Search

In their classic experiments, Neisser and his collaborators (Neisser, 1963; Neisser, Novick, & Lazar, 1963) studied the ability of subjects to find a particular target character or characters embedded in long lists of randomly chosen characters. Subjects searched lists from top to bottom and made a manual response when they detected the target. Neisser *et al.*'s fastest reported search times were on the order of 20 msec per distractor (nontarget) character. For example, if the target were the thousand and first character on the list, it would take the subject about 20 seconds longer to discover the target than if it were the first character on the list. Unfortunately, Neisser *et al.*'s calculated search times per character were not consistent between lists having different spatial arrangements of characters.

Eye Movements in Visual Search To investigate the conjecture that eye movements might have been a limiting factor in Neisser *et al.*'s visual search, a computer-driven display was devised to enable visual search to proceed without

[3]The term information processing resource was first introduced by Norman and Bobrow (1975).

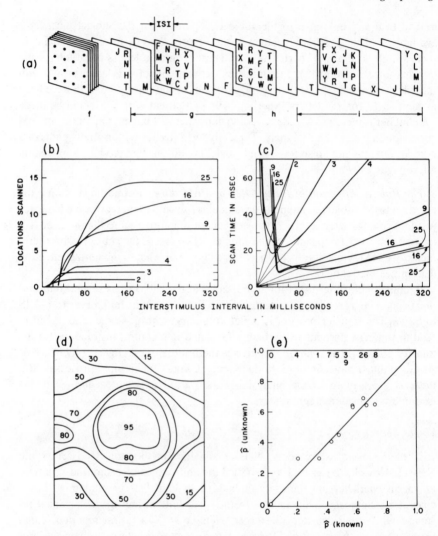

Figure 4.2 Visual search without eye movements in computer-generated displays. (a) The stimulus—fixation point (f), random number (6–12) of displays containing only letters (g), critical display containing a numeral target (h), and 12 more nontarget displays (i). (b) Number of locations (ℓ) searched as a function of interstimulus interval (ISI), the parameter is the number of letters in the display, ℓ is corrected for guessing. (c) The scan time T derived from (b): T = ISI/ℓ. (d) Search-field contours in a 7 × 7 array. The parameter shown is search accuracy at the contour. (e) Comparison of search accuracy with known numeral targets [p̂ (known)] to search with unknown numeral targets [p̂ (unknown)]. Numerals at the top indicate the identity of the target points plotted, and the line through the data has a slope of 1.0, accounting for 97% of the variance. (Panel d based on Sperling and Melchner, 1978b; Panels a–c, and e based on Sperling, Budiansky, Spivak and Johnson, 1971.)

eye movements (Budiansky & Sperling, Note 3). In the sequential search procedure, a sequence of briefly flashed letter arrays is presented on a cathode-ray tube (CRT) display screen, with each new array falling on top of its predecessor. A critical array containing a lone numeral target is embedded somewhere in the middle sequence. The target's spatial location (within the array) and its identity are chosen randomly on each trial. The task of the subject is to detect the location and to identify the target (see Figure 4.2).

In rapid, natural, visual search through simple material, the eyes make about four saccadic eye movements per second, each movement lasting a few tens of milliseconds (depending on the distance transversed), with the eyes relatively motionless between saccades (Woodworth & Schlosberg, 1954). To approximate this natural search mode, the computer-generated arrays are exposed for durations of 200 msec with brief 40-msec blank periods between arrays. Such a stimulus sequence to the stationary eye approximates the stimulus sequence produced by saccadic eye movements. In fact, data obtained with 200-msec exposures followed by 40-msec blank periods are not different from data obtained with 10-msec exposures and 230-msec blank periods (Sperling, 1973; Sperling & Melchner, 1978b, p. 676). The computer-generated sequence has many information processing advantages over the natural sequence. For example, in natural search, when the eyes do not move quite far enough between fixations, some of the same material falls within the eyes' search area in successive fixations and is searched twice, which is wasteful. Even when redundant material on the retina is ignored, the redundant material still usurps space within the search area that could have been occupied by new material. If the eyes move too far between fixations, they leave unsearched lacunae in the stimulus.

In natural search, there are two unknown factors: (1) the eye movement strategy and (2) the attentional field around the eye fixations. Eye movement strategy must be known to determine the attentional factors. In the computer-generated sequence, eye movements are effectively eliminated[4] so that the attentional field around fixation can be determined.

Experimental Investigations of Visual Search in Computer-Driven Visual Displays Visual search was studied with many different presentation rates in addition to those that most closely approximated natural search (Sperling 1970a;

---

[4]Subjects reported no difficulty in maintaining fixation in the center of the display sequences. In briefly flashed arrays, eye movements during the array are not a problem because subjects would require several tenths of a second to initiate a movement and the array is exposed only for 0.01 second (10 msec) or less. That the stimulus is radially symmetric around the intended fixation in the center of the display negates the utility of altering the fixation point, and the rapid succession of displays encourages oculomotor passivity. When Sperling and Reeves (1980) observed and Murphy, Kowler, & Steinman (1975) and Murphy (1978) carefully measured fixation stability in similar situations, it has been found that subjects can and do maintain stable fixation.

Sperling *et al.*, 1971). The most rapid visual search actually occurred when new arrays were presented every 40 msec—five times faster than the fastest possible saccade rate (Figure 4.2c). At these artifically high presentation rates, search proceeded at a rate of one background character per 10 msec, about twice as fast as Neisser's (1963) maximum rate and twice as fast as in the 240-msec presentation rate that simulated Neisser's conditions. In fact, there was only a small difference in detection accuracy between interarray times of 120 and 240/sec (Figure 4.2b); suggesting that in some natural searches, the motor control of the eye is the limiting factor. In Neisser *et al.*'s (1963) search task, if their subjects' eyes had executed saccades every 120 msec, search rate might have doubled with little loss of accuracy. The second half of many fixation pauses seems to have been wasted waiting for the eyes to move.

In contrast to Neisser *et al.*'s lists, the computer-generated arrays of different sizes are searched at similar rates (characters/sec). Further, there is a considerable trade-off possible between scanning characters in one array or in several; thus, almost as many background characters can be scanned in 1 array presented for 120 msec (12 characters) as in 3 arrays each presented for 40 msec (4 characters/array). This is best seen by looking at the scan times per character (Figure 4.2c), which dip just below 10 msec/character throughout the 40- to 120-msec interval.

The attentional search field around fixation is defined by the proportion of targets detected at various points within it, as shown in Figure 4.2d for search of 7 × 7 letter arrays. The search field is approximately concentric, centered slightly above fixation. However, locations with fewer neighbors or with adjacent blank space are easier to search (Bouma, 1978; Harris, Shaw, & Bates, 1979; Shaw, 1969), so that the measured search field is distorted by the boundaries of the 7 × 7 stimulus. The subject in Figure 4.2d tends to concentrate search more in the left than in the right half of the stimulus.

The search field depends on the stimuli used to measure it; extremely rapid presentations or extremely small-sized characters shrink the search field. However, these parameter variations do not necessarily alter the shape of the search field. That means, except for a task-dependent monotonic transformation, the search field would appear to be an invariant property of the visual system. Attention is distributed gracefully, like Fujiyama, high in the center and tapering gradually towards the periphery. Attractive though this picture of attention may be, in the next section it is shown to be false by evidence that the spatial distribution of attention can be voluntarily altered.

The Role of Attention in the Visual Search for Multiple Targets Among the most interesting questions concerning this aspect of attention (see also Schneider, Dumais & Shiffrin, Chapter 1, this volume) is: Can a subject search as quickly for a known target, for example say a *5*, as for an unknown numeral that is a member of a set of potential targets, for example say *0, 1, . . 9*? Neisser (1963) conjectured that the answer was yes, but he did not test the hypothesis correctly. The correct test requires comparing performance for the *same* target in known and unknown conditions.

In the sequential-search procedure, comparing detection accuracy for known and unknown targets requires comparing accuracy of the location judgments (*Where* in the critical array did the target occur?) in the two conditions: A typical *numeral-known* condition is a block of 100 trials in which only the target 5 occurs. The corresponding *numeral-unknown* condition is a mixed list of 1000 trials in which the numeral targets *0, 1, . . . 9* occur with equal probability. From this mixed list, the subset of 100 trials (on each of which the target 5 occurred) is extracted for comparison with the known condition. Obviously it would have made no sense to compare identification responses between two conditions because the subject knew in advance the identity of the target in the numeral-known condition. Location judgments are used to compare numeral-known and numeral-unknown conditions. Sperling *et al.* (1971) found that accuracies of location judgments for each of the numerals *0, 1, . . . 9* were nearly the same for target-known and target-unknown conditions and were highly correlated (0.97; see Figure 4.2e), providing strong evidence that the same search processes were executed in the two conditions. Any difference in search processes would suggest that a numeral that was relatively easy in one condition (e.g., known) would be relatively more difficult in the other condition (e.g., unknown), but this was not observed.

One can conceive of the search for a particular target numeral, for example, the numeral *1*, as a search task, for example, Task 1. One can conceive of search for the numeral *2* as Search Task 2. It is known that a subject who has to execute both searches simultaneously (i.e., either target may occur), does so with negligible loss in either search and is thus able (in classical terminology) to *attend* to 2 (or even 10) numerals at once. This is a case of apparently lossless division of attention, or better, of multiplication of attention. To describe this situation in contemporary jargon, the subject can execute 10 searches (for the 10 numerals) in parallel.

There is a technical problem in the interpretation of simultaneous search for two possible targets as the carrying out of two simultaneous tasks. Recall the prototypical concurrent tasks mentioned earlier: driving and listening to the radio. The search for Target 1 is analogous to driving the car, and the search for Target 2 is analogous to listening to the radio. Sometimes a driver encounters a road obstacle and a radio news item simultaneously, but Sperling *et al.*'s (1971) subjects never encountered Target 1 and Target 2 simultaneously in the same display. This is symptomatic of an important, real difference. Before resolving this difference, Example 3, in which two search tasks occur simultaneously, is considered.

Concurrent Search for Two Targets

Target Size Matched to Information-Processing Capacity The visual search experiments of Sperling *et al.* (1971) just described were directed at the question of finding optimal stimuli for visual search. How should characters in an array be arranged so that search can proceed as efficiently as possible? In the course of subsequent experiments with arrays of characters composed of different sizes, it quickly became apparent that it was inefficient to compose arrays of characters of just that size. For example, although it was efficient to image many small characters in the foveal area where acuity is good, these characters were below the acuity limit of peripheral vision, and thus most of the peripheral visual field was wasted. Conversely, composing an array of large characters that are resolvable in peripheral vision caused central acuity to be squandered because the fovea was fully occupied by a mere fragment of a character. The obvious solution seemed to be to compose an array of characters of different sizes, ranging from small characters in the center to large characters in the periphery, in which each size of character was matched to the information-processing capacity of the retinal area on which it was imaged. Anstis (1974) independently developed remarkably similar displays, which he used for demonstrating letters that are equally above their acuity threshold in different areas of the retina.

The investigation of spatially matched arrays was begun by the author in collaboration with Melvin Melchner. As before, test sequences were constructed in which only one target numeral occurred in a critical array that was otherwise composed entirely of letters (see preceding description). This target might occur at peripheral locations that received large-sized targets or central locations that

Figure 4.3 Search array matched to the information-processing capacity of the visual system. There is one numeral target.

received smaller targets. Figure 4.3 shows one of several array configurations that were tested.[5] To our astonishment, Melchner was unable to search arrays simultaneously for large and small targets (e.g., a large 9 or a small 9). This was especially astonishing because in earlier experiments, he had been able to search simultaneously for ten numeral targets (0, 1, . . . 9) when they were all the same size. Was a large 9 more different from a small 9 than from a large 3 or 4? We set about to devise an appropriate search task to test this possibility.

Concurrent Search for Large and Small Targets To investigate how well subjects can search for targets of two different sizes concurrently, arrays were constructed as follows: an outer frame contained 16 letters of the same large size as the earlier Sperling *et al.* (1971) experiments. A central interior contained 4 small letters. A long sequence of briefly flashed arrays was presented at a rate of 4/sec. A critical array embedded in the middle of the sequence contained a randomly chosen numeral target at one of the 16 outside locations and another randomly chosen numeral at one of the 4 inside locations.

In the main experimental conditions, the subjects' task was to detect both targets: the subjects had to state the identity, location, and their confidence level for each of the two targets. In some blocks of trials, they were told to give 90% of their attention to the inside target and 10% to the outside target; in other blocks, the instructions were reversed; and in still other blocks, subjects were instructed to give equal attention to both classes of targets.

Some useful methodological innovations were incorporated in the analysis of these data. Responses on which the lowest confidence was used (zero, "guessing") were found by chi-square tests to indeed be statistically independent of the stimuli. This means the subjects really knew when they really didn't know (Sperling and Melchner, 1976b, p. 209). Further, analysis of verifiable location errors showed that more than 95% of the time when a target was mislocated, it was mislocated at an adjacent horizontal or vertical (not diagonal) position. Thus, a more rigorous criterion for true identifications could be used, namely, correct identification response *and* confidence greater than zero *and* mislocation not greater than one adjacent position. The data are displayed in Figure 4.4a.

The abscissa and ordinate represent the percent of correct identifications of outside and inside targets, respectively, and each data point represents the average of 70–150 trials. The data fall along a line of slope approximately −1, indicating that as probability of identifying one class of target increases (according to the instructional demand), it is compensated by an almost exactly equivalent decrease in identification probability for the other class of targets. The locus of all achievable joint performances on the two tasks (approximated by the straight-line segments connecting the data points) is called an *attention operating*

---

[5]In all these experiments, stimuli are flashed very briefly and are disposed symmetrically around the fixation point to induce subjects to maintain eye fixation and move attention rather than move their eyes. See also footnote 4.

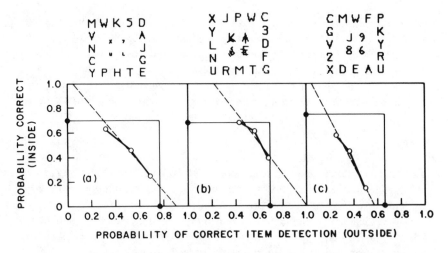

Figure 4.4 Attention operating characteristics for three pairs of concurrent tasks. In (a), concurrent detection of large and small numeral targets is shown. The abscissa indicates the percentage of correct identifications of the outside target; the ordinate indicates the percentage of correct identifications of the inside target. Isolated control conditions are indicated by darkened circles on coordinate axes; the independence point is defined by the meeting of the perpendiculars drawn through these control points. Concurrent performance is indicated by open circles. Data are shown for one subject (MJM) with two (or occasionally three) blocks of trials averaged for each data point. Attention conditions, ordered from upper left to lower right, respectively, are 90% to the inside, equal, and 90% to the outside. The heavy line connecting the data points is the AOC. The broken line represents the best-fitting straight line to the data. In (b), coordinates are the same as in (a), the outside task is the same as in (a). The inside task is detection of a noise-obscured numeral target of the same size as the outside target. In (c), the coordinates and the outside task are the same as in (a). The concurrent inside task is detection of a letter target among three numeral distractors, instead of vice verse as in (a) and (b). (Subject MJM, from Sperling and Melchner, 1978a.)

characteristic (AOC; Sperling & Melchner, 1976, 1978a),[6] following the terminology of signal detection theory. (For the history of receiver operating characteristics [ROCs] see Swets, 1964.) The AOC is a particular instance of the performance operating characteristic (POC) proposed by Norman & Bobrow (1975).

[6]The first to use the term "Attention Operating Characteristic" appears to have been Kinchla in 1969 in the title of an unpublished talk in rural Netherlands and in a privately circulated document (cited in Kinchla, 1980). Curiously, his subsequent publications (Kinchla, 1977; Kinchla and Collyer, 1974) argued against an AOC, proposing instead that attentional manipulations had no effect on the subjects' allocation of their information-processing resources, only on their decision criteria. The attention allocation data of Figure 4.4, the AOC and its relation to the ROC, the attention-switching model, and attendance theory were first reported at the Psychonomic Society, St. Louis, November 1975 (Sperling, 1975) and subsequently more completely at the Seventh Conference on Attention and Performance, Gordes, France, and the International Congress of Physiology, Leningrad, USSR, November 1976. Because of unanticipated publication delays, the data actually were published in the

Control Conditions Two control conditions are especially important.

1. Control for memory overload: A series of trials was run in which the letter distractors were replaced by dots. This made target identification trivially easy, and subjects never failed to report both targets correctly. Thus, any errors subjects may make in experimental conditions are due to their inability to detect the targets among distractors, not to their inability to report targets once detected.

2. Isolation condition, report of only one class of targets: In some blocks of trials, subjects were instructed to report only outside targets and to ignore inside targets; and in other blocks, they received the reverse instruction. These control data are graphed directly on the coordinate axes in Figure 4.4a. That the probability of report is nearly equal in the two control tasks (inside, outside) is not a coincidence; the character sizes and array sizes were chosen to match the tasks in difficulty.

Can Subjects Search Simultaneously for Large and Small Targets? If subjects could search for both targets concurrently without loss, their performance in all experimental conditions would fall on the *independence point,* the point at which subjects identify both large and small targets concurrently as accurately as they do in the corresponding control condition. (This is the upper right point of the square in Figure 4.4a). Clearly, this point is not achieved; there always is some loss.

Three Concurrent Pairs of Search Tasks In order to gauge the amount of loss, it is informative to investigate other, related pairs of concurrent tasks. In all, three pairs of tasks were studied. One task in each pair remained precisely the same throughout: detection of a numeral among the outside letters. Three different inside tasks were matched to this task in difficulty: (1) detection–identification of a small inside target, (2) detection–identification of a normally-sized inside numeral (where every inside character was obscured by a randomly chosen "noise squiggle"), and (3) detection–identification of a single target *letter* among inside numerals.

The same control and experimental conditions as before were conducted with these stimuli. Figure 4.4 shows the AOCs generated by these three pairs of tasks. The distance of the AOC from the independence point is a measure of the incompatibility of two tasks. *Perfectly compatible* tasks—performed as well concurrently as in isolation—would fall on the independence point. Perfectly incompatible tasks would fall somewhere on the straight line connecting the isolated control performances.

The percent of isolated performance achieved by concurrent performance provides an index of compatibility between two tasks. Concurrent performance is averaged over the component tasks under conditions of equal attention, that is, at the point where the AOC curve—or surface in higher dimensional space—crosses the line connecting the origin and the independence point. (Area under the AOC is a better, but more complex, measure considered later in this chapter.)

Soviet Union (Sperling & Melchner, 1976a) 2 years earlier than in the United States (Sperling & Melchner, 1978a, 1978b). These are the first published AOCs.

For subject MJM, the most incompatible pair of tasks consists of (1) searching for a numeral among letters concurrently with (2) searching for a letter among numerals. These tasks are almost mutually exclusive, average concurrent performance being about 54% of isolated performance. (By doing only one task or the other, never both—even under concurrent instructions—50% of isolated performance would be achieved, by definition.) The most compatible tasks are searching for a numeral (on the outside) concurrently with searching for a numeral of the same size obscured by noise (on the inside). Concurrent performance is about 82% of isolated performance. The original pair of tasks (searching for a large numeral concurrently with searching for a small numeral) falls between with a concurrent performance of 66% of isolated performance.

We have distinguished implicitly between the process by which performance moves from one AOC to another (changing the component tasks) and the process by which performance moves along a given AOC (increasing the amount of attention allocated to one member of a concurrent task pair at the expense of the other). To compare the compatibility of two pairs of tasks, we generally need two AOCs (not just one point on each AOC). The situation is analogous to signal detection theory in which, to compare the detectability of two signals, in general two ROCs are needed, not just one point on each. The relation of AOC to ROC is developed fully in subsequent sections of this chapter.

Concurrent versus Compound Tasks

Concurrency in Partial-Report Procedures

AOC Graph

Consider the partial report procedure just described in which a subject views a brief flash of a 2 × 4 letter array. The coordinates of an AOC graph are accuracy of report of the top row versus accuracy of report of the bottom row.

Control Conditions

The isolated control condition would consist of a block of trials in which only one particular row of the stimulus is presented. Unfortunately, there is a technical problem with this task. The problem with conducting blocks of trials or cuing the subject too far in advance of the stimulus presentation is that his or her visual fixation will drift involuntarily—if not actually jump—toward the requested row (Kowler & Steinman, 1979, 1981), and such trials are thus not strictly comparable to ones in which the eyes remain fixated between the two rows. An equiv-

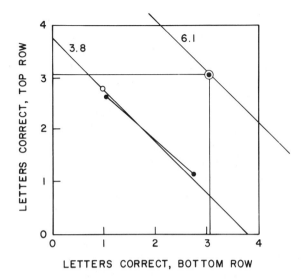

Figure 4.5 Concurrent reports of the top and the bottom row in a whole-report procedure. Filled circles indicate data from one subject for two conditions: (1) give attention to and report the top row first; and (2) give attention to and report the bottom row first. The light diagonal lines indicate equal capacity contours (equal numbers of letters). Open circle indicates data from unconstrained whole reports. Partially filled circle indicates data from partial reports of one row only. The extrapolation of the partial-report data to the coordinate axes represents a lower bound on the performance that might have been observed in an isolated control task. (Subject JC, from Sperling, 1959.)

alent but better isolated control task is telling the subject just 150 msec in advance of each stimulus presentation which row to report. Either form of the isolated control task leads to nearly perfect performance.

Concurrent Tasks

The concurrent condition would be a full report of both rows, with the instruction to direct attention primarily to the top row in some conditions and to the bottom row in others. Sperling (1959, 1960) studied a closely related condition that was interpreted by some subjects as the concurrent condition described here. Data are shown in Figure 4.5 for one such subject.[7] This subject has a memory capacity of 3.8 letters in whole reports. In unconstrained whole reports, the subject normally reports the top row first (achieving 2.8 of 4 letters) and then the

[7]The AOC and partial report data of Figure 4.5 are averaged over four cue delays (0, 0.15, 0.30, 0.50 seconds) because performance did not vary between these short delays due to the strategy the subject used. For partial reports (partially filled circle, Figure 4.5), accuracy is assumed to be equally divided between top and bottom rows because the breakdown by row is no longer available. (Data from Sperling, 1959, app. I, Tables 8, 11, 12.)

bottom row (achieving 1.0 of 4). When requested, the subject can, remarkably, allocate most of this capacity either to the top or to the bottom row, with residual capacity falling to the remaining row without any loss. These data define subject's AOC. Data from partial reports (reports of only one row) represent a lower bound on the performance that might have been observed in an isolated control task, and these data are illustrated in Figure 4.5, on the coordinate axes. (Looked at in another way, the independence point, defined by the intersection of the isolated control data on a graph like Figure 4.5, would lie on or beyond the partial report point.) In making whole reports, subjects show enormous loss relative to the independence point because they can remember barely one row of 4 letters and independence would require them to remember 1.5 rows.

The whole report task is a concurrent task requiring concurrent reports of top and bottom rows. In the component (control) task, the subject is prepared for and reports only one row. This control task is equivalent to a partial report task in which the signal indicating which row to report is given long in advance of the stimulus presentation (prestimulus cue.) How are data of partial report tasks with post-stimulus cues interpreted—a task in which the subject must be prepared for both rows?

To represent partial-report data on an AOC graph as in Figure 4.5, the accuracy of partial reports on the top row is graphed as the y coordinate and reports of the bottom row as the x coordinate, even though x and y values represent different trials rather than the same trial as in concurrent tasks. The control tasks (theoretically, blocks of partial reports of only the top row or only the bottom row but, in practice, partial reports with prestimulus cues) are the same as for the concurrent task of reporting both rows.

The partial report data are interpreted as indicating that the subject has a memory capacity of 6.1 letters, almost twice the whole report of 3.8 letters. Unlike the whole report task, in the partial report task there is no trial in which the subject actually reports 6 letters—the inference of a memory capacity of 6 letters is based on trials on which the subject reports only 3. Thus, the interpretation of the partial report task requires a theory about an assumed mental process—visual memory.

Compound Tasks

Partial report is an example of an attention task that is only partially concurrent. Stimuli of *both* component tasks (upper row, lower row) are presented, and only *one* component response (report of only one row) is made. A functionally different type of task is involved in the search for one of two possible targets. The stimulus from just one of the component tasks is presented (one target) and the subject responds with a response chosen from just one of the component tasks (a target name). This is an example of a compound task.

The analysis of compound tasks is fundamentally different from concurrent tasks. To characterize the difference, it is necessary first to define a task. A task is a triple (S, R, U) of two sets (Stimulus, Response) and a Utility function that assigns a real value to every stimulus–response pair (see Sperling, 1983, for details). A concurrent tasks is the *sum* of its component tasks. A stimulus and response are chosen from every component task. In concurrent tasks, such as driving a car and simultaneously listening to a newscast, performance on each concurrent task is compared to performance on the same task in isolation.

A compound task is the *union* of its component tasks. Only a single stimulus selected from any one of all the component tasks is presented on each trial, and the subject responds with any response selected from any of the component tasks. In concurrent tasks, the context that makes a particular task difficult is the other task being performed on the *same* trial. In compound tasks, the context occurs on *other* trials. The detection of Target 1 in the detection task is difficult because, on other trials, Target 2 is presented and the subject must be prepared for both. In the following, it will become clear that, to interpret data from compound tasks, one needs first, a theory of *stimulus uncertainty loss* (loss that a statistically ideal detector with perfect memory and attention would exhibit) and second, a theory of mental processing to deal with any residual, intrinsically human loss.

Concurrency, Compounding, and Processing Stages

Normally, information processing by an organism is regarded as reflecting the operation of a chain of internal processes (a sequence of processing stages.) By definition, concurrent tasks measure the throughput—from stimulus to response—of the whole organism, that is, the whole chain. Compound tasks are usually implicitly interpreted as being concurrent tasks for some subset of the processing chain. Compound tasks are usually interpreted as being concurrent tasks for some subset of the processing chain. For example, compound search for two targets is described (incorrectly) as concurrent within a comparison stage that matches stimuli against remembered targets.

The interpretation of concurrent tasks is easier than that of compound tasks. With concurrent tasks, one observes performance on the task in isolation and then again on precisely the same task in the concurrent context (e.g., driving in isolation and then driving plus listening to the radio). In concurrent tasks, the input and output for all component tasks are observable on every trial.

In compound tasks, only one component task is presented on each trial. Nevertheless, all the compound tasks under consideration here (varieties of signal detection, target localization, stimulus identification, choice reaction times) are interpretable as being concurrent for a subset of the processing chain. This is a favorable circumstance that simplifies interpretation of the performance of the subset, but it is not the whole answer. The input or output of a subset of the processing chain—not both—can be observed because either or both are interior to the organism and therefore unobservable. Ergo, to interpret such a compound task, a theory is needed, no matter how trivial—a theory that (1) asserts which subset is assumed to be concurrently exercised by the compound task and (2) bridges the gap between the exercised subset and the rest of the processing chain. When the compound task is not interpretable as being concurrent within the critical stage, it will be even more cumbersome to relate performance of the compound task to performance of component subtasks; and the theoretical burden will be correspondingly greater.

Concurrency and Compounding in Search Tasks

Simultaneous Search for Different Alternative Targets

Search for Targets 1 and *2 versus Search for 1* or *2* Recall the search experiment in which an observer searched for a numeral target (0, 1, 2, . . . , 9) among letter distractors. This search can be regarded as 10 simultaneous searches. Previously, two of these tasks were considered: (1) search for a *1* and (2) search for a *2*. If performance of Task 1 versus Task 2 is plotted on an AOC graph, the same problem arises as with partial report: searching for *1 or 2* is not the same as searching for *1 and 2*. In searching for *1 or 2*, there are no trials on which both Targets 1 and 2 are presented. Furthermore, the distractor items for Target 1 are also the distractors for Target 2. Contrast this to Sperling and Melchner's (1978a) concurrent search for large and small numerals in which each class of targets had its own distractor—large distractor letters for the large numeral targets and small ones for the small targets.

A Model for Search The purpose of these examples is to illustrate first, that a compound task and a concurrent task require basically different processing mechanisms even when much of the same processing is involved; and second, that a compound task is *necessarily* more difficult than the isolated control, whereas performing two tasks concurrently is not necessarily more difficult than performing an isolated control task.

Consideration is restricted here to the most favorable case for equivalence in the compound–concurrent comparison; namely, to a perception component for which the compound task, search for *1 or 2*, is concurrent (i.e., a component that performs the same operations whether confronted with searching for *1 or 2* or *1 and 2*. Consider, for example, a "perception" component that executes comparisons between a feature list that represents a stimulus item (distractor or target) and the feature lists in memory that represent the eligible target items (0, 1, 2, . . . , 9). It might sensibly program the same sequence of comparisons whether it is confronted with *1 or 2* or *1 and 2* when the task ultimately is to discover the location of *1 and/or 2*.

In order to analyze a subsequent decision component that acts on the output of the perception component, this output must be defined. The required response in both the concurrent and compound tasks is a location judgment. Therefore, it is assumed that the output of the perception component consists of the best estimate of the location of each possible target (*1, 2*), for example, *1* lower left and *2* upper right. In the concurrent task (search for *1 and 2*), this is exactly what is needed for a response, and the decision component merely needs to transmit the location information for the eligible targets (*1 and 2*) to a response mechanism. In the compound task, this is inadequate information because there are two possible responses (e.g., lower left, upper right). Thus, a sensible decision component would ask the perception component to rate its outputs in terms of confidence. Then, the decision component could choose the one among the alternatives that maximized the expected payoff. Only if the a priori probabilities of target occurrence were equal for all targets, and the payoffs were equal for all correct responses and equal for all errors, would the highest confidence output necessarily be chosen for response. Note that the confidence information— essential to the compound task—is irrelevant to the concurrent task.

Performance in the compound task is inevitably inferior to performance in the isolated control condition—even when there is no attentional loss of information. This occurs because of occasional confusion of a distractor with an unpresented target. For example, in a trial on which Targets 1 and 2 were eligible for presentation, and Target 1 was presented, the subject might think Target 2 occurred somewhere in the search field and respond accordingly. The response, a location judgment, would probably be wrong. This kind of error is avoided in the isolated control condition when the subject knows that only Type 1 targets can appear.

In both examples (partial report and visual search), the concurrent and the compound versions of the tasks were interpreted as making similar demands on an early stage (VIS or sensory memory in one case and perception or recognition in the other) and making enormously different demands on later stages of memory and decision. This is hardly surprising given that these compound tasks were invented in order to study early stages of information processing.

Conclusions The conclusions from the analysis thus far of concurrent and compound tasks are

1. There necessarily is at least some loss in compound search for multiple targets compared to search for a simple target.[8] It requires a detection theory to determine whether or not experimental data exhibit an additional loss due to attention.

2. Concurrent search does not necessarily show a loss compared to an isolated control.

3. In concurrent tasks, a task performed in isolation is the standard against which performance is measured for precisely the same task in different concurrent combinations. Concurrent tasks can be

[8]Duncan (1980) makes similar observations of the performance losses that are inherent in increases in the number of stimulus alternatives, increases that inevitably occur in going from an elementary task to a compound task (of which the elementary task is a component).

analyzed without resort to any information-processing theory. In this respect concurrent tasks are the ideal tool for studying the splitting of attention between competing task demands because concurrent tasks measure the input–output characteristics of the whole organism. There are two cautionary provisions: (1) To avoid degenerate cases, the component tasks of a concurrent task must be completely discriminable—the subject must be able to correctly say which task he or she has performed. (2) Alternatives to attentional loss—such as response incompatibility—must be ruled out in control experiments.

4. Performance in compound tasks cannot be analyzed without a theory about the intermediate stages of information processing. When the assumptions, model, or theory about intermediate stages are not controversial, they may be a small price to pay for learning about intermediate stages. In fact, the focus of compound tasks is inherently on the input–output characteristics of intermediate stages of processing, and cleverly designed compound tasks (together with concurrent tasks) are the ideal tool for unravelling the components of information processing.

Thus, concurrent tasks are appropriate for either macroscopic or microscopic analysis, whereas compound tasks are inherently microscopic in analysis.

Compound and Concurrent Search of Multiple Locations

In this section, these principles are applied to one of the most studied problems of visual attention—the ability (or lack of ability) of observers simultaneously to monitor different locations in the visual field for the occurrence of some event. Over how many locations in the visual field can attention be spread before performance suffers in each local area? This question has already been considered in the numeral detection experiments (Figure 4.2 and 4.4). It is demonstrated here that attempts to answer this question with classical incremental stimuli run afoul of insidious methodological traps.

Mertens One of the first serious experimental attempts to measure the spread of visual attention was by Mertens (1956). He required his observers to maintain fixation faithfully on a central fixation mark. He then presented them with very weak flashes of light to be detected. When subjects detected a flash, they indicated so by pressing a button. In some blocks of trials, the flashes could occur at any of four locations around fixation (northwest, southwest, southeast, or northeast); in others, at only one (e.g., northeast; see Figure 4.6).

Mertens's observers seemed to have slightly lower detection thresholds at an unknown one of four locations than at one predetermined location. He concluded, gamely, that it was more effective for the subject to allow visual attention to spread out over four locations than "to stress himself continually not to look in the direction of attention" (p. 1070). Unfortunately, Mertens was unaware of the rudiments of signal detection theory, and so there were flaws in his procedure. His strange result was replicated once by Schuckman (1963) in an experiment with the same difficulties as Mertens' and by Howarth and Lowe (1966), who found no effect of any kind of uncertainty—not of stimulus location, size, or time of occurrence. Since then, the opposite result has been obtained.

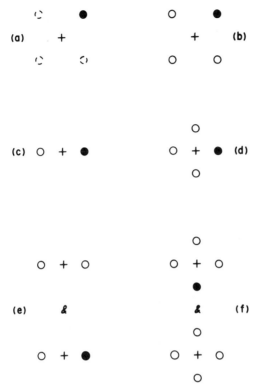

Figure 4.6 Stimulus configurations in spread of attention studies: left column, focused configurations; right column, spread-out configurations. Plus signs indicate fixation marks. Filled circles indicate targets. Open circles indicate other locations at which a target can occur on other trials. (a) Mertens' display for yes–no detection judgments; the dashed circles indicate locations that, in some conditions, contain visible pedestals (baseline illumination) even though no targets will appear there. (b) Mertens' display in which the target may occur in any of four locations; a particular target in the northeast location is indicated. (c and d) Displays for, respectively, two-alternative and four-alternative forced-location judgments. (e and f) Cohn and Lasley's displays for two-interval forced-choice judgments; the ampersand lies between the display that occurs in the first interval (above) and in the second interval (below).

Some contemporary approaches to spatial uncertainty in detection are now considered in order of increasing complexity.

Forced-Location Judgments Consider the following *Gedanken* experiment. A flash can occur in either of two locations[9] (east or west) in some sessions and in any of four locations (Figure 4.6c and d) in other sessions. The accuracy of naming the target location is measured and found to be higher in two-location

[9]See Footnotes 4 and 5.

than in four-location sessions. Unfortunately, it requires a theory of guessing to estimate the attention effect because visual detection accuracy is higher in two-location than four-location stimuli even when the observer's eyes are shut; and for low-intensity stimuli, the guessing effect is predominant. This forced-location judgment, for example, is the one used by Sperling et al. (1971) in the search tasks described in a previous section (Figure 4.2).

Two-Interval Forced Choice To obviate guessing analysis, a two-alternative forced-choice paradigm may be used (Cohn & Lasley, 1974). All trials are composed of two intervals, and a target always occurs in one or the other of the intervals. In some sessions, there are two possible locations in which the target may occur; in others, there are four possible locations for the target.[10] Subjects correctly identify the interval containing the target in the two-location trials. Because chance guessing is the same in both kinds of trials, and four locations usually are not monitored as accurately as two, there is an attentional loss in attempting to monitor four locations. Simple? Wrong!

The problem in interpreting the results of the two-versus four-location experiments is that, according to the most widely accepted theory, even a theoretically ideal detector (one without attention or memory loss) would do worse on the four-location trials than on the two-location trials. An attentional deficit is proved only when the human's loss is larger than the ideal detector's loss. Thus, the interpretation of these experiments hinges on the theory of ideal detectors.

An *ideal detector* operates according to a rule that has been proved optimal for some desired outcome; for example, maximizing the percentage of correct responses. An ideal detector does not forget information and is limited only by the quality of data it receives. The ideal detector concept may be extended to the case in which the detector has internal noise, provided the noise does not vary as a function of signals or tasks. How do ideal detectors apply to the present experiment?

Detection Theory Assume that each location (i) being monitored produces an amount of sensory noise n_i on each trial where n_i is a random variable. At the target location (i_T) there is an additional signal (s) producing a net input of $n_i + s$. The ideal detector would choose the location that had the largest net input: If $n_i + s$ were greater than all other n_i ($i \neq T$), a correct detection would occur; if some other n_i ($i \neq T$) happened to be the largest, false detection would occur. A false detection might still, by chance, produce a correct response in a two-interval forced choice if the false detection happened to occur in the same interval as (but at another location than) the target. So stated, the theory is simple. As soon as realistic complications are added—such as, (1) unequal signal

---

[10]Actually, Cohn and Lasley compared one versus four locations (not two versus four), but this has no significance for the discussion here.

probabilities, (2) unequal rewards for the various locations, (3) signal parameters not known exactly, and (4) multiple observations (within an interval) at each location—matters become more complex.[11]

Largest Noise Sample I propose a simple way to grasp the statistical complexity involved in multiple-location paradigms. Consider how an ideal detector comes to make a mistake: the noise at some particular location exceeds the signal plus noise at the target. It is necessary only to consider the location i that produced the largest noise sample (n_i) because this is the one that, if it exceeds n_T + s, produces the error. The largest noise sample will be the largest of three (in the four-location monotiring task, Figure 4.6d) or the largest of seven (in the two-interval, four-location monitoring task, Figure 4.6f). This compares to the largest of one (Figure 4.6c) or the largest of three (Figure 4.6e) in the two-location monitoring tasks. The greater the number of equally distributed random variables, the larger the maximum of the sample tends to be, and thus the more likely it is to be the cause of an error. A response based on noise is not necessarily wrong, but it is always less likely to be correct than a response based on signal, which is correct by definition. The more locations there are to be monitored, the more noise samples there will be; the more noise samples there are, the more errors there will be. The particular advantage of looking at the largest noise sample is that, although the distribution of the noise random variable may be unknown, there are only three possible distributions of maxima (Gumbel, 1958; Galambos, 1978). Thus when the number of locations is large, the distribution of the maximum noise sample may be better known than that of any individual sample.

Consequences of Stimulus Uncertainty The point of the preceding discussion is that it is not possible to interpret the loss of accuracy in detection with increases in the number of stimulus locations being monitored unless one has a theory to determine whether the loss is greater than would be exhibited by an ideal detector. This dependence on a theory (ideal detectors) is not surprising; a little reflection shows that the paradigms considered here were exemplars of compound tasks. The complexities of compound tasks can be avoided by concurrent tasks that have different, perhaps more tractable, problems. In the case of N locations being monitored, concurrent means that each location has the same probability of containing a target when it is viewed in the context of the other N − 1 locations as it does in isolation. It also means that 0, 1, 2, . . . n targets may occur in a presentation instead of just 0 or 1 as in most compound tasks. Obviously, a large number of targets would pose memory and recognition problems as well as detection problems; fortunately, there are paradigms to provide

---

[11]Some of these complexities are dealt with, for example, by Swets (this volume), Green and Swets (1966), and Shaw and Shaw (1977).

the data to estimate these sources of interference. Furthermore, the occurrence (or detection) of a target makes the detection of a second target more difficult (Gilliom & Sorkin, 1974; Pohlmann & Sorkin, 1976; Sorkin, Pastore & Pohlmann, 1972; Sorkin, Pohlman & Gilliom, 1973; Sorkin, Pohlmann & Woods, 1976; Schneider & Shiffrin, 1977; Sperling & Melchner, 1978b, p. 681).

Concurrent versus Compound Tasks: Summary and Conclusions

Concurrent and compound are just two categories of tasks. It is certainly easy to create new tasks that are neither concurrent nor compound and that are arbitrarily close to either one or the other category. Clearly the concurrent–compound distinction could be obscured or made unimportant. Nevertheless, the paradigms that are in use today do fall into these categories. What of practical importance can be concluded about the four cases generated by the two paradigms (concurrent and compound) and the two outcomes (loss or no loss relative to the control task)?

No Loss

When there is an insignificant amount of loss in either paradigm, the conclusion is simple: there is no loss. That is, the component tasks of the concurrent combination of tasks can be carried out without loss; and the asserted component processes underlying performance in compound tasks could be carried out without loss.

Loss in Concurrent Tasks

Loss in concurrent tasks means an actual, human performance loss in one or more of the concurrent tasks. We emphasize *human* loss because ideal detectors would not show a loss. In a driving–listening task, the performance loss itself is the datum of interest. In concurrent psychophysical tasks, the fact of a loss often is not in itself of interest—the underlying processes are. Thus we may want to know whether the real performance loss is due to an overburdening of detection, recognition, memory, or response processes. Such questions are not answered in just one experiment. For example, Sperling and Melchner's four variations in targets and distractors greatly helped to eliminate memory or response processes as the determinants of performance loss in their concurrent tasks. Usually, more than just one paradigm is needed; and because compound tasks deal with inferred processes, they can be useful in arriving at answers about component processes.

Loss in Compound Tasks

The null hypothesis for compound tasks is the performance loss shown by an ideal detector. To infer an attention deficit, recognition failure, a memory lapse, response interference, or any intrinsically human loss requires first rejecting the null hypothesis. On the other hand, the null hypothesis for concurrent tasks is that there is no loss; observation of any loss is informative about intrinsic human functions.

To this summary two provisos must be added: (1) Concurrent tasks lose their good properties when the component tasks become indiscriminable from each other (a degenerate case). (2) The parameters of a human sensory system—even when it is behaving like an ideal detector—are intrinsically human and may even interest more people than just the psychophysicists. But the distinction between ideal detectors and theories that postulate additional losses is crucial, as is the relation of these theories to the tasks (concurrent and compound) that give rise to them. The purpose of the metaphors and examples of this section has been to emblazon these distinctions in the mind of the reader so that they may serve as guideposts in his or her encounters with the frequently confusing literature on attention.

Optimization Theory

The Interpretation of Performance Operating Characteristics

Attending Example

Nonoverlapping Classes Consider a student who wishes to attend two classes: a class in Nursing, offered between noon and 2:00 p.m., and a class in Spanish offered between 3:00 and 5:00 p.m. The classes are offered in two different classrooms that are adjacent to each other. The student can run from one class to another in a negligible amount of time, but once the student leaves a classroom, the student may not return. At the end of the semester, the student takes a final examination in each class. Each instructor asks one question about each lecture on the examination. The times within a lecture during which the tested material was discussed are distributed randomly and uniformly over the lecture period. If the student happened to be present at the instant the relevant material was presented, the student will be able to answer the question correctly, otherwise the student will fail that question.

The student's only strategic option is the choice of switching time from one class to the other. Clearly, if the student switches from Class 1 to Class 2 anytime between 2:00 and 3:00 p.m., he or she will score 100% on both examinations.

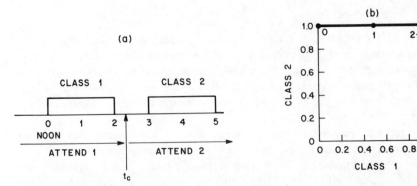

Figure 4.7 Attendance example, nonoverlapping classes. (a) Scheduled times for two classes, (1) and (2). The height of the Class 1 and Class 2 functions represents the instantaneous density of information being offered in each class. The abscissa represents time (in hours), and a particular class-switching time (2:30) is indicated by t_c under the abscissa. (b) Joint performance (performance operating characteristic—POC) for the two classes in (a). The ordinates indicate performance on examinations for each class, 1 and 2, respectively, and the classroom-switching times are indicated near the points on the POC that represent the joint performance on the two examinations.

Figure 4.7a illustrates the two class periods, and Figure 4.7b the attendance operating characteristic, which is another instance of a performance operating characteristic (POC). Joint performance for a switch between 2:00 and 3:00 p.m. is represented at the independence point. The student's expected performance[12] as a function of switch times is illustrated in Figure 4.7b.

The independence point represents the only reasonable strategy for this class schedule. The top and the right hand limbs of the POC represent foolish strategies. The left side and bottom of Figure 4.7b represent perverse strategies. By sitting in Classroom 2 from noon to 2:30 (while nothing is happening there) and then switching over to Classroom 1 and spending the remainder of the time there, the student could achieve a score of exactly zero on both examinations! Having acknowledged that perverse strategies exist, their study is now relegated to another branch of psychology, and attention here is focused on the search for optimal strategies.

Overlapping Classes: Iso-utility Contours Consider now a more perplexing example: Class 1 is scheduled from noon to 3:00 p.m., and Class 2 is scheduled from 2:00 to 4:00 p.m.; the classroom-switching rule and examinations remain as

---

[12]In this example, information is viewed as though it is presented at an instant in time and the stochastic variability in responses is neglected, thereby treating expected outcomes as though they were actual outcomes. These are technical details that would unnecessarily complicate the exposition for those readers who are not fluent in probability theory and that are not essential for those readers who are.

before. Now there is a real scheduling conflict. The attending operating characteristic in Figure 4.8 shows the outcome of the various allowable switching strategies. The student cannot expect to perform perfectly on both examinations. The student can perform perfectly in Class 1 and achieve a score of 50% in Class 2, perform perfectly in Class 2 and achieve a score of 66.7% in Class 1, or achieve something in between. Again, the student can devise strategies, but these are not considered here. How is the student to decide among the reasonable strategies?

To choose a strategy, it is necessary to know the utility of the strategy. For example, suppose that these two classes contribute equally to the student's overall grade point average—the higher the average is, the greater the utility will be. The utility function is

$$u(x_1, x_2) = \frac{100(x_1 + x_2)}{2} , \qquad (4.1)$$

where x_1 is score on Class 1 and $u(x_1, x_2)$ is utility. (Because utility is known only to an arbitrary, strictly increasing monotonic transformation; the concern with scale factors here is only to clarify the example.)

The optimal strategy is to attend all of Class 2 and as much of Class 1 as possible, thereby achieving an average of 83.3%. This and other implications of the particular utility function 4.1 are made intuitively obvious by plotting the utility function together with the operating characteristic[13] as in Figure 4.8. The utility of each strategy can now be computed. That is, utility can now be written as a function of the class-switching time (t_c) by writing the examination scores as a function of t_c. Therefore,

$$u(t_c) = 50\left[\frac{\min(t_c, 3)}{3} + \frac{\min(4 - t_c, 2)}{2} \right] , \qquad 0 \leq t_c \leq 4,$$

where $\min(a, b)$ is defined as the smaller (minimum) of a and b, and t_c is measured in hours (with noon taken as zero).

The diagonal lines in Figure 4.8b represent iso-utility contours. Utility (u) can be computed for every point in the joint performance space (x_1, x_2) whether or not that point is achievable. The parameters used to label iso-utility contours

[13]Graphs displaying operating characteristics together with iso-utility contours have long been widely used in economic theory and were introduced to psychology via the study of attention by Navon and Gopher (1979). The concept of utility is central to signal detection theory (e.g., Swets, Tanner, & Birdsall, 1961), and ROCs have been graphed together with various performance criteria (Swets, 1973); but the only prior graph of an ROC together with iso-utility contours is in Metz, Starr, Lusted, and Rossman (1975, Figure 5, p. 420). The attendance example was proposed by Sperling and Melchner (1978b).

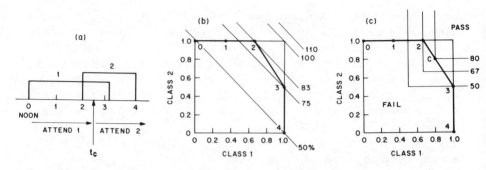

Figure 4.8 Attendance example, overlapping classes: (a) density of information offered in Classes 1 and 2 as a function of time; (b) joint performance (POC) for the classes in (a). The iso-utility contours represent the loci of equal contributions to the cumulative grade point average. (c) Same POC as (b). The contours divide the space into pass–fail regions and the parameter represents the minimum passing grade required in both courses.

indicate their utility. The attendance operating characteristic can be followed as it crosses these contours until it touches the maximum utility contour it can reach. The highest contour reached is 83.3%; this occurs with a class-switching time of 2:00 p.m. and results from a perfect score in Class 2 jointly with 66.7% in Class 1. The reason for the relative neglect of Class 1 is that useful information has higher density per unit time in Class 2 than in Class 1, and therefore the *marginal utility* of attending Class 2 is greater than that of Class 1. The student should exchange time in Class 1 for time in Class 2 whenever possible.

Suppose that what matters is not grade point average but simply passing all the courses. The utility is 1.0 if both courses are passed, and 0 otherwise. Figure 4.8c illustrates utility graphs for three minimum required passing grades (50%, 67%, and 80%). The curves in Figure 4.8c are not iso-utility contours as before, but divisions of the graph into two regions: pass and fail. For convenience, the three boundaries under consideration are represented on one graph. All the reasonable strategies suffice when the minimum passing grade is 50%; two-thirds of the reasonable strategies are adequate with a minimum passing grade of 67%; only one strategy will achieve 80%, which is the highest grade simultaneously achievable in both courses. To achieve a grade of 80%, the student attends 80% of each class;[14] that is, he or she switches from Class 1 to Class 2 after 2.4 hours in Class 1 (at 2:24 p.m.). Ironically, this strategy, which is the only one that will able the student to pass both courses when a passing grade of 80% is required, is the only strategy that would cause the student to *fail* both courses when a passing grade of 80.1% is required.

[14]See Footnote 12.

Signal Detection Theory: Receiver Operating
Characteristic

In the classroom example, the assumption that information is transmitted by the instructor uniformly over the whole scheduled class period is unrealistic. More realistic assumptions would be that instructors take a while to ''warm up'' before they reach their maximum exposition rate; and, having once reached this rate, they begin to tire, at first slowly, and then severely. Figure 4.9a shows estimated instructor information rates for two classes: Nursing from noon to 5:00 p.m. and Spanish from 1:00 p.m. to 4:00 p.m. Figure 4.9b shows the attendance operating characteristic for the student who attempts to take both classes. With these more realistic assumptions, the previously straight-lined POCs now describe smooth curves. The information rate during class period i, $P_i(t)$, is assumed to be zero when class is not in session and to be nonnegative during class. The total amount of information (E_i) presented in a class $[E_i = \int_{\text{start}}^{\text{finish}} p_i(t)\, dt]$ is assumed to exist and be bounded. For the attending strategy, in which a student attends Class 1 from its start until time c and then attends Class 2 until its finish, the amount of information E_i accumulated in each class is given by

$$E_1 = \int_{-\infty}^{c} p_1(t)\, dt \quad\text{and}\quad E_2 = \int_{c}^{\infty} p_2(t)\, dt.$$

Information accumulates only from the starting time t_0 of the class; however, because $E_1(t)$ is zero for $t < t_0$, it is convenient to write the integral from $-\infty$ to c rather than from t_0. The same holds true for Class 2. The POC is a graph of E_2 versus E_1 as c varies.

The information rates for Nursing (n) and Spanish (s) shown in Figure 4.9a are analogous to the conditional probability distributions given noise n, $p_n(t)$, and signal plus noise, $s + n$, $p_s(t)$, in signal detection theory (Green & Swets, 1966). Typically, these conditional distributions are assumed to be normal probability density functions, but this is not essential to the theory. On any trial k, the stimulus produces an effect t_k described by a sample from the appropriate distribution (p_s, p_n), and the observer reports ''signal'' if $t_k > c$ and ''noise'' otherwise. In signal detection theory, c is called the criterion. The probabilities of hits P_s and of false alarms Q_n are given by

$$P_s = \int_{c}^{\infty} p_s(x)\, dx, \quad\text{and}\quad Q_n = \int_{c}^{\infty} p_n(x)\, dx.$$

A graph of P_s versus Q_n (Figure 4.9c) is called a receiver operating characteristic (ROC).

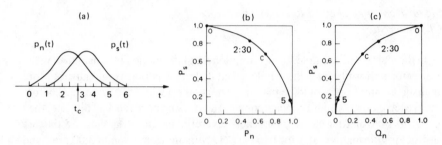

Figure 4.9 (a) Normal assumptions for information density in two classes, Nursing (n) and Spanish (s) as a function of time (t) in hours after noon. (b) Attendance Operating Characteristic for a student who switches from Class *n* to Class *s* at various times. Representative values of switching times are indicated adjacent to the POC, and the abscissa P_n and ordinate P_s indicate performance (examination scores) in the two classes, Nursing (n) and Spanish (s), respectively. (c) A Receiver Operating Characteristic (ROC) for the distributions illustrated in (a). The density functions $p_n(t)$ and $p_s(t)$ are interpreted as the conditional distributions of noise alone and of signal plus noise on the sensory continuum *t*, and the abscissa Q_n and ordinate P_s represent false alarms and hits, respectively. Panel b, the mirror image of Panel c, is now interpreted as a decision operating characteristic, when it is applied to a discrimination or to a signal detection experiment. See text for details.

Decision Operating Characteristic

The ROC and POC graphic conventions produce mirror images of each other (compare Figures 4.9b and 4.9c). In fact, the ROC uses a counter-intuitive convention: it plots good performance on signal trials (hits) versus bad performance on noise trials (false alarms). The mirror image graph of an ROC (1) is mathematically equivalent; (2) plots good performance on signal trials versus good performance on noise trials; (3) follows the usual convention of graphing good performance up and to the right; and, therefore, (4) is psychologically easier to grasp. Let $P_n = 1 - Q_n$. A graph of P_s versus P_n, correct detections (hits) versus correct rejections, is the graph that illustrates good performance in the conventional way and is mathematically isomorphic to the AOC. Although signal detection theory originally was applied to the discrimination of signals from noise, the formalism of the theory applies equally well to other cases. For example, signal detection theory applies well to discrimination experiments in which an observer's task is to discriminate two stimuli (e.g., tones of 1000 Hz and 1001 Hz) as opposed to discriminating one stimulus from zero. Because the general case is discrimination (of which discrimination from zero—detection—is a subcase) the P_s versus P_n representation is appropriately called a discrimination operating characteristic (cf. Sperling & Melchner, 1978b) or a decision operating characteristic (DOC). The AOC, ROC, and DOC are members of a much more general category, that of performance operating characteristics, POCs (Norman & Bobrow, 1975).

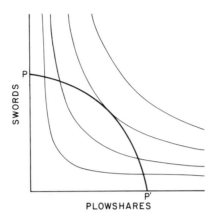

Figure 4.10 Production possibility frontier $(p - p')$ and iso-utility contours for the primitive swords–plowshares economy. The nearly flat utility contours at the extreme right indicate that large changes in (surplus) plowshares can be compensated by small changes in (scarce) swords; similarly, the nearly vertical contours at the upper left indicate that large amounts of (surplus) swords would be traded for just a few (scarce) plowshares.

Economic Analogy

Consider a primitive society in which there are two occupations, agriculture and war. All the farmers could in principle become warriors, and all the warriors could in principle be farmers; although obviously there are some persons who would be better farmers than warriors, and vice versa. The strength of the army is measured in units of "swords" and the productivity of the agricultural sector in units of "plowshares." Consider the joint productivity (swords, plowshares) as the fraction of the labor force that devotes itself to farming varies from 1.0 to 0. The graph of swords versus plowshares has various names; here, it is designated a *production possibility frontier* (Samuelson, 1980). When graphed as in Figure 4.10, the production possibility frontier is concave *toward* the origin. This means, for example, that if the society were to alter the fraction of farmers from 1.0 to 0.95, it would decrease plowshares by less than the increase in swords (see lower right portion of production possibility frontier in Figure 4.10). It is assumed that the first persons to change occupations would be among the worst farmers; that is, persons who were relatively more efficient as warriors than as farmers. Similarly, if the fraction of warriors were to increase from 0.95 to 1.0, it would increase the number of swords only slightly because the very last to join the army would be the least efficient. This tendency to concavity toward the origin is a general property of POCs, which is discussed in more detail later in the chapter.

The production possibility frontier is something that is computed by the systems analysts and economic experts in the society—the technocrats. Insofar as such things can be measured, the production possibility frontier has the status of an objective fact: A particular allocation of resources leads to a corresponding output. On the other hand, the *utility* of any joint combination of swords and plowshares is something that people express through their politicians. In this instance, utility has the status of a preference or an opinion, although it may be formed on the basis of a logical examintion of objective facts. Suppose, for example, the society were devoted entirely to agriculture. This would tempt some of the more opportunistic neighbors to expropriate the agricultural produce by force, and so the industrious citizens might starve in spite of (or perhaps because of) their efficient production. Converting even a few farmers to warriors might create an effective deterrent. The notion of utility applies not only to production that is possible but also to any production. Suppose a society had a thousand times more plowshares than could be consumed and not a single warrior. It would gladly trade many surplus plowshares for just a few swords. Similarly, a society that had an enormous surplus of swords but no plowshares— to avert possible starvation in case the neighbors had the same paucity of plowshares—would be willing to trade many swords for a few plowshares. From these considerations, it follows that equal utility contours are concave *away* from the origin.

The solution for the society—once it has decided on its utility function—is to maximize utility, which it can do by moving along the production possibility frontier until it touches the highest iso-utility contour. At this optimal point, the utility contour and the production contour will be tangent to each other and have the same slope. This is classical economic theory. Modern macroeconomic theory deals with many complex additions to this model that may prevent an optimum from being achieved, but these are beyond the scope of the present discussion. Note, however, that the guns versus butter trade-off just described has numerous other economic analogies. For example, should an automobile company manufacture large or small cars? Should a scarce resource be consumed now or saved for later? Finding the optimum point along various trade-offs is at the heart of economic theory, and specialized branches of mathematics (such as linear programming) have been developed to deal with the problems of optimization. In the next section, the equivalences between trade-offs and optimization in signal detection, in concurrent tasks, and in economic theory are explored.

Optimization in Signal Detection, Attending, Attention, Economics, and Motivation

Signal Detection Theory

Consider the conditional distributions of noise and of signal plus noise in classical signal detection theory. Let the likelihood ratio (lr) for an observation

($x;$ the internal sensory representation of the stimulus on a particular trial) be the conditional probability of signal given x divided by the conditional probability of noise given $x;$ that is,[15]

$$lr(x) = \frac{p_{s+n}(x)}{p_n(x)} .$$

In the examples considered here, the conditional density functions p_{s+n} and p_n are arranged in order of increasing likelihood ratio on the sensory continuum (x). Figure 4.11 shows p_{s+n} and p_n as normal density functions—the usual assumptions of classical signal detection theory. The criterion c represents the value of x corresponding to the lr below which the observer responds "noise," and above which the observer responds "signal." The DOC (mirror image ROC) at the upper right of Figure 4.11 represents the joint performance on n trials and $s + n$ trials as c is varied from $-\infty$ to ∞.

The logorithm of the likelihood ratio is illustrated in Figure 4.11, column 3. The reason for illustrating the log lr rather than lr itself is that log lr is symmetric around $lr = 0$, which reflects the actual symmetry of treatment of lr and lr^{-1}, and that log lr occurs in many statistical treatments.

The normalized distance between the mean of n and of $s + n$ density functions is the d' statistic of signal detection theory. The area under the DOC, Area(DOC), is a more general statistic, which is simply related to d' for those special cases where d' makes sense, but is itself useful in more cases. The interpretation of Area(DOC) is

$$Area(DOC) = P\ (x_{s+n} > x_n).$$

That is, Area(DOC) is the probability that a random sample drawn from the distribution p_{s+n} exceeds a sample drawn from p_n. According to a simple signal detection theory model, Area(DOC) is the probability of a correct choice in a two-alternative, forced-choice task (Green & Swets, 1966). More generally, Area(DOC) is a nonparametric measure of the amount by which the $s + n$ distribution dominates (is to the right of) the n distribution. Statistics for Area(DOC) are given in Bamber (1975).

Signal detection theory and decision theory differ only in nomenclature—not in any critical conceptual or substantive way. Both are special cases of theories

---

[15]The statement defining lr is correct for discrete probabilities but needs to be technically elaborated for the continuous probability density functions. The equation is correct for either the discrete or continuous case with appropriate interpretation of p_{s+n}, p_n. In the formal treatment of signal detection theory, the sensory variable x usually is discarded as quickly as possible and replaced by lr (because all decisions are based on the value of lr). However, when the emphasis is on the sensory continuum under investigation, it is more useful to formulate the theory directly in terms of this continuum—the approach taken here.

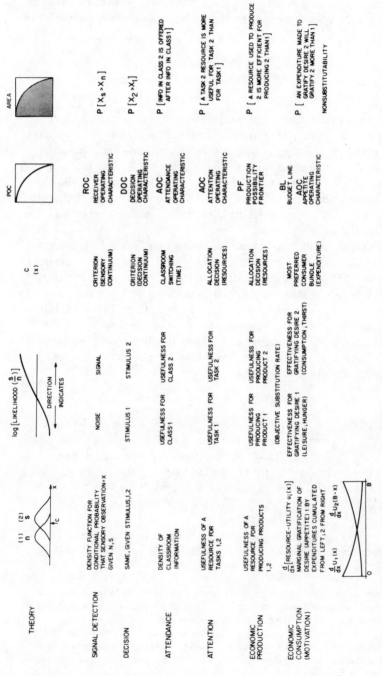

Figure 4.11 Summary of isomorphisms among six theories: signal detection, decision, attendance, attention, economic production, and economic consumption (motivation). Density functions are indicated by $n(x)$, $s(x)$; log likelihood ratio is $\log [s(x)/n(x)]$; c indicates the decision criterion; and (x) is the dimensional interpretation of the decision variable, x. The performance operating characteristic (POC) is the curve indicated in the graph; the area under the operating characteristic is the shaded area in the rightmost graph. In economic consumption and in motivation theory, the shape of the n, s density functions is usually assumed to be different than in the other theories, as is illustrated.

for compound tasks. The remaining theories outlined in Figure 4.11 are resource theories for concurrent tasks.

Attendance Theory

Attendance Theory deals with two or more classes offered during overlapping time periods. The conditional distributions represent the usefulness of information offered at a time x for each of the courses, respectively. The decision axis of signal detection theory becomes a time axis in attendance theory. At early times, information is more useful for Course 1; at later times, it becomes more useful for Course 2.

The likelihood ratio (lr) of signal detection theory is now interpreted as a usefulness ratio—the higher lr is, the more useful information for Course 2 will be relative to Course 1—whereas criterion and DOC of signal detection theory become the classroom-switching time and AOC of attendance theory. The area under the DOC has an interesting interpretation in attendance theory. Let t_1 be the time when a bit of information sampled randomly from Class 1 was offered, and t_2 the corresponding time for Class 2. Then, the area under the AOC is given by $Area(AOC) = p[t_1 > t_2]$. The Area(AOC) is a measure of how much later Class 2 is than Class 1 in terms of the time at which classroom information actually is offered. In order for Area(AOC) to have this useful interpretation in resource theories, the coordinates of the operating graph must be normalized to maximum possible performance, which is equivalent to normalizing the density functions to unit area.

Economic Production Theory

In economic theory, the signal detection theory decision axis of "observations" (ordered in terms of their likelihood of indicating n or $s + n$) is replaced by an ordering of resources (ordered according to their usefulness for the competing production goals of the economy). For example, in the swords–plowshares example, the decision axis might represent an ordering of all the laborers in the country. Those whose usefulness as farmers (relative to warriors) was greatest would be represented at the left side of the axis; those whose usefulness as warriors was greatest would be represented on the right side.

The economic analog to the likelihood ratio of signal detection theory is sometimes called the *objective substitution rate*; in this example, it represents the rate at which swords (or warriors) can be substituted for or converted into plowshares (or farmers). The distribution $p_n(x)$ represents the net effectiveness as farmers of all the laborers whose objective substitution rate (or usefulness ratio) was x. The function $p_{s+n}(x)$ represents the effectiveness of this same group of laborers as warriors. The decision criterion c corresponds to the decision to assign all laborers with usefulness ratio less than c to farming and the remainder to fighting. The DOC of signal detection theory, generated as c varies from $-\infty$ to $+\infty$, corresponds to the production possibility frontier of economic theory, similarly generated.

The decision axis in economic theory need not represent merely labor. In the present example, it could represent some other resource—such as mining and manufacturing operations. For example, mines and other industries could be ordered according to how effective their production was in the manufacture of swords relative to the manufacture of plowshares. Or a single factory could make such an ordering of its internal production facilities. In all these cases, as the decision criterion c to allocate resources to plowshares or to swords varies over its full range, it will trace out the production possibility frontier.

These economic examples show that the concept of resource can be quite general; it may refer to labor, to production facilities, to available capital, or to some combination of all these and other resources. When many resources are involved, matters can be quite complex; and the discovery of an ordering may be nontrivial. Some of the complexities are considered later in the chapter, but they should not obscure the general principles elaborated here about how resources are allocated.

Finally, the area under the production possibility frontier has a similar interpretation to the areas under the DOC and AOC: it represents the probability that a randomly chosen sword-resource will be more useful for sword production than a randomly chosen plowshare resource would be for sword production. It is a measure of the extent to which skills or facilities (e.g., for farming, for fighting) are segregated into different people or facilities as opposed to coexisting in the same person or facility.

Motivation Theory and Economic Consumption Theory

The terms used in studies of animal motivation and consumer economics are quite parallel. Economic consumption theory is somewhat different from production theory because, in consumption, there is only one resource (money) that can be allocated to satisfy various different desires. Similarly, in the typical animal motivation experiment (see Rachlin & Burkhard's, 1978, review), the single resource is time; a hungry and thirsty rat has to allocate its limited session time to working for food rewards or for water rewards.

In the usual case, the satisfaction value (marginal utility) of each additional reward increment diminishes with the amount x already consumed, at least for large x. This nonlinear resource-utility function $u(x)$ leads to a curved POC. Let the resource-utility function $u_i(x)$ represent the utility for reward system i of an amount x of the disposable resource. It is assumed that the $u_i(x)$ are monotonic, nondecreasing functions of x and that x is bounded ($0 \leq x \leq B$). The bound B is the budget limit; for example, the rat's total session time or the human's total disposable money. The aim is to find a critical quantity c of the resource such that when c is allocated to Reward 1 and the remainder $B - c$ is allocated to Reward 2, the total utility $u_1(c) + u_2(B - c)$ is maximized. This expenditure yields the most preferred consumer bundle. The density functions, $p_1(x)$, $p_2(x)$, of Figure 4.11 can be interpreted as marginal utilities—the derivatives (d/dx) $u_1(x)$, (d/dx) $u_2(B - x)$ of the resource-utility functions. Note that, as drawn in Figure 4.11 the marginal utility function (d/dx) $i_1(x)$ is cumulated from left to right and (d/dx) $u_2(x)$ is cumulated from right to left. In consumption theory, the likelihood ratio represents the ratio of marginal utilities of an incremental expenditure for Rewards 1 and 2 at the budget allocation x. The performance operating characteristic is called a *budget line* or an *appetite operating characteristic*. It represents the joint utilities $u_1(x)$ and $u_2(B - x)$ of expenditures x, $B - x$, respectively, for the two rewards. The particular formulation given in the preceding—in terms of (d/dx) $u_1(x)$, (d/dx) $u_2(B - x)$—is only one of several ways of generating the budget line.[16] More natural ways to generate the same budget line using nonlinear resource-utility functions are considered later in this chapter (see Figures 4.21 and 4.22 and the subsequent discussion under the subheading "Single-Resource Pool" on p. 166).

The area under the budget line or under the appetite operating characteristic represents the nonsubstitutability of the competing rewards (e.g., food and water). The minimum area (area under the negative diagonal) indicates completely substitutable rewards (e.g., waters with different but equally acceptable flavors); the maximum area indicates nonsubstitutable rewards (e.g., water and dry food). That is, rewards are *nonsubstitutable* if, in a control experiment in which an animal is offered only reward A or only reward B for $\frac{1}{2}$ hour, it consumes them in the same ratio as in a 1-hour concurrent session in which it is offered access to both (cf. classroom example of Figure 4.7). Rewards are *substitutable* to the extent that, in the concurrent experimental session, the animal can be induced to vary the proportion of alternative rewards consumed from the proportion consumed in the isolated control sessions.

Attention Theory

Concurrent Tasks The allocation of mental resources (attention) determines which of several concurrent cognitive tasks are performed more or less well; just

---

[16]See Coombs and Avrunin (1977) for various sets of conditions that generate trade offs.

as in economic theory, the allocation of economic resources—labor, capital, raw materials, and the like—determines which manufacturing goals are achieved. This analogy of attention to economic production theory was proposed by Navon and Gopher (1979). The critical aspect of the attention analogy is the interpretation of the decision axis x as an ordering of resources—in the case of attention, mental processing resources. The mental resources for which the usefulness ratio x (usefulness for Task 2 divided by usefulness for Task 1) is lowest are represented at the extreme left of the resource axis (Figure 4.11). Thus, the resource axis is directly analogous to a likelihood decision axis of signal detection theory. The conditional density function $p_1(x)$ represents the usefulness to Task 1 of resources as a function of their usefulness ratio x; $p_2(x)$ represents the usefulness of resources to Task 2. The decision criterion c represents the decision by the subject to allocate mental resources with usefulness ratio less than c to Task 1 and the remainder to Task 2. The attention operating characteristic is traced out as c is varied over its range. The area under the AOC represents the probability that a resource, chosen at random from all those useful for Task 2, really is more useful for Task 2 than a randomly chosen Task 1 resource would have been. It is a nonparametric measure of the extent to which separate—as opposed to interchangeable—resources are involved in performing the two tasks.

Compound Tasks Attentional manipulations (e.g., instructions to attend to Task 1 versus Task 2) can be interpreted as controlling resource allocation only in concurrent tasks. In compound tasks, because of the effects of stimulus uncertainty, the attentional manipulation must first be viewed as a decision manipulation (as in signal detection or decision theory). The starting hypothesis for compound tasks is that precisely the same resources are used under all conditions of attention; the quality of data input to and output by these processes does not vary with selective attention, only the decision made on the basis of the data output varies. If, after stimulus uncertainty has been accounted for, there is a residual effect of attention in a compound task; then, obviously, resource analysis would be appropriate for this residual effect.

What Are Mental Resources? There are two approaches to this question. The first is that it is not necessary to know what mental resources are. They have the status of a random variable much like the decision variable of signal detection theory. All the power and prediction of signal detection theory work whether or not the psychological (mental) dimensions of the decision variable are known precisely. All the power of optimization theory is available to predict and describe performance in concurrent tasks even when it is not known precisely where these tasks conflict. On the other hand, I would not be a cognitive psychologist if I did not have a very special interest in learning precisely what particular mental resources were involved in cognitive functions.

With respect to particular mental resources, the critical resources for which there is competition vary with the task. In the partial–whole report tasks, the critical resource was short-term memory (STM); it had a limited capacity, and that capacity was allocated to items from one stimulus row or the other according to the task demand. This memory resource seems to be quite interchangeable.

In search tasks, the critical resource probably is a processing resource involved in making comparisons. A stimulus item at one location in the visual field *can* be compared to a memory representation of a target at the same time that another item in another part of the field is being compared to a representation of another target (Sperling, *et al.*, 1971). However, the extent to which such comparisons can occur simultaneously and the extent to which they draw from a common pool of resources depends on many factors, among the most important of which is the familiarity of the target and the extent to which special resources have been developed for highly specific targets (see also Schneider *et al.*, this volume). Later in this chapter, a powerful technique to investigate whether resources from a common pool can be evenly shared by two tasks or whether they are switched in all-or-none fashion from one task to the other on different trials is examined. First, however, consequences of the unified decision theory that has been presented here are examined further.

Iso-Utility Contours

Iso-utility contours are a powerful heuristic device for studying optimization; that is, for investigating which of a number of alternative procedures or parameters produces the maximum utility or most preferred outcome. Iso-utility contours have long been commonplace in economic theory.[17] Navon and Gopher (1979) introduced iso-utility contours into the study of attention; in this chapter, they were introduced in the classroom example. Here, their use to signal detection theory experiments (DOC, ROC) and to related situations is introduced.

In a typical signal detection task, a 2 × 2 payoff matrix describes the utility of stimulus–response (S–R) outcomes. Let the payoff values be *a* and *j* respectively, for "signal" and "noise" responses on noise trials, and *h* and *m*, respectively on signal trials, representing false *a*larms, correct re*j*ections, *h*its, and *m*isses. If the fraction of signals is α (thus the fraction of noise trials is 1 − α), and probability of an "*s*" response given *s* is $p(``s"|s)$, and analogously for the other conditional probabilities; the expected utility *Eu* is

---

[17]Iso-utility contours are also referred to as "equal-utility contours" and "indifference curves" (Samuelson, 1980). According to Due (1951, p. 92), the indifference curve approach "was suggested in writings of Pareto (1909) and by the Russian economist Slutzky (1915)," and popularized by Hicks and Allen (1934).

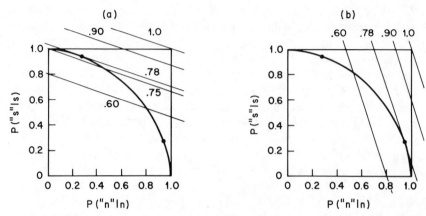

Figure 4.12 (a and b) Iso-utility contours in a signal detection task. In (a), the abscissa indicates the probability of a correct rejection response, given the stimulus was noise, and the ordinate indicates the probability of a correct detection response, given the stimulus was signal. In this example, the a priori probability α of a signal stimulus is 0.75; $1 - \alpha$, the a priori probability of a noise stimulus, is 0.25; the utility is 1.0 for correct responses and zero for wrong ones; and the expected (utility) payoff for the joint performances—$p(\text{``}S\text{''}|S)$ and $p(\text{``}N\text{''}|N)$—is represented by the labeled iso-utility contours. The DOC illustrated is for equal variance normal distributions with a d' of 1.0 (cf., Figure 4.10). Panel b is the same as Panel a, except $\alpha = 0.25$.

$$Eu = \alpha \, [hp(\text{``}s\text{''}|s) + mp(\text{``}n\text{''}|s)$$
$$+ (1 - \alpha) \, [ap(\text{``}s\text{''}|n) + jp(\text{``}n\text{''}|n)]. \qquad (4.2)$$

Given a particular payoff matrix, Equation 4.2 gives the expected utility for every possible performance level—$p(\text{``}s\text{''}|s)$ and $p(\text{``}n\text{''}|n)$. (See Equation 4.1 in the attendance example.) In fact, the limits of achievable performance levels are described by the DOC, which is a graph of $p(\text{``}s\text{''}|s)$, $p(\text{``}n\text{''}|n)$ pairs obtained as some *nonstimulus* parameter of the experiment that is varied. (The phrase "limit of performance" is used here because the subject can always do worse by making deliberate errors or by following a nonoptimal decision strategy.)

To illustrate the effect of α on performance, a particular payoff matrix is chosen; for example, wrong responses a and m earn zero and correct responses j and h earn V dollars per trial. In brief: $a = m = 0$ and $j = h = V > 0$. Figure 4.12a illustrates iso-utility contours for $\alpha = .75$ and Figure 4.12b illustrates iso-utility contours for $\alpha = .25$. The parameter on the contours is the expected utility per trial. Expected utility as defined by the payoff matrix and Equation 4.2 is computable for all values of $p(\text{``}s\text{''}|s) \, p(\text{``}n\text{''}|n)$, not just achievable values. The iso-utility contours are straight lines with slope S easily calculable from Equation 4.2:

$$S = \left[\frac{h - m}{j - a} \right] \left[\frac{1 - \alpha}{\alpha} \right].$$

Suppose the outcomes of a trial are symmetrical with respect to s and n for both errors and correct responses. Then the iso-utility slope is simply the ratio of the two a priori stimulus probabilities, $-(1 - \alpha)/\alpha$. In the two examples in Figure 4.12a and b, the slopes are -3 and $-1/3$.

A typical DOC based on the assumption of equal-variance Normal distributions for n, $s + n$ is also illustrated in Figure 4.12. It is quite obvious graphically that the criterion should be adjusted quite differently to achieve the optimal performance with $\alpha = 0.25$ and $\alpha = 0.75$. The expected utility of each strategy (criterion value) can also be estimated from the graph so that the cost of, for example, not changing the criterion (c) when α changes can be quickly assessed. The optimal strategy has an expected utility of 0.78 per trial. This is only marginally better than 0.75, the utility that could be achieved by simply naming the a priori more probable stimulus on each trial without actually observing the stimulus. For Normally distributed signal and noise, it always pays to observe the stimulus because the likelihood ratio varies between 0 and ∞. But there are many distributions—such as the logistic distribution, which is very similar to the Normal—for which the likelihood ratio is bounded. For stimuli characterized by such distributions, when the a priori probabilities are very asymmetrical, it would be better *not* to observe the stimulus but merely to use the a priori information.

The *value* of a priori information is the expected value of a trial with this information minus the value of a trial without it. In the example in Figure 4.12, suppose that an observer has no information about the a priori stimulus probabilities and therefore sets the decision criterion symmetrically (at a likelihood ratio equal to 1.0). The expected probability of a correct response would be 0.69, which (in this example) is also the number of utility units (V) the observer would expect to earn on each trial. Note that 0.69 is the highest achievable expected probability of a correct response with equally probable stimuli or with unequally probable stimuli when the probability is unknown. The a priori information that one stimulus is three times more probable than the other enables the observer to achieve an expected probability of a correct response of 0.75 without even observing the stimulus and 0.78 if he or she chooses to actually observe it. The a priori information alone is thus worth more (0.75) than the opportunity of viewing the stimulus without a priori information (0.69). In the present example, therefore, the a priori information about stimulus probabilities is worth at least 0.25 utility units (0.75 − 0.50) per trial when the observer does not bother to look at the stimulus, and is worth 0.09 units (0.78 − 0.69) if the observer bothers to observe the stimulus. Finally, it is obvious that good detection of signal stimuli $p(``S"|s) = 1$, can be profitably traded off for good detection of noise stimuli, $p(``n"|n) = 1$, when there are more noise than signal stimuli, and vice versa.

All these properties and relations of variables in signal detection are, of course, derivable algebraically; and they are well known. The aim here is to illustrate them in a new way so that previously unobserved similarities between optimization in the various situations (detection, discrimination, attendance, attention, economics, etc.) will be made obvious.

Reaction-Time Trade-Offs

Simple Reaction Time with Alternative Stimuli

Consider the following experiment by Posner, Nissen, and Ogden (1978). A subject views a fixation point between two locations, left and right, where a light flash may appear on a given trial. Whichever flash appears, the subject is to respond as quickly as possible by pressing a key. Occasional blank trials (no flash) are introduced to reduce anticipatory responses (responses before the flash). This is a go/no-go reaction-time experiment in which the subject must respond ("go") when any stimulus is presented and must not respond ("no-go") on catch trials. The experimental manipulation of concern here is the fraction α of stimulus-containing trials on which the left stimulus appears. Posner *et al.* investigated three conditions—trials in which α was, respectively, 0.80, 0.50, and 0.20. Although trials with different α traditionally have been run in separate blocks (Audley, 1973; Falmagne, Cohen & Dwivedi, 1975; Link, 1975; Welford, 1980), Posner *et al.* ran them mixed together, using a pre-cue before each trial to inform the subject of α. The pre-cue procedure (with varying interval of pre-cue to reaction stimulus) is used to determine how quickly the pre-cue can influence the subjects' response. When the pre-cue is given well in advance, as in the present experiment, the mixed procedure is equivalent to the traditional, blocked procedure.

Posner *et al.*'s experiment is analyzed here as a two-task compound experiment in which the two component tasks are (1) press the key when the left flash appears, and (2) press the (same) key when the right flash appears. The outcome of the experiment, the reaction time for each of the two component tasks in the three conditions, is represented in Figure 4.13a. (Except for a slowing of reaction time, there was no important difference between the reaction times in this Donders Type 3 experiment and in a disjunctive reaction-time experiment in which the subject had to press a left key in response to the left flash and a right key in response to the right flash.) So far, the only measure of performance considered here has been accuracy—usually, the fraction of correct detections, correct identifications, or correct answers. In the following, the dependent measure is mean reaction time; errors that occur when the observer responds before the stimulus

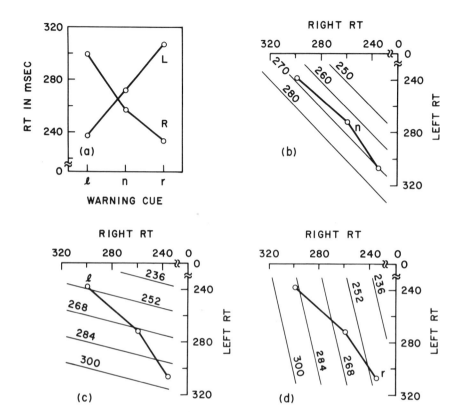

Figure 4.13 Simple reaction times for two alternative stimuli. The same data (from Posner *et al.* 1978, Figure 5) are represented in all panels. (a) Conventional representation of simple reaction times (*RT*) to a flash of a Left (L) or a Right (R) stimulus light with three different warning cues: l and r, indicating 80% probability of Left and Right lights, respectively, and n, indicating a neutral (uninformative) cue. In Panels b, c, and d, the data of (a) are regraphed as a POC. The coordinates represent simple reaction times to the Left and Right stimuli, respectively, and are oriented to show good performance up and to the right. The iso-utility contours in panels b, c, and d each represent equal mean reaction times as indicated; that is, each point along the contour represents a joint performance to Left and Right stimuli for which the overall mean reaction time is the value indicated on the contour, $u = \alpha RT_{Left} + (1 - \alpha)RT_{Right}$. In (b), the iso-utility contours represent a weighting of performance appropriate to the stimulus probabilities in effect with cue l: $u = 0.8[RT_{Left} + 0.2RT_{Right}]$. (c), the iso-utility contours represent a weighting of performance appropriate to the stimulus probabilities in effect with cue n: $u = 0.5[RT_{Left} + RT_{Right}]$. In (d), the iso-utility contours represent a weighting of performance appropriate to the stimulus probabilities in effect with cue r: $u = 0.2RT_{Left} + 0.8RT_{Right}$.

occurs, fails to respond within a reasonable time period, or responds on a catch trial are ignored for the moment. Fast reaction times represent good performance; following the convention of this chapter, they are represented up and to the right in Figure 4.13.

Iso-Utility Contours for Reaction Times What are the utilities in Posner *et al.*'s experiment? Unfortunately, the authors did not define these explicitly for the subjects, so it is necessary to guess. Suppose that utility varies in direct inverse proportion to the reaction time: The faster the reaction is, the higher the utility will be; and vice versa. With this assumption, the utility u of any performance—pair of reaction times (RT_{left}, RT_{right})—can be computed as a function of α, the proportion of left stimuli:

$$u = -[\alpha RT_{left} + (1 - \alpha)RT_{right}]. \tag{4.3}$$

The utility function (Equation 4.3) is defined in terms of minus one times the reaction times because smaller values of reaction time represent better performance, and utility, by definition, increases as performance improves. Iso-utility functions based on Equation 4.3 are illustrated in Figure 4.13b, c, and d for the three values of α for which data are available. Note that the utility functions (Figure 4.13b, c, and d) are similar to those in typical signal detection tasks, but the data are not, in that the data seem to fall on a straight rather than a curved line. Straight-line data in this experiment, as in Sperling and Melchner's (1978a) attention study, have special significance: They suggest that a mixture of just two states rather than a continuum of states is sufficient to account for the data. This point is taken up in detail later in the chapter.

Posner *et al.*'s observers seem to operate sensibly with respect to the utility function (Equation 4.3) optimizing their performance in each case (Figure 4.13b, c, and d). Note that informative precues enable the observers to shorten their mean reaction times substantially over the mean reaction time to uninformative cues. A valid cue (e.g., left warning followed by left light) "benefits" reaction time (by speeding it up) by about the same amount as in invalid cue "costs" reaction time (by slowing it down). The important point—overlooked by Posner *et al.*—is not that the costs and benefits of knowing α when α equals 0.2 or 0.8 happen to be approximately symmetrical, but that the benefits are available on 80% of the trials, whereas the costs are paid only on 20%. Thus, the mean reaction time improves with unsymmetrical stimulus probabilities in a way that is completely analogous to the improvement of s/n detection accuracy with asymmetric stimulus probabilities, as considered in the preceding section.[18]

---

[18]The cost and benefits in choice (as opposed to simple) reaction-time tasks have been extensively analyzed by numerous investigators. For a review of experiments, see Audley (1973); for a review of the random walk model's (RWM) predictions, see Link (1975); for examples of other models, see Green and Luce (1973).

Simple Reaction Time with Alternative Stimuli: A Compound Task Finally, the careful reader will have observed that Posner *et al.*'s task, like the signal detection tasks, is a compound task. On one trial, the observer never receives both a left and right stimulus to which independent responses must be made. A closely related task, which would be concurrent, is responding with the left hand to left stimuli and with the right hand to right stimuli when both stimuli could occur on the same trial. The concurrent tasks would make it possible to determine whether an observer can simultaneously perform two tasks concurrently as readily as one by providing the opportunity to compare concurrent performance to performance in single-task control experiments. This is the ideal task for studying attention, although it may present problems when conflicts arise in the motor system (Kantowitz, 1974). Posner *et al.*'s compound task does not enable us to come to any such conclusion about the ability to perform two tasks simultaneously. The compound reaction-time situation in which either a left or right signal occurs on each trial is analogous to signal detection in which either noise or signal plus noise occurs on each trial. Recall that signal detection theory assumes there is no loss of information by the observer; an ideal detector (matched to the observer's performance on the simple task) would show a loss similar to the observer's when presented with the compound task. In the ideal detector, only the decision criterion changes as the payoff matrix and the a priori signal probability are varied rather than the quality of the information. Is it possible, in Posner *et al.*'s task, that performance varies with instructions and payoffs and yet the quality of perceived information remains invariant? The following question arises: Is a subject slower to react when there are two locations to monitor because the subject cannot process information as efficiently from two as from one location, or does the subject's slower reaction merely reflect the same loss that an ideal detector with no information loss would show in the same situation? As with all compound tasks, a theory is necessary to decide these questions.

Before going on to a theory, it is worth noting that if any performance deficit is observed in a compound task (relative to any of the component tasks) then a full POC could be generated (i.e., a range of costs and benefits observed). To illustrate this point, consider the two-choice reaction-time experiment. This is a compound task with two component tasks, each a simple reaction-time task. (Each simple reaction-time Task *i* requires Response *i* for Stimulus i). Suppose it is known that simple reaction times are faster than choice reaction times for at least one set of a priori probabilities of the occurrence of the component tasks in the compound. That is, suppose Task 1 is slowed in the choice reaction time relative to simple reaction time. Let the a priori probability of Task 1 in the compound be increased to, for example, .9999. A Gedanken experiment is performed using this new compound task. A session consist of 1000 trials. Only once in any 10 sessions will the subject experience a component task other than Task 1. This is a very slow way to gather data about Task 2, but it is as efficient for Task 1 as the simple reaction-time Task 1. Moreover, the data from this compound Task 1 will not differ significantly from the simple Task 1 data because in more than 9 of 10 sessions the simple and compound task have exactly the same stimuli and required responses. Insofar as simple reaction times and choice reaction times are ever different, manipulating a priori probability allows a smooth transition over this range of differences. Thus once it has been observed that choice reaction time is slower than simple reaction time, the POC and costs/benefits for choice reaction times are not a discovery, but rather follow immediately from the procedure for measuring them. Probability manipulations in choice reaction time have been extensively analyzed in the literature (Audley, 1973; Link, 1975; Welford, 1980); therefore the discussion here focuses on a theory for the simple reaction time with alternative stimuli, which has not been so extensively treated.

Random Walk Model for Simple Reaction Time with Alternative Stimuli A simple theory for reaction time, closely related to signal detection theory, is the random walk model (RWM) (Link & Heath, 1975; see also Laming, 1968). Signal detection theory is a theory for the perception and decision component in detection tasks; the RWM is a theory for the perception and response-decision component in reaction-time tasks. Without going into full detail, the principle of the RWM can be summarized as follows: An ideal detector accumulates information from the start of a trial. When the information exceeds a threshold, the appropriate response is made. Each new increment of information is assumed to be somewhat unreliable so that the cumulative balance of all the information may waver between the alternatives—that is, execute a random walk. A strategy consists of a choice of response threshold (the distance from the starting point to the absorbing boundary) for each of the alternative responses.

The response threshold is adjusted so that an optimum compromise is made between several incompatible criteria. The response threshold is set high to avoid accidental incorrect responses (due to some randomness in the incoming information), but not so high that the reaction time is too long. (The higher the threshold is, the longer it will take, on the average, to reach it.) These relations are illustrated in Figure 4.14. A priori information that a stimulus is probable will cause the threshold for the corresponding response to be set lower (thereby decreasing reaction time) without a corresponding loss in accuracy. A priori information that a stimulus is unlikely forces the threshold to be raised in order to avoid errors. (The response threshold is changed by changing A or C or both together.)

In order to apply a RWM to Posner's task, it is necessary to choose one from among the many candidate configurations. For a single location being monitored in a go/no-go reaction time, I propose a RWM with two boundaries: a near one for the "go" responses and another; much further boundary for the occasional

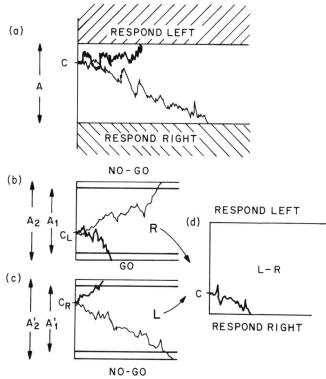

Figure 4.14 Random walk models for reaction-time paradigms. In (a), an illustration of a random walk model (RWM) for a choice reaction time with two alternative stimuli (Left, Right) is shown. A possible random walk that leads to initiation of a Left response is represented by the heavy jagged line; a possible random walk that leads to initiation of a Right response is represented by the light jagged line. When a random walk reaches a boundary, the reaction-time (RT) response is initiated. The sensitivity of the process is controlled by the parameter A (which is set in accordance with the penalties for errors and the rewards for speed, etc.). The bias is reflected in the starting point C (which is determined primarily by the expectation of Left versus Right stimuli). When C is in accordance with the expectation of predominantly Left stimuli (as illustrated), then RTs to Left stimuli will be faster than to Right stimuli (as illustrated). In (b), a random walk for a GO/NO GO RT experiment with a RIGHT stimulus light is shown. The inner, heavy boundaries A_1 are used when this is the only active RW. The outer boundaries A_2 are used when there is one other active random walk (such as [c]); that is, when both LEFT and RIGHT stimulus lights are being monitored. A possible RW that initiates a GO response is shown as a heavy line; and a possible RW that leads to a no response, NO-GO, is shown as a light line. In (c), a random walk for a GO/NO-GO RT experiment with a LEFT stimulus light is shown. Posner, Nissen, and Ogden's (1978) experiment involves both left and right stimulus lights; the first RW to reach the A_2 or A'_2 boundary initiates the response. In (d), a random walk for a Left–Right choice reaction time involving the same stimuli as in (b) and (c). The starting point indicates a strong Right bias; otherwise, the L minus R random walk in (d) is similar to that in (a).

"no-go" response. The no-go boundary has little influence on the simple go/no-go experiment: Catch (no-go) trials are rare, the subject is not rewarded for a quick no-go decision (in fact, this decision speed is not explicitly measured); and if the boundary is very far, only very seldom will it be crossed on go trials. Monitoring two locations is modeled by two simultaneous, independent go/no-go random walks; the response being triggered by the first completion. Because two random walks would produce more false reactions (on catch trials or premature responses) than one walk, the boundaries must be moved away (A_1 to A_2) to maintain the same accuracy in performance. Therefore, monitoring two locations produces slower decisions than monitoring just one. The explanation is exactly analogous to the previous explanation of the difficulty in searching for two targets (*1* or *2*) instead of one target. Recall that the concurrent task of searching for *1* and *2* did not have this problem. Nor would the concurrent task of presenting stimuli independently for responses with the left and right hands. The concurrent reaction-time task is composed of two simple component reaction-time tasks: (1) respond with the left hand to a left stimulus, and (2) respond with the right hand to a right stimulus. The concurrent reaction-time task—in which both left and right stimuli might occur on any given trial—is quite different from the usual choice reaction-time task, which is a compound task: Either the left or the right stimulus occurs, but never both together. The concurrent task is modeled by two independent random walks. The choice (compound) reaction-time task can be modeled in a manner equivalent to Link's (1975) by taking as the RW the difference of the two individual right and left walks considered here (see Figure 4.14).

The point of this discussion is not to provide a definitive model of trade-offs in multistimulus go/no-go reaction times, but to demonstrate a particular class of ideal detectors (RWMs) that exhibit trade-offs similar to those of the subjects in Posner *et al.*'s combined task. In the RWM, a loss of information quality is represented as a slowing of the random walk—it takes longer to accumulate the same amount of information. The attentional question is: When subjects monitor two locations instead of one, do they show more of a performance loss than the simple RWM predicts—a loss that must be described as a slowing of the walk rather than merely an adjustment of the response thresholds? Obviously, this is a very difficult question to answer—so difficult, it suggests that the concurrent task analog to Posner *et al.*'s (1978) experiment should be reconsidered—the concurrent task requires no model for its interpretation.

Conclusion To study attention (the allocation of processing resources) without the burden of a model, use concurrent tasks and abhor compound tasks. To study decision making under uncertainty (the otpimal compromise between incompatible goals when the incoming data are noisy or incomplete), compound tasks are appropriate. Optimization theory (POCs, iso-utility contours, etc.) is applicable in formally similar ways whether the problem is resource allocation (concurrent tasks) or noise (compound tasks).

Speed–Accuracy Trade-Off (SATO)

Consider the following kinds of reaction-time experiments. On each trial, a subject is presented a stimulus that he or she must classify into one of two (or more categories) as quickly as possible. For example, the subject may be shown a letter string and asked to press a reaction key with the left hand if it is a word or another key with the right hand if it is not a word (*lexical decision task;* Rubenstein, Garfield, & Millikan, 1970; Rubenstein, Lewis, & Rubenstein, 1971a, 1971b). Or the subject may be asked to classify as red or green a colored patch that has an irrelevant color name written on it (*Stroop effect;* Stroop, 1935; Kahneman & Treisman, this volume). Or the subject may be asked to classify stimuli by means of a card-sorting task, placing cards as quickly as possible into different piles according to category. Note that all these tasks are compound (not concurrent) tasks; the subject is presented only one of the possible stimuli and makes only one of the alternative responses on any one trial.

In all reaction-time tasks, subjects typically have been asked to respond as quickly as possible while making as few mistakes as possible. These are clearly incompatible goals; subjects could go faster by accepting more mistakes, or they could reduce errors by increasing their reaction times. The ambiguity of the "fast and accurate" instruction is well known: and, in contemporary experiments, the subject is rewarded according to a well-specified payoff matrix for quick correct responses and penalized for errors.

In addition to the straightforward, classical reaction-time procedure two variations should be considered: the *deadline procedure* and the Reed–Wickelgren–Dosher cued-response procedure. In the former the subject is given a time limit (the deadline) within which he or she must respond in order to avoid an explicit penalty (Fitts, 1966). In the *Reed–Wickelgren–Dosher cued-response procedure* (Dosher, 1976; 1981; Reed, 1973; Wickelgren, Corbett, & Dosher, 1980); a "respond now" cue follows the stimulus with a variable delay, with the subject having to respond within a brief interval (deadline) thereafter.

To induce the subject to respond more quickly in the three procedures (classical reaction-time, deadline, and cued-response), the rewards for fast responses and the penalties for slow responses are increased, the deadline is shortened, or the delay of the response cue is decreased. To induce the subject to be more accurate, the penalty for errors is increased, the response deadline is increased, or the delay of the "respond now" cue is increased. Thus, given precisely the same stimuli, subjects can be induced to be either fast and inaccurate or slow and accurate. The range of performance of which a subject is capable defines his or her speed–accuracy trade-off (SATO).

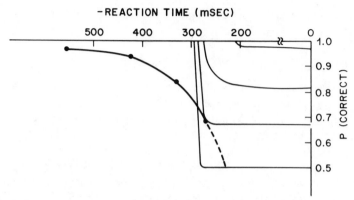

Figure 4.15 A speed-accuracy trade-off (SAT) in a two-alternative reaction-time experiment with various deadlines. The abscissa is the speed (zero minus reaction time), and the ordinate is the probability of a correct response. Iso-utility contours are illustrated for a deadline of 300 msec, corresponding to the rightmost data point. They are equally appropriate for a cued-response procedure. (Data are computed from Pachella and Fisher, 1972.)

Example of a Speed–Accuracy Trade-off and Utility Function A typical SATO is illustrated in Figure 4.15. Data are from a two-choice reaction-time experiment (Pachella & Fisher, 1972) with deadlines of 300, 400, 700 msec, and infinity. Both accuracy and speed are averaged over all responses; accuracy is represented by the proportion of correct responses, and speed is represented by zero minus the mean reaction time. Notice that good performance (fast, accurate) is again represented up and to the right. Whenever payoffs are defined in terms of individual responses rather than in terms of averages over a session, to represent the utility functions along with the SATO on a graph of accuracy versus speed requires additional information about the distribution of individual reaction times and errors. However, for the deadline or cued-response procedures, the form of the utility function is so simple that it will not be much influenced by the reaction-time distribution. A representative utility function[19] is illustrated in Figure 4.15. Utility is proportional to the number of correct responses, with a very high penalty for late responses (i.e., responses that exceed the deadline in the deadline procedure or that fall beyond the "respond now" deadline in the

[19]Pachella and Fisher (1972) used a tone to indicate to subjects that they had responded within the deadline and visual feedback (an arrow) to indicate the correctness of their response, but they did not explicitly assign values to the various outcomes of the trial. At least some of their subjects failed to follow instructions to be as accurate as possible; responding far in advance of the deadline, presumably because of an incorrect (but quite natural) assumption that quicker reaction times were better than slow ones or (equivalently) because of impatience. Therefore, the right halves of the actual utility functions in Figure 4.15 are not quite horizontal. The data in Figure 4.15 are derived from Pachella and Fisher's measure of information transmitted by assuming complete symmetry between alternative responses.

"respond now" procedure). A high utility is achieved by combining high accuracy with a very small fraction of late responses. Responding sooner than required yields no additional award; thus, the iso-utility contour is horizontal for short reaction times. A small increase in late responses must be compensated by a large increase in accuracy; thus, the iso-utility function is almost vertical near deadline time (in the deadline procedure) or the cue plus deadline time in the cued-response procedure.

In all nonpathological cases, the POC is concave down, the iso-utility contour is concave up, and the two curves are tangent to each other at the optimum point. In the deadline and cued-response procedures, the corners of the iso-utility contours (where the tangent point will be) tend to be almost vertically above each other; demonstrating the overriding importance of speed (relative to accuracy) in determining the operating point on the SATO.

According to optimization theory—even with the ordinary, ambiguous "speed plus accuracy" instruction—the subject operates at the optimal point on his or her SATO; with ambiguous instructions, the optimum is determined by the subject's *implicit* utility function. Insofar as different points on a SATO can be measured, the reasoning just described can be reversed and the tangent relation between the SATO and the iso-utility contour can be used to discover the shape of the subject's implicit iso-utility contours.

Finally, it should be noted that multiresponse reaction-time experiments cannot be represented completely in a single, one-dimensional SATO. For example, the speed and accuracy of particular response alternatives can be varied inversely even as overall performance remains relatively unaffected—the problem to which RWMs are addressed. However, in symmetrical situations, where the difficulty and payoffs for the various alternative responses in the compound task are approximately equal; the SATO as defined here has interesting and useful properties—some of which are considered in the next section.

Strategy Mixture in Operating Characteristics

On all the operating characteristics considered so far, a strategy is defined as the choice by which a subject or an economy arrives at a particular point on the operating characteristic. In attendance theory, strategy is the choice of classroom-switching time; in signal detection theory, it is the criterion above which a sample will be called a "signal"; in attention theory and economics, it is the choice of how to allocate resources between competing tasks or industries; and in speed accuracy trade-offs, it is the choice of speed and accuracy level (which, according to random walk theory, is mediated by the choice of boundaries—see Figure 4.14). Consider two strategies, S_a and S_b, represented by two distinct points a, b on an operating characteristic (Figure 4.16b). Suppose on some

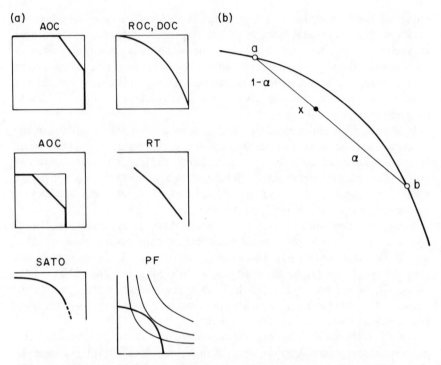

Figure 4.16 (a) Six Performance Operating Characteristics: (AOC) Attendance: (ROC) Receiver, (DOC), Discrimination or Decision; (AOC) Attention; (RT) Reaction Time Trade-off; (SATO) Speed Accuracy Trade-off; and (PF) economic Production Possibility Frontier. (b) Close-up view of a curved segment of an operating characteristic—the points **a** and **b** represent performance achieved by Strategies S_a and S_b, and the point **x** represents performance on a mixture of occasions on which S_a and S_b are used, with S_a being used on a fraction (α) of occasions and S_b on the remaining fraction ($1 - \alpha$) of occasions.

fraction (α) of the trials, the subject uses Strategy S_a and on the remaining fraction ($1 - \alpha$) of trials used Strategy S_b. The observed performance **x** would lie along the straight line connecting Performances **a** and **b**. The distance from **b** to **x** is proportioned to α; that is,

$$\frac{|\mathbf{x} - \mathbf{b}|}{|\mathbf{a} - \mathbf{x}|} = \frac{\alpha}{1 - \alpha}$$

and of course $\mathbf{x} = \mathbf{a}$ for $\alpha = 1$.

The property of strategy mixtures, that they lie along the line connecting them in a POC graph, can easily be generalized: The net result of a mixture of strategies is a point that represents the center of gravity of the mixture. That is, let $S_1, S_2, \ldots, S_N$ represent N strategies each of which produces a performance on each of M tasks ($P_{11}, \ldots, P_{ij}, \ldots, P_{MN}$). Let α_j, $\alpha \geq 0$, and $\sum_{j=1}^{N} \alpha_j = 1$ represent the proportion of trials on which strategy S_j is engaged. Then the

mixture of strategies $S = \Sigma\alpha_j S_j$ produces the performance $P_1., P_2., \ldots, P_M.$
where

$$(P_1., P_2., \ldots, P_M.) = \sum_{j=1}^{N} \alpha_j(P_{1j}, P_{2j}, \ldots)$$

$$= (\Sigma\alpha_j P_{1j}, \Sigma\alpha_j P_{2j}, \ldots)$$

Primarily, the interest here is in mixtures of just two strategies; so, higher dimensional generalizations can be dispensed with, and the equation can be simply summarized as: The mixture of two strategies lies on the straight line connecting them.

Contingency Analysis: Attendance Example

To explore the properties of strategy mixtures, consider an extreme attendance example. Two courses are offered at precisely overlapping time periods, for example, noon until 1:00 p.m. Suppose a student attends only Course 1 (S_1). The student's performance is perfect on examinations for Class 1, and zero for Class 2. Another student who attends only Class 2 (S_2) has perfect performance for Class 2, and zero for Class 1. To produce an equal mixture of the strategies ($S_{1\wedge2}$), a third student flips a fair coin each day before class to determine which class to attend. The third student's performance with $S_{1/2}$ is 50% on examinations for each course. On the other hand, a fourth student attends Class 1 from noon to 12:30 and Class 2 from 12:30 to 1:00—a pure strategy. The fourth student also scores 50% on each class's examinations. How can the third student's mixture of strategies be discriminated from the fourth student's pure strategy?

When a POC is strictly concave, then a mixture of strategies lies on a straight line away from the curved POC. Insofar as an intermediate point **y** on a POC lies above the line representing the mixture of its neighbors (**a** and **b**) it cannot represent the mixture of strategies that gave rise to **a** and **b** but represents a new strategy. This procedure can be generalized. Suppose it is established that at least N straight-line segments are required to generate a curved POC. Then there are at least $N + 1$ different strategies. In the limit (for example, in the usual signal detection case with normal distributions assumed for noise and signal plus noise and with a continuously variable criterion), an infinite number of strategies is assumed.

The problem with using the shape of the POC to infer the number or existence of possible intermediate strategies is that it is a statistically weak test when the POC is not very curved, and it is useless when the POC is straight (as it is in the classroom example just described). Nevertheless, a strong differentiation of the mixed and intermediate pure strategy is possible by considering joint performance on the two tasks. Consider the examination questions asked about the material covered on a particular day in each classroom. For simplicity, assume

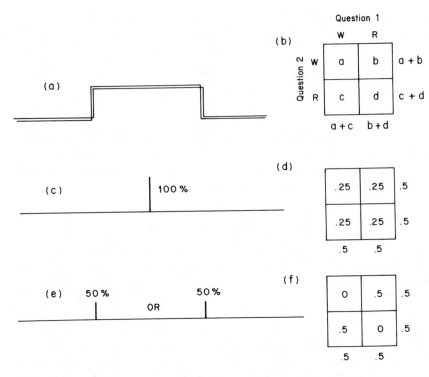

Figure 4.17 Contingency analysis of strategy mixture in a classroom attendance example. (a) Representation of information being offered in two classes scheduled at precisely the same time. (b) Contingency table representing the joint probability of answering two examination questions correctly. Question 1 is drawn at random from material offered in Class 1 and Question 2 from material offered in Class 2 on the same day. W and R represent wrong and right answers, respectively. It is assumed that if the student was in the classroom at the time the material was presented, he or she would answer the examination question correctly. (c) Representation of a (pure) strategy in which, on each day, a student switches from one classroom to the other midway through the class period. (d) Contingency table for the strategy in (c). (e) Representation of a mixture of strategies in which a student attends either one class or the other on each day (i.e., the student switches from Class 1 to Class 2 either in the first or at the last instant of each class). (f) Contingency matrix for the mixed strategy in (e).

that just one question is asked by each instructor. There are four possible outcomes of the joint response to these questions: A student can correctly answer both, neither, or one question from either one of the two classes. These outcomes are represented in the 2 × 2 contingency table shown in Figure 4.17a and b. In the mixed strategy, in which the third student attends all of one class or the other, the student always answers the question from the attended class correctly and fails the other question. Over the whole examination with questions asked about many days, the student's performance will average out to 50% in each class, but the student never answers both or misses both (Figure 4.17 e and f).

On the other hand, if it is assumed that instructors construct their examination questions independently and that they are equally likely to probe information offered in the first half as in the second half of the class period, then the fourth student (who switches classes halfway through the period) is as likely to answer any examination question as any other. This student's pure strategy results in a contingency matrix in which all cells have equal probability. Thus, the pure strategy results in a contingency matrix in which there is statistical independence and zero correlation between the two performaances. The mixed strategy results in a contingency matrix with statistic dependence and maximum negative correlation. In summary, the classroom example shows that a pure and a mixed strategy can be powerfully discriminated even when they fall on precisely the same point of a POC.

Generalized Mixtures of Statistics

The preceding argument can be generalized somewhat: The mixture of two strategies results not only in a mixture of the probabilities of a correct response in each strategy, but also in a linear combination of all the statistics that characterize the two strategies being mixed. In the classroom example, there was a matrix characterizing each component (S_1, S_2) of the mixed strategy; the mixed strategy itself was characterized by the mixture (combination) of the matrices characterizing the components (Figure 4.17). Strategy mixture is mixture indeed.

Strategy Mixture in Attention Operating Characteristics

The AOCs (Figure 4.14) reported by Sperling and Melchner (1978a) are nearly straight lines. The extreme strategies are "give 90% of your attention to the inside" and "give 90% of your attention to the outside," respectively. The equal attention strategy is near the midpoint of these extremes. One may ask, can the contingency matrix tell us whether the "equal attention" strategy is a pure strategy (attention sharing) or whether it is a mixture of switching between the extremes.

The answers differ a little for the different task combinations: In no case are the data powerful enough to reject the switching (mixture) hypothesis; the sharing hypothesis can be rejected for concurrent search for large and for small targets, and for concurrent search for numerals and for letters. For the concurrent search of noise-masked and normal numerals, performance is so close to the independence point that the mixed strategy and pure strategy predictions of the equal-attention matrix do not differ enough to make a discrimination feasible. Although mixture cannot be rejected for any individual subject or condition, all the data deviate somewhat from the pure mixture predictions in the direction of sharing. Thus, the most likely conclusion is that strategies entering into the mixture in the equal-attention conditions are not quite as extreme as the strategies

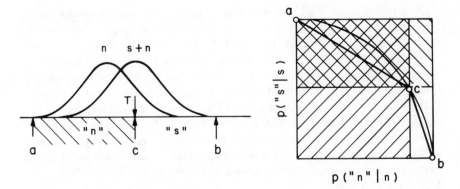

Figure 4.18 (a) Representation of a threshold in signal detection theory. The decision criterion c cannot be moved to the left of the point on the abscissa indicated by T. Shaded area indicates forbidden criteria. Of course the observer can always respond "signal" even without observing the stimulus; this is represented by a criterion at a. A response of "noise" to all stimuli is represented by a criterion at b. In (b) the decision operating characteristic (DOC) representation of the three decision criteria (a, b, and c) in (a) is shown. The shaded area indicates portions of the DOC along which threshold theory asserts no pure strategy can exist; performance within the shaded area is achievable only by strategy mixtures.

employed in the give-90%-of-your-attention conditions. In other words, there are more than two strategies: Equal attention is achieved by switching between strategies that allocate more resources to one or the other class of target, but not such an extreme allocation as is the case with the instruction, "give 90% of your attention" to one class of target.

Strategy Mixture in Signal Detection Theory

The threshold model is the most common source of the (implicit) assertion of strategy mixture in signal detection experiments. Essentially, an observer threshold means that the subject cannot adopt the full range of criteria; small values of n or $s + n$ on the subject's "internal sensory continuum" are all treated alike (Figure 4.18). Whether this is due to a decision criterion that cannot normally be induced below the high threshold or whether it is due to a sensory process that simply transmits the value zero whenever the summed value of input plus process-noise falls below the threshold is immaterial for the present analysis. The net outcome is that the DOC would have an interruption (shaded area, Figure 4.18b) unless the subject employed a mixture of strategies to bridge the gap between the strategy, "always say 'signal,'" and the strategy, "say 'signal' if the decision variable is above threshold."

In its strongest form, threshold theory also asserts that all signals above threshold are treated alike—for the purposes of detection, that is, the unshaded area of Figure 4.18b between b and c also is forbidden. The strong form of high threshold theory is an assertion that the DOC consists of three points derived from pure strategies: two degenerate extremes and one intermediate point. All other points that may be observed on a DOC are based on strategy mixtures that lie on the straight-line segments connecting pure strategies. More complicated forms of threshold models (such as two thresholds: low and high) are equivalent to assertions that the DOC consists of more than two straight-line segments, or of some straight lines plus some curved sections, etc. Still more complicated models (e.g., Krantz, 1969), which include both probabilistic thresholds (a stimulus confusion process) and probabilistic responses (a response confusion process) are not considered here and, in fact, are better considered in a more general scaling context (Shepard, 1958).

Any curve can be approximated by straight-line segments, and smooth curves—such as DOCs typically are—can be well approximated by very few line segments. From a DOC alone, it is impossible in practice to distinguish a threshold theory (N pure strategies plus mixtures) from an infinitely variable criterion theory (only pure strategies). The difficulty arises because the signal detection experiment is a compound (not concurrent) paradigm. There is only one stimulus presented on each trial; therefore, there is no possibility of a contingency analysis such as that which distinguished pure from mixed strategies in the concurrent tasks of attendance and attention theory.

The Objective Study of Strategy Mixture

Phenomenological Approach To resolve the issue of pure versus mixed strategies in signal detection (and similar compound tasks) requires going beyond the data that are usually collected. I propose three methods of resolution: phenomenological, mathematical, and experimental. The phenomenological approach is the simplest: Ask the subjects directly whether they are mixing strategies. This method does not convince skeptics who argue that subjects' answers could be uninformed, misinformed, or (worst of all) deliberately deceitful.

Mathematical Approach The proposed mathematical approach relies on confidence ratings: Instead of a simple yes or no, the subject uses one of J (typically, 5 ± 2) responses ranging from "certain n," to "probably n," to "certain s" (Egan, 1975). Consider a mixed-list detection experiment in which, on each trial, either noise (n) or a signal of intensity i (s_i) is presented, and the subject makes a confidence rating response j. The signal intensity on each trial is chosen randomly from a set of $I - 1$ different, nonzero intensity values so that, with noise, there are I different stimuli. The data consist of the $I \times J$ response matrix, $R_i(j)$ (the proportion of trials on which stimulus i elicits response j). A row of this matrix represents the *profile (distribution) of confidences elicited by stimulus i*.

Let k be the state of the subject produced by stimulus $i;$ for example, k is the value produced by the stimulus on the subject's internal sensory continuum.

Threshold theory asserts that (1) there is a small number K of internal states, and the probability that stimulus i produces state k is $p_i(k)$; (2) each internal state k is characterized by a profile $f_k(j)$ of confidence ratings that the subject produces at random when the subject is in state k; (3) the observed confidence rating profile $R_i(j)$ elicited by a stimulis i will be the mixture of profiles f_k that represents the proportion of times the observer is in state k when i is presented.

$$R_i(j) = \sum_{k=1}^{K} p_i(k)f_k(j)$$

Thus, threshold theory is an assertion about the rank of the matrix R. For example, for $K = 3$, it asserts that even if the experimenter had used 10 different stimuli ($i = 10$), the apparently different observed confidence profiles $R_i(j)$ would be derivable from just 3 fundamental profiles $f_k(j)$ that represent the K internal states.

This formulation of threshold theory makes it equivalent to some of the most studied problems of psychology and mathematics. For example, in test theory, row i of the matrix (which represented a stimulus) becomes a subject, i. And the column j (which represented the proportion of times the confidence rating j was used) becomes a score on Test j. Internal states k become factors $f_k(j)$, and K-state threshold theory becomes the assertion that scores of the subjects on the various tests are explained by a small number K of factors, for which the loadings of tests $f_k(j)$ and the loadings of subjects $p_i(k)$ on the factors are required. From this vantage point, factor analysis of confidence ratings is an appropriate method for analyzing internal states, the number of internal states being at least as large as the number of factors needed to account for the data. Alternative approaches for deriving the minimum number of internal states in discrete-state models have been proposed by Bamber and van Santen (1983) and by van Santen and Bamber (1981), who derive statistical methods (unavailable in factor analysis) for testing the models.

With a small but important modification in the confidence rating procedure, other powerful analytic methods can be brought into play. The confidence rating method uses an arbitrary number of confidence rating levels that are unrelated, and uses no explicit correction method to reinforce the subject for using ratings optimally. Suppose the number of confidence levels is made equal to the number of stimuli. Then the confidence experiment becomes so nearly equivalent to an identification experiment that the confidence scale might as well be replaced with the stimulus names (i.e., their relative intensities). For example, with 9 signals and noise, the confidence ratings 0, 1, . . . 9 are equivalent to noise followed by the stimulus names, in order of increasing intensity. The subject does essentially the same thing whether stating a confidence or stating a belief that some particular stimulus occurred (Sperling, 1965). The resulting S–R confusion matrix can be analyzed, for example, by multidimensional scaling to yield a representation of the threshold stimuli embedded in Euclidian space (see Sperling, Figure 12, p. 160, in Levitt, 1972). The multidimensional representation does not directly answer the theoretical question of how many discrete internal states there are, but it does provide a means of answering many questions relating to discriminability of threshold stimuli.

Experimental Approach: The Contrived Control Finally, one may study the subject's ability to perform in accordance with an N-threshold theory in a case where the N-discriminable thresholds are not in doubt. That is, two experiments that should produce equivalent results if the threshold theory were correct are conducted. The first experiment is the original signal detection experiment, for example, presentation of either a weak stimulus or noise with equal probability on each trial. The subject is required to give confidence ratings on a 7-point scale. Suppose that the analysis by high-threshold theory suggests that the signal exceeds the high threshold 0.7 of the time, and noise exceeds the threshold 0.1 of the time.

A control experiment can now be contrived that is matched in all respects to the original threshold experiment except one: The control has a highly visible stimulus, say 10 *jnds* over threshold. The subject would unfailingly detect this stimulus; so it can safely be assumed that when the stimulus is presented, it exceeds the subject's high threshold. Because in the original experiment, the subject's high threshold was exceeded on 0.7 of the signal trials, in the contrived control experiment, the strong stimulus is presented on 0.7 of the signal trials, and a blank is presented on the remaining signal trials. (A signal trial means that the subject is told (after responding) that a signal was presented.) On 0.9 of the noise trials, the blank is presented; and on the remaining 0.1 of the noise trials, the strong stimulus is presented (to correspond to the subject's internal state following a false detection). For equal probabilities of signal and noise trials, this means that after $0.25 = 0.3/(0.9 + 0.3)$ of the blanks, the subject is told that the signal had been presented (to correspond to the misses in the original experiment). After $0.125 = 0.1/(0.7 + 0.1)$ of the strong stimuli, the subject is told that noise had been presented. To make this feedback plausible, the subject is told that the apparatus does not work reliably, and that the task is to base responses—a confidence level—on what the apparatus had been programmed to do, not on what it actually did (because the apparatus failures are manifest).

The contrived control experiment yields a subject whose internal states, given "signal" or "noise," are known. The subject's strategy in the use of confidence ratings, for example, can be studied directly and not merely inferentially. For that matter, a three-state or even an N-state threshold theory can be mimicked by an appropriately contrived control experiment with three or with N highly discriminable stimuli. Insofar as subjects behave similarly in contrived control experiments and in the actual signal detection experiments, it substantiates the N-

state threshold models; insofar as subjects are unable to maintain the complex strategies ascribed to them by the N-state theorists, it defeats such N-state models. In either case, these procedures provide an objective experimental approach to the study of strategy and strategy mixtures.

Strategy Mixture in Speed–Accuracy Trade-Offs

The assertion of strategy mixture in SATOs comes most commonly in the guise of the fast-guess model. This model applies, for example, to two-choice reaction-time experiments in which the subject is presented on each trial with one of two alternative stimuli and is required to make the corresponding one of two responses as quickly as possible. For example, in Ollman's (1966) and Yellott's (1967, 1971) theory, the subject is asserted to respond to the stimulus with a normal reaction time on some fraction $1 - \alpha$ of the trials, and on the remaining trials α the subject responds as quickly as possible (simple reaction time) according to a predetermined guess at what the stimulus might be. On fast-guess trials, the subject is correct with only chance accuracy ($p = 0.5$) but with very short reaction times; on the remaining trials, the subject has long reaction times and a correspondingly higher percentage of correct responses. When the experimenter demands from the subject an even lower average reaction time, the subject complies by increasing the proportion α of fast guesses.

The fast-guess model is equivalent to the assertion that the SATO is composed of a straight-line segment the end points of which represent the two strategies, the honest strategy and the fast-guess strategy. An alternative hypothesis to fast guess would be that the subject chooses a pure strategy appropriate to each payoff matrix—a process that could be modeled, for example, by boundary changes in a random walk model. This alternative strategy might generate either a curved or a straight-line SATO. As in all the previous cases, it is not efficient to discriminate pure from mixed strategies by close examination of the curvature of the operating characteristic. In the case of the SATO, associated with each point on the SATO are not only the mean reaction-time and mean accuracy (which define the point), but also two reaction-time distributions—one for correct responses and one for errors.[20] The fast-guess model not only requires the SATO to be a straight line, but also requires the reaction-time distributions associated with each point to be a mixture of the reaction-time distributions associated with the extreme points. This is a powerful test to discriminate between strategy mixtures and pure strategies[21] that is formally similar to the test for mixture of

---

[20]In the case of unsymmetric stimuli or responses, there are even more reaction-time distributions to be considered; but that is beyond the scope of the present treatment (see, for example, Link and Heath, 1975).

[21]Mixtures of two probability density functions $p(x) = p_1(x) + (1 - \alpha)p_2(x)$ have the interesting property (Falmagne, 1968) that there is at least one value—x_0, the fixed point of the random

strategies in confidence ratings discussed in the preceding. Furthermore, contingency matrices also apply to the SATO. In a pure strategy, reaction speed and accuracy are uncorrelated or weakly related. In a mixed strategy, however, there is a strong negative correlation of accuracy with speed exactly analogous to the negative correlation of performance on Task 1 with Task 2 in the attendance and in the attention contingency matrices.

Mixed Strategies in Production

Consider the primitive plowshares–swords economy. Suppose it is decided to devote half of the economy to each goal. Does it make any difference whether on every odd-numbered day of the year, the whole economy is devoted to agriculture, and on every even-numbered day, the economy is devoted to defense production (mixed strategy) versus the case in which on all days, the resources are divided in half and equally devoted to each goal (pure strategy)? Certainly! The pure strategy is far more efficient in terms of the production facilities needed. But even if production facilities were not at issue and only the availability of labor was, it would still be more efficient to divide labor equally on every day than to alternate days. The reason is that if even one laborer were more efficient at making plowshares than swords, it would be efficient to assign this laborer to the task for which he or she were better suited. By similar reasoning regarding any resource, a pure strategy is preferable whenever resources are not completely equal and interchangeable with respect to the economic goals. This is the line of argument used previously to demonstrate that economic production possibility frontiers are always concave toward the origin. A mixed strategy does not take advantage of the curvature; it always lies closer to the origin and is of lower utility than the corresponding pure strategy (Figure 4.16b). There is inherent superiority in a pure strategy—optimal for the situation—over a mixture of less than optimal strategies.

Given the economic superiority of pure over mixed strategies, it is pertinent to ask, What limitation in allocation of mental processing resources prevents the utilization of pure strategies in human divided attention tasks? One possible answer is that there is a single processor or process involved in concurrent tasks, and that there is a changeover delay incurred in switching this resource from task to task. Switching the resource within a trial produces unacceptable costs. An analogous problem occurs in computer time-sharing systems in switching from one user to another. There is an overhead cost (time and memory) incurred in swapping a second user's program into the central processor unit (CPU), and the

---

variable—for which the associated probability density does not change as the mixture ratio α varies. Whenever this occurs $p_1(x_0) = p_2(x_0)$. The existence of a fixed point in probability distributions is analogous to a fixed point in the absorption spectra of a putative mixture of two chemicals formed, for example, by decomposition of one into the other.

first user's program out into a buffer until it again gains access to the CPU. Trying to divide time too finely results in too many swaps per second with a corresponding, disproportionately high overhead cost. In the limit, no useful work is accomplished—only swapping is achieved. Changeover costs have some interesting consequences in other economies as well; these are considered in the next section.

Path Dependence in Performance Operating Characteristics

Path Dependence in Classroom Attendance

The simplest situation in which to discover effects of changeover costs is the classroom example. Suppose that when a student was ready to run from Class 1 to Class 2, the second class were located not in an adjacent room but in a different building, and the trip between classes would consume 5 minutes. Clearly, there would be no point in switching from Class 1 to Class 2 unless the information being offered in Class 2 were so much more valuable that it could compensate for the lost time.

The effect of a changeover cost is to maintain the status quo. The student remains in the present classroom, even when another class would be slightly more useful, because the additional utility is insufficient to compensate for the changeover cost. The student's presence in current classroom reflects not only the current utility of the competing classes, it also reflects the past history that brought the student to the class in the first place. A class that was useful in the recent past holds students even after its utility has slipped below that of its competitors. This phenomenon is called *path dependence*. It is ubiquitous in psychology, although only since the 1970s has it begun to be appreciated outside the realm of clinical psychology. It is sometimes referred to as *hysteresis*—a reference to the electromagnetic phenomenon in which a magnetic substance tends to retain its previous magnetic orientation even after an oppositely directed external magnetic field has been applied, a field that—had the previous magnetic orientation been neutral—would have been sufficient to induce a change. Of course, hysteresis can be overcome; it simply requires a stronger external magnetic field. Energy is lost in a hysteresis cycle related to the amount of path dependence, with no energy being lost when there is no hysteresis (see Figure 4.19a). The classroom dilemma is analogous. Students can be induced to switch classes, provided the required differential benefit is sufficient to overcome the cost. The classroom-switching cost—lost information during changeover—is somewhat analogous to lost energy in hysteresis. (A better analogy with magnetic hysteresis is the loss in information due to the student's being in a nonoptimal classroom (see Figure 4.19b). When classes are adjacent and there is no

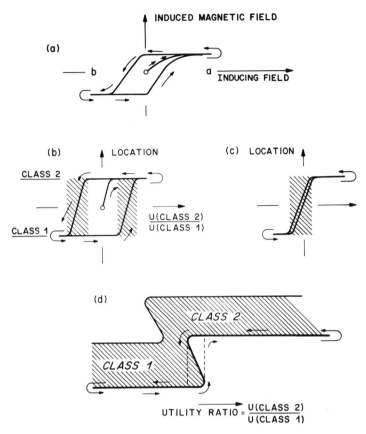

Figure 4.19 Examples of path-dependence. In (a), hysteresis in a piece of magnetized iron is shown. The electric field is initially neutral (open circle) and then varies back and forth between *a* and *b*, indicated on the abscissa. The ordinate indicates the induced magnetic orientation of the microcrystals in the iron. The curved arrows indicate the flow of time. In (b), hysteresis in the classroom is shown. Two courses are offered; the ratio of their utility to the student u(Class 2)/u(Class 1) is varied periodically during a very long class period. Initially (open circle), the inexperienced student is midway between classes. As the information being offered in Class 2 is becoming more valuable than in Class 1, the student runs to Class 2 and remains there; subsequently, Class 1 becomes more valuable so the student runs to it; when the utility of Class 1 subsides, the student returns to Class 2; etc. Information is completely lost during transit (heavily shaded area) and partially lost during the time the student lingers in the less informative class (clear center rectangle). In (c), the classroom strategy of the upperclassman is shown. Being smarter than an iron crystal or a freshman, this student anticipates the future course of events. When in Class 2, as its utility diminishes, he or she leaves while it is still more valuable than Class 1, knowing that by the time of arrival in Class 2 the relative utility will have reversed. This student loses information only as a result of transit (shaded area), never by being in the wrong classroom. In (d), the catastrophe theory representation of the events in (b) is shown. The upper surface represents Class 2, the lower surface Class 1. The abscissa represents the control parameter, the utility ratio u(Class 2)/u(Class 1). When u is varied and a fold in the surface is reached, the student cannot reverse direction. So, the student jumps to the other surface and continues there. The jump is the "catastrophe" of catastrophe theory.

changeover delay, there also is no path dependence, no hysteresis, and no lost information. The student's strategy at any and every instant of time can be optimal for that instant.

There is an interesting heuristic representation of path-dependent effects in *catastrophe theory* (Thom, 1975a; 1975b; Zeeman, 1976). The student's current classroom may be thought of as the dependent variable, which is under the control of an independent variable—the utility ratio of the material offered in the two competing classes. As the utility ratio changes, the state changes—as described in the preceding and as illustrated in Figure 4.19d. The "catastrophe" occurs when the student switches from one surface (classroom) to the other at a fold in the surface. A useful aspect of the catastrophe theory representation is that all possible equilibrium states and the relations between them are clearly shown. A limitation of the catastrophe theory representation is that neither the dynamic aspects of the situation nor the underlying processes are represented. By itself, a catastrophe theory representation is an insufficient description of a dynamic system (Sussman & Zahler, 1978).[22]

Path Dependence in Economics

I do not know of an analog to changeover costs in signal detection theory; but in economic theory, changeover costs (obviously) are extremely significant. For example, according to the preceding argument, it would be expected that as demand for small cars began to grow in the 1970s, the American automobile manufacturers would have continued to make too many large cars because of the retooling expense and risks involved in changing over from the manufacture of large to small cars (see Figure 4.19b). In fact, contemporary economic decisions seldom can afford to wait until they are caused by events themselves; almost always, it is the anticipation of predicted events and of trends that drives economic decisions (see Figure 4.19c). The incorporation of expectations into economic theory so complicates the theory that it can hardly serve as a simple illustrative example. Whether automobile manufacturers retooled early or late depended on their expectations of future market forces. Because it is not known what these expectations were nor how they were derived, the automobile retooling problem is hardly the simple changeover analogy that it superficially appears to be.

Path Dependence in Attention

The moral from economics for the study of human attention is that sophisticated performance requires correspondingly sophisticated theory. Sperling and

---

[22]See Sperling (1970b) for illustrative examples of the relations between path dependence and multiple stable states. See Sperling (1981) for the relation of catastrophe theory to the just-discussed phenomena and for references.

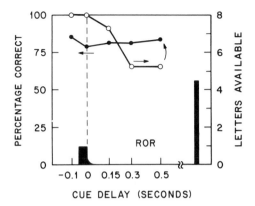

Figure 4.20 Path-dependence in a partial report experiment. Accuracy of partial reports for 10 blocks of trials conducted in one session. Arrows indicate the sequence of blocks. Bar at right indicates accuracy of whole reports. Stimulus exposure is indicated at lower left. Descending cue-delay series (open circles) corresponds to the strategy, "attend equally to both rows", and ascending series (closed circles) corresponds to the strategy, "attend primarily to the top row." The loop is not closed at the left in these data because the session ended; but from other data, it is clear that with continued exposure to prior cues (−0.10 seconds) the subject will switch to "equal attention," that is, jump to top curve. (Subject ROR from Sperling, 1960.)

Melchner's (1976, 1978b) observation that visual attention tended to be switched rather than shared suggested that there was a single, serial central processor that avoided switching between tasks within a trial in order to avoid the changeover cost; and thus, within a trial, the processor was devoted almost entirely to one task or the other. The single processor hypothesis is the most ubiquitous theory of attention. However, in this instance, it is too simple and leaves too many questions unanswered. How does one account for the imperfect but nonetheless substantial performance on the secondary task? Further, in follow-up experiments in which different sizes of targets occurred in the same or in nearby places, Sperling and Harris (Note 4) failed to find significant effects of attention instructions; performance was at the independence point. A similar result is reported by Hoffman and Nelson (1981). In case it is not already obvious, the reader is reminded that not all questions are answered in this chapter.

    Rather than close this section on a question, it seems useful to remind the reader that path dependence between trials has an honorable, but sporadic, history in the experimental psychology of attention under the pseudonyms of "set" and "Einstellung." In the realm of the examples of visual attention discussed here, for example, Sperling (1960) exhibited data from a subject with textbook hysteresis who failed to switch soon enough between "equal attention" strategies and "guessing" strategies as the conditions favoring one or the other of these strategies were gradually altered between blocks (Figure 4.20). Figure 4.1 showed this subject earlier in training using a single (pure) strategy.

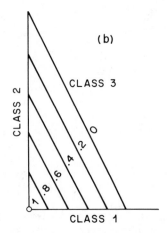

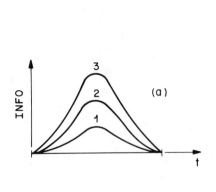

Figure 4.21 A two-dimensional strategy covers an *area* in operating space. (a) Three classes that draw on precisely the same resource pool. In an extension of previous examples, the density of information offered in each class (ordinate, INFO) is allowed to differ although the three information density functions differ only by a scale factor. (b) The amount of information a student acquires from Class 1 and Class 2 as the classroom-switching time from Class 1 to 2 is varied (the student also spends some units of time, indicated as the parameter, in Class 3 during which the student attends neither Class 1 nor 2).

Single and Multiple Resources

Single-Resource Pool

Multidimensional Strategies In the attendance analogy, a single-resource pool is exemplified by a set of competing courses offered at a particular time (e.g., noon to 1:00 p.m.) in all of which there is the same temporal distribution of information. Thus, all the competing courses use the same resource pool (the time from noon to 1:00 p.m.) with the same effectiveness, except possibly for an arbitrary scale factor that reflects the fact that performance measurements in different tasks may be incommensurate (Figure 4.21a). If the distribution of information over time $f(t)$ were not uniform, it would be possible to monotonically transform time from seconds into new units—resource units—which have the property that $\frac{1}{1000}$ of the daily lesson is covered in each resource milliunit. Insofar as a student's performance in a course is directly proportional to the number of resource milliunits for which the student has attended that course (the only assumption so far), it is trivial to compute performance when the student divides the total time between N classes. We simply add up the milliunits spent in each classroom i to determine the performance P_i in that class.

Dimensions The dimensionality of operating space equals the number of independent performance measurements. In nearly all the examples of this chapter, performance was measured on two tasks and operating space was two-dimensional. In the three-class example of Figure 4.21, operating space is three-dimensional. In two-alternative choice reaction-time experiments, operating space is four-dimensional (two speeds, two accuracies), although only the most significant two of the four dimensions have been considered in this chapter.

The trade-off between performance on two tasks—determined by a single decision criterion or a single resource-allocation parameter—is one-dimensional, a line—the POC—in two-dimensional operating space. When there are two independent strategy decisions, as in the allocation of time to three overlapping classes, the POC is a two-dimensional area in operating space—a plane in this example. Figure 4.21b illustrates various possible POCs as one strategy is varied and the other is held constant. When two strategies both vary as a consequence of an experimental manipulation, the experimentally determined POC can be almost any regular or irregular curve, being restricted only to lying on the POC surface, (e.g., the right triangle in the bottom left of Figure 4.21b).

Nonlinear Resource–Performance Function A slightly more complicated, realistic condition in which performance is monotonic with—but not directly proportional to—the number of resource units is represented by a nonlinear resource–performance function. These are the considerations introduced by Norman and Bobrow (1975) in their resource–performance function. For example, suppose the instructor tends to repeat material at random intervals. If it is assumed that listening to the repetition is wasted time, the student's performance increases slower than a linear function of milliunits because repetitions become more probable the more class units are accumulated (Figure 4.22). With repetition permitted, the marginal utility of a milliunit of class participation is a positively decreasing function of the amount of participation already accumulated. This assumption leads to a curved AOC.[23] The monotonic but nonlinear increase of performance with resource milliunits of participation is dealt with by several analytical methods, most notably conjoint measurement (Krantz, 1969) and monotonic analysis of variance (Carroll, 1972; Kruskal, 1965). These derive the nonlinear resource–performance transformation and ferret out the underlying additive structure in resource milliunits. In conclusion, when there is only one

---

[23]If the instructor repeats material *between* classes (on different days) as well as *within* a single class period, even the mixture of strategies would not be represented as a straight line. This would correspond to dependent trials in attention or in signal detection experiments. Although dependent trials do occur in psychophysical methods such as in the method of limits or in threshold tracking, the discussion here is confined to independent trials or, equivalently, independent topics covered in different class periods.

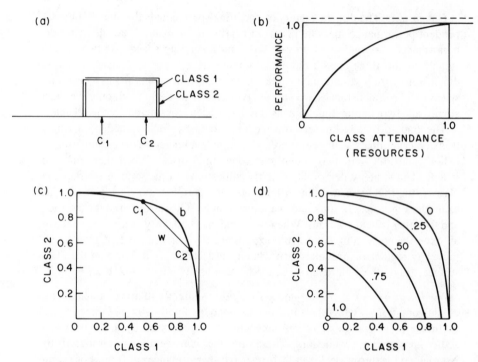

Figure 4.22 Consequences of a nonlinear resource–performance function. (a) Two classes are offered at precisely the same time. In (b), the resource–performance function in which an instructor repeats himself or herself within a class period is shown. When the student attends the entire class (attendance is 1.0), the performance also is 1.0. If the class were longer, performance would asymptote at the dashed horizontal line. In (c), the Attendance Operating Characteristic generated as classroom-switching time c varies is shown. When the student mixes two strategies, switching some days at c_1 and other days at c_2, the student's performance lies along the straight-line segment w (within-day repetition). If the instructor were equally likely to repeat material between days as within a day, the mixed strategy would actually lie along the segment b because the whole term would be, in effect, one long class period rather than a sequence of independent periods or trials. In (d), a third class is offered at precisely the same hours as the first two. If the student did not attend Class 3, the POC for Class 2 versus Class 1 will be unchanged from (c) as indicated by the POC labelled "0". If the student's participation in Class 3 increased (the curve parameter in (d), the POC would become straighter and be shifted toward the origin.

underlying resource pool shared in the same relative proportions by all the competing tasks, then, with linear resource–performance functions, description is perfectly straight forward; with nonlinear resource–performance functions, adequate methods exist for discovering and describing this situation.

Multiple-Resource Pools: Substitutability and Interference

Consider two tasks, Task 1 and Task 2. Let $u_i(r)$ be the utility of the resource r for Task i. For example, in the attendance example, a resource r is a particular time interval $[t_a, t_b]$. In the single-resource pool, the utility ratio $u_2(r)/u_1(r)$ is exactly the same for all r. In the multiple-resource pool, $u_2(r)/u_1(r)$ varies with r—the situation considered in most of the previous examples of this chapter. How can the existence of multiple-resource pools be demonstrated formally.

Demonstration of Multiple Resources   As has been shown in the previous sections, curvature of the POC is not a sufficient condition for concluding that there are multiple-resources; curvature could result from a nonlinear resource–performance function.

The most direct demonstration of multiple-resource pools is by way of an interaction involving the differential effect of a third task on performance in the first two tasks (see Wickens, Chapter 3, this volume). An excellent analysis and totally different kinds of examples are provided by Rachlin, Green, Kagel, and Battallo (1976) and Rachlin and Burkhardt (1978). Consider a rat given access to a dry solid food $S1$ and a liquid food $L1$. The rat spends, let us say, an equal amount of time consuming $S1$ and $L1$. Eating and drinking, respectively, can be regarded as two tasks, and consumption time as the dependent performance variable similar to a performance in attention or in classroom attendance tasks. The food and liquid dispensers are at different locations so the rat cannot simultaneously eat and drink; it has to choose to perform either one "task," or the other, or neither. When a second solid food $S2$ (a third task) is introduced, it interferes with consumption of $S1$ but not with $L1$. Similarly, a second liquid $L2$ interferes with consumption of $L1$ but not with $S1$ or $S2$.

It is hardly news that solid foods and fluids satisfy different appetites. However, casting a rat's motives into formal economic terms was an original and useful contribution by Rachlin and his co-workers (Rachlin, Batallio, Kagel, & Green, 1981; Rachlin & Burkhardt, 1978; Rachlin, Kagel, & Battalio, 1980). The subsequent treatment here differs somewhat from theirs. Figure 4.23 illustrates the three POCs appetite operating characteristics, for food $S1$ versus liquid $L1$ with the parameters: no competing task, competing $L2$, and competing $S2$. To generate points along an appetite operating characteristic, the relative amounts of deprivation (hunger or thirst) are varied. The POCs of Figure 4.23 cross each other in striking contrast to the POCs of Figures 4.21 and 4.22, which are parallel. The crossed POCs would require an interaction term in the analysis of variance, as can be seen from the more usual representation of such data in Figure 4.23b, and such data defeat any single-factor model.

The key economic concept is substitutability. Two different solid foods can substitute for each other, but eating and drinking are relatively nonsubstitutable (Rachlin *et al.*, 1976). Nonsubstitutability was treated earlier in this chapter. It occurred in the first attendance example (Figure 4.8c) in which a student had to pass each of two courses in order to graduate. This was contrasted to the case of grade point average (Figure 4.8b) in which courses are completely substitutable;

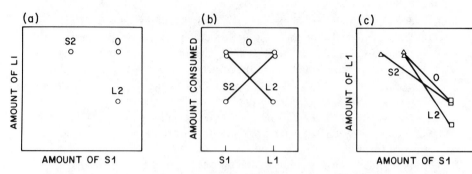

Figure 4.23 A demonstration of performance as a function of utility and interference, specifically, dry food and liquid consumption as determined by hunger and thirst and by alternative food and drink. In (a), the abscissa indicates the quantity of a dry, solid food $S1$; and the ordinate indicates the amount of liquid ($L1$) consumed by a hungry and thirsty rat. The open circle labeled zero (0) indicates that $S1$ and $L1$ were the only offerings, the circle labeled $S2$ indicates a second solid food $S2$ was offered along with $S1$ and $L1$, and the circle labeled $L2$ indicates a second liquid ($L2$) was offered with $S1$ and $L1$. In (b), a conventional representation of the data in (a) is illustrated to show interaction. The abscissa indicates what was being consumed ($S1$, $L1$), the ordinate indicates the amount consumed (of $L1$ or $S1$), and the parameter indicates the third alternative (zero, $S2$, $L2$). In (c), the appetite operating characteristics is shown. Coordinates are the same as in (a). Animals are offered $S1$, $L1$, and one of 0, $S2$, or $L2$ in different sessions. Triangles indicate hypothetical data from animals that are more thirsty (water deprived) than hungry (food deprived), and squares indicate more food than water deprivation.

a high grade in one can compensate for a low grade in the other. In the case of pass–fail, courses are completely nonsubstitutable because both have to be passed and good performance on one cannot compensate for failing performance in the other.

Interference In these examples, substitutability is a property of the utility function. Interference ultimately affects the utility that is achieved, but interference is best considered at the level of individual performance in each of the concurrent tasks. For example, in the animal experiments, eating and drinking interfere with each other in a physical sense; the animal would need two heads at opposite ends of its body to simultaneously eat and drink. Interference between two classes has been the point of all the classroom examples; attending one class totally interferes with attendance at the other. To see the interference effects of a third class, consider first two classes, one from noon until 1:00 p.m. and the other from 1:00 until 2:00 p.m. A third class scheduled from noon until 1:00 would interfere only with performance on Class 1; a class scheduled from 1:00 until 2:00 p.m. would interfere only with Class 2; a class scheduled between 12:30 and 1:30 would interfere with both Classes 1 and 2. This last class is analogous to a liquid food, such as milk, that depresses both eating of $S1$ and drinking of $L1$.[24]

Beyond variations in the content of a course itself, the classroom analogy admits two operations to manipulate the time spent in a classroom: (1) varying the relative utilities of the courses being offered and (2) varying the particular assortment of courses offered. These operations are referred to here as *varying utility* and *interference,* respectively. In the case of specific appetites, varying utility is most easily accomplished by specific deprivation; food has greater utility for a hungry animal than a sated one. Interference is accomplished by varying the assortment of foods and activities offered. The interference-generated data by themselves are somewhat cumbersome, both in collection and in utilization; so it is preferable to have access to both utility and interference data in constructing a resource model.

Interference data are probably the most widely collected data in analyzing mental processing resources. The AOC is an elementary interference method involving just two tasks. The extension to a full-fledged interference method would involve additional tasks. In detection experiments, such as Sperling and Melchner's (1978a) visual search task for numerals and/or letters, appropriate third tasks might involve memory loads (items that the subject was required to maintain in memory for subsequent recall during the search phase of the trial), irrelevant targets (targetlike items to be ignored that appear outside of the delimited search area), irrelevant auditory stimuli, etc. The various Stroop phenomena discussed by Kahneman and Treisman (Chapter 2, this volume) represent exhaustive studies of interference phenomena.

For exploiting interference data, factor analysis is an appropriate mathematical model. The appetite preference test is analogous to a battery of test items, such as the component tests of an IQ test. Each combination of competing tasks (e.g., $L1, S1, S2$) is analogous to a subject who has certain traits and abilities (e.g., $L1$, $S1, S2$). The factor analysis attempts to arrive at the minimum number of underlying factors needed to represent these abilities (appetites) and test items (foods and drinks). Even though factor analysis is a far more formidable technique than is demanded by any of the data currently available, it is useful to keep the interference methods and the corresponding analyses in mind when confronting these data.

---

[24]To complete the analogy between specific appetites and classroom attendance, additional assumptions are necessary. For example, assume classes offered between 12:00 and 1:00 are science classes, classes offered between 1:00 and 2:00 are language classes, and the student must ultimately pass both a science and a language examination. Assume it matters little to the student's performance which particular combination of classes in a category are elected. Science classes (solid food) are then substitutable for each other as are language classes (liquid foods).

Measuring the Reaction Time of a Shift
of Attention

Previous sections of this chapter have been concerned with the spatial distribution of attention during stable periods when the spatial distribution is not changing. This section is concerned with the dynamics of changing attention and with the comparison of attentional dynamics to the dynamics of motor responses. The reaction time of a motor response is the time from the onset of the reaction stimulus to the onset of the required response. Both the stimulus, for example, a light flash, and the response, for example, pressing a key, are trivial to measure. In the case of attention, the stimulus is easy to measure; but measuring the attention response requires ingenuity. Attention is the allocation of mental processing resources; hence, an attention response is a shift in resource allocation. The shift is not directly observable, but it can be inferred from its consequences. Because the concern here is with an attention response that involves "grabbing" an item from a list, the attention procedure is introduced with an analogous procedure for measuring the reaction time of a motor "grabbing" response.

Measuring the "Grabbing" Response

Imagine a subject who is seated adjacent to a conveyor belt on which balls are passing by while observing a screen on which stimuli are flashed. As soon as a visual target appears on the screen, the subject reaches through a small opening that permits access to the conveyor belt and grabs the first possible ball. The balls are numbered and arranged such that, for example, the ball numbered 1 passes the opening exactly 0.1 seconds after the target, the ball numbered 2 passes the opening exactly 0.2 seconds after the target, and so on. From the number of the ball that the subject grabbed, the reaction time of the grabbing response can be inferred exactly. Of course, the subject also would know the reaction time. Imagine a long sequence of trials on which the subject has consistently grabbed Ball 5. On the next trial, the subject grabs Ball 6 or perhaps even Ball 7. When the subject is asked the number of the ball, the subject might be ashamed to tell the truth and might say 5. To keep the subject honest, the numbers must be scrambled on the balls so that the experimenter can know from the number what the grabbing time was, but the subject cannot. In fact, a random one of the numbers could even be omitted on each trial. If the subject ever reported grabbing a ball with that number, the experimenter would know immediately there was a flaw in the procedure.

The subject reports the number on the ball only seconds after it actually was grabbed. The reaction time of the response, which actually had occurred much earlier, can be inferred from the reported number. The latency of the subject's verbal report has little to do with the latency of the grabbing response; the content of the verbal report is what reveals the grabbing reaction time. Obviously, this is an indirect method of measuring a reaction time. A high-speed film of the subject's movements could have been made. From a study of the film, it could have been determined directly when the subject's hand first began to move, when it first made contact with the passing ball, when the ball first was lifted from the conveyer, and so on. These are direct measures.

In the case of motor reaction times, there is a choice of direct or indirect measures of reaction time. In the case of attention responses, there is no visible response—nothing that can be photographed; there are only indirect measures. On the other hand, little is lost in the indirect measurement. Not only the mean, but also the variance and, in fact, the whole reaction-time distribution are obtained by the indirect method. The responses are perforce quantized into discrete times—there are balls passing only every 0.1 seconds—but this is neither a serious problem nor a necessary aspect of the indirect procedure.

Attention Reaction Time Distributions

To measure the reaction of a shift of visual attention, Sperling and Reeves (1980)[25] used the following procedure. The subject maintained fixation on a fixation mark throughout a trial (see Sperling & Reeves, 1980, p. 349). To the left of fixation, a target appeared. In one series of experiments, the target was chosen at random from a letter C, a letter U, or an outline square. The target was embedded in a stream of distractors (consisting of the other letters of the alphabet) that were flashed briefly, one on top of the other, at a rate of one character/218 msec. At the right of fixation, a stream of numerals occurred (one on top of the other) at either a fast rate of from one numeral/75 msec; or, in other conditions, at rates as slow as one numeral/240 msec (see Figure 4.24).

The subject's task was to detect the target in the letter stream and then to report the first numeral he or she could from the numeral stream. The task implicitly required the subject to attend to the letter stream until the target was detected and then to shift attention to the numeral stream in order to "grab" the earliest numeral. The identity of the reported numeral is important only insofar as—like the number on the billiard ball—it indicates the numeral's temporal position. The time from the onset of the target to the onset of the named numeral defines the attention reaction time on that trial. From a block of trials, an entire attention reaction-time distribution is obtained.

[25]Many investigators have attempted to measure the speed of attentional processes. Sperling and Reeves (1976, 1978, 1980) were the first to pose the problem as one of measuring the reaction time of an attention response, to formally propose the indirect procedure, to use this indirect procedure to generate the reaction-time distribution of an attentional response, to publish an attention reaction-time distribution, and to present side-by-side comparisons of attention reaction-time and motor reaction-time distributions made in response to the same stimuli.

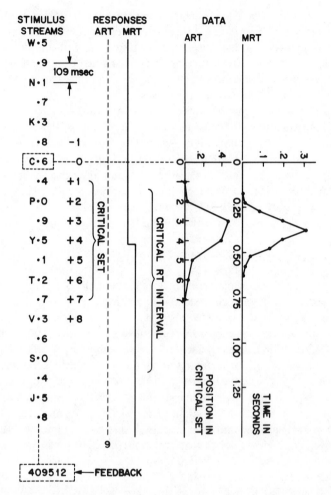

Figure 4.24 Measuring the reaction time of a shift of visual attention: procedures and typical results. Stimulus streams are shown at the left. The subject sees only the letters, the fixation dots, and the numerals. Each row represents a single display, briefly flashed and superimposed on the preceding display. The target letter is a C. The critical set of numerals and the critical reaction-time periods are indicated. The finger (motor) reaction-time key is indicated by MRT, and the attention-shift reaction (9) is indicated by ART. Feedback indicates the answer display (first six numerals of the critical set) shown to the subject after the ART response. The results show the actual observed MRT distribution and the observed ART distribution (proportion of times a numeral corresponding to each position is named) for 414 trials in this particular condition; that is, a letter stream rate of 4.6/sec, target C, and a numeral rate of 9.1/sec, in which report of one letter is tested in subject AR. (After Sperling and Reeves, 1980, Figure 17.1.)

There are certain important procedural considerations. In measuring a simple motor reaction time, for example, the interval between the warning stimulus or trial initiation and the occurrence of the target is varied randomly so that the reaction-time experiment does not degenerate into an experiment in time estimation. Moreover, the experimenter cannot simply instruct the subject to "respond as quickly as possible." There must be explicit contingencies so that responses that occur before the target stimulus are punished as premature "anticipations," and responses occurring too late are punished for being "slow." The effect of such restrictions is to define a critical interval within which the response is supposed to occur, (e.g., from 100 to 800 msec after target occurrence), and to reward the subject for responding as early as possible within the critical interval.

Similarly, in measuring an attention reaction time, one cannot simply instruct the subject to name the earliest numeral possible. Rather, a critical interval is defined; and the subject is instructed to grab the earliest possible numeral from that interval. As with the motor reaction-time procedure, the beginning of the critical interval is placed so early that it cannot be achieved by a legitimate response. An additional complication in the attention reaction-time procedure is that the numerals within the critical interval, as well as the one or two before and after it, are all arranged to be different so that the numeral's identity unambiguously indicates its position in the stream.

Using the motor reaction-time and attention reaction-time methods as outlined, Reeves (1977) simultaneously measured motor reaction times and attention reaction times for 3 subjects in 17 conditions, obtaining a total of over 50 pairs of attention reaction-time and motor reaction-time distributions. A representative pair of motor reaction-time and attention reaction-time distributions is illustrated in Figure 4.24. Although they are measured in completely different ways—motor reaction time by a direct method and attention reaction time by an indirect method—they are quite comparable in terms of their mean and variance. These data are typical of the attention reaction-time procedure when the numeral stream occurs at a high rate (7/sec or faster); with slow numeral rates, attention reaction times become shorter than motor reaction times. Attention reaction times respond similarly to motor reaction times with manipulations of target difficulty (motor reaction times and attention reaction times get slower for hard-to-detect targets) or target probability (motor reaction times and attention reaction times get faster as the likelihood of a target increases). The interested reader will find a theory for these and other interesting features of motor reaction-time and attention reaction-time distributions in Sperling and Reeves (1980).

The point of the present discussion is that the indirect method yields measures of attention reaction times—unobservable responses—that are no less reliable and no more difficult to obtain than directly observable motor reaction times. Unobservable does not mean unmeasurable. The way to measure a reallocation of mental processing resources is by its effect—by how soon the reallocated resources have an effect. This indirect method can, in principle, be extended to any of the attentional tasks described in this book.

Optimization: A Last Word

Optimization—finding the most favorable compromise between conflicting goals or demands—has been the unifying principle throughout this chapter. It is a Darwinian principle. In the classroom attendance example, optimization involved the best choice of which class to attend when there were schedule conflicts. In signal detection tasks, it was the choice of a criterion that optimized the expected rewards for correct responses minus the expected costs for errors. It is essential to recognize that in all real situations there is imperfect information, and errors are possible. The signal detection theory of optimization is applicable far beyond the case of humans detecting threshold auditory signals in noise. The same optimization principles apply, for example, to seeds that must decide whether to sprout now or to wait for a better time, to juries that must balance the risk of punishing an innocent person against the risk to society of releasing a criminal, or to a human body's immunological system that must decide whether an unknown substance is a dangerous germ to be fought off or a part of itself to be left alone. The principles of optimum decision making transpose to cases of optimum resource allocation in selective attention—such as the optimal location of mental processing resources to one of several competing tasks, or of economic behavior—such as that of animals in motivation and reinforcement experiments; or, originally and ultimately, of economic issues—such as the optimal allocation of resources by consumers, by industries, and by entire societies.

With respect to psychology, application of the calculus of optimization represents an explicit reintroduction of *purpose* to the explanation of human performance by once again explaining behavior in terms of its goals. Explicit knowledge of the utility function is necessary to understand the decision process in signal detection tasks or the allocation of mental processing resources in attentional tasks—decisions that are governed by utility. In this respect, optimization theory is a link between many branches of psychology, and it will link the psychology of the future to the neglected psychology of the past in which purpose once had been an essential ingredient of psychological theory.

Reference Notes

1. Sperling, G. *Measuring Attention*. Invited address presented at the meeting of the American Psychological Association, Montreal, Quebec, September 4, 1980.

2. Sperling, G. *A unified theory of attention and signal detection.* Invited address presented at the fifteenth annual meeting of the Society for Mathematical Psychology, Princeton University, Princeton, N.J., August 8, 1982.
3. Budlansky, Judy T., and Sperling, G., *GS Letters: A general purpose system for producing visual displays in real time and for running psychological experiments on the DOP24 computer.* Unpublished technical memorandum, 1969. Bell Laboratories, Murray Hill, N.J..
4. Sperling, G., and Harris, J. R. Unpublished experiments, 1976–1977, Bell Laboratories, Murray Hill, N.J.

References

Anstis, S. M. A chart demonstrating variations in acuity with retinal position. *Vision Research,* 1974, *14,* 589, 592.

Audley, R. J. Some observations on theories of choice reaction time: Tutorial review. In S. Kornblum (Ed.), *Attention and performance IV.* New York: Academic Press, 1973.

Bamber, D. The area above the ordinal dominance graph and the area below the receiver operating characteristic graph. *Journal of Mathematical Psychology,* 1975, *12,* 387–415.

Bamber, D., and van Santen, J. P. H. How many parameters can a model have and still be testable? *Journal of Mathematical Psychology,* 1983, in press.

Bouma, H. Visual search and reading: Eye movements and functional visual field: A tutorial review. In J. Requin (Ed.), *Attention and performance VI.* Hillsdale, N.J.: Erlbaum, 1978, 115–147.

Carroll, J. D. Individual differences and multidimensional scaling. In R. N. Shepard, A. K. Romney, and S. Nerlove (Eds.), *Multidimensional scaling: Theory and applications in the behavioral sciences,* (Vol. 1, Theory). New York: Seminar Press, 1972.

Cohn, T., & Lasley, D. Detectability of a luminance increment: Effect of spatial uncertainty. *Journal of the Optical Society of America,* 1974, *64,* 1715–1719.

Coombs, C. H., & Avrunin, G. S. Single-peaked functions and the theory of preference. *Psychological Review,* 1977, *84,* 216–230.

Dosher, B. A. The retrieval of sentences from memory: A speed–accuracy study. *Cognitive Psychology,* 1976, *8,* 291–310.

Dosher, B. A. The effects of delay and interference: A speed–accuracy study. *Cognitive Psychology,* 1981, *13,* 551–582.

Due, J. F. *Intermediate economic analysis.* Chicago: Irwin, 1951.

Duncan, J. The demonstration of capacity limitation. *Cognitive Psychology,* 1980, *12,* 75–96.

Egan, J. P. *Signal detection theory and ROC analysis.* New York: Academic Press, 1975.

Falmagne, J. C. Note on a simple property of binary mixtures. *British Journal of Mathematical and Statistical Psychology,* 1968, *21*(1), 131–132.

Falmagne, J. C., Cohen, S. P., and Swivedi, A. Two-choice reactions as an ordered memory scanning process. In P. Rabbitt and S. Dornic (Eds.), *Attention and performance V.* London: Academic Press, 1975. Pp. 296–344.

Fitts, P. M. Cognitive aspects of information processing (Vol. 3): Set for speed versus accuracy. *Journal of Experimental Psychology,* 1966, *71,* 849–857.

Galambos, J. *The asymptotic theory of extreme order statistics.* New York: Wiley, 1978.

Gilliom, J. D., & Sorkin, R. D. Sequential and simultaneous two-channel signal detection: More evidence for a high level interrupt theory. *Journal of the Acoustical Society of America,* 1974, *56,* 157–164.

Green, D. M., & Luce, R. D. Speed–accuracy tradeoff in auditory detection. In S. Kornblum (Ed.), *Attention and performance IV*. New York: Academic Press, 1973. Pp. 547–569.

Green, D. M., & Swets, J. A. *Signal detection theory and psychophysics*. New York: Wiley, 1966.

Gumbel, E. J. *Statistics of extremes*. New York: Columbia University Press, 1958.

Harris, J. R., Shaw, M. L., & Bates, M. Visual search in multicharacter arrays with and without gaps. *Perception & Psychophysics*, 1979, *26*(1), 69–84.

Hicks, J. R., & Allen, R. G. D. A reconsideration of the theory of value. *Economica*, 1934, *1*, 52–76, 196–219.

Hoffman, J. E., & Nelson, B. *Spatial selectivity in visual search*. Perception and Psychophysics, 1981, *30*, 283–290.

Howarth, C. I., & Lowe, G. Statistical detection theory of Piper's Law. *Nature*, 1966, *212*, 324–326.

Kantowitz, Barry H. Double stimulation. In B. H. Kantowitz (Ed.), *Human information processing: Tutorial in performance and cognition*. Hillsdale, N.J.: Erlbaum, 1974. Pp. 83–131.

Kinchla, R. A. The role of structural redundancy in the detection of visual targets. *Perception & Psychophysics*, 1977, *22*, 19–30.

Kinchla, R. A. The measurement of attention. In R. S. Nickerson (Ed.), *Attention and performance VIII*. Hillsdale, N.J.: Erlbaum, 1980.

Kinchla, R. A., & Collyer, C. E. Detecting a target letter in briefly presented arrays: A confidence rating analysis in terms of a weighted additive effects model. *Perception & Psychophysics*, 1974, *16*, 117–122.

Kowler, E., & Steinman, R. M. The effect of expectations on slow oculomotor control—II: Single target displacements. *Vision Research*, 1979, *19*, 633–646.

Kowler, E., & Steinman, R. M. The effect of expectations on slow oculomotor control (Vol. 3): Guessing unpredictable target displacements. *Vision Research*, 1981, *21*, 191–203.

Krantz, David H. Threshold theories of signal detection. *Psychological Review*, 1969, *76*, 308–324.

Kruskal, J. B. Analysis of factorial experiments by estimating monotone transformations of the data. *Journal of the Royal Statistical Society*, series B, 1965, *27*, 251–263.

Laming, D. R. *Information theory of choice-reaction times*. New York: Academic Press, 1968.

Levitt, H. Decision theory, signal detection theory, and psychophysics. In E. E. David and P. B. Denes (Eds.), *Human communication: A unified view*. New York: McGraw-Hill, 1972, 114–174.

Link, S. W. The relative judgment theory of two-choice response time. *Journal of Mathematical Psychology*, 1975, *12*, 114–135.

Link, S. W., & Heath, R. A. A sequential theory of psychological discrimination. *Psychometrika*, 1975, *40*, 77–105.

Mertens, J. J. Influence of knowledge of target location upon the probability of observation of peripherally observable test flashes. *Journal of the Optical Society of America*, 1956, *46*, 1069–1070.

Metz, C. E., Starr, S. J., Lusted, L. B., & Rossmann, K. Progress in evaluation of human observer visual detection performance using the ROC curve approach. In C. Raynaud and A. Todd-Pokropek, Eds., *Information processing in scintigraphy*. Orsay, France: Commissariat a l'Energie atomique, Departement de Biologie, Service Hospitalier Frederic Joliot, 1975. Pp. 420–439.

Murphy, B. J. Pattern thresholds for moving and stationary gratings during smooth eye movements. *Vision Research*, 1978, *18*, 521–530.

Murphy, B. J., Kowler, E., & Steinman, R. M. Slow oculomotor control in the presence of moving backgrounds. *Vision Research*, 1975, *15*, 1263–1268.

Navon, D., & Gopher, D. On the economy of the human-processing system. *Psychological Review*, 1979, *86*,(3), 214–255.

Neisser, U. Decision time without reaction time: Experiments in visual scanningl *American Journal of Psychology*, 1963, *76*, 376–385.

Neisser, U. *Cognitive psychology*. New York: Appleton-Century-Crofts, 1966.

Neisser, U., Novick, R., & Lazar, R. Searching for ten targets simultaneously. *Perceptual and Motor Skills*, 1963, *17*, 955–961.

Norman, D. A., & Bobrow, D. G. On data-limited and resource-limited processes. *Cognitive Psychology*, 1975, *7*, 44–64.

Ollman, Robert. Fast guesses in choice reaction time. *Psychonomic Science*, 1966, *6*, 155–156.

Pachella, R. G., & Fisher, D. Hick's Law and the speed–accuracy trade-off in absolute judgment. *Journal of Experimental Psychology*, 1972, *92*, 378–384.

Pareto, V. *Manuel d'economie politique*. 1909.

Pohlman, L. D. & Sorkin, R. D. Simultaneous three-channel signal detection: Performance and criterion as a function of order of report. *Perception and Psychophysics*, 1976, *20*, 179–186.

Posner, M. I., Nissen, M. J., & Ogden, W. C. Attended and unattended processing modes: The role of set for spatial location. In H. I. Pick, Jr., & E. Saltzman (Eds.), *Modes of perceiving and processing information*. Hillsdale, N.J.: Erlbaum, 1978.

Rachlin, H., Battalio, R., Kagel, J., & Green, L. Maximization theory in behavioral psychology. *The Behavioral and Brain Sciences*, 1981, *4*, 371–417.

Rachlin, H., & Burkhardt, B. The temporal triangle: Response substitution in instrumental conditioning. *Psychological Review*, 1978, *85*, 22–47.

Rachlin, H., Green, L., Kagel, J. H., & Battalio, R. C. Economic demand theory and psychological studies of choice. In G. Bower (Ed.), *The psychology of learning and motivation*, (Vol. 10). New York: Academic Press, 1976.

Rachlin, H., Kagel, J. H., & Battalio, R. C. Substitutability in time allocation. *Psychological Review*, 1980, *87*, 355–374.

Reed, A. V. Speed–accuracy trade-off in recognition memory. *Science*, 1973, *181*, 574–576.

Reeves, A. *The detection and recall of rapidly displayed letters and digits*. Unpublished doctoral dissertation, City University of New York, 1977.

Rubenstein, H., Garfield, L., & Millikan, J. A. Homographic entries in the internal lexicon. *Journal of Verbal Learning and Verbal Behavior*, 1970, *9*, 487–494.

Rubenstein, H., Lewis, S. S., & Rubenstein, M. A. Evidence for phonemic recoding in visual word recognition. *Journal of Verbal Learning and Verbal Behavior*, 1971a, *10*, 645–657.

Rubenstein, H., Lewis, S. S., & Rubenstein, M. A. Homographic entries in the internal lexicon: Effects of systematicity and relative frequency of meanings. *Journal of Verbal Learning and Verbal Behavior*, 1971b, *10*, 57–62.

Samuelson, P. A. *Economics* (11th ed.). New York: McGraw-Hill, 1980.

Schneider, W., and Shiffrin, R. M. Controlled and automatic human information processing: I Detection, search, and attention. *Psychological Review*, 1977, *1*, 1–66.

Schuckman, H. Attention and visual threshold. *American Journal of Optometry and Archives of the American Academy of Optometry*, 1963, *40*, 284–291.

Shaw, P. Processing of tachistoscopic displays with controlled order of characters and spaces. *Perception & Psychophysics*, 1969, *6*, 257–266.

Shaw, M. L., and Shaw, P. Optimal allocation of cognitive resources to spatial locations. *Journal of Experimental Psychology: Human Perception and Performance*, 1977, *3*, 201–211.

Shepard, R. N. Stimulus and response generalization: Tests of a model relating generalization to distance in psychological space. *Journal of Experimental Psychology*, 1958, *55*, 509–523.

Sorkin, R. D., Pastore, R. E., & Pohlmann, L. D. Simultaneous two-channel signal detection: II. Correlated and uncorrelated signals. *Journal of the Acoustical Society of America*, 1972, *51*, 1960–1965.

Sorkin, R. D., Pohlmann, L. D., & Gilliom, J. D. Simultaneous two-channel signal detection: III. 630- and 1400-Hz signals. *Journal of the Acoustical Society of America,* 1973, *53,* 1045–1050.

Sorkin, R. D., Pohlmann, L. D., & Woods, D. D. Decision interaction between auditory channels. *Perception and Psychophysics,* 1976, *19,* 290–295.

Sperling, G. *Information available in a brief visual presentation.* Unpublished doctoral dissertation, Department of Psychology, Harvard University, 1959.

Sperling, G. The information available in brief visual presentations. *Psychological Monographs,* 1960, *74*(11, whole No. 498).

Sperling, G. A model for visual memory tasks. *Human Factors,* 1963, *5,* 19–31.

Sperling, G. Temporal and spatial visual masking. I. Masking by impulse flashes. *Journal of the Optical Society of America,* 1965, *55,* 541–559.

Sperling, G. Extremely rapid visual scanning. *Bulletin of the British Psychological Society,* 1970a, *23,* 58.

Sperling, G. Binocular vision: A physical and a neural theory. *American Journal of Psychology,* 1970b, *83,* 461–534.

Sperling, G. The search for the highest rate of search, *Symposium on Attention and Performance,* August 1973, *5* Saltsjobaden, Stockholm, Sweden.

Sperling, G. Multiple detections in a brief visual stimulus: The sharing and switching of attention. *Bulletin of the Psychonomic Society,* 1975, *9,* 427. (Abstract)

Sperling, G. Mathematical models of binocular vision. In S. Grossberg (Ed.), *Mathematical psychology and psychophysiology.* American Mathematical Association (SIAM–AMS) Proceedings, 1981, *13,* 281–300.

Sperling, G. Unified theory of attention and signal detection. *Mathematical Studies in Perception and Cognition.* New York University, Department of Psychology, 1983, *83*(3), 1–64.

Sperling, G., Budiansky, J., Spivak, J. G., and Johnson, M. C. Extremely rapid visual search: The maximum rate of scanning letters for the presence of a numeral. *Science,* 1971, *174,* 307–311.

Sperling, G., & Melchner, M. J. Visual search and visual attention. In V. D. Giezer (Ed.), Information processing in visual system. *Proceedings of the Fourth Symposium of Sensory System Physiology.* Leningrad, U.S.S.R.: Academy of Sciences, Palov Institute of Physiology, 1976a, 224–230.

Sperling, G., & Melchner, M. J. Estimating item and order information. *Journal of Mathematical Psychology,* 1976b, *13,* 192–213.

Sperling, G., & Melchner, M. J. The attention operating characteristic: Some examples from visual search. *Science,* 1978a, *202,* 315–318.

Sperling, G., & Melchner, M. J. Visual search, visual attention, and the attention operating characteristic. In J. Requin (Ed.), *Attention and performance VII.* Hillsdale, N.J.: Erlbaum, 1978b, 675–686.

Sperling, G., & Reeves, A. Reaction time of an unobservable response. *Bulletin of the Psychonomic Society,* 1976, *10,* 247. (Abstract)

Sperling, G., & Reeves, A. Measuring the reaction time of a shift of visual attention. *Investigative Ophthalmology and Visual Science,* (ARVO Supplement), 1978, *17,* 289. (Abstract)

Sperling, G., & Reeves, A. Measuring the reaction time of a an unobservable response: A shift of visual attention. In R. Nickerson (Ed.), *Attention and Performance VIII.* Hillsdale, N.J.: Erlbaum, 1980, 347–360.

Stroop, J. R. Studies of interference in serial verbal reactions. *Journal of Experimental Psychology,* 1935, *18,* 643–662.

Sussman, H. J., & Zahler, R. S. Catastrophe theory as applied to the social and biological sciences: A critique. *Synthese,* 1978, *38,* 117–216.

Swets, J. A. (Ed.), *Signal detection and recognition by human observers: Contemporary readings.* New York: Wiley, 1964.

Swets, J. A. The relative operating characteristic in psychology. *Science,* 1973, *182,* 990–1000.

Swets, J. A., Tanner, W. P., & Birdsall, T. G. Decision processes in perception. *Psychological Review,* 1961, *68,* 301–340.

Thom, R., & Zeeman, E. Catastrophe Theory: Its Present State and Future Perspectives. In A. Manning (Ed.), *Dynamical Systems—Warwick 1974: Proceedings of a Symposium Held at the University of Warwick 1973/74.* Berlin: Springer-Verlag, 1975b.

Wald, A. *Statistical decision functions.* New York: Wiley, 1950.

van Santen, J. P. H., and Bamber, D. Finite and infinite state confusion models. *Journal of Mathematical Psychology,* 1981, *24,* 101–111.

Welford, A. T. (Ed.), *Reaction time.* London: Academic Press, 1980.

Wickelgren, W. A., Corbett, A. T., & Dosher, B. A. Priming and retrieval from short-term memory: A speed accuracy analysis. *Journal of Verbal Learning and Verbal Behavior,* 1980, *19,* 387–404.

Woodworth, R. S., & Schlosberg, H. *Experimental psychology* (rev. ed.). New York: Holt, 1954, Ch. 17, 492–527.

Yellot, John I. Correction for guessing in choice reaction time. *Psychonomic Science,* 1967, *8,* 321–322.

Yellott, John I. Correction for fast guessing and the speed–accuracy tradeoff. *Journal of Mathematical Psychology,* 1971, *8,* 159–199.

Zeeman, E. C. Catastrophe theory. *Scientific American,* April 1976, *234,* 65–83.

5

Mathematical Models of Attention

John A. Swets

Introduction

A characterization of the terms in this chapter's title will indicate the scope of the chapter. By *attention* I mean behavioral processes that evidence an increment or decrement in the effectiveness with which an organism handles current information from a given source in its environment. The difference in effectiveness may be a matter of choice or necessity. It may be a matter of receiving full information from that source or none at all, or it may be instead a quantitative difference in the received information. The difference may arise because the organism is considering two or more sources—and attention may be *selective* (all attention devoted to one of the competing sources) or *divided* (attention distributed among more than one of the competing sources)—or because it is considering a source over a relatively long time—and attention may be more or less well *sustained.* In either case, a question arises regarding the allocation of the organism's information-handling resources; especially in the case of selective attention, questions arise concerning the switching and time-sharing of attentive focus. The existence of attentive processes is obvious in the richest environments, but interesting cases of attention can be demonstrated for alert observers in very simple environments as well.

In this chapter, I include normative as well as descriptive representations as *models* of attentive processes and consider experimental data only to the extent that they help to justify inclusion here of a particular model or aid in understanding a model or a general concept. Indeed, my primary concern is not the closeness of fit of a model to data or whether a model seems, or once seemed, to be correct, but whether it is, or has been, useful. Because models guide as well as follow our general conceptions, models are considered here if only their place in history is secure, and they are considered in an at least roughly chronological order. (A 30-year history should not strain us much in that respect). Naturally, some models of nonattention are also discussed as foils.

Mathematical models are those stated essentially in quantitative terms. The use of a mathematical system to analyze data in a given line of research does not

183

qualify that research for inclusion here. Thus, the use of information theory primarily to quantify a limit on capacity, or the use of signal detection theory primarily to achieve a criterion-free measure of sensitivity, does not involve mathematical models sufficiently to meet present requirements. In my experience, mathematical models are generated more readily for process conceptions that are reduced to a simple level than for those in which the real complexity of the processes is given a large amount of conceptual rein. For example, an hypothesized loss of stimulus information in an early perceptual stage is more likely to be modeled mathematically than a view of attentive processes as controlling overall the flow of information in and among perceptual, memory, and response stages. In any case, this chapter deals primarily with what appear to be perceptual effects, stopping short of effects accounted for primarily in terms of memory or response.

Consideration in this chapter of particular models begins with the first and the simplest, which deal with elementary signals (tones, lights) and fundamental tasks (detection, simple recognition). The concern of these models is with more than one signal and selective or divided attention. These models were developed explicitly for frequency selectivity in audition, and they incorporate sensory *filters* that pass energy in limited ranges or *bands* of the frequency spectrum. A basic contrast is between *filtering,* or reception in only a single narrow band, and reception throughout the wider band that defines the ear's outer structural limits. Another contrast is between *successive* reception in selected bands, via the temporal scanning or switching of a single narrow filter from one band to another, and *simultaneous* reception of information in several selected bands, via a widened filter or the conjunction of multiple filters. For instances of successive reception, mathematical models exist for structurally determined temporal parameters as well as for adjustable balances of attention to different bands. These filter concepts were soon extended to analogous mechanisms that may be tuned, for example, to different visual locations and to tuning mechanisms that heighten sensitivity to one kind of stimulus or stimulus property at the expense of sensitivity to others. In such cases, the term *channel* is often used instead of band, as is *attentive focus* instead of filter. Some of the studies considered near the end of this section treat elementary signals in extensions of the fundamental tasks—for example, in tasks involving combined detection and recognition.

The focus in the second main section of this chapter, entitled "Aggregation over Channels," is the process by which stimulus information in multiple bands, or channels, is brought together—a process termed the *aggregation* of information *across separate bands.* Two classes of models—also applied first to the simplest stimuli and tasks—contain alike the assumption that the organism can rather freely choose which bands to attend to, and differ with respect to how the stimulus information in those bands is processed further. In one class of models, fine-grained evidence concerning signal existence—for example, the posterior probability of a signal—is combined across bands in one way or another and enters an overall decision in a manner that preserves most of the information in the several bands. In the other class of models, whether or not such fine-grained evidence is present in each band, only binary decisions about signal existence in each band are processed further in arriving at an overall decision.

In the third section, entitled "Visual Form Perception," more complex versions of the models identified previously and other more extensive models developed since are discussed. These models are applied to more complex stimuli (e.g., letters) and more complex perceptual tasks (e.g., search for a particular letter). These models elaborate the issue of successive versus simultaneous observation—in terms of *serial* versus *parallel processing*—and ramify conceptions about the allocation of attentional resources and the aggregation of stimulus information. These models reflect an attempt to cope with intricate experimental paradigms and may incorporate relatively broad and sophisticated conceptions of behavioral processes, involving memory and reaction time as well as interactions among various stages of information processing.

In the fourth section, entitled "Sustained Attention," consideration shifts from selective or divided attention to sustained attention, or at least to tasks and models in which the distribution of attention over time plays a larger role than the distribution of attention over bands or channels. One class of models treats the *accumulation* of sensory information *over time*—either that accumulated from a continuous observation or an observation broken into discrete pieces. The length of the observation or the number of observation pieces may be constant as fixed by the experimenter or variable as determined on a trial-by-trial basis by the observer. For both constant and variable durations of observation, the models of accumulation over time are (to a large extent) the models mentioned earlier for the aggregation over bands or channels. For observer-terminated trials, consideration is also given to decision-theory models—with the variables of prior probability of signal, values and costs of correct and incorrect decisions, and cost of additional observation time—and to the trade-off of speed and accuracy. Another class of models for sustained attention refers to detection tasks with little temporal structure—that is, those in which some *uncertainty* exists *about the temporal location* within each trial of the interval, or intervals, that may contain a signal; or in which those intervals, or the trials themselves in a much longer period, are left altogether undefined. All of these models point toward the so-called *vigilance* task, in which the time on task is long and the signal rate is low, and toward the more complex tasks, as described in the succeeding section, that combine vigilance with manual or supervisory control.

The succeeding and final section, entitled "Multiple Complex Tasks," brings together the concepts of sustained attention and selective or divided attention. It is concerned with tasks more realistic than those usually studied in the laboratory, with respect to both dimensions of attention. Its models are directed at performance of multiple tasks that go beyond simple detection and recognition of singular targets and beyond a simple replication of nearly identical and independent trials. These models also reflect the importance of values and costs in the realistic tasks. Here, the emphasis is on the human monitor who must react differentially and quickly to quite different stimuli, on the human controller who must share attention among skilled motor tasks as well as perceptual and cognitive tasks, and on the human supervisor who must monitor and control and communicate about a multiprocess dynamic system. Some of the key words in this discussion are visual sampling, tracking, dynamic decisions, mental workload, effort, observation cost, expected value, and optimal *resource allocation*.

A last word of introduction: like most other secondary sources on topics in mathematical psychology, this one contains little mathematics. The exclusion of other than a few summary formulas stems both from the breadth of the audience sought for the chapter and limitations on space. However, the chapter's objective should suffer little if the reader interested in the mathematical derivations and particulars must pursue original sources through the references supplied. Its objective is to provide a reasonably general review of how certain techniques and theories developed in mathematics have articulated with psychological conceptions in the experimental study of attention. The editors and author believe that in tracing the history of mathematical models of attention, one often follows and sometimes leads major efforts in the field, and sees a substantial part of the flow of the field's conceptions and experimentation.

Simple Sensory Filters

This section treats first the filter models developed for attention to frequency bands in audition, as reflected in the simplest tasks. It then considers similar models for other modalities and tasks, primarily for dimensions of visual stimuli and tasks involving combined detection and recognition or other complexities. It proceeds to a discussion of models for active deployment of a sensory filter—for scanning or switching times between bands and for the balance of choice between different bands. It concludes with models for the shape and width of sensory filters.

Auditory Frequency

A dual mechanism for the detection of tones, consisting of a single narrow-band filter that can be tuned to any portion of the frequency spectrum and a wide-band receiver simultaneously sensitive to all audible frequencies, was proposed by Tanner and Norman (1954) and further developed by Tanner, Swets, and Green (Note 1). The two parts of the mechanism—the one attentive and the other nonattentive, the one able to recognize which frequency is present and the other able to convey only that some signal energy is present—were viewed as operating under the observer's adaptive control and as following immediately a fixed preattentive stage (a "multiplexing" system) that serves only to register information throughout the audible range.

A narrow-band receiver is presumably optimal for detection when the signal has a single frequency or a small range of frequencies; whereas the listener must presumably pay the price of more masking noise in the wide-band receiver if listening simultaneously for signal frequencies across their total possible range. A multiple-band receiver, permitting the observer to select the number and frequency locations of two or more operative filters, would also be useful; and the authors mentioned gave passing consideration to such a mechanism. The following pages describe the predictions of the single-band (SB) and wide-band (WB) models and of various forms of the multiple-band (MB) model for three observing tasks—detection with signal uncertainty, detection of multicomponent signals, and signal recognition. In each case the predictions are relative to control conditions that present a signal having a single known frequency.

Detection with Signal Uncertainty

Simple mathematics for the SB mechanism were specified for an experimental condition in which the signal was equally likely to be at either of two specified and widely separated frequencies, relative to the control condition of a single known frequency. In either condition, the signal would occur in one and only one of four temporal intervals in a forced-choice trial. It was assumed that if the observer could not attend, or chose not to attend, to both frequencies during the signal's duration, and so selected one frequency band or the other on each trial, then the percentage correct across trials would equal one-half that for the single known frequency (resulting from the one-half of the trials in which attentive focus and signal frequency happened to coincide) plus one-half times the chance probability of one-quarter (resulting from the remaining trials in which the tuning was inappropriate and all information was lost):

$$P(C)_{1 \text{ of } 2} = \tfrac{1}{2} P(C)_i + \tfrac{1}{2}(\tfrac{1}{4}).$$

The top curve in Figure 5.1 shows the theoretical relationship between percentage correct, $P(C)$, and the detectability index d' for a single known frequency (Tanner and Swets, 1954). If the observer could act only as a wide-band receiver, this same curve would give the WB prediction for both known and uncertain frequency; if the top curve (on the other hand) represents the performance of a narrow-band receiver, then the WB prediction would be much lower,

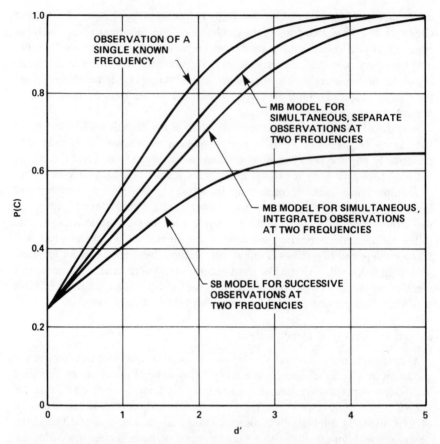

Figure 5.1 Predictions of wide-band (WB), multiple-band (MB), and single-band (SB) models for a signal equally likely to be at either of two specified and widely separated frequencies. Percentage of correct responses $P(C)$ in a four-alternative forced-choice task is plotted as a function of the detection index, d'.

perhaps near the chance value of .25. Point by point for the top curve, the bottom curve gives the SB prediction for "successive" observation at two frequencies. As another comparison, the second curve from the top shows predicted performance for "simultaneous" observation at two frequencies by an MB observer who takes eight measures of signal likelihood (one for each frequency in each interval) and chooses the interval containing the greatest measure.

In presenting the three curves in Figure 5.1 so far described, Tanner and Norman (1954) referred to relevant data as supportive of the SB model but did not report data. The first published data were presented on such a graph by Tanner *et al.* (Note 1) and sampled in an article by Tanner (1956), and they were given in tabular form in a later review article by Swets (1963). The original graphs, reproduced in Figure 5.2, show two-frequency data for three or four pairs of frequencies, and for two signal durations and three observers as indicated in the legends. The data points for groups of trials containing two frequencies are placed on the graphs directly below the average $P(C)$ for the two groups of trials containing just one of the frequencies; the sigma values listed are standard deviations calculated on the assumption of binomial variance. Performance is seen to fall off monotonically as the separation of the two frequencies is increased from 50 to 300 or 350 Hz and approximates the SB (successive) prediction at the larger separations. The authors concluded, "The data establish only that a price must be paid for observing signals at different frequencies. Strictly from the data reported above, it is impossible to say whether the price is paid in terms of definition, or in terms of noise, or in terms of time as suggested by the model" (Tanner *et al.*, Note 1, p. 89).

The curve in Figure 5.1 remaining to be described represents the most widely considered form of the MB model, as advanced by Green (1958). According to this model, the price for observing different frequencies is paid primarily in terms of noise rather than time—and, in a way, in terms of definition. Specifically, this MB model assumes for the uncertain-frequency condition an integration of the outputs of two filters centered on the two frequencies. Hence the observer is exposed to twice as much masking noise (for nonoverlapping filters) as when listening at just one frequency, and he or she loses the ability to deal separately with observations at each frequency. I call this model here the *integrated MB* model, and the one described earlier the *maximum-output MB* model. As indicated by Green (1958) and spelled out by Swets, Shipley, McKay, and Green (1959), this MB model predicts that the detection index d' for one of two sufficiently separated (and equally detectable) frequencies will equal the single-frequency d' divided by the square root of two (or the number of possible frequencies); that is,

$$d'_{1 \text{ of } 2} = \frac{d'_i}{2^{1/2}} \ .$$

Several experiments undertaken to compare the SB and MB models for uncertain frequency are reviewed elsewhere (Swets, 1963; Green & Swets, 1966/1974; Swets & Kristofferson, 1970). As far as the predictions just described go, the result is a standoff, as one might imagine when realizing that the effective experimental range in Figures 5.1 and 5.2 has an upper limit of d' equal to about 2.5. The single study reporting reaction times was also consistent with both models (an unpublished study by Swets, Schouten, and Lopes-Cardozo conducted in 1958 and described by Green & Swets 1966/1974). Data on trial-to-trial dependencies (Swets, Shipley, McKay, and Green, 1959; Pastore and Sorkin, 1971; Macmillan & Schwartz, 1975) and on precueing and postcueing of

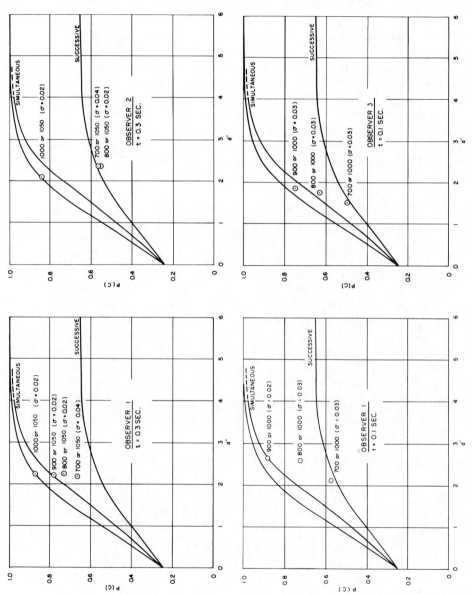

Figure 5.2 Detection of one of two frequencies. (Data reported by Tanner *et al.*, Note 1)

frequency (Swets and Sewall, 1961; Johnson and Hafter, 1980) lend support to the SB model. And, as will be discussed in a subsequent section, data on multiple observations over time indicate that the observer can zero in on an initially uncertain frequency. Other types of experiments and analysis, however, support the MB model; and there is evidence to suggest that observers can choose to use either type of mechanism (Swets, 1963).

Green (1961) studied larger degrees of uncertainty, among 50 possible signals, and observed much smaller decrements than predicted for such conditions by the SB and integrated MB models. In that paper, he considered again the maximum-output MB model in which likelihood ratios are taken separately on the output of each filter and then compared. Johnson and Hafter (1980) reviewed extensions of this model in which the widths of the filters are also under the observer's control.

Detection of Multicomponent Signals

Marill (Note 2) obtained data on signals consisting of two frequencies that supported the SB model—if sufficiently separated, the second frequency contributed nothing to detectability—though Schafer and Gales (1949) had observed some, but less than perfect, summation of power at widely separated frequencies. Marill further found a simple linear summation of d' for frequencies close together. Green (1958) proposed the integrated MB model in this context, which predicted that d' for multiple frequencies, if sufficiently separated, would be the square root of the sum of the squares of d' for the individual frequencies. If the M individual frequencies are equally detectable, then

$$d'_M = M^{1/2} d'_i .$$

Green spoke to the issue of "sufficient separation" by considering two effects of signals so close that their appropriately placed filters overlap. One effect is a correlation of outputs that is introduced by energy common to the two filters, denoted here as r. The second effect is an influence on one filter output of the energy put into the other filter, also ranging from 0 to unity, denoted here as k. He derived the equation for two equally detectable frequencies:

$$d'_{1 \text{ and } 2} = 2^{1/2} d'_i \frac{1 + k}{(1 + r)^{1/2}} .$$

If the two frequencies are close, k and r are nearly unity and

$$d'_{1 \text{ and } 2} = 2d'_i .$$

If they are far apart, k and r are nearly zero and

$$d'_{1 \text{ and } 2} = 2^{1/2} d'_i .$$

The relation between k, r, and frequency separation is not known and depends on the shape of the filter.

Each of these three models for multicomponent signals—for no summation, partial ($M^{1/2}d_i'$) summation, and linear (Md') summation—finds one or more sets of data in close agreement, and models of other sorts (based on combinations of binary decisions about filter outputs, as described in a subsequent section) exist to predict various other degrees of summation. Green's (1958) 2-frequency data fit well with the integrated MB model, as did Green, McKay, and Licklider's (1959) 16-frequency data, in both cases for widely separated frequencies. For 2-point vibrotactile stimuli, Craig (1968) found varying degrees of summation depending on conditions, whereas Franzén, Markowitz, and Swets (1970) found no summation. Fidell (1970) found agreement with the integrated MB model for simultaneous visual and auditory signals. And so on. The general conclusion is that detectability is likely to suffer when stimulus energy is divided (i.e., when components of a signal are sufficiently separated on some physical dimension that they may be regarded as falling in separate filters or bands) or when signals are presented simultaneously to separate sensory systems or channels.

Signal Recognition

Tanner (1956) presented a model for the recognition d' between two signals, when the observer's task is to decide which signal was presented in a given interval. In particular, he assumed that outputs of overlapping filters would be correlated and outputs of widely separated filters would be uncorrelated. The recognition predictions were expressed in terms of the vector difference of the separate detectabilities as determined in control conditions. In general, according to the law of cosines,

$$(d'_{1 \text{ versus } 2})^2 = (d'_1)^2 + (d'_2)^2 - 2\cos \Theta \, d'_1 \, d'_2 \, ,$$

where Θ is the angle between the detection vectors, and $\cos \Theta$ is a coefficient of correlation. For separate filters, $\Theta = 90°$, $\cos \Theta = 0$, and

$$d'_{1 \text{ versus } 2} = [(d'_1)^2 + (d'_2)^2]^{1/2};$$

whereas for completely overlapping filters, $\Theta = 0°$, $\cos \Theta = 1$, and

$$d'_{1 \text{ versus } 2} = |d'_1 - d'_2|.$$

He elaborated the recognition model to take into account the earlier results consistent with the single-band model (Figure 5.2), predicting that Θ would increase from 0 to 90° as the frequency difference increased from 0 to about 100 Hz, and then would decrease to an apparent 60° as the frequency difference further increased to about 300 Hz. The apparent 60° does not represent a correlation but rather a loss due to the observer's attending to only one frequency on a trial.

Dimensions of Visual Stimuli

Tanner suggested that the vector model just described might be applied to wavelength differences in vision to identify the independent receptor mechanisms mediating color vision—a possibility pursued by Swets (Notes 3 and 4), Guth (1967), Guth, Donley, and Marrocco (1969). In the same vein, Swets (Notes 3 and 4) found the detectability of two-color signals to decline as a function of wavelength separation, and Greenhouse and Cohn (1978) found detection of one-color signals to suffer from color uncertainty. Both studies examined versions of the MB model.

Tanner (Note 5) sought also to extend the concept of attentive focus for auditory frequency to a similar kind of focusing for visual location—that is, to shifts in attention not mediated by eye movements. He conducted experiments on uncertain location using the paradigm for uncertain frequency described above (in the subsection beginning on page 187). Using a light signal 1 minute in diameter, he found detectability for one of two locations to decrease monotonically to a separation of 5° and to remain constant for wider separations up to 16°. He suggested a narrow-beam (single-band) scanning mechanism for separations up to 5°, and—because the detectability at larger separations was greater than the prediction of successive observation (Figure 5.1)—invoked a wide-beam mechanism (essentially an integrated multiple-beam mechanism) to handle the larger separations. He pointed up the biological utility of a dual mechanism, with the wide-beam portion serving as ''a detector of signals sufficiently strong to justify search at the expense of stopping concentration . . . [and providing] the possibility of detection without continuous search of the narrow-beam receiver'' (Tanner, Note 5, p. 8).

In the same paper, Tanner defined the minimum area observable by the single-beam mechanism, and the maximum area observable by an integrative process, in terms of the growth of the detection index d' as a function of area. He developed the ideas that d' would increase in direct proportion to area up to the minimum area observable, then increase as the square root of area up to some maximum of integration, and then show no further increase beyond that point. Plotting log d' against log area, he showed that slopes of 1, $\frac{1}{2}$, and 0 could be reasonably fitted to three successive portions of the empirical function, at each of five eccentricities from the center of the visual field along a single radial axis. The areal extent at the intersection of the slopes of 1 and $\frac{1}{2}$, taken as an estimate of the minimum area observable, increased regularly with increases in eccentricity.

Cohn and Lasley (1974) pursued this line of research on uncertain location by considering four locations and an extension of the maximum-output MB model advanced by Nolte and Jaarsma (1967). The model's prediction that d' would be halved from certainty to uncertainty conditions was borne out by the data. These investigators introduced several methodological and analytical controls to eliminate alternative explanations of their result.

Posner, Nissen, and Ogden (1978) studied uncertainty about visual location in a detection paradigm in which one third of the trials presented a signal with equal likelihood 7° to the right or left of fixation and were cued to indicate the even probability; the remaining trials presented a cue pointing to the right or left, which was valid on 80% of those trials. They found that relative to the equal-likelihood condition, reaction time under the second cue was decreased by about 25 msec when the cue was valid and increased by about 40 msec when the cue was invalid. Trials in which the subject's eyes moved were not included in this analysis. The experimenters concluded that attention can be directed to locations other than the point of fixation.

Bashinski and Bacharach (1980) repeated the experiment of Posner *et al.*, except that they substituted an analysis of detection probabilities via the relative, or receiver, operating characteristic (ROC) for the measurement of reaction time. They obtained similar results and drew the same conclusion. They found facilitation in the absence of shifts in the decision criterion, suggesting a locus of the effect in early perceptual stages.

Kristofferson reanalyzed data on two-point visual signals collected by Dember and him, as reported by Green and Swets (1966/1974). For separations up to 8 minutes, these data approximated linear d' summation, suggesting that two points within that distance fall within a single filter or channel. For separations from 12 to 64 minutes, these data approximated the integrated MB prediction—which is consistent with the idea that points that far apart are relayed in separate channels. Kristofferson's data on binocular summation, similarly reanalyzed and reported, showed approximately a linear d' summation.

Davis (1981) applied the SB model and the integrated and maximum-output MB models to uncertainty about the spatial frequency of visual patterns. Her data were most consistent with the maximum-output MB model. Davis, Kramer, and Graham (1983) further examined the effects of uncertainty about spatial frequency and included location uncertainty. Using the experimental paradigm described above in the section on detection with signal uncertainty, they reported an uncertainty effect for both spatial frequency and location consistently smaller than predicted by the SB model and approximating the sizes predicted by the integrated and maximum-output MB models. They added a condition in which signals with a variable parameter were preceded by a cue that indicated which parameter value would occur and found the cueing to be fully effective: performance under the cue condition was indistinguishable from that under the condition of fixed signal parameters.

Sekuler and Ball (1977) used the basic paradigm to measure the effects of uncertainty about direction and speed of motion of visual targets. They reported substantial decrements in $P(C)$—similar, I might add, to those predicted by the integrated MB model. Reaction-time measurements for strong signals also showed an uncertainty effect. Ball and Sekuler (1981b) showed that cue effectiveness depended on the amount of time by which the cue preceded the signal, reaching full effectiveness for a long enough interval. Ball and Sekuler (1980) developed a model for two-direction uncertainty in which a single filter is centered on a direction midway between the two, and reported that seven experiments favored this midway SB model over competing SB and MB models. Ball and Sekuler (1981a) found that practice reduced the uncertainty decrement; they also found new evidence for the propositions (Swets, 1963) that observers can manipulate attention during a sufficiently long signal, that individual differences exist in the ability to use different attentional mechanisms, and that observers can exert adaptive control over the filtering mechanisms they employ as task variations make adaptation appropriate.

Regan (1982) has given a general review of evidence for filtering effects in vision, including the dimensions of color, spatial frequency, motion, and depth.

Simple Signals in More Complex Tasks

Filter-based or similar models for elementary stimuli have been employed in connection with tasks more complex than those of detection and simple recognition. Examples are tasks presenting noise alone or one of M signals and calling for both detection and recognition; tasks like the preceding except that the M signals may also be presented together; tasks presenting M signals differentially through two earphones, thereby adding to frequency uncertainty a channel uncertainty with channels defined by the earphones; tasks calling for simultaneous discrimination along different stimulus dimensions in different sensory modalities; and tasks in which each of M signals could occur only in its own assigned observation interval of a multi-interval trial, to allow comparison of successive and simultaneous observation.

Combined Detection and Recognition

In a detection-and-recognition task, the observer must say whether a signal occurred and, if one did, which one. A model that extends to this task the recognition model described by Tanner (1956; discussed in a previous section) was presented by Swets and Birdsall (1956). A model developed by Nolte (1967) can be described as an extension of the maximum-output (MB) model. He assumed that likelihood ratios are continually updated for each band as observation time increases, and that the largest of the M values is continually compared with a decision criterion for a detection response. Detection and recognition are clearly part of the same process in this model, and grow apace. The basis for a recognition response is always present, and specifically whenever a detection response is made.

Starr, Metz, Lusted, and Goodenough (1975) developed a model allowing prediction of a "joint detection-and-recognition" ROC from the simple detection ROC. In essence, a quantity is subtracted from the ordinate (proportion of true detections) of the empirical curve for detection of one of M orthogonal signals, the exact quantity depending on M, to obtain a predicted ordinate for the joint ROC (proportion of signals correctly detected *and* correctly recognized). Green and Birdsall (1978) further related the model of Starr *et al.* to the model for detection of one of M orthogonal signals (Nolte and Jaarsma, 1967) and to concepts of signal uncertainty.

In an experiment varying tonal frequency, Green, Weber, and Duncan (1977) showed quite good agreement with the predicted joint ROC for two tones sufficiently separated in frequency, and a systematic decrease in performance relative to the prediction as the frequency separation was decreased. Swets, Green, Getty, and Swets (1978) supported the model for eight signals consisting of single, vertical lines that differed in horizontal location across a display, and for five signals consisting of different spatial patterns of three such lines. Swensson and Judy (1981) supported the models of Nolte (1967) and of Nolte and Jaarsma (1967), and the model of Starr *et al.* as related by Green and Birdsall (1978), for one to eight possible signal locations in visual displays that simulated the images of computed tomography as used in diagnostic radiology.

The General Two-Signal Paradigm

The general paradigm for two signals or channels is the one in which neither, either, or both signals may occur; and the observer has four choices. Eijkman and Vendrik (1965) used this paradigm with simple auditory and visual signals and concluded that their observers were observing the two channels simultaneously. Sorkin, Pohlman, and Gilliom (1973) and Gilliom and Sorkin (1974) drew the same conclusion for tonal signals of different frequency on the same basis: detection of a given signal is as accurate in a series of trials in which either or both of two signals may occur as in a series in which only one of the signals can occur—if only trials in which the other signal does not occur are considered.

Ears as Channels

The most widely regarded work on attention has been on speech stimuli presented differentially to the ears, in the Broadbent (1958, 1971) tradition. Moray (1970), Moray, Fitter, Ostry, Favreau, and Nagy (1976), and Ostry, Moray, and Marks (1976) have used tonal stimuli to examine the general issues arising in that work. In a similar vein, Pastore and Sorkin (1972) began an extensive line of research with tonal signals and perceptual channels defined by earphones, applying the filter models described in the preceding and extensions of them.

Sorkin and Pohlman (1973) reviewed five models for the two-signal detection-and-recognition task: (1) the observer can monitor just one channel and makes a yes–no decision for it; (2) both channels are monitored and the difference between their output measures is compared to two decision criteria; (3) two output measures are compared to their respective decision criteria, and the channel having the greater measure is chosen if both measures exceed their criteria; (4) a coin is flipped to decide between the two measures if both measures exceed their criteria; and (5) like the previous model except that only one channel is monitored at a time, with each monitored during half of the observation interval. A review of the decade's research in this area was given by Puleo and Pastore (1978). They questioned the procedure of using earphones to define channels, on the grounds that the earphone outputs may be perceptually fused. Thus, performance decrements may reflect a reduced ability to determine the source of the signals rather than a reduced ability to detect signals.

Multidimensional Discrimination

Taylor, Lindsay, and Forbes (1967) and Lindsay, Taylor, and Forbes (1968) used the additive properties of $(d')^2$ to quantify the proportion of processing capacity devoted to discrimination when discriminations are called for in two modalities simultaneously, relative to that used for any single discrimination performed alone. They found a constant 85% when two auditory, two visual, one auditory and one visual, or two auditory and two visual discriminations were attempted simultaneously. They drew the implication that 15% of the finite capacity of the discrimination processor is required to control the procedure for sharing the processor between the different tasks.

Successive Presentation

Shiffrin, Craig, and Cohen (1973) devised a novel procedure to permit a comparison of detectabilities under simultaneous and successive observation. In the *simultaneous* case, any one of M signals could occur in the single observation interval of a trial; in the *successive* case, a single trial had M observation intervals, with a particular interval assigned to each signal. They found, with tactile stimuli to three skin loci, that performance was identical in the two conditions. Shiffrin, Gardner, and Allmeyer (1973) reported the same result for visual dot patterns, as did Shiffrin and Grantham (1974) for signals in three sensory modalities. Shiffrin and Grantham interpreted this result as disconfirming the single-channel model and as indicating that "selective allocation to sensory modalities does not affect the early stages of perceptual processing" (p. 460).

As stated by Shiffrin and Grantham, "The successive condition allowed S to give his full attention to each sensory modality in turn'' (p. 460). The assumption that S was able to do so—that is, that an observer can control the attentive focus so precisely in time—was not tested by a comparison of the successive condition with conditions in which a single known signal was presented throughout a group of trials. The advisability of that control was indicated by the earlier finding that a precue indicating which of two tones would occur on a given forced-choice trial—the precue being the tone itself but at a greater amplitude—was insufficient to bring detectability to the same level observed in series of trials in which only one of the tones occurred (Swets and Sewall, 1961). Johnson and Hafter (1980) found that tonal precues in a sequential condition like that of Shiffrin and his associates (Shiffrin et al., 1973; Shiffrin & Grantham, 1974) increased detectability in that condition significantly. Another assumption of the sequential procedure is that the observer's memory is fully adequate to the task.

Switching Times and Attention Allocation

Considered now are models for the process of shifting attention from one source (filter, band, channel, signal) to another and for the distribution of attention between two sources.

A Model for Scanning Time

Tanner and Norman (1954) estimated attainable scan speeds for the narrow-band receiver discussed earlier. They summarized experiments in which a signal could occur anywhere in the range of 400–1100 Hz (in one condition) and 1000–1700 Hz (in another condition). Relative to the average $P(C)$ for several signals of known frequency in each range presented with a duration of 0.1 seconds, signals of unknown frequency had to be increased to approximately 0.3 seconds for the lower range and 0.2 seconds for the higher range to reach the same $P(C)$. Taking the differences of 0.2 seconds and 0.1 seconds as scanning times for the two ranges, respectively, and assuming a linear scan within each range, these authors associated a rate of 3500 Hz/sec/sec with the midfrequency of 700 Hz and 7000 Hz/sec/sec with the midfrequency of 1400 Hz. They then approximated the scan rate by the equation $df/dt = 5f$ and postulated a rate of change in scan rate that is a linear function of frequency.

A Model for Switching Rate

Considering only independent channels, as defined by the auditory and visual modalities, Schmidt and Kristofferson (1963) postulated a mechanism that requires no time to shift attention, but can make the shift only at certain equally spaced points in time. From two kinds of experiments, successiveness discrimination and reaction time, Kristofferson (1967a, 1967b) derived three temporal parameters that agreed in indicating that the switching points occur at a rate of about 20/sec. The first parameter is the time difference between the ends of two signals required for them to be discriminated as successive with $P(C) = 1.0$. The second parameter is a function of the mean and variance of the increments in reaction time that are added by uncertainty as to which signal will occur. The third parameter is the quantum of delay in processing a signal that is added when attention must be shifted and the shift must await the next time point. The three parameters were found to be equal in average value, about 50 msec; to vary similarly across individuals; to be the same for the two modalities, or input channels; and to be correlated between channels.

Baron (1971) had his subjects make second choices in a three-signal successiveness-discrimination task and found that these choices were made with greater-than-chance probability. He interpreted these data as contradictory to "psychological moment theory" in general and the attention-switching model in particular. Kristofferson (Note 6) and Allan (1975) disagreed with Baron's interpretation, and pointed up a distinction between the switching model and classical moment theory. Extensions and applications of the switching model were reported by Kristofferson and Allan (1973) and Allan and Kristofferson (1974).

Attention Operating Characteristic

Kalsbeek and Sykes (1967) plotted performance on a secondary task versus performance on a primary task, showing the covariation as the demands of the primary task were increased. The primary task consisted of responding with two keys to two lights and was paced. The secondary task was to respond with two pedals to two tones and was unpaced. Performance on the secondary task decreased linearly with linear increases in the informational output of the primary task, which was varied by manipulating the rate of the lights.

Kinchla (Note 7) proposed that such a plot, representing the allocation of attentive focus between two sources, be called an attention operating characteristic (AOC). In his experiment, signals consisting of brief off periods could occur with equal probability on neither, either, or both of two laterally displaced lights; and the subject was to respond "yes" if he or she detected a signal on either or both lights. In different groups of trials, the subject was instructed to attend only to the left light, mostly to the left light, equally to both lights, mostly to the right light, or only to the right light. On an AOC plot of the probability of detection given a signal on the left versus the probability of detection given a signal on the right, the five conditions produced five points ranging along a nearly straight line approximately from the upper left corner to the lower right corner—that is,

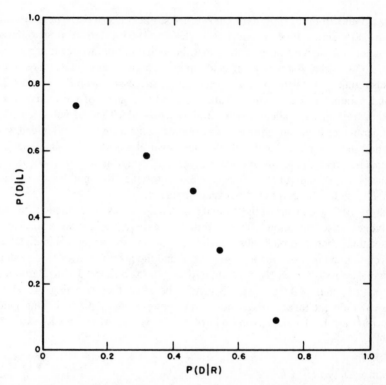

Figure 5.3 Probability of detection given a signal on the left, $p(D|L)$, versus probability of detection given a signal on the right, $p(D|R)$, under five sets of instructions about relative attention (average of 3 observers; data from Kinchla, Note 7, 1980).

approximately from $(0.10, 0.80)$ to $(0.80, 0.10)$. These data are shown in Figure 5.3.

The model reported by Kinchla to fit data of this general form was an all-or-none, or single-channel, model in which the observer attends only to the left light on some trials, only to the right light on the remaining trials, and responds "yes" or "no" relative to his or her decision criterion for that light. The extreme points on the AOC reflect pure strategies, whereas the intermediate points represent mixed strategies of allocation of attentive focus. A version of the multiple-band model, termed the *weighted-integration* model, was shown to predict a curvilinear function, and to predict a smaller reduction in accuracy relative to conditions of signal certainty than was actually obtained.

To avoid a misimpression about the history of the AOC concept that might stem from the organization of this chapter, I mention here that Kinchla anticipated in his unpublished technical note in 1969 a much fuller theoretical and empirical development discussed at conferences by Sperling and Melchner in

1975 and 1976 and published by them in 1978 (1978a, 1978b). Also at that time
Norman and Bobrow published a related theoretical paper (1975). Kinchla's
publication on the subject appeared in 1980, and the data of Figure 5.3 are taken
from that paper. Sperling and Melchner used "complex" signals (letters, numerals) rather than "elementary" signals (lights), and hence their work is alluded to
in a subsequent section of this chapter entitled "Visual Form Perception." A
fuller discussion of their work appears in Sperling (Chapter 4, this volume).
Norman and Bobrow were oriented more toward performance, therein defining a
performance operating characteristic (POC), and their work is alluded to in the
section of this chapter entitled "Multiple Complex Tasks." A fuller discussion
of their work appears in Wickens (Chapter 3, this volume).

Shapes and Widths of Auditory Filters

Considered now are models for the shape of an attention filter for frequency,
and several ways to estimate the filter's width, and then a model that relates
frequency attention to loudness attention.

Varying the Bandwidth of Masking Noise

Using bands of noise of various widths centered about a pure tone, Fletcher
(1940) found that only noise components in a narrow band are effective in
masking the tone. Termed the *critical band,* its width was estimated to be about
65 Hz at 1000 Hz, increasing to 500 Hz at 8000 Hz. A similar estimate of width
at the lower frequencies was obtained by Schafer, Gales, Shewmaker, and
Thompson (1950).

Whereas Fletcher had assumed the response characteristic of the critical band,
or internal filter, to be rectangular, Schafer *et al.* considered it to have the shape
of a "single-tuned," or "universal-resonance" filter. Tanner *et al.* (Note 1; see
also Swets, Green, & Tanner, 1962) collected new data at 1000 Hz and compared those two hypotheses to two more—both referring to Gaussian-shaped
filters, one with width measured at the half-power points and one with width
measured at the one-sigma points. These authors recognized, of course, that
what they were dealing with was simply a convenient mathematical model,
though the filters with sloping skirts were thought to be better representations of
the excitatory effect of a weak tone on the basilar membrane.

Knowing the shape and various widths of their external filter, Tanner *et al.*
calculated the reduction of noise power that would occur if their external filter
were combined in series with each of the four shapes considered for an internal
filter. Based on an empirical determination of detectability as a function of the
power of a broad-band noise, they estimated the effect on detectability of external filtering and so calculated critical widths for each hypothetical filter. Those

widths were 40 Hz for the universal-resonance filter, 80 Hz for the Gaussian-shaped (half-power) filter, and 95 Hz for the other two. The authors noted that the estimate of width is highly dependent on assumed shape, but observed that the real width and shape might well vary from one sensory task to another under intelligent control.

Varying a Notch in Masking Noise

Webster, Miller, Thompson, and Davenport (1952) devised a way to determine the shape of the internal filter by direct measurement. They filtered out a portion of a masking noise (from 600 to 1200 Hz), thus producing a notch in the noise, and varied the frequency of a pure tone relative to the frequency location of the notch. They compared the observed variation in the stimulus threshold for the tone to the shapes of a universal-resonance filter and a rectangular filter. As seen in Figure 5.4, the data points (circles) are fitted noticeably better by the dashed line, representing the universal-resonsance filter, than by the dotted line, representing the rectangular filter.

The solid line in Figure 5.4 represents a symmetrical filter and was suggested as a good fit to the data of Webster, *et al.* by Patterson (1974). In a first experiment, Patterson varied the position of the edge of a sharply filtered low- or high-pass noise and obtained such a shape, symmetrical on a linear frequency scale. He calculated half-power widths ranging from 30 Hz at a signal frequency of 500 Hz, through 75 Hz at 1000 Hz and 150 Hz at 2000 Hz. Patterson (1976) used a notched noise in a second experiment and determined that the Gaussian curve provides a good approximation to the obtained filter shape. He then calculated filter widths about twice as large as before, equal to 0.13 of their center frequency. Patterson and Henning (1977) obtained similar results with two tones as maskers. The last three articles mentioned give an excellent summary of an extensive literature on this general topic.

The Probe-Signal Technique

Greenberg and Larkin (1968) and Greenberg (1969a, 1969b) used "probe signals" in another attempt to obtain a direct measurement of the human's frequency-response characteristic. In such an experiment, the main signal is presented at a fixed frequency with high probability; and the probe signals are presented at various other frequencies with low probability. The frequency of the main signal is assumed to define the center of the band of attention, or internal filter; and the observed lower detectabilities of the outlying frequencies are taken as reflecting the filter's shape and width. This particular technique of attracting attention by features of the signal probability distribution is a refinement of methods used by Tanner and Norman (1954) and Karoly and Isaacson (see Swets & Kristofferson, 1970, p. 349). Greenberg and Larkin observed a detectability

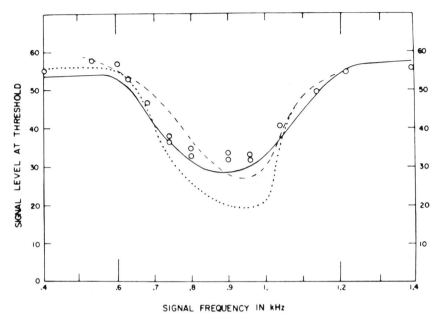

Figure 5.4 Threshold signal power in the region of a noise notch. (Data from Webster *et al.* 1952.) Dotted, dashed, and solid lines represent thresholds predicted by the rectangular, universal-resonance, and symmetric filters, respectively. (Reproduced from Patterson, 1974.)

function suggestive of an internal filter with sloping skirts, and they estimated half-power widths for different observers ranging from nearly 80 Hz to about 140 Hz at 1000 Hz. With the same technique, Macmillan and Schwartz (1975) estimated widths ranging from nearly 60 Hz at 700 Hz to values centered about 150 Hz at 1600 Hz.

Attention Model for Intensity and Frequency

Considering the absolute identification of loudnesses, Green and Luce (1974) proposed an attention model for intensity. The location of the hypothesized attention band can be varied under central control, with possible changes in width as location varies; the average bandwidth is calculated to be between 10 and 20 db. The neural representation of a signal falling within the band is interpreted as having a larger sample size, allowing greater precision in estimating signal parameters. Such a model accounts for the capacity effect for more than 7 ± 2 signals, and the range effect that comes into play at about 20 db. Luce and Green (1978) later suggested that the attention band for intensity and the critical band for frequency are manifestations of a single neural process and represent a differential monitoring of groups of neural fibers. Each group transmits both frequency and intensity information; the observer selects one group to be monitored fully and takes a sample in remaining groups estimated to be about $\frac{1}{10}$ of the fibers in a group.

To date, attention bands of intensity have been studied only by techniques that rest on attracting attention by features of the signal probability distribution. Luce and Green (1978) used a two-frequency identification design in which intensities were chosen at random from several distributions of the following general type. Six levels were clustered within a 10-db band and two other levels were either 20 or 40 db from the nearest edge of the cluster. The assumptions that attention focuses on clustered frequencies and that there is a 10:1 ratio in sample size lead to a prediction of a substantially lower percentage correct for the outlying intensities than for the clustered intensities. This prediction was found to hold for some but not all of the data.

Aggregation over Channels

Considered in this section are models for how, and for how well, the human observer handles information arriving at once from multiple sources in different bands or channels.

Three general questions arise: Can the observer attend to any set of bands of his or her choice while ignoring all others? Is aggregation of information in separate bands perfectly efficient? Is the manner of storing information from a given band, and/or the manner of further processing that information, different when attention is directed to several bands rather than one—perhaps changed in a way to relieve the added demand on memory or further processing?

Observation Integration and Decision Combination

Two classes of models may be identified here. One class, introduced in a previous section under the rubric of "multiple-band" models, assumes that the observation made in each band is related in some way to the observation made in each of the other bands considered. In the most common of these models, identical to the integrated MB model described previously, an observation in each band concerning signal presence is assumed to be encoded in a fine-grained form, as posterior probability or likelihood ratio, and then simply summed with those in other relevant bands. In another variant of the models based on a combination of the observations, the observations are weighted in the summing. These models are called here *observation-integration* (OI) models.

The second class of models assumes that either the information about signal presence in each band is inherently binary, as it would be with a threshold mechanism; or that continuous information is mapped into a binary ("yes–no") decision, and only the decision is available for further processing. These models are termed here *decision-combination* (DC) models.

For simple signals in random noise, the OI models assume that relevant bands (and only relevant bands) are selected for observation. The same assumption is made by DC models that take into account false-positive responses or the possibility of guessing. Both the OI and DC models predict that aggregation over bands is less than perfect. So although these models are sometimes referred to as nonattentional when contrasted with the single-band model, particularly in the context of letter detection (as discussed in a later section), there are also grounds for thinking of them as attentional.

Specification of Observation-Integration and Decision-Combination Models

Pirenne (1943) usually receives credit for introducing the DC model in psychology. That is to say, he first adduced the independence theorem of probability theory as a perceptual model, in the context of binocular summation. A simple application of that theorem gives a model that asserts that if an overall positive decision is made when either of two independent detectors makes a positive (detection) response, then the overall probability of a positive decision equals the sum of the individual probabilities minus their product. Alternatively, one can multiply the individual probabilities of detection failures for any number of independent detectors to calculate the combined probability of detection failure; the complement is the probability that one or more of the detectors will yield a detection response. The equation is often expressed for two detectors as

$$p_{1 \text{ and } 2} = p_1 + p_2 - p_1 p_2;$$

alternatively,

$$p_M = 1 - \prod_{i=1}^{M} (1 - p_i).$$

The kind of summation predicted by this model has been termed *probability summation,* and the amount of summation it predicts has been regarded as a baseline that a "neural summation" would have to exceed (Blake and Fox, 1973). This is so despite the fact that the predicted summation is quite large. For example, for detectors each having a detection probability of .50, two yield .75, three yield .88, and four yield .94. As another example, for detectors with a probability of .80, three of them yield .99. This simple version of the DC model has been criticized on the grounds that it depends on a two-state high-threshold model of sensory information; Eriksen (1966) has shown that a sensory model incorporating multiple states of signal likelihood predicts less summation.

Green (1958) observed that various rules of decision combination are possible (e.g., a majority rule for more than two detectors) and that DC predictions could be developed under various models of sensory information (e.g., a two-state low-threshold model). Birdsall (Note 3) developed DC predictions under the continuous model of sensory information for two combination rules: the one described in the preceding and one in which an overall positive decision is made if and only if all individual responses are positive—in other words, for the "union" and "intersection" rules. These two DC predictions are shown relative to the OI prediction for two detectors and three values of d' in Figure 5.5.

For two detectors, it can be seen that both rules predict less summation than the OI prediction of $2^{1/2}d_i$. (The latter prediction is less than that of the original union-rule version of the DC rule in which false-positive responses are ignored or in which the correction for guessing is applied.) Birdsall's (Note 8) calculations indicated that a perfect power summation for two auditory frequencies ($2d_i'$) is approximately 3 db; that the OI model at $2^{1/2}d_i'$ predicts an effect of about 1.5 db; and that the two DC rules predict, on average, an effect of about 0.75 db. The latter value can be seen to be an average with respect to the variable of false-positive probability and to represent both the intersection and union rules reasonably well only at relatively strong signal levels. At lower signal levels, and at lower values of the false-positive probability, the intersection rule predicts a summation effect very similar to that predicted by the particular OI model under consideration, and the union rule predicts a nearly zero effect of adding a second detector.

In examining the relation of the predictions of these models to data, it is helpful to plot d' against the number of observations (M) on logarithmic scales and note the slope of the function. The OI model's square-root prediction, of course, yields a slope of one half. Taking the DC predictions along the negative diagonal of Figure 5.5, where the two rules yield the same prediction, gives a slope of about one third. This point is returned to in later sections of this chapter.

Some Applications of These Models

Few, if any, experimental studies have considered both OI and DC models—including a DC version based on a continuous or multistate model of sensory information; and few studies have been designed with regard to the varying effects on the DC predictions of signal level and false-positive probability. So the relative validities of the various models are by no means clear. The interested reader can consult Schafer and Gales (1949), who considered the simple DC model for multiple frequencies in audition; Pollack (1961) and Corcoran (1967), who considered both classes of models for the combination of intensity and frequency discriminations in audition, though with a different experimental para-

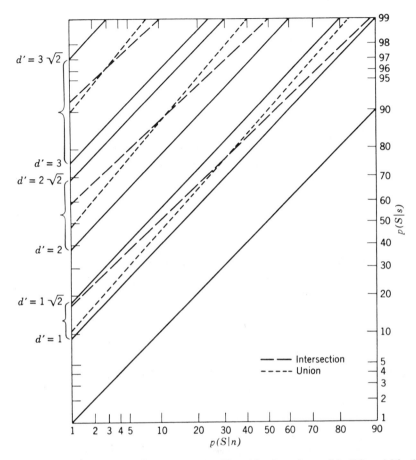

Figure 5.5 Comparison of predictions from the OI model and two forms of the DC model for the combination of two observations. The comparisons are made in terms of ROC curves—hits $p(S|s)$ versus false alarms $p(S|n)$—shown here on probability scales. The lower solid lines in each of the three bands represent three levels of equal individual detectabilities, and the upper solid lines are the corresponding predictions of the OI model, $2^{1/2}d'_i$. The dashed lines represent two rules of decision combination (see key), as discussed in the text. (After Birdsall, Note 8; reproduced from Green and Swets, 1966/1974, p. 241.)

digm than discussed here; Wickelgren (1967), who considered adequate versions of both classes of models for widely spaced black dots on a white field, though with a different control condition than discussed here; Loveless, Brebner, and Hamilton (1970), who considered the simple DC model and the most common OI model for auditory and visual signals; Sachs, Nachmias, and Robson (1971) and Graham (1977), who considered a simple form of DC model for spatial-frequency channels in vision; and Zagorski (1975), who examined intensity and frequency in audition, with the experimental paradigm implied here, with respect to a simple DC model and the OI model.

Several of these studies indicate that a version of the simple DC model, in which the detection probabilities are corrected for chance success, fits the data rather well. This finding raises the possibility that observers encode signal information continuously, or in several states, when attending to one band, and in just two states when attending to more than one band. As mentioned earlier, such a strategy would be one way of dealing with the increased demands on memory and processing that are introduced by signals with components in more than one band. Consistent with this possibility is the fact that the experimental paradigms in two of these studies, the one analyzed by Pollack (1961) and the one used by Corcoran (1967), placed still further demands on memory.

Extensions of These Models

The OI and DC models of aggregation have been extended in an attempt to treat a possible correlation among sensory channels, and the predictions of some of the models have been amplified.

Correlation among Channels

Fidell (1970) reviewed the vector model for correlation (as summarized in a previous section) in connection with his study of auditory (A) and visual (V) signals. He found the integrated MB or OI model that assumes independence of the two detection systems, that is,

$$[(d'_A)^2 + (d'_V)^2]^{1/2},$$

to fit the data quite well; and concluded, along with Eijkman and Vendrik (1965), that intensity discriminations in the two modalities are uncorrelated. He achieved these results under conditions of both independence and complete correlation of the external noises masking the two signals, though bimodal performance was slightly better when the external noises came from independent sources.

Craig, Colquhoun, and Corcoran (1976) reviewed four models of the sort under discussion, including a DC model for correlated channels. They concluded that this model fitted their data on auditory and visual signals better than either the DC or OI models based on independent detectors, and inferred a correlation between the two sensory systems.

Further Development of Model Predictions

Mulligan and Shaw (1980) reexamined the union-rule version of the DC model in combination with the sensation–decision model of modern detection theory (see also Shaw, 1980). According to the latter model, a positive or negative decision is made depending on whether a continuous sensory variable (X) exceeds or fails below some decision criterion (β). They also considered a contrasting SB model (of the sort described earlier), similarly combined with the detection-theory view of continuous sensory information and variable decision criterion. They applied these two models, along with the weighted-integration form of the OI model (Kinchla & Collyer, 1974), to combined auditory and visual detection. Their experimental paradigm presented at random one of four stimuli—noise alone, visual signal, auditory signal, auditory and visual signals—and called for one of two responses—"no" (noise alone) or "yes" (any of the three signal stimuli).

The dependent variable they consider for all three models is the conditional probability of a "no" response given the stimulus pattern i, denoted p_i. The subscript i can take on the value A, V, B, or N for auditory, visual, bimodal, or noise-alone trials, respectively. For the SB model, assuming that attention is directed to the auditory modality with probability α and to the visual modality with probability $1 - \alpha$,

$$p_i = \alpha p(X_A < \beta_A) + (1 - \alpha)p(X_V < \beta_V).$$

The DC model under the union rule has

$$p_i = p(X_A < \beta_A)p(X_V < \beta_V).$$

In the OI model, the sensory variables for the A and V modalities are summed with weights (w and $1 - w$), respectively; and the sum is compared to a decision criterion:

$$p_i = p[wX_A + (1 - w)X_V < \beta].$$

Shaw (1980) has shown that these three models predict additivity of certain response probabilities, each under a different transformation. Specifically, if the two modalities are independent; the SB model predicts

$$p_A + p_V = p_N + p_B,$$

and the DC model makes the following prediction (in terms of the natural logarithm of the probabilities):

$$\ln p_A + \ln p_V = \ln p_N + \ln p_B.$$

If, further, the observer's signal and noise distributions are Gaussian and of equal variance; then the OI model predicts

$$z_A + z_V = z_N + z_B,$$

where z is the inverse Gaussian or z transformation of p_i.

Mulligan and Shaw (1980) concluded that their experimental results favor the DC model and are inconsistent with the OI model. Fidell (1982) suggested in a published letter that their study was not up to a definite conclusion, and they (Shaw & Mulligan, 1982) came to their defense in an accompanying letter. Space is not available here to attempt to sort out the many issues raised. Suffice to say that detection theorists would generally prefer the simpler experimental paradigm previously used—in which three pairs of stimuli (N–A, N–V, and N–B) are presented in three separate conditions—to the one used by Mulligan and Shaw—in which the four stimuli are presented at random in a single condition. As Nolte and Jaarsma (1967) have pointed out, the latter paradigm entails testing a "composite" signal hypothesis, instead of "simple" signal hypotheses, via a rather complicated form of likelihood ratio that is the average of the likelihood ratios for the three subhypotheses. A complete analysis would require measuring all of the d' distances—here, six distances for four stimulus hypotheses—as in Tanner's (1956) work described earlier. One might avoid such extensive measurement by invoking some sort of independence, as Nolte and Jaarsma did; but one could clearly not use here the further assumption of those authors that all signals are equally detectable. In brief, though detection theorists laid the foundation for optimal decisions in the paradigm used by Mulligan and Shaw (1980), they did not reach a prediction for performance, even in the subcase of orthogonal signals.

For the simpler, straightforward paradigm, the models underlying Figure 5.5 are appropriate. Those models possess the generality sought by Shaw and Mulligan (1982) in incorporating both low-threshold and continuous conceptions of sensory processes and in allowing decision criteria to vary from unimodal to bimodal tasks. As the figure indicates, contrary to Shaw and Mulligan's assertion, the OI and DC models are identifiable on the basis of the relation between bimodal and unimodal d' values.

Union Rule and Properties of Extrema

Wandell and Luce (1978) observed that the process of deriving a decision statistic from a sum (or average) of random variables is relatively well understood, depending on the central limit theorem; whereas the behavior of the maximum of a set of random variables, which is the process assumed in the union-rule version of the DC model, is known but less familiar. They reviewed the literature on properties of extrema (going back to von Mises in 1923) and used the main results to extend certain psychophysical detection models. Specifically, they developed extreme-value forms of both counting and timing models of detection to compare with the OI forms of those models considered in previous work. They were able to calculate the models' predictions for response probabilities, Weber functions, speed–accuracy trade-off (SATO) in reaction-time experiments, and ROC curves. At the present stage of modeling, the extremum model works well in a counting context and fails in a timing context. The authors concluded that secondary assumptions of the models need review.

Visual Form Perception

In this section, various models for attention to visual forms are considered. Though the stimuli are more complex than the tones and lights discussed to this point, and although the experimental tasks are often more complex, the questions encountered are very similar. Thus, the principal questions have to do with whether the observer scans successively from one channel to another or makes simultaneous observations in multiple channels; with shifts in attention versus divided attention; and with the mode of aggregating sensory information over multiple channels.

The main line of research treated here was stimulated by modern work on the span of apprehension. Sperling (1960, 1963) asked his subjects to report as many of a set of briefly flashed letters as they could, or to report the letters in certain cued positions, and proposed a model in which iconic memory traces of the letters were successively scanned. Estes and Taylor (1964) devised a letter-recognition task to emphasize perceptual aspects and reduce memory aspects, and also proposed a scanning model. Variants of that perceptual task, and variants of and alternatives to that model, have appeared in a steady flow ever since.

Other lines of research mentioned here include searching for signals in radiographs, switching a single band of attention, analysis via AOCs, and tuning of the weights placed on perceptual dimensions.

Letter Detection or Recognition

The detection of a specified letter, or the recognition of one of two specified letters, in either a spatial or temporal array of other unspecified letters, was modeled as a serial process (Estes and Taylor, 1964), as a mixed serial–parallel process (Rumelhart, 1970), as a parallel process with decision combination (Eriksen and Spencer, 1969; Gardner, 1973), and as parallel process with observation integration (Kinchla, 1974; Kinchla & Collyer, 1974).

According to the terminology developed earlier, these models can be classified as in Table 5.1. The first two models represent processes of limited capacity in that a central scanning process attempts successively to reach and encode rapidly fading representations of the signals in iconic memory. The remaining models have been described as representing processes of unlimited capacity, but we might note again that a combination of binary decisions loses sensory informa-

TABLE 5.1

Models for Letter Detection or Recognition

	Observation		Aggregation	
Model	Single band (SB)	Multiple band (MB)	Decision combination (DC)	Observation integration (OI)
Serial or scanning process (Estes & Taylor, 1964)	X			
Feature extraction (Rumelhart, 1970)	X	X	X	
Parallel process, DC (Eriksen & Spencer, 1969) (Gardner, 1973)		X	X	
Parallel process, OI (Kinchla, 1974) (Kinchla & Collyer, 1974)		X		X

tion relative to an integration of fine-grained observations and that integration is not always optimal. The chronology reflected in the table is the replacement of SB models by MB models; and within the latter category, a shift from DC models to an OI model.

I shall very briefly review these models and relate them to the major experimental findings. Although the concern in the first two models was to reflect data on latency, the empirical effects usually regarded as the main ones are stated in terms of accuracy. The first of these is the *set-size* effect: the fact that the percentage of correct responses, $P(C)$, or a detection index such as d' decreases with increasing numbers of noise letters per trial. The second is the *redundancy* effect: the fact that these two accuracy measures increase with the number of signal letters per trial. A third main effect is that decreasing the relative confusability of signal and noise letters decreases the set-size effect. These three effects are neatly shown in data reported by Estes (1972) and reproduced here as Figure 5.6.

Serial or Scanning Model

The task devised by Estes and Taylor (1964) presented with equal probability either of two signal letters in a horizontal line of four letters (that is, along with three noise letters) and required the subject to state only which signal letter was present. (They referred to this task as one of detection. Had they required the subject only to state a signal's location, the status of the task as one of detection or recognition would have been ambiguous; but the task they used would more commonly be called a recognition task.) Assuming that the subject can success-

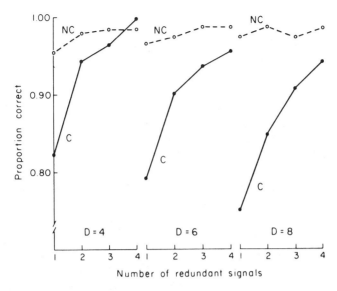

Figure 5.6 Proportion of correct detections versus number of signal letters, with relatively confusable (C) and nonconfusable (NC) noise letters and with set or display size (D) as parameters. (Reproduced from Estes 1972.)

fully recognize an average of R letters, and generalizing to M letters per display, Estes and Taylor suggested that the probability of a correct recognition is expressed by

$$p(C) = R/M + (1 - R/M)\tfrac{1}{2},$$

namely, the probability that the R letters recognized include the signal letter, plus the complement of that probability times the chance of a correct guess.

The serial model developed in connection with this task was responsive to the set-size effect expressed both in terms of (decreasing) accuracy and (increasing) latency. The scan was regarded as stopping either when the memory traces of the letters faded below a threshold or when a signal trace was reached. The first basis for scan termination was later discarded in light of the result that incorrect response times are relatively constant over different set sizes (Estes and Wessel, 1966), and the second basis for scan termination foundered on the result that correct latencies are invariant when redundant signal elements are added (Bjork and Estes, 1971; Wolford, Wessel, & Estes, 1968). Another finding that contributed to rejection of the original model (though perhaps it should not have) is the considerable reduction in the set-size effect when noise letters are made less confusable with signal letters (Estes, 1972; Gardner, 1973). Estes and Taylor (1965) considered a model with serial and parallel aspects, employing the DC union rule of aggregation for redundant signals.

Feature-Extraction Model

Rumelhart (1970) also proposed a mixed model and adduced the DC union model for redundant signals. In this model, all letters are attended to simultaneously, though with different weights or amounts of attention; but features of the letters are extracted serially as the letter traces fade, letters are recognized serially when enough of their features are recognized, and letters are transferred serially into short-term memory (STM). Rumelhart showed this model to fit Sperling's data on whole and partial report, some of Estes' data on letter recognition, and data on effects of backward masking. Gardner (Note 9) also found results favoring this model. Like the first serial model mentioned, this one does not handle findings on redundant signals and confusability of signal and noise elements.

Parallel-Processing Model with Decision Combination

The first thoroughgoing parallel-processing model advanced in this context was described by Eriksen and Spencer (1969). They used a yes–no detection task in which a single signal letter was present in a temporal sequence of letters. One result opposing a serial model was that the rate of presentation had little or no effect on accuracy (as measured by a variant of the index d') over a wide range of rates. A second finding was that the false-alarm proportion increased more than the hit proportion as set size increased. This finding suggested that increasing set size served to offer more opportunities for confusion of signal and noise letters in the decision process rather than to require more time to perceive more letters. At this point, as Kinchla (1974) put it, modeling emphasis shifted from a "race to code a rapidly decaying iconic memory" to a "statistical decision among multiple noisy samples" (p. 149).

Eriksen and Spencer (1969) applied the DC model to aggregate information over the multiple channels. They used both the intersection and union rules, and treated false alarms as well as hits. This model was found consistent with the three main effects mentioned in the preceding. Gardner (1973) extended this decision-theory model from the yes–no detection task to the recognition task of Estes and Taylor (1964) and considered additional rules for decision aggregation, including a majority rule. At the same time, Gardner reported results inconsistent with Rumelhart's (1970) model, and related the parallel-process model favorably to other experimental findings.

Parallel-Processing Model with Observation Integration

Kinchla (1974) related the set-size and redundancy effects to an expanded version of the integrated MB model, or the OI model, (discussed earlier). As is discussed in the next main section of this chapter, he had done so in a 1969 paper for the case of successive presentation of stimuli and anticipated then the applica-

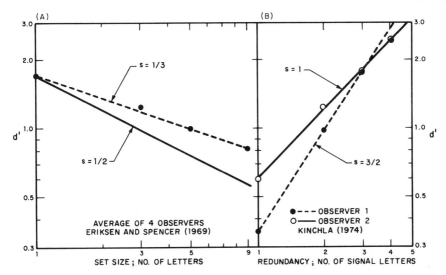

Figure 5.7 (A) d' versus set size, on logarithmic scales. The dashed line is fitted to the data by eye with a slope of one-third. The solid line shows a slope of one-half for comparison. (B) d' versus redundancy, on logarithmic scales. Data for A: average of four observers; from Eriksen and Spencer (1969). Data for B from Kinchla (1974): the lines are fitted by eye to the data of two observers, with slopes of three halves and one, respectively.

tion discussed here to simultaneous presentation. In the simple form previously discussed, the integrated MB model predicts that the accuracy index d' will decrease as the square root of the number of noise elements increases, and increase as the square root of the number of signal elements increases. However, Eriksen and Spencer's (1969) data on set size showed d' to decrease less rapidly than did the square root; rather, it decreased as the cube root of the number of noise elements increased. Kinchla and Collyer's (1974) data on redundant signals, presented by Kinchla (1974), showed d' to increase more rapidly than did the square root: one observer showed a linear summation of d' and another observer's d' increased approximately as the three-halves power of the number of signals. The two sets of data are replotted in Figure 5.7 as drawn from Kinchla's (1974) two tables, to show the effects just mentioned. It may be noted here in connection with the discussion of Figure 5.5 earlier in the chapter, that the set-size data are consistent with the DC model and that the redundancy data are inconsistent with both the DC and OI models for independent channels, insofar as those models have been described to this point.

To compare these data to a form of OI model, Kinchla fitted to them an extended version of the OI model, one having two variance parameters associated with the underlying detection model. He associated the first parameter with the variance in the observation of each letter and described it as a measure of confusability that makes a contribution to perceptual noise in proportion to the number of letters. Fitting this parameter is equivalent to fitting d', which is routinely done in one way or another in applications of the MB or OI model. He introduced a second parameter to reflect any fixed source of perceptual noise, but which he preferred to think of as reflecting variation in the observer's criterion for a positive response. The second parameter enabled him to handle the variation in slopes seen in Figure 5.7 and to fit very well the data shown there.

Comment

I have replotted in Figure 5.8 Estes's (1972) data, shown previously in Figure 5.6, in order to compare them with the simple (square-root) form of the OI model. Conversion from proportion correct to d' was made by Elliott's (1964) table for two-alternative forced choice ($M = 2$). A few arbitrary lines with slope of (plus or minus) one half are shown to facilitate the comparison with the square-root prediction. Figure 5.8A indicates that d' increases more than the prediction in moving from one to two signals but follows the prediction reasonably well for larger numbers of redundant signals. Figure 5.8B suggests that the square-root model is reasonably adequate for variation in set size. To be sure, fitting Kinchla's second parameter—variation in the response criterion—would probably provide a still better match of model and data.

With effort, one might account for differences in rate of growth and decline in d', as seen in Figures 5.7 and 5.8, in terms of what may well be substantial differences among the displays presented, the memory demanded, and the responses required in various studies of letter detection or recognition. Recall that Eriksen and Spencer's (1969) task called for a yes–no decision as to whether a single signal letter (an A) was present or absent in a temporal sequence of letters. Kinchla's and Collyer's (1974) task called for a confidence rating that a 4-letter spatial array contained one or more signal letters (Fs). And Estes' task called for a forced choice relative to 2 sets of signal letters (A, B, C, D, and S, T, U, V) presented in spatial array with 10 noise letters; in different conditions the choice was between 2 specified letters (A versus T), between two pairs of letters (A or B versus S or T), and between the sets as wholes (A or B or C or D versus S or T or U or V).

The next main section, of this chapter, which treats studies of multiple observations over time, shows instances of effects on rate of change in d' that were attributed to task variations of the sort just described. Specifically, Figure 5.9 (cited in the subsubsection entitled ''Fixed Number of Observations'') and the corresponding text discussion show an effect of the degree of initial uncertainty about the signal similar to that seen in Figure 5.8A; Figure 5.10 (cited in the subsubsection entitled ''Observer-Terminated Observation'') and the corresponding text discussion show an effect of the nature of the response used in training, contrasting a confidence rating and a yes–no response. With those

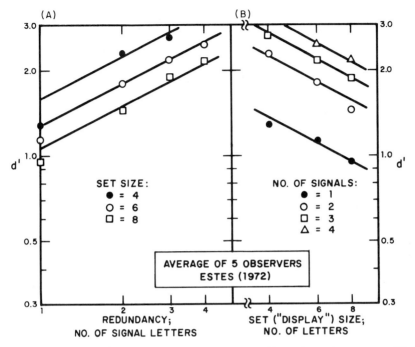

Figure 5.8 (A) Detection index (d') versus redundancy, with set size as the parameter. (B) d' versus set size, with redundancy as the parameter. Arbitrary lines of slope one-half provide a comparison with the one-parameter OI model, which predicts square-root growth and decline of d'. (Replotting of data from Estes 1972, shown in Figure 5.6.)

kinds of variation in mind, the relatively good fit of the simple OI model to Estes' data strikes me as little more than a coincidence.

On prior grounds, it could hardly be expected that the simple OI model— expressed in terms of d' and therefore based on Gaussian signal and noise distributions of equal variance—would fit the many variants of letter detection or recognition tasks that have been invented. Those distributions are usually found to be of unequal variance even for simple visual signals, and the distortion in assigning a value of d' to an ROC curve that is better described by another index grows in size with increases in the level of detectability. Hence, the slope of the function relating d' to set size or redundancy may be systematically affected. I would note, however, that plotting the log of d' or of some other ROC index against the log of the number of signals or noises does provide a way to compare and contrast data from different experiments.

Related Models

A few related models are briefly characterized here. In one, the main elements of the models just summarized—parallel processing, feature extraction, scanning, and statistical decisions—were brought together by Shiffrin and Geissler (1973). This model is nonattentional at the perceptual stage, with parallel processes operating largely automatically; the scanning occurs in a short-term-storage stage after the stage of iconic memory. In the second respect, the model articulates with a large body of work on memory scanning (e.g., Sternberg, 1966). The authors apply the model to predict accuracy and latency results, as obtained by Estes (1972), on covariation of set size, redundant signals, number of signal alternatives, and signal–noise confusability.

Harris, Shaw, and Bates (1979) proposed a model in which processing of individual items can overlap in time, with the amount of overlap ranging from none (serial processing) to all (parallel processing). A fixed-rate scanner is followed by an encoder, the efficiency of which decreases with the number of items being processed, and, in turn, by an item comparator or tester, the efficiency of which is constant over the number of items it processes. This model predicts observed serial-position results in letter arrays and reaction times for arrays with gaps.

Lupker and Massaro (1979) asked whether the limitations of memory and decision processing observed in the work on span of apprehension leave room also for limitations and selective attention at the perceptual stage. In their model, visual features are detected and placed in a preperceptual visual storage, and then a primary recognition process integrates the features into a percept. They develop the mathematics for the time course of the second process under various conditions; they develop the implications for selective attention; and they report data consistent with the model.

Shaw and Shaw (1977) applied to letter recognition a theory of optimal search developed in the 1950s in military operations research. This model quantifies the effects of capacity limitations without attempting to assign a locus for them and treats the allocation of available capacity. Shaw (1978) generalized the model to deal with reaction times as well as accuracy.

Lesion Search or Nonsearch

Swensson (1980) studied radiologists attempting to detect manifestations of lesions in chest radiographs and reported the "counter-intuitive result" that detectability was greater in a task requiring search than in one not requiring search. That is to say, the ROC curve calculated when the observer made a (three-category) confidence-rating response in relation to radiographic "features" he both located and identified as abnormal was to the left of the curve calculated when he made a (six-category) rating response relative to features located for him by the experimenter. The features consisted of a certain number of "signals" reflecting abnormalities and a certain number of instances of "noise" selected because they resembled signals. To account for the experimental finding, the author developed mathematics for a two-stage perceptual model in which (1) a preattentive filter automatically selects features for later attention and explicit evaluation, (2) the filter stage has a greater capacity to discriminate signal and noise features than the evaluation stage, and (3) the greater discrimination capacity of the filter stage cannot be applied once a feature has been selected for attention.

An alternative explanation is that observers performed more accurately in the search than in the nonsearch condition because in the former they could select the subset of features on which they would be scored. To put some fine structure on this suggestion, it may be noted that the observers' nonresponses to designated features in the search condition were scored as selections of a fourth rating category (a lower category beyond the three actually used by the observers). Thus, to the extent those features were noises, the search observers were scored as being "correct"; and the ratio of noise to signal features was on the order of three to one in one experiment and four to one in a second experiment. Ordinary variability would suggest that when the observers were in the nonsearch condition and were forced to respond to features not meeting their criterion for a positive response, some of the actual ratings of those features would be in categories above the lowest. The majority of those ratings would apply to the higher frequency or noise event and so would be scored as "incorrect" (false-positive) in varying degrees depending on the ROC point being calculated. My calculations indicate that if about two thirds of the nonresponses are assigned to the higher categories in sharply declining amounts as one departs from the lowest category, then the observed search ROC shifts over to the observed nonsearch ROC. Because the false-positive probabilities for the search observers were very small, only a few nonresponses need be assigned to the upper three categories to achieve the required shift.

One might further imagine that many of the features not responded to in the search condition were among the more equivocal ones and so would more likely be assigned middle than lower ratings, thus exaggerating the penalty of the forced response in the nonsearch condition. Finally, it should be noted that the features designated as noise by the experimenter were defined by a kind of observer consensus rather than by truth external to observer performance (in particular, they were all of the features that at least one search observer called signal), and that a stricter experimenter's criterion for designating a feature as noise would reduce the observed difference between the search and nonsearch conditions.

Attention Switching

Baron (1973) extended the predictions of the single-band model to a setting in which the subject is called on to make two perceptual discriminations at once.

The model predicts the maximum probability of being correct on both discriminations given fixed probabilities of being correct on each, under both "strong" and "weak" assumptions. When applied to tasks of successiveness discrimination between pairs of letters, the weaker form of the model was rejected. An analysis of the data's implications for switching times were interpreted as evidence against the attention-switching model described earlier in the chapter, but the task's complexity does not recommend it as a sharp test of theory.

The SB model was applied to simultaneous tone and letter recognition by Massaro and Kahn (1973) and Massaro and Warner (1977). They presented results showing a decrement under simultaneous presentation approaching the SB prediction (discussed in a previous section) and a larger decrement under simultaneous than under sequential presentation (also discussed in a previous section). Both outcomes were taken to indicate perceptual attention.

Attention Operating Characteristics

Sperling and Melchner (1978a, 1978b) applied an AOC analysis of the general sort introduced earlier in the chapter to tasks involving letters and numerals. In three pairs of tasks, these signals varied in size and clarity and in position on the inside or outside of an array. The authors concluded that movement along the AOC resulted primarily from switching attention but also, to some degree, from dividing or sharing attention. (See Sperling, Chapter 4, this volume, for a review of work on the AOC.)

Kinchla (1977) applied the weighted form of the integrated MB model (defined earlier in this section) and the AOC analysis to "structural redundancy" in visual forms. The displays consisted of small letters arranged to form large letters, and the subject's task was to state whether a small signal letter was contained in either of two large letters. The results were consistent with an integration of information in the large letters, with more weight placed on the one more likely to contain the signal letter. Experimental variation of the relative likelihoods produced an AOC function suggesting an appropriate division of attention between the large letters. In a review of attention measures, Kinchla (1980) relates the AOC to the work of Posner et al. (1978) and Estes and Taylor (1964, 1965) discussed previously, and to the work of Norman and Bobrow (1976) and Navon and Gopher (1979, 1980) discussed later. He has begun a new line of research in which a concept analogous to the ROC and AOC—called the *organizational operating characteristic*—is used to study alternative figure–ground organizations (Kinchla, Note 10).

Weighting Perceptual Dimensions

Some studies have suggested that observers allocate emphasis among the perceptual dimensions of a set of stimuli so as to maximize the probability of a correct identification of singly presented members of the set. Howard, Ballas, and Burgy (Note 11) reported this result using complex acoustic patterns. Manipulation of dimensional weights was achieved with visual spectrograms of acoustic patterns (1) by calling for identification only of individual members of a · subset of the total set of stimuli presented and varying the composition of that subset (Getty, Swets, Swets, and Green, 1979), and (2) by reducing the relative value of a dimension to identification through decreasing its range of variation (Getty, Swets, and Swets, 1980).

Sustained Attention

Reviewed in this section are models for (1) temporal accumulation of information in trials with multiple observation intervals, and for termination of such trials by the observer; (2) temporal uncertainty, including uncertainty about which intervals of a trial contain signals and about the definition of a trial; and (3) long periods of observation, with either defined or undefined trials. (Parasuraman treats sustained attention in more detail in Chapter 3 of this volume.)

Temporal Accumulation

The processes of accumulation over a fixed number of observation intervals and of observer-terminated successions of observations (both discussed in the following) are similar to, respectively, accumulation over a single short fixed interval and observer termination of a single short interval. Treatment of the latter processes—dealing respectively with signal duration and reaction time—is beyond the focus of this chapter. To see, however, the relations of models in those areas to the models that are considered here, the reader can consult Green, Birdsall, and Tanner (1957) on signal duration and Laming (1973) on reaction time. The purpose of breaking continuous observations into pieces by experimental procedure is to permit overt responses after each of the pieces and thereby to track more sensitively the processes that develop over time.

Fixed Number of Observations

The basic OI model discussed earlier was applied by Swets, Shipley, McKey, and Green (1959) in an experimental paradigm similar to one used by Schafer and Shewmaker (Note 12). Specifically, a trial consisted of five observations, and an observation consisted of four temporal intervals; a signal was present in the same interval throughout the trial; and the observer made a cumulative forced-choice response after each observation. (For the discussion of this experiment only, "observations" and "intervals" are distinguished from one another; in other experiments they coincide.)

The OI model predicts $d'_m = m^{1/2}d'_1$, where m is the number of observations. This model was found to fit the data reasonably well when the samples of noise were independent from one observation to the next, and substantially overestimated the increase found when the samples of noise were the same on each observation of a given trial. The independent-noise data fell short of the union-rule prediction of the DC model, but that model was not clearly rejected.

The improvement of $m^{1/2}$ in d' is consistent with Schafer and Shewmaker's finding that the signal power required to reach some fixed level of detectability declined linearly as $m^{1/2}$ increased. Incidentally, the ubiquity of the square root of time was noted by Taylor (1966). He drew examples from figural aftereffects, motion aftereffects, vigilance, motion neutralization, visibility of the stabilized retinal image, effects of contours on visibility, and fluctuations in the perception of ambiguous figures to show perceptual changes progressing linearly with the square root of time, changes that for the most part represented a decrease in perceptual efficiency. He commented that devoting less attention, or information-processing capacity, to stimulus information that is highly correlated from moment to moment, or increasingly redundant, makes adaptive sense.

In the multiple-observation experiment of Swets et al. (1959), conditions in which the signal could be at either of 2 frequencies on a trial, at any of 16 frequencies, or comprised of all 16 frequencies showed systematic differences as well as individual differences relative to the OI-model prediction and led the authors to conclude that their observers could choose to follow either a single-band (SB) or multiple-band (MB) strategy for attending to different frequencies.

The problem of frequency uncertainty in multiple observations over time was attacked again later, with more theoretical ammunition, by Swets and Birdsall (1978). In the meantime, work carried out in Birdsall's laboratory had developed several models for the "adaptive optimum receiver," namely that by Nolte (1967), Nolte and Jaarsma (1967), Spooner (1969), and Birdsall and Gobien (1973). In their experiment, Swets and Birdsall used the "yes–no" stimulus–response procedure, 12 observations per trial, and 8 frequencies. They added to the primary control condition, which presents a signal at a single known frequency across observations and trials, another control condition in which the signal could assume any of 8 frequencies and varied from one observation to another *within* a trial. In the experimental condition, the signal frequency was constant within a trial and varied *across* trials. Following the language of hypothesis testing, the second control condition presented a *simple* signal, whereas the experimental condition presented a *composite* signal.

The ideal-observer model for the simple signal is an MB observer that adds together over observations the largest of the M filter outputs on each observation and successively compares the sum to criteria for a "yes" response, with these criteria changing appropriately over observations. The predicted growth from this model is the familiar $m^{1/2}d'_1$. The ideal-observer model for the composite signal keeps the M filter outputs separate; adds the new outputs of each filter to the cumulative value of the preceding outputs for that filter; and after each observation, compares the largest of the M individual sums to a criterion for a "yes" response (Nolte, 1967). The predicted growth from this composite-signal model is greater than $m^{1/2}d_1'$ for the early observations of a trial because this ideal observer can adapt—can tune to the frequency—as the frequency uncertainty is reduced over time. In later observations, after the signal's frequency is established by the observer, the MB observer becomes effectively an SB observer; and the predicted growth is then at the rate of $m^{1/2}$.

As seen in Figure 5.9, the experimental results confirmed this prediction for the composite signal of an early growth of d' exceeding $m^{1/2}$ and a later growth approximating that rate. Looking at the average data, it is clear that for the signal at a single known frequency—designated signal specified exactly (SSE)—d' grows at a rate a little less than $m^{1/2}$. Simple-signal performance is close to the multiband prediction and consistently below the simple-signal prediction. Composite-signal performance exceeds both of the predictions based on no adaptation. And the composite-signal prediction (drawn point by point from the observed SSE data) exceeds the composite-signal performance by what amounts to 1 db of signal energy. The authors concluded that human observers can accumulate information over time in a near optimal manner and can adjust the band of attention in accordance with their changing knowledge of the stimulus.

Observer-Terminated Observation

Wald's (1947) theory of sequential analysis was used by Swets and Green (1961) as a model for observer termination of a series of observations. According to this model, a form of OI model, the observer adds together over observations the values of a decision variable—posterior probability of signal or likelihood ratio of signal to noise—and continues making observations until the sum of the values crosses a decision boundary or response criterion (i.e., until it either exceeds a criterion for a "yes" response or falls below a criterion for a "no" response). (This is the model used by Stone, 1960, for reaction time.) Under the DC model for this situation, a trial would be terminated if and only if the value of a single observation crosses a boundary.

Swets and Green compared the OI and DC models for accumulation by analyzing the number of trials terminated at each stage of observation in relation to the error rates at each stage. They concluded that their observers behaved in accordance with the DC model when left to their own devices and behaved in accordance with the OI model when specifically urged to integrate across observations. Concerning the decision model for termination, they found (approximately as predicted) that the error rates and mean numbers of observations to termination varied with each other and with the payoff values assigned to correct and incorrect responses.

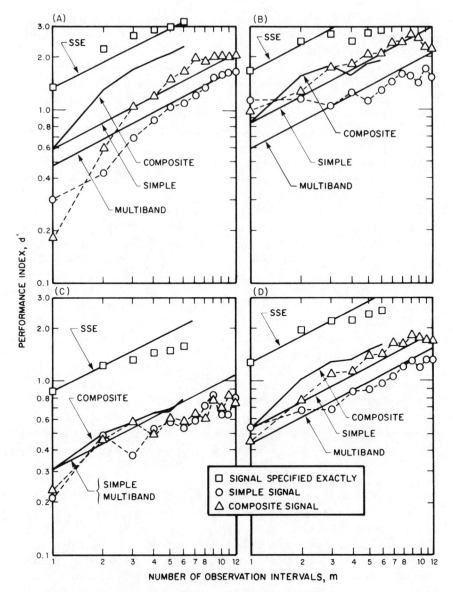

Figure 5.9 Detection index d' versus number of observations, for three signal conditions, relative to four models, as discussed in the text: (A–C), Observers 1–3, respectively, and (D), average of Observers 1–3. (Reproduced from Swets and Birdsall 1978.)

These problems were reexamined by Swets and Birdsall (1967) in relation to some revisions of Wald's theory advanced by Birdsall and Roberts (1965a, 1965b). Whereas Wald's theory applied to open-ended trials, the newer theory applied to trials having some maximum number of observations. The newer theory also treated the nonsequential process by which the observer sets the number of observations on each trial in advance of making any.

Swets and Birdsall (1967) asked experimentally whether pretraining with a yes–no response would incline observers to follow a DC model of accumulation, whereas pretraining with a confidence-rating response—stressing a fine-grained analysis of sensory informatin—would incline observers to follow the OI model. Their answer was a qualified "yes." As seen in Figure 5.10, the rating group

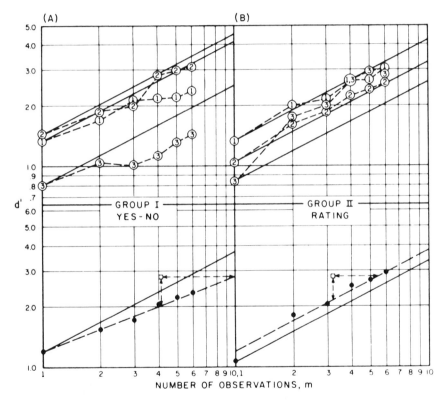

Figure 5.10 Value of d' versus number of observations m: individual results (above) and average result for three observers (below). (A) data from observers trained with a yes–no response, and (B) data from observers trained with a rating response. Solid lines are fitted to the point at $m = 1$ with a slope of one-half, to represent the OI model. Darkened circles represent data from a condition in which all trials have a fixed m; the two squares represent data from a condition in which the observers terminated each trial at will. (Reproduced from Swets and Birdsall 1967.)

improved at a rate of $d' = m^{1/2}$, whereas the yes–no group improved at a lower rate, one generally consistent with the predictions shown in Figure 5.5. Furthermore, the rating group reached given error rates in fewer observations. An analysis of response criteria, however, showed that the yes–no group did not follow the union-rule version of the DC model.

Concerning the process of termination as separate from the accumulation process, it was found that the observers did not predetermine the termination stage in advance of making an observation; rather, they used sensory information obtained sequentially throughout a trial. In a related result, the economy of the sequential-analysis, or deferred-decision, procedure—relative to the procedure with a fixed number of intervals—was evidenced by approximately a 50% savings in the number of observations required to reach a given error probability. This result is indicated by the open-square data point in Figure 5.10 relative to the curve fitted there to the closed circles.

In an analysis of decision boundaries, or response criteria, the observers were shown to use boundaries that were stable for a few observations and then converged in anticipation of the maximum number of observations allowed on each trial; in this manner, they followed qualitatively the optimal process. In a final analysis, the observers were seen to respond appropriately to changes in the prior probability of a signal. When this probability was offset one way or the other from .50, they took fewer observations to respond in favor of the more likely stimulus alternative and more observations to respond in favor of the less likely alternative.

Temporal Uncertainty

A model incorporating both temporal accumulation and temporal uncertainty is discussed in the following. Then considered are models for temporal uncertainty with observation intervals defined. Lastly, several models for temporal uncertainty in the *free-response* situation, in which observation intervals and trials are undefined, are considered.

Accumulation and Uncertainty

Kinchla (1969) developed a model for an experimental paradigm proposed by Schreitmueller (Note 13; see also Swets, *et al.*, 1959): Any of several observation intervals of a trial may contain a signal; and at the conclusion of the trial, the observer states whether or not at least one of the intervals did. In other terms, either 0 or $y = 1, \ldots m$ of m intervals actually contain a signal; the observer responds "no" for 0 signals and "yes" for y signals.

Kinchla followed the uncertainty and integration models discussed earlier in this chapter and suggested that d' would decrease as $m^{1/2}$ increased and increase as $y^{1/2}$ increased. He went further in allowing the ratio of the standard deviations of the signal and noise distributions (denoted b) to vary. The model was found consistent with the data over a wide range of m and y values. A second experiment fixed $y = 1$, let m assume the values 1, 3, and 6 in three separate conditions, and varied signal probability across groups of trials within those conditions. Here, focusing on temporal uncertainty, the empirical ROC curves were predicted exceptionally well with regard to both the sensitivity parameter (d') and the slope parameter (b).

Uncertainty with Defined Observation Intervals

Green and Weber (1980) devised a trial structure in which each of two observation periods contained either 1, 5, or 10 separate observation intervals. One or the other of the two observation periods contained one signal on every trial, and the observer selected one of the two observation periods. Five models were considered, three based on a discrete sensory model and two based on a continuous sensory model. One was a high-threshold model with the union rule for decision combination of both hits and false alarms. Another was a two-state model with a provision for counting the detect states and choosing the observation period with the greatest number. A third model was a one-parameter version of the discrete model that assumed equal error rates. One continuous model was the optimal signal detection model based on Nolte and Jaarsma's (1967) calculations, and the other was a one-parameter version of Luce's (1959) choice theory. The two continuous models and the one-parameter discrete model failed to fit the data acceptably. The remaining discrete models provided good fits, though using one more parameter.

Undefined Observation Intervals and Trials

In an experimental paradigm that has evolved to represent certain aspects of realistic detection settings, signals are presented in quantities and at times that are not made known to the observer, and the observer makes a positive response whenever he or she chooses. Thus, the only data available are the two time series of signal and response. A problem is therefore posed for the experimenter who desires to categorize responses as hits or false alarms in the interests of plotting an ROC and obtaining a measure of detectability that is independent of the observer's decision criterion.

Egan, Greenberg, and Schulman (1961) identified the problem and offered the first of the four or five models that have been proposed as solutions. Their approach was to determine rates of responding in two time intervals associated with each signal presentation—one interval immediately after the signal's occurrence and the other longer after the signal's occurrence but before the next signal—and to regard these response rates as proportional to the probabilities of hits and false alarms, respectively. They demonstrated that the relationship between these two response rates, as the observer's decision criterion varies, is described by a power function. They treated this power function as a form of ROC curve, and derived from it a detection index (d_s or d'_e) often associated with empirical ROC curves. Strong support for the model came from their finding, in an undefined-trials experiment, that this index is linearly related to the detection-theory measure of signal-to-noise ratio (E/N_0, see Green & Swets, 1966/1974), as it is in experiments with defined trials.

Watson and Nichols (1976) chose to estimate the hit and false-alarm probabilities from response latencies rather than response rates. They obtained one latency density function for the first response following a signal and a second such function for the first response following randomly selected instances of background noise. Detection performance was indexed by the maximum separation between the two overlapping functions, with a value of d' calculated much as it is for discrete responses in a defined-trials paradigm. Empirical values of d' so calculated were found to be about 2 db greater than values of d' obtained in defined-trials experiments—a result in agreement with a finding by Egan et al. (1961).

Egan et al. had assumed that the observer quantizes time into a series of subjective observation intervals of constant length, after each of which a decision is made. Watson and Nichols (1976) avoided that assumption. Lucas (1967) emphasized that the assumption of Egan et al. was one of subjective intervals synchronized with the signal-generation process and proposed to remove the assumption of synchronous observation. He developed an asynchronous extension of signal detection theory, according to which the observer obtains an average value of likelihood ratio over some time period t, by summing the information in all values of likelihood ratio for t seconds in the past. In his model, certain statistical properties of that average likelihood ratio are related to three observable response variables: (1) the probability distribution of interresponse intervals for long periods of noise alone; (2) the probability of a response in a given time interval, equal to the duration of the signal, when noise alone is present; and (3) the probability of a response while the signal is present. These relations may be used to generate a form of ROC curve.

Luce (1966) proposed a way of separating sensitivity from response bias in the free-response paradigm that does not attempt to estimate hit and false-alarm probabilities. It is based on a two-state threshold model of sensory information, and derives signal-induced and noise-induced sensitivity parameters from analysis of observed distributions of interresponse and signal-response times. Green and Luce (1967) conducted experiments to test the model and exposed needed changes in both the model and the experimental procedure. These changes were pursued by Luce and Green (1970) and Green and Luce (1971). The main procedural change was to keep each signal on until a response was made, thus approximating a reaction-time paradigm. Continuing problems for the model include an inability to solve for the distribution of times associated with residual processes after assumptions are made about sensory and decision times, and unaccountable differences in results obtained with the weak signals of the detection task and the strong signals of the reaction-time task. However, the experiments did provide estimates of the ratios of Poisson signal and noise parameters and showed their regular growth with signal intensity.

Long Watches

Long periods of observation, measured in hours, occur in military vigils for signals of the enemy and in industrial monitoring for defects in products. Broadbent (1971) gives an excellent review of vigilance concepts and research, and Mackie (1977) has collected 35 papers from a conference on the subject. Drury and Fox (1975) have presented 20 papers from a conference on industrial monitoring.

The basic mathematical models applied to long watches are the two that have been applied generally to detection or discrimination. Taking historical precedence was the high-threshold model, which allows consideration of the probability of a true-positive response, $p(\text{TP})$, as the only datum and as an index of sensitivity. Serving to call attention to vigilance as a worthy psychological problem was the result that this probability decreased markedly with time on watch, even for relatively short watches (Mackworth, 1948). The subsequent application of signal detection theory considered $p(\text{TP})$ in relation to the probability of a false-positive response, $p(\text{FP})$, and thereby provided independent indices of sensitivity and of the decision or response criterion. In later experiments, the drop in $p(\text{TP})$ was seen to be accompanied by a drop in $p(\text{FP})$, implicating an increasing conservatism of the response criterion as a substantial factor in the decline of $p(\text{TP})$ (Broadbent & Gregory, 1963; Mackworth & Taylor, 1963). A minority of experiments showed a decline in sensitivity as well as an increasing conservatism of the response criterion. These experiments were identified by Parasuraman and Davies (1977) and Parasuraman (1979) as having both a high event rate and successive presentation of the events to be discriminated. (See a further discussion in Parasuraman's chapter in this volume.)

An aspect of detection theory that can be used in modeling the observed change in the decision criterion is the expected-value definition of the optimal decision criterion. According to this definition, the optimal value of the decision criterion, β, is related to the prior probabilities of signal, $p(s)$, and noise, $p(n)$, and to the values and costs of true- and false-positive responses, $V(\text{TP})$ and $C(\text{FP})$, and true- and false-negative responses, $V(\text{TN})$ and $C(\text{FN})$, by the formula

$$\beta = \frac{p(n)}{p(s)} \left[\frac{V(\text{TN}) + C(\text{FP})}{V(\text{TP}) + C(\text{FN})} \right] .$$

The main thing to note in relation to the vigilance findings just reviewed is that β will decrease—that is, the criterion will become more conservative—as $p(s)$ declines. It is easy to imagine that the observer's estimate of $p(s)$ declines during an experimental session. Less clear is the possibility that the observer's response values and costs when a signal is present (denominator) decline relative to those when no signal is present (numerator). However, Smith (1968) proposed a model in which the average cost of a decision is a linear sum of the probability densities of noise alone and signal plus noise that underlie the ROC curve. The cost function is thus bimodal with maxima at the means of the distributions. Smith assumes that observers try to reduce cost over time in a vigilance situation and so accounts for the finding of Broadbent and Gregory (1963) that cautious criteria (greater than the mean of the signal distribution) become more cautious, whereas lax criteria (between the means) do not.

An interest in controlling the observer's criterion arises in the military-vigilance setting because commanders would probably like that criterion at least to be constant if not appropriately adjusted to the threat at hand. This interest in the industrial-monitoring setting arises obviously from the desire to establish the criterion that will satisfy management's specific objectives for the quality of the product.

Signal probability was manipulated in vigilance studies by Baddeley and Colquhoun (1969), Williges (1969, 1971, 1973), and Johnston, Howell, and Williges (1969), and in monitoring studies by Murrell (1975), Fox and Haslegrave (1969), Drury and Addison (1973), Zunzanyika and Drury (1975), Smith and Barany (1970), and Embrey (1975). I have summarized these studies elsewhere (Swets, 1977) and concluded that the observer changes his or her criterion in an appropriate direction as signal probability changes, that he or she approaches the optimal value for moderate optima, and that he or she shies away (as in ordinary detection studies, Green and Swets, 1966/1974) from extreme optima.

Values and costs of correct and incorrect responses were manipulated in vigilance studies by Levine (1966), Davenport (1968, 1969), Williges (1971), and Guralnick (1972), and in a monitoring environment by Smith and Barany (1970). In my earlier review (Swets 1977), I observed that the first three of these studies showed a substantial and appropriate effect, and the last three studies showed either a weak effect or no effect. Values, I think, are harder to instill (particularly in an artificial setting) and harder to change (particularly in a realistic setting).

Jerison, Pickett, and Stenson (1965) devised a model that described three types of vigilance observing in terms of their typical values of d' and β. One is *alert observing*, having the d' and β of a standard psychophysical experiment; the second is *blurred observing*, having a lower d'; and the third is *distraction*, having a very high β. They showed how various mixtures of these observing modes were consistent with different results in their several experimental conditions. Perhaps this approach will provide a response to a question recently directed to a colleague of mine. A letter to him from a research laboratory read in full: "May we have your opinion on the question: 'What percent of the time is a person inattentive to his or her task?' Your response would be greatly appreciated."

Multiple Complex Tasks

Were this chapter to be self-contained, there would now be a concluding section as large and full as any of the preceding ones. Such a section is unnecessary, however, because the material it would cover is covered very well by two other chapters in this volume (those by Wickens and Moray). This material is, however, briefly characterized here, with constructive references to the other two chapters. Those chapters, for the most part, treat two separate lines of work that we would consider together in the context of this chapter.

One line of work on multiple complex tasks traces back to Senders's (1955, 1964) papers on the sampling of information sources by human monitors. The theme of his models and experiments is that sources are attended to for amounts of time in proportion to the amount of information (or the bandwidth) they provide.

These ideas about sampling behavior were brought together with models for manual control (for example, of aircraft), and applied to tasks in which sampling behavior was influenced by control consequences, by Senders, Elkind, Grignetti, and Smallwood (Note 14), Carbonell (1966), Carbonell, Ward, and Senders (1968). An extension of this development is represented by applications of optimal control theory in the articles of Baron and Kleinman (1969), Levison, Baron, and Kleinman (1969), and Levison, Elkind, and Ward (Note 15). Levison (1979) reviewed the decade of research with emphasis on time-sharing of attention among control and noncontrol tasks, or capacity sharing, and presented a model of mental workload.

Sheridan (1970) focused on the division of attention between sampling and control functions in his treatment of supervisory control (for example, of a power plant). He brought to bear Howard's (1966) concept of information value and the economic concepts of decision theory, and developed a model centered on the payoff or expected value of the supervisor's decisions (see also Kiguchi & Sheridan, 1979; Tulga & Sheridan, 1980). Other research of this type was reported by Kvålseth (1977, 1979). In the general picture that has evolved (Moray, 1976), the system operator uses probabilities and values in establishing response strategies that govern the decisions he or she makes about signal data obtained from observations and also about when and where to observe, with the goal of predicting and adapting well enough to reduce reaction time and information-processing load. Some papers in this field appear in a volume edited by Sheridan and Johannsen (1976).

The line of work just described is relatively unfamiliar to psychologists because it is being conducted by engineering psychologists whose basic training is in engineering and who publish in engineering journals. Moray has sought diligently to bridge the gap and does so in Chapter 13 of this volume.

A related body of work, conducted by experimental psychologists and reported for psychologists, is reviewed in Chapter 3 of this volume by Wickens. Newer and less extensive, these studies are similar in using a tracking task as the basic task and in assessing the effects on tracking performance of attention given to a second task (Wickens, 1976, 1980; Wickens & Gopher, 1977; Navon & Gopher, 1979, 1980). They are also similar in giving economic concepts a central position in the models. The strong focus on dual-task performance and resource allocation has led to extensive use of the POC, advanced by Norman and Bobrow (1975). The POC is closely related to the AOC discussed in this chapter and by Sperling (Chapter 4, this volume).

Conclusions

There are many more mathematical models of attention than I, for one, had surmised. But it will be more useful to observe that despite their large number, they hang together rather well. A few basic concepts serve to organize most of the material.

For selective attention, the working concept is that of a filter, channel, or band of attention. Converging operations exist to give it meaning. Thus, in certain settings, one can measure the degree of attentiveness that characterizes a given band, the width of a band, the scanning speed or switching rate when only single bands are maximally sensitive, the relative allocation of attentiveness to competing bands, and the numbers and locations of individual bands that are yoked effectively to widen the range of attentiveness.

Ample evidence indicates that the observer will sometimes work with a single band. My conjecture is that the observer is most likely to do so when attempting to make fine distinctions (detect weak signals) within a single band, and that doing so is at bottom a matter of choice. Attending at once to multiple bands is clearly possible and is no doubt the process of choice when interesting stimuli are spread across several bands, which they usually are.

Given the observer's desire and ability to attend to several bands, the second fundamental concept is that of the aggregation of stimulus information in different bands. This concept takes on added scope because one can think in the same way of the aggregation of stimulus information over time and thus make a link to sustained attention. However, on asserting the centrality of this concept, it must be granted that there is not as yet a satisfactory handle on it.

There are two classes of aggregation models, decision combination and observation integration, and no standard and good way to pit them against each other. For 25 years researchers have tried primarily to distinguish these models by their predicted rates of growth, but it should be acknowledged that almost any rate can probably occur under either mode depending on a host of conditions and that almost any rate can probably be modeled under either mode given a second parameter. My current hope, not backed by demonstration, is that analysis of the different response criteria implied by the different models will give a sharper test. Issues of continuity versus discontinuity have persisted throughout the study of sensory processing more generally, and they may be no easier to resolve in the study of attention.

The last two sections of this chapter indicate that the ideas of probability and utility, as united in decision theory, can play a modeling role in attention as they have in sensory processing. Decision theory may therefore qualify as the third of the organizing concepts in the material reviewed here. Admittedly, it was not much of a thread through the first three sections, but this is a deficit that could be corrected. I believe it would pay to keep an eye on the lines of research characterized here in the two main sections preceding this one, especially in the section entitled "Multiple Complex Tasks," for leads that may be useful in other lines. Such a tactic would coincide well with increasing interest in the control processes, as opposed to the structural components, of attention.

Acknowledgments

I dedicate this chapter to the memory of Wilson P. Tanner, Jr.

I appreciate the counsel of Raja Parasuraman, readings of a draft by David M. Green and Ronald A. Kinchla, a helpful conversation with William P. Banks, manuscript preparation by Mildred C. Webster, and copyediting by Judith R. Harris. My appreciation is also due the 20 or so active investigators who responded to my request for reprints of their relevant articles. Preparation of this chapter was supported by Bolt Beranek and Newman Inc.'s Science Development Program.

Reference Notes

1. Tanner, W. P., Jr., Swets, J. A., and Green, D. M. Some general properties of the hearing mechanism (Tech. Rep. 30). Ann Arbor, Mich.: University of Michigan, 1956.
2. Marill, T. Psychophysics and signal detection theory (Tech. Rep. 319). Cambridge, Massachusetts: Massachusetts Institute of Technology, 1956.
3. Swets, J. A. A psychophysical approach to wavelength analysis. Paper presented at a meeting of the Eastern Psychological Association, New York, April 15 and 16, 1960.

4. Swets, J. A. *Signal detection by human observers: Color vision* (Quarterly Progress Report No. 51). Cambridge, Mass.: Research Laboratory of Electronics, Massachusetts Institute of Technology, April 15, 1960, pp. 127–136.
5. Tanner, W. P., Jr. *Visual detection when location is not known exactly.* Unpublished Manuscript, 1955.
6. Kristofferson, A. B. Personal communication, December, 1981.
7. Kinchla, R. A. *An attention operating characteristic in vision* (Tech. Rep. 29). Hamilton, Ontario, Canada: McMaster University, Department of Psychology, 1969.
8. Birdsall, T. G. Unpublished research, 1955.
9. Gardner, G. T. *Spatial processing characteristics in the perception of brief visual arrays* (Tech. Rep. 23). Ann Arbor: University of Michigan, 1970.
10. Kinchla, R. A. *"Figure–ground" processing in vision: An organizational operating characteristic* (Research Rep. 22). Princeton N.J.: Princeton University, Department of Psychology, 1978.
11. Howard, J. H., Jr., Ballas, J. A., & Burgy, D. C. *Feature extraction and decision processes in the classification of amplitude-modulated noise patterns.* (Tech. Rep. ONR-78-4). Washington, D.C.: The Catholic University of America, Human Performance Laboratory, 1978.
12. Schafer, T. H., & Shewmaker, C. A. *A comparative study of the audio, visual and audio–visual recognition differentials for pulses masked by random noise* (Tech. Rep. 372). San Diego, Calif.: U.S. Naval Electronics Laboratory, 1953.
13. Schreitmueller, R. F. *Effect of repeated presentations on the detection of signals in noise.* Unpublished master's thesis, Massachusetts Institute of Technology, 1952.
14. Senders, J. W., Elkind, J. I., Grignetti, M. E., & Smallwood, R. D. *An investigation of the visual sampling behavior of human observers* (Report No. 434). Washington, D.C.: National Aeronautics and Space Administration, 1966.
15. Levison, W. H., Elkind, J. I., & Ward, J. L. *Studies of multi-variable manual control systems: A model for task interference* (Report No. CR-1746). Washington, D.C.: National Aeronautics and Space Administration, May 1971.

References

Allan, L. G. Second guesses and the attention-switching model for successiveness discrimination. *Perception & Psychophysics,* 1975, *17*(1), 65–68.
Allan, L. G., & Kristofferson, A. B. Successiveness discrimination: Two models. *Perception & Psychophysics,* 1974, *15*(1), 37–46.
Baddeley, A. D., & Colquhoun, W. P. Signal probability and vigilance: A reappraisal of the "signal-rate" effect. *British Journal of Psychology,* 1969, *60*(2), 169–178.
Ball, K., & Sekuler, R. Models of stimulus uncertainty in motion perception. *Psychological Review,* 1980, *87*(5), 435–469.
Ball, K., & Sekuler, R. Adaptive processing of visual motion. *Journal of Experimental Psychology: Human Perception and Performance,* 1981, *7,* 786–794. (a).
Ball, K., & Sekuler, R. Cues reduce direction uncertainty and enhance motion detection. *Perception & Psychophysics,* 1981, *30*(2), 119–128. (b)
Baron, J. The threshold for successiveness. *Perception & Psychophysics,* 1971, *10*(4A), 201–207.
Baron, J. Division of attention in successiveness discrimination. In S. Kornblum (Ed.), *Attention and performance IV.* New York: Academic Press, 1973, 703–711.
Baron, S., & Kleinman, D. L. The human as an optimal controller and information processor. *IEEE Transactions on Man–Machine Systems,* 1969, *MMS-10*(1), 9–17.

Bashinski, H. S., & Bacharach, V. R. Enhancement of perceptual sensitivity as the result of selectively attending to spatial locations. *Perception & Psychophysics,* 1980, *28*(3), 241–248.

Birdsall, T. G., & Gobien, J. O. Sufficient statistics and reproducing densities in simultaneous sequential detection and estimation. *IEEE Transactions on Information Theory,* 1973, *IT-19*(6), 760–768.

Birdsall, T. G., & Roberts, R. A. On the theory of signal detectability: An optimum nonsequential observation–decision procedure. *IEEE Transactions on Information Theory,* 1965, *IT-11*(2), 195–204. (a)

Birdsall, T. G., & Roberts, R. A. Theory of signal detectability: Deferred-decision theory. *Journal of the Acoustical Society of America,* 1965, *37*(6), 1064–1074. (b)

Bjork, E. L., & Estes, W. K. Detection and placement of redundant signal elements in tachistoscopic displays of letters. *Perception & Psychophysics,* 1971, *9*(5), 439–442.

Blake, R., & Fox, R. The psychophysical inquiry into binocular summation. *Perception & Psychophysics,* 1973, *14*(1), 161–185.

Broadbent, D. E. *Perception and communication.* New York: Pergamon, 1958.

Broadbent, D. E. *Decision and stress.* New York: Academic Press, 1971.

Broadbent, D. E., & Gregory, M. Division of attention and the decision theory of signal detection. *Proceedings of the Royal Society, B,* 1963, *158,* 222–231.

Carbonell, J. R. A queuing model of many-instrument visual sampling. *IEEE Transactions on Human Factors in Electronics,* 1966, *HFE-7*(4), 157–164.

Carbonell, J. R., Ward, J. L., & Senders, J. W. A queueing model of visual sampling: Experimental validation. *IEEE Transactions of Man–Machine Systems,* 1968, *MMS-9,* 82–87.

Cohn, T. E., & Lasley, D. J. Detectability of a luminance increment: Effect of spatial uncertainty. *Journal of the Optical Society of America,* 1974, *64*(12), 1715–1719.

Corcoran, D. W. J. Perceptual independence and recognition of two-dimensional auditory stimuli. *Journal of the Acoustical Society of America,* 1967, *42*(1), 139–142.

Craig, A., Colquhoun, W. D., & Corcoran, D. W. J. Combining evidence presented simultaneously to the eye and ear: A comparison of some predictive models. *Perception & Psychophysics,* 1976, *19*(6), 473–484.

Craig, J. C. Vibrotactile spatial summation. *Perception & Psychophysics,* 1968, *4*(6), 351–354.

Davenport, W. G. Auditory vigilance: The effects of costs and values on signals. *Australian Journal of Psychology,* 1968, *20,* 213–218.

Davenport, W. G. Vibrotactile vigilance: The effects of costs and values on signals. *Perception & Psychophysics,* 1969, *5*(1), 25–28.

Davis, E. T. Allocation of attention: Uncertainty effects when monitoring one or two visual gratings of noncontiguous spatial frequencies. *Perception & Psychophysics,* 1981, *29*(6), 618–622.

Davis, E. T., Kramer, P., & Graham, N. Uncertainty about spatial frequency, spatial position, or contrast of visual patterns. *Perception & Psychophysics,* 1983, *33*(1), 20–28.

Drury, C. G., & Addison, J. L. An industrial study of the effects of feedback and fault density on inspection performance. *Ergonomics,* 1973, *16,* 159–169.

Drury, C. G., & Fox, J. G., (Eds.) *Human reliability in quality control.* New York: Halsted, 1975.

Egan, J. P., Greenberg, G. Z., & Schulman, A. I. Operating characteristics, signal detectability, and the method of free response. *Journal of the Acoustical Society of America,* 1961, *33*(8), 993–1007.

Eijkman, E., & Vendrik, A. J. H. Can a sensory system be specified by its internal noise? *Journal of the Acoustical Society of America,* 1965, *37*(6), 1102–1109.

Elliott, P. B. Tables of *d'*. In J. A. Swets (Ed.), *Signal detection and recognition by human observers.* New York: Wiley, 1964, 651–684.

Embrey, D. E. Training the inspector's sensitivity and response strategy. In C. G. Drury and J. G. Fox (Eds.), *Human reliability and quality control.* New York: Halsted, 1975, 189–195.

Eriksen, C. W. Independence of successive inputs and uncorrelated error in visual form perception. *Journal of Experimental Psychology*, 1966, *72*, 26–35.

Eriksen, C. W., & Spencer, T. Rate of information processing in visual perception: Some results and methodological considerations. *Journal of Experimental Psychology Monograph*, 1969, *79*(2), 1–16.

Estes, W. K. Interactions of signal and background variables in visual processing. *Perception & Psychophysics*, 1972, *12*(3), 278–286.

Estes, W. K., & Taylor, H. A. A detection method and probabilistic models for assessing information processing from brief visual displays. *Proceedings of the National Academy of Sciences*, 1964, *52*(2), 446–454.

Estes, W. K., & Taylor, H. A. Visual detection in relation to display size and redundancy of critical elements. *Perception & Psychophysics*, 1965, *1*, 9–16.

Estes, W. K., & Wessel, D. L. Reaction time in relation to display size and correctness of response in forced-choice visual signal detection. *Perception & Psychophysics*, 1966, *1*, 369–373.

Fidell, S. A. Sensory function in multimodal signal detection. *Journal of the Acoustical Society of America*, 1970, *47*(4), 1009–1015.

Fidell, S. A. Comments on "Multimodal signal detection: Independent decisions vs. integration." *Perception & Psychophysics*, 1982, *31*(1), 90.

Fletcher, H. Auditory patterns. *Review of Modern Physics*, 1940, *12*, 47–65.

Fox, J. G., & Haslegrave, C. M. Industrial inspection efficiency and the probability of a defect occurring. *Ergonomics*, 1969, *12*, 5, 713–721.

Franzén, O., Markowitz, J., & Swets, J. A. Spatially-limited attention to vibrotactile stimulation. *Perception & Psychophysics*, 1970, *7*(4), 193–196.

Gardner, G. T. Evidence for independent parallel channels in tachistoscopic perception. *Cognitive Psychology*, 1973, *4*, 130–155.

Getty, D. J., Swets, J. A., Swets, J. B., & Green, D. M. On the prediction of confusion matrices from similarity judgments. *Perception & Psychophysics*, 1979, *26*(1), 1–19.

Getty, D. J., Swets, J. B., & Swets, J. A. The observer's use of perceptual dimensions in signal identification. In R. S. Nickerson (Ed.), *Attention and performance VIII*. Hillsdale, N.J.: Erlbaum, 1980, 361–380.

Gilliom, J. D., & Sorkin, R. D. Sequential vs. simultaneous two-channel signal detection: More evidence for a high-level interrupt theory. *Journal of the Acoustical Society of America*, 1974, *56*(1), 157–164.

Graham, N. Visual detection of aperiodic spatial stimuli by probability summation among narrowband channels. *Vision Research*, 1977, *17*, 637–652.

Green, D. M. Detection of multiple component signals in noise. *Journal of the Acoustical Society of America*, 1958, *30*(1), 904–911.

Green, D. M. Detection of auditory sinusoids of uncertain frequency. *Journal of the Acoustical Society of America*, 1961, *33*(7), 897–903.

Green, D. M., & Birdsall, T. G. Detection and recognition. *Psychological Review*, 1978, *85*(3), 192–206.

Green, D. M., Birdsall, T. G., & Tanner, W. P., Jr. Signal detection as a function of signal intensity and duration, *Journal of the Acoustical Society of America*, 1957, *29*(4), 523–531.

Green, D. M., McKey, M. J., & Licklider, J. C. R. Detection of a pulsed sinusoid in noise as a function of frequency. *Journal of the Acoustical Society of America*, 1959, *31*(11), 1446–1452.

Green, D. M., & Luce, R. D. Detection of auditory signals presented at random times. *Perception & Psychophysics*, 1967, *2*(1), 441–450.

Green, D. M., & Luce, R. D. Detection of auditory signals presented at random times: III. *Perception & Psychophysics*, 1971, *9*(3A), 257–268.

Green, D. M., & Luce, R. D. Variability of magnitude estimates: A timing theory analysis. *Perception & Psychophysics*, 1974, *15*(2), 291–300.

Green, D. M., & Swets, J. A. *Signal Detection Theory and Psychophysics*. Huntington, N.Y.: Krieger, 1974. (Originally published, New York: Wiley, 1966.)

Green, D. M., & Weber, D. L. Detection of temporally uncertain signals. *Journal of the Acoustical Society of America*, 1980, *67*(4), 1304–1311.

Green, D. M., Weber, D. L., & Duncan, J. E. Detection and recognition of pure tones in noise. *Journal of the Acoustical Society of America*, 1977, *62*(4), 948–954.

Greenberg, G. Z. Frequency-selection detection at three signal amplitudes. *Perception & Psychophysics*, 1969a, *6*(5), 297–301.

Greenberg, G. Z. Frequency selectivity during amplitude discrimination of signals in noise. *Journal of the Acoustical Society of America*, 1969b, *45*(6), 1438–1442.

Greenberg, G. Z., & Larkin, W. D. Frequency-response characteristic of auditory observers detecting signals of a single frequency in noise: The probe-signal method. *Journal of the Acoustical Society of America*, 1968, *44*(6), 1513–1523.

Greenhouse, D. S., & Cohn, T. E. Effect of chromatic uncertainty on detectability of a visual stimulus. *Journal of the Optical Society of America*, 1978, *68*(2), 266–267.

Guralnick, M. M. Observing responses and decision processes in vigilance. *Journal of Experimental Psychology*, 1972, *93*(2), 239–244.

Guth, S. L. Nonadditivity and inhibition among chromatic luminances at threshold. *Vision Research*, 1967, *7*, 319–328.

Guth, S. L., Donley, N. J., & Marrocco, R. T. On luminance additivity and related topics. *Vision Research*, 1969, *9*, 537–575.

Harris, J. R., Shaw, M. L., & Bates, M. Visual search in multicharacter arrays with and without gaps. *Perception & Psychophysics*, 1979, *26*(1), 69–84.

Howard, R. A. Information value theory. *IEEE Transactions on Systems Sciences and Cybernetics*, 1966, *SSC-2*, 22–26.

Jerison, H. J., Pickett, R. M., & Stenson, H. H. The elicited observing rate and decision processes in vigilance. *Human Factors*, 1965, *7*, 107–128.

Johnson, D. M., & Hafter, E. R. Uncertain-frequency detection: Cuing and condition of observation. *Perception & Psychophysics*, 1980, *28*(3), 143–149.

Johnston, W. A., Howell, W. C., & Williges, R. C. The components of complex monitoring. *Organizational Behavior & Human Performance*, 1969, *4*, 112–114.

Kalsbeek, J. W. H., & Sykes, R. N. Objective measurement of mental load. *Acta Psychologica*, 1967, *27*, 253–261.

Kiguchi, T., & Sheridan, T. B. Criteria for selecting measures of plant information with application to nuclear reactors. *IEEE Transactions on Systems, Man, and Cybernetics*, 1979, *SMC-9*(4), 165–175.

Kinchla, R. A. Temporal and channel uncertainty in detection: A multiple observation analysis. *Perception & Psychophysics*, 1969, *5*(3), 129–136.

Kinchla, R. A. Detecting target elements in multielement arrays: A confusability model. *Perception & Psychophysics*, 1974, *15*(1), 149–158.

Kinchla, R. A. The role of structural redundancy in the perception of visual targets. *Perception & Psychophysics*, 1977, *22*(1), 19–30.

Kinchla, R. A. The measurement of attention. In R. S. Nickerson (Ed.), *Attention and performance VIII*. Hillsdale, N.J.: Erlbaum, 1980, 213–237.

Kinchla, R. A., & Collyer, C. E. Detecting a target letter in briefly presented arrays: A confidence rating analysis in terms of a weighted additive effects model. *Perception & Psychophysics*, 1974, *16*(1), 117–122.

Kristofferson, A. B. Attention and psychophysical time. *Acta Psychologica*, 1967a, *27*, 93–100.

Kristofferson, A. B. Successiveness discrimination as a two-state quantal process. *Science*, 1967b, *158*, 1337–1339.

Kristofferson, A. B., & Allan, L. G. Successiveness and duration discrimination. In S. Kornblum (Ed.), *Attention and performance IV*. New York: Academic Press, 1973, 737–749.

Kvålseth, T. O. A decision-theoretic model of the sampling behavior of the human process monitor. *IEEE Transactions on Systems, Man, and Cybernetics*, 1977, *SMC-7*, 810–813.

Kvålseth, T. O. A decision-theoretic model of the sampling behavior of the human process monitor: Experimental evaluation. *Human Factors*, 1979, *21*(6), 671–686.

Laming, D. *Mathematical psychology*. New York: Academic Press, 1973.

Levine, J. M. The effects of values and costs on the detection and identification of signals in auditory vigilance. *Human Factors*, 1966, *8*, 525–537.

Levison, W. H. A model for mental workload in tasks requiring continuous information processing. In N. Moray (Ed.), *Mental workload: Its theory and measurement*, New York: Plenum, 1979, 189–219.

Levison, W. H., Baron, S., & Kleinman, D. L. A model for human controller remnant. *IEEE Transactions on Man–Machine Systems* 1969, *MMS-10*, 4, 9–17.

Lindsay, P. H., Taylor, M. M., & Forbes, S. M. Attention and multidimensional discrimination. *Perception & Psychophysics*, 1968, *4*(2), 113–117.

Loveless, N. E., Brebner, J., & Hamiltion, P. Bisensory presentation of information. *Psychological Bulletin*, 1970, *73*(3), 161–199.

Lucas, P. A. Human performance in low-signal-probability tasks. *Journal of the Acoustical Society of America*, 1967, *42*(1), 158–178.

Luce, R. D. *Individual choice behavior*. New York: Wiley, 1959, 58–67.

Luce, R. D. A model for detection in temporally unstructured experiments with a poisson distribution of signal presentations. *Journal of Mathematical Psychology*, 1966, *3*, 48–64.

Luce, R. D., & Green, D. M. Detection of auditory signals presented at random times: II. *Perception & Psychophysics*, 1970, *7*(1), 1–14.

Luce, R. D., & Green, D. M. Two tests of a neural attention hypothesis for auditory psychophysics. *Perception & Psychophysics*, 1978, *23*(5), 363–371.

Lupker, S. J., & Massaro, D. W. Selective perception without confounding contributions of decision and memory. *Perception & Psychophysics*, 1979, *25*(1), 60–69.

Mackie, R. R. (Ed.) *Vigilance: Theory, operational performance, and psychological correlates*. New York: Plenum, 1977.

Mackworth, J. F., & Taylor, M. M. The *d'* measure of signal detectability in vigilance-like situations. *Canadian Journal of Psychology*, 1963, *17*(3), 302–325.

Mackworth, N. H. The breakdown of vigilance during prolonged visual search. *Quarterly Journal of Experimental Psychology*, 1948, *1*, 6–21.

Macmillan, N. A., & Schwartz, M. A probe-signal investigation of uncertain-frequency detection. *Journal of the Acoustical Society of America*, 1975, *58*(5), 1051–1058.

Massaro, D. W., & Kahn, B. J. Effects of central processing on auditory recognition. *Journal of Experimental Psychology*, 1973, *97*(1), 51–58.

Massaro, D. W., & Warner, D. S. Dividing attention between auditory and visual perception. *Perception & Psychophysics*, 1977, *21*(6), 569–574.

Moray, N. Time sharing in auditory perception: Effect of stimulus duration. *Journal of the Acoustical Society of America*, 1970, *47*(2), 660–661.

Moray, N. Attention, control, and sampling behavior. In T. Sheridan and G. Johannsen (Eds.), *Monitoring behavior and supervisory control*. New York: Plenum, 1976, 221–244.

Moray, N., Fitter, M. Ostry, D., Favreau, D., & Nagy, V. Attention to pure tones. *Quarterly Journal of Experimental Psychology*, 1976, *28*, 271–283.

Mulligan, R. M., & Shaw, M. L. Multimodal signal detection: Independent decisions vs. integration. *Perception & Psychophysics,* 1980, *28*(5), 471–478.

Murrell, G. A. A reappraisal of artificial signals as an aid to a visual monitoring task. *Ergonomics,* 1975, *18,* 693–700.

Navon, D., & Gopher, D. On the economy of the human-processing system. *Psychological Review,* 1979, *86*(3), 214–255.

Navon, D., & Gopher, D. Task difficulty, resources, and dual-task performance. In R. S. Nickerson (Ed.), *Attention and performance VIII.* Hillsdale, N.J.: Erlbaum, 1980, 297–315.

Nolte, L. W. Theory of signal detectability: Adaptive optimum receiver design. *Journal of the Acoustical Society of America,* 1967, *42*(4), 773–777.

Nolte, L. W., & Jaarsma, D. More on the detection of one of *M* orthogonal signals. *Journal of the Acoustical Society of America,* 1967, *41*(2), 497–505.

Norman, D. A., & Bobrow, D. G. On data-limited and resource-limited processes. *Cognitive Psychology,* 1975, *7,* 44–64.

Ostry, D., Moray, N., & Marks, G. Attention, practice, and semantic targets. *Journal of Experimental Psychology,* 1976, *2*(3), 326–336.

Parasuraman, R. Memory load and event rate control sensitivity decrements in sustained attention. *Science,* 1979, *205,* 924–927.

Parasuraman, R., & Davies, D. R. In R. R. Mackie (Ed.), *Vigilance: Theory, operational performance, and physiological correlates.* New York: Plenum, 1977, 559–574.

Pastore, R. E., & Sorkin, R. D. Adaptive auditory signal processing. *Psychonomic Science,* 1971, *23*(4), 259–260.

Pastore, R. E., & Sorkin, R. D. Simultaneous two-channel signal detection. I: Simple binaural stimuli. *Journal of the Acoustical Society of America,* 1972, *51*(2), 544–551.

Patterson, R. D. Auditory filter shape. *Journal of the Acoustical Society of America,* 1974, *55*(4), 802–809.

Patterson, R. D. Auditory filter shapes derived with noise stimuli. *Journal of the Acoustical Society of America,* 1976, *59*(3), 640–654.

Patterson, R. D., & Henning, G. B. Stimulus variability and auditory filter shape. *Journal of the Acoustical Society of America,* 1977, *62*(3), 649–664.

Pirenne, M. H. Binocular and uniocular thresholds in vision. *Nature,* 1943, *152,* 698–699.

Pollack, I. On the combination of intensity and frequency differences in auditory discrimination. *Journal of the Acoustical Society of America,* 1961, *33*(8), 1141–1142.

Posner, M. I., Nissen, M. J., & Ogden, W. C. Attended and unattended processing modes: The role of set for spatial location. In H. I. Pick, Jr. & E. Saltzman (Eds.), *Modes of perceiving and processing information.* Hillsdale, N.J.: Erlbaum, 1978, 137–157.

Puelo, J. S., & Pastore, R. E. Critical-band effects in two-channel auditory signal detection. *Journal of Experimental Psychology, Human Perception and Performance,* 1978, *4*(1), 153–163.

Regan, D. Visual information channeling in normal and disordered vision. *Psychological Review,* 1982, *89*(4), 407–444.

Rumelhart, D. E. A multicomponent theory of the perception of briefly exposed visual displays. *Journal of Mathematical Psychology,* 1970, *7,* 191–218.

Sachs, N. B., Nachmias, J., & Robson, J. G. Spatial-frequency channels in human vision. *Journal of the Optical Society of America,* 1971, *61*(9), 1176–1186.

Schafer, T. H., & Gales, R. S. Auditory masking of multiple tones by random noise. *Journal Acoustical Society of America,* 1949, *21*(3), 392–398.

Schafer, T. H., Gales, R. S. Shewmaker, C. A., & Thompson, P. O. The frequency selectivity of the ear as determined by masking experiments. *Journal of the Acoustical Society of America,* 1950, *22*(4), 490–496.

Schmidt, M. W., & Kristofferson, A. B. Discrimination of successiveness: A test of a model of attention. *Science*, 1963, *139*, 112–113.

Sekuler, R., & Ball, K. Mental set alters visibility of moving targets. *Science*, 1977, *198*, 60–62.

Senders, J. W. Man's capacity to use information from complex displays. In H. Quastler (Ed.), *Information theory in psychology*. Glencoe, Ill.: Free Press, 1955.

Senders, J. W. The human operator as a monitor and controller of multidegree of freedom systems. *IEEE Human Factors in Electronics*, 1964, *HFE-5*, 2–5.

Shaw, M. L. A capacity allocation model for reaction time. *Journal of Experimental Psychology: Human Perception and Performance*, 1978, *4*(4), 586–598.

Shaw, M. L. Identifying attentional and decision-making components in information processing. In R. S. Nickerson (Ed.), *Attention and performance VIII*. Hillsdale, N.J.: Erlbaum, 1980, 277–295.

Shaw, M. L., & Mulligan, R. M. Models for bimodal signal detection: A reply to Fidell. *Perception & Psychophysics*, 1982, *31*(1), 91–92.

Shaw, M. L., & Shaw, P. Optimal allocation of cognitive resources to spatial locations. *Journal of Experimental Psychology: Human Perception and Performance*, 1977, *3*(3), 201–211.

Sheridan, T. On how often the supervisor should sample. *IEEE Transactions on Systems Sciences and Cybernetics*, 1970, *SCC-6*, 140–145.

Sheridan, T., & Johannsen, G. *Monitoring behavior and supervisory control*. New York: Plenum, 1976.

Shiffrin, R. M., Craig, J. C., & Cohen E. On the degree of attention and capacity limitation in tactile processing. *Perception & Psychophysics*, 1973, *13*(2), 328–336.

Shiffrin, R. M., Gardner, G. T., & Allmeyer, D. H. On the degree of attention and capacity limitations in visual processing. *Perception & Psychophysics*, 1973, *14*(2), 231–236.

Shiffrin, R. M., & Geisler, W. S. Visual recognition in a theory of information processing. In R. L. Solso (Ed.), *Contemporary issues in cognitive psychology: The Loyola Symposium*. New York: Halsted, 1973, 53–101.

Shiffrin, R. M., & Grantham, D. W. Can attention be allocated to sensory modalities? *Perception & Psychophysics*, 1974, *15*(3), 460–474.

Smith, L. A., & Barany, J. W. An elementary model of human performance on paced visual inspection tasks. *AIEE Transactions*, 1970, *2*(4), 298–308.

Smith, P. T. Cost, discriminability, and response bias. *British Journal of Mathematical and Statistical Psychology*, 1968, *21*, 35–60.

Sorkin, R. D., & Pohlmann, L. D. Some models of observer behavior in two-channel auditory signal detection. *Perception & Psychophysics*, 1973, *14*(1), 101–109.

Sorkin, R. D., Pohlman, L. D., & Gilliom, J. D. Simultaneous two-channel signal detection. III. 630- and 1400-Hz signals. *Journal of the Acoustical Society of America*, 1973, *53*(4), 1045–1050.

Sperling, G. The information available in brief visual presentations. *Psychological Monographs: General and Applied*, 1960, *74*(11), 1–29.

Sperling, G. A model for visual memory tasks. *Human Factors*, 1963, *5*, 19–31.

Sperling, G., & Melchner, M. J. The attention operating characteristic: Examples from visual search. *Science*, 1978, *202*, 315–318. (a)

Sperling, G., & Melchner, M. J. Visual search, visual attention, and the attention operating characteristic. In J. Requin (Ed.), *Attention and performance VII*. Hillsdale, N.J.: Erlbaum, 1978, 675–686. (b)

Spooner, R. L. Comparison of receiver performance: The ESP receiver. *Journal of the Acoustical Society of America*, 1969, *45*(1), 233–236.

Starr, S. J., Metz, C. E., Lusted, L. B., & Goodenough, D. J. Visual detection and localization of radiographic images. *Radiology*, 1975, *116*, 533–538.

Sternberg, S. High-speed scanning in human memory. *Science*, 1966, *153*, 652–654.
Stone, M. Models for choice–reaction time. *Psychometrika*, 1960, *25*, 251–260.
Swensson, R. G. A two-stage detection model applied to skilled visual search by radiologists. *Perception & Psychophysics*, 1980, *27*, 11–16.
Swensson, R. G., and Judy, P. F. Detection of noisy visual targets: Models for the effects of spatial uncertainty and signal-to-noise ratio. *Perception & Psychophysics*, 1981, *29*(6), 521–534.
Swets, J. A. Central factors in auditory frequency selectivity. *Psychological Bulletin*, 1963, *60*(5), 429–440.
Swets, J. A. Signal detection theory applied to vigilance. In R. R. Mackie (Ed.), *Vigilance: Relationships among theory, physiological correlates and operational performance*. New York: Plenum, 1977, 705–718.
Swets, J. A., and Birdsall, T. G. The human use of information, III: Decision-making in signal detection and recognition situations involving multiple alternatives. *Transactions of the Institute of Radio Engineers, Professional Group on Information Theory*, 1956, *IT-2*, 138–165.
Swets, J. A., and Birdsall, T. G. Deferred decision in human signal detection: A preliminary experiment. *Perception & Psychophysics*, 1967, *2*(1), 15–28.
Swets, J. A., and Birdsall, T. G. Repeated observations of an uncertain signal. *Perception & Psychophysics*, 1978, *23*(4), 269–274.
Swets, J. A., and Green, D. M. Sequential observations by human observers of signals in noise. In C. Cherry, (Ed.), *Information Theory*. London: Butterworths, 1961, 177–195.
Swets, J. A., Green, D. M., Getty, D. J., and Swets, J. B. Signal detection and identification at successive stages of observation. *Perception & Psychophysics*, 1978, *23*(4), 275–289.
Swets, J. A., Green, D. M., and Tanner, W. P., Jr. On the width of critical bands. *Journal of the Acoustical Society of America*, 1962, *34*(1), 108–113.
Swets, J. A., and Kristofferson, A. B. Attention. *Annual Review of Psychology*, 1970, *21*, 339–366.
Swets, J. A., and Sewall, S. T. Stimulus vs response uncertainty in recognition. *Journal of the Acoustical Society of America*, 1961, *33*(11), 1586–1592.
Swets, J. A., Shipley, E. F., McKey, M. J., and Green, D. M. Multiple observations of signals in noise. *Journal of the Acoustical Society of America*, 1959, *31*(4), 514–521.
Tanner, W. P., Jr. Theory of recognition. *Journal of the Acoustical Society of America*, 1956, *28*(5), 882–888.
Tanner, W. P., Jr., and Norman, R. Z. The human use of information: II. Signal detection for the case of an unknown signal parameter. *Transactions of the Institute of Radio Engineers, Professional Group on Information Theory*, 1954, *PGIT-4*, 222–227.
Tanner, W. P., Jr., and Swets, J. A. A decision making theory of visual detection. *Psychological Review*, 1954, *61*, 401–409.
Taylor, M. M. The effect of the square root of time on continuing perceptual tasks. *Perception & Psychophysics*, 1966, *1*, 112–119.
Taylor, M. M., Lindsay, P. H., and Forbes, S. M. Quantification of shared capacity processing in auditory and visual discrimination. *Acta Psychologica*, 1967, *27*, 223–229.
Tulga, M. K., and Sheridan, T. B. Dynamic decisions and work load in multitask supervisory control. *IEEE Transactions on Systems, Man, and Cybernetics*, 1980, *SMC-10*(5), 217–232.
Wald, A. *Sequential Analysis*. New York: Wiley, 1947.
Wandell, B., and Luce, R. D. Pooling peripheral information: Averages versus extreme values. *Journal of Mathematical Psychology*, 1978, *17*(3), 220–235.
Watson, C. S., and Nichols, T. L. Detectability of auditory signals presented without defined observation intervals. *Journal of the Acoustical Society of America*, 1976, *59*(3), 655–667.
Webster, J. C., Miller, P. H., Thompson, P. O., and Davenport, E. W. The masking and pitch shifts of pure tones near abrupt changes in a thermal noise spectrum. *Journal of the Acoustical Society of America*, 1952, *24*(2), 147–152.

Wickelgren, W. A. Strength theories of disjunctive visual detection. *Perception & Psychophysics,* 1967, *2*(8), 331–337.

Wickens, C. D. The effects of divided attention on information processing in manual tracking. *Journal of Experimental Psychology: Human Perception and Performance,* 1976, *2*(1), 1–13.

Wickens, C. D. The structure of attentional resources. In R. S. Nickerson (Ed.), *Attention and performance VIII.* Hillsdale, N.J.: Erlbaum, 1980, 239–257.

Wickens, C. D., and Gopher, D. Control theory measures of tracking as indices of attention allocation strategies. *Human Factors,* 1977, *19,* 349–366.

Williges, R. C. Within-session criterion changes compared to an ideal observer criterion in a visual monitoring task. *Journal of Experimental Psychology,* 1969, *81*(1), 61–66.

Williges, R. C. The role of payoffs and signal ratios in criterion changes during a monitoring task. *Human Factors,* 1971, *13*(3), 261–267.

Williges, R. C. Manipulating the response criterion in visual monitoring. *Human Factors,* 1973, *15*(3), 179–185.

Wolford, G. L., Wessel, D. L., and Estes, W. K. Further evidence concerning scanning and sampling assumptions of visual detection models. *Perception & Psychophysics,* 1968, *3*(6), 439–444.

Zargorski, M. Perceptual independence of pitch and loudness in a signal-detection experiment: A processing model for 2ATFC (2IFAC) experiments. *Perception & Psychophysics,* 1975, *17*(6), 525–531.

Zunzanyika, X. K., and Drury, C. G. Effects of information on industrial inspection performance. In C. G. Drury, and J. G. Fox (Eds.), *Human reliability in quality control.* New York: Halsted, 1975, 189–195.

6

Sustained Attention in Detection and Discrimination

Raja Parasuraman

Introduction

Sustained Attention and Vigilance

Many perceptual and cognitive activities demand sustained attention if they are to be executed successfully and efficiently. Maintaining attention to a single source of information for an unbroken period of time is relatively easy for intrinsically interesting activities or for those carried out in a rich environment, such as solving a challenging problem or watching an absorbing play. But if the problem resists solution, or if the play is dull, remaining attentive is much more difficult. The difficulty is compounded if attention has to be maintained on some source for the occurrence of infrequent but critical events. The processes that govern the ability to maintain attention and remain vigilant for such events for sustained periods of time forms the focus of research on sustained attention or vigilance.

The terms sustained attention and vigilance are used interchangeably in this chapter. Neurologists and physiologists, however, tend to use *vigilance* as a synonym for either "physiological efficiency" or "arousal," following the example of the British neurologist Sir Henry Head (1923), and indeed the French word *vigilance* does have the latter meaning. Head (1926) defined vigilance as "a state of high grade efficiency of the central nervous system" (p. 361). The concept of vigilance as a central process is retained in this chapter, but vigilance is considered an aspect of attention rather than arousal. As discussed further in the section entitled "Arousal and Sustained Attention," arousal and vigilance are distinct, albeit related, concepts. *Arousal* is a general state of the organism that affects the ability of the organism to carry out various functions of attention, including remaining vigilant. Attention possesses both an intensive and a selective dimension (Kahneman, 1973; Posner & Boies, 1971); thus, vigilance is sustained attention (Broadbent & Gregory, 1963a; Jerison, 1977; Mackworth, 1970), specifically sustained attention over a period of time (from seconds to hours) for targets that appear infrequently and unpredictably. This was emphasized in N. H. Mackworth's (1957) definition of vigilance: "A state of readiness to detect and respond to certain small changes occurring at random time intervals in the environment" (pp. 389–390).

Overview of the Chapter

This chapter reviews studies of sustained attention and vigilance in detection and discrimination tasks. The chapter focuses on the role of attention in the extraction and accumulation over time of stimulus information, and the efficiency with which this information is utilized in signal detection and discrimination over sustained periods of time. A variety of tasks will be examined: tasks with signals presented in well-defined observation intervals and at predictable times, or continuously and at random times; tasks with either brief signals or signals that remain until some response is made (referred to by Broadbent, 1958, as *limited-hold* and *unlimited-hold* signals, respectively); signals presented either in single- or multiple-observation intervals; and tasks of either short or long duration.

The chapter begins by examining how the accumulation of information regarding an uncertain stimulus proceeds over a short observation interval, and whether information accumulation is affected by changes in prestimulus alertness. This section also examines how information is utilized for the purposes of detection and identification when the signal may be one of several different signals. The discussion then turns to the influence of momentary fluctuations in attention and of temporal uncertainty on the efficiency with which stimulus information is utilized (perceptual sensitivity). The sections entitled "Arousal and Sustained Attention," "The Decision Criterion," and "Sensitivity Decrement in Sustained Attention" examine sustained attention over longer periods of time. Here the major concern is with the explanation of changes from the beginning to the end of a continuous period of performance, specifically with performance decrement, or the so-called vigilance decrement; although explanations of the overall level of performance, or the "level of vigilance" are also important. A distinction is drawn between the vigilance decrement and the level of vigilance, the latter being shown to be closely regulated by arousal, whereas two functionally distinct mechanisms are shown to be responsible for the vigilance decrement— criterion shifts and sensitivity decrement. The final section discusses the theoretical implications of this functional dissection of vigilance.

Information Accumulation and Attention

Phasic Alertness

In its broadest sense, *alertness* involves a change in the receptivity of the nervous system to external or internal information (Posner, 1978). Repetitive presentation of the same stimulus, for example, may temporarily inhibit receptivity to that stimulus, a phenomenon known as *habituation*. On the other hand, receptivity to all or a broad class of stimuli may be affected because the individual's general state, or arousal, has been altered. A person may be sober or intoxicated, sleepy or fully refreshed, sick or healthy; all these factors will affect a general state of receptivity (Davies & Parasuraman, 1982). These two causes of changes in receptivity may loosely be identified as the *phasic* and *tonic* aspects of alertness, respectively; although, as Posner (1975) has cautioned, an overly strict division of alertness into phasic and tonic components poses a number of difficulties of interpretation. To avoid additional difficulties of terminology, the term *arousal* will be used to refer to general state, and *alertness* to phasic alertness.

Changes in phasic and tonic alertness can affect detection and discrimination performance in a number of ways. Fluctuations in phasic alertness could, for example, affect the buildup of stimulus information in the nervous system. However, Posner (1975, 1978) has shown that alertness has only a negligible influence on the rate of accumulation of such information; rather, changes in phasic alertness, as induced by a warning signal, for example, influence how this information is evaluated and utilized in making responses. In reaction-time tasks, phasic changes in alertness affect the criterion for responding. The observer who adopts a risky criterion responds quickly but at the expense of making errors; a conservative criterion reduces errors but prolongs reaction time (Davies & Parasuraman, 1982). Generally, therefore, fast responses are based on less accumulative information and are therefore error prone. However, this is true only for unlimited-hold signals that are present until the subject responds. For limited-hold or transient signals, a fast response may be based on more accumulative information than a slower response, because there is a decay in the quality of the accumulated information once the signal is terminated. Thus, fast responses may be more accurate than slow responses (Posner, Klein, Summers, & Buggie, 1973).

These results suggest that the buildup of stimulus information in the nervous system is unaffected by changes in prestimulus alertness, although reaction time and response criteria are affected. The effects on reaction time are particularly marked when prolonged and brief signals are compared. In the former case, further sampling of the stimulus may reduce error but increase reaction time; in the latter, it may increase both errors and reaction time. Changes in reaction time can reflect variations in either sampling or decision time, and a variety of sequential-decision models of reaction time have been developed to account for such changes (Laming, 1968, 1973). The data support sequential-decision models for cases in which performance can be improved by successive sampling of the input, as in tasks with unlimited-hold signals or multiple-observation intervals. In such tasks, a sequential sampling strategy is more accurate than one based on a fixed number of samples (Wald, 1947), although there are trade-offs as far as response speed is concerned (Laming, 1968). The relationship between reaction time and response criteria is examined further in the subsection entitled "Reaction Time and Criterion Shifts."

Detection and Identification

Once stimulus information has been accumulated, responses to signals can begin to be initiated. This section briefly examines how the buildup of stimulus information is utilized in making detection and identification responses regarding an uncertain signal. The relevant evidence comes from studies of signal detection over multiple observation intervals (Swets, Chapter 5, this volume; Swets & Kristofferson, 1970). In such tasks, the observer's observation interval for a signal is divided into successive temporal blocks in which the signal, which may be one of several different types, may appear.

Swets and Birdsall (1978) had subjects detect a signal that could be one of 8 possible tones differing in frequency across 12 successive observation intervals (a *trial*). A yes–no detection response was required at the end of each interval. The signal frequency was varied either within a trial (a *simple* signal) or across trials (a *composite* signal). Assuming that the observer can attend to and monitor the outputs of either one or all of 8 filters corresponding to the 8 possible signals, how is this information accumulated and used? If all filter outputs are monitored simultaneously, the observer can optimize detection by accumulating the largest of the outputs (over observations) and successively comparing the sum to a criterion for a positive (yes) response. Swets, Shipley, McKey, & Green (1959) showed that the ideal observer in this case would show a growth in detectability over observations, compared to the one-signal case, proportional to $\sqrt{N}$, where N is the number of observations. The growth in detectability over five observation intervals conformed to this prediction, as shown in Figure 6.1.

The ideal observer for the composite signal in the Swets and Birdsall (1978) study should show a growth in detectability higher than $\sqrt{N}$ for the initial observations because all filter outputs are monitored separately and the observer can attend adaptively to (tune in to) the signal of the appropriate frequency. Swets and Birdsall (1978) found these predictions to be followed fairly closely. Alternative models for the multiple observation detection task are considered in more detail by Swets (Chapter 5, this volume).

Thus, it appears that observers can accumulate information about an uncertain signal over time in a nearly optimal manner. By requiring the observer to make both detection and identification responses based on this information, one can examine how the information is used. One question that then arises is whether information pertaining to identification is extracted and encoded at the same time as the detection code; or more, generally, whether in such combined detection and identification tasks detection and identification are sequential, cascaded, or concurrent temporal processes. Nolte (1967) first suggested that an ideal ob-

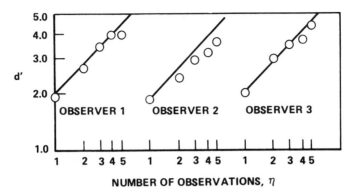

Figure 6.1 Growth in detectability (d') over five successive observations for a pure tone signal presented against background noise. A straight line representing a square root function provides a good fit to the data points. (The data are plotted on logarithmic axes, with the scale of the ordinate twice the scale of the abscissa; thus a square root function appears as a straight line with unit slope). (From Swets *et al.*, 1959.)

server in such a task would store, over the course of the observation period, updated probability estimates of each possible signal; these estimates represent the accumulative information on which either detection and identification responses can be based. Thus detection and identification can be considered to proceed together as the nervous system gathers probabilistic information about the uncertain stimulus. A study by Swets, Green, Getty, and Swets (1978) provides support for this view. In this study, concerned with the perception of simulated sonar images, signals were presented on a spectrographic display that was exposed progressively more completely over successive observation intervals, as in the Swets and Birdsall (1978) study, except that a confidence rating response was required. Swets *et al.*, (1978) found that detection and identification accuracy increased together over observation intervals in a manner consistent with Nolte's (1967) model.

Studies have traced the temporal course of processing that a stimulus that has to be detected and identified undergoes in the nervous system by recording the associated brain event-related potentials (Parasuraman & Beatty, 1980; Parasuraman, Richer, & Beatty, 1982). In these studies, observers listened to signal tones presented against background noise and reported both whether a signal had occurred and whether the signal was one of a set of signal tones differing in frequency. Signals elicited a complex of temporally overlapping brain potentials, each of which was related to different aspects of processing: an early (100-msec) potential that varied in amplitude only with processing related to the detection of the stimulus; a later (300-msec) potential that varied with both detection and identification; and a final (400+-msec) slow positive shift that was unaffected by detection and varied only with identification (Parasuraman *et al.*, 1982).

These results suggest that detection and identification are partially concurrent processes, but that processing for detection begins before that for identification. Depending on factors that influence the observer's attention over the observation interval, such as signal probabilities and instructions on speed–accuracy trade-off, either process may terminate before or after the other; thus, identification does not necessarily have to follow detection, or detection follow identification.

Temporal Distribution of Attention

In the preceding section, evidence was provided for the view that observers can attend to a signal and extract information pertaining to either detection or identification in a nearly optimal manner. When the exact properties of the signal are known, perceptual sensitivity is improved; and models of the ideal observer for this case show that almost all aspects of the signal are processed by the nervous system in such detection tasks (Green and Swets, 1966). However, the observer's performance still generally falls short of that of an ideal detector. Attentional fluctuations either within or across observation periods may be one of many possible factors limiting observer performance. This section briefly examines the possible effects of such fluctuations in the temporal distribution of attention on detection performance.

Thus far, this chapter has discussed the detection and discrimination of signals that are presented in well-defined observation intervals and at relatively predictable times. Signals in the real world often do not have this property. Modeling some of the qualities of detection and discrimination in real settings leads to a consideration of tasks incorporating temporal uncertainty. Egan, Greenberg, and Schulman, (1961a, 1961b) developed one such experimental task, the free-response task, in which signals are presented at times unknown to the observer, who is free to respond at any time (hence, the connotation, "free-response").

In the studies described in the preceding section (entitled "Information Accumulation and Attention") sensitivity was found to grow over defined observation intervals with each presentation of the signal. If, however, only one signal is presented at an unpredictable time during a similar observation period, detectability is impaired. Egan *et al.* (1961a) varied the interval during which the signal could be present from 0 to 8 seconds, and found that detectability (d') decreased progressively as the interval was increased. In a second study, Egan *et al.* increased the observation period further; signals were presented at random times in continuous 2-minute observation periods, with 15-second rest intervals between periods. Egan *et al.* plotted the response rate as a function of time following a signal and found that the rate rose sharply immediately following a signal and then fell to a low (but measurable) level a few seconds after the signal.

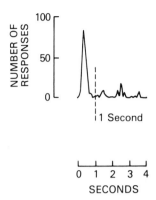

Figure 6.2 Distribution of detection responses as a function of time since the previous target for a visual discrimination task. The interstimulus interval was 1 second (dotted line), and targets appeared with a probability of .25. Most responses to a target are made before the presentation of the next stimulus. (From Nuechterlein *et al.* 1983.)

They identified these two portions of the response rate function as proportional to the probabilities of hits and false alarms respectively. By inducing observers to adopt different criteria for reporting signals, they were able to generate pairs of hit and false alarm probabilities and generate the receiver operating characteristic (ROC) that is routinely obtained in detection tasks with defined observation intervals.

The analytical technique developed by Egan *et al.* for free-response tasks can be extended to vigilance tasks with discrete signal and nonsignal events. Specifying a valid "observation interval" may pose a problem in such tasks and make it difficult to distinguish false-alarm responses from hits. If reaction-time data are available Egan *et al.*'s method can be used to validate the choice of the observation interval. Figure 6.2 shows a plot of the detection response rate to signals as a function of time since signal onset from a study by Nuechterlein, Parasuraman, and Jiang (1983; see also subsection in this chapter entitled "Rapid Sensitivity Decrements over Time"). The interstimulus interval (ISI) was 1 second in this study, and thus there was a potential danger in classifying "late" hits (longer than 1 second) as false alarms. As Figure 6.2 shows, however, the response-rate function peaks well within 1 second, and the function is relatively flat and low for longer latencies; thus the use of a 1-second observation interval can be justified. Watson and Nichols (1976) extended this approach, but they omitted the assumption made by Egan *et al.* that false alarms occur after a fixed (and arbitrary) interval following signal onset. Watson and Nichols assumed instead that the total observation period can be divided into imaginary measurement intervals containing either signal or noise and that only the first response following a signal is in fact a response to that signal. The response rate to signals was estimated from the distribution of reaction times of first responses, whereas the response rate to noise was estimated from the identically sampled distribution of reaction times in measurement intervals containing only noise.

Watson and Nichols (1976) applied their method to the estimation of d' and β in a 30-minute auditory detection (free-response) task. Their analysis indicated that there was a slight but nonsignificant drop in d' over the 30-minute observation period, whereas β increased. Thus in this particular task, observers were able to sustain attention over a relatively long period without an appreciable loss in perceptual sensitivity, but their criterion for reporting targets became increasingly stringent. In other tasks, however, sensitivity does decline over time. The distinction between sensitivity and criterion shifts underlying the vigilance decrement is discussed in further detail in subsequent sections of this chapter.

Arousal and Sustained Attention

This section examines the influence on performance of tonic alertness, or arousal, when attention has to be maintained for relatively longer periods of time than in the studies considered thus far. Two aspects of performance are discussed here, the vigilance decrement and the level of vigilance.

Reaction Time and the Vigilance Decrement

The *vigilance decrement* generally refers to the decline over time in the rate of correct detection of infrequently presented signals. However, reaction-time measures have also been used, not only in free-response tasks, but also in tasks with discrete signal and nonsignal events. A typical result in these studies is that the speed of reaction to critical signals declines over time on task (see Davies & Tune, 1969). Thus when both measures are recorded the general finding is that there is a deterioration over time in both detection accuracy and detection speed.

Changes in tonic arousal could lead to this pattern of increasingly sluggish and error-prone responding over time. However, the results of studies using reaction-time measures suggest that arousal does not directly control such performance changes (Davies & Parasuraman, 1976, 1977; Parasuraman & Davies, 1975, 1976). Reaction-time data can be obtained either for only the observer's detection responses or for all categories of response. Consider a detection or discrimination task in which the observer is required to respond overtly to both signals and nonsignals. This allows one to record reaction times for all possible stimulus–response (S–R) categories, correct detections, false detections (false alarms), correct rejections, and omission errors (incorrect rejections). Parasuraman and Davies (1976) obtained such data for an auditory intensity-discrimina-

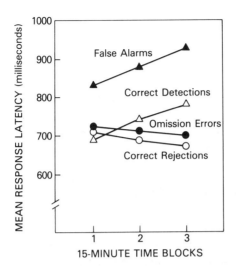

Figure 6.3 Mean response latencies for all possible stimulus–response (S–R) outcomes in a 45-minute intensity discrimination task, as a function of consecutive 15-minute blocks of the task. (From Parasuraman and Davies 1976.)

tion task lasting 45 minutes. Response latencies were obtained for consecutive 15-minute blocks in the task. (Accuracy rather than speed was emphasized in the instructions to the subject; this has a bearing on the types of response latency models appropriate for such tasks; see subsection entitled "Reaction Time and Criterion Shifts"). The results are shown in Figure 6.3. The latencies of positive responses (correct detections and false alarms) increased over successive blocks of time, indicating a vigilance decrement in detection speed. The latencies of negative responses (correct rejections and omission errors), on the other hand, decreased or remained stable. The latter finding suggests that the increase in correct detection latency cannot simply reflect a decrement in response speed but must involve other processes.

Buck (1966) proposed that the decrement in detection rate in vigilance tasks is determined by the relationship of the initial "vigilance level" to some critical level below which performance degradation occurs. The critical level is set by parameters such as signal intensity and signal duration. If the critical level is low, as in unlimited-hold tasks, the decline in "perceptual vigilance" over time results in an increment in detection latency; but so long as the vigilance level exceeds the low critical level, there is no decrement in detection accuracy. A decline in both accuracy and speed occurs only when the critical level is high, that is, when the signal is brief or otherwise weak.

In Buck's model, temporal changes in performance are directly influenced by a decline in "perceptual vigilance," or arousal. Thus the latencies of all response categories should increase with time, a prediction that is falsified by the results of Parasuraman and Davies (1976). However, the changes in reaction time can be interpreted if it is assumed that the observer's criterion for responding positively increases over time (resulting in a corresponding decrease in the criterion for negative responses) and that response latency is inversely related to the strength of the evidence (the accumulated stimulus information) received by the observer relative to the criterion level differentiating positive from negative responses. As discussed further in a subsequent section, the existence of such criterion increments over time has been confirmed in a number of studies.

Psychophysiological Measures of Arousal

A number of studies have used physiological measures to investigate the effects of arousal on vigilance performance. In general, changes in both autonomic and central nervous system (ANS and CNS) activity during the performance of vigilance tasks show that the vigilance decrement is accompanied by a decrement in physiological arousal over time. However, physiological arousal declines quite freely in almost any situation of prolonged testing, not just in vigilance tasks. As Table 6.1 indicates, measures of both ANS and CNS activity show that declines in physiological arousal are ubiquitous; they are found irrespective of the type of task being performed and the behavioral outcome. For example, arousal declines whether a vigilance decrement occurs (Davies & Krkovic, 1965) or not (Hink, Fenton, Tinklenberg, Pfefferbaum, & Kopell, 1978), whether the decrement can be attributed to such independent mechanisms as a decline in perceptual sensitivity or a criterion increment (Davies & Parasuraman, 1977), and even when the observer relaxes and performs no task for a comparable period (Fruhstorfer & Bergstrom, 1969). The only prerequisite for obtaining a decrement in physiological arousal is that the experimental situation be prolonged and relatively monotonous (Davies, Shackelton, & Parasuraman, 1983).

These findings suggest that although arousal does decline during a period of sustained performance of a detection or discrimination task, the vigilance decrement does not necessarily result from lowered arousal. In subsequent sections of this chapter evidence is presented that the vigilance decrement is not a unitary process (see also Warm, 1977). This may explain why it has proved difficult to account for the vigilance decrement in terms of a unitary-state concept of arousal. Several researchers have therefore proposed the need for a multistate arousal model in which for example, a distinction is made between autonomic and electrocortical arousal or between internal and external sources of arousal (Gale, 1977; Loeb & Alluisi, 1977); and such an elaboration of arousal theory

TABLE 6.1

Physiological Signs of Lowered Arousal Associated with Continuous Performance[a]

Physiological index of lowered arousal	Task performed and behavioral outcome
Mean heart rate—decrease	Vigilance—decrement
Heart rate variability—increase	Vigilance—no decrement
Skin conductance—decrease	Vigilance—sensitivity decrement
Respiration rate—decrease	Vigilance—criterion increment
EEG alpha power—increase	Pursuit motor tracking
EEG theta power—increase	Serial reaction time
N100 amplitude—decrease	No task—passive listening

[a] Arousal declines over time irrespective of the task performed, of the behavioral outcome of the task, and even of the nonperformance of the task. (The table should be read column by column; items in a given row are not necessarily associated.)

has also been proposed in the evaluation of the effects of environmental stressors on human performance (Hamilton, Hockey, & Rejman, 1977; see also Hockey, Chapter 12, this volume). This may well be useful, but the elements of such a model as applied to vigilance remain to be worked out.

Arousal and the Level of Vigilance

Changes in tonic arousal have more direct effects on the level of vigilance than on the vigilance decrement. If the observer's arousal level is particularly low, vigilance performance is likely to be poor throughout the task, irrespective of whether performance declines with time on task. Several studies have examined the effects on vigilance of various environmental and state factors known to influence the observer's level of arousal (see Davies & Parasuraman, 1982, for a review). Overall, the evidence points to a monotonic relationship between the level of vigilance and the level of arousal.

Detection efficiency is imparied by a number of stressors thought to lower arousal, such as moderate heat (Poulton, 1977). Alcohol-induced drowsiness also lowers the overall level of vigilance, there being little or no effect on the vigilance decrement (Erwin, Wiener, Linnoila, & Truscott, 1978). On the other hand, stressors that increase arousal, such as low-frequency vibration (Poulton, 1978), improve the level of vigilance. Naturally occurring changes in arousal due to the diurnal rhythm alter the overall level of vigilance but do not significantly affect the vigilance decrement (Blake, 1967; Davies, Toh, & Parasuraman, Note 1; see also concluding section of this chapter). The evidence for a nonmonotonic relationship (for example, the "inverted-U") between arousal and performance is, however, less convincing, and will not be discussed here (Davies & Parasuraman, 1982; Näätänen, 1973).

The evidence suggests, therefore, that changes in arousal primarily affect the overall level of vigilance rather than the vigilance decrement. This generalization may not hold when the changes in arousal are relatively more extreme, for example after sleep deprivation or alcohol intoxication, or when the stressor is likely to reduce attentional capacity in addition to affecting arousal level. Under these conditions, the vigilance decrement may be more pronounced, particularly if the task places a particularly high demand on the allocation of attentional resources (see concluding section of this chapter).

The Decision Criterion

Whereas changes in arousal primarily affect the level of vigilance, two factors, criterion shifts and sensitivity decrement, seem to be responsible for changes in vigilance over time. This section examines the role of criterion shifts in vigilance.

Reaction Time and Criterion Shifts

The detection rate in vigilance tasks may decline because the observer's criterion for responding positively to signals may increase over time, although the observer's ability to detect signals, or perceptual sensitivity, remains stable (Broadbent & Gregory, 1963b). The work of Egan et al. (1961a, 1961b) and Watson and Nichols (1976), discussed previously, also suggests criterion rather than sensitivity changes as the basis of the vigilance decrement, and the reaction-time experiment of Parasuraman and Davies (1976) supports the idea of criterion shifts during vigilance.

Parasuraman and Davies (1976) found that the latency changes over time for positive and negative responses were consistent with the assumption that the observer's criterion for positive responses increased. They assumed a simple model in which response latency is inversely proportional to the "distance" from the current response criterion (Audley, 1973; Carterette, Friedman, & Cosmides, 1965; Gesheider, Wright, & Evans, 1968; Kopell, 1976). Decision latency is a function of the "evidence" (the current accumulative information) favoring a positive response; the observer decides between alternative responses by comparing the likelihood ratio associated with the current evidence with some decision criterion. The closer the likelihood ratio is to the criterion, the less "evidence" there will be on which responses can be based; thus the closer the relative distance between observation and criterion is, the weaker the evidence will be, and, hence, the longer the response time.

Parasuraman and Davies (1976) found that, consistent with these predictions, reaction times were positively correlated with the decision criterion (log β) for positive responses (correct detections and false alarms) and negatively correlated with log β for negative responses (correct rejections and omission errors). This pattern of correlations was the same irrespective of whether criterion shifts were induced by time on task or by a change in the a priori signal probability.

Expectancy and Subjective Probability

Changes in reaction time and the detection parameter β provide evidence for the existence of criterion shifts over time during vigilance. Several variables that influence criterion placement in vigilance have been identified, such as signal probability, instructions, feedback, and the costs and values of S–R outcomes (see Davies & Parasuraman, 1982). The most consistent effects have been obtained with signal probability and time on task, both variables having significant but opposing effects on the criterion (Baddeley & Colquhoun, 1969; Broadbent & Gregory, 1963b, 1965). Furthermore, these variables interact; the higher the signal probability is, the lower will be the criterion increment over time (Williges, 1969, 1973).

The effects of signal probability suggest a role for expectancy in the interpretation of the criterion increment if expectancy is related to apparent shifts in the observer's subjective probability of signal occurrence over time. Colquhoun and Baddeley (1964, 1967) have shown that expectancies established during a training session can significantly influence the course of the vigilance decrement. They found a greater decrement in hits and false alarms over time for observers trained with an inappropriately high signal rate than for those trained with a signal probability appropriate to that actually used in the task. The subjects trained with an inappropriately high signal rate tend to find that signals occur much less frequently than they expected, and consequently revise their criteria towards greater strictness. Craig and Colquhoun (1975) suggest that a major part of the decrement observed in many vigilance studies may be due to inappropriate expectancies developed in the pretask period (see also MacFarland & Halcomb, 1970).

However, a decrement in detections (and a criterion increment) has still been obtained in studies in which subjects were given appropriate training or allowed to have practice sessions to stabilize their criterion (Milosevic, 1975; Parasuraman, 1976, 1979; Parasuraman & Davies, 1976; Williges, 1973). A form of expectancy theory that incorporates a normative signal detection model can account for these results. An ideal observer in a vigilance task should set the detection criterion β at or near the value $(1 - p)/p$, where p is the a priori signal probability. Because the observer is monitoring a low-probability event, p will be much less than .5, and thus the observer's (positive) response rate will be less than the signal rate. The observer who monitors responses to signals in an attempt to estimate the future occurrence of signals will always underestimate the true signal probability. If, as proposed by expectancy theory (Deese, 1955), the observer's self-feedback influences subsequent performance, the criterion will subsequently be made more stringent to conform to the (lower) estimate of signal probability. Making the criterion more stringent will result in a lower hit and false-alarm rate, leading to further revision of the criterion, and so on in a "vicious circle" (Baker, 1959; Broadbent, 1971). The result is a steady increase in the response criterion.

Craig (1978) proposed an alternative explanation of the criterion increment. He suggested that criterion shifts do not reflect changes in expectancy and subjective probability but in *probability matching*—that is, the observer attempting to match his or her response rate to the signal rate. In a review of 30 studies of vigilance, Craig found that in 14 out of 20 studies reporting within-session data, the response rate was greater than the signal rate at the beginning of a session but approached the signal rate at the end of the session, suggesting probability matching. However, when the response rate to signal rate ($R:S$) ratio was less than 1 initially, the ratio also declined (but not significantly) thereafter. If probability matching is used, then presumably observers should adjust their response rates either downwards (when $R:S > 1$) or upwards (when $R:S < 1$). Furthermore, in discrimination tasks, Dusoir (1974) and Thomas (1975) found that although group subject data were indicative of the possible use of probability matching, the data of individual subjects showed large deviations from probability matching. Thomas (1975) proposed a modification of the basic probability-matching model to account for a systematic deviation from probability matching (for example, undermatching); but Dusoir (1980) has shown that in a threshold detection task, subjects did not consistently probability match, undermatch, or overmatch, so that neither the original nor modified versions of the model fitted more than a proportion of the subjects tested.

The Ideal Observer

The results of the studies examined in the previous subsection provide strong evidence for an expectancy model of the criterion increment. Williges (1973, 1976) has further elaborated this model by suggesting that the observer's behavior over time approaches that of the *ideal* observer as prescribed by normative signal detection theory. Such an interpretation assumes a "strong" form of signal detection theory in which decision rules are considered to be compatible with the maximization of expected value. Williges suggested that because the obtained value of β approaches the optimal β value towards the end of a vigilance session, the observer's performance actually represents an attempt to reach optimal behavior; this he termed the *vigilance increment* (Williges, 1976).

This novel interpretation raises a number of issues, but three methodological difficulties should also be considered. First, the β measure of the criterion depends on the assumption that the underlying signal and noise distributions have equal variance; Williges did not report whether this assumption was met or not. In low signal probability tasks, the confidence limits on β values are so large that although the trends in the criterion may be reliably assessed using this index, attaching a meaning (i.e., comparing it to an ideal criterion) to absolute values of β is rather tenuous. Some investigators have therefore recommended that β should not be used as a criterion measure for vigilance tasks (Craig, 1977; Mackworth & Taylor, 1963; Taylor, 1967); and unfortunately, a satisfactory alternative to β, parametric or nonparametric, has yet to be developed (Davies and Parasuraman, 1982; see also Dusoir, 1975). Second, most detection and discrimination studies have found that observers almost always have decision criteria that are not as extreme as those prescribed for an ideal observer who maximizes expected value (Green & Swets, 1966; for an exception, see Murrell, 1975). Hence, for $p < .5$, the increase in β with time will always make it approach β_{opt}, because $\beta < \beta_{opt}$; and the reverse is true for $p > .5$, when β decreases over time and $\beta > \beta_{opt}$. Third, the ideal observer's decision criterion should take into account both the a priori signal probability and the payoff matrix. However, many studies have found that manipulations of the payoff matrix do not affect β in the manner predicted by the expected value model for the ideal observer, in magnitude or in direction (Levine, 1966; Swets, 1977; Williges, 1971).

Williges's interpretation suggests that if observers are provided with sufficient exposure to the task and given training to develop appropriate expectancies about signal occurrence, they will eventually adopt response criteria that are nearly optimal; and then the chance of any further vigilance decrement will be minimized. Moray, Fitter, Ostry, Favreau, and Nagy (1976) found that for a task requiring the detection of weak signals in either one or both ears, observers' response criteria were very close to the optimal value after about 10 hours of performance (see also Ostry, Moray, & Marks, 1976). And, on the whole, the idea that response criteria can be stabilized given appropriate training and sufficient practice provides a useful general principle with application not only to vigilance performance but also to performance on a range of other tasks in which criterion shifts are obtained over both short and long intervals of time, as in tasks involving monitoring and supervisory control (Moray, 1976).

Sensitivity Decrement in Sustained Attention

The vigilance decrement may result not only from shifts in the observer's response criterion, but also from a decrement in the observer's perceptual sensitivity over time. Because targets appear infrequently at unpredictable times in vigilance tasks, and because temporal uncertainty has been shown to reduce sensitivity (see subsection entitled "Signals Appearing at Unpredictable Times"); one might expect that a sensitivity decrement should be obtained in certain tasks. In fact, since the early studies of Mackworth and Taylor (1963)— who found a sensitivity decrement, a number of studies have reported the existence of such decrements (see Swets, 1977). This section briefly considers the factors responsible for the sensitivity decrements over time.

Event Rate

As discussed previously, Egan et al. (1961a) showed that an observer's sensitivity in detecting a simple auditory signal (d') declines progressively as the interval of time uncertainty (the interval of time in which the signal can occur) is increased. This finding was replicated in a vigilance situation by Mackworth and Taylor (1963). Both studies indicate the importance of the interval of time in which a signal may occur, the event interval or event rate, in determining changes in sensitivity over time.

Jerison and Pickett (1964) first showed that for subjects monitoring a cathode-ray tube (CRT) display for occasional targets, detection rate was high (about 90%) and stable over time when the event rate was low (5/min). When the event rate was increased to 30/min, detection rate declined dramatically to about 30% and deteriorated sharply over time. Such potent effects of the event rate on the detection rate have since been confirmed in a number of other studies (Jerison, 1967; Loeb & Binford, 1968; Parasuraman & Davies, 1976).

Task Characteristics

Several studies have attempted to identify factors other than the event rate that might produce sensitivity decrements. It was originally thought that sensitivity decrements occur only for visual displays, especially those demanding a high rate of observation (Mackworth, 1970). However, there are examples of auditory tasks showing sensitivity decrements; conversely, there are tasks with high event rates that do not show reductions in sensitivity over time (Swets, 1977).

Parasuraman (1976, 1979; Parasuraman & Davies, 1977) suggested a division of vigilance tasks into simultaneous- and successive-discrimination tasks. In *simultaneous discrimination*, the target is specified fully within a stimulus event, as in the detection of a target item in a display containing other distractor items. In Colquhoun's (1961) study, for example, the observer had to detect a disk of different hue in a display of many disks. In *successive discrimination*, the target is specified as a change in some feature of a repetitive, standard stimulus (non-target), the standard feature being absent when the nonstandard feature (target) is presented; thus a successive comparison of a change in a standard value held in memory has to be made. In a study reported by Hatfield and Loeb (1968), for example, subjects had to detect an increase in the intensity of a repetitive flashing light. Tasks that require the detection of a sequence of items presented over successive events or display states, such as the Bakan task (Bakan, 1959), also fall in this category.

Parasuraman and Davies (1977) suggested that only tasks requiring successive discrimination will be likely to show sensitivity decrements. Studies conducted in the 1950s that found a greater increase over time in sensory "thresholds" with a successive than with a simultaneous discrimination threshold procedure anticipate this suggestion (Bakan, 1955; Berger and Mahneke, 1954). Parasuraman (1979) carried out two experiments that examined the effects of target discrimination type and event rate on performance decrements in visual and auditory vigilance tasks. In the first experiment, the successive-discrimination task required the detection of an increase in the intensity of an intermittent 1000-Hz tone; whereas in the simultaneous-discrimination task, the same tone had to be detected within an intermittent noise burst. The event rate was either low (15 events/min) or high (30 events/min). Four groups of subjects were assigned to one of the four conditions, combining target discrimination type and event rate, and performed the task for a period of 45 minutes. Although a vigilance decrement (in detection rate) was obtained in all four conditions, as Figure 6.4 shows, a decrement in mean values of sensitivity (d_a) was obtained only for the successive-discrimination task run at a high event rate.

A second experiment was carried out to confirm and extend these results. It could be argued that the auditory tasks in the first experiment differed in respects other than the need for contact with memory (threshold detection in the simultaneous task and intensity discrimination in the successive task). Two adjacent sources of visual signals were used in each of three high-event rate tasks used in this study. If intermittently flashing lights are presented over both sources and the target is defined as a decrease in the intensity of both sources, successive discrimination is required. If, however, the target (dimmer flash) is presented on

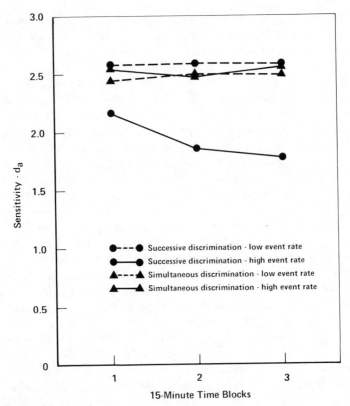

Figure 6.4 Mean values of sensitivity (d_a) in successive 15-minute blocks of a 45-minute vigilance task, for successive and simultaneous discriminations at low and high event rates. Sensitivity declines over time only for the successive discrimination task at a high event rate. (From Parasuraman, 1979.)

only one source, simultaneous discrimination is possible because the two sources may be compared within a stimulus event. From the results of the first experiment one would predict that although both tasks require intensity discrimination, only the first should exhibit a sensitivity decrement over time. For comparison purposes, a third task requiring a different simultaneous discrimination was also run; subjects had to detect a small circle appearing at the center of one of the sources in this task. The three tasks were performed by independent groups of subjects. Table 6.2 summarizes the findings. Although the detection rate declined over time in all three tasks, only the successive-discrimination task showed a decline in d'.

TABLE 6.2

Mean Values of Correct Detection Rate and Sensitivity (d') for
Each Target Type in Consecutive 15-Minute Time Blocks of a
45-Minute Period

	Blocks		
Target type	1	2	3
Detection Rate			
Successive	.68	.45	.36
Simultaneous 1	.64	.59	.58
Simultaneous 2	.63	.63	.58
d'			
Successive	2.42	2.11	1.81
Simultaneous 1	2.30	2.37	2.37
Simultaneous 2	2.34	2.34	2.37

Rapid Sensitivity Decrements over Time

The results of the studies discussed thus far indicate that for a subset of vigilance tasks, the vigilance decrement is associated with a decrement in perceptual sensitivity over time. The sensitivity decrement, although reliable, is generally quite small in magnitude. Moreover, the decrement occurs only after 30 to 45 minutes of time on the task. A study by Nuechterlein et al. (1983), however, found that under certain conditions extremely rapid decrements in sensitivity can be obtained, after only about 2–5 minutes.

In this study, digit stimuli were presented at a fast event rate (one per second); the subject had to detect the presence of the digit 0 among nontarget digits 1–9. Large declines in sensitivity, independent of changes in the response criterion, were found within 5 minutes of the 8-minute task when the digits were highly degraded but not when they were moderately degraded or undegraded. Figure 6.5 shows the mean values of two sensitivity indices, d_a and A_z, as a function of time on task for the high and moderate image degradation conditions. Repeated testing (4 sessions on consecutive days) did not abolish the decrement.

These results suggest that the sensitivity decrements results from excessive demands on the limited capacity system of attention. When the demand of a high stimulus processing rate is coupled either with a memory load or a perceptual load from degraded stimuli, sensitivity is likely to decline over time. The finding that a marked decrement in sensitivity can occur over a period of time in which organismic arousal cannot be expected to decline significantly provides further evidence against an arousal theory of the decrement. Rather, attentional factors must be implicated, and the short time constant of the decrement suggests that

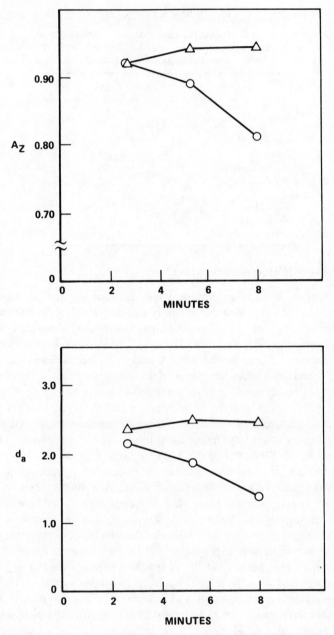

Figure 6.5 Mean values of sensitivity (A_Z and d_a) as a function of time on task for a visual discrimination task at high (○) and moderate (△) levels of visual degradation of stimuli. (From Nuechterlein *et al.*, 1983.)

the distinction between the attentional studies considered in the first and second halves of this chapter is an arbitrary one and serves only to organize the treatment of studies with somewhat different areas of focus.

Discussion and Conclusions

The interpretation of performance decrements over time has been a primary focus for theories of vigilance. A number of such theories have been postulated, including ones based on constructs of arousal, expectancy, habituation, motivation, and inhibition. As recent reviews have pointed out, however (Davies & Parasuraman, 1982; Loeb & Alluisi, 1977; Parasuraman, 1983, in press; Warm, 1977), none of the theories can account satisfactorily for all the results; and at least one source of conflicting evidence can be brought to bear against each theory. But the failure of these theories may reflect less on the inadequacy of these constructs than on the inappropriateness of viewing vigilance as a unitary phenomenon (see also Warm, 1977). As noted previously, the vigilance decrement is not a unitary process and can be attributed to one of two functionally distinct mechanisms; and a further distinction must be made between the level of vigilance and the vigilance decrement, each being regulated by different processes.

This functional dissection grew out of a taxonomic analysis of vigilance that indicated many vigilance effects are intimately related to the particular cognitive processes involved in target discrimination (Parasuraman, 1976, 1979; Parasuraman & Davies, 1977). Many different tasks have been used in vigilance studies, but until the late 1970s not too much attention was paid to what these tasks had and did not have in common. The implicit assumption was that a particular theory should explain performance on any "vigilance" task. Indeed, for many years the common finding that intertask correlations in vigilance performance are often low prompted doubts as to the construct validity of vigilance as a central process (Buckner & McGrath, 1963).

The approach adopted here argues instead that different vigilance tasks impose different information-processing demands on the observer; thus different processes may be responsible for the vigilance decrement and the level of vigilance, and performances on different tasks need be correlated only if the tasks share certain processing demands in common. Lowered arousal over time is clearly a concomitant of the vigilance decrement; but apart from extremes of arousal induced by such factors as sleep deprivation, arousal primarily affects the level of vigilance rather than the decrement. It has been shown that stimulus information can be accumulated in an efficient manner that is not significantly affected by changes in prestimulus alertness. Alertness does, however, influence the criterion for responding. This suggests that in prolonged vigilance tasks, fluctuations in alertness will primarily affect decision criteria and not the efficiency with which stimulus information is accumulated and utilized; or, in other words, that time-on-task effects should be seen in β rather than d'. This has been confirmed in many studies. In many vigilance tasks, changes in the observer's subjective probability of the occurrence of critical signals can account for performance changes over time; and individual differences in the decrement function may reflect different adopted strategies for responding to infrequent events. These within-task changes in subjective expectancy can be minimized with appropriate training; and because in most such tasks there is little or no drop in perceptual sensitivity, the vigilance decrement can be more or less eradicated. As discussed in the preceding section, however, sensitivity does drop in certain tasks. The sensitivity decrement is generally obtained when the required processing rate is high as a result of a high event rate. This can be interpreted to mean that the usage of stimulus information becomes less efficient with time only when stimuli cannot be encoded easily (given the required processing rate) because they are degraded, or when target discrimination loads memory.

The differences between successive and simultaneous discrimination outlined previously indicate that the former places a greater load on memory because not only does information have to be integrated over events, but also the value of nonsignal events on some dimension (for example, intensity, pitch, or duration) has to be remembered. With weak or difficult signals, the processing resources of attention that must be consistently allocated to detection may not meet the level needed for stable performance when the processing demands of a memory load are combined with those of a high stimulus event rate. Kahneman (1973) suggested that processing resources (or, to use his term, *effort*) are mobilized in response to task demands, and that there is a fixed allocation of effort for each task; time pressure, which is inherent in the structure of the task, increases processing demands. In Kahneman's words, "the investment of less than this standard effort causes a deterioration of performance, but in most tasks it is impossible to completely eliminate errors by a voluntary increase in effort. . . . Time pressure is a particularly important determinant of monetary effort. Tasks that impose a heavy load on short-term memory necessarily impose severe time pressure" (p. 27). Successive-discrimination tasks run at high event rates fall into the category of tasks for which attentional resources must be consistently maintained for efficient performance; although this is possible for short periods of time, it becomes difficult over longer periods, and performance declines due to an effective loss in detectability.

Schneider and Shiffrin (1977; see also Schneider, Dumais, & Shiffrin, Chapter 1, this volume) have argued that only what they call *control processes* are limited by the amount of resources allocated to processing, whereas *automatic* processes require little or no processing resources. The sensitivity decrement in vigilance has been attributed to a decline in the allocation of processing resources to detection over time. The automatic–control processing analytical framework suggests that under conditions in which attentional resources are likely to decline over time, only tasks requiring control processing will show a decrement; whereas sensitivity will be stable for a task in which automatic processing has been developed. Fisk and Schneider (1981) confirmed this prediction in a study using a modification of a high event rate, visual discrimination task used by Schneider and Shiffrin (1977). Subjects detected specified digit or letter stimuli in briefly presented displays containing nontarget letters. In the consistent mapping (CM) condition, digits were targets and letters were nontargets; in the variable mapping (VM) condition, subjects had to detect letters (among distractor letters) that previously had been or subsequently could be nontargets—the required target being specified on a "memory-set" display. The vigilance session lasted 50 minutes and consisted of 30-second detection periods each preceded by the memory-set display. A decrement in sensitivity over the 50-minute task was obtained only for the VM condition.

The implications of Fisk and Schneider's (1981) study for the interpretation of the vigilance decrement are somewhat unclear, for two reasons. First, the significance of the results rests on the distinction between CM and VM, but *all* previous vigilance studies have used only CM. Second, significant performance decrements over time have been reported for subjects—both college students and military personnel, performing both laboratory and simulated tasks—even after several repeated sessions; these studies used tasks in which stimuli and responses were consistently mapped (Binford & Loeb, 1966; Colquhoun, 1977; see also Davies & Parasuraman, 1982). Fisk and Schneider (1981) suggest that this is because the standard vigilance task, with its lack of speed stress and low signal probability, hinders the development of automaticity. At present, there is little converging evidence for this assertion. Nevertheless, Fisk and Schneider's suggestion that maximizing automatic processing development may provide a technique for reducing vigilance problems in the field is one that needs to be explored further.

The view that sensitivity may fall in vigilance tasks because the level of processing resources needed to detect targets cannot be maintained over a prolonged period (Parasuraman, 1979) would carry greater weight if one could independently measure processing resources or effort. One such independent measure is the task-evoked pupillary response (TEPR), which has been found to increase in amplitude with increased effort (Beatty, 1982b). It might be expected, therefore, that a decrement in the amplitude of the TEPR would be obtained in a vigilance task in which sensitivity declined. Beatty (1982a) recorded TEPRs to auditory signals in a 40-minute successive–discrimination task. A small but reliable decrement in perceptual sensitivity was found, accompanied by a decrement in the amplitude of the TEPR. As discussed in earlier sections, a decrement in a physiological index could be interpreted as indicating a decline in arousal over time. However, Beatty (1982a) measured both the (phasic) pupillary dilation and the (tonic) absolute pupillary size; the latter measure, which in other studies has been shown to be a sensitive indicator of the overall level of arousal (Yoss, Moyer, & Hollenhorst, 1970), did not change significantly with time on task. These results confirm the view that sensitivity declines during a vigilance task due to the combined demand on processing resources of short-term memory (STM) and a high event rate. They also provide additional confirmation for the view expressed previously that tonic changes in arousal over time are unrelated to the vigilance decrement.

As also discussed previously, however, tonic changes in arousal do affect the overall level of performance. A study by Davies et al. (Note 1) provides further support for this view and at the same time indicates the importance of the successive–simultaneous dimension in vigilance. Davies et al. (Note 1) found that the overall level of performance (as assessed by the sensitivity index d_a) improved from morning to afternoon testing for an auditory simultaneous-discrimination task. For a successive-discrimination task, however, performance deteriorated from morning to afternoon. In addition, the sensitivity decline over time on task for the successive-discrimination task occurred both in the morning and in the afternoon. It has been shown that tonic arousal level increases from the morning to the afternoon and evening as part of the diurnal rhythm; the increase in arousal is associated with an improvement in performance on tasks requiring a direct response to stimulus input, as in signal detection and choice reaction-time tasks (Blake, 1967; see also Posner, 1975). However, STM performance typically declines from morning to afternoon testing (Baddeley, Hatter, Scott, & Snashall, 1970; Folkard, 1979). This has been interpreted to be consistent with the view that although increased tonic arousal facilitates the immediate processing of information, it impairs processing utilizing stored information (Colquhoun, 1971; Folkard, 1979). These time-of-day results thus support the distinction between successive- and simultaneous-discrimination tasks in terms of memory load; vigilance for low-probability targets is better in the afternoon and evening than in the early morning unless target discrimination loads memory, in which case afternoon performance is superior. Moreover, changes in arousal due to the diurnal rhythm have their principal effect on the overall level of performance rather than on the performance decrement.

The functional distinction made in this chapter among the level of vigilance, criterion shifts underlying the vigilance decrement, and sensitivity decrements in vigilance can account for a number of findings in the literature on sustained attention and vigilance. The development of a comprehensive theoretical account of different aspects of vigilance must build on this and related efforts (Warm, 1977) aimed at identifying the specific perceptual and cognitive processes involved in detection and discrimination during sustained attention.

Reference Note

1. Davies, D. R., Toh, K., and Parasuraman, R. *Time of day, memory load, and vigilance performance*. Unpublished manuscript, University of Aston, Birmingham, 1981.

References

Audley, R. J. Some observations on choice reaction time: Tutorial survey. In S. Kornblum (Ed.), *Attention and performance IV*. New York: Academic Press, 1973.

Baddeley, A. D., & Colquhoun, W. P. Signal probability and vigilance: A reappraisal of the 'signal rate' effect. *British Journal of Psychology*, 1969, *60*, 165–178.

Baddeley, A. D., Hatter, J. E., Scott, D., & Snashall, A. Memory and time of day. *Quarterly Journal of Experimental Psychology*, 1970, *22*, 605–609.

Bakan, P. Discrimination decrement as a function of time in a prolonged vigil. *Journal of Experimental Psychology*, 1955, *50*, 387–390.

Bakan, P. Extraversion–introversion and improvement in an auditory vigilance task. *British Journal of Psychology*, 1959, *50*, 325–332.

Baker, C. H. Towards a theory of vigilance. *Canadian Journal of Psychology*, 1959, *13*, 352.

Beatty, J. Phasic not tonic pupillary responses vary with auditory vigilance performance. *Psychophysiology*, 1982, *19*, 167–172. (a)

Beatty, J. Task-evoked pupillary responses, processing load, and the structure of processing resources. *Psychological Bulletin*, 1982, *91*, 276–292. (b)

Berger, C., & Mahneke, A. Fatigue in two simple visual tasks. *American Journal of Psychology*, 1954, *67*, 509–512.

Binford, J. R., & Loeb, M. Changes within and over repeated sessions in criterion and effective sensitivity in an auditory vigilance task. *Journal of Experimental Psychology*, 1966, *72*, 339–345.

Blake, M. J. F. Time of day effects in a range of tasks. *Psychonomic Science*, 1967, *9*, 349–350.

Broadbent, D. E. *Perception and communication*. New York: Pergamon, 1958.

Broadbent, D. E. *Decision and stress*. New York: Academic Press, 1971.

Broadbent, D. E., & Gregory, M. Division of attention and the decision theory of signal detection. *Proceedings of the Royal Society*, 1963, *158B*, 221–231. (a)

Broadbent, D. E., & Gregory, M. Vigilance considered as a statistical decision. *British Journal of Psychology*, 1963, *54*, 309–323. (b)

Broadbent, D. E., & Gregory, M. Effects of noise and of signal rate upon vigilance analysed by means of decision theory. *Human Factors*, 1965, *7*, 155–162.

Buck, L. Reaction time as a measure of perceptual vigilance. *Psychological Bulletin*, 1966, *65*, 291–308.

Buckner, D. N., & McGrath, J. J. (Eds.) *Vigilance: A symposium*. New York: McGraw-Hill, 1963.

Carterette, E. C., Friedman, M. P., & Cosmides, R. Reaction-time distributions in the detection of weak signals in noise. *Journal of the Acoustical Society of America*, 1965, *38*, 531–542.

Colquhoun, W. P. The effect of unwanted signals on performance in a vigilance task. *Ergonomics*, 1961, *4*, 41–52.

Colquhoun, W. P. (Ed.) *Biological rhythms and human performance*. London: Academic Press, 1971.

Colquhoun, W. P. Simultaneous monitoring of a number of sonar outputs. In R. R. Mackie (Ed.),

Vigilance: Theory, operational performance, and physiological correlates. New York: Plenum 1977, 163–188.

Colquhoun, W. P., & Baddeley, A. D. The role of pre-test expectancy in vigilance decrement. *Journal of Experimental Psychology,* 1964, *68,* 156–160.

Colquhoun, W. P., & Baddeley, A. D. Influence of signal probability during pretraining on vigilance decrement. *Journal of Experimental Psychology,* 1967, *73,* 153–155.

Craig, A. Broadbent & Gregory revisited: Vigilance and statistical decision. *Human Factors,* 1977, *19,* 25–36.

Craig, A. Is the vigilance decrement simply a response adjustment towards probability matching? *Human Factors,* 1978, *20,* 441–446.

Craig, A., & Colquhoun, W. P. Vigilance: A review. In C. G. Drury and J. G. Fox (Eds.), *Human reliability in quality control.* London: Taylor and Francis, 1975.

Davies, D. R., & Krkovic, A. Skin conductance, alpha-activity, and vigilance. *American Journal of Psychology,* 1965, *78,* 304–306.

Davies, D. R., & Parasuraman, R. Vigilanz, Antwortlatenzen, und kortikae evozierte Potentiale. *Probleme und Ergebnisse der Psychologie,* 1976, *59,* 95–99.

Davies, D. R., & Parasuraman, R. Cortical evoked potentials and vigilance: A decision theory analysis. In R. R. Mackie (Ed.), *Vigilance: Theory, operational performance, and physiological correlates.* New York: Plenum, 1977, 285–306.

Davies, D. R., & Parasuraman, R. *The psychology of vigilance.* London: Academic Press, 1982.

Davies, D. R., Shackelton, V. J., & Parasuraman, R. Monotony and boredom. In G. R. J. Hockey (Ed.), *Stress and fatigue.* London: Wiley, 1983.

Davies, D. R., & Tune, G. S. *Human vigilance performance.* New York: American Elsevier, 1969.

Deese, J. Some problems in the theory of vigilance. *Psychological Review,* 1955, *62,* 359–368.

Dusoir, A. E. Thomas and Legge's matching hypothesis for detection and recognition tasks: Two tests. *Perception and Psychophysics,* 1974, *16,* 466–470.

Dusoir, A. E. Treatments of bias in detection and recognition models: Review. *Perception and Psychophysics,* 1975, *17,* 167–178.

Dusoir, A. E. Some evidence on additive learning models. *Perception and Psychophysics,* 1980, *27,* 163–175.

Egan, J. P., Greenberg, G. Z., & Schulman, A. I. Interval of time uncertainty in auditory detection. *Journal of the Acoustical Society of America,* 1961, *33,* 771–778. (a)

Egan, J. P., Greenberg, G. Z., & Schulman, A. I. Operating characteristics, signal detectability and the method of free response. *Journal of the Acoustical Society of America,* 1961, *33,* 993–1007. (b)

Erwin, C. W., Wiener, E. L., Linnoila, M. I., & Truscott, T. R. Alchohol induced drowsiness and vigilance performance. *Journal of Studies of Alchohol,* 1978, *39,* 565–576.

Fisk, A. D., & Schneider, W. Control and automatic processing during tasks requiring sustained attention: A new approach to vigilance. *Human Factors,* 1981, *23,* 737–750.

Folkard, S. Time of day and level of processing. *Memory and Cognition,* 1979, *7,* 247–252.

Fruhstorfer, H., & Bergstrom, R. M. Human vigilance and auditory evoked potentials. *Electroencephalography and Clinical Neurophysiology,* 1969, *27,* 346–365.

Gale, A. Some EEG correlates of sustained attention. In R. R. Mackie (Ed.), *Vigilance: Theory, operational performance, and physiological correlates.* New York: Plenum, 1977, 263–283.

Gesheider, G. A., Wright, J. H., & Evans, M. B. Reaction time in the detection of vibrotactile signals. *Journal of Experimental Psychology,* 1968, *77,* 501–504.

Green, D. M., & Swets, J. A. *Signal detection theory and psychophysics.* New York: Wiley, 1966.

Hamilton, P., Hockey, G. R. J., & Rejman, M. The place of the concept of activation in human information processing theory: An integrative approach. In S. Dornic (Ed.), *Attention and performance VI.* Hillsdale, N.J.: Erlbaum, 1977, 463–486.

Hatfield, J. L., & Loeb, M. Sense mode and coupling in a vigilance task. *Perception and Psychophysics*, 1968, *4*, 29–36.

Head, H. The conception of nervous and mental energy. II. Vigilance: A physiological state of the nervous system. *British Journal of Psychology*, 1923, *14*, 126–147.

Head, H. *Aphasia and kindred disorders of speech*. New York: Macmillan, 1926.

Hink, R. F., Fenton, W. H., Tinklenberg, J. R., Pfefferbaum, A., & Kopell, B. S. Vigilance and human attention under conditions of methylphenidate and secobarbital intoxication: An assessment using brain potentials. *Psychophysiology*, 1978, *15*, 597–605.

Jerison, H. J. Activation and long-term performance. In A. F. Sanders (Ed.), *Attention and performance*. Amsterdam: North-Holland, 1967.

Jerison, H. J. Vigilance: Biology, psychology, theory and practice. In R. R. Mackie (Ed.), *Vigilance: Theory, operational performance, and physiological correlates*. New York: Plenum, 1977, 27–40.

Jerison, H. J., & Pickett, R. M. Vigilance: The importance of the elicited observing rate. *Science*, 1964, *143*, 970–971.

Kahneman, D. *Attention and effort*. Englewood Cliffs, N.J.: Prentice-Hall, 1973.

Kopell, S. Latency function hypothesis and Pike's multiple observations model for latencies in signal-detection. *Psychological Review*, 1976, *83*, 308–309.

Laming, D. R. J. *Information theory of choice-reaction times*. New York: Academic Press, 1968.

Laming, D. R. J. *Mathematical psychology*. New York: Academic Press, 1973.

Levine, J. M. The effects of values and costs on the detection and identification of signals in auditory vigilance. *Human Factors*, 1966, *8*, 525–537.

Loeb, M., & Alluisi, E. A. An update of findings regarding vigilance and a reconsideration of underlying mechanisms. In R. R. Mackie (Ed.), *Vigilance: Theory, operational performance, and physiological correlates*. New York: Plenum, 1977, 719–749.

Loeb, M., & Binford, J. R. Variation in performance on auditory and visual monitoring tasks as a function of signal and stimulus frequencies. *Perception and Psychophysics*, 1968, *4*, 361–366.

MacFarland, B. P., & Halcomb, C. G. Expectancy and stimulus generalization in vigilance. *Perceptual and Motor Skills*, 1970, *30*, 147–151.

Mackworth, J. F. *Vigilance and attention*. Baltimore: Penguin, 1970.

Mackworth, J. F., & Taylor, M. M. The d' measure of signal probability in vigilance-like situations. *Canadian Journal of Psychology*, 1963, *17*, 302–325.

Mackworth, N. H. Some factors affecting vigilance. *Advancements in Science*, 1957, *53*, 389–393.

Milosevic, S. Changes in detection measures and skin resistance during an auditory vigilance task. *Ergonomics*, 1975, *18*, 1–18.

Moray, N. Attention, control and sampling behavior. In T. Sheridan and G. Johannsen (Eds.), *Monitoring behavior and supervisory control*. New York: Plenum, 1976.

Moray, N., Fitter, M., Ostry, D., Favreau, D., & Nagy, V. Attention to pure tones. *Quarterly Journal of Experimental Psychology*, 1976, *28*, 271–283.

Murrell, G. A. A reappraisal of artificial signals as an aid to a visual monitoring task. *Ergonomics*, 1975, *18*, 693–700.

Näätänen, R. The inverted-U relationship between activation and performance: A critical review. In S. Kornblum (Ed.), *Attention and performance IV*. New York: Academic Press, 1973, 155–174.

Nolte, L. W. Theory of signal detectability: Adaptive optimum receiver design. *Journal of the Acoustical Society of America*, 1967, *42*, 773–777.

Nuechterlein, K. Parasuraman, R., & Jiang, Q., Visual sustained attention: Image degradation produces rapid sensitivity decrement over time. *Science*, 1983, *220*, 327–329.

Ostry, D., Moray, N., & Marks, G. Attention, practice and semantic targets. *Journal of Experimental Psychology: Human Perception and Performance*, 1976, *2*, 326–336.

Parasuraman, R. Consistency of individual differences in human vigilance performance: An abilities classification analysis. *Journal of Applied Psychology*, 1976, *61*, 486–492.

Parasuraman, R. Memory load and event rate control sensitivity decrements in sustained attention. *Science*, 1979, *205*, 924–927.

Parasuraman, R. Vigilance, arousal and the brain. In A. Gale and J. Edwards (Eds.), *Physiological correlates of human behavior: Attention and performance*. London: Academic Press, 1983, 1–32.

Parasuraman, R. The psychobiology of sustained attention. In J. S. Warm (Ed.), *Sustained attention and human performance*. London: Wiley, in press.

Parasuraman, R., & Beatty, J. Brain events underlying detection and recognition of weak sensory signals. *Science*, 1980, *210*, 80–83.

Parasuraman, R., & Davies, D. R. Response and evoked potential latencies associated with commission errors in visual monitoring. *Perception and Psychophysics*, 1975, *17*, 465–468.

Parasuraman, R., & Davies, D. R. Decision theory analysis of response latencies in vigilance. *Journal of Experimental Psychology: Human Perception and Performance*, 1976, *2*, 569–582.

Parasuraman, R., & Davies, D. R. A taxonomic analysis of vigilance performance. In R. R. Mackie, (Ed.), *Vigilance: Theory, operational performance, and physiological correlates*. New York: Plenum, 1977, 559–574.

Parasuraman, R., Richer, F., & Beatty, J. Detection and recognition: Concurrent processes in perception. *Perception and Psychophysics*, 1982, *31*, 1–12.

Posner, M. Psychobiology of attention. In M. S. Gazzaniga and C. Blakemore (Eds.), *Handbook of psychobiology*. New York: Academic Press, 1975, 441–480.

Posner, M. *Chronometric explorations of mind*. Hillsdale, N.J.: Erlbaum, 1978.

Posner, M., & Boies, S. J. Components of attention. *Psychological Review*, 1971, *78*, 391–408.

Posner, M., Klein, R., Summers, S., & Buggie, J. On the selection of signals. *Memory and Cognition*, 1973, *1*, 2–12.

Poulton, E. C. Arousing stresses increase vigilance. In R. R. Mackie (Ed.), *Vigilance: Theory operational performance, and physiological correlates*. New York: Plenum, 1977, 423–459.

Poulton, E. C. Increased vigilance with vertical vibration at 5 Hz: An alerting mechanism. *Applied Ergonomics*, 1978, *9*, 73–76.

Schneider, W., & Shiffrin, R. M. Controlled and automatic human information processing: I. Detection, search, and attention. *Psychological Review*, 1977, *84*, 1–66.

Swets, J. A. Signal detection theory applied to vigilance. In R. R. Mackie (Ed.), *Vigilance: Theory, operational performance, and physiological correlates*. New York: Plenum, 1977, 705–718.

Swets, J. A., & Birdsall, T. G. Repeated observation of an uncertain signal. *Perception and Psychophysics*, 1978, *23*, 269–274.

Swets, J. A., Green, D. M., Getty, D. J., & Swets, J. A. Signal detection and identification at successive stages of observation. *Perception and Psychophysics*, 1978, *23*, 275–289.

Swets, J. A., & Kirstofferson, A. B. Attention. *Annual Review of Psychology*, 1970, *21*, 339–366.

Swets, J. A., Shipley, E. F., McKey, M. J., & Green, D. M. Multiple observations of signals in noise. *Journal of the Acoustical Society of America*, 1959, *31*, 514–521.

Taylor, M. M. Detectability theory and the interpretation of vigilance data. In A. F. Sanders (Ed.), *Attention and performance*. Amsterdam: North-Holland, 1967.

Thomas, E. A. C. Criterion adjustment and probability matching. *Perception and Psychophysics*, 1975, *18*, 158–162.

Wald, A. *Sequential analysis*. New York: Wiley, 1947.

Warm, J. S. Psychological processes in sustained attention. In R. R. Mackie (Ed.), *Vigilance: Theory, operational performance, and physiological correlates*. New York: Plenum, 1977, 623–644.

Watson, C. S., & Nichols, T. L. Detectability of auditory signals presented without defined observation intervals. *Journal of the Acoustical Society of America*, 1976, *59*, 655–667.

Williges, R. C. Within session criterion changes compared to an ideal observer criterion in a visual monitoring task. *Journal of Experimental Psychology*, 1969, *81*, 61–66.

Williges, R. C. The role of payoffs and signal ratios on criterion changes during a monitoring task. *Human Factors*, 1971, *13*, 261–267.

Williges, R. C. Manipulating the response criterion in visual monitoring. *Human Factors*, 1973, *15*, 179–185,

Williges, R. C. The vigilance increment: An ideal observer hypothesis. In T. B. Sheridan and G. Johannsen (Eds.), *Monitoring behavior and supervisory control*. New York: Plenum, 1976, 181–190.

Yoss, R. E., Moyer, N. J., & Hollenhorst, R. W. Pupil size and spontaneous pupillary waves associated with alertness. *Neurology*, 1970, *201*, 545–554.

7

The Control of Attention in Visual Search

Patrick Rabbitt

Introduction

Many discussions of visual selective attention have been unhelpful because they have implied that people passively take in visual information in order to recognize any objects that may happen to be there. Visual search is, rather, an active interrogation of the visual world during which people systematically detect and use meaningful patterns of relationships to decide where to look first and in what sequence to seek for further information. People also actively look for some things rather than others. This chapter reviews what is known about these two types of active control—control of where to look, and control of what to look for next. It also considers what functional mechanisms these types of control must involve, and how control may be learned and optimised.

Knowing Where to Look

Very simple experiments show that people can rapidly learn to inspect spatial locations on a display in an optimal order to detect targets that may be present. For example, Rabbitt (1979) asked subjects to search for letter targets on displays that also contained other background letters. Targets appeared with different probabilities in different locations. Young people (ages 18–30 years) very rapidly recognized these constraints and used the information to guide their scans and to find targets most rapidly when they occurred at the most frequent locations. It is a point of interest that even this simple control of direction and order of scan is, apparently, not attainable by all humans. Fit, active, 70-year-old people could describe relative target probabilities at different display locations as accurately as could the 18–30-year-olds. But they apparently could not use this information to guide their visual search, because they could detect targets no faster when they occurred at frequent than at rare locations.

Moray (1978) lucidly discusses empirical work by Senders (1973) who recorded head movements to show that young adults systematically adopt very subtle search strategies to adapt to the different absolute and contingent probabilities of signals from different sources. Moray (1978) points out that human search strategies approximate to the theoretical optimum search strategies worked out by Sheridan and Johannsen (1976) for multisource monitoring behavior (see also Moray, Chapter 13, this volume).

We thus know that people can recognize and adopt optimal search strategies. But, in everyday life, different situations demand different strategies of search. Evidently a person must have a repertoire of different search strategies, each of them optimal for a specific situation. In order to succeed one must first recognize the kind of display or scenario being looked at and then, very rapidly, access an appropriate search strategy from long-term memory (LTM) and deploy it as required.

Rabbitt, Bishop, and Vyas (described in Rabbitt, 1981a) showed this by an experiment in which subjects scanned displays of 26 letters searching for designated targets. Each such display was generated by randomly positioning target and background symbols among the 900 possible cells of an invisible 30 × 30 matrix on a computer visual display unit. For each subject, one, particular, intrinsically random pattern of display locations recurred on 50% of all trials during experimental runs of 150 display presentations. On all other trials, different display patterns occurred. Note that when the frequent display pattern occurred subjects did not know whether or not a target letter was present, where the target letter was if it was present, or in what relative positions the background letters might appear. Nevertheless young people located targets faster when they occurred on frequent than on unique displays. Analysis of the rank order of their detection times across target locations showed that this was because they learned and adopted a particular, fixed, optimal sequential scan across display locations whenever one of these familiar display patterns appeared. It seemed that they made two, successive, independent decisions about each display. First they decided whether it was a familiar pattern or not. If it was not, they searched as best they could. But if it was familiar, they initiated a particular, efficient scan that they had developed and learned. This experiment may offer insight into cases in everyday life in which a person recognizes that a particular "scenario" is one for which a particular, learned search strategy is appropriate. The person then recalls and "plugs in" this particular optimal search routine. If recognition of the scenario takes too long, or if retrieval of an appropriate scanning strategy is too slow, the total time consumed in deciding what it is best to do may be so great that ordered search is no faster than random, undirected search. In everyday life people do not deal with abstract random patterns of letters, but rather with scenes that may be broken up into meaningful units. In the following section we consider how people may use this fact to guide their investigation of the world.

Breaking Up a Display into Meaningful Subsections

The idea that people first make a preliminary, global analysis of a display and only then guide their subsequent analysis contingently on it is implicit in Neisser's (1967) distinction between "pre-attentional" and "attentional" processing of the visual world. In Neisser's words, after preattentional processing a subject has "extracted global characteristics of the display such as figure, background and contour" (p. 89). Neisser envisages these decisions as global, parallel processes that precede and guide subsequent, slower, more analytical, and perhaps serial processes. It is argued here that in some tasks, such two-stage, successive, contingent processing does, in fact, occur but also that such processing takes more diverse and perhaps more complex forms than Neisser appeared to envisage. Considered first are experiments that precisely confirm Neisser's insight that global "gestalt" processing of a display may precede and guide later, more detailed scanning and analysis.

Banks and Prinzmetal (1976) showed that when background items on a display were clustered into groups that showed "good figure," in the sense of having definable external contours or in the senses described by Gestalt theorists (see Helson, 1933), subjects detected targets very rapidly if they fell outside these configurations as "outliers" and more slowly if they fell within their boundaries. Prinzmetal and Banks (1977) extended these demonstrations to show that targets are detected more slowly when they exhibit "good continuation," with contours formed by strings of background items than when they stand apart from these, imaginary, figures.

It must be borne in mind that the human visual system can segregate display items into discrete clusters in a number of different ways. Cahill and Carter (1976) found that when subjects were set to search for some three-digit numbers among others, they took longer as the number of different colors in which display items were printed was increased. This was true even when subjects knew in advance in which color the target items would appear and when the number of items in the target color were held constant across displays. But, very evidently, Cahill and Carter would not have obtained this result if the numbers on their displays had been grouped together in columns of the same color. For example, Neisser (Note 1) and Willows and McKinnon (1973) found that when alternate lines of text were printed in red and in black, subjects could read lines in one color with no interference from lines in the other. Consider if Cahill and Carter's display numerals had been arranged to form the outlines of familiar shapes. Here rapid location of clusters or of contours of items of the same color would have been followed by fast and efficient inspection of its members, and only of its members.

Neisser and Becklen (1975) have done the most imaginative experiment to date. They arranged that two videotaped scenarios involving movement were superimposed in their subjects' field of view and found that people could easily follow either with little distraction from the other. This remarkable ability to relate together complex, moving contours as part of a pattern, and to use the appreciation of the entire pattern as a guide to localization of its components clearly underlines the power of the visual system to extract and use wholistic characteristics of displays as an initial guide to further processing.

The use of clustering, or grouping, to guide visual search is apparent even on static displays in which symbols are grouped in terms of a complex common attribute such as shape. Marken and Patterson (1979) reported that variation in the size of the vocabulary of different background symbols used in visual search experiments had less effect when they are grouped together into sets of identical items, for example, AAACCCEEEDDD, than when they were randomly alternated, for example, ACAEDCEDAECD. Farmer and Taylor (1980) also make this general point. They used stimuli differing in hue and brightness and showed that search was faster when items with symbols with similar values on a dimension are grouped together than when they were randomly scattered.

Thus, it is no longer in question that subjects may, by initial processing, detect various types of "structures" in a display and contingently use them to guide their further search. The discussion has shifted to more interesting points. Broadbent (1977) has suggested that the detection of larger figures, contours and clusters on a display may involve operation of a detection and coding system for lower spatial frequencies, whereas a second, subsequent, and possibly independent stage of analysis involving smaller stimulus features may require the separate operation of a high spatial frequency analyzer channel. This insight demands further investigation, but the important question seems to be precisely *which* particular common features or attributes of stimuli on a display may be detected and used by the visual system to identify grouping or overall "structure." In experiments described by Julesz (1975), by Frisby and Mayhew (in Frisby, 1979, pp. 114–115), and by others, subjects have been asked whether or not they detect contours or gradients of texture on displays in which particular common features, or patterns of common orientation among symbols, are systematically varied. It is by no means clear that such detection of contour or gradient must involve use of low-frequency detector systems prior to, and independent of, high-frequency detector systems. Indeed, it is hard to see how large outline shapes can be resolved until the common characteristics of smaller symbols have been detected and recognized by high-frequency analyser systems.

We have considered cases in which the detection of particular physical characteristics of symbols on a display may allow a subject to discover an efficient scanning strategy and then to recognize rapidly situations in which it can be usefully deployed. The basic assumption is that such initial processing may guide subsequent more detailed processing that leads to the subsequent discovery of the "meaning" of a scenario or of particular elements within it. Data collected since 1967, suggest that, in fact, much more interesting and efficient processes occur. It seems that people may sometimes be able to recognize the overall "meaning" or "semantic context" of displays and scenes *before* they resolve all details within them. They may use this rapid recognition of the "meaning" of a display, or of a pattern of regular relationships within it, to guide their further interrogation of its component features.

Recognition of Meaning May Precede and Guide Identification of Detail; Rapid Access and Use of "Knowledge of the World" Can Guide Visual Search

It may seem implausible that people can *first* recognize the taxonomic class or category to which an object belongs and *then* deploy this knowledge to guide their subsequent scanning in order to identify it completely. However, brief consideration of the way in which people recognize high-contrast puzzle pictures shows that this must be the case. When photographs of complex objects or scenes are processed to achieve high-contrast "whitewash" effects, so that undifferentiated black blobs stand out against a white background, it may be quite impossible to recognize what these blobs represent until a cue is provided—at which point all details immediately fall into place. Thus a picture presented by Frisby (1979, p. 20) may be quite unrecognizable until one is told that it is a treated photograph of a dog. At this point not only this main object (a Dalmatian) becomes visible, but also other, peripheral, parts of the scene such as a curb and a tree are immediately recognizable.

More formal experiments by Mackworth and Morandi (1967) have used television monitoring of pictures inspected by subjects with superimposed traces of their momentary ocular fixation points to illustrate that people identify and use local clusters of relationships ("pictures within pictures") to decide where to look next. Biederman, Glass, and Stacey (1973) and Biederman, Rabinowitz, Glass, and Stacey (1974) have shown that people can both scan faster and remember better scenarios in which conventional or meaningful relationships between familiar objects are preserved than they can scan and remember montages in which pictures of the same objects appear in random juxtapositions. In other words, scanning of familiar scenes appears to be guided by previous experience ("knowledge of the world"). Clearly, it is not necessary to question whether people scanning familiar scenes or objects are guided by their previous experience. Evidently they are, and the only question is whether this recognition and subsequent guidance is rapid enough to make identification by controlled search faster than identification by systematic, but otherwise undirected and inflexible scanning strategies.

Experiments to check the speed with which "knowledge of the world" can be accessed and deployed to facilitate recognition have typically used "priming" paradigms in which pictures or words are presented in advance of other semantically related or semantically unrelated words or pictures. For example, Carr, Davidson, and Hawkins (1978) and McCauley, Parmelee, Sperber, and Caw (1980) showed that brief presentation of higher order, contextual information can guide and facilitate the subsequent, efficient, coding of lower order, featural information necessary for complete identification. This higher-order information can, apparently, be very rapidly recognized and used to facilitate further identification. Meyers and Rhoades (1978) showed that subjects may require as little as 500 msec to maximize benefits when primed by a word before presentation of an associated picture, or vice versa.

The speed of recognition of overall semantic attributes of objects is illustrated by a particularly elegant experiment by Potter (1975), who presented series of 12 different pictures in immediate succession at rates ranging from 1/125 msec to 1/133 msec. Her subjects either were told verbally in advance to scan for the presence or absence of a picture of any examplar of a large class of different objects (e.g., "Is there *any* picture of a boat?"); or, before the pictures were presented, were actually shown a particular line drawing that might, or might not, appear. Correct identifications were possible at presentation rates of 1/125 msec, and subjects reached ceiling accuracy at rates of 1/167 msec. The point of interest is that targets were almost as readily detected when they were cued only by category name as when they were visually inspected before a run. It must be concluded that, under some circumstances, people need no longer than 167 msec to decide that a picture is a representation of "some sort of a boat" and that (if Meyers and Rhoades's 1978 data are taken into account) within a further 500 msec, or less, they can use this decision to optimize their further scanning and information selection and better identify a complex display. As Potter (1975) remarks: "It is apparent that a scene is processed rapidly to an abstract level of meaning before intentional selection occurs" (p. 966). To put this another way, it is apparent that people can very rapidly decide whether or not something that they briefly glimpse is the sort of thing they are looking for. The remainder of this chapter considers how they manage to do this.

Categorization and Identification in Visual Search

We have begun to consider how preliminary, categorical, decisions may allow people to locate and inspect those, and only those, symbols or objects in a display that may repay further inspection. Jonides and Gleitman (1976) have neatly made this point with the observation that one can locate a cowboy among a herd of cows before one can further identify him as John Wayne or Henry Fonda. This may mean that one preliminary, identification process based on feature extraction ("Wayne or Fonda") may be independent of, successive to, and contingent on the outcome of another identification process ("Cowboy or Cow") that precedes it. But, as will become clear in the following, the data available also suggest other models. One possibility is that many different categorical decisions may be made simultaneously and in parallel, that they may be based on independent or on overlapping kinds of evidence, that they may involve similar or different levels of analysis, and that some of these parallel decisions may be completed faster than others. A different possibility is that in some cases categorizations are not successive, or independent, approximations to complete identification; but that all possible categorizations of symbols on a display may be achieved simultaneously so that choices among them may be the outcomes of "late selections" among these various responses (Deutsch, 1977). In considering the evidence, it is important to bear in mind that these models are not mutually exclusive, and that a highly successful, and adaptive, perceptual processing system might be expected to use each and any of them that may be best suited to a particular task. There is an unfortunate tradition in cognitive psychology that models of human information-processing should be validated by elimination, and that some ill-defined principles of parsimony preclude the postulate that information can be processed in more than one way. It seems that the perceptual systems studied are, paradoxically, much less limited and more eclectic than the theories put forward by the people who study them.

Categorization When All Members of a Target Class Possess a Single, Identifiable, Common Perceptual Property

It is easy to understand how categorization may precede identification when all stimuli in a target class share some common perceptual attribute, cue, or feature that is not shared by other, irrelevant background stimuli. Here initial recognition of class membership will only require detection and identification of this property. Any further decision as to *which* member of the class has been identified may then continue by analysis of quite different features. There is clear evidence that people do use such successive, contingent, decisions to improve their search. But it is important to recognize that efficiency differs between cases in which categorization and identification involve separate decisions on different perceptual features or perceptual dimensions, and those in which categorization and identification involve decisions on the basis of the same dimensions or features.

Corcoran and Jackson (1979) provide an excellent demonstration that decisions can be based on single critical features. Their subjects searched for the symbol Ø, either among sets of straight-line letters (e.g., N, K, and Y or A, V, and X) or among sets of curved-line letters (e.g., O, C, and G or Q, S, and U). Transfer from one straight-line set to another, from one curved-line set to another, or, indeed, from a straight-line to a curved-line set did not affect performance. In all cases, subjects could always use only one of the two possible components (0 or /) to make their discrimination. But there was marked negative transfer when they switched to search for Ø among a mixture of straight- and curved-line letters (e.g., O, K, X, C, Q, G, and V). It is apparent that subjects could search very efficiently if they could use *either* the / or the 0 cue alone, but could search very much less efficiently when they had to detect both cues to make their discriminations, and neither cue alone could suffice.

Neisser (1963) and Rabbitt (1962, 1967) had earlier made this point less precisely. If subjects are trained to search for straight-line letters (e.g., A and X) among curved-line letters (such as O, C, and Q), they do not slow when transferred to search for the same target among different background letters. However, if they are trained to search for straight-line targets among straight-line background letters, they apparently must learn particular cues that are no longer valid when they have to look for the same targets among *other* straight-line background letters.

Few experiments have investigated when targets and background items differ only in terms of a single critical difference along a single perceptual dimension. Exceptions are studies by Bloomfield (1979) and Howarth and Bloomfield (1969), who have derived mathematical models to predict variations in search speed with the magnitude of differences between target and background stimuli (e.g., search among circles differing in diameter). Apart from these elegant pioneering studies, most experiments on search among "unidimensional" stimuli have involved decisions about sets of familiar symbols such as letters and digits. These tasks do not really reveal much about perceptual classifications of stimuli along a single dimension; for example, they cannot reveal much about the dimension of shape because shape is hardly a single dimension.

Attempts to apply multidimensional scaling to describe the mutual discriminability of sets of letters have not been very successful. Descriptions of confusability in terms of the theory of fuzzy sets (e.g., by Oden, 1979) have not yet influenced the design of experiments. With rare exceptions (e.g., Townsend, 1971) matrices for particular typefaces, fonts, or symbol sets have not been obtained; so the basic data to test theories are not available. The general assumption that has been the most popular since the mid 1970s is that people discriminate symbols from each other in terms of the presence, absence, or relative salience of particular discriminative features such as the riser that distinguishes a *Y* from a *V* (Naus and Schillman, 1976). Thus the experimental results available on search among symbols are still conveniently reviewed by separating them into three cases: (1) those in which all target symbols or stimuli have in common a single discriminative feature that is not possessed by any background stimulus or symbol; (2) those in which target symbols are defined by, but do not necessarily share with each other, an indeterminably large set of distincitve features—none of which are possessed by any background symbol; and (3) those in which target symbols are evidently recognized by wholistic comparisons in which all features are simultaneously considered and in which no single feature or set of features may, alone, be critical for the discrimination.

Categorization When Members of a Target Class May Each Possess One or More of a Set of Critical Common Features

It is very rare that discriminations between sets of symbols can be made in terms of any single, common identifying feature. Rabbitt (1967) trained subjects to search for either two or eight target-letters among one set of background symbols and then transferred them to search for the same targets among new background sets. When background sets were switched, subjects who had searched for eight targets showed more set-specific improvement and greater negative transfer than subjects who had searched for only two targets. This suggests that discriminations between target and background items involves many different features and that, in general, the larger is the number of symbols for which people search, the greater will be the number of distinctive features they must learn and use to optimize target detection.

Rabbitt (1978, 1981b) pointed out that the number of critical cues to be taken into consideration and so, also, the efficiency of search, will vary depending on whether subjects have only to distinguish all target items from all background items or on whether they must distinguish each target item from every other. Thus a person who has to locate and make a different response to each of two targets, A and B, in effect categorizes a stimulus population into three sets—A, B, and all background items. If he or she has to make different responses to each of the eight targets A, B, C, D, E, F, G, and H; he or she will, in effect, have to discriminate the symbols on the display into nine sets—A, B, C, D, E, F, G, H, versus all background items. Rabbitt (1959) and Pollack (1963) have both shown that categorization times increase as a multiplicative function of the number of categories discriminated and the number of items within each of these categories. This is, no doubt, because the number of cues necessary to discriminate between stimuli must rise more sharply with the number of stimulus categories to be discriminated than with the number of stimuli in any one of these categories.

In considering under what circumstances a person can recognize that a stimulus is a member of a category *before* he or she recognizes which particular stimulus it is, it is useful to consider limiting cases of overlap in the cues used to make these two different kinds of discriminations. Let us suppose that there is a set of features or characteristics $(T_1^B, T_2^B, \ldots T_N^B)$ that discriminate all members of a set of target symbols from all members of a set of background symbols. Let us further suppose that there is a set of features $(T_1^T, T_2^T, \ldots T_N^T)$ that discriminate each target symbol from every other target symbol. In one limiting case, there will be no overlap whatever between these two sets of features. Here, if only T^B features are considered, it will be possible for a person to recognize that a symbol is *some* member of the target set without recognizing *which* member of the set it is. In the other limiting case the set of T^T and T^B cues will completely overlap. Here categorization and identification of symbols will be equivalent decisions and a person will completely identify each target by virtue of the same comparisons by means of which he or she detects it. Between these limits are cases in which the sets of T^T and T^B cues partially overlap. Here it may be possible for a person to recognize that *some* target stimuli are members of the T set without identifying them. But for other target stimuli the same cues will be used for both categorization and identification and these will therefore be equivalent decisions. It is useful to bear these points in mind when considering a wide range of experiments on discriminations between overlearned subsets of symbols (e.g., letters and digits) that have been undertaken to test whether categorization can precede identification.

Early experiments by Ingling (1971) and Rabbitt (1962) showed that digits are detected faster and more accurately among letters than they are among other digits, and vice versa. A neat experiment by Brand (1971) showed that subjects could search as efficiently for letters among digits under instructions to locate "any letter" as they could when asked to find any single, specified letter (e.g., *K*). This result, with later experiments by Gleitman and Jonides (1976), Jonides and Gleitman (1976), and Egeth, Atkinson, Gilmore, and Marcus (1973), suggest that subjects can sometimes recognize that a symbol on a display is a letter, or a digit before they recognize which *particular* letter or digit it is. This has led to the idea that categorical recognition may be used to locate members of a class of symbols that can then be further analyzed and identified as particular items. In such situations, it is claimed that members of the target class subjectively appear to "pop out" from among background items on a display (Neisser, 1963). Digits can certainly be recognized remarkably rapidly among background letters. Sperling, Budiansky, Spivak, and Johnstone (1971) estimated scanning rates of 8 to 13 msec/symbol for rapid, serial visual presentation of displays on which subjects searched among letters for a numeral.

In spite of evidence indicating that efficiency may not be as great as was once thought (Francolini & Egeth, 1979) letter–digit classification tasks provide a provocative suggestion that sometimes, at least for very highly learned symbol sets, categorization and identification may be separable, serial contingent processes that involve consideration of different types of perceptual evidence. Thus far, categorizations considered have been those based on single idiosyncratic characteristics and those based on constellations of several features all of which relate to a particular stimulus dimension—in this case, symbol shape. The next case is one in which recognition of the category to which target symbols belong involves a decision based on one stimulus dimension; and subsequent identification of particular symbols within the category may require a different, subsequent decision based on another, different dimension.

Categorization and Identification on Separate Dimensions

The classic experiments are by Green and Anderson (1956), whose subjects searched for a target of designated color (e.g., "a red triangle") among background symbols printed in several different colors. They found that search speed was unaffected by the range of *shapes* of symbols in other colors. It seemed that subjects first scanned a display to locate symbols printed in the relevant color and only then, when they were located, subsequently and contingently analyzed their shapes. Green and Anderson (1955) also showed that people can make similar, successive and contingent decisions on target shape and size. Neisser (Note 1) and Willows and McKinnon (1973) have shown that if alternate lines of text are printed in different colors people can read words in one color without any interference from words in the other.

Rabbitt (1978) has pointed out that such, highly efficient serial, contingent scanning strategies are only possible when stimulus dimensions are "separable" in the sense coined by Garner and Felfoldy (1971; Garner and Felfoldy 1970). These authors found that although some pairs of dimensions, such as color and shape, can be independently processed; others, such as color and brightness are apparently "integral" and must be processed together. An experiment by Farmer and Taylor (1980), though not intended to make this specific point, shows that subjects cannot carry out serial contingent scans to locate stimuli on one of a pair of integral dimensions (color and shape) in order to subsequently identify them completely on the other. Both dimensions must, apparently, be simultaneously rather than successively processed.

Thus if serial, contingent scanning is considered as the exercise of a particular, efficient control strategy in visual search, it requires successful integration at least two separate, complex lower level processes. First, people must recognize which among all the available pairs of stimulus dimensions are separable, and so allow contingent search. They must then recognize which dimension in each pair allows the maximum, initial reduction of the field of search. For example, if symbols may be any of five different colors but only either of two different shapes, maximum reduction of the number of symbols *completely* inspected will *theoretically* be achieved by searching first on color and then on shape. For five shapes and two colors the converse strategy will *theoretically* be optimal. The word *theoretically* is stressed because as yet nothing is known of the trade-offs that are *practically* possible for human beings in these situations. The relative ease of discriminations among shapes and among colors, and the consequent relative ease and difficulty of these decisions on other grounds than information reduction will certainly have a bearing on what people actually choose to do. Further we do not know whether there are trade-offs between the relative possible complexities of an initial and a subsequent decision, or what these trade-offs may be. The present argument is that subjects do, very rapidly, recognize and operate optimal search strategies so as to allow contingent decisions whenever possible; and that it is worthwhile to try to discover the means by which these strategies are recognized, deployed, learned, and stored for later appropriate use.

In the preceding sections it has been assumed that people making discriminations among complex symbols or objects always actively strive to detect and use the minimum range of distinctive features necessary to make the choices required of them. Work carried out since 1968 suggests that this is not always the case and that other, contingent, decisions may be based on an initial, wholistic comparison across *all* features and dimensions simultaneously.

Categorization by Wholistic Matching To Detect Identity or Change

Many experiments have shown that complex symbols are very rapidly recognized when they are immediately repeated on successive trials (e.g., Bertelson, 1965; Rabbitt, 1968). This also happens with visual search tasks, in which a target is very rapidly detected if it is repeated on immediately successive displays. Further, if the same target is immediately repeated at the same spatial position on a display, the time taken to detect it does not increase with the variance of the range of background items also presented (Rabbitt, Cumming, and Vyas, 1977, 1979b). It seems that subjects begin their analysis of each new display by making a rapid, wholistic comparison to determine whether or not it is identical to the last one they saw. If it is, they can very rapidly repeat the same response. If it is not they then, contingently, extend their analysis and make further comparisons to detect the presence of any target.

This was shown by Jordan and Rabbitt (1977), who required subjects to make one response to all displays containing a cross (+) and another response to all displays containing a bar (−). Crosses and bars might occur against red, green, or amber colored patches. The color of the patch was always irrelevant to the choice of response. When, at random, both symbol and color were repeated on immediately successive displays (e.g., red cross followed by red cross), responses were some 50 msec faster than when the relevant symbol recurred but the color changed (e.g., red cross followed by amber cross). An experiment by Fletcher and Rabbitt (1978) points to the same model. Their subjects made one response to every occurrence of the letter A and another response to every occurrence of the letter B during a fast, self-paced serial two-choice response task. Very occasionally, a random dot pattern appeared instead of an A or a B. Subjects were told that this dot pattern was a programming mistake and that they should, as fast as possible, press either key to remove it and then respond to whichever symbol came next. Early in practice subjects almost invariably disposed of the random dot pattern by pressing the same key as they used to make their last response. Later in practice they invariably pressed the *alternate* key to that used for the last response (e.g., A appears, and right hand responds; then dot pattern appears, and left hand responds). Fletcher and Rabbit found evidence that this happens because highly practiced subjects cease to try to identify each symbol as a particular entity (A or B) and instead set themselves to detect identity or change between successive symbols. If identity is detected, the same response is repeated. If *any* change is detected, the alternate response is made. Thus control in this task does not only involve an initial wholistic comparison between successive symbols on a display to detect identity or change; subjects must also have some memory record for what the last response was because the new response must be chosen in relation to the previous response (alternation or repetition; that is, change or no change).

Evidence for Other, Wholistic, Discrimination Strategies Developed After Extensive Practice

An early demonstration that people discover and learn to use particular sets of optimal cues was reported by Rabbitt (1967). In this experiment, subjects showed negative transfer when after having practiced detecting target symbols among one set of background symbols, they were then transferred to search for the same targets among a new background set. Rabbitt, Cumming, and Vyas (1979a) showed that this specific cue learning was retained, after initial practice, for as long as 4 weeks but not for as long as 6 weeks. It follows that information about a particular, optimal set of cues for discriminations between particular target and background symbols can be retained in LTM for several weeks and deployed effectively as soon as it is recognized that such a display has recurred. However several studies carried out since 1970 show that it is dangerous to assume that specific cue learning is the *only* way by which subjects improve their performance with practice. Prinz (1979) described experiments in which subjects who were practiced on particular target and background sets and were then transferred to various new tasks in which the old target set became the new background set, the old background set became the new target set, target and background sets were switched or new targets were sought among new background items. Prinz appears to have found maximum negative transfer for the case in which target and background symbols were reversed after initial training. He cogently argues that this must mean that subjects must have learned to recognize completely target items at some level of perceptual analysis, and that they do not merely search for a subset of cues (e.g., T^B cues) that distinguish target items from background items but that do not distinguish target items from each other.

The amount, and kind, of negative transfer obtained after initial training appears to vary with practice in an interesting way. Very early in the practice, subjects who have been asked to look for a randomly selected subset of target letters have difficulty remembering which letters they have been asked to search for. Until this initial learning is complete, they have to identify completely all items, target and background alike, as individual, named symbols in order to decide whether these items are targets or not. At intermediate levels of practice, as in experiments by Corcoran and Jackson (1979), Neisser (1963), and Rabbitt (1967), people learn to select out optimal T^B cues that distinguish members of a particular target set from a particular background set. Transfer deprives them of this learned advantage, and they regress to a lower level of performance until new learning has taken place. But Rabbitt *et al.* (1979a) found that when subjects were given very extensive practice (30 days), they ceased to show negative transfer when they searched for a familiar target set among an unfamiliar background set. At these levels of practice it seems that subjects have changed their detection strategy. This result is supported by similar data from two-choice categorization tasks reported by Kristofferson (1977). An interesting possibility is that if subjects practice for sufficiently long periods, they can recognize target items by simultaneously testing for each and all of a very wide range of different features. Apparently some subset of these features is usually adequate to allow rapid target detection among any of a variety of different subsets of background symbols. In brief, very extended practice seems to increase the number of different, alternative ways in which target items can be identified so that use of any, particular, set of T^B features becomes unnecessary.

Whatever new processes further research may reveal, the point of the current argument is that practice at visual search does not simply bring about improvement in the speed and accuracy with which passive processes may be completed. Subjects do not simply learn to do the same things in the same way ever faster and ever more accurately. Rather, they actively seek out and try new ways to do things. As they practice, they continually develop new techniques that allow them actively to control where they look and what they look for. A demonstration of this comes from a clever experiment by Bruce (1979) who used a sequential decision task to investigate the way in which subjects searched for faces of well-known politicians (that is, stimuli familiar from long experience in daily life). In one of her experiments (Experiment II), subjects searched for the faces of Heath, Douglas-Home, Wilson, and Callaghan among distractor faces that might be either visually similar to these targets—but were not faces of politicians—or faces of other well-known politicians who might or might not resemble any of the target group. Bruce's subjects took longer to reject visually similar distractors, but were also slower to reject visually dissimilar but categorically related faces (i.e., of other politicians). Her key finding was that these two distracting effects were *independent* because the category-relation effect was as marked for visually similar as for visually dissimilar faces.

It seems that when people search among very familiar stimuli, they may simultaneously and, if Bruce's results are confirmed, *independently* make judgments on the basis of perceptual features and of taxonomic class. A number of experiments on visual search for some words among others also show the effects of higher-order (semantic) as against lower-order (graphemic or featural) effects. For example, Karlin and Bower (1976) and Henderson and Chard (1978) found that target words were found more slowly if they were embedded among distractors that were semantically related to them than if they were embedded among words of unrelated meanings.

Fletcher (Note 2) has also found that target words are located faster when all distractors come from a different, and homogeneous, background semantic class than when they are drawn at random from a variety of different semantic classes. He also found separate effects of graphemic and semantic similarity of distractor to target items in searches of word lists. Bruce (in press) has extended her earlier study to show that when subjects search among words, the effects of semantic and featural (graphemic) distraction are independent and additive. Thus, after practice, people develop different options of categorization. At high levels of skill control of search must involve selection of the optimal categorical *option* (whether feature-analytical or semantic) to maximally reduce distraction and to improve efficiency.

Conclusions

People scan the visual world actively and purposively. They know where to look and they know what to look for. It has been shown in this chapter how they improve both these kinds of control with practice. Learning control of search may require mastery of very complex information as when people use their acquired "knowledge of the world" to guide their search. It may only require very simple learning as when people systematically seek, and discover, specific cues that are optimal to distinguish target from background symbols. But even this simple learning of cue systems apparently marks a stable addition to the range of control strategies that a person may have at his or her command. Rabbitt *et al.*, (1979a) found that learning of a specific cue system apparently can persist without any intervening experience for as long as 4 weeks.

This gives us a new insight into the constraints under which systems exercising control of visual search must operate. Evidently, when confronted with a new display, scene, or scenario, a person can recognize, within a very few milliseconds (Potter, 1975) whether or not it is of a kind that has been previously encountered. Within a very few further milliseconds the person can then retrieve from LTM a particular, appropriate, search strategy and deploy it to optimize scanning and speed detection of the information required. Note that unless these processes take place very rapidly indeed they will be of no use at all. Rather than choosing scenarios a person might well choose to use the same, stereotyped, scanning strategy for all occasions. The advantage of this procedure would be that no time would be consumed in recognizing the scene as a member of a class to which a specific strategy was appropriate or in selecting the appropriate strategy out of a large number of different strategies held in memory. Search might not proceed in the optimal way, but at least it could *start* at once. Thus, unless access and deployment of optimal scanning strategies is very swift, they can never allow a person to "catch up" with an instantly initiated, stereotyped, strategy for all occasions. As human beings, it is pleasant to find that we do something so complicated so fast and so well. As scientists, it is intensely exciting to find that we have such richly intriguing processes to study.

Reference Notes

1. Neisser, U. *Selective reading: A method for the study of visual attention.* Conference abstracts, 19th International Congress of Psychology. London: Butterworths, 1969.
2. Fletcher, C. D. Philosophy thesis, University of Oxford, 1981.

References

Banks, W. P., and Prinzmetal, W. Configurational effects in visual information processing. *Perception and Psychophysics*, 1976, *19*, 361–367.

Bertelson, P. Serial choice reaction time as a function of response versus signal-and-response repetition. *Nature*, 1965, *206*, 217–218.

Biederman, I., Glass, A. L., and Stacey, E. W. Searching for objects in real-world scenes. *Journal of Experimental Psychology*, 1973, *97*, 22–27.

Biederman, I., Rabinowitz, J. C., Glass, A. L., and Stacey, W. E., Jr. On the information extracted at a glance from a scene. *Journal of Experimental Psychology*, 1974, *103*, 587–600

Bloomfield, J. R. Visual search with embedded targets: Colour and texture differences. *Human Factors*, 1979, *21*, 317–330.

Brand, J. Classification without identification in visual search. *Quarterly Journal of Experimental Psychology*, 1971, *23*, 178–186.

Broadbent, D. E. The hidden pre-attentive processes. *American Psychologist*, 1977, *32*, 109–118.

Bruce, V. Searching for politicians: An information processing approach to face recognition. *Quarterly Journal of Experimental Psychology*, 1979, *31*, 373–395.

Bruce, V. Visual and semantic effects in a serial word classification task. *Current Psychological Research*, in press.

Cahill, M. C., and Carter, R. C. Color code size for searching displays of different density. *Human Factors*, 1976, *18*, 273–280.

Carr, T. H., Davidson, B. J., and Hawkins, H. L. Perceptual flexibility in word recognition: Strategies affect orthographic computation but not lexical access. *Journal of Experimental Psychology, Human Perception and Performance*, 1978, *4*, 674–690.

Corcoran, D. W., and Jackson, A. Flexibility in the choice of distinctive features in visual search with random cue blocked designs. *Perception*, 1979, *6*, 629–633.

Deutsch, J. A. On the category effect in visual search. *Perception and Psychophysics*, 1977, *21*, 590.

Egeth, H., Atkinson, J., Gilmore, G., and Marcus, N. Factors affecting processing rate in visual search. *Perception and Psychophysics*, 1973, *13*, 394–462.

Farmer, E. W., and Taylor, R. M. Visual search through colour displays: Effects of target-background similarity and background uniformity. *Perception and Psychophysics*, 1980, *27*, 267–272.

Felfoldy, G. L., and Garner, W. R. The effects on speeded classification of implicit and explicit instructions regarding stimulus dimensions. *Perception and Psychophysics*, 1971, *9*, 289–292.

Fletcher, C. E., and Rabbitt, P. M. A. The changing pattern of perceptual and analytic strategies and response selection with practice in a two-choice reaction time task. *Quarterly Journal of Experimental Psychology*, 1978, *30*, 417–427.

Francolini, C. M., and Egeth, H. E. Perceptual selectivity is task dependent. The pop-out effect poops out. *Perception and Psychophysics*, 1979, *25*, 99–110.

Frisby, J. *Seeing: Illusion, brain and mind*. Oxford, Oxford University Press, 1979.

Garner, W. R., and Felfoldy, G. L. Integrality of stimulus dimensions in various types of information processing. *Cognitive Psychology*, 1970, *1*, 225–241.

Gleitman, H., and Jonides, J. The cost of categorisation in visual search: Incomplete processing of targets and field items. *Perception and Psychophysics*, 1976, *20*, 281–288.

Green, B. F., and Anderson, L. K. Size coding in a visual search task. *M.I.T. Research Reports*, 1955, No. 16.

Green, B. F., and Anderson, L. K. Color coding in a visual search task. *Journal of Experimental Psychology*, 1956, *51*, 19–24.

Helson, H. The fundamental propositions of Gestalt psychology. *Psychological Review*, 1933, *40*, 13–32.

Henderson, L., and Chard, J. Semantic effects in visual word detection with visual similarity controlled. *Perception and Psychophysics*, 1978, *23*, 290–298.

Howarth, C. I., and Bloomfield, J. R. A rational equation for predicting search times in simple inspection tasks. *Psychonomic Science*, 1969, *17*, 226.

Ingling, N. W. Categorisation: A mechanism for rapid information processing. *Journal of Experimental Psychology*, 1971, *94*, 239–243.

Jonides, J., and Gleitman, H. The benefit of categorization in visual search: Target localization without identification. *Perception and Psychophysics*, 1976, *20*, 289–298.

Jordan, T. C., and Rabbitt, P. M. A. Response times to stimuli of increasing complexity as a function of ageing. *British Journal of Psychology*, 1977, *68*, 189–201.

Julesz, B. Experiments in the visual perception of texture. *Scientific American*, 1975, *232*(April), 34–43.

Karlin, M. B., and Bower, G. H. Semantic category effects in visual word search. *Perception and Psychophysics,* 1976, *19,* 417–424.

Kristoffersen, M. W. The effects of practice with one positive set in a memory scanning task can be completely transferred to a new set. *Memory and Cognition,* 1977, *5,* 177–186.

Mackworth, J. H., and Morandi, A. J. The gaze selects informative details within pictures. *Perception and Psychophysics,* 1967, *2,* 547–552.

Marken, R., and Patterson, J. Effects of sequence and variety of irrelevant items in visual search. *Perceptual and Motor Skills,* 1979, *49,* 315–318.

McCauley, C., Parmelee, C. M., Sperker, R. D., and Caw, T. H. Early extraction of meaning from pictures and its relation to conscious identification. *Journal of Experimental Psychology,* 1980, *6,* 265–275.

Meyers, L. S., and Rhoades, R. W. Visual search of common scenes. *Quarterly Journal of Experimental Psychology,* 1978, *30,* 297–310.

Moray, N. The strategic control of information processing. In G. Underwood (Ed.), *Strategies of information processing.* New York: Academic Press, 1978.

Naus, M. J., and Schillman, R. J. Why a Y is not a V: A new look at the distinctive features of letters. *Journal of Experimental Psychology: Human Perception and Performance,* 1976, *2,* 394–400.

Neisser, U. Decision time without reaction time: Experiments in visual scanning. *American Journal of Psychology,* 1963, *76,* 376–385.

Neisser, U. *Cognitive psychology.* New York: Appleton-Century-Crofts, 1967.

Neisser, U., and Becklen, R. Attending to visually specified events. *Cognitive Psychology,* 1975, *7,* 450–494.

Oden, G. C. A fuzzy logical model of letter identification. *Journal of Experimental Psychology: Human Perception and Performance,* 1979, *5,* 336–352.

Pollack, I. Speed of classification of words into superordinate categories. *Journal of Verbal Learning and Verbal Behaviour,* 1963, *2,* 159–165.

Potter, M. C. Meaning in visual search. *Science,* 1975, *187,* 965–966.

Prinz, W. Locus of the effect of specific practice in continuous visual search. *Perception and Psychophysics,* 1979, *25,* 137–142.

Prinzmetal, W., and Banks, W. P. Good continuation affects visual detection *Perception and Psychophysics,* 1977, *21,* 389–395.

Rabbitt, P. M. A. Effects of independent variations in stimulus and response probability. *Nature,* 1959, *183,* 1212.

Rabbitt, P. M. A. *Perceptual discrimination and the choice of responses.* Unpublished doctoral dissertation, University of Cambridge, 1962.

Rabbitt, P. M. A. Learning to ignore irrelevant information. *American Journal of Experimental Psychology,* 1967, *80,* 1–13.

Rabbitt, P. M. A. Repetition effects and signal classification strategies in serial choice response tasks. *Quarterly Journal of Experimental Psychology,* 1968, *20,* 232–240.

Rabbitt, P. M. A. Sorting, categorisation and visual search. In E. C. Carterette, and M. Friedman (Eds.), *Handbook of perception,* (Vol. 10). New York: Academic Press, 1978.

Rabbitt, P. M. A. Some experiments and a model for changes in attentional selectivity with old age. In F. Hoffmeister and C. Muller (Eds.), *Brain function in old age.* Berling: Springer-Verlag, 1979.

Rabbitt, P. M. A. Cognitive psychology needs models for changes in performance with old age. In J. Long and A. D. Baddeley (Eds.), *Attention and performance, IX.* Hillsdale, N.J.: Erlbaum, 1981. (a)

Rabbitt, P. M. A. Visual selective attention. In C. R. Puff (Ed.), *Handbook of research methods in human memory and cognition.* New York: Academic Press, 1981. (b)

Rabbitt, P. M. A., Cumming, G., and Vyas, S. M. An analysis of visual search: Entropy and sequential effects. In S. Dornic (Ed.), *Attention and performance, VI*. Potomac, Md: Erlbaum, 1977.

Rabbitt, P. M. A., Cumming, G., and Vyas, S. M. Improvement, learning and retention of skill at visual search. *Quarterly Journal of Experimental Psychology*, 1979, *31*, 441–459. (b)

Rabbitt, P. M. A., Cumming, G., and Vyas, S. M. Modulation of selection attention by sequential effects in visual search tasks. *Quarterly Journal of Experimental Psychology*, 1979, *31*, 305–317.

Senders, J. W. Visual scanning behaviour in visual search. Washington, D.C.: New York Academy of Sciences, 1973.

Sheridan, T., and Johannsen, G. (Eds.) *Monitoring behavior and supervisory control*. New York: Plenum Press, 1976.

Sperling, G., Budianski, J., Spivak, J. G., and Johnstone, M. L. Extremely rapid visual search: The maximum rate of scanning letters for the presence of a numeral. *Science*, 1971, *174*, 307–310.

Townsend, J. T. Theoretical analysis of an alphabetic confusion matrix. *Perception and Psychophysic*, 1971, *9*, 40–50.

Willows, D. M., and McKinnon, G. E. Selective reading: Attention to the "unattended" lines. *Canadian Journal of Psychology*, 1973, *27*, 292–304.

8

Brain Mechanisms of Visual Selective Attention[1]

M. Russell Harter and Cheryl J. Aine

Introduction

For the purposes of this chapter, *selective attention* is defined as the predisposition of an organism to process selectively relevant, as compared to irrelevant, environmental information. From a neurophysiological perspective, this selection is assumed to occur at synapses between neurons. More specifically, the processing of afferent neural information through the synapse is modulated (enhanced or suppressed) by efferent activity. Such activity may be initiated prior to stimulation as a consequence of task-relevance instructions stored in memory, or after stimulation as a consequence of information derived from the stimulus per se. In studying selective attention from a neurophysiological perspective, therefore, three basic questions need to be answered: (1) At what level of the nervous system is the efferent modulation of synaptic activity taking place? (2) What type of sensory information is represented or coded by the postsynaptic neurons, the activity of which is being modulated at different levels of the nervous system? (3) What is the nature of the mechanisms that control the efferent modulation? These questions correspond generally with issues raised in the cognitive psychology literature concerning (1) the stage of the selection, (2) the specificity of the selection, and (3) the directing of attention.

At first glance, these questions may appear straightforward. The situation becomes complex, however, when one considers that there are billions of neurons and synapses in the central nervous system (CNS). In the visual system, there are at least five to six levels of synapses involved before sensory information arrives at a cortical level, not counting the indeterminable number of synapses involved at the cortical level. Each postsynaptic neuron may receive inputs from as many as 1000 presynaptic neurons. In addition, there are serial and

[1]Supported by NINCDS Grant 1-R01-NS19413-01 NEUB and the University of North Carolina Research Council 0-2-110-218-65300-7529. We thank Dr. Robert Eason for his editorial comments during the preparation of this chapter.

parallel projection systems, with efferent activity at virtually all levels of each system feeding back from higher to lower levels of the system (Van Essen, 1979; Wilson, 1978).

In this chapter, event-related potentials (ERPs) of the brain are considered as indices of neurophysiological mechanisms of selective attention. Given the complexity of the mechanisms and the fact that ERPs reflect neural activity from large areas of the nervous system, one should anticipate that ERP correlates of the selection process will be complex. Furthermore, the degree of complexity may be expected to exceed considerably that suggested by the cognitive literature on selective attention, which conceptualizes the selection process as consisting of a relatively few discrete stages—for example, stimulus set and response set (Broadbent, 1971; Treisman, 1969).

The area of selective attention has been reviewed recently from both a behavioral (Posner, 1980, 1982; Treisman & Gelade, 1980) and brain potential (Hillyard & Picton, 1979; Näätänen, 1982) perspective. Posner (1982) discussed both electrophysiological and behavioral evidence that suggested involvement of regional activation of the nervous system in the directing and sustaining of attention, particularly with regard to space. The present chapter, in attempting to answer the three questions formulated above, emphasizes the work of the authors and other investigators whose efforts have focused on identifying and assessing the neurophysiological mechanisms involved in visual selective attention.

Neural Specificity Model of Selective Attention

The Receptive Field as a Functional Unit of Selection

The properties of the receptive field of a neuron suggest a conceptual framework or model, within which the answers to the first two questions may be approached. A *retinal receptive field* is defined as that area of the retina that must be stimulated to influence the activity of a single neural unit. Receptive fields are organized at higher levels of the nervous system in a manner that make the neural unit selectively responsive to specific types of stimulation, for example, a specific orientation or spatial frequency of a pattern. The activity of a specific neuron might therefore represent a particular type of information. Aggregates of neurons with identical receptive field properties, all of which are capable of encoding a given feature of a stimulus, are referred to as neural channels. It is the premise of this paper and our previous ones (Harter, Aine, & Schroeder, 1982; Harter & Previc, 1978; Harter & Guido, 1980; Previc & Harter, 1982) that selective neural processing due to attention is mediated by the efferent modulation of such neural channels and that the specificity of selection is determined by the information-processing properties of each neural channel subjected to modulation.

Selection in the Inferior Temporal and Posterior Parietal Systems

The anatomical arrangement of information-processing channels in the nervous system varies with the nature and complexity of the information they process. In the visual system, there reportedly are two main cortical projection systems (geniculostriate and tectopulvinar) and cortical regions (inferior temporal and posterior parietal). They differ in terms of the nature of information channels they contain.

The geniculostriate and tectopulvinar projection systems have been described by Rodieck (1979), Schneider (1969), Van Essen (1979), and Wilson (1978). In higher primates, including humans, the major connections and projections of the geniculostriate system are the following: retina, lateral geniculate nucleus of the thalamus, striate cortex (Area 17), prestriate cortex (Areas 18 and 19), and inferotemporal cortex (Areas 20 and 21). Centrifugal connections from higher to lower areas are evident throughout this system (Singer, 1977; Updyke, 1975; Van Essen, 1979). In the monkey, this system has a heavy representation of the central retina (Van Essen, 1979). Neurons at the retinal (ganglion cells) and lateral geniculate nucleus (LGN) levels have receptive fields that enable them to respond selectively to wavelength (color), contrast, changes in luminance, and spatial frequency (DeValois & DeValois, 1975; Enroth-Cugell & Robson, 1966).

The geniculostriate system consists of both slowly conducting sustained or X-type cells and fast conducting transient or Y-type cells, both of which remain relatively segregated throughout the system (Dreher, Fukada, & Rodieck, 1976). Sustained or X-type cells have receptive fields that make them more sensitive to slowly moving or flashing edges of specific orientations in a restricted portion of the visual field and to spatial frequencies ranging from 0.3–3 cycles/degree. In contrast, transient or Y-type cells have larger receptive fields that require a fast moving or flashing stimulus, are directionally sensitive, and prefer lower spatial frequencies (Braddick, Campbell, & Atkinson, 1978; Breitmeyer & Ganz, 1976; Maffei, 1978; Tolhurst, 1975).

In the cat, 90–99% of the cells in the central retina are estimated to be of the sustained type, with the number of transient cells steadily increasing toward the periphery (Fukada & Stone, 1974; Hoffmann, Stone, & Sherman, 1972; Wright & Ikeda, 1974). As an alternative to Hubel and Wiesel's (1962, 1965) hierarchical model of cortical organization in the cat, it has been proposed by Hoffman and Stone (1971) that sustained and transient LGN cells project to simple and complex cells, respectively. The predominance of X-cell input to Area 17 and a predominance of Y-cell input to Area 18 suggest different functional roles for Areas 17 and 18 in the cat, especially because these pathways remain segregated (Movshon, Thompson, & Tolhurst, 1978). These data have led Movshon *et al.* (1978) to conclude that Area 17 subserves the role of "pattern" detection, whereas Area 18 subserves "movement" detection in parallel with Area 17. The function of the Y-cells appears related to that of posterior parietal cortex (discussed below). Both striate and prestriate cells have receptive fields that are limited to the contralateral retina.

Cells in inferotemporal cortex generally have large bilateral receptive fields that usually include the fovea and are sensitive to pattern parameters such as spatial frequency and orientation (Gross, Rocha-Miranda, & Bender, 1972; Ungerleider & Mishkin, 1982). In addition, some inferotemporal cells will respond only if the pattern is task relevant; that is, the pattern is attended or discriminated (Bolster & Crowne, 1979; Nuwer & Pribram, 1979). Ungerleider and Mishkin proposed that this system identifies "what" an object is regardless of its spatial location.

In summary, the portion of the geniculostriate system that projects to inferotemporal cortex appears to be primarily involved in the identification of patterned stimuli that are presented to the central retina and is not involved in localizing the visual field or specific location of the pattern. Selective attention to a specific pattern, therefore, should influence processing in this system.

The tectopulvinar system reportedly originates from transient cells that bifurcate en route to the LGN. The major connections and projections of the tectopulvinar system are the following: retina, superior colliculus, pulvinar and lateral posterior nuclei of the thalamus, parietal cortex (Area 7) and prestriate Areas 18 and 19 (Kasdon and Jacobson, 1978; Mesulam, Van Hoesen, Pandya, & Geschwind, 1977; Rodieck, 1979; Van Essen, 1979; Wilson, 1978). This system contains centrifugal connections from higher to lower centers down to at least the level of the superior colliculus (Goldberg & Robinson, 1978; Rodieck, 1979; Wilson, 1978). Collicular cells receive only a weak projection from foveal areas (Hubel, LeVay, & Wiesel, 1975), and parietal cells generally do not receive foveal projections (Yin & Mountcastle, 1977). The receptive fields of parietal cortex are relatively large (receptive fields of parietal cells are greater than $60 \times 60°$), have contralateral projections, and are particularly sensitive to the spatial locus and movement of stimuli in reference to the fovea and whether or not that locus is attended (Bushnell, Goldberg, & Robinson, 1981; Ungerleider & Mishkin, 1982; Yin & Mountcastle, 1977). These characteristics are somewhat different from those of striate cells, which also receive input from Y-cells but which are less sensitive to location in reference to the fovea and less influenced by task relevance.

Because the tectopulvinar system consists of transient cells and because transient cells respond 50–100 msec more quickly than sustained cells (Breitmeyer & Ganz, 1976; Dow, 1974), this system as a whole responds more quickly than the geniculostriate system. Parietal cells have reaction times as short as 40 msec. (Bushnell *et al.,* 1981).

It should be noted that, in primates, the posterior parietal system appears to originate primarily in striate cortex. Ungerleider and Mishkin (1982) present and review considerable data supporting this conclusion. Parietal cortex, therefore, receives some input from both the tectopulvinar and geniculostriate systems.

In summary, the parietal systems primarily are concerned with the processing of the location and movement of peripheral stimuli in the contralateral visual field in relationship to the fovea. It is reasonable to assume, therefore, that attention to a transient flash at a specific region in visual space, particularly in the peripheral visual field, would be mediated by the activity of these parietal systems.

Breitmeyer and Ganz (1976) have suggested that Neisser's (1967) two-stage model of perception could be mediated by sustained and transient channels. The faster conducting transient cells may mediate preattentive processes, which serve to direct attention and visual fixation to the location of the stimulus; whereas the slower conducting sustained cells may mediate focal processes, which identify the stimulus on the basis of figural information. At the cortical level, these functions may be associated primarily with the parietal and inferotemporal regions, respectively. Similar interpretations, whether from a physiological or cognitive perspective, have been reported by a number of investigators (Alwitt, 1981; Goldberg & Robinson, 1978; Holtzman, Volpe, & Gazzaniga, Chapter 12, this volume; Humphreys, 1981; Schiller, Stryker, Cynader, & Berman, 1974; Schneider, 1969; Todd & Van Gelder, 1979; Wurtz & Goldberg, 1972). It should be emphasized, however, that the data do not indicate either a structural or functional dichotomy between these systems. The differences are a matter of degree; there is considerable overlap in both structure and function, particularly at the cortical level.

Event-Related Potential Measures of Selective Neural Processing in Inferior Temporal and Posterior Parietal Cortex

The differences in the structural and functional properties of these two cortical areas, as suggested by the above electrophysiological data from monkeys and cats, may be used as a basis for predicting how different kinds of selective attention will be manifested in ERP measures of selective neural processing in humans. Given that posterior parietal cortex is particularly sensitive to spatial location in the contralateral peripheral visual field and that information is processed relatively quickly in this system, selective processing in this system should be most involved in mediating attention to points in peripheral visual space and should be primarily reflected by early ERP measures of processing in the parietal areas. Given that inferior temporal cortex is sensitive primarily to stimulus configuration in the central retina and that information is processed more slowly in this system, selective processing in this system should be most involved in mediating attention to pattern configuration in the central visual field and should be primarily reflected by later ERP measures of processing in the striate areas.

It is not a purpose of this chapter to consider critically the relationship between surface recorded ERPs and the electrical activity of different brain regions. We presume that ERPs reflect the slow dendritic potentials of aggregates of neurons and that the polarity, amplitude, and latency of an ERP measure from a given pair of electrodes indicates, respectively, the orientation of the voltage source in relationship to the electrodes, the magnitude and/or number of graded potentials, and the latency of the graded potentials. Readers are referred to a review paper by Wood and Allison (1981) for a complete discussion of the anatomical and neurophysiological substrates of ERPs.

Interlocation versus Intralocation Selection

We tested the above hypotheses by assessing interlocation and intralocation attention effects on ERPs measured over the left and right central and occipital cortical regions. Attention was directed toward a particular type of stimulus (green circle versus white ring) at a particular location (central visual field versus $20°$ in the left and right peripheral visual fields) by requiring the subject to give a reaction time response to a particular stimulus. The stimuli were flashed at a rate of $\frac{1}{520}$ msec in random order to the left, central, and right visual fields. ERPs to a given stimulus were obtained when both the location and type of stimulus was attended (A_{LT}), when the location but not the type of stimulus was attended (A_{Lt}), and when neither the location nor type of stimulus was attended (A_{lt}). The results from the peripheral stimuli (left and right visual field) have been published by Harter et al. (1982).

The quantified ERP waveform, derived from six subjects, in response to both foveal and peripheral stimulation is shown in Figure 8.1. The interlocation attention effects are indicated by the enhancement of ERP amplitude first as an increased negativity between about 126 and 300 msec (selection negativity) and then as an increased positivity between 300 and 500 msec (P3 or P300). These enhancements occurred whenever the flash was at the relevant location, regardless of whether the type of flash was relevant (A_{LT}) or irrelevant (A_{Lt}), as

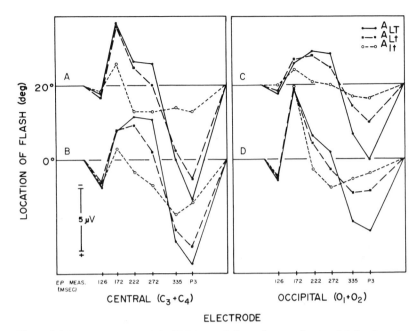

Figure 8.1 Event-related potentials (ERPs) recorded over the central and occipital scalp regions in response to flashes presented in the central (0°) and peripheral (20°) visual fields. Data are averaged across hemispheres (left and right), stimulus type (white ring and solid green circle), subjects (six), and replications (three). In addition, the peripheral data have been averaged across the left and right visual field.

compared when it was at an irrelevant location (A_{lt}). As predicted, these enhancements were greatest under those conditions that should most optimally
reflect selection in the posterior parietal projection areas; they were evident in
very early activity (starting at 130 msec) and were greatest when the peripheral
visual field was attended and ERPs were measured from extrastriate cortex
(central electrodes; Figure 8.1A). In contrast, this effect was smaller and started
later in time (at about 172 msec) under those conditions that should most optimally reflect selection in the inferior temporal areas—central stimulation and
recording over the lateral occipital cortex (Figure 8.1D). These interlocation
effects corroborate previous ERP (Eason, Harter & White, 1969; Van Voorhis
and Hillyard, 1977) and behavioral (Posner, Cohen, & Rafal, 1982; Posner,
Snyder & Davidson, 1980) data that show attention to a point in space increases
the sensitivity to all stimuli presented to that point.

  The *intralocation* attention effect is indicated by the additional enhancement
of ERP amplitude when the type of flash was also relevant (A_{LT}), as compared to
irrelevant (A_{Lt}). It reflects the selection of the relevant type or configuration of

information within the relevant location. In comparison to the centrally recorded interlocation attention effects (8.1A), the intralocation effects started later in time (at about 172 msec), were proportionately greater when the central visual field was attended and were statistically significant only for ERPs recorded over occipital cortex (Figure 8.1D). These trends were particularly evident for P3. This pattern of results is consistent with the prediction that intralocation selection is mediated primarily within the inferior temporal projection region. It may be noted that the occipital electrodes also reflected interlocation attention effects. This is consistent with the anatomical data that indicate Y-type cells also project to occipital cortex. Intralocation selection is discussed in more detail in a subsequent section of this chapter.

In summary, the enhancement of ERP amplitude due to selective attention is consistent with the hypothesis that the location of the stimulus was initially selected in the posterior parietal projection system, as reflected by the interlocation attention effects on ERPs recorded over central cortex. The selection of the particular type of stimulus at that location occurred later in time and presumably in the inferior temporal projection systems, as reflected by the intralocation attention effects on ERPs recorded over occipital cortex.

Hemispheric Differences in Selection

Another finding of Harter et al.'s (1982) was that the interlocation and intralocation attention effects reflected by the selection negativity over the left and right occipital hemispheres, in response to left and right visual field stimulation, reflected three types of hemispheric asymmetries and presumably three different generators. These asymmetries are shown in Figure 8.2 as difference potentials that reflect the enhancement of ERPs due to interlocation and intralocation attention effects.

1. The interlocation attention effect, reflected by enhanced selection negativity from 126 to 222 msec poststimulus, was greater over the occipital hemisphere *contralateral* to the visual field of the evoking flash; it was greater over the right hemisphere when attending flashes in the left visual field (Figure 8.2A) and vice versa (Figure 8.2B). Hillyard (Note 1) reported a similar type of contralateral enhancement for both interlocation and intralocation (color) attention effects. This contralateral enhancement may be attributed to selective processing in the geniculostriate projection system because, under the conditions of the experiment, each hemisphere of striate cortex received input selectively from the contralateral visual field and because the effect was evident only over occipital cortex. Behavioral enhancement of both striate (Wurtz & Mohler, 1976) and prestriate (Robinson, Baizer, & Dow, 1980) neurons in monkeys has been reported. However, the contralateral selection also could reflect the activity of

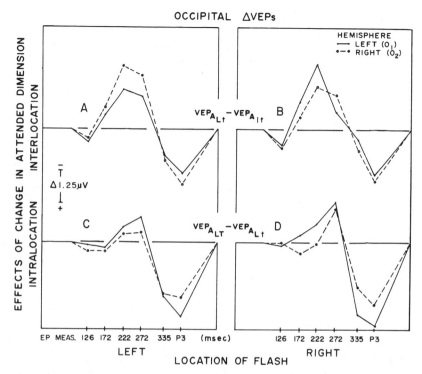

Figure 8.2 Occipital difference ERPs (ΔVEPs) reflecting the change in the ERP amplitude measured at different latencies (*x* axis) in response to a given stimulus when a dimension of that stimulus was attended as compared to ignored. Interlocation effects: the ERP to a given stimulus when its location is attended (A_{Lt}) minus the ERP to that same stimulus when the opposite location was attended (A_{lt}), the type of evoking stimulus always being ignored. Intralocation effects: the ERP to a given stimulus when it is attended (A_{LT}) minus the ERP to that stimulus when the other type of stimulus was attended (A_{Lt}), the location of the evoking stimulus always being attended. The location of the flash was 20° to the left and right of the fixation point. Data have been averaged across the two types of stimuli, six subjects, and three replications. (From Harter *et al.*, 1982.)

parietal cortex that has been implicated in contralateral attentional neglect (Heilman, 1979; Posner *et al.*, 1982). This latter interpretation is questionable since the contralateral effect was not reflected in ERPs from the central electrodes.

2. A second later asymmetry was noted in the interlocation attention effect on occipital ERPs. Enhancement of ERP amplitude 272 msec poststimulus was greater over the right hemisphere regardless of the area of the visual field attended. This enhancement may be attributed to the right hemisphere specialization for processing spatial location that has been reported in the parietal (Heilman & Van Den Abell, 1980) and temporal (Kolb & Whishaw, 1980, p. 266) regions in other studies. It did not approach statistical significance, however, in centrally recorded ERPs.

3. The intralocation effects reflected a left hemisphere specialization. The enhanced selection negativity from 126 to 272 msec poststimulus, associated with attending the particular type of stimulus at a particular location, was greater over the left occipital hemisphere regardless of the visual field attended (Figure 8.2C and 8.2D). Aine and Harter (in press) have reported a similar left hemisphere effect in a color- and word-attention task (discussed here in a subsequent section). Bolster, Harrington, & Pribram (Note 2) presented behavioral data from humans indicating left hemisphere superiority in detecting the conjunctions of features. It is unclear whether this left hemisphere effect is associated with only intralocation selection, with the selection of feature conjunctions, and/or with target selection per se. Data from monkeys indicate that this type of differential processing, due to task relevance of pattern and configural cues, occurs in inferotemporal cortex (Bolster & Crowne, 1979; Nuwer & Pribram, 1979; Rothblat & Pribram, 1972). The occipital electrodes possibly reflected activity both from the temporal as well as occipital areas.

Subcortical versus Cortical Selection

It is difficult to identify precisely, using surface recorded ERPs, at what level or where within the visual system selective neural processing occurs. Both local and far field activity may contribute to ERPs depending on the magnitude and orientations of the generators in relationship to the recording electrode. The level of neural selection reflected by ERPs typically is inferred indirectly by the latency and/or scalp distribution of the ERP components from humans and by reference to electrophysiological data from nonhumans. As noted in the initial section of this chapter, two conditions must be met before selection, due to attention, can occur at a particular level of the nervous system: (1) the particular type of information being attended must be coded at that level, and (2) there must be centrifugal modulation of the mechanisms representing the information at that level.

The receptive field properties of single units in cats and monkeys indicate that a number of features are coded subcortically: color by ganglion and LGN cells (DeValois & DeValois, 1975), location by retinotopic organization throughout the subcortical visual projection systems (Benevento & Rezak, 1976; Goldberg & Robinson, 1978), movement by superior colliculus cells (Goldberg & Robinson, 1978), and stimulus element size or spatial frequency by ganglion cells (Enroth-Cugell & Robson, 1966).

Efferent projections to subcortical visual structures are retinotopically organized (Goldberg & Robinson, 1978; Rodieck, 1979; Singer, 1977; Wilson, 1978). Attention to a particular area in space, therefore, is a likely candidate for causing subcortical priming and modulation of the neural processing of informa-

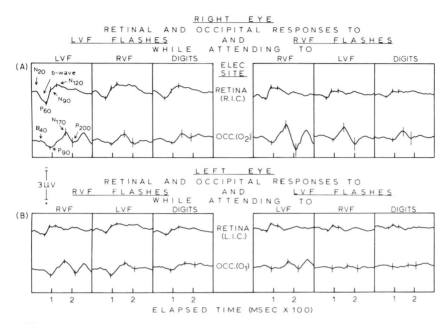

Figure 8.3 Retinal potentials—ERGs measured from the right and left internal canthus of the (A) right and (B) left eye, respectively; and occipital responses—ERPs measured from the right hemisphere (O_2). Each waveform is a superaverage based on 16 subjects. Changes in waveform from left to right are due to whether the left or right visual field (LVF or RVF) was attended or whether digits presented in the central visual field (Digits) were attended (From Eason *et al.* 1983).

tion presented to that point in space. The earliest components of visual evoked cortical potentials (VEPs) (40–80 msec poststimulation) presumably reflect the arrival of afferent information at the cortical level. It has been demonstrated that these early components are influenced by whether the location of the evoking stimulus is attended or not (Eason, 1981; Eason *et al.*, 1969; Eason, Oakley, & Flowers, 1983; Harter *et al.*, 1982; Van Voorhis & Hillyard, 1977), which provides indirect support for subcortical selection. These very early attention effects are found when the peripheral retina is stimulated and are greatest over central–parietal cortical areas; thus, they most likely reflect the modulation of activity in the parietal projection systems.

The electroretinogram (ERG) data presented by Eason *et al.* (1983) more directly indicates subcortical modulation of sensory information in humans. The primary purpose of their experiment was to test the hypothesis that cortically induced centrifugal influences, associated with voluntary sustained selective attention, result in filtering of sensory information prior to its arrival at the cortex. An important secondary purpose was to test further the question of whether or not centrifugal fibers project to the retina in humans.

Surface electrodes were placed at the internal canthus of the right eye (ERGs) and at occipital scalp position O_2 (ERPs). The right earlobe served as a reference. Averaged ERGs and ERPs were obtained to peripherally presented flashes when subjects attended the left, right and central visual fields. Group results obtained from 16 subjects during left and right visual field (LVF and RVF) stimulation of the left and right eye are summarized in Figure 8.3. Upper tracings are group averaged ERGs; lower tracings are occipital ERPs. The largest ERGs and ERPs were obtained when the evoking flashes were attended (left segment of each quadrant). The responses were of intermediate size when attention was directed toward flashes in a homologous location in the opposite field (middle segment of each quadrant). The smallest responses were obtained when foveally presented numerals (digits) were attended (right segment of each quadrant). Eason et al. (1983) reported that both the b-wave of the ERG and the early positive component of the occipital ERP (B40–P90) were significantly affected by the attention manipulations, along with later components of the ERG (P60–N90 and P60–N120) and ERP (P90–N170 and N170–P200).

The authors interpreted these results as providing support for the centrifugal filtering hypothesis as well as providing further evidence for the existence of centrifugal optic nerve fibers. The conditions of their experiment utilized stimulus parameters that optimize the involvement of the posterior parietal projection systems. For a detailed discussion of thalamic mechanisms, which possibly are involved in the selection of location and sensory modality, the reader is referred to the neural model proposed by Skinner and Yingling (1977).

Cortical Selection of Visual Features Other Than Spatial Location

The Selection of Size or Spatial Frequency

Both psychophysical (Blake and Levinson, 1977; Blakemore & Campbell, 1969) and VEP (Campbell and Maffei, 1970; Harter, Towle, & Musso, 1976) data from humans indicate there are cortical size channels. These channels have $\frac{1}{2}$ bandwidths at $\frac{1}{2}$ amplitude of 0.25–1.25 octaves. Harter and Previc (1978) tested the hypothesis that selective attention to a specific check size modulates the sensitivity of those channels processing the attended check size. If this was the case, the size-specific attention effects on ERPs should (1) reflect the same bandwidth as the sensory-size channels, and (2) be indicated by the same components reflecting the sensory-size channels. This hypothesis was tested by obtaining ERPs in response to randomly presented checkerboards of different check sizes and determining the effects of selective attention to a given stimulus (diffuse flashes, 12′ or 35′ checked flashes) on the resulting ERPs.

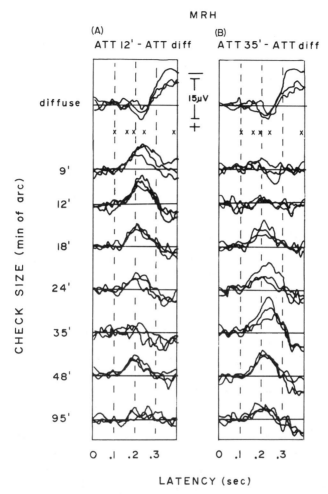

Figure 8.4 Difference ERPs from subject MRH reflecting size-specific attention: (A) ERPs to each of the 8 stimuli (indicated on the left) when the 12′ check was attended minus ERPs to the same 8 stimuli when diffuse light was attended; (B) same as (A) except that the 35′ checks were attended. Each of the three superimposed tracings is a replication ($N > 32$). The Xs indicate the latencies at which ERP amplitude was measured. (From Harter and Previc, 1978.)

The increase in ERP amplitude to checks due to attending either 12′ or 35′ checks, as compared to when the diffuse flashes were attended, is reflected by the difference potentials in Figure 8.4. The difference ERPs to checkerboards were negative between about 100 and 300 msec poststimulus (selection negativity) and positive between about 300 and 400 msec (P3 or P300). These efforts were independent of the nature of the response made by the subject, the reaction time, or the count; and thus they cannot be attributed to motor processes. The

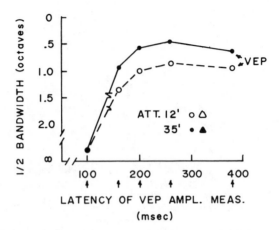

Figure 8.5 Bandwidth of the size-specific tuning functions derived by measuring the amplitude of the difference potentials (VEPs) shown in Figure 8.4 at different latencies (100, 160, 200, 260, and 380 msec). Ordinate indicates $\frac{1}{2}$ bandwidth at $\frac{1}{2}$ amplitude. Data have been averaged across 6 subjects and 3 replications. (From Harter and Previc, 1978.)

enhancement was not significant for the earliest component of the pattern VEP and therefore apparently did not involve the earliest size channels (subcortical channels mentioned previously).

The enhancement was greatest when the flashed and attended checks were identical, 12'/12' or 35'/35', and progressively decreased as they became less similar. The bandwidth of the functions between ERP enhancement and the degree of similarity between flashed and attended check size depended on the latency of the enhancement. It progressively decreased from between 0.87 and 1.35 octaves at 160 msec to between 0.43 and 0.96 octaves at 260 msec (Figure 8.5). The bandwidth indicated by the late portion of the selection negativity (260 msec) is similar to that of sensory-size channels (just noted), and thus, the hypothesis of attentional modulation of sensory-size channels was supported.

The progressive narrowing of the tuning functions reflected by successive portions of selection negativity is of particular interest. It could indicate either that a series of different channels were activated in the selection process, successive channels being more finely tuned, or that a given channel became more finely tuned over time.

The Selection of Orientation

Orientation specificity is another characteristic of striate neurons, as indicated by both psychophysical (Maudarbocus & Ruddock, 1973; Tolhurst & Thompson, 1975) and evoked potential (Campbell & Maffei, 1970; Harter, Conder, &

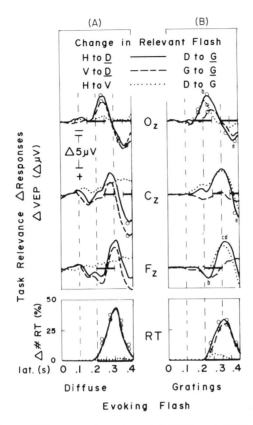

Figure 8.6 Difference ERPs measured over the occipital (O_z), central (C_z) and frontal (F_z) scalp regions and reaction-time frequency distributions (RT) following diffuse (A) and grating (B) flashes. The grating difference ERPs have been averaged across the vertical and horizontal gratings. The difference waveforms are due to changing the relevant flash. In conditions D, H, and V, the relevant flash was diffuse light, horizontal grating, and vertical grating, respectively. Conditions G and G̲ refer to ERPs to gratings when a grating was relevant, G when the flashed and relevant gratings had different orientations and G̲ when they had the same orientation. The underline indicates the ERP was to a target stimulus. Data have been averaged across 6 subjects and 3 replications. See text for further information. (From Harter and Guido, 1980.)

Towle, 1980) data from humans. Harter and Guido (1980) tested the hypothesis that selective attention to pattern orientation modulates the activity of occipital orientation-specific channels. It was predicted that the scalp distribution of orientation-specific attention effects would be the same as that of pattern components of the ERP, which are of occipital origin (Jeffreys, 1977). Three stimuli were flashed in random order: a diffuse light, a vertical grating, or a horizontal grating. ERPs to each grating (for example, vertical) were obtained as a function of three attention conditions: D, attend diffuse flashes (gratings are irrelevant), G, attend the grating of a different orientation (attend horizontal grating), and G̲, attend the grating of the same orientation (attend vertical grating). The difference potentials illustrated in Figure 8.6 show the change in ERP waveform associated with the different attention conditions: D to G, or contour-specific attention effects; G to G̲, or orientation-specific attention effects; and D to G̲, or the total effects of both contour and orientation.

The occipital ERPs (O_z) reflect the time course of the selection process (Figure 8.6B, top). The earliest selection negativity, starting at about 150 msec post-stimulus, was an enhanced response to a grating of one orientation (for example, vertical) when either orientation—the same (G̲ or vertical) or different (G or horizontal)—was attended as compared to when diffuse light (D) was attended. This contour-specific enhancement is reflected by the D to G and D to G̲ difference potentials in Figure 8.6. Later in time, starting at about 200 msec poststimulus, the enhancement became specific to the orientation of the relevant grating (Figure 8.6, conditions G to G̲). In summary, selective attention to a vertical grating first enhanced the response to all gratings, as compared to diffuse light (contour-specific selection), and then enhanced the response to vertical gratings, as compared to horizontal gratings (orientation-specific selection).

The scalp distribution of the orientation-specific effect is consistent with the hypothesis that it originated from occipital cortex. This effect (dashed lines in right portion of Figure 8.6) was reflected by an increased negativity over occipital cortex, a small increase in positivity at C_z and larger positivity at F_z. The inversion in polarity from O_z to C_z–F_z is consistent with an occipital source and is similar to the scalp distribution of pattern-specific VEPs assumed to be of prestriate origin (Jeffreys, 1977).

Multifeature Selection (Size and Orientation)

The studies cited above suggest that selection negativity, the increased negativity of ERP amplitude from about 100 to 300 msec due to attention, does not reflect a unitary underlying process and is not specific to the relevant stimulus per se. When subjects attended patterns, the response to contours was enhanced before the response to specific features was enhanced. Furthermore, comparison across studies indicates that spatial frequency or size is selected before orientation.

Previc and Harter (1982) investigated the nature of spatial frequency and orientation selection when the relevant stimulus was defined as a conjunction of features. In addition, they tested the hypothesis that feature-specific selection occurs before the selection of the conjunctions of features. Four gratings were presented in random order. They contained either 9′ or 36′ black and white bars

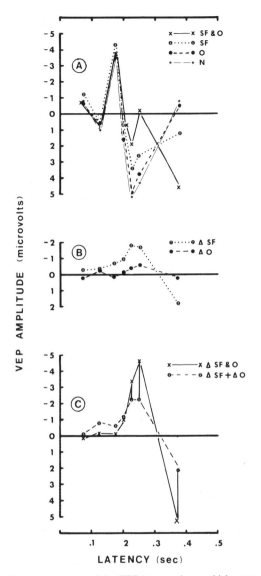

Figure 8.7 (A) Event-related potentials (ERPs) to gratings, which were obtained when four different gratings were relevant: SF & O, when the spatial frequency and orientation of the relevant grating were the same as the flashed grating; SF, when only the spatial frequency of the relevant grating was the same as the flashed grating; O, when only the orientation of the relevant grating was the same as the flashed grating; and N, when neither the spatial frequency nor orientation of the relevant grating was the same as the flashed grating. Data have been averaged across two flashed gratings, 8 subjects, and 4 replications. (B) Difference ERPs based upon the ERPs shown in (A), revealing the increase in amplitude due to having only spatial frequency (SF − N = ΔSF) or only orientation (O − N = ΔO) common to both the relevant and flashed gratings. (C) The additional effect of having the conjunction of spatial frequency and orientation (SF&O − N = ΔSF & O) common to the flashed and relevant gratings as compared to the sum of the feature-attention effects shown in (B) (ΔSF + ΔO). This conjunction effect is indicated by the difference between the two functions (vertical bars). (From Previc and Harter, 1982.)

(fundamental spatial frequencies of 3.3 and 0.83 cycles/degree, respectively) of either vertical or horizontal orientation. These gratings are referred to here as 9V, 9H, 36V, 36H. Attention was directed to one of these gratings (the conjunction of a specific size and orientation) by requiring a reaction-time response to that grating.

The change in ERP waveform in response to gratings, as a function of whether the evoking and attending grating had the same spatial frequency and orientation (SF & O), the same spatial frequency only (SF), the same orientation only (O), or neither the same spatial frequency nor orientation (N), are shown in Figure 8.7. For example, if the ERPs were to the 9V grating, these conditions would be to attend 9V, 9H, 36V, and 36H, respectively. Figure 8.7B shows the change in ERP waveform reflecting feature-specific selection; ERP amplitude increased from when neither feature was common to when only spatial frequency (ΔSF) or only orientation (ΔO) was common. For example, if ERPs were obtained to the 9V grating, these increases would be associated with changes in attention from the 36H to 9H gratings (changes in size selection) and from the 36H to 36V grating (changes in orientation selection). Note that the increases in amplitude shown in Figure 8.7B are all associated with irrelevant gratings.

Consistent with our previous attention studies, spatial-frequency selection started before orientation selection (150 versus 225 msec poststimulus). Spatial-frequency selection also was greater in magnitude, which is consistent with the greater saliency of this feature in visual search (Keren, 1976). The onsets of these selection processes are consistent with single-unit data from animals, which indicate spatial frequency is represented earlier in the projection system than is orientation (discussed in a previous section). As discussed in the subsection preceding this, such feature-specific selection most likely takes place in occipital cortex. Hansen and Hillyard (1983) similarly have shown that different "attributes" of auditory stimuli are selected at different times.

The selection of the conjunction of size and orientation is illustrated in Figure 8.7c. This effect may be defined as that portion of the overall attention effect (ΔSF & O) that exceeds the sum of the feature-specific effects (ΔSF + ΔO). The excess started at about 225 msec and increased up to 375 msec. The similarity of its time course with the orientation selection suggests this selection took place in occipital cortex. The pattern-recognition and target-selection functions of inferotemporal cortex (Bolster & Crowne, 1979; Mishkin, 1972; Nuwer & Pribram, 1979; Sahgal & Iversen, 1978), however, also make this cortical area a possible source of the conjunction selection effects.

The Selection of Colors and Words

Aine and Harter (in press) investigated the time course and scalp distribution of color and word processing. It is generally accepted that words are represented in the temporal–parietal regions of the left hemisphere (Geschwind, 1972; Kolb

OCCIPITAL DIFFERENCE POTENTIALS (ΔERPs)

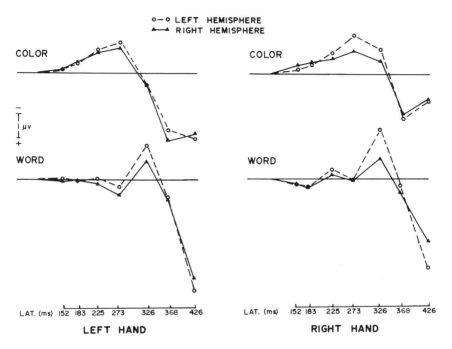

Figure 8.8 Occipital difference ERPs measured over the left (O₁) and right (O₂) hemispheres. Subjects gave a reaction time with their left or right hand to either a specific color or word. The difference ERPs reflect the increase in amplitude due to attending the flashed color, as compared to the nonflashed color, or the flashed word, as compared to the nonflashed word. ERPs are averaged across Stroop and non-Stroop stimuli, the two words, and the two colors.

& Whishaw, 1980). It is also generally accepted that color is represented in the striate and extrastriate visual areas (DeValois and DeValois, 1975; Zeki, 1973, 1980), although it is unclear as to whether hemispheric specialization exists for color or if color is represented bilaterally. This theoretical framework served as a basis for predicting that selection negativity associated with attending color would occur relatively early in time and would be greatest over occipital regions; whereas, selection negativity associated with attending words would occur relatively late in time and would be greatest over the left central cortex.

These hypotheses were tested by flashing the words *red* and *blue* in red or blue colors randomly to the central visual field. The words were presented in upper and lower case to minimize configural differences in the words and the letter *e* was omitted from the word *blue* so that both words contained three letters. Occipital (O₁ and O₂) and central (C₃ and C₄) ERPs (referenced to linked ears) were obtained to the four color–word combinations. Changes in ERP waveform were investigated as a function of two color-attention conditions (attend color red versus blue) and of two word-attention conditions (attend word red versus blue).

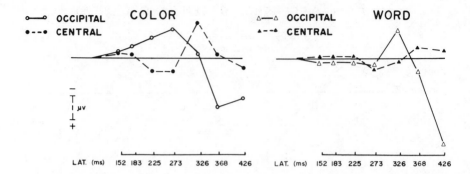

Figure 8.9 Difference ERPs measured over the occipital (O_1 + O_2) and central (C_3 + C_4); cortical areas reflecting color and word processing. See Figure 8.8 and text for how color and word difference ERPs were obtained. ERPs are averaged across hemispheres, hands, Stroop and non-Stroop stimuli, and the two color or word stimuli.

Attention was directed toward a particular color or word by making it relevant to a reaction-time task.

The occipital difference potentials in Figure 8.8 reflect the time course and hemispheric asymmetry of the selection negativity associated with attending colors and words. Data from subjects behaviorally responding with their left and right hands are shown to illustrate that these effects are independent of the responding hand. The increased negativity due to attending colors, for example the increase to the color red when the color red as compared to blue was attended, started around 150 msec, peaked at 273 msec, and was followed by a positivity peaking at about 370 msec. The increased negativity due to attending words, for example the increase to the word *red* when the word *red* as compared to *blue* was attended, occurred later in time as predicted. It started at about 273 msec, peaked at about 326 msec, and was followed by an increased positivity that peaked at about 426 msec. The behavioral reaction-time data reflected this same trend; mean reaction time for color was 387 msec as compared to 421 msec for words.

Also as predicted, the selection of words was greater over the left than the right hemisphere. A left hemisphere advantage was reflected for color processing as well, although to a lesser extent. This is consistent with the left hemisphere intralocation effect reported by Harter *et al.* (1982; see also discussion of their work in a previous section of this chapter).

The occipital–central scalp distribution of the color and word selection effects indicate that these two types of processing are mediated by different cortical regions (Figure 8.9). As predicted, the early color selection negativity was greater over the occipital than central region. In fact, the activity associated with color selection between 183 and 300 msec inverted from negativity over the occipital cortex to positivity over the central regions. Such an inversion also was noted for orientation selection by Harter and Guido (1980) and was interpreted by them as reflecting an occipital source. This conclusion also is consistent with single-unit data from rhesus monkeys (Zeki, 1973, 1980) that indicate that color processing is localized in the poststriate region of occipital cortex.

Contrary to the prediction that word processing would be greater over central than occipital cortex, the central electrodes did not reflect a significant word-selection effect, whereas the occipital electrodes did. Possibly the late activity of the occipital electrodes, which did reflect word processing, originated from temporal areas; and/or the central electrodes were not optimally placed for reflecting activity in temporal cortex. Subsequent pilot data suggest that the latter may be true. Effects due to matching words appeared to invert in polarity from occipital to frontal areas suggesting that the central electrodes may have been over a null point of the voltage dipole.

Summary and Conclusions

This chapter has focused on the increased negativity of the ERP, between about 100 and 300 msec (following stimuli that are attended or that share features common to the attended stimulus), which we have termed *selection negativity*. Selection negativity is a measure of the relative increase in the neural response to a stimulus when it does versus when it does not have specified features in common with the relevant stimulus. It presumably reflects the enhanced response of aggregates of neurons with similar receptive field properties (sensory channels) due to efferent modulation by higher mechanisms involved in directing attention prior to stimulus presentation. It may reflect enhanced responsiveness to the relevant information and/or suppressed responsiveness to irrelevant information.

The data presented indicate that selection negativity does not reflect a single underlying process but many functionally different processes in different projection systems. The modulation of processing in two general classes of channels was discussed: those identified primarily in terms of spatial location and included in the posterior parietal projection systems, and those identified primarily in terms of spatial frequency, orientation, and color and included in the inferior temporal projection system. The time of onset and overlapping nature of selection negativities to different stimulus features suggests the different types of channels are activated in series; but once activated, such activations continue in parallel. The overall amplitude and duration of the negativity presumably will be determined by the summation of the selection negativities associated with processing the different features and conjunctions of features defining the relevant stimulus. The relative order of the onset of the various types of neural channel selection discussed was the selection of location, contour, color, spatial frequency, orientation, conjunction of features, and/or the relevant stimulus per se. The selection negativity varied in cortical asymmetry depending on the nature of information being selected. Location selection, as reflected by the occipital electrodes, was greater first in the hemisphere contralateral to the attended visual field and then in the right hemisphere, regardless of the attended visual field. These two effects were related to other electrophysiological data implicating the striate–prestriate and parietal areas in spatial attention. The selection of shape, color, words, and the conjunction of features occurred later in time and was greater in the left hemisphere regardless of the visual field attended. These intralocation effects were related to other electrophysiological data implicating the occipital and temporal cortex in the selection and identification of color and pattern.

It may be noted that our data and conclusions, related to the nature of the selection process, differ in a number of respects from some of the conclusions made in the papers by Hansen and Hillyard (1983) and Näätänen (1982).

Hansen and Hillyard (1983) concluded that their negative difference potentials, due to selective attention, were not specific to any one configuration of cues. A number of exceptions to this conclusion should be noted. First, auditory cues result in greater negative potentials over the anterior central cortical regions (Hansen and Hillyard, 1983), whereas visual cues result in greater negativity over posterior cortical regions (Harter and Guido, 1980). Second, within the visual modality, different types of visual cues, for example, inter- versus intralocation cues (Harter et al., 1982) and foveal versus peripheral locations (see discussion in a previous section of this chapter), result in different scalp distributions of selection negativity. Our data and other neurophysiological data suggest that there are as many selection negativities as there are functionally distinct neural aggregates involved in the processing of the relevant stimulus. It appears that the similarity of selection negativities to different cues depends on the similarities of the voltage sources, in terms of location and orientation, of the mechanisms involved in the different selection processes.

Hansen and Hillyard also concluded that the ''selection of the hard dimension was contingent on the prior negativity associated with the selection of the easy dimension'' (p. 15). This proposal is not supported by Previc and Harter (1982; see also discussion in a previous section of this chapter) who found that the spatial frequency dimension, although harder to discriminate than the orientation dimension, as indicated by false-alarm data, was nevertheless selected first. Previc and Harter proposed that the order in which dimensions are selected is determined by which dimension is first coded or represented.

Näätänen (1982) proposed that processing negativity is dependent on the development of an attentional trace, which in turn is dependent on the frequent presentation of the target stimulus. Data, however, have been presented indicating that a decrease in the frequency of both targets and nontargets increases the amplitude of the negativity (Fitzgerald & Picton, 1981; Squires, Squires, & Hillyard, 1975). These data are in direct conflict with the conclusion that the negativity increases in amplitude with an increase in frequency of the relevant stimulus. The fact that rare, task-relevant information is associated with large negativities also suggests the importance of selective inhibition in the selection process. It appears that the frequent presentation of irrelevant information is necessary for the inhibition of processing of that information because such suppression is not apparent with novel stimuli.

The neural specificity model of the selection process presented above differs conceptually in a number of aspects from the models proposed by Hansen and Hillyard (1983) and by Näätänen (1982). First, Näätänen's attentional trace model of selection involves only the internal representation of task-relevant information. The neural specificity model, in contrast, incorporates both the increased processing of task-relevant information (*facilitation*) and the decreased processing of task-irrelevant information (*inhibition*). The latter mechanism was not considered by Näätänen.

Second, in the neural specificity model, emphasis is placed on the efferent excitation (or inhibition) of the neural aggregates that process the features of the relevant (or irrelevant) stimulus *prior* to stimulation. Selection negativity presumably reflects the enhanced responsivity of a neural aggregate when it is excited or primed, as compared to inhibited, by the task-relevance instructions represented in memory. In the self-terminating model accepted by Hansen and Hillyard, emphasis is placed on the accumulation of information after stimulus presentation. Näätänen suggests that there must be a bias in the sensory system toward the attended stimulus before or during stimulus presentation to account for such early-onset latencies. But, this bias begins to develop *after* the first presentation of the stimulus as a result of selective rehearsal of the task-relevant features.

Third, the neural specificity model does not assume an initial analysis of all attributes or dimensions, whereas the self-terminating model of Hansen and Hillyard and the model presented by Näätänen do. Hansen and Hillyard describe the self-terminating model as follows: ''Selective attention to a multidimensional tone involves parallel analyses of its attributes in separate 'analyzers.' Each tone is processed until sufficient evidence accrues from any of the dimensional analyzers that the tone fails to match the target in one or more dimensions, at which time all processing of that stimulus ceases'' (p. 16). Näätänen subscribes to a similar view: ''All the input during a selective attention state is somehow processed against some internal representation of the stimulus to be attended'' (p. 631). This process continues until either a match or a mismatch is made against this sensory–perceptual template. The neural specificity model does not assume that all information is initially represented. For example, the initial enhancement following both orientations when only one is task relevant does not necessarily indicate that both orientations were being analyzed and processed at that time. It could originate from aggregates of neurons in the early portion of the neural processing sequence that are not involved in the analysis of orientation (that is, their receptive fields are not orientation specific). The early enhancement following both relevant and irrelevant orientations most likely reflects the analysis and selection of the features common to both the relevant and irrelevant stimuli. In this example, it would be spatial frequency, because both the relevant and irrelevant orientations had the same spatial frequencies and because the receptive fields of neurons selective for spatial frequency are represented early in the neural information-processing sequence. In other words, the early negativity associated with multidimensional stimuli having just one dimension in common with the relevant stimulus reflects the processing of just that one dimension rather than the preliminary processing of all of the dimensions.

Fourth, if a dimension, such as orientation, is not represented initially, it would be incorrect to say that the initial processing of that dimension or orientation can be terminated (due to a mismatch) and that the shorter duration of the negativity reflects this termination, as suggested by both Hansen and Hillyard (1983) and by Näätänen (1982). The shorter duration of negativity following stimuli with only one, as compared to two, features in common with the relevant stimulus most likely reflects the fact that the later selection of the second relevant dimension did not occur because that dimension was not present in the stimulus. In this sense, the late decrease in negativity or shorter duration of negativity does not reflect the termination of a prior selection process but reflects the absence of a subsequent second selection process.

Inspection of the data in Figure 8.1 supports this interpretation. The negativity starting between 172 and 222 msec associated with the wrong type of stimulus at the correct location (ALt) does not terminate. In fact, it reflects continued processing on through P3. This negativity simply does not reflect the additional enhancement associated with the correct stimulus at the correct location (ALT).

Finally, the terms *channel* and *attentional trace* have been used to refer to the unit of selection by Hansen and Hillyard and Näätänen. They did not carefully define these terms neurophysiologically. Hansen and Hillyard use the term *channel* to refer to "a specific source of stimuli in the environment, a zone of receptor surface, or a region in sensory 'input space'" (1983, p. 2). Yet, the neurophysiological mechanisms constituting a channel or determining the zone or region was not considered. Näätänen described the attentional trace as an internal representation, a channel, and the facilitated part of the receiving system. Yet, these terms were not given clear neurophysiological definition, other than suggesting that the attentional trace resides in secondary sensory areas.

The neural specificity model proposed here asserts that the receptive field organization of sensory neurons is the structural and functional neurophysiological unit of the selection process and that aggregates of neurons with similar receptive field properties constitute neural channels. This conceptualization is not consistent with the notion that selection takes place only in the secondary sensory areas of the cortex. If the activity of a neuron, with a receptive field organization that makes it respond selectively to a specific type of stimulation, is considered to be an internal representation of that information, then such representations are located throughout the sensory projection systems. The nature of the information they represent depends on their location in the projection system. The selection negativities recorded by cortical electrodes could reflect the modulation of activity in neural channels as peripheral as the thalamic level (for "location" cues, for example) and as central as the temporal lobes (for "shape" cues, for example). The location and number of negativities contributing to the ERP would depend on the nature of information in the stimulus and, in turn, the nature of neural channels activated.

Reference Notes

1. Hillyard, S. A. *Selective attention: Color and spatial cues.* Paper presented at the second International Conferende on Cognitive Neuroscience, Kingston, Ontario, September–October, 1982.
2. Bolster, R. B., Harrington, M. J., & Pribram, K. H. *Hemispheric processing of visual targets in multidimensional displays.* Unpublished manuscript, Stanford University. 1982.

References

Aine, C. J., & Harter, M. R. Hemispheric differences in event-related potentials to stroop stimuli: Attention and color/word processing. In R. Karrer, J. Cohen, and P. Tueting (Eds.), *Sixth international conference on event-related slow potentials of the brain.* New York: Academy of Sciences, in press.

Alwitt, L. F. Two neural mechanisms related to modes of selective attention. *Journal of Experimental Psychology: Human Perception and Performance,* 1981, *7,* 324–332.

Benevento, L. A., & Rezak, M. The cortical projections of the inferior pulvinar and adjacent lateral pulvinar in the rhesus monkey (*Macaca mulatta*): An autoradiographic study. *Brain Research,* 1976, *108,* 1–24.

Blake, R., & Levinson, E. Spatial properties of binocular neurones in the human visual system. *Experimental Brain Research,* 1977, *27,* 221–232.

Blakemore, C., and Campbell, F. W. On the existence of neurons in the human visual system selectively sensitive to the orientation and size of retinal images. *Journal of Physiology,* 1969, *203,* 237–260.

Bolster, B., & Crowne, D. P. Effects of anterior and posterior inferotemporal lesions on discrimination reversal in the monkey. *Neuropsychologia,* 1979, *17,* 11–20.

Braddick, O., Campbell, F. W., & Atkinson, J. Channels in vision: Basic aspects. In R. Held, H. W. Leibowitz, & H. Teuber (Eds.), *Handbook of sensory physiology* (Vol. 8). New York: Springer–Verlag, 1978.

Breitmeyer, B. G., & Ganz, L. Implications of sustained and transient channels for theories of visual pattern masking, saccadic suppression, and information processing. *Psychological Review,* 1976, *83,* 1–36.

Broadbent, D. E. *Decision and stress.* New York: Academic Press, 1971.

Bushnell, M. C., Goldberg, M. E., & Robinson, D. L. Behavioral enhancement of visual responses in monkey cerebral cortex (Pt. 1): Modulation in posterior parietal cortex related to selective visual attention. *Journal of Neurophysiology,* 1981, *46,* 755–772.

Campbell, F. W., & Maffei, L. Electrophysiological evidence for the existence of orientation and size detectors in the human visual system. *Journal of Physiology,* 1970, *207,* 635–652.

DeValois, R. L., & DeValois, K. K. Neural coding of color. In E. C. Carterette & M. P. Friedman (Eds.), *Handbook of perception* (Vol. 5). New York: Academic Press, 1975, 117–166.

Dow, B. M. Functional classes of cells and their laminar distribution in monkey visual cortex. *Journal of Neurophysiology,* 1974, *37,* 927–946.

Dreher, B., Fukada, Y., & Rodieck, R. W. Identification, classification, and anatomical segregation of cells with X-like and Y-like properties in the lateral geniculate nucleus of old-world primates. *Journal of Physiology,* 1976, *258,* 433–452.

Eason, R. G. Visual evoked potential correlates of early neural filtering during selective attention. *Bulletin of the Psychonomic Society,* 1981, *18,* 203–206.

Eason, R. G., Harter, M. R., & White, C. T. Effects of attention and arousal on visually evoked cortical potentials and reaction time in man. *Physiology and Behavior,* 1969, *4,* 283–289.

Eason, R. G., Oakley, M., & Flowers, L. Central neural influences on the human retina during selective attention. *Physiological Psychology,* 1983, *11,* 18–28.

Enroth-Cugell, C., & Robson, J. G. The contrast sensitivity of retinal ganglion cells of the cat. *Journal of Physiology,* 1966, *187,* 517–552.

Fitzgerald, P. G., & Picton, T. W. Temporal and sequential probability in evoked potential studies. *Canadian Journal of Psychology: Review of Canadian Psychology,* 1981, *35,* 188–200.

Fukada, Y., & Stone, J. Retinal distribution and central projections of Y-, X- and W-cells of the cat's retina. *Journal of Neurophysiology,* 1974, *37,* 749–772.

Geschwind, N. Language and the brain. *Scientific American,* 1972, *226,* 76–83.

Goldberg, M. E., & Robinson, D. L. Visual system: Superior colliculus. In R. B. Masterton (Ed.), *Handbook of Behavioral Neurobiology.* New York: Plenum, 1978, 119–164.

Gross, C. G., Rocha-Miranda, C. E., & Bender, D. B., Visual properties of neurons in inferotemporal cortex of the macaque. *Journal of Neurophysiology,* 1972, *35,* 96–111.

Hansen, J. C., & Hillyard, S. A. Selective attention to multidimensional auditory stimuli. *Journal of Experimental Psychology: Human Perception and Performance,* 1983, *9,* 1–19.

Harter, M. R., Aine, C., & Schroeder, C. Hemispheric differences in the neural processing of stimulus location and type: Effects of selective attention on visual evoked potentials. *Neuropsychologia,* 1982, *20,* 421–438.

Harter, M. R., Conder, E. S., & Towle, V. L. Orientation-specific and luminance effects: Interocular suppression of visual evoked potentials. *Psychophysiology,* 1980, *17,* 141–145.

Harter, M. R., and Guido, W. Attention to pattern orientation: Negative cortical potentials, reaction time, and the selection process. *Electroencephalography and Clinical Neurophysiology,* 1980, *49,* 461–475.

Harter, M. R., & Previc, F. H. Size-specific information channels and selective attention: Visual evoked potential and behavioral measures. *Electroencephalography and Clinical Neurophysiology,* 1978, *45,* 628–640.

Harter, M. R., Towle, V. L., & Musso, M. F. Size specificity and interocular suppression: Monocular evoked potentials and reaction times. *Vision Research,* 1976, *16,* 1111–1117.

Heilman, K. M. Neglect and related disorders. In K. M. Heilman, & E. Valenstein (Eds.), *Clinical neuropsychology.* New York: Oxford University Press, 1979, 268–307.

Heilman, K. M., & Van Den Abell, T. Right hemisphere dominance for attention: The mechanism underlying hemispheric asymmetries of inattention (neglect). *Neurology,* 1980, *30,* 327–330.

Hillyard, S. A., & Picton, T. W. Conscious perception and cerebral event-related potentials. In J. E. Desmedt (Ed.), *Cognitive components in cerebral event-related potentials and selective attention* (Progress in Clinical Neurophysiology, Vol. 6). Karger: Basel, 1979, 1–52.

Hoffman, K. P., & Stone, J. Conduction velocity of afferents to cat visual cortex: A correlation with cortical receptive field properties. *Brain Research,* 1971, *32,* 460–466.

Hoffmann, K. P., Stone, J., & Sherman, S. M. Relay of receptive-field properties in dorsal lateral geniculate nucleus of the cat. *Journal of Neurophysiology,* 1972, *35,* 518–531.

Hubel, D. H., LaVay, S., & Wiesel, T. N. Mode of termination of retinotectal fibers in Macaque monkey. An autoradiographic study. *Brain Research,* 1975, *96,* 25–40.

Hubel, D. H., & Wiesel, T. N. Receptive fields, binocular interaction and functional architecture in the cat's visual cortex. *Journal of Physiology,* 1962, *160,* 106–154.

Hubel, D. H., & Wiesel, T. N. Receptive fields and functional architecture in two nonstriate visual areas (18 and 19) of the cat. *Journal of Neurophysiology,* 1965, *28,* 229–289.

Humphreys, G. W. On varying the span of visual attention: Evidence for two modes of spatial attention. *Quarterly Journal of Experimental Psychology,* 1981, *33A,* 17–31.

Jeffreys, D. A. The physiological significance of pattern visual evoked potentials. In J. E. Desmedt (Ed.), *Visual evoked potentials in man: New developments.* Oxford: Clarendon, 1977, 134–167.

Kasdon, D. L., & Jacobson, S. The thalamic afferents to the inferior parietal lobule of the rhesus monkey. *Journal of Comparative Neurology,* 1978, *177,* 685–706.

Keren, G. Some considerations on two kinds of selective attention. *Journal of Experimental Psychology: General,* 1976, *105,* 349–374.

Kolb, B., & Whishaw, I. Q. *Fundamentals of human neuropsychology.* San Francisco: Freeman, 1980.

Maffei, L. Spatial frequency channels: Neural mechanisms. In R. Held, H. W. Leibowitz, & H. Teuber (Eds.), *Handbook of sensory physiology* (Vol. 8). New York: Springer–Verlag, 1978.

Maudarbocus, A. Y., & Ruddock, K. H. The influence of wavelength on visual adaptation to spatially periodic stimuli. *Vision Research,* 1973, *13,* 993–998.

Mesulam, M. M., Van Hoesen, G. W., Pandya, D. N., & Geschwind, N. Limbic and sensory connections of the inferior parietal lobule (area PG) in the rhesus monkey: A study with a new method for horseradish peroxidase histochemistry. *Brain Research,* 1977, *136,* 393–414.

Mishkin, M. Cortical visual areas and their interaction. In A. G. Karczmar & J. C. Eccles (Eds.), *The brain and human behavior.* Berlin: Springer-Verlag, 1972, 187–208.

Movshon, J. A., Thompson, I. D., & Tolhurst, D. J. Spatial and temporal contrast sensitivity of neurones in areas 17 and 18 of the cat's visual cortex. *Journal of Physiology.* 1978, *283,* 101–120.

Näätänen, R. Processing negativity: Evoked-potential reflection of selective attention—review and theory. *Psychological Bulletin,* 1982, *92,* 605–640.

Neisser, U. *Cognitive psychology.* New York: Appleton-Century-Crofts, 1967.

Nuwer, M. R., and Pribram, K. H. Role of inferotemporal cortex in visual selective attention. *Electroencephalography and Clinical Neurophysiology,* 1979, *46,* 389–400.

Posner, M. I. Orienting of attention. *Quarterly Journal of Experimental Psychology*, 1980, *32*, 3-25.

Posner, M. I. Cumulative development of attentional theory. *American Psychologist*, 1982, *37*, 168-179.

Posner, M. I., Cohen, Y., & Rafal, R. D. Neural systems control of spatial orienting. *Philosophical Transactions of the Royal Society, London, 1982, B298*, 187-198.

Posner, M. I., Snyder, C. P. R., & Davidson, B. J. Attention and the detection of signals. *Journal of Experimental Psychology: General*, 1980, 109, 160-174.

Previc, F. H., & Harter, M. R. Electrophysiological and behavioral indicants of selective attention to multifeature gratings. *Perception and Psychophysics*, 1982, *32*, 465-472.

Robinson, D. L., Baizer, J. S., & Dow, B. M. Behavioral enhancement of visual responses of prestriate neurons of the rhesus monkey. *Investigative Ophthalmology*, 1980, *9*, 1120-1123.

Rodieck, R. W. Visual pathways. *Annual Review of Neurosciences*, 1979, *2*, 193-225.

Rothblat, L., & Pribram, K. H. Selective attention: Input filter or response selection? An electrophysiological analysis. *Brain Research*, 1972, *39*, 427-436.

Sahgal, A., & Iversen, S. D. The effects of foveal prestriate and inferotemporal lesions on matching to sample behavior in monkeys. *Neuropsychologia*, 1978, *16*, 391-406.

Schiller, P. H., Stryker, M., Cynader, M., & Berman, N. Response characteristics of single cells in the monkey superior colliculus following ablation or cooling of visual cortex. *Journal of Neurophysiology*, 1974, *37*, 181-194.

Schneider, G. E. Two visual systems. *Science*, 1969, *163*, 895-902.

Singer, W. Control of thalamic transmission by corticofugal and ascending reticular pathways in the visual system. *Physiological Review*, 1977, *57*, 386-420.

Skinner, J. E., & Yingling, C. D. Central gating mechanisms that regulate event-related potentials and behavior. In J. E. Desmedt (Ed.), *Attention, voluntary contraction and event-related cerebral potentials* (Progress in Clinical Neurophysiology Vol. 1), Basel: Karger, 1977, 30-69.

Squires, N. K., Squires, K. C., & Hillyard, S. A. Two varieties of long-latency positive waves evoked by unpredictable auditory stimuli in man. *Electroencephalography and Clinical Neurophysiology*, 1975, *38*, 387-401.

Todd, J. T., & Van Gelder, P. Implications of a transient-sustained dichotomy for the measurement of human performance. *Journal of Experimental Psychology: Human Perception and Performance*, 1979, *5*, 625-638.

Tolhurst, D. J. Reaction times in the detection of gratings by human observers: A probabilistic mechanism. *Vision Research*, 1975, *15*, 1143-1149.

Tolhurst, D. J., & Thompson, P. G. Orientation illusions and after-effects: Inhibition between channels. *Vision Research*, 1975, *15*, 967-972.

Treisman, A. M. Strategies and models of selective attention. *Psychological Review*, 1969, *76*, 282-299.

Treisman, A. M., & Gelade, G. A feature-integration theory of attention. *Cognitive Psychology*. 1980, *12*, 97-136.

Ungerleider, L. G., & Mishkin, M. Two cortical visual systems. In D. J. Ingle, M. A. Goodale & R. J. Mansfield (Eds.) *Analysis of visual behavior*, MIT Press, Cambridge, 1982, pp. 549-586.

Updyke, B. V. The patterns of projection of cortical areas 17, 18, and 19 onto the laminae of the dorsal lateral geniculate nucleus in the cat. *Journal of Comparative Neurology*, 1975, *163*, 377-396.

Van Essen, D. C. Visual areas of the mammalian cerebral cortex. *Annual Review of Neurosciences*, 1979, *2*, 227-263.

Van Voorhis, S., & Hillyard, S. A. Visual evoked potentials and selective attention to points in space. *Perception and Psychophysics*, 1977, *22*, 54-62.

Yin, T. C. T., & Mountcastle, V. B. Visual input to the visuomotor mechanisms of the monkey's parietal lobe. *Science,* 1977, *197,* 1381–1383.

Wilson, M. Visual system: Pulvinar-extrastriate cortex. In R. B. Masterton (Ed.), *Handbook of behavioral neurobiology* (Vol. 1) New York: Plenum, 1978, 209–247.

Wood, C. C., & Allison, T. Interpretation of evoked potentials: A neurophysiological perspective. *Canadian Journal of Psychology: Review of Canadian Psychology,* 1981, *35,* 113–135.

Wright, M. J., & Ikeda, H. Processing of spatial and temporal information in the visual system. In F. O. Schmitt, & F. G. Worden (Eds.), *The neurosciences.* (Third Study Program). Cambridge, Mass.: MIT Press, 1974, 115–122.

Wurtz, R. H., & Goldberg, M. E. The primate superior colliculus and the shift of visual attention. *Investigative Ophthalmology,* 1972, *11,* 441–450.

Wurtz, R. H., & Mohler, C. W. Enhancement of visual responses in monkey striate cortex and frontal eye fields. *Journal of Neurophysiology,* 1976, *39,* 766–772.

Zeki, S. M. Colour coding in rhesus monkey prestriate cortex. *Brain Research,* 1973, *53,* 422–427.

Zeki, S. M. The representation of colours in the cerebral cortex. *Nature,* 1980, *284,* 412–418.

9

The Orienting Reflex: Performance and Central Nervous System Manifestations

John W. Rohrbaugh

Introduction

It has been long recognized that occasional stimuli obtrude on awareness by virtue of their inherent unexpectedness or significance. William James, to whom the title of the present volume pays tribute, included a characterization of this rudimentary sort of attention in his taxonomy, according it an equal status with other varieties described there. To it he ascribed several important properties, which save for some elaboration might serve to represent contemporary thought: it is reflexive (i.e., "involuntary"); it is elicited in response to stimuli that are "intense, voluminous, or sudden" or are intrinsically salient (i.e., "instinctive"); it is to some degree a nonspecific response; and it is an immediate and transient response (James, 1890). Pillsbury (1908), a contemporary of James, also emphasized with remarkable prescience the importance of novelty as a precondition for its elicitation and the adaptive significance of the ensuing behavioral and autonomic nervous system (ANS) responses.

Despite this distinguished heritage, however, the concept of reflexive attention is generally not well represented in contemporary cognitive psychology. It remains largely the domain of psychophysiologists, much of whose work has been patterned after that of Pavlov (1927), Sokolov (1960, 1963b), and other Russian neuroscientists. During conditioning experiments, Pavlov noted reflexive attentional reactions in response to occasional environmental distractions. The ensuing behavioral response was described by him as the "what's that?" or the "orienting" reflex (OR) and, following his lead, Russian investigators have given the OR a central position in the study of mental processes. Since the early 1960s the importance of the OR in a variety of perceptual, conditioning, and attentional processes has attracted the interest of Western investigators (primarily psychophysiologists) as well.

This chapter provides a selective description of the OR, with particular emphasis on its relevance to the study of cognitive processes, but departs from the customary treatment in several ways. Instead of the usual emphasis on the feature of habituation, this chapter stresses the likelihood that the OR is a persistent response when elicited by salient stimuli, and is thus likely to accompany a great variety of experimental situations. A second departure is an emphasis on the functional significance of the OR for sensory and cognitive processes, in keeping with positions espoused by Kahneman (1973), Posner (1978), Pribram and McGuiness (1975), and others, in contrast to the more usual emphasis on the stimulus characteristics or antecedent conditions responsible for its elicitation. Yet another departure is that attention is drawn to work using event-related brain potentials as an indicator of the OR as a complement to the usual reliance on autonomic measures.

General Features of the Orienting Reflex

The general features of the OR are well known and have been described in detail elsewhere (see Graham, 1973; Kimmel, Van Olst, & Orlebeke, 1979; Lynn, 1966; Van Olst, 1971; Venables, 1973). Accordingly, they are only briefly summarized here.

Most OR investigation has been inspired by the characteristization provided by Sokolov (1960, 1963a, 1963b, 1966, 1969, 1975). Despite refinements in instrumentation and techniques, and the use of statistical evaluation, it may be concluded that this characterization has proved remarkably durable. Sokolov provides a comprehensive examination of the conditions responsible for elicitation of the OR, the neural mechanisms involved in its elicitation, the functional changes associated with it, and the adaptive significance of these changes.

The Neuronal Model

Sokolov describes a number of conditions responsible for the elicitation of the OR. Of these, the quality of novelty as the effective agent has, without question, received the major share of emphasis. The agent of novelty is detected, it is hypothesized, through a matching process of any given stimulus against a library of internal representations (*neuronal models*) of previous stimulations. These neuronal models are usually held to incorporate a number of features pertaining to the quality of stimulation, rate of presentation, associated behavioral responses, and contextual information. A failure to find a neuronal model as a match for a current stimulus gives rise to an OR.

It is important to note that this mechanism of OR elicitation does not depend critically on whether or not the stimulus is presented in the focus of attention, but rather on whether the stimulus is novel, has adaptive value, violates expectations, or is associated with biologically noteworthy accompaniments. Thus it is possible, for example, to obtain an OR to the offset of a stimulus (the "terminal OR") that presumably is in the focus of attention during its presentation (e.g., Greene, Dengerink, & Staples, 1974).

Habituation of the Orienting Reflex

As novelty dissipates with repeated presentations of a stimulus (i.e., as a neuronal model becomes established), the OR diminishes, or habituates. Habituation differs from fatigue or adaptation in that any change in the stimulus, including a decrease in intensity, is sufficient to lead immediately to recovery of the OR. This phenomenon of OR recovery, in addition to distinguishing habituation from fatigue, has come commonly to be accepted as a sufficient definition of habituation itself. Following recovery to a changed stimulus, responses to the original stimulus may be dishabituated for a period as well.

A number of factors have been found to influence habituation of the OR (Graham, 1973; O'Gorman, 1977; Thompson & Spencer, 1966; Van Olst, 1971). These include stimulus intensity, modality, duration, rate of presentation, predictability, and significance, as well as a number of subject factors and background arousal level.

Manifestations of the Orienting Reflex

The OR is accompanied by a transient increase in skin conductance, and by diphasic skin potential activity. Western investigators have emphasized the electrodermal components of the OR, to the extent that skin activity is often accepted operationally as a sole and sufficient criterion for identifying the OR. The OR is held, however, to incorporate a number of other features, including the inhibition of ongoing activity, gross realignment of head and receptor orientation, and postural adjustments. Also present in this constellation of responses are pervasive changes in the nervous, vegetative, and somatic systems, the adaptive significance of which has been emphasized by Sokolov. In addition to the changes in skin electrical potential and conductance are pupil dilation, heart rate deceleratory (and possibly acceleratory) phases, respiratory pause or lability, peripheral vasoconstriction and cephalic vasodilation, nonspecific electromyographic (EMG) activity, desynchronization of electroencephalographic (EEG) rhythms, and patterned changes in spinal and blink reflexes. The OR also is held to have a role in the establishment of a conditioned bond between the signal stimulus and subsequent stimuli and to lead to a temporary decrease in sensory threshold. With the notable exception of the deceleratory heart rate response and some question as to the pattern of vasomotor responses, the responses in the ANS may be characterized as a pattern of sympathetic excitation.

As has been noted (Mackworth, 1969), however, the OR differs from Cannon's (1936) "fight or flight" mechanism by virtue of the parasympathetic components (as well as the investigatory nature of the behavioral response). A consideration of the functional significance of these responses and some speculations regarding effects on cognitive strategies appear in a later section of this review.

Other Reflexes

The OR must be distinguished from several other nonspecific responses, primary among these being the adaptation, defense, and startle responses. The adaptation response invokes homeostatic mechanisms and may be demonstrated by the application of heat or cold to the peripheral skin. The initial response to heat is an OR-mediated vasoconstriction. On repeated applications, the OR habituates and the vasoconstriction gives way to an vasodilation adaptation response, which is resistant to extinction.

The response to intense or noxious stimuli is the *defense reflex* (DR), conceptualized by Sokolov as a protective mechanism that yields decreased sensitivity in the sensory systems (as opposed to the increase in sensitivity associated with the OR). An important criterion used by Sokolov in distinguishing the OR and DR is that the DR is accompanied by cephalic vasoconstriction, rather than by cephalic dilation as is the OR (although it must be noted that Western investigators generally have not replicated this effect [Cook, 1970; Skolnick, Walrath, & Stern, 1979]). Graham (1979; Graham & Clifton, 1966) proposes a number of other criteria for distinguishing the OR and DR. One is that, unlike the DR, the OR can be elicited by the offset of a stimulus, or by the omission of an expected stimulus, and is thus less critically dependent on stimulus intensity. Additionally, the DR habituates more slowly than the OR, and is accompanied by heart rate acceleration rather than deceleration. Graham proposes that the primary function of the DR is to subserve motor readiness (as opposed to the sensory facilitation associated with the OR).

Graham (1979) also notes several features according to which the startle reflex may be distinguished from other responses. The more important of these is that startle is associated primarily with the abruptness of stimulation (not solely with intensity) and has associated with it widespread convulsive contraction of flexor muscles. The function attributed to the startle reflex by Graham is primarily that of an interruption of on-going motor activities.

Problems with a Unitary Orienting Reflex Construct

Typically it is observed that the course of habituation proceeds at different rates for the different OR measures. Whereas electrodermal responses often habituate to criterion within the first few trials, other responses, such as EEG desynchronization or vasomotor responses, appear on occasion to be resistant or immune to habituation. This is but one of many instances in which the various measures show loose coupling. Additionally, definitional problems associated with the OR construct must be acknowledged. The salient features of the eliciting stimulus have been reported to range from intensity to semantic properties, and the effects of the OR have been reported to be manifest in behaviors as varied as infant sucking and control over the span of apprehension. It is difficult to reconcile such diverse experimental operations, and such assorted effects, with any single construct.

Based on such considerations, a number of investigators have been led to assert that a unitary OR construct as envisaged by Sokolov is beset with problems identical to those that plague arousal theory, and to question its usefulness. (e.g., Donchin, Ritter, & McCallum, 1978; Furedy & Arabian, 1979). In part, the separability of OR measures may be ascribed to an interplay of OR manifestations with metabolic or homeostatic exigencies (Obrist, Webb, Sutterer, & Howard, 1970). In some situations, the OR may compete with (or be supplanted by) defensive, adaptation, or startle reflexes; and additionally, it is possible that several varieties of ORs may be distinguished. During the course of habituation, the generalized OR gives way to (or unmasks) a local OR, involving responses only in the systems specific to the modalities of stimulation and effector action (Sokolov, 1963b; Stern, 1968). Further distinctions may be drawn on the basis of the duration of the OR (Sokolov identifies tonic and phasic varieties) and between the initial OR and a subsequent OR that is reevoked after a period of overextinction.

In larger part, it is possible that the different behavioral and autonomic responses are differentially responsive to separate stages involved in OR production and manifestation. Bagshaw and her associates (Bagshaw & Benzies, 1968: Bagshaw, Kimble, & Pribaum, 1965) have distinguished the autonomic components of the OR from behavioral components on such a basis. They observed that bilateral amygdalectomy in monkeys abolished autonomic reactivity but not behavioral or EEG signs of orienting. It was concluded that the autonomic responses are manifestations not of orienting per se, but rather of the registration of novel stimuli. This registration process presumably is that which is abolished by amygdalectomy; and because the accrual of a neuronal model is thereby prevented, the overt behavioral signs of orienting do not habituate. A number of other investigators, in a similar vein, have ascribed selected measures to initial evaluative processes and other measures to active behavioral stages in the OR sequence (e.g., Näätänen, in press; Roth, 1983; Verbaten, Woestenburg, & Sjouw, 1980).

Further distinctions among the autonomic response systems are advocated by Barry (1977a, 1977b, 1978, 1979, 1981, 1982a, 1982b; Barry & James, 1981; James & Barry, 1980), who has noted fractionation (i.e., differential responsiveness) among the various autonomic measures as a function of the factors of intensity, novelty, significance, signal value, and repetition. He has proposed a comprehensive scheme involving a number of "registers" each responsive to various stimulus properties and each associated with specific OR manifestations. All registers are assumed to represent preliminary processes, the culmination of which are the perceptual, cognitive, and behavioral manifestations of the OR.

In sum, the OR may be characterized as a cluster of loosely coupled physiological, sensory, and mental changes that are subject to dissociation in the face of vegetative, adaptive, or stimulus factors. The diversity and fractionation of these factors may be held not so much to asperse the value of a broadly construed OR concept, as to indicate the presence of multiple registers and independent systems of action leading to, and perhaps embodied within, that response.

Orienting Reflex Elicitation: An Information-Processing Perspective

As noted earlier, the OR has not been well integrated into the mainstream of cognitive psychology. This situation may reflect the traditional concern of OR research with short-term habituation processes and assessment of effects in the ANS. The significance of these traditional concerns must not be understated; they have raised a number of important issues about the adequacy of the neuronal model hypothesis and the factors governing habituation, as well as patterns of integration among the various physiological systems.

It must also be noted, however, that these traditional emphases disserve the OR in that they distract from its relevance to the study of cognitive processes within a broader context. In the following sections, a number of OR characteristics relating to its broader relevance are highlighted. Evidence is summarized in support of contentions that the OR is a ubiquitous and persistent response when elicited by information-bearing stimuli, the behavioral ramifications of which are considerable. In so doing, the speculative nature of these contentions must be acknowledged. The accompanying caveats should not be viewed as discrediting the likelihood that the OR has great functional significance or that its origins are amenable to information-processing description. Rather they should be taken to indicate simply that these factors have received relatively little systematic empirical investigation.

The Neuronal Model Hypothesis

According to the customary rendering of Sokolov's (1963b) thought, the OR is generated in response to a mismatch between a stimulus and internalized representations of previous stimulations (neuronal models). Habituation is presumed to reflect the establishment or updating of a neuronal model on repeated applications of a given stimulus. This general notion has guided a major share of OR research, and its allure is obvious. It proposes a very powerful form of selective effect to otherwise equipotent stimuli differing only in their history of exposure to the individual subject.

The strength of an OR elicited by a change in stimulation is assumed to depend in large measure on the similarity between the new stimulus and previous stimuli for which neuronal models are available. That is, habituation is generalized according to a gradient of similarity, and new stimuli lying within the gradient will elicit a smaller or more rapidly habituating OR than will stimuli that are greatly discrepant from previously habituated stimuli. The steepness of this gradient is assumed to be a function of the length of habituation training. These assumptions have been examined for a number of stimulus dimensions, with conflicting results. O'Gorman (1973) concluded that only an intensity increase, or a change in stimulus modality, is effective in eliciting a test-stimulus OR. Other investigators, however, have obtained results more in keeping with the neuronal model hypothesis (see review by Graham, 1973). Orienting reflex recovery has been shown to be inversely related to degree of change in such factors as intensity (Siddle & Heron, 1977), pitch (Siddle & Heron, 1976), and semantic content (Siddle, Kyriacou, Heron, & Matthews, 1979).

Despite an alluring simplicity, the neuronal model hypothesis has limitations. The neuronal model is traditionally construed as a reflexive mechanism that shares little with the dynamic, evaluative processes central to contemporary models of attention and information processing. Problems with the neuronal model hypothesis have been reviewed by Velden (1978), who also has traced progressive refinements in Sokolov's theoretical formulations.

One elaboration proposes that the comparison is not between an incoming stimulus and representations of past stimuli, but between an incoming stimulus and predictions of possible stimuli. Thus the "model involves extrapolation in time of the expected value of the stimulus" (Sokolov, 1963a, p. 562). Although this elaboration of the neuronal model hypothesis permits it to encompass a wider range of findings, it does so at some sacrifice in simplicity. As noted by Velden (1978), it seems an unwieldy proposition that a complex system of neuronal models for possible alternative stimuli, each with its respective probability, would be so constructed and so maintained.

The neuronal model is less essential to an hypothesis (Sokolov, 1966) derived from formal information theory constructs. Here it is proposed that uncertainty is introduced by a stimulus at its onset and is resolved throughout the stimulus presentation. The amount of uncertainty introduced by the stimulus determines the strength of the OR, which persists until the uncertainty is resolved. In stressing the information value of the stimulus, and residual levels of entropy, the physical characteristics of the eliciting stimuli are considered important primarily insofar as they are effective at transmitting this information.

Effects of Significance

More recent formulations have tended to emphasize the confluence of stimulus novelty or information with such factors as the relevance or significance of the information. Suggestions of a significance effect were provided by Bernstein and his associates (Bernstein, 1968; Bernstein, Taylor, Austen, Nathanson, Scarpelli, 1971), whose findings point up shortcomings in the neuronal model concept in its simplest form. It was noted that OR strength depended not only on the degree of change, but also on the direction of change as well, with intensity increases having a greater effect than intensity decreases (Bernstein, 1968). In a subsequent experiment (Bernstein et al., 1971), it was determined that visual stimuli apparently moving toward the observer elicited a stronger OR than did stimuli apparently moving away from the observer. Bernstein (1981) proposes that the common factor for effective stimuli in these experiments is an apparent approach toward the observer (presumably of greater significance than apparent retreat). A second consideration pointing to the existence of a significance factor stems from demonstrations that the perception of stimulus change is, in and of itself, not adequate for OR elicitation (as reviewed by Bernstein, 1981; O'Gorman, 1973). This appears to be true for a number of OR components in various response systems. Yet another consideration with respect to the influence of significance is the argument put forth by Bernstein (1979, 1981) that a significance-appraisal stage in the OR serves an adaptively valuable function of limiting the OR only to "those signals whose information carries some relevance for the organism" (Bernstein, 1981, p. 179).

"Significance" has been experimentally defined in a number of ways. Some purported demonstrations have relied more on post hoc rationalization than any attempt at denotative definition, the inadequacies of which have been noted elsewhere (O'Gorman, 1979; Siddle, 1979). In other instances, however, more satisfactory operational definitions have been used, including hortatory instructions to attend stimuli (Brown, Morse, Leavitt, & Graham, 1976), to count them (Luria & Homskaya, 1970), to assign ratings of subjective impact (Maltzman & Boyd, Note 1), to make a perceptual judgment (Bernstein, Taylor, & Weinstein, 1975; Greene et al., 1974), or, most frequently, to give some overt response (Bernstein & Taylor, 1979; Ray & Piroch, 1976). Another effective means of making a stimulus significant is to make it a conditional stimulus in a classical conditioning paradigm or as a warning stimulus in a forewarned response task (Pendry & Maltzman, 1977).

Although the existence of significance effects is generally acknowledged, debate has arisen as to their interpretation and the extent to which they may be reconciled with traditional OR theory. A variety of interpretations, some complementary and some competing, have been offered. O'Gorman (1979) has proposed two interpretations, one being that the introduction of a significance-imparting operation may increase background levels of arousal in anticipation of the significant stimuli, which in turn may yield larger or more persisting ORs (see also Siddle, 1979). A second proposed interpretation, aimed specifically at situations in which significance is achieved by requiring an overt response, is that the neuronal model incorporates response-related kinesthetic cues as well as stimulus features and that stimuli requiring a motor response thus are likely to fare differently in the match–mismatch process (Germana, 1968).

Bernstein (1979, 1981) and Maltzman (1979b) have argued that these interpretations are inadequate based on evidence that the opportunity for heightened prior arousal is not prerequisite for a significance effect and that a significance effect can be obtained even when independent measures of arousal (such as skin conductance levels) indicate no consistent basal differences in the various experimental conditions. Neither is an immediate overt response required, as is indicated by the appearance of an OR in response to signal (conditional) stimuli in conditioning paradigms. The interpretation proposed by Maltzman (1979b) is one of conditioning (verbal conditioning in the case of instructionally imparted significance), whereby "dominant foci" or states of "cortical set" are established for selected stimuli (see also Barry, 1982b). According to this interpretation, the process of conditioning links previously unrelated brain centers in patterns of synchronous activity, a condition which in turn leads to OR generation.

Bernstein (1979) argues that the significance effect reflects an active process of appraisal, whereby "scanning is thought to be continuously biased toward the detection of significant stimuli. . . . The actual detection of significant stimuli within the field triggers an increase in information scanning coupled with a lowering of OR criterion levels" (p. 267). Bernstein notes that some evaluation of "importance," "pertinence," or significance is a feature common to virtually all theories of attention.

Affinities among traditional OR conceptions and models of information processing have been noted elsewhere. Venables (1973), for example, has pointed out close parallels between the neuronal model hypothesis and Norman's (1968) concept of "representations in storage," which are activated by stimuli on the basis of a factor of "pertinence" (which in turn is a product of contextual and expectancy factors). The OR is incorporated in Kahneman's (1973) model of attention as a special case among more general situations in which demands are placed upon processing capacity, provoked in the case of the OR when preliminary analyses of "novel, complex, or barely discernible" stimuli indicate that more extensive processing is warranted.

The general notions put forth in these analyses are elaborated in Öhman's (1979) ambitious model, which places the OR within a broader context of attentional, learning, and memory theory. An OR, it is hypothesized, reflects a call for controlled processing in a central capacity-limited channel (see Schneider,

Dumais, & Shiffrin, Chapter 1, this volume). This call may be initiated via one of two routes, one associated with nonsignal stimuli and the other associated with signal or significant stimuli. A nonsignal OR is elicited under conditions in which "preattentive mechanisms fail to identify a stimulus because there is no matching representation in short-term memory." The second route, associated with signal stimuli, is activated when the stimulus "matches a memory representation that has been primed as 'significant'" (Öhman, 1979, p. 445). Once a stimulus is admitted to the central channel a search of a long-term memory (LTM) store may be initiated for "associated representations" and "plans for actions." Öhman indicates how elaborations on these basic postulates may account for a wide variety of conditioning, short- and long-term habituation, and attention phenomena.

If there exists any unanimity of opinion with respect to these issues, it is that the effects of significance are appreciable, and that the OR associated with signal stimuli warrants closer examination than it has received. Or, as summarized more pithily by Maltzman (1979b), "As long as the OR is studied in research with human subjects by manipulating the same kinds of parameters as those used with dogs or spinal cats, it is unlikely that we will obtain results that appear too different from those obtained with dogs and spinal cats" (p. 281). Given the great emphasis on ORs to signal stimuli in the writing of Sokolov (e.g., 1963b) and the fact that signalization effects comprise one of the most critical distinctions between Sokolov's model and other models of habituation (Thompson & Spencer, 1966), the relative neglect of significance or signal factors is surprising. As is apparent from the preceding discussion, the critical factors with respect to the eliciting conditions have yet to be characterized with certainty.

Even less certain are the respective natures of the signal versus nonsignal ORs themselves and any differences that might distinguish them from one another. The usual, and perhaps prudent, conclusion is that the two are structurally identical, differing only in intensity or resistance to habituation (see Bohlin & Kjellberg, 1979). On the other hand, Näätänen (1979) urges that the two be distinguished on the basis of eliciting mechanisms, reserving the term *reflex* for situations characterized by novelty and *reaction* for ORs to signal stimuli that require effortful processing. There have been occasional reports suggesting that the two might differ with respect to the associated patterns of autonomic responses as well, but the evidence is fragmentary. Sokolov (1963b) suggests that the signal OR may initially represent a mixture of local and generalized ORs, and that the generalized OR components (e.g., electrodermal responses) might habituate at a more rapid rate than those specifically associated with the local OR (e.g., occipital alpha blockade). A number of reports (e.g., Coles & Duncan-Johnson, 1975) have reported that signal stimuli, particularly stimuli requiring an immediate response, are associated with a greater heart rate acceleratory component than are nonsignal stimuli. There are some difficulties, however, in relating such findings to the signal–nonsignal distinction per se, because OR-related effects must be distinguished from superimposed effects reflecting the increased processing requirements or somatic demands often associated with signal stimuli (Barry, 1979; Kahneman, 1973; Öhman, 1979).

Other evidence derives from examination of individual differences in responsiveness to signal and nonsignal stimuli, which again provides some indication that the respective ORs may be mediated by separate systems. Barham and Boersma (1975) have presented findings that the respective amplitudes of the electrodermal ORs to signal and nonsignal stimuli are only weakly correlated, suggesting that different mechanisms may be involved. Whereas it is commonly observed that the process of signalization protracts the course of habituation, Berggren, Öhman, and Frederikson (1977) obtained this effect only in subjects showing a high "internal control" psychometric profile. Luria and Homskaya (1970) present neuropsychological evidence that the frontal cortex may be involved in the regulation of the OR to signal stimuli but less critical in regulation of it to nonsignal stimuli.

Hemispheric Factors

A number of authors have proposed that the OR is asymmetrically determined, and that the nature of the OR follows from the hemisphere of origination (Demina & Khomskaya, 1976; Luria, 1973). Maltzman (1979b) explicitly proposed, for example, that *involuntary ORs* (i.e., those elicited in response to a novel or unexpected stimulus) originate in the right hemisphere. In contrast, *voluntary ORs* (i.e., those mediated by factors of significance or "noteworthiness") are predominantly left hemisphere in function. The rationale for this dichotomy lies principally in observations that the verbal and reasoning processes presumed to underlie a significance factor are largely functions of the left hemisphere. Unfortunately, little empirical evidence is available to support this sort of bilateral dichotomy in OR generation (Maltzman, 1979a; Venables, 1980).

More convincing evidence exists to suggest that some forms of attention, particularly the OR, are predominantly functions of the right hemisphere. Several lines of evidence support this view, including the clinical sequelae of damage to left and right hemispheres, respectively. As noted by Mesulam and Geschwind (1978), global deficits of attention (including derangement of selective attention) tend to be associated with lesions of the right frontal and parietal cortices. This appears particularly to be the case for the hemineglect syndrome, in which ORs are deficient and which, according to one interpretation, may be considered to be an attentional or activation deficit (as opposed to a sensory or perceptual deficit; see Heilman & Watson, 1977). The hemineglect syndrome is appreciably more common and more severe with right hemisphere lesions of frontal and parietal cortices than with left (Friedland & Weinstein, 1977). Howes and Boller (1975) have presented related data from a mixed series of left and right lesioned patients indicating an overall trend for reaction times (a measure usually held to include an attentional component) to be disproportionately slower in patients with right hemisphere lesions than in those with left. A right hemisphere deficit has also been posited as the underlying cause of electrodermal OR nonresponsiveness in certain classes of schizophrenic patients (Venables, 1980).

Supporting data are available from normal subjects, as well. Heilman and Van Den Abell (1980) have demonstrated that the EEG alpha desynchronization component of the OR is more widespread following visual signal stimuli presented to the right hemisphere than following presentation of stimuli to the left, and Hugdahl, Wahlgren, and Wass (1982) report similar findings for the strength of the electrodermal OR. Elsewhere, Heilman and Van Den Abell (1979) have made the related observation that signal stimuli in a forewarned reaction-time experiment are more efficacious at reducing reaction time when projected to the right hemisphere.

Habituation: An Obligatory Characteristic of the Orienting Reflex?

The emphasis customarily placed on habituation as the cardinal feature of the OR has been noted earlier in this review. Kahneman (1973), for example, asserts that "habituation with repetition is the most important characteristic of the OR" (p. 43). Similarly, Siddle (1979) gives the "major definitional requirements of an OR [as] habituation as a function of stimulus repetition and recovery to stimulus change" (p. 307).

The stress on habituation as the quintessence of the OR presents an obvious impediment confronting any attempt to integrate the OR within a general information-processing context. In a few areas of study, for example, learning (Öhman, 1979) or vigilance (Blakeslee, 1979), habituation of the OR may be exploited for some explanatory benefit. It is more often the case that cognition and performance are studied without regard to serial or time effects within the experimental session. Indeed, it is customary to minimize such effects through use of practice, familiarization, and counterbalancing procedures. It is to these situations that the process of habituation, and thereby the OR, bears little apparent relevance.

Some question may be raised, however, as to whether this emphasis on habituation as an inescapable or defining characteristic of the OR is warranted (Bernstein, 1981; Donchin, 1981; Roth, 1983). The theoretical emphasis on habituation may be related to the customary experimental emphasis on two procedural factors: (1) Because habituation is the variable under study in the majority of OR experiments, these experiments are designed so as to ensure rapid habituation, with innocuous stimuli presented under little or no task and instructional rigor (Iacono & Lykken, 1979). (2) The major emphasis has been placed on the electrodermal component as the OR measure because it is the most "sensitive," meaning in large part that it is the fastest habituating component in the OR constellation of responses. Whether or not these procedures are appropriate, or at least the generality of the conclusions that may be drawn from them, is subject to debate on both counts.

As indicated in earlier sections of this review, the eliciting conditions are too often narrowly construed so as to include only nonsignal stimuli, in which case rapid habituation is inevitably observed. As also noted, however, the factor of significance yields potent additional effects, which according to some formulations (Siddle, 1979; O'Gorman, 1979; Öhman, 1979) combine additively with nonsignal factors. The assumption of additivity is introduced to accommodate situations in which an OR is elicited by nonsignal stimuli, the sole effective agent of which is novelty or unexpectedness. The obverse to this assumption, which is less frequently the subject of comment, is that so long as significance or signal value is maintained, or so long as the required stimulus processing resists automatization; there is no preordained reason to expect the OR to habituate. This was clearly noted some time ago by Worden (1973), who interprets habituation as referring to "a progressive loss of behavioral responsivity to a stimulus as its lack of adaptive significance is discovered. . . . The import of repetition of the stimulus is that it affords repeated opportunities for assessment of the stimulus and its possible reinforcement contingencies. Loss of behavioral responses and attention to the stimulus is attributed to its assigned inconsequentiality" (p. 121).

Commensurate with this observation there are a number of situations, including those described by Sokolov (1963b), in which ORs to signal stimuli habituate very slowly or imperceptibly. Graham, Putnam, and Leavitt (1975), for example, observed no detectable habituation over 9 trials for the heart rate deceleratory OR response to signal stimuli. Even in the normally rapidly habituating electrodermal system, instances are available in which little or no habituation is obtained for signal stimuli. In a differential conditioning paradigm, Gale and Ax (1968) observed some initial decrement in the electrodermal OR component during the first few trials but no further extinction over 150 stimulus repetitions. Additional examples of little or no electrodermal response habituation, or any asymptote in the habituation curve at substantial levels of response, have been reported (Bernstein & Taylor, 1979; Bernstein et al., 1975; Dawson, Schell, Beers, & Kelly, 1982; Luria and Homskaya, 1970; Van Olst, 1971; Van Olst, Heemstra, & Ten Kortenaar, 1979).

The claim that the electrodermal response is the most adequate or sensitive component of the OR (e.g., Ginsberg & Furedy, 1974) also needs examination. Other OR responses generally habituate more slowly, or sometimes, as in the

case of EEG desyncrhonization (Voronin, Bonfitto, & Vasilieva, 1975) or vasomotor responses (see Furedy & Arabian, 1979), not at all. The extent to which
electrodermal responses are favored over responses in these other systems depends in large measure on the debatable extent to which rapid habituation is
deemed a priori to be a defining characteristic of the OR. In some regards, other
systems may be preferable. Maher and Furedy (1979) note instances in which
pupillary dilation meets a number of definitional criterial more satisfactorily (cf.
Stelmack & Siddle, 1982), and Verbaten (1983) suggests that eye movements
may on occasion be more sensitive.

More significantly, there exists very little empirical evidence pertaining to the
most important OR response systems, namely those involved in the perceptual,
cognitive, and behavioral manifestations. Although these are routinely deferred
to as the most critical components of the OR, there is no strong evidence to
indicate that their courses of habituation are coextensive with that of electrodermal responses. Nor, given evidence that behavioral and electrodermal responses
are subject to dissociation (Bagshaw, Kimble, & Pribaum, 1965), is there strong
reason to suspect a priori that the courses ought to be parallel. If anything, the
evidence favors a greater resistance to habituation for behavioral and perceptual
manifestations (Sanders, 1977).

Intensity

The magnitude and resistance to habituation of the OR are sensitive to stimulus intensity, albeit in a complex way. The relationship was described by
Sokolov (1963b) as a "J curve," with greater OR strength near threshold (less
than 20 db above threshold in the case of acoustic stimuli) and again at loud
intensities. Above 75 db or so the response also incorporates DRs in varying
degree. Graham (1973) reviews a number of studies that have provided general
support for this relationship. On the other hand, various discrepancies may be
noted, depending in part on procedural variables (Barry, 1975; Graham, 1973).
The most usual exception is the finding of a strictly monotonic growth in OR
strength or persistence with increasing intensity (Barry, 1975; Turpin & Siddle,
1979; cf. Jackson, 1974). It should further be noted that the effects of intensity
may not be equally represented in all response systems. Barry (1978) has found a
monotonic relationship for electrodermal, peripheral vasomotor, and reaction-
time measures, but no effect for heart rate, respiratory, and cephalic pulse
measures. Electroencephalographic alpha desynchronization is weakly nonmonotonic with intensity (Barry, 1976). There have been attempts to interpret
the effect of intensity as a transmutation of a noveltylike factor (Asafov, 1965) or
in terms of intrinsic salience (Öhman, 1979). Another possibility is that it reflects
activity in an OR "amplifying" system, whereby stimulus "power" interacts
with other eliciting characteristics (see Siddle & Spinks, 1979).

Stimulus Modality

Stimulus modality is another factor that has been found, on occasion, to have important effects on OR magnitude and persistence. The traditional assumption is that acoustic stimuli are favored over others, particularly visual stimuli. Figar (1965) summarizes animal research from which the following order of effectiveness for eliciting an OR may be derived: "a) intense acoustic, b) intense olfactory, c) tactile, d) intense thermic, e) optical, and f) weak acoustic" (p. 1996). For humans, unfortunately, the effects of modality on traditional OR indexes have not been comprehensively examined and the few studies available do not disclose a consistent picture (Mefford, Sadler, & Wieland, 1969; Pfurtscheller, Waibel, & Schuy, 1976; Smith & Strawbridge, 1969; Ziegler & Graham, note 2).

For performance measures, to whatever extent they may be held to be manifestations of the OR (discussed in the following), the situation is quite different. Here, the fundamental OR or activation prepotency of acoustic stimuli is supported by a broad spectrum of evidence (reviewed by Posner, Nissen, & Klein, 1976). These modality-related differences are nontrivial in that they do not follow in any obvious way from the specific mechanical natures of the receptors and analyzer systems. The differences are evident in diverse experimental paradigms: (1) Acoustic stimuli result in a more rapid response than do visual stimuli. Trumbo and Gaillard (1975) have concluded that the effect transcends differences in conduction velocity in the two systems. (2) Acoustic warning stimuli are more effective at reducing reaction times than visual warning stimuli (see review by Niemi & Näätänen, 1981). (3) Reaction times to acoustic imperative stimuli are relatively more impervious to the effects of forewarning than are reaction times to visual imperative stimuli (Sanders & Wertheim, 1973). (4) Acoustic "accessory stimuli" (i.e., those coming either shortly before, simultaneously, or shortly after a reaction-time signal) are more effective in reducing reaction time than are visual accessory stimuli (see review by Nickerson, 1973). (5) The vigilance decrement is less for acoustic than for visual (or cutaneous) stimuli (Baker, Ware, & Sipowicz, 1962; Colquhoun, 1975; Davenport, 1969). (6) Acoustic prestimuli are more effective at variously inhibiting or facilitating (depending on prestimulation time) the startle response than are visual prestimulations (e.g., Ziegler & Graham, Note 2).

These findings must be interpreted cautiously. First, it is difficult to ensure that stimuli are psychophysically of equivalent intensity in the different modalities (Niemi & Lehtonen, 1982), although attempts were made to do so using psychophysical matching procedures in many of the relevant studies. A second consideration is that acoustic (and possibly tactile) stimuli may elicit an early effect variously called "automatic alerting" (Posner et al., 1976), or "immediate arousal" (Sanders, 1977). Van der Molen and Orlebeke (1980) argue that this factor affects primarily the preparedness of the motor system, thus linking it more with the DR than the OR (Graham, 1979). Schiers and Brunia (1982) provide additional support for this notion. They found that intense acoustic stimuli are followed by a short period (peaking at about 100 msec) during which spinal reflexes are enhanced in comparison to the responses following visual stimuli.

Another consideration is that visual stimuli vary along a number of unique dimensions, such as color and form, that have been largely unexplored as possible sources of the OR or activation differences. Neuropsychological evidence points to a type of vision, presumably mediated by extrastriate pathways, particularly attuned to moving stimuli presented in the peripheral fields. Lesions in the primary and association visual cortices paradoxically spare the ability to orient to such stimuli, despite the loss of ability to report their detection (Koerner & Teuber, 1973; Perenin & Jeannerod, 1975; Weiskrantz, Warrington, Sanders, & Marshall, 1974; see also Holtzman, Volpe, & Gazzaniga, Chapter 10, this volume). Perhaps stimuli designed expressly to capture this secondary system are more effective at eliciting ORs than are stationary stimuli presented to the fovea. Possibly related observations are those of Niemi and Lehtonen (1982) that area of visual subtense is an important factor above and beyond intensive factors related to areal summation of energy.

Rate of Stimulation

The effects of rate are so well established that they have assumed definitional status in models of habituation (Thompson & Spencer, 1966). In general, the slower the rate, the more resistant is the OR is to habituation. Due to the slow onset and protracted recovery times of responses in the electrodermal system, examination of this effect has been confined to intervals of at least several seconds. Several interpretations for the effect may be offered, one being that the neuronal model or internal representation of the stimulus has a very short life of only a few seconds (Näätänen & Gaillard, 1983) or minutes (Öhman, 1979). A second interpretation, advocated by Maltzman, Vincent, & Wolff, (1982; also Geer, 1966), is that ORs may be actively inhibited for a period following a previously elicited OR. Yet another interpretation stresses the temporal uncertainty associated with slow rates and the associated difficulties in the neuronal modeling process (Voronin et al., 1975).

Functional Properties

It is unfortunate that any consideration of the ORs functional significance must be prefaced with a lament about sizable gaps in the relevant empirical evidence— despite the common gesture of acknowledgement that the effects are great. This situation contrasts remarkably with the wealth of information available regarding antecedent conditions and autonomic responses. The lament is not a new one, having been expressed in 1963 by Sokolov (1963b): "A serious defect in work done on the orientation reflex has been that its autonomic and motor manifestations have usually been studied quite apart from its most important function, the enhancement of analyzer sensitivity" (p. 13).

In this section, evidence relating to the ORs functional properties is briefly surveyed, followed by some speculations concerning the supraordinate strategies disclosed by this evidence. Much of the evidence must be adduced from related bodies of literature, such as those relating to the effects of accessory stimuli on forewarned reaction time, which do not explicitly invoke the OR concept but do share paradigmatic similarities with studies of the OR. The conclusion from this survey may be stated at the outset: that the OR may exert an influence on activities in sensory, perceptual, cognitive, and motor systems that must be reckoned with in any general theoretical account of information processing and performance. These effects are tapped in varying degree, depending on such frequently encountered variables as information content, predictability, history of exposure, response demands, complexity, significance, modality, intensity, rate, and hemisphere of stimulation. Moreover, because the effects of the OR pervade a number of systems, they are likely to transcend individual stages in the information-processing sequence. These effects will be manifest in the processing of both the stimulus eliciting the OR and subsequent stimuli delivered within the temporal course of the OR. The implications for models of information processing, particularly additive factors models, are obvious (as noted in a different context by Nissen, 1977; Van der Molen & Orlebeke, 1980).

Temporal Course of the Orienting Reflex

The Russian literature, in particular, distinguishes a variety of ORs on the basis of their duration (e.g., "phasic," "tonic," and "anticipatory" ORs). The distinctions between tonic and phasic ORs have been summarized by Barham and Boersma (1975), who note that the tonic OR is similar to the traditional concepts of arousal or activation. Additional complexities with respect to the time course of the OR arise when the eliciting stimuli are prolonged. Also, there are some difficulties in inferring temporal properties from autonomic responses because in some cases these may be serially activated or interact recursively with one another (Brooks & Lange, 1982). Yet another consideration is that humoral factors may yield aftereffects that outlive the more immediate OR manifestations (Bonvallet, Dell, & Hiebel, 1954).

Although acknowledging these possible exceptions and complications, it may be concluded that the OR as typically envisaged is a transient response, the manifestations of which first become apparent within 200 or 300 msec, peak within 0.5 or 1.5 seconds, and last for no more than a few seconds (perhaps 3–5 seconds). Evidence in support of this time course may be drawn from diverse sources. In the faster acting autonomic systems, a time course approximating this has been reported for the pupillary (Beatty & Waggoner, 1978), respiratory (James & Barry, 1980), and heart rate deceleratory (Graham, 1979) responses. Even in the generally more sluggish electrodermal and vasomotor systems, the eliciting burst of impulses in the peripheral sympathetic nerves occurs 0.5 to 1.0 seconds following stimulation (Wallin, 1981). In the case of the alpha blockade response, the peak again is at about 0.5 to 1.0 seconds, commensurate with the maximum facilitation in forewarned reaction time (Lansing, Schwartz, & Lindsley, 1959). The relatively transient nature of the reaction time facilitation is attested to by Gottsdanker's (1975) assertion that preparation is an aversive state that cannot be held for more than a few seconds. A similar time course appears to hold individually for sensory facilitation effects, as manifested in forewarned detection performance (Klein & Kerr, 1974), as well as for responses in the motor systems, as reflected in elicited EMG bursts (Gogan, 1970) and reflexive eye-blink facilitation (Graham et al., 1975). Finally, of possible relevance, it may be noted that intervals of 0.5 to 1.5 or 2 seconds are generally regarded as optimum for conditioning (Jones, 1962). All of these behaviors have been linked in some way with the OR, and the coherence among them with respect to temporal course is remarkable.

Functions of Autonomic Responses

Sokolov emphasizes the behavioral importance of the autonomic responses, suggesting that they underlie the ultimate goal of enhancement of analyzer sensitivity. Accordingly, the electrodermal and peripheral vasomotor responses are presumed to increase tactile sensitivity (Edelberg, 1961). Sokolov couples the peripheral cephalic vasodilation with a concomitant increase in the supply of blood intracranially, but (as noted by Cook, 1970) there is little physiological support for this assertion. The pupillary dilation response is held to increase sensitivity to light, although any such gain is likely to be offset by degradations in image quality caused by refractive errors (Kahneman, 1973).

Several functions have been attributed to the cardiac deceleratory response. One possibility is that it may be related to a baroreceptor-mediated alteration in cortical tone (Graham, 1979). Alternatively, as proposed by Kahneman (1973), it may reflect a period of somatic quietude associated with the inhibition of ongoing activity. Mandler (1979) proposes yet another interpretation, relating it to the damping of distracting heart rate acceleratory feedback cues that are normally associated with states of arousal.

Conditioning and Learning Effects

The OR has traditionally been held to play an important role in conditioning, particularly the early stages. These effects have been well reviewed elsewhere and need be mentioned only briefly here (see Lynn, 1966; Martin & Levey, 1969). Too strong an OR is considered inimical to the formation of a conditioned reflex, presumably because of competition among OR and conditioned responses. For this reason, conditioning procedures are often preceded by habituation training for the individual conditional (CS) and unconditional (UCS) stimuli. On subsequent pairing of these stimuli, the OR is again elicited by the CS in response to the change in stimulus situation. This newly instated OR is deemed particularly helpful in facilitating the bond between the CS and UCS, the solidification of which is presumed to be reflected in OR extinction. For cases in which prior habituation training to the CS is so extensive as to delay the reappearance of the OR on CS–UCS pairing, the acquisition of the conditioned bond will be commensurately retarded. It must be acknowledged that there are a number of complexities in this picture, particularly in the electrodermal conditioning literature, with respect to the associative status of various responses (see Prokasy, 1977).

A number of investigators have emphasized the role of the OR within a broader context of learning and memory. Maltzman (1979a) identifies the conditioned electrodermal response as an OR elicited by the CS, associated with the discovery or learning of the CS–UCS contingency. The difficulties encountered in conditioning thoroughly habituated stimuli has prompted the observation from Kahneman (1973) that "when one no longer pays attention to the occurrence of an event, it is difficult to learn anything new about it" (p. 46). Similarly, Öhman (1979) specifies that "we learn primarily about novel and unexpected events" (p. 450) for which there exist no well-defined internal representations. Consistent with these assertions are data from a number of studies that have found recall performance to be greater for items that elicited large ORs during their initial presentation (see Craik & Blankstein, 1975).

Sensory Effects

The primary function of the OR is held by Sokolov (1963b) to be increased sensitivity in the sensory "analyzers," by which is meant a comprehensive system including "the whole of receptor, projection system, the specific cortical area and the efferent system which provides feedback to the analyzer" (Van Olst, 1971, p. 19). The increase in sensitivity is thus presumed to be subserved by a number of processes, including the autonomic responses described in the preceding and by gross body, head, and receptor reorientation. Also brought into play are efferent control of the receptor organs and central changes in excitability.

The problem has received comparatively little direct attention in the Western literature, although a fair amount of information may be adduced from the related literatures concerning heteromodal stimulation effects. Experimentally, the problem has been investigated using variants of double-stimulation paradigms, in which the effects of one stimulus on a succeeding stimulus are investigated. The most pertinent studies are those in which a suprathreshold stimulus (which may be presumed to elicit an OR) is accompanied or followed at various intervals by a test stimulus requiring a detection or other perceptual judgment (see reviews by Klayman, 1973; London, 1954; Loveless, Brebner, & Hamilton, 1970). These studies suggest that, under selected conditions, a facilitating effect of one stimulus on a successive stimulus may be observed, and persists at least for several hundred milliseconds.

Unfortunately, the apparent simplicity of this paradigm is deceiving in that OR (or activation) effects must be disentangled from a variety of possible facilitating and interference effects (Loveless *et al.*, 1970). Some investigators (Egan, Schulman, & Greenberg, 1961; Treisman, 1964) have argued that the facilitating effects of the accessory stimulus are due to a cuing function that delimits the test-stimulus observation interval.

Others, however, have discerned a separate effect related to an alerting or activation function, as is commonly associated with the OR. Watkins and Feehrer (1965), for example, report that facilitation is greater when the accessory stimulus is an increase in intensity rather than a decrement—an effect that seems difficult to reconcile with a simple interpretation in terms of temporal marking. Horn and Venables (1964) have described an experiment in which two-flash fusion threshold was lowered by accessory stimulation, peaking at a 600-msec lead time between accessory and test stimuli. The results were tentatively ascribed to arousing activity of the reticular activating system.

Perhaps the most methodologically satisfactory demonstration of the effects of phasic activation (conceivably OR-linked) on sensitivity is that described by Klein and Kerr (1974), wherein the effects of a tone accessory stimulus on visual detection were studied at several intervals. The experiment incorporated a number of methodological refinements designed to obviate the contribution of temporal cuing or temporal uncertainty effects, and to isolate sensitivity changes from judgment criterion factors. The course of facilitation showed some immediate improvement (in comparison to no accessory stimulation) with a foreperiod of 50 msec, and a steady rise in sensitivity, peaking at 500 msec. Considerable improvement was evident still at the longest interval of 1000 msec. The authors considered the effects to reveal the influence of phasic activation, and thought it to be identical to the process manifest in forewarned reaction-time studies. For both types of studies, the effects were presumed to reflect central processes, specifically the urgency with which a decision mechanism polls the accumulation of test-stimulus representations in a "memory system."

Motor Effects

Commensurate with the investigatory nature of the OR, its motor effects presumably subserve an enhancement of sensitivity (Sokolov, 1963b). The gross manifestations thus are held to be movements associated with receptor orientation toward the stimulus or anticipated source of future information. Another facet is the inhibition of ongoing activity, the effectiveness of which may lie in minimizing the distraction of competing environmental and endogenous stimuli (Näätänen & Michie, 1979; Obrist, 1976). Consistent with this speculation are results from a number of studies that have found somatosensory ERPs to be reduced in magnitude during active or passive movement (e.g., Abbruzzese, Ratto, Favale, & Abbruzzese, 1981).

It is difficult, however, to derive specific experimental predictions from these simple postulates. Does the "inhibition of ongoing activity" entail an active arrest or a passive cessation of movement? Does behavioral stillness consist of isometric rigidity or flaccid relaxation? Does the motor system enter a state of covert preparedness or one of genuine hyporesponsiveness? Are there patterned changes in excitation or inhibition so that suppression of irrelevant movements is accompanied by a simultaneous excitation in motor systems subserving specific, adaptively appropriate or task-relevant movements? In part, the difficulties in addressing these problems lie in the artificial nature of laboratory situations, wherein there is little ongoing behavior in need of inhibition, nor is there usually any need to reorient the receptors physically or to make postural adjustments (Kahneman, 1973).

Despite these conceptual and methodological problems, some OR effects that may be characterized as distinctly motor may be discerned. These effects indicate the existence of a period of increased generalized motor excitability during the temporal course of the OR. A common effect is the widespread appearance of adventitious and nonspecific EMG activity (Davis, 1948, 1950) in the form of a series of transient bursts, in which a number of separate components, varying in their sensitivity to intensity and in their courses of habituation, may be detected. Gogan (1970) describes two distinct EMG responses from a variety of nonspecific sites, the early one peaking within 20 to 40 msec after stimulus onset. This early burst was considerably greater for loud stimuli and was related by the author to a startle mechanism. A later burst was postulated to be a component of the OR; in contrast to the early EMG response, it was elicited by both strong and weak stimuli and showed a more rapid course of habituation than the early response.

Motor effects may be detected also by the method of reflex elicitation, either electrically or mechanically, during the presumed course of the OR. The course of reflex facilitation appears to have an early peak at 100 to 200 msec, and then to be followed by a later peak at 400 to 500 msec, which has been attributed by Beale (1971) to activity in the gamma system. An alternative interpretation, suggesting that the late peak may be an OR-mediated effect, is provided by the findings of Schiers and Brunia (1982) that its magnitude is responsive to the signal value of the warning stimulus but relatively less sensitive to its intensity or modality than the early peak.

A special case seems to be the eye-blink reflex, which is facilitated during the course of the OR. An initial hypothesis that both sensory and motor effects are evinced in blink amplitude and latency, respectively (Silverstein, Graham, & Bohlin 1981), has more recently been disclaimed. The facilitatory effects are now believed to reflect solely an OR-linked sensory facilitation effect for the blink-eliciting stimulus (Bohlin, Graham, Silverstein, & Hackley, 1981).

Reaction-Time Effects

An experimental paradigm that may well hybridize the separate OR-related sensory and motor effects, as well as central effects, is the familiar forewarned reaction-time task. (See Niemi & Näätänen, 1981; Sanders, 1980). As with other measures, care must be taken to distinguish OR-related effects from a variety of other effects reflecting the respective processing demands of warning and imperative stimuli, specific priming processes, and particularly the effects of temporal cuing and expectancy factors. These effects appear to be complex, depending on the range and distribution of possible foreperiods as well as sequential factors from one trial to the next, and are rather difficult to parse completely from OR- or activation-related effects. When the effects of temporal expectancy are diminished by using an irregular foreperiod duration or by requiring selective response, facilitation follows the familiar course of an early peak within the first 1 to 3 seconds and a duration of apparently no more than several seconds.

Several aspects of this literature that are specifically relevant to the present context may be highlighted. Some evidence for a specific OR- or activation-related effect on reaction time may be derived from the aforementioned consequences of the intensity or modality of the warning stimulus, which appear on occasion to be appreciable (particularly at foreperiods less than 1 or 2 seconds). The reflexive character of these effects has been emphasized by Posner (1978), who summarizes evidence that "voluntary effort on the part of the subject seems unable to compensate for the absence of a warning signal" (p. 130). Additional factors, above and beyond intensive properties or activity in an "amplifying system," seem also to be involved, as shown by Adams and Behar (1966), who found that a warning signal that was a decrement in intensity was equally effective, if not more so, in facilitating reaction time as was an increase in intensity. Moreover, the amount of facilitation was proportional to the degree of change, whether increment or decrement, so that changes of 60 or 90 db were progressively more efficacious than a change of 30 db.

There are unfortunately few studies that permit direct comparison of the effectiveness of a warning signal with the magnitude of autonomic OR components elicited by it that use foreperiods short enough that the OR might be expected to have some influence on reaction-time performance. Dawson *et al.* (1982), however, reported a study in which electrodermal responses were examined in a differential conditioning paradigm with a 7-second interval. Reaction times were obtained to auditory probe tones introduced unpredictably throughout the interval. Following a brief period of reaction-time inhibition (peaking at 300 msec following the CS), reaction times were facilitated in proportion to the magnitude of the first interval electrodermal response.

Central and Supraordinate Effects

Tantalizing as these scattered glimpses into the functional properties of the OR are, they provide insufficient information from which to assemble, with conviction, a comprehensive overview of the functional character of the OR. Several fundamental questions pertaining to the central effects and strategic properties of the OR can be identified, many of which have been the subject of thoughtful review by Siddle and Spinks (1979) and Spinks (Note 3).

Is the Primary Locus of Effects Sensory, Motor, or Central?

Although the literature cited in the preceding provides some evidence for sensory and motor, as well as possible central effects, there is no consensus as to where the primary effects are found. Consistent with Sokolov's (1963b) emphasis on sensory and perceptual facilitation are the theoretical stances of Skinner (1978), Graham (1979), and others who view this as the principal function of the OR. In contrast, other investigators have argued that the principal effects are on motor outflow or performance. Sanders (1980), for example, asserts that "immediate arousal," which elsewhere (Sanders, 1977) is tentatively equated with the OR, affects a terminal "motor adjustment stage by reducing the distance to the 'motor action limit.' " This reduction would lead to effects quite different from perceptual enhancement because it "carries the obvious danger that errors are made when some sort of choice is involved, since the central computational stages of identification and response choice are bypassed" (p. 346).

Other theorists have ascribed to the OR a role in central information processing. Kahneman (1973), while acknowledging effects on sensory and motor systems, attributes primary significance to "effort" and a capacity "allocation policy" that is called on to facilitate the analysis of the eliciting stimulus. According to Öhman (1979) the OR reflects the "call" for processing capacity itself, although the OR might be expected under normal circumstances to be closely linked with the attendant devotion of central capacity to the eliciting stimulus. The OR is linked with a phasic "arousal" process by Pribram and McGuiness (1975), but explicitly dissociated from somatomotor readiness processes embodied in "activation" states. The OR-linked arousal is purported to reflect the registration of the eliciting stimulus, and has associated with it enduring "changes in the organization of central mechanisms" (p. 122) that affect the way stimuli, presumably subsequent stimuli, are processed. Specifically, arousal and activation processes are yoked via an "effort" component, whereby "the internal redundancy in the input channels is increased so that all of the information being simultaneously processed becomes chunked into one unit" (p. 136). Posner's (1978) theorizing also grants the OR an important role in central processing, describing it as a form of set whereby attention is turned, either covertly or overtly, toward fresh sources of stimulation. The "phasic alertness" process is apparently not subsumed within the OR process per se, although it is considered relevant to its generation.

One possibility is that terminal motor or action stages may be relatively more prominent for signal than nonsignal ORs. Germana (1968, 1969) has presented evidence that signal stimuli requiring an overt response yield larger ORs than nonsignal stimuli, from which he concludes that the neuronal model incorporates characteristics of the associated behavioral responses; the OR, thus "asks 'what is it?' only insofar as it is concerned with 'what's to be done' " (1969, p. 85).

Does the Orienting Reflex Affect Processing of the Eliciting Stimulus or Anticipated Stimuli?

In part, this distinction may be an artifact of the typical laboratory situation in which discrete stimuli, having no compelling or intrinsic association with one another, are used in contrast to natural situations in which the sources of stimulation are less likely to be intermittent and in which various stimuli might cluster in some ecologically significant way. Insofar as the OR is believed to exert an influence on laboratory tasks, however, the distinction is important.

A complication is that the character of the OR with respect to this issue may depend on whether the stimulus is signal or nonsignal. Sokolov (1963b), speaking of the nonsignal OR, describes it as a "response which mobilizes all [the body's] resources for the perception of the stimulus" (p. 64). In contrast, the OR to a signal stimulus is described as belonging to a class of reactions "in anticipation of external agents likely to appear in the future" (p. 163).

If the OR reflects an enhancement in processing of the eliciting stimulus, it might be expected to be larger for stimuli that are complex or that convey large amounts of information. Siddle and Spinks (1979) have reviewed studies in which information is varied by different means and have concluded that the evidence is equivocal. The characteristic pattern of results is that increasing information content may delay the course of OR habituation but not affect its initial amplitude (Spinks & Siddle, 1976). More recent evidence has been inconsistent, with some investigators finding no effects of information on the electrodermal OR amplitude or habituation (Connolly & Frith, 1978; Verbaten, 1983; Verbaten, Westenburg, & Sjouw, 1979;) and others (Verbaten et al., 1980; Frederickson & Öhman, 1979) discerning effects on initial amplitude and course of habituation. Verbaten (in press) noted an anomaly in these findings in that stimulus information generally has no effect on the OR to nonsignal stimuli, wherein the salient information is carried by the stimulus itself rather than some anticipated event, but, paradoxically, has a more pronounced effect on ORs to signal stimuli. Bernstein and Taylor (1979) interpret such findings as indicating a multiplicative relationship between stimulus information and its significance.

Siddle and Spinks (1979) advocate an interpretation of the OR as reflecting the anticipation of future information and have presented evidence that electrodermal responses following a warning stimulus are greater when it signals high information than when it signals low information. On the basis of this evidence the authors conclude that "the functional significance of the OR can be viewed with reference to facilitation of perception of future stimuli rather than facilitation of perception of the eliciting stimulus" (p. 491). Certainly this interpretation is consistent with a broad spectrum of evidence indicating that the OR incorporates a period of sensory–motor facilitation that applies to stimuli, even heteromodal stimuli, that arrive via channels different from those entailed in the analysis of the eliciting stimulus (for example, Ziegler & Graham, note 2).

It must also be noted, however, that an important component of the OR is the analysis of the eliciting stimulus itself, with the associated processes of updating the neuronal model, orienting receptors to the source of stimulation, and responding (due to an innate tendency) toward the direction of stimulation (Simon, Craft, & Small, 1970). And contrary to James' (1890) characterization of "involuntary attention" as "effortless," it is likely that the analysis of information critical for OR generation is resource and time consuming. Accordingly, responses either to the eliciting stimulus itself (Van Olst, 1971) or to immediately subsequent stimuli (Dawson et al., 1982) may be impeded if the prior processing stages are complex. Related to this observation is Mandler's (1979) hypothesis that the "organism's conscious perception of autonomic activity . . . automatically demands attentional capacity." (p. 187).

Is Attention Narrowed or Broadened?

The customary assumption is that the OR entails a narrowing of the focus of attention. This interpretation is consistent with Pavlov's initial characterization of the OR as a "focusing" reaction (according to Figar, 1965) and with a much broader tradition (reviewed by Eysenck, 1982) relating arousal to a narrowing in attentional breadth or a restriction in cue utilization (Easterbrook, 1959). More recent espousals of this point of view may be found, for example, in Koepke and Pribram (1966), who assert that the OR "prepares and focuses the organism for optimal perception" (p. 447); in Jeffrey (1968), who presumes the OR "to sharpen perception, i.e. focus attention on that cue or subset of cues that is most salient" (p. 323); or in Maltzman et al. (1982), who propose that the stimulus eliciting the OR attracts "a voluntary and effortful focusing of attention" (p. 226). In contrast, Bernstein (1979) argues against the notion of attentional narrowing in its simplest form, insisting that the stimulus or cue-selection process is according to relevance or significance, and that an OR increases scanning processes rather than restricts them.

There is some suggestion that the breadth of attention is a function of the signal–nonsignal dimension. Siddle (1979) speculates that "responses elicited by signal stimuli serve to maximize the gathering of particular information by focusing attention on one particular aspect of the perceptual field while those elicited by nonsignal stimuli may serve to maximize the gathering of information from all aspects of the field" (p. 307). Neurophysiological evidence in support of this interpretation has been presented by Skinner (1978), who contrasts two modes of sensory modulation in thalamic nuclei. One is mediated by the mesencephalic reticular formation, is associated with novel or intense (i.e., nonsignal) stimuli, and exerts a nonspecific facilitatory effect on sensory transmission through thalamic nuclei. A second system, involving frontal cortex and medial thalamic nuclei, is responsive to conditioned (i.e., signal) stimuli and exerts a selective gating influence consistent with a narrowed focus of attention.

Precisely the opposite proposal has been advanced by Floru (1979), who asserts that signal stimuli are accompanied initially by a state of "diffuse expectancy" for "something after the stimulus, . . . which indicates more of a general readiness than a specific orientation" (p. 302). Floru argues that by the time a signal is familiar enough to allow the accurate prediction of its consequences (i.e., to permit a narrowing of attention), the OR to that stimulus is habituated and replaced with a conditioned response.

Is the Orienting Reflex an Arousal Reaction?

A common assumption is that the effects of the OR are universally facilitatory, and that they may be ascribed to generalized arousal (phasic in the case of the OR). In many respects, however, this interpretation is inadequate. The concept of arousal as a unidimensional energizing agent seems no longer tenable. It is too amorphous to predict, or adequately describe, the specific strategies or mechanisms whereby behavior in the face of an OR is altered or improved, as alluded to previously with particular reference to motor aspects of the OR. These shortfalls are discussed by Eysenck (1982), who identifies various ways arousal might affect attention. These include "changes in attentional selectivity, attentional capacity, speed of functioning of attentional mechanisms and susceptibility to attentional distraction" (p. 7). Moreover, distinctions must also be drawn between the forms of arousal inherent in the OR and the forms associated with other reactions, such as DRs or startle reactions. Nor is there universal consensus that the effects of ORs are singularly beneficial. Waters, McDonald, and Koresko (1977) emphasize the converse, whereby the creation of neuronal models, and habituation of the OR's distracting and interruptive effects, allow a powerful sort of selective attention that minimizes the perturbing effects of monotonous or insignificant stimulation.

A major difficulty confronting the study of the OR is that it is a transitory response that, at least when elicited by nonsignal stimuli, may habituate quickly. These features yield rather brief periods in which to assay the OR's functional effects, imposing experimental constraints on the types of tasks that may be examined. For heuristic purposes, it may be profitable to consider the possibility that some central effects can be modeled on those seen with more sustained forms of arousal, especially those associated with environmental stress. In particular, the effects of sustained noise, which have received extensive scrutiny (see Hockey, Chapter 12, this volume), may offer a valuable analogue. Sustained noise is associated with a pattern of autonomic arousal characterized by sympathetic dominance not unlike that seen transiently during the OR. Several factors may be considered to grant legitimacy to such an enterprise: (1) The effects are exogenously induced, as is the case with the OR, in contrast to other forms of arousal associated with incentive, motivation, or anxiety. (2) A further level of conceptual similarity between noise and OR eliciting conditions is witnessed by Mandler's (1979) definition of stress as the "result of interruption" (p. 186) of "some action, thought sequence, plan or processing structure" (p. 185). The interruption of ongoing activity is universally held to be an important feature of the OR. (3) In harmony with the distinction between the OR and the DR, some measures of performance show improvement under moderate levels of noise but impairment under high levels.

The effects of noise on performance are complex, causing mixed patterns of facilitation and interference (see Eysenck, 1982; Hockey, 1979, this volume). Many of these effects share affinities with functional properties that have been ascribed to the OR or have an intuitive plausibility as being adaptively desirable characteristics of the OR. A primary effect of noise is believed to be the narrowing of attention; so that performance on main tasks is maintained or improved, but subsidiary tasks may suffer (e.g., Broadbent, 1978; Hockey, 1979). The attentional selection may be accorded disproportionately to "highly dominant or high-priority stimulus features" (Millar, 1979, p. 236). There appear to be alterations in the allocation of processing resources as well; so that speeded processes are emphasized over more ruminative processes, and analysis of physical features is emphasized relative to the analysis of semantic features (Hockey, 1979). Such stimuli are subject to a "stronger registration" which, in turn, leads to a more durable representation in memory. Long-term memory seems particularly to be facilitated, whereas the effects of noise on short-term memory (STM) are equivocal—an effect in accord with Corteen's (1969) finding that the magnitude of the electrodermal OR on initial presentation of stimulus items is more closely associated with long-term recall than with short-term recall. Additionally, subjects eschew intermediate levels of judgment confidence in favor of more emphatic decisions or actions (Broadbent, 1978).

Event-Related Potential Manifestations
of the Orienting Reflex

Introduction

This final section is concerned with the study of the OR in the central nervous system (CNS), as manifested in scalp-recorded EEG activity. It is suggested that EEG measures offer a valuable complement to autonomic and behavioral measures in that they are dimensionally complex responses that encode unique sorts of temporal and localizing information that is unavailable in other response systems, and they are relatively impervious to the metabolic and homeostatic influences that complicate measurement of peripheral or visceral responses. This proposition is stated more colorfully by Darrow (1967):

> The domain of the GSR is thus a hierarchy wherein the "cortical-most-high" speaks only from the secrecy of the cerebral sanctum sanctorum through his ministers, and they through their emissaries, and they through their mouthpieces in the epidermis, including the orifices of the sweat glands. The "voice from on high" is never heard except by the whim and disposition of his ministers, and of their emissaries, and of their mouthpieces, and they may sometimes be prompted to speak on their own. They may respond on their own initiative to external stimulation without the word even getting through to the cortical-most-high. And by the same token, silence of the emissaries or of their mouthpieces is no proof that the "most high" has not spoken (p. 394).

It is with this "cortical-most-high," and its "voice," that the following is concerned.

Two general classes of EEG phenomena have been associated with the OR; one being the traditional alpha desynchronization measures, and the second being derived from the event-related potential (ERP). It is the latter class that is the principal subject of this review, primarily because of the potentially great amount of information ERP measures offer about the time courses of OR processes and their neural representations. This is not, of course, to denigrate the importance of OR measures based on the blockade of intrinsic EEG rhythms, which have been the subject of a very large and influential literature since the pioneering observations by Beck in the 1890s. The alpha-blockade response is given great significance as a measure of the OR and conditioning by Sokolov and other Russian investigators. Although the response is broadly parallel in some respects to autonomic OR components, several important differences may be noted. It is apparently less sensitive than the electrodermal component to intensity (Barry, 1978) and stimulus significance (Bernstein, Taylor, Starkey, Juni, Lubowsky, & Paley, 1981), and may be more closely allied with "an efferent part of the orienting reflex arc" than with stimulus registrations (Sokolov, 1963a, p. 551; see also Bagshaw & Benzies, 1968). A constraining factor in much of the relevant work has been the use of a limited number of EEG recording sites and the general reliance on occipital or parietal alpha measures. Although posterior alpha blockade is often interpreted as a component of the generalized OR, it may in fact reflect much more specialized processes related specifically to visual or visuomotor processes (Mulholland, 1973), which are held to be a component of the OR, albeit an early, "primary phase" (Verbaten *et al.*, 1979). Thus, the posterior alpha-blockade response may appear only insofar as the eliciting stimulus engages visual and visuomotor processes.

Russian investigators value the alpha-blockade response particularly with respect to the distinction between local and generalized ORs (described earlier in this review). Sokolov (1963b) provides a number of examples of local ORs reflecting the respective activity in occipital cortex following visual stimulation, and Rolandic areas for somatosensory stimulation. The distinction between local and generalized ORs, as reflected in EEG rhythms, has received very little investigation in Western laboratories, with the most explicit recent investigation of the distinction yielding negative results (Barry, 1975). This neglect is a pity, given the advances in the analysis of EEG signals and the ready availability of multichannel EEG instruments. Although not explicitly concerned with the OR concept, a number of studies have provided ample evidence that there are a variety of topographically distinct rhythms within the alpha band, and that these may undergo regional patterns of desynchronization (e.g., Grünewald-Zuberbier, Grünewald, Rasche, & Netz, 1978; Pfurtscheller, 1981; Pfurtscheller & Aranibar, 1977).

In addition to these alterations in background rhythms, ERP complexes are, as is well known, elicited by the stimuli. In view of the emphasis placed on habituation in traditional OR theory, the averaging procedures commonly employed in ERP analysis would seem to provide an obstacle to their interpretations within an OR context. For several reasons, however, this problem is not intractable. One is that, as discussed previously, there likely are many tasks associated with significant stimuli in which the OR shows little or no habituation. Also, there are procedural means whereby the course of ERP habituation is made

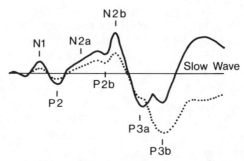

Figure 9.1 Schematized event-related potential (ERP) associated with tone stimuli, and suggested component structure. Separate waveforms are depicted from midline frontal (Fz; solid line) and parietal (Pz; dotted line) sites. The interval between N1 and N2b is stretched for illustrative purposes. (Adapted from Näätänen *et al.*, 1982, with permission.)

accessible to study, including averaging by ordinal position across several runs (Ritter, Vaughan, & Costa, 1968) or a "sliding average" within runs (Laurian & Gaillard, 1976). Moreover, some ERP components, particularly late components, are large enough to permit single-trial measurement, which may be refined variously using cross-correlation or covariance estimates or adaptive filtering of the ERP signals (e.g., Wastell & Kleinman, 1980; Woestenburg, Verbaten, & Slangen, 1981). Using such techniques, it has become well established that some ERP components habituate, particularly a complex involving a negative component at about 100 msec (N1) and the immediately subsequent positive peak (P2), and that this habituation may on occasion closely parallel the course of electrodermal or heart rate OR habituation (Rust, 1977; see reviews by Callaway, 1973; Öhman & Lader, 1977). The functional significance of the N1 component, and its habituation, remains in question; a suggestion has been made that it is related to the initial OR seen on first presentation of a stimulus (Näätänen & Gaillard, 1983), and it may be noted that its habituation displays the general characteristics of recovery to change, generalization of habituation, effects of rate, and spontaneous recovery. Öhman and Lader (1977) conclude that N1 is not an OR component, based on the apparent insensitivity of its habituation course to attentional factors (although this conclusion is challenged by the demonstration of such an effect reported by Donald & Little, [1981]).

In any case, the focus of the remainder of this review is on ERP components that are linked to the OR by their relationship to the neuronal mechanisms presumably involved in OR generation and its hypothesized functional consequences, rather than solely by their susceptibility to habituation. Although most, if not all, nonspecific ERP components have on occasion been linked with OR processes, the emphasis here is on ERP components for which the case can be made with conviction. Evidence relating to the earlier of these has been reviewed by Näätänen and Gaillard (1983) and Roth (1983), who place particular emphasis on the relationship of ERP components to the OR; so the descriptions here need not be extensive. These components, and their interrelationships with one another, are depicted in the stylized ERPs plotted in Figure 9.1. The N1–P2 complex, and its susceptibility to habituation, is described above. N1–P2 is succeeded by several individual components, which are considered separately in the following.

The N2a Component as a Manifestation of Stimulus Change

Evidence pertaining to N2a (also called mismatch negativity) has been reviewed by Näätänen and Gaillard (1983). The N2a component occurs in close temporal contiguity with N2b, and it is often difficult to disentangle from it, but the two are believed to exhibit quite different properties. Näätänen and Gaillard (1983) argue that N2a appears only under conditions in which the nervous system detects that a stimulus is deviant from immediately prior stimuli. The effective deviations are strictly in physical properties, such as frequency or intensity, and not in semantic or informational properties; and the wave is believed, on the basis of topographical evidence, to be generated in the relevant sensory cortical area. It is usually seen to have its onset at about 100 msec, with the subsequent duration and peak latency depending on the magnitude of stimulus deviation. Large deviation yields an earlier peak and shorter duration. Some element of the wave is reported to appear even when the stimulus deviation is so small as not to be consciously detected. Whether or not attention is directed to the eliciting stimulus apparently has no effect. Amplitude of N2a is a strong function of rate, being largest at a rate of 1 stimulus/sec. and decayed greatly at a rate of 1/8 sec. It shows no long-term habituation.

On the basis of these properties, Näätänen and Gaillard propose that the wave represents a "preperceptual" and "automatic cerebral process which is a necessary, but not a sufficient condition for the conscious perception of stimulus deviance" (p. 132). The process is one that occurs "without attention and conscious effort, at a high level of the central nervous system" (p. 138). This process is postulated to be identical with the match–mismatch processes in the neuronal modelling system as hypothesized by Sokolov, particularly in a version emphasizing physical features of stimulation (Sokolov, 1975), although it is held not to be a sufficient condition for OR elicitation. A notable ramification of this identity, suggested by findings that N2a occurs only under rapid rates of stimulation, is that the neuronal model may be very short-lived, no more than 10 seconds. This characterization is, of course, substantially different from that implicit in classical OR research, which generally assumes a life of minutes (for short-term habituation) or days or weeks (for long-term habituation). To account for OR habituation and recovery using slow rates of stimulation, Näätänen (Note 4) has invoked a more cognitively oriented concept of "template" matching. A second point, related to that just mentioned, is that the initial stimulus in a run does not elicit an N2a, from which Näätänen and Gaillard (1983) infer that different mechanisms are involved in the genesis of initial ORs and ORs to stimulus change.

The N2b–P3a Complex as a Manifestation of Attended Stimulus Change

The immediately succeeding negative wave, N2b, is postulated by Näätänen and Gaillard (1983) to be part of a complex that includes also P2b, or "P165" (Goodin, Squires, Henderson, & Starr, 1978), and a following P3a component (Squires, Squires, & Hillyard, 1975). This complex, too, is held to be elicited by stimulus deviance, but only when the deviant stimulus is in an attended channel. The amplitude of N2b is greater for large deviations, and possibly the latency is decreased as well. In contrast to N2a, N2b distribution over the scalp is fronto-central and its modality is nonspecific. Noting the sensitivity of the OR to attentional factors, Näätänen and Gaillard (1983) suggest that the classical full-scale OR is only likely to emerge when the N2b–P3a complex occurs. On the basis of topographical similarities between N2b and N1, it is also suggested that the two components may represent the activation of a common system of OR generation, accessed through the initial OR system in the case of N1 and through the detection of stimulus change in the case of N2b.

The P3b Component as a Manifestation of Stimulus Processing

The P3b component has been the subject of a substantial literature (reviewed by Donchin et al., 1978; Pritchard, 1981), which has demonstrated convincingly a close connection between it and stimulus-processing requirements. The specific literature linking P3b to the OR concept also is substantial, as reviewed by Friedman (1978), Donchin (1981), and Roth (1983). An interpretive problem with much of this literature lies in the difficulty of separating P3b from P3a, with which P3b is likely to overlap; so some of the effects attributed to P3b may well represent a composite effect of both waves. With this precaution in mind, a number of remarkable similarities between P3b and more traditional OR indexes may be noted. One striking similarity is in the eliciting conditions, which may be characterized in the customary terms of novelty, signal value, relevance, intensity, rate and variability of stimulation, and deviation from expected stimulation

(Roth, 1983). Also, trends may be noted for the magnitude of P3b to be coextensive with the magnitude of simultaneous autonomic measures, such as pupil
dilation (Friedman, Hakerem, Sutton, & Heiss, 1973), heart rate (Steinhauer,
Jennings, Aubin, & Heldom, Note 5), and electrodermal responses (Schandry,
Sparrer, & Elton, Note 6); although there are also examples of poor association
(e.g., Becker & Shapiro, 1980; Chattopadhyay, Cooke, Tonne, & Lader, 1980;
Roth, Ford, Krainz, & Kopell, 1978), and some of the results may be attributable
to P3a rather than to P3b (Schandry *et al.*, Note 6). P3b also shows a clear
propensity for habituation when the eliciting stimuli are nonsignificant (Courchesne, 1978; Ritter *et al.*, 1968).

As noted in a previous section, a number of theorists have suggested that the
OR reflects the devotion of central processing to a stimulus (Kahneman, 1973) or
a call for additional processing (Öhman, 1979). Whatever the nature of this
processing may be, it would seem to be that which is manifested by P3b as well.
The most explicit proposal has been made by Donchin (1981), who relates P3b to
the processes involved in updating the neuronal model and experimental expectancies. The importance of this process is emphasized by Sokolov (1969), who
stresses that "the neuronal model of a stimulus cannot be thought of as some
static imprint. Rather, it constantly undergoes revisions in order to account for
the characteristics of the stimulus which is operating at a given moment" (p.
677). As a test of this interpretation of P3b, Donchin postulates that stimuli
eliciting a large P3b will be better remembered, a postulate that has received
experimental support (Karis, Baghor, Fabiani, & Dorchin, Note 7). The similarities between this finding and comparable findings relating electrodermal OR
amplitude to subsequent memory have been noted by Roth (1983).

Slow Waves as Manifestations of the Functional Effects of the Orienting Reflex

The stylized ERP depicted in Figure 9.1 shows the P3a and P3b components to
be followed by slow potentials that are of opposite polarity at frontal and parietal
sites. This late wave is generally called the *slow wave* (after Squires *et al.*, 1975;
see review by Ruchkin & Sutton, 1983). It appears to be part of a complex of late
waves that includes a positive component as depicted in Figure 9.1, but includes
predominantly negative aspects as well. Collectively this complex of late waves
is referred to here as the *O wave* (after Loveless & Sanford, 1974), to denote an
hypothesized link with the OR. Evidence in support of this identity is summarized on a number of counts in the following; it may be noted at the outset that
Sokolov (1963a) has established a precedent for linking slow negative waves
with the OR. Reviewing animal evidence relating to a surface negative shift
associated with stimulation, Sokolov concludes that the wave "may play a role

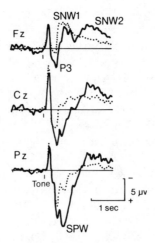

Figure 9.2 ERPs obtained to low- ($p = .25$; solid line) and high- ($p = .75$; dotted line) probability tone stimuli, delivered at a variable rate averaging 1 tone/6 sec. Subjects were instructed to
count silently the number of low-probability tones. Waveforms are depicted from midline frontal
(Fz), central (Cz), and parietal (Pz) sites, and are averaged over 6 subjects.

in the mechanisms of EEG activation and participate in the fixation of traces. As
a response to novel stimuli, this shift is a component of the orienting reflex'' (p.
553). More recent evidence from humans linking the O wave to the OR has been
reviewed by Loveless (1979) and by Rohrbaugh and Gaillard (1983), and is
elaborated briefly below:

Structure, Topography, and Temporal Course

A representative O wave, associated with acoustic stimuli, is depicted in
Figure 9.2. These data were obtained under conditions in which subjects listened
to a randomly ordered sequence of rare ($p = .25$) and frequent ($p = .75$) tones,
and were asked to keep a silent count of the rare tones. A number of late
components, each responsive to the probability variable, may be distinguished.
The earliest is a P3 component, which is positive at all electrode sites, and seems
predominantly to be the P3b component. This is followed by an intermediate
component that is simultaneously negative at frontal sites and positive at parietal
sites and can be identified with the ''slow wave'' component described in the
preceding. There is some question as to whether or not the frontal negative and
posterior positive aspects can be legitimately considered to be a single component; a variety of evidence suggests that the separate aspects appear free to vary
independently in amplitude (see reviews by Rohrbaugh & Gaillard, 1983;
Ruchkin & Sutton, 1983). For this reason, the two aspects are given separate
labels here: *slow negative wave 1* (SNW1) to denote the frontal negative aspect,

and *slow positive wave* (SPW) to denote the posterior positive aspect. These components are followed by yet another wave, which is uniformaly negative at all electrode sites, but tends to be predominant at frontal or central sites. This wave is here labeled *slow negative wave 2* (SNW2).

The representation of the O wave over frontal areas of the brain (dorsolateral frontal in the case of SNW2, as described below) is consistent with interpretations ascribing to the frontal cortex important roles in both intensive and directional properties of the OR (Luria & Homskaya, 1970; Skinner, 1978), and in stimulus registration (Pribram & McGuiness, 1975). Equally suggestive is its temporal course, which reaches a peak (in the case of SNW1) at about 500–700 msec, and can persist (in the form of SNW2) for several seconds. As noted earlier, this temporal course follows *pari passu* the temporal course of a variety of performance manifestations. Whatever specific functional role is eventually assigned the O wave, however, it is important to note that it is complicated by the existence of at least two (perhaps three) distinct components within the complex.

Eliciting Conditions

The O wave can be elicited under a diverse array of conditions, including nonsignal conditions (Loveless, 1976; Rohrbaugh, Syndulko, & Lindsley, 1978). Its magnitude is increased appreciably by any of a variety of manipulations for ascribing signal value, including counting and discrimination tasks; and it is greater for low-probability stimuli than for high-probability stimuli (Rohrbaugh *et al.*, 1978).

The most frequent conditions of observation have been signal conditions in which the O wave is elicited by a warning stimulus in a forewarned reaction-time task, wherein it forms a part of the contingent negative variation (CNV) (see reviews by Rockstroh, Elbert, Birbaumer, & Lutzenberger, 1982; Tecce & Cattanach, 1982). It is most clearly observed when the foreperiod is long enough to prevent overlap with anticipatory activity, although its presence may be detected at short foreperiods as well (McCarthy & Donchin, 1978; Rohrbaugh, Syndulko, Sanquist, & Lindsley, 1980). In this situation, it is responsive to the informative properties of the warning stimulus, in a manner paralleling the differences seen with autonomic responses between differential and simple conditioning situations (Gaillard & Perdok, 1979, 1980; Kok, 1978). The interpretation of the O wave in this situation as an OR to the warning stimulus—rather than as a conditioned or associative response reflecting the contingency—can be made with conviction. Comparison of the O wave following the warning stimulus with that generated in response to nonpaired stimuli, on a number of amplitude, temporal, and topographic criteria, indicates almost certainly that the two are identical responses (Rohrbaugh & Gaillard, 1983). Additionally, O waves elicited by paired and nonpaired stimuli are responsive in like manner to a number of task, modality, and intensity properties.

As a related matter, it is generally found that only under exceptional circumstances is an O wave elicited by the imperative stimulus in a forewarned reaction-time task. (The "post-imperative negative variation" has been reviewed by Dongier, Dubrovsky, & Engelsman, 1977.) This is in general accord with typical findings from electrodermal conditioning studies that have shown reduced responsiveness to UCS in comparison to unsignaled stimuli (see Kimmel, 1966; Öhman, 1979).

Concomitants in Other Systems

This problem has received relatively little attention, with most studies more concerned with assaying possible sources of artifact in O wave or CNV recording than with relating the waves to other psychophysiological variables (Papakostoupolos, 1973). As a result of this work, electrodermal, electrooculographic, and respiratory effects have been acknowledged as possible sources of artifact in the O wave, but are not considered responsible for its production.

The available evidence points to some parallels between O wave amplitude and the cardiac deceleratory component of the OR, as a function of such variables as intensity, signal value, and discrimination difficulty (Connor & Lang, 1969; Klorman, 1975; Lacey & Lacey, 1973; Lang, Gatchel, & Simons, 1975; Lang, Öhman, & Simons, 1978; Simons & Lang, 1976). One study has found, in adults but not in children, parallel courses of habituation in the O wave and cardiac OR components over the course of the experiment (Klorman, 1975). Other measures have received scant attention within this context. There is some evidence that pupil dilation may accompany the growth of the CNV (Michalewski, 1975), that electrodermal responses may covary in amplitude with O wave amplitude (Klorman & Bentson, 1975), that eye blinks and movements are especially prevalent during the time of the O wave (Weerts & Lang, 1973), and that the O wave is accompanied by a regionally specific desynchronication of frontal EEG rhythms (Grünewald-Zuberbier et al., 1978).

Intensity Effects

As is the case with other OR components, there is some evidence to indicate that O-wave amplitude is a function of intensity, both in signal (Loveless & Sanford, 1975) and in nonsignal situations (Rohrbaugh & Gaillard, 1983). Although many of the relevant studies have used fairly intense stimuli, unpublished evidence from our laboratory indicates clearly that the O wave can be elicited effectively by low-intensity stimuli; some subjects, in fact, yield the "J-shaped" intensity function prescribed by Sokolov (1963b).

Laterality Effects

The O wave, particularly the late, SNW2 component, appears to be distinctly asymmetric in its bilateral representation (Rohrbaugh, Newlin, Varner and

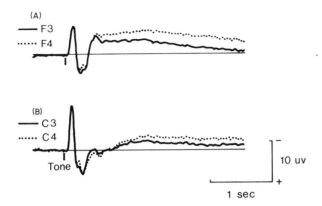

Figure 9.3 ERPs obtained in a pitch discrimination task in which subjects were instructed to count silently the number of standard pitch tones, intermingled in random sequence with other tones entailing either a difficult or easy frequency discrimination. Tones were delivered at a variable rate averaging 1 tone/15 sec. Waveforms are averaged over trial type and 22 subjects. Separate waveforms are depicted for (A) left and right frontal (F_3, F_4) and (B) central (C_3, C_4) sites.

Ellingson, in press). This feature is illustrated in Figure 9.3, which depicts records from bilateral frontal (F_3 and F_4) and central (C_3 and C_4) sites. These records are averaged over 22 subjects and display a degree of asymmetry that is remarkably large by surface EEG standards, which is essentially undiminished at the end of the 3-second epoch. The asymmetry predominates at frontal sites, and is apparently confined to the SNW2 component (suggesting that it is not artifactual or related to some such trivial factor as bilateral inequalities in skull impedance). The data displayed here were obtained in a discrimination task in which subjects were required to maintain a silent count of standard tone stimuli presented in a mixed sequence with other tones differing in pitch by small or large amounts (see Rohrbaugh *et al.*, in press, for details). Varying degrees of asymmetry were obtained in different tasks for nonsignal and nondiscriminatively counted stimuli as well. Most individual subjects show the direction of asymmetry indicated in Figure 9.3; some subjects show a diminution or reversal in asymmetry, and over all subjects, there was a weak tendency for the direction and degree of O wave asymmetry to be correlated ($r = 0.40$) with the strength and direction of the propensity to make lateral eye movements on reflective thought (as measured with the procedure and test items described by Schwartz, Davidson, & Maer, 1975). Electrooculographic activity cannot be considered as the source of this asymmetry, however, because control procedures essentially eliminated this artifact. The predominance of the O wave over the right side of the scalp agrees remarkably well with evidence, reviewed in an earlier section, indicating a right hemisphere predominance for the OR and attentional processes.

Modality Effects

Evidence favoring an OR prepotency for acoustic stimulation, particularly with regard to a variety of performance measures, is described in a earlier section of this review. It is notable that the O wave shows a corresponding effect, both for signal (Gaillard, 1976; Sanquist, Beatty, & Lindsley, 1981) and nonsignal stimuli (Rohrbaugh, Syndulko, & Lindsley, 1979), although the difference apparently can be overcome under stringent task requirements (Rohrbaugh et al., 1978). The difference is preserved at a variety of intensities, suggesting the effect is not related simply to a psychophysical mismatch in intensity (Rohrbaugh et al., 1979).

Rate Effects

As is the case with other OR components (see above), the O wave is a strong function of rate, being fairly difficult to observe at rapid rates of stimulation (Rohrbaugh et al., 1979).

Habituation Effects

Habituation effects have not been adequately characterized, with some studies finding the anticipated habituation (Klorman, 1975; Rockstroh et al., 1982, p. 36; Simons, Öhman, & Lang, 1979; Weerts & Lang, 1973) and others either noting no decrement (Gaillard, 1976; Klorman & Bentsen, 1975; Zappoli, Denoth, & Navona, 1980) or observing a growth in O wave amplitude (Rohrbaugh, Syndulko, & Lindsley, 1976). The extent to which these discrepant results rule against an interpretation of the O wave as an OR component is not clear; these observations have all been made under signal conditions, in which case habituation of the OR may be protracted or nonexistent. In the absence of habituation data from nonsignal conditions, and in the absence of converging evidence from some more traditional measure of the OR; no strong inference can be drawn.

Relationship with the K Complex

If a habituation sequence is allowed to continue for some time after the OR has habituated completely or to asymptotic values, it may eventually reappear at a level equal to, or exceeding the original strength. The reevoked OR then is somewhat more resistant (Johnson, Townsend, & Wilson, 1975; McDonald & Carpenter, 1975; Sokolov, 1963b) or immune (Johnson & Lubin, 1967; Williams, Morlock, Morlock, & Lubin, 1964) to habituation than was the initial OR, depending on the particular measure and the rate or intensity of stimulation. Sokolov (1963b) contends that this OR reevocation is due to inhibition within the cortex itself and a consequent relaxation of its usual inhibitory influence over the collaterals to the brain-stem activation systems; and he implicates this process in sleep onset. It should be noted that the autonomic manifestations of the sleeping

OR differ in several important respects from the waking OR (McDonald & Carpenter, 1975), and the response is suggested by Graham (1979) to be a DR rather than an OR.

If indeed the O wave is a manifestation of the OR, then it ought to have some representation during the sleeping state. The most conspicuous EEG sign of the OR during sleep is the *K complex,* which is a large transient response that can be easily seen in the unaveraged record (see Roth, Shaw, & Green, 1956, for a more thorough description). It may be elicited by external stimulation, or may occur spontaneously (presumably in response to some endogenous stimulation). Spontaneous K complexes recur with some degree of regularity (Johnson and Karpan, 1968), and there is some evidence that their appearance is timed to the cardiac cycle (Fruhstorfer, Partanen, & Lumino, 1971). Evidence linking the K complex to the OR is substantial. Both the K complex and visceral indicators of the OR tend to be elicited during the same stage of sleep (Stage 2) and only those stimulations that elicit a K complex also elicit the autonomic signs of the OR (Berg, Jackson, & Graham, 1975; Johnson & Lubin, 1967; Johnson et al., 1975). Moreover, the K complex is associated with behavioral and EEG signs of activation (Oswald, Taylor, & Treisman, 1960; Sassin & Johnson, 1968).

The case for considering the K complex to be a varient of the O wave cannot be made with certainty, although several suggestive parallels may be noted. Although the K complex is generally not recorded with long time-constant amplification, its morphology and scalp representation seem nevertheless to be similar to that of the O wave. Both are characterized by a prominent positive wave at parietal sites, and a subsequent, very broad negativity over frontal and precentral sites (Brazier, 1949; Bremmer, Smith, & Karacan, 1970; Roth et al., 1956; Weitzman & Kremen, 1965). The K complex, moreover, can be discerned in the waking EEG of some subjects, being somewhat smaller and of shorter latency but otherwise similar to the sleeping K complex (Roth et al., 1956). This response seen in the waking state may well be an unaveraged O wave.

Relationship with Performance Measures

A final bit of evidence linking the O wave to the OR is that it apparently is accompanied by changes in sensory and motor performance. Loveless (1975) has explored the possibility that the lowering of sensory threshold elicited by an accessory stimulus (discussed in the preceding) mirrors the course of the O wave by requiring an acoustic detection at various times after an acoustic accessory signal. Peak detection sensitivity and the O wave peak both occurred 1.0 seconds following the accessory tone, and thereafter declined at a commensurate rate. Loveless (1973) elsewhere has observed a close correspondence between O wave growth and reaction-time facilitation, under conditions in which the foreperiod was irregular so as to minimize the contribution from temporal expectancy factors. These findings raise the intriguing possibility that the O wave may earmark the strength and temporal course of the functional characteristics of the OR.

Acknowledgments

Preparation of this chapter was supported in part by National Institute of Mental Health Grant No. R02 MH 35742. The helpful comments of Robert J. Ellingson and Stephen Paige, and the preparation of the manuscript by Pamela Unruh, are gratefully acknowledged.

Reference Notes

1. Maltzman, I., & Boyd, G. *Stimulus significance and bilateral SCRs to "potential phobic" stimuli.* Paper presented at the annual meeting of the Society for Psychophysiological Research, Minneapolis, October, 1982.
2. Zeigler, B. L., & Graham, F. K. *Priming (match–mismatch) and alerting (modality) effects on reflex startle and simple reaction time.* Paper presented at a meeting of the Society for Psychophysiological Research, Minneapolis, October, 1982.
3. Spinks, J. A. *The attentional nature of the orienting response.* Paper presented at meeting of the Society for Psychophysiological Research, Vancouver, October, 1980.
4. Näätänen, R. *Mechanisms of the orienting reflex as reflected by ERPs.* Paper presented at the Second International Conference on Cognitive Neuroscience, Kingston, Ontario, September, 1982.
5. Steinhauer, S. R., Jennings, J. R., Aubin, J., & Heidorn, P. B. *Pupillary dilation, P300 and heart rate are influenced by conditional probability.* Paper presented at the annual meeting of the Society for Psychophysiological Research, Vancouver, October, 1980.
6. Schandry, R., Sparrer, B., & Elton, M. *Correlations between P300 and SCR in a habituation experiment.* Paper presented at the annual meeting of the Society for Psychophysiological Research, Minneapolis, October, 1982.
7. Karis, D., Bashor, T., Fabiani, M., & Donchin, E. *P300 and memory.* Paper presented at the annual meeting of the Society for Psychophysiological Research, Washington, D.C., October, 1981.

References

Abbruzzese, G., Ratto, S., Favale, W., & Abruzzese, M. Proprioceptive modulation of somatosensory evoked potentials during active or passive finger movements in man. *Journal of Neurology, Neurosurgery, and Psychiatry*, 1981, *44*, 942–949.

Adams, C. K., & Behar, I. Stimulus change properties of the RT ready signal. *Psychonomic Science*, 1966, *6*, 389–390.

Asafov, B. D. Change in the dynamics of autonomic components of the orienting reflex with employment of sound stimuli of progressively increasing intensity. In: L. G. Voronin, A. N. Leontiev, A. R. Luria, E. N. Sokolov, & O. S. Vinogradova (Eds.), *Orienting reflex and exploratory behavior*. Washington, D.C.: American Institute of Biological Sciences, 1965, p. 155–162.

Bagshaw, M. H., & Benzies, S. Multiple measures of the orienting reaction and their dissociation after amygdalectomy in monkeys. *Experimental Neurology*, 1968, *20*, 175–187.

Bagshaw, M. H., Kimble, D. P., & Pribram, K. H. The GSR of monkeys during orienting and habituation and after ablation of the amygdala, hippocampus, and inferotemporal cortex. *Neuropsychologia*, 1965, *3*, 111–119.

Baker, R. A., Ware, J. R., & Sipowicz, R. R. Vigilance: A comparison in auditory, visual, and combined audio-visual tasks. *Canadian Journal of Psychology*, 1962, *16*, 192–198.

Barham, R. M., & Boersma, F. J. *Orienting responses in a selection of cognitive tasks*. Rotterdam: Rotterdam University Press, 1975.

Barry, R. J. Low-intensity auditory stimulation and the GSR orienting response. *Physiological Psychology*, 1975, *3*, 98–100.

Barry, R. J. Failure to find the "local" EEG OR to low-level auditory stimulation. *Physiological Psychology*, 1976, *4*, 171–174.

Barry, R. J. The effect of "significance" upon indices of Sokolov's orienting response: A new conceptualization to replace the OR. *Physiological Psychology*, 1977, *5*, 209–214. (a)

Barry, R. J. Failure to find evidence of the unitary OR concept with indifferent low-intensity auditory stimuli. *Physiological Psychology*, 1977, *5*, 89–96. (b)

Barry, R. J. Physiological changes in a reaction time task: Further problems with Sokolov's dimension of stimulus "significance." *Physiological Psychology*, 1978, *6*, 438–444.

Barry, R. J. A factor analytic examination of the unitary OR concept. *Biological Psychology*, 1979, *8*, 161–178.

Barry, R. J. Signal value and preliminary processes in OR elicitation. *Pavlovian Journal of Biological Science*, 1981, *16*, 144–150.

Barry, R. J. Anticipatory changes in state, dual-process theory, and preliminary OR processes. *Physiological Psychology*, 1982, *10*, 209–214. (a)

Barry, R. J. Novelty and significance effects on the fractionation of phasic OR measures: Synthesis with traditional OR theory. *Psychophysiology*, 1982, *19*, 28–35. (b)

Barry, R. J., & James, A. J. Fractionation of respiratory and vascular responses with simple visual stimulation. *Physiological Psychology*, 1981, *9*, 96–101.

Beale, D. K. Facilitation of the knee jerk as a function of the interval between auditory and stretching stimuli. *Psychophysiology*, 1971, *8*, 504–508.

Beatty, J., & Wagoner, B. L. Pupillometric signs of brain activation vary with level of cognitive processing. *Science*, 1978, *199*, 1216–1218.

Becker, D. E., & Shapiro, D. Directing attention toward stimuli affects the P300 but not the orienting response. *Psychophysiology*, 1980, *17*, 385–389.

Berg, W. K., Jackson, J. C., & Graham, F. K. Tone intensity and rise–decay time effects on cardiac responses during sleep. *Psychophysiology*, 1975, *12*, 254–261.

Berggren, T., Öhman, A., & Fredrikson, M. Locus of control and habituation of the electrodermal orienting response to nonsignal and signal stimuli. *Journal of Personality and Social Psychology*, 1977, *35*, 708–716.

Bernstein, A. S. The orienting response and direction of stimulus change. *Psychonomic Science*, 1968, *12*, 127–128.

Bernstein, A. S. The orienting response as novelty *and* significance detector: Reply to O'Gorman. *Psychophysiology*, 1979, *16*, 263–273.

Bernstein, A. S. The orienting response and stimulus significance: Further comments. *Biological Psychology*, 1981, *12*, 171–185.

Bernstein, A. S., & Taylor, K. W. The interaction of stimulus information with potential stimulus significance in eliciting the skin conductance orienting response. In H. D. Kimmel, E. H. Van Olst, & J. F. Orlebeki (Eds.), *The orienting reflex in humans*. Hillsdale, N.J.: L

Bernstein, A. S., Taylor, K. W., Austen, B. G., Nathanson, M., & Scarpelli, A. Orienting response and apparent movement toward or away from the observer. *Journal of Experimental Psychology*, 1971, *87*, 37–45.

Bernstein, A. S., Taylor, K. W., Starkey, P., Juni, S., Lubowsky, J., & Paley, H. Bilateral skin conductance, finger pulse volume, and EEG orienting response to tones of differing intensities in chronic schizophrenics and controls. *The Journal of Nervous and Mental Disease*, 1981, *169*, 513–528.

Bernstein, A. S., Taylor, K. W., & Weinstein, E. The phasic electrodermal response as a differentiated complex reflecting stimulus significance. *Psychophysiology*, 1975, *12*, 158–169.

Blakeslee, P. Attention and vigilance: Performance and skin conductance response changes. *Psychophysiology*, 1979, *16*, 413–419.

Bohlin, G., Graham, F. K., Silverstein, L. D., & Hackley, S. A. Cardiac orienting and startle blink modification in novel and signal situations. *Psychophysiology*, 1981, *18*, 603–611.

Bohlin, G., and Kjellberg, A. Orienting Activity in two-stimulus paradigms as reflected in heart rate. In H. D. Kimmel, E. H. Van Olst, & J. F. Orlebeke (Eds.), *The orienting reflex in humans*. Hillsdale, N. J.: Erlbaum, 1979, 169–197.

Bonvallet, M., Dell, P., & Hiebel, G. Tonus sympathique et activite electrique corticale. *Electroencephalography and Clinical Neurophysiology*, 1954, *6*, 119–144.

Brazier, M. A. B. The electrical fields at the surface of the head during sleep. *Electroencephalography and Clinical Neurophysiology*, 1949, *1*, 195–204.

Bremer, G., Smith, J. R., and Karacan, I. Automatic detection of the K-complex in sleep electroencephalograms. *IEEE Transcations on Bio-medical Engineering*, 1970, *BME-17*, 314–323.

Broadbent, D. E. The current state of noise research: Reply to Poulton. *Psychological Bulletin*, 1978, *85*, 1052–1067.

Brooks, C. M., & Lange, G. Patterns of reflex action, their autonomic components, and their behavioral significance. *Pavlovian Journal of Biological Science*, 1982, *17*, 55–61.

Brown, J., Morse, P., Leavitt, L., & Graham, F. Specific attentional effects reflected in the cardiac orienting response. *Bulletin of the Psychonomic Society*, 1976, *7*, 1–4.

Callaway, E. Habituation of averaged evoked potentials in man. In: H. V. S. Peeke & M. J. Herz (Eds.), *Habituation* (Vol. 2). New York: Academic Press, 1973, 153–174.

Cannon, W. B. *Bodily changes in pain, fear and rage*. Appleton-Century-Crofts, 1936.

Chattopadhyay, P., Cooke, E., Tonne, B., & Lader, M. Habituation of physiological responses in anxiety. *Biological Psychiatry*, 1980, *15*, 711–721.

Coles, M. G. H., & Duncan -Johnson, C. C. Cardiac activity and information processing: The effects of stimulus significance, and detection and response requirements. *Journal of Experimental Psychology: Human Perception and Performance*, 1975, *1*, 418–428.

Colquhoun, W. P. Evaluation of auditory, visual, and dual-mode displays for prolonged sonar monitoring in repeated sessions. *Human Factors*, 1975, *17*, 425–437.

Connolly, J. F., & Frith, C. D. Effects of stimulus variability on the amplitude and habituation of the electrodermal orienting response. *Psychophysiology*, 1978, *15*, 550–555.

Connor, W. H., & Lang, P. J. Cortical slow-wave and cardiac rate responses in stimulus orientation and reaction time conditions. *Journal of Experimental Psychology*, 1969, *82*, 310–320.

Cook, M. R. *The cutaneous vasomotor orienting response and its habituation*. Unpublished doctoral dissertation, Health Sciences Center, University of Oklahoma, Okalhoma City, 1970.

Corteen, R. A. Skin conductance changes and word recall. *British Journal of Psychology*, 1969, *60*, 81–84.

Courchesne, E. Changes in P3 waves with event repetition: Long-term effects on scalp distribution and amplitude. *Electroencephalography and Clinical Neurophysiology*, 1978, *45*, 754–766.

Craik, F. I. M., & Blankstein, K. R. Psychophysiology and human memory. In: P. H. Venables & M. J. Christie (Eds.), *Research in psychophysiology*, New York: Wiley, 1975, 389–417.

Darrow, C. W. Problems in the use of the galvanic skin response (GSR) as an index of cerebral function: Implications of the latent period. *Psychophysiology*, 1967, *3*, 389–396.

Davenport, W. G. Vigilance for simultaneous auditory cutaneous signals. *Canadian Journal of Psychology*, 1969, *23*, 93–100.

Davis, R. C. Motor effects of strong auditory stimuli. *Journal of Experimental Psychology*, 1948, *38*, 257–275.

Davis, R. C. Motor responses to auditory stimuli above and below threshold. *Journal of Experimental Psychology,* 1950, *40,* 107–120.

Dawson, M. E., Schell, A. M., Beers, J. R., & Kelly, A. Allocation of cognitive processing capacity during human autonomic classical conditioning. *Journal of Experimental Psychology: General,* 1982, *111,* 273–295.

Demina, L. D., & Khomskaya, E. D. Interhemispheric asymmetry of visual evoked potentials during involuntary and voluntary attention. *Human Physiology,* 1976, *2,* 617–623.

Donald, M. W., & Little, R. The analysis of stimulus probability inside and outside the focus of attention, as reflected by the auditory N1 and P3 components. *Canadian Journal of Psychology,* 1981, *35,* 175–187.

Donchin, E. Suprise! . . . Surprise? *Psychophysiology,* 1981, *18,* 493–513.

Donchin, E. Ritter, W., & McCallum, W. C. Cognitive psychophysiology: The endogenous components of the ERP. In: E. Callaway & S. H. Koslow (Eds.), *Event related brain potentials in man.* New York: Academic Press, 1978, 349–411.

Dongier, M., Dubrovsky, B., & Englesmann, F. Event-related slow potentials in psychiatry. In: C. Shagass, S. Gershon, & A. J. Friedhoff (Eds.), *Psychopathology and brain dysfunction.* New York: Raven, 1977, 339–352.

Easterbrook, J. A. The effect of emotion on cue utilization and the organization of behavior. *Psychological Review,* 1959, *66,* 183–201.

Edelberg, R. The relationship between the galvanic skin response, vasoconstriction, and tactile sensitivity. *Journal of Experimental Psychology,* 1961, *62,* 187–195.

Egan, J. P., Schulman, A. I., & Greenberg, G. Z. Memory for waveform and time uncertainty in auditory detection. *Journal of the Acoustical Society of America,* 1961, *33,* 779–781.

Eysenck, M. W. *Attention and arousal.* Berlin: Springer-Verlag, 1982.

Figar, S. Conditional circulatory responses in men and animals. In W. F. Hamilton & P. Dow (Eds.), *Handbook of physiology* (Sect. 2, Vol. 3: *Circulation.* Washington, D.C.: American Physiological Society, 1965, 1991–2035.

Floru, R. F. Unconditioned and conditioned orienting reflex: Psychophysiological investigations. In H. D. Kimmel, E. H. Van Olst, & J. F. Orlebeke (Eds.), *The orienting reflex in humans.* Hillsdale, N.J.: Earlbaum, 1979, 289–303.

Fredrikson, M., & Öhman, A. Heart-rate and electrodermal orienting responses to visual stimuli differing in complexity. *Scandinavian Journal of Psychology,* 1979, *20,* 37–41.

Friedland, R. P., & Weinstein, F. A. Hemi-inattention and hemisphere specialization: Introduction and historical review. In E. A. Weinstein, & R. P. Friedland (Eds.), *Advances in neurology* (Vol. 18). New York: Raven, 1977, 1–31.

Friedman, D. The late positive component and orienting behavior. In D. A. Otto (Ed.), *Multidisciplinary perspectives in event-related brain potential research.* Washington, D.C.: Government Printing Office, 1978, EPA-600/9-77-043, 178–180.

Friedman, D., Hakerem, G., Sutton, S., & Fleiss, J. Effect of stimulus uncertainty on the pupillary dilation response and the vertex evoked potential. *Electroencephalography and Clinical Neurophysiology,* 1973, *34,* 475–484.

Fruhstorfer, H., Partanen, J., & Lumino, J. Vertex sharp waves and heart action during the onset of sleep. *Electroencephalography and Clinical Neurophysiology,* 1971, *31,* 614–617.

Furedy, J. J., & Arabian, J. M. A Pavlovian psychophysiological perspective on the OR: The facts of the matter. In H. D. Kimmel, E. H. Van Olst, & J. F. Orlebeke (Eds.), *The orienting reflex in humans.* Hillsdale, N.J.: Erlbaum, 1979, 353–372.

Gaillard, A. Effects of warning-signal modality on the contingent negative variation (CNV). *Biological Psychology,* 1976, *4,* 39–154.

Gaillard, A. W. K., & Perdok, J. Slow cortical and heart rate correlates of discrimination performance. *Acta Psychologica,* 1979, *43,* 185–198.

Gaillard, A. W. K., & Perdok, J. Slow brain potentials in the CNV-paradigm. *Acta Psychologica,* 1980, *44*, 147–163.

Gale, E. N., and Ax, A. F. Long term conditioning of orienting responses. *Psychophysiology,* 1968, *5*, 307–315.

Geer, J. H. Effect of interstimulus intervals and rest-period length upon habituation of the orienting response. *Journal of Experimental Psychology,* 1966, *72*, 617–619.

Germana, J. Response characteristics and the orienting reflex. *Journal of Experimental Psychology,* 1968, *78*, 610–616.

Germana, J. Central efferent processes and autonomic-behavioral integration. *Psychophysiology,* 1969, *6*, 78–90.

Ginsberg, S., & Furedy, J. J. Stimulus repetition, change, and assessments of sensitivities of and relationships among an electrodermal and two plethysmographic components of the orienting reaction. *Psychophysiology,* 1974, *11*, 35–43.

Gogan, P. The startle and orienting reactions in man: A study of their characteristics and habituation. *Brain Research,* 1970, *18*, 117–135.

Goodin, D. S., Squires, K. C., Henderson, B. H., & Starr, A. An early event-related cortical potential. *Psychophysiology,* 1978, *15*, 360–365.

Gottsdanker, R. The attaining and maintaining of preparation. In: P. M. A. Rabbitt & S. Dornic (Eds.), *Attention and performance.* London: Academic Press, 1975, 33–49.

Graham, F. K. Habituation and dishabituation of responses innervated by the autonomic nervous system. In H. V. S. Peeke & M. J. Herz (Eds.), *Habituation: Behavioral studies and physiological substrates* (Vol. 1). New York: Academic Press, 1973, 163–218.

Graham, F. K. Distinguishing among orienting, defense, and startle reflexes. In H. D. Kimmel, E. H. van Olst, & J. F. Orlebeke (Eds.), *The orienting reflex in humans.* Hillsdale, N.J.: Erlbaum, 1979, 137–168.

Graham, F. K., & Clifton, R. K. Heart rate change as a component of the orienting response. *Psychological Bulletin,* 1966, *65*, 305–320.

Graham, F. K., Putnam, L. E., Leavitt, L. A. Lead stimulation effects on human cardiac orienting and blink reflex. *Journal of Experimental Psychology: Human Perception and Performance,* 1975, *104*, 161–169.

Greene, R. L., Dengerink, H. A., & Staples, S. L. To what does the terminal orienting response respond? *Psychophysiology,* 1974, *11*, 639–646.

Grünewald-Zuberbier, E., Grünewald, G., Rasche, A., & Netz, J. Contingent negative variation and alpha attentuation responses in children with different abilities to concentrate. *Electroencephalography and Clinical Neurophysiology,* 1978, *44*, 37–47.

Heilman, K. M., & Van Den Abell, T. Right hemispheric dominance for mediating cerebral activation. *Neuropsychologia,* 1979, *17*, 315–321.

Heilman, K. M., & Van Den Abell, T. Right hemisphere dominance for attention: The mechanism underlying hemispheric asymmetries of inattention (neglect). *Neurology,* 1980, *30*, 327–330.

Heilman, K. M., & Watson, R. T. Mechanisms underlying the unilateral neglect syndrome. In E. A. Weinstein & R. P. Friedland (Eds.), *Hemi-attention and Hemispheric Specialization (Advances in Neurology;* Vol. 18). New York: Raven, 1977.

Hockey, R. Stress and the cognitive components of skilled performance. In V. Hamilton & O. M. Warburton (Eds.), *Human stress and cognition.* New York: Wiley, 1979, 141–177.

Horn, G., & Venables, P. H. The effect of somaesthetic and acoustic stimuli on the threshold of fusion of paired light flashes in human subjects. *The Quarterly Journal of Experimental Psychology,* 1964, *16*, 289–296.

Howes, D., and Boller, F. Simple reaction time: Evidence for focal impairment from lesions of the right hemisphere. *Brain,* 1975, *98*, 317–332.

Hugdahl, L., Wahlgren, C., & Wass, T. Habituation of the electrodermal orienting reaction is dependent on the cerebral hemisphere initially stimulated. *Biological Psychology*, 1982, *15*, 49–62.

Iacono, W., & Lykken, D. The orienting response: Importance of instructions. *Schizophrenia Bulletin*, 1979, *5*, 11–14.

Jackson, J. C. Amplitude and habituation of the orienting reflex as a function of stimulus intensity. *Psychophysiology*, 1974, *11*, 647–659.

James, A. L., & Barry, R. J. Respiratory and vascular responses to simple visual stimuli in autistics, retardates, and normals. *Psychophysiology*, 1980, *17*, 541–547.

James, W. *The principles of psychology* (Vol. 1). New York: Holt, 1890.

Jeffrey, W. E. The orienting reflex and attention in cognitive development. *Psychological Review*, 1968, *75*, 323–334.

Johnson, L. C., & Karpan, W. E. Autonomic correlates of the spontaneous K-complex. *Psychophysiology*, 1968, *4*, 444–452.

Johnson, L. C., & Lubin, A. The orienting reflex during waking and sleeping. *Electroencephalography and Clinical Neurophysiology*, 1967, *22*, 11–21.

Johnson, L. C., Townsend, R. E., & Wilson, M. R. Habituation during sleeping and waking. *Psychophysiology*, 1975, *12*, 574–584.

Jones, J. E. Contiguity and reinforcement in relation to CS–UCS intervals in classical aversive conditioning. *Psychological Review*, 1962, *69*, 176–186.

Kahneman, D. *Attention and effort*. Englewood Cliffs, N.J.: Prentice-Hall, 1973. Kimmel, H. D. Inhibition of the unconditioned response in classical conditioning. *Psychological Review*, 1966, *73*, 232–240.

Kimmel, H. D. Inhibition of the unconditioned response in classical conditioning. *Psychological Review*, 1966, *73*, 232–240.

Kimmel, H. D., Van Olst, F. H., & Orlebeke, J. F. (Eds.), *The orienting reflex in humans*. Hillsdale, N.J.: Erlbaum, 1979.

Klayman, B. E. Heteromodal cueing and auditory–visual interaction: A literature review. *The Journal of Psychology*, 1973, *83*, 173–199.

Klein, R. M., & Kerr, B. Visual signal detection and the locus of the foreperiod effects. *Memory and Cognition*, 1974, *2*, 431–435.

Klorman, R. Contingent negative variation and cardiac deceleration in a long preparatory interval: A developmental study. *Psychophysiology*, 1975, *12*, 609–617.

Klorman, R., & Bentsen, E. Effects of warning-signal duration on the early and late components of the contingent negative variation. *Biological Psychology*, 1975, *3*, 263–275.

Koepke, J. E., & Pribram, K. H. Habituation of GSR as a function of stimulus duration and spontaneous activity. *Journal of Comparative and Physiological Psychology*, 1966, *61*, 442–448.

Koepke, J. E., & Pribram, K. H. Habituation of the vasoconstriction response as a function of stimulus duration and anxiety. *Journal of Comparative and Physiological Psychology*, 1967, *64*, 502–504.

Koerner, F., & Teuber, H. L. Visual field defects after missile injuries to the geniculo-striate pathway in man. *Experimental Brain Research*, 1973, *18*, 88–113.

Kok, A. The effect of warning stimulus novelty on the P300 and components of the contingent negative variation. *Biological Psychology*, 1978, *6*, 219–233.

Lacey, J. I., & Lacey, B. C. Experimental association and dissociation of phasic bradycardia and vertex-negative waves: A psychophysiological study of attention and response-intention. In W. C. McCallum & J. R. Knott (Eds.), Event-related slow potentials of the brain. *Electroencephalography and Clinical Neurophysiology* (Suppl.) 1973, *33*, 281–285.

Lang, P. J., Gatchel, R. J., & Simons, R. F. Electro-cortical and cardiac rate correlates of psychophysical judgment. *Psychophysiology*, 1975, *12*, 649–655.

Lang, P. J., Öhman, A., & Simons, R. F. The psychophysiology of anticipation. In J. Requin (Ed.), *Attention and performance VII*. New York: Erlbaum, 1978, 460–485.

Lansing, R. W., Schwartz, E., & Lindsley, D. B. Reaction time EEG activation under alerted and nonalerted conditions. *Journal of Experimental Psychology*, 1959, *58*, 1–7.

Laurian, S., & Gaillard, J. Habituation of visually evoked responses in man: A study of its time course. *Neuropsychobiology*, 1976, *2*, 297–306.

London, I. D. Research on sensory interaction in the Soviet Union. *Psychological Bulletin*, 1954, *51*, 531–568.

Loveless, N. E. The contingent negative variation related to preparatory set in a reaction time situation with variable foreperiod. *Electroencephalography and Clinical Neurophysiology*, 1973, *35*, 369–374.

Loveless, N. E. The effect of warning interval on signal detection and event-related slow potentials of the brain. *Perception and Psychophysics*, 1975, *17*, 565–570.

Loveless, N. E. Distribution of responses to non-signal stimuli. In W. C. McCallum & J. R. Knott (Eds.), *The responsive brain*. Bristol: John Wright, 1976, 26–29.

Loveless, N. E. Event related slow potentials of the brain as expressions of orienting function. In H. D. Kimmel, E. H. Van Olst, & J. F. Orlebeke (Eds.), *The orienting reflex in humans*. Hillsdale, N. J.: Erlbaum, 1979, 77–100.

Loveless, N. E., Brebner, J., & Hamilton, P. Bisensory presentation of information. *Psychological Bulletin*, 1970, *73*, 161–199.

Loveless, N., & Sanford, A. Effects of age on the contingent negative variation and preparatory set in a reaction-time task. *Journal of Gerontology*, 1974, *29*, 52–63.

Loveless, N., & Sanford, A. The impact of warning signal intensity of reaction time and components of the contingent negative variation. *Biological Psychology*, 1975, *2*, 217–226.

Luria, A. R. *The working brain*. New York: Basic Books, 1973.

Luria, A. R., & Homskaya, E. D. Frontal lobes and the regulation of arousal processes. In D. I. Mostofsky (Ed.), *Attention: Contemporary theory and analysis*. New York: Appleton-Century-Crofts, 1970, 303–330.

Lynn, R. Attention, arousal and the orienting reaction. London: Pergamon, 1966.

Mackworth, J. F. *Vigilance and habituation*. Baltimore: Penguin, 1969.

Maher, T. F., & Furedy, J. J. A comparison of the pupillary and electrodermal components of the orienting reflex in sensitivity to initial stimulus presentation, repetition, and change. In H. D. Kimmel, E. H. Van Olst, & J. F. Orlebeke (Eds.), *The orienting reflex in humans*. Hillsdale, N.J.: Erlbaum, 1979, 381–391.

Maltzman, I. Orienting reflexes and classical conditioning in humans. In H. D. Kimmel, E. H. Van Olst, & J. F. Orlebeke (Eds.), *The orienting reflex in humans*. Hillsdale, N.J.: Erlbaum, 1979, 323–351. (a)

Maltzman, I. Orienting reflexes and significance: A reply to O'Gorman. *Psychophysiology*, 1979, *16*, 274–282. (b)

Maltzman, I., Vincent, C., & Wolff, C. Verbal conditioning, task instructions, and inhibition of the GSR measure of the orienting reflex. *Physiological Psychology*, 1982, *10*, 221–228.

Mandler, G. Thought processes, consciousness, and stress. In V. Hamilton & D. M. Warburton (Eds.), *Human stress and cognition*. New York: Wiley, 1979, 179–201.

Martin, I., & Levey, A. B. *The genesis of the classical conditioned response*. Oxford: Pergamon, 1969.

McCarthy, G., & Donchin, E. Brain potentials associated with structural and functional visual matching. *Neuropsychologia*, 1978, *16*, 571–586.

McDonald, D. G., & Carpenter, F. A. Habituation of the orienting response in sleep. *Psychophysiology*, 1975, *12*, 618–623.

Mefford, R. B. Sadler, T. J., & Wieland, B. A. Physiological responses to mild heteromodal sensory stimulation. *Psychophysiology*, 1969, *6*, 186–196.

Mesulam, M. M., & Geschwind, N. On the possible role of the neo-cortex and its limbic connections in attention in schizophrenia. In L. C. Wynne, R. L. Cromwell, & S. Matthyse (Eds.), *The nature of schizophrenia*. New York: Wiley, 1978, 161–166.

Michalewski, H. J. *Lateralized cerebral processing and the development of hemispheric slow scalp potentials—the CNV*. Unpublished doctoral dissertation, Simon Fraser University, Burnaby, B.C., 1975.

Millar, K. Word recognition in loud noise. *Acta Psychologica*, 1979, *43*, 225–237.

Mulholland, T. B. Objective EEG methods for studying covert shifts of visual attention. In F. J. McGuigan & R. A. Schoonover (Eds.), *The psychophysiology of thinking*. New York: Academic Press, 1973, 109–151.

Näätänen, R. Orienting and evoked potentials. In H. D. Kimmel, E. H. Van Olst, & J. F. Orlebeke (Eds.), *The orienting reflex in humans*. Hillsdale, N.J.: Erlbaum, 1979, 61–75.

Näätänen, R. The N2 component of the evoked potential: A scalp reflection of neuronal mismatch of orienting theory? In J. Strelau, F. Farley, & A. Gale (Eds.), *Biological foundations of personality and behavior*. Washington, D.C.: Hemisphere, in press.

Näätänen, R., & Gaillard, A. W. K. The orienting reflex and the N2 deflection of the event-related potential (ERP). In A. W. K. Gaillard & W. Ritter (Eds.), *Tutorials in ERP research: The endogenous components*. Amsterdam: North-Holland, 1983, 114–141.

Näätänen, R., & Michie, P. T. Different variants of endogenous negative brain potentials in performance situations: A review and classification. In D. Lehmann & E. Callaway (Eds.), *Human evoked potentials*. New York: Plenum, 1979, 251–267.

Näätänen, R., Simpson, M., & Loveless, N. E. Stimulus deviance and evoked potentials. *Biological Psychology*, 1982, *14*, 53–98.

Nickerson, R. S. Intersensory facilitation of reaction time. *Psychological Review*, 1973, *80*, 489–509.

Niemi, P., & Lehtonen, E. Foreperiod and visual stimulus intensity: A reappraisal. *Acta Psychologica*, 1982, *50*, 73–82.

Niemi, P., & Näätänen, R. Foreperiod and simple reaction time. *Psychological Bulletin*, 1981, *89*, 133–162.

Nissen, M. J. Stimulus intensity and information processing. *Perception and Psychophysics*, 1977, *22*, 338–352.

Norman, D. A. Toward a theory of memory and attention. *Psychological Review*, 1968, *75*, 522–536.

Obrist, P. A. The cardiovascular–behavioral interaction—as it appears today. *Psychophysiology*, 1976, *13*, 95–107.

Obrist, P. A., Webb, R. A., Sutterer, J. R., & Howard, J. L. The cardiac–somatic relationship: Some reformulations. *Psychophysiology*, 1970, *6*, 569–587.

O'Gorman, J. G. Change in stimulus conditions and the orienting response. *Psychophysiology*, 1973, *10*, 465–470.

O'Gorman, J. G. Individual differences in habituation of human physiological responses: A review of theory, methods, and findings in the study of personality correlates in non-clinical populations. *Biological Psychology*, 1977, *5*, 257–318.

O'Gorman, J. G. The orienting reflex: Novelty or significance detector? *Psychophysiology*, 1979, *16*, 253–262. '

Öhman, A. The orienting response, attention and learning: An information-processing perspective. In H. D. Kimmel, E. H. Van Olst, & J. F. Orlebeke (Eds.), *The orienting reflex in humans*. Hillsdale, N.J.: Erlbaum, 1979, 443–471.

Öhman, A., & Lader, M. Short-term changes of the human auditory evoked potentials during repetitive stimulation. In: J. E. Desmedt (Ed.), *Auditory evoked potentials in man: Progress in clinical neurophysiology* (Vol. 2). Basel: Karger, 1977.

370   John W. Rohrbaugh

Oswald, I., Taylor, A. M., & Treisman, M. Discriminative responses to stimulation during human sleep. *Brain*, 1960, *83*, 440–453.

Papakostopoulos, D. CNV and autonomic function. In W. C. McCallum & R. Knott (Eds.), *Event-related slow potentials of the brain: Electroencephalography and Clinical Neurophysiology.* (Suppl.) 1973, *33*, 269–280.

Pavlov, I. P. *Conditioned reflexes: An investigation of the physiological activity of the cerebral cortex.* London: Oxford University Press, 1927.

Pendery, M., & Maltzman, I. Instructions and the orienting reflex in "semantic conditioning" of the galvanic skin response in an innocuous situation. *Journal of Experimental Psychology*, 1977, *106*, 120–140.

Perenin, M. T., & Jeannerod, M. Residual vision in blind hemifields. *Neuropsychologia*, 1975, *13*, 1–8.

Pfurtscheller, G. Central beta rhythm during sensorimotor activities in man. *Electroencephalography and Clinical Neurophysiology*, 1981, *51*, 253–264.

Pfurtscheller, G., & Aranibar, A. Event-related cortical desynchronization detected by power measurement of scalp EEG. *Electroencephalography and Clinical Neurophysiology*, 1977, *42*, 817–826.

Pfurtscheller, G., Waibel, R., and Schuy, S. Changes of the EEG during a CNV paradigm. *Medical and Biological Engineering*, 1976, *14*, 199–206.

Pillsbury, W. B. *Attention.* New York: MacMillan, 1908.

Posner, M. I. *Chronometric explorations of mind.* Hillsdale, N.J.: Erlbaum, 1978.

Posner, M. I., Nissen, M. J., & Klein, R. Visual dominance: An information-processing account of its origins and significance. *Psychological Review*, 1976, *83*, 157–170.

Pribram, K. H., & McGuiness, D. Arousal, activation, and effort in the control of attention. *Psychological Review*, 1975, *82*, 116–149.

Pritchard, W. S. Psychophysiology of P300. *Psychological Bulletin*, 1981, *89*, 506–540.

Prokasy, W. F. (Ed.). Symposium: Skin conductance response conditioning. *Psychophysiology*, 1977, *14*, 333–367.

Ray, R. L., & Piroch, J. F. Orienting responses to a change in stimulus significance. *Bulletin of the Psychonomic Society*, 1976, *8*, 82–84.

Ritter, W., Vaughan, Jr., H. G., & Costa, L. D. Orienting and habituation to auditory stimuli: A study of short-term changes in average evoked responses. *Electroencephalography and Clinical Neurophysiology*, 1968, *25*, 550–556.

Rockstroh, B., Elbert, T., Birbaumer, N., & Lutzenberger, W. *Slow brain potentials and behavior.* Baltimore: Urban & Schwarzenberg, 1982.

Rohrbaugh, J. W., & Gaillard, A. W. K. Sensory and motor aspects of the contingent negative variation. In A. W. K. Gaillard & W. Ritter (Eds.), *Tutorials in ERP research: Endogenous components.* Amsterdam: North-Holland, 1983, 269–310.

Rohrbaugh, J. W., Newlin, D. B., Varner, J. L., & Ellingson, R. J. Bilateral distribution of the O wave. In R. Karrer, J. Cohen, & P. Tueting (Eds.), *Brain and information: Event related potentials.* New York Academy of Sciences Monograph 12, in press.

Rohrbaugh, J. W., Syndulko, K., & Lindsley, D. B. Brain wave components of the contingent negative variation in humans. *Science*, 1976, *191*, 1055–1057.

Rohrbaugh, J. W., Syndulko, K., & Lindsley, D. B. Cortical slow negative waves following non-paired stimuli: Effects of task factors. *Electroencephalography and Clinical Neurophysiology*, 1978, *45*, 551–567.

Rohrbaugh, J. W., Syndulko, K., & Lindsley, D. B. Cortical slow negative waves following non-paired stimuli: Effects of modality, intensity, and rate of stimulation. *Electroencephalography and Clinical Neurophysiology*, 1979, *46*, 416–427.

Rohrbaugh, J. W., Syndulko, K., Sanquist, T. F., & Lindsley, D. B. Synthesis of the contingent negative variation brain potential from noncontingent stimulus and motor elements. *Science,* 1980, *208,* 1165–1168.

Roth, M., Shaw, J., & Green, J. The form, voltage distribution, and physiological significance of the K-complex. *Electroencepahlography and Clinical Neurophysiology,* 1956, *8,* 385–402.

Roth, W. T. A comparison of P300 and the skin conductance response. In A. W. K. Gaillard & W. Ritter (Eds.), *Tutorials in ERP research: Endogenous components.* Amsterdam: North-Holland, 1983, 177–199.

Roth, W. T., Ford, J. M., Krainz, P. L., & Kopell, B. S. Auditory evoked potentials, skin conductance response, eye movement, and reaction time in an orienting response paradigm. In D. A. Otto (Ed.), *Multidisciplinary perspectives in event-related brain potential research.* Washington, D.C.: Government Printing Office, 1978, EPA-600/9-77-043, 209–214.

Ruchkin, D. S., & Sutton, S. P300 and slow wave—association and dissociation. In A. W. K. Gaillard & W. Ritter (Eds.), *Tutorials in ERP research: Endogenous components.* Amsterdam: North-Holland, 1983, 233–250.

Rust, J. Habituation and the orienting response in the auditory cortical evoked potential. *Psychophysiology,* 1977, *14,* 123–126.

Sanders, A. F. Structural and functional aspects of the reaction process. In S. Dornic (Ed.), *Attention and performance* (Vol. 6). New York: Wiley, 1977, 3–25.

Sanders, A. F. Stage analysis of reaction processes. In G. E. Stelmach & J. Requin (Eds.), *Tutorials in motor behavior.* Amsterdam: North-Holland, 1980, 331–354.

Sanders, A. F., & Wertheim, A. H. The relation between physical stimulus properties and the effect of foreperiod duration on reaction time. *Quarterly Journal of Experimental Psychology,* 1973, *25,* 201–206.

Sanquist, T. F., Beatty, J. T., & Lindsley, D. B. Slow potential shifts of human brain during forewarned reaction. *Electroencephalography and Clinical Neurophysiology,* 1981, *51,* 639–649.

Sassin, J. F., & Johnson, L. C. Body motility during sleep and its relation to the K-complex. *Experimental Neurology,* 1968, *22,* 133–144.

Scheirs, J. G. M., & Brunia, C. H. M. Effects of stimulus and task factors on achilles tendon reflexes evoked early during a preparatory period. *Physiology and Behavior,* 1982, *28,* 681–685.

Schwartz, G. E., Davidson, R. J., & Maer, F. Right hemisphere lateralization for emotion in the human brain: Interactions with cognition. *Science,* 1975, *190,* 286–288.

Siddle, D. A. T. The orienting response and stimulus significance: Some comments. *Biological Psychology,* 1979, *8,* 303–309.

Siddle, D. A. T., & Heron, P. A. Effects of length of training and amount of tone frequency change on amplitude of autonomic components of the orienting response. *Psychophysiology,* 1976, *13,* 281–287.

Siddle, D. A. T., & Heron, P. A. Effects of length of training and amount of tone intensity change on amplitude of autonomic components of the orienting response. *Australian Journal of Psychology,* 1977, *29,* 7–16.

Siddle, D. A. T., Kyriacou, D., Heron, P. A., & Matthews, W. A. Effects of changes in verbal stimuli on the skin conductance response component of the orienting response. *Psychophysiology,* 1979, *16,* 34–40.

Siddle, D. A. T., & Spinks, J. A. Orienting response and information-processing: Some theoretical and empirical problems. In H. D. Kimmel, E. H. Van Olst, & J. F. Orlebeke (Eds.), *The orienting reflex in humans.* Hillsdale, N.J.: Erlbaum, 1979, 473–497.

Silverstein, L. D., Graham, F. K., & Bohlin, G. Selective attention effects on the reflex blink. *Psychophysiology,* 1981, *18,* 240–247.

Simon, J. R., Craft, J. L., & Small, A. M. Manipulating the strength of a stereotype: Interference effects in an auditory information processing task. *Journal of Experimental Psychology*, 1970, *86*, 63–68.

Simons, R. F., & Lang, P. J. Psychophysical judgment: Electro-cortical and heart rate correlates of accuracy and uncertainty. *Biological Psychology*, 1976, *4*, 51–64.

Simons, R. F., Öhman, A., & Lang, P. J. Anticipation and response set: Cortical, cardiac, and electrodermal correlates. *Psychophysiology*, 1979, *16*, 222–233.

Skinner, J. E. A neurophysiological model for regulation of sensory input to cerebral cortex. In D. A. Otto (Ed.), *Multidisciplinary perspectives in event-related brain potential research*. Washington, D.C.: Government Printing Office, 1978, EPA-600/9-77-043, 616–625.

Skolnick, B. E., Walrath, L. C., & Stern, J. A. Evaluation of temporal vasomotor components of orienting and defensive responses. In H. D. Kimmel, E. H. Van Olst, & J. F. Orlebeke (Eds.), *The orienting reflex in humans*. Hillsdale, N.J.: Erlbaum, 1979, 269–276.

Smith, D. B. D., & Strawbridge, P. J. The heart rate response to a brief auditory and visual stimulus. *Psychophysiology*, 1969, *6*, 317–329.

Sokolov, E. N. Neuronal models and the orienting reflex. In M. A. B. Brazier, (Ed.), *The central nervous system and behavior*. Madison, N.J.: Madison Printing, 1960, 187–276.

Sokolov, E. N. Higher nervous functions: The orienting reflex *Annual Review of Physiology*, 1963, *25*, 545–580. (a)

Sokolov, E. N. *Perception and the conditioned reflex*. New York: Pergamon, 1963. (b)

Sokolov, E. N. Orienting reflex as information regulator. In A. Leontiev, A. Luria, & S. Smirnov (Eds.), *Psychological research in the USSR* (Vol. 1). Moscow: Progress, 1966, 334–360.

Sokolov, E. N. The modeling properties of the nervous system. In A. I. Berg (Ed.), *Cybernetics, thought, life*. Moscow: Izd Mysl', 1964. (Reprinted in M. Cole, & I. Maltzman (Eds.), *A handbook of contemporary soviet psychology*. New York: Basic Books, 1969).

Sokolov, E. N. The neuronal mechanisms of the orienting reflex. In E. N. Sokolov & O. S. Vinogradova (Eds.), *Neuronal mechanisms of the orienting reflex*. New York: Wiley, 1975, 217–235.

Spinks, J. A., & Siddle, D. A. T. Effects of stimulus information and stimulus duration on amplitude and habituation of the electrodermal orienting response. *Biological Psychology*, 1976, *4*, 29–39.

Squires, N., Squires, K. C., & Hillyard, S. A. Two varieties of long-latency positive waves evoked by unpredictable auditory stimuli in man. *Electroencephalography and Clinical Neurophysiology*, 1975, *38*, 387–401.

Stelmack, R. M., & Siddle, D. A. T. Pupillary dilation as an index of the orienting reflex. *Psychophysiology*, 1982, *19*, 701–705.

Stern, J. A. Toward a developmental psychophysiology: My look into the crystal ball. *Psychophysiology*, 1968, *4*, 403–420.

Tecce, J. J., & Cattanach, L. Contingent negative variation. In E. Niedermeyer & F. Lopes da Silva (Eds.), *Electroencephalography: Basic principles, clinical applications, and related fields*. Baltimore: Urban & Schwarzenberg, 1982, 543–562.

Thompson, R. F., & Spencer, W. A. Habituation: A model phenomenon for the study of neuronal substrates of behavior. *Psychological Review*, 1966, *73*, 16–43.

Treisman, M. The effect of one stimulus on the threshold for another: An application of signal detectability theory. *The British Journal of Statistical Psychology*, 1964, *17*, 15–35.

Trumbo, D. A., & Gaillard, A. W. K. Drugs, time uncertainty, signal modality, and reaction time. In P. M. A. Rabbit & S. Dornic (Eds.), *Attention and performance V*. New York: Academic Press, 1975, 441–454.

Turpin, G., & Siddle, D. A. T. Effects of stimulus intensity on electrodermal activity. *Psychophysiology*, 1979, *16*, 582–591.

Van Der Molen, M. W., & Orlebeke, J. F. Phasic heart rate change and the U-shaped relationship between choice reaction time and auditory signal intensity. *Psychophysiology*, 1980, *17*, 471–481.

Van Olst, E. H. *The orienting reflex*. The Hague: Mouton, 1971.

Van Olst, E. H., Heemstra, M. L., & ten Kortenaar, T. Stimulus significance and the orienting reaction. In H. D. Kimmel, E. H. Van Olst, and J. F. Orlebeke (Eds.), *The orienting reflex in humans*. Hillsdale, N.J.: Erlbaum, 1979, 521–547.

Velden, M. Some necessary revisions of the neuronal model concept of the orienting response. *Psychophysiology*, 1978, *15*, 181–185.

Venables, P. H. Input regulation and psychopathology. In M. Hammer, K. Salinger, & S. Sutton (Eds.), *Psychopathology: Contributions from the social, behavioral, and biological sciences*. New York: Wiley, 1973, 261–284.

Venables, P. H. Primary dysfunction and cortical lateralization in schizophrenia. In M. Koukkou, D. Lehmann, & J. Angst (Eds.), *Functional states of the brain: Their determinants*. Amsterdam: Elsevier North-Holland, 1980, 243–264.

Verbaten, M. N. The influence of information on habituation of cortical, autonomic, and behavioral components of the orienting response (OR). In A. W. K. Gaillard & W. Ritter (Eds.), *Tutorials in ERP research: Endogenous components*. Amsterdam: North-Holland, 1983, 201–216.

Verbaten, M. N., Woestenburg, J. C., & Sjouw, W. The influence of visual information on habituation of the electrodermal and the visual orienting reaction. *Biological Psychology*, 1979, *8*, 189–201.

Verbaten, M. N., Woestenburg, J. C., & Sjouw, W. The influence of task relevance and stimulus information on habituation of the visual and the skin conductance orienting reaction. *Biological Psychology*, 1980, *10*, 7–19.

Voronin, L. G., Bonfitto, M., & Vasilieva, V. M. The interrelation of the orienting reaction and conditioned reflex to time in man. In E. N. Sokolov & O. S. Vinogradova (Eds.), *Neuronal mechanisms of the orienting reflex*. New York: Wiley, 1975, 252–263.

Wallin, B. G. Sympathetic nerve activity underlying electrodermal and cardiovascular reactions in man. *Psychophysiology*, 1981, *18*, 470–476.

Wastell, D. G., & Kleinman, D. Potentiation of the habituation of human brain potentials. *Biological Psychology*, 1980, *10*, 21–29.

Waters, W. F., McDonald, D. G., & Koresko, R. L. Habituation of the orienting response: A gating mechanism subserving selective attention. *Psychophysiology*, 1977, *14*, 228–236.

Watkins, W. H., & Feehrer, C. E. Acoustic facilitation of visual detection. *Journal of Experimental Psychology*, 1965, *70*, 332–333.

Weerts, T., & Lang, P. The effects of eye fixation and stimulus and response location on the contingent negative variation (CNV). *Biological Psychology*, 1973, *1*, 1–19.

Weiskrantz, L., Warrington, E. K., Sanders, M. D., & Marshall, J. Visual capacity in the hemianopic field following a restricted occipital ablation. *Brain*, 1974, *97*, 709–728.

Weitzman, E. D., & Kremen, H. Auditory evoked responses during different stages of sleep in man. *Electroencephalography and Clinical Neurophysiology*, 1965, *18*, 65–70.

Williams, H. L., Morlock, H. C., Morlock, J. V., & Lubin, A. Auditory evoked responses and the EEG stages of sleep. *Annuals of the New York Academy of Sciences*, 1964, *112*, 172–181.

Woestenburg, J. C., Verbaten, M. N., & Slangen, J. L. The influence of information on habituation of the "Wiener" filtered visual event related potential and the skin conductance reactions. *Biological Psychology*, 1981, *13*, 189–201.

Worden, F. G. Auditory habituation. In H. V. S. Peeke, & M. J. Herz (Eds.), *Habituation* (Vol. 2). New York: Academic Press, 1973, 109–137.

Zappoli, R., Denoth, F., & Navona, C. Changes of vertex–CNV and parieto–occipital alpha activity under closed- and open-eye conditions. In H. H. Kornhuber & L. Deecke (Eds.), *Motivation, motor, and sensory processes of the brain: Electrical potentials, behavior, and clinical use*. Amsterdam: Elsevier, 1980, pp. 57–61.

10

Spatial Orientation following Commissural Section[1]

Jeffrey D. Holtzman, Bruce T. Volpe, and
Michael S. Gazzaniga

Introduction

The human visual system transmits an abundance of sensory information that,
ultimately, is used for the coordination of behavior within the environment.
Despite the overwhelming richness of the optic array, human information-processing capacity is profoundly limited—only a small fraction of the sensory
world is available to conscious awareness at a given moment. If the conscious
appreciation of a stimulus were a prerequisite for directed behavior, orientation
to singificant sensory events would be severely impaired. Thus, although conscious activity coincides with certain visual functions, much of our behavior
must depend on visual processing that does not have access to conscious
awareness.

This "two-visual-systems" hypothesis, (i.e., that a functional distinction can
be made between two kinds of visual information) is not a new one. Supportive
evidence has been accumulated from electrophysiological, neuroanatomical, and
clinical sources. This chapter is concerned primarily with the third source of
evidence: patients with focal neurological damage whose behavior suggests that
visual information that is used to orient to a stimulus is distinguishable from
visual information underlying explicit stimulus identification. A general review
of the clinical evidence in support of this distinction is provided in this chapter.
Following this review, we summarize some observations from our laboratory on
attentional control after disconnection of the cerebral hemispheres.

The data we present were collected from two patients who have undergone
complete midline transection of the corpus callosum for the control of intractable
epilepsy, so-called "split-brain" surgery (see Wilson, Reeves, & Gazzaniga,
1980 for a review). In both instances, callosal section did not include the anterior
commissure. Our data describe several characteristics of the control of visual
attention in humans that may reflect the functional role of the secondary visual

[1]The authors were aided in preparing this chapter by United States Public Heath Service grants
numbers R01 NS 17936-01, and R01 NS 15053-02 and by the Alfred P. Sloan Foundation.

375

system. First, we demonstrate that, whereas callosal section results in independent processing in the separated hemispheres with respect to stimulus identification, callosal surgery does not produce two independent orienting systems. Second, we show that, despite the interhemispheric disconnection of visual cortex, a spatial representation of both visual half-fields is available for visual orienting. Finally, we argue that the control of orienting can be unlinked from associated motor function.

Clinical Evidence for Two Visual Systems

In the late 1960s, several researchers proposed that there are two anatomically and functionally distinguishable subsystems that use visual information for different purposes (Diamond & Hall, 1969; Ingle, 1967; Schneider, 1969; Trevarthen, 1968). Although their empirical findings were limited to infrahuman species, and their positions differed in detail, their observations have been interpreted to support the existence of "two visual systems" in humans. In general, the primary geniculostriate visual pathway is thought to subserve the analysis of visual pattern underlying stimulus identification, whereas the secondary colliculus–pulvinar–parietal visual pathway is concerned with visual information as it exists for the control of spatial orientation. It was further proposed by Trevarthen (1968) that secondary visual processes, which he characterized as "ambient vision," in large part are not mediated by conscious awareness. He notes, "Vision in the lateral fields remains efficient in low light, is highly sensitive to motion, and produces little impression in consciousness" (p. 302).

Clinical evidence from which the functional role of secondary visual pathways can be inferred dates from patients with isolated missile wounds incurred during World War I. Holmes (1918) described impairments in visual orientation, visual localization of objects, and oculomotor and praxic control arising from focal lesion of the posterior parietal region. In contrast, Riddoch (1917) described patients with focal occipital damage who could consistently report movement within the affected area of the visual field. Riddoch stressed the elusiveness of these perceptions, indicating that patients had great difficulty in describing the nature of the movement they saw, characterizing it as "vague and shadowy." He emphasized that such perceptions of motion arose from stimulation within a field that was entirely blind to stationary objects.

More recent reports of residual visual function following focal occipital damage have emphasized both its role in orienting to visual stimulation and the unconscious nature of this visual process (termed *blind-sight* by Weiskrantz, Warrington, Sanders, & Marshall, 1974). Thus, whereas damage to primary visual cortex results in visual field deficits (e.g., an inability to identify stimuli in the area of the scotoma), the magnitude of voluntary saccadic eye movements to visual stimuli briefly flashed in the affected area increases monotonically with target eccentricity (Poppel, Held, & Frost, 1973). This result has been confirmed by Weiskrantz *et al.* (1974) and Perenin and Jeannerod (1975). Analogous results have been obtained for pointing movements of the hand by these authors as well as by Williams and Gassel (1962). It should be pointed out, however, that some residual perceptual capacities also have been reported in "blind" visual areas. These include large-scale pattern discriminations, discriminations of stimulus orientation, color discriminations, and figural identification (Richards, 1973; Torjussen, 1978; Weiskrantz *et al.*, 1974). Except under unusual stimulus situations, however, perception is limited to the detection of gross changes in a large portion of the visual field. Therefore, such information may not be of sufficient resolution to account for the accuracy of elicited motor responses into the same areas, especially for pointing movements of the hand.

On the other hand, studies of residual function following focal damage to parietal cortex, and more recently the superior colliculus and pulvinar, reveal intact sensory capacities but a constellation of attentional deficits in response to contralateral stimulation. These include deficiencies in spatial orientation, directed saccadic eye movements, and smooth pursuit eye movements (Cogan, 1965; Hecaen & De Ajuriaguerra, 1954; Heywood and Ratcliff, 1975; Oxbury, Campbell, & Oxbury, 1972; Zihl & Von Cramon, 1979); inaccurate pointing movements of the hand (Teuber, 1963); and a general reluctance to acknowledge stimuli in the impaired field. This latter syndrome, termed *hemiinattention* or *hemineglect* (see Weinstein & Friedland, 1977, for a review) has been characterized by Mountcastle (1978) as a "reluctance or inability to direct visual attention to the contralateral half-field of behavior space, or to make stereotaxic exploration within it" (p. 18).

Relevant observations of neurologically intact subjects have produced somewhat conflicting results. On the one hand, several studies have demonstrated that observers can accurately localize visual targets with a motor response despite gross perceptual mislocalizations. This has been noted for pursuit eye movements by Dichgans, Kerner, and Voigt (1969), Festinger, Sedgwick, and Holtzman (1976), Herman (1972), Mack and Stoper, (1967), and Wyatt and Pola (1979); for saccadic eye movements by Hallit and Lightstone (1976) and Wong (1981); and for ballistic arm movements and manual pointing by Bridgeman, Lewis, Heit, and Nagle (1979) and Hanson and Skavinski (1976). Bridgeman *et al.* speculate as to a possible organization of such performance:

> Two levels of the visual system might process different kinds of information, so that spatially oriented motor activity might have access to accurate position information even when that information is not available at a cognitive level that mediates symbolic decisions such as button presses or vocal responses (p. 693).

In contrast, other findings reveal the importance of perceptual information for the control of pursuit eye movements (Holtzman & Sedgwick, Note 1; Holtzman, Sedgwick, & Festinger, 1978; Steinbach, 1976; Wyatt & Pola, 1979) and saccadic eye movements (Miller, 1980; White & Holtzman, Note 2), even when such information is erroneous. Overall these data seem to imply that, although perceptual information is used for the control of visual–motor behavior, visual and motor information that is not consciously perceived also plays an important role in motor function associated with the control of visual orientation.

Conclusions regarding the functional specialization of two visual systems in humans based on lesion studies are subject to criticisms on both theoretical and methodological grounds. First, although such observations have demonstrated that one visual function can be spared when the other is lost, they do not substantiate the coexistence of two visual systems simultaneously subserving different visual functions in the intact brain. Instead, residual visual function following the critical lesion may reflect compensatory processes rather than basic visual organization. Sprague (1966), for example, has noted in cats that if Areas 17, 18, and 19 are lesioned, there are transient periods of hemianopsia that recover after several days. When the ipsilateral superior colliculus is lesioned as well, hemianopsia is permanent, implying that ancillary visual structures may compensate for cortical blindness. Mohler and Wurtz (1977) have noted comparable findings in monkeys with regard to elicited saccadic eye movements. Analogously, Zihl (1980) has noted that in patients with occipital lesions, repeated saccadic eye movements to targets within a blind hemifield improve in accuracy; and that some patients come to report the ability ''to 'feel' the correspondence between target and eye position.'' Zihl and von Cramon (1982) also report restitution of perceptual function in visual scotomas following practice at detecting lights in these regions.

Such functional reorganization need not take place, however. Meienberg, Zangemeister, Rossenberg, & Hoyt, and Stark (1981), for example, have demonstrated an alternative strategy used by patients with occipital lesions to foveate stimuli appearing within visual scotomas: a large initial saccade that repositions the stimulus in the intact field followed by a smaller saccade that brings the stimulus to fovea. Thus, unless required to do otherwise, these patients tend to rely on perceptual information for the programming of saccadic eye movements.

Second, and most importantly, the assessment of attentional capacities in patients with parietal or occipital damage has focused primarily on overt motor behaviors associated with changes in the locus of attention (e.g., the presence or absence of elicited saccadic eye movements, reaching or pointing movements of the hand) rather than on attentional control per se. Although visually elicited motor behavior depends on an observer's capacity to orient to visual stimulation, the absence of such behavior does not necessarily imply a deficit in the antecedent attentional processes (Robinson, Goldberg, & Stanton, 1978). Furthermore, with regard to oculomotor and praxic localizations of visual stimuli appearing within visual scotomas, it is surprising that pointing responses were more accurate than saccadic eye movements (see Perenin and Jeannerod, 1975; Weiskrantz et al., 1974) because eye movements to briefly flashed targets are normally quite accurate (Miller, 1980). It is unfortunate that eye movements to stimuli appearing in the intact field were not reported because such data would be useful in calibrating the accuracy of their recording technique, particularly because electrooculography was used. This technique is of limited accuracy and is subject to a number of recording artifacts (see Robinson, 1968). It is also significant that, on pointing trials, Perenin and Jeannerod (1975) report that subjects always turned their eyes to the target position each time it had to be localized. Thus, pointing responses may have represented manual alignments with the direction of gaze rather than praxic components of secondary visual processes.

Finally, for methodological reasons, the assertion that a dissociation has been demonstrated between visual information used for the control of visual orienting and that used for stimulus identification is questionable. This is the case for the movement studies described in the preceding in which observers could accurately "guess" the location of a flashed target in a "blind" field with a motor response but, in no instance, were observers also required to localize targets with a forced-choice perceptual "guess." In fact, Barbur, Ruddock, & Waterfield (1980) have shown that patients with visual scotomas are better able to perceptually localize a visual target appearing within a blind area than they are able to report its occurrence. Unfortunately, these authors did not measure eye movements to subthreshold visual targets. Thus, it cannot be concluded that accurate eye movements into blind visual areas necessarily require perceptual information.

Reports by Trevarthen and Sperry (1973) of the cross-integration of "ambient" visual half-fields, but not "focal" half-fields in commissurotomy patients raise similar questions. These authors provide impressive evidence of perceptual access to both visual half-fields in these patients when stimuli appear in the far periphery. They contrast this performance, however, with established findings of a perceptual disconnection of the visual half-fields in and around the fovea rather than recreating their stimulus conditions with focal visual targets. Thus, it cannot be determined whether their findings reflect intact visual processes that are limited to ambient visual space, whether cross-integration occurs for some visual stimuli but not for others, or whether these patients represent instances in which the delayed emergence of a form of perceptual access to both visual half-fields coincided with the testing period (see Gazzaniga, Siditis, Volpe, Smylie, Holtzman, & Wilson, 1982).

Studies of Spatial Orientation

The data described in the following were collected from two commissurotomy patients in an attempt to examine the relationship between spatial orientation and explicit stimulus identification in more detail. Initially, we assessed performance at perceptual tasks that required the manipulation of the locus of visual attention. We attempted to measure attentional control separately from motor control by using a paradigm that measured the capacity to manipulate spatial attention independent of overt orienting movements. We then contrasted the ability of these patients to orient to visual targets with their ability to explicitly identify the same stimuli. Our results imply that, whereas the control of orienting is relatively unaffected by callosal section, profound limitations in the capacity to identify visual targets are present. Finally, we assessed the extent to which visual information that is available for attentional control also is available for directed motor responses.

Attentional Control and the Commissurotomy Patient

A subset of commissurotomy patients are unable to perform perceptual comparisons of stimuli briefly presented on both sides of the visual midline, such as whether two stimuli are the same or different (see Gazzaniga, 1970; Gazzaniga and LeDoux, 1978). This occurs because direct visual input to each hemisphere is predominantly contralateral; ipsilateral information is provided only indirectly through the interconnections between the hemispheres via the corpus callosum. Therefore, for example, because speech is a left hemisphere function, visual stimuli presented to the right hemisphere via left visual field exposure typically cannot be named by the commissurotomy patient. However, though mute, the right hemisphere can direct the left hand to retrieve the correct stimulus from an array of objects placed in front of the patient.

Such observations raise several possibilities concerning the commitment of attentional resources for a cognitive task. One possibility is that sectioning the callosum provides each hemisphere with its own private resource pool. If so, one might expect that the commissurotomy patient would show enhanced performance at dual tasks, one of which is lateralized to one hemisphere and the other to the other hemisphere. There is some evidence for such enhancement (Gazzaniga and Young, 1967); but in general, performance is rarely superior to that of normal observers (Kreuter, Kinsbourne, & Trevarthen, 1972; Teng & Sperry, 1974), and facilitation effects tend to reflect reduced interference between two tasks rather than an increase in overall information-processing capacity (Ellenberg & Sperry, 1980; Gazzaniga & Hillyard, 1973; Springer & Gazzaniga, 1975). Observations reported by Holtzman and Gazzaniga (1982) suggest that, whereas the separated hemispheres do not share access to a common data base, thus accounting for the absence of perceptual interference between the hemispheres, they do utilize common processing resources, which, under conditions of bilateral stimulation, are distributed between the hemispheres.

Hemispheric disconnection effects also raise questions concerning the control of spatial orientation following commissural section. For example, do the hemispheres have independent orienting systems? How do the hemispheres interact in specifying the locus of attention? Because each hemisphere receives unilateral visual information and is capable of stimulus acquisition, storage, and retrieval as well as of the initiation of directed movement, it might be expected that as a consequence, coordinated behavior outside the laboratory would be severely disrupted. If, for example, a single hemisphere dominated behavior, a state of unilateral neglect would be anticipated. On the other hand, if the hemispheres vied for the control of behavior, instances of response competition would be expected, with the hemispheres attempting to direct the patient toward disparate goals. In fact, instances of both response competition and unilateral neglect occur very infrequently. Instead, commissurotomy patients are able to direct action within the environment with little overt difficulty or hesitation (e.g., walk, run, avoid obstacles, and in one instance operate a motorcycle; see Gazzaniga, 1970).

These observations suggested to us that, although visual information is not transferred between brain areas subserving explicit stimulus identification, the hemispheres use visual information from both hemifields for the control of selective visual attention. Such integration could account for the absence of overt indications of visual neglect and response competition in commissurotomy patients as well as the overall integrity of coordinated visual-motor behavior within the normal environment.

In order to test this hypothesis, we needed a means of manipulating visual attention and measuring its spatial locus. The method we used for these purposes was based on a "facilitation" paradigm originally developed by Posner and his colleagues (see Posner, 1980; Posner, Snyder, & Davidson, 1980). These authors determined that the response latency to a peripheral visual target is reduced when observers have prior information regarding its spatial locus, even when eye movements to the cued location are prohibited. Presumably, the spatial cue allows observers to direct their attention to the appropriate location prior to the onset of the target. In the present context, this paradigm was used to measure the extent to which such attentional cues affected performance under a variety of conditions. We determined that, despite the perceptual segregation of the visual fields for explicit stimulus identification in split-brain patients, the separated hemispheres are not strictly independent in the control of spatial orientation. These patients rely on a common orienting system that serves to maintain a single focus of attention, a system that makes use of visual information from both hemifields.

Commissurotomy Does Not Result in Dual Attentional Systems

In our first experiment, we employed a facilitation paradigm to examine whether the hemispheres can simultaneously orient to different spatial locations

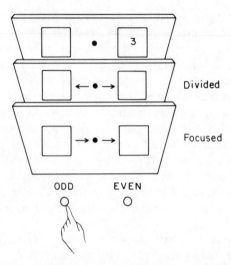

Figure 10.1 Spatial cues for the focused and divided attention trials. On each trial, the spatial cue appeared for 150 msec, followed by a 1.5-second lapse, and then the target appeared again for 150 msec. For description of additional trials, see text.

within the visual environment. Although there are data to indicate that normal observers can distribute attentional resources over a relatively small area (Jonides, 1980; Shaw & Shaw, 1977), for the stimulus conditions used here, it has been determined that normal observers are unable to direct attention simultaneously to disparate points in space (Posner *et al.*, 1980). If, unlike the performance of normal observers, each hemisphere of the commissurotomy patient has its own orienting system, orienting to disparate spatial locations would be possible.

The background visual display for this study, generated by a microprocessor and displayed on a video monitor, is depicted in Figure 10.1. It consisted of two 3° square boxes, presented 7° on either side of a central dot on which the observer fixated at all times. On each trial, a target digit briefly appeared in one of the boxes and the observer indicated with a forced-choice key press whether the digit was even or odd. On each trial one of four spatial cue configurations briefly appeared 1.5 seconds before the onset of the target. On "focused attention" trials (approximately 44% of the total trials), two arrows—one in each field— pointed to the box in which the target would appear; on "divided attention" trials (22%), the arrows pointed in opposite directions; on neutral-cue trials (22%), two noninformative *X*s appeared in place of the arrows; and on invalid-cue trials (11%), two arrows pointed to the wrong box.

If the separated hemispheres have completely independent attentional systems, response latencies on focused and divided-attention trials should be similarly

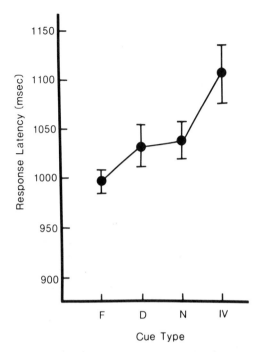

Figure 10.2 Average response latencies (±1 standard error) for (F) Focused-attention, (D) Divided-attention, (N) Neutral-cue, and (IV) Invalid-cue trials. All data were collected from commissurotomy patient JW.

facilitated. If spatial attention is restricted to one area, then performance on divided-attention trials should more closely resemble performance on neutral-cue trials.

The results of 720 total trials collected from patient JW are summarized in Figure 10.2. Approximately 6% of the trials were rejected from the analysis because of an incorrect response or a response latency in excess of 2.5 seconds. It can be seen that performance on divided-attention trials was most similar to performance on neutral-cue trials. These results imply that commissurotomy does not result in separate orienting systems that can be manipulated independently and concurrently by each hemisphere. Thus, like neurologically intact observers, split-brain patients are unable to prepare for events in two spatially disparate locations; that is, their attention is unifocal. This may be one factor that minimizes the potential for interhemisphere rivalry in these patients.

If attention is unifocal, the question then arises as to how attention is directed when the hemispheres receive conflicting spatial cues (e.g., on divided-attention trials). One possibility is that, on each such trial, a decision is made to orient to either the left or right box. When the target appears in the attended location, response latencies would be similar to those on focused-cue trials; when it appears in the unattended location, latencies would be similar to those on invalid-cue trials. Under such circumstances, the decision regarding where to direct attention would be consistent with the spatial cue from either the left or right visual half-field, with a single hemisphere dominating behavior on each trial.

This interpretation would predict that the sum of these two distributions of latencies would produce a third distribution with a mean intermediate between that for focused- and invalid-cue trials, and the data appearing in Figure 10.2 show just this. It would also predict that the variability of the latency distribution for divided-attention trials would exceed that for both focused and invalid-cue trials. This was not the case; the variability of the response latencies on divided-attention trials ($s.d.$ = 253 msec) was *less* than that for both focused- and invalid-cue trials ($s.d.$ = 271 msec and 310 msec, respectively). Thus, in both instances, this difference is opposite to the increase in variability that would occur if divided-attention trials were comprised of a combination of focused- and invalid-cue trials. On the other hand, the variability on divided-attention and neutral-cue trials was quite similar ($s.d.$ = 253 msec and 248 msec, respectively). Thus, it appears that, on the whole, divided-attention and neutral-cue trials were regarded by JW as equally uninformative.

One possible explanation for these data is that visual information from both hemifields was used to direct the locus of attention. On divided-attention trials, when *conflicting* and therefore uninformative spatial cues were presented to the two hemifields, JW adopted an allocation strategy identical to that used on neutral-cue trials in which *consistent* and uninformative spatial cues were presented. This interpretation would predict that because bilateral visual information is available for attentional control, the hemifield in which the spatial cue appears would not differentially effect response latencies. Our next experiment verified this prediction.

Attention Can Be Directed Across the Visual Midline

This experiment examined whether the hemispheres cooperate in the manipulation of the locus of attention. Specifically, we asked whether a spatial cue presented to one hemisphere can be used to direct attention into the sensory field corresponding to the other hemisphere, that is, across the visual midline. The background visual display and temporal parameters for this study were identical to those described in the preceding. As in the prior experiment, central fixation was maintained throughout each trial, a target digit appeared in one of the boxes, and an odd–even discrimination was required. As can be seen in Figure 10.3, however, a different set of cue configurations was used. On directionally cued trials, a single arrow appeared either in the left or right visual field. Valid within-field and between-field cue trials (approximately 66% of the total trials) were

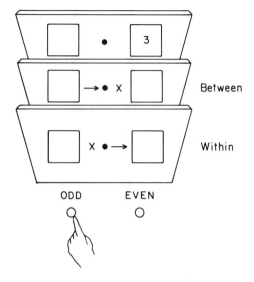

Figure 10.3 Valid spatial cues for within-field and between-field trials. For description of additional trials, see text.

those in which the cue and target appeared in the same visual field or different fields, respectively; on neutral-cue trials (17%), the cue consisted of two *X*s; and invalid-cue trials (17%) were those in which the target appeared in the uncued location. Thus, between-field trials required the observer to orient to a spatial location that presumably lacked sensory representation in the visual cortex of the cued hemisphere.

The average of 352 total trials collected from patients JW and PS are summarized in Figure 10.4. Approximately 10% of the trials were rejected from the analysis because of an incorrect response or a response latency in excess of 2.5 seconds for JW or 2.0 seconds for PS. The similarity of performance on within-field and between-field trials indicates that either hemisphere can direct attention into either visual half-field. Despite this, the performance of both patients did not exceed chance when they were required to indicate whether two arrows, one in each visual field, pointed in the same or different directions.

Thus, information about a stimulus presented to one hemisphere, in this case the spatial location of an impending target, facilitates processing of that stimulus by the other hemisphere. Because in this study the target could only appear in one location in each field, however, we could not conclude that our findings reflected a shift in attention across the midline to a specific location. Similar results also would be expected if the primed hemisphere were globally activated and, thus, more sensitive to any stimulus appearing in its sensory field.

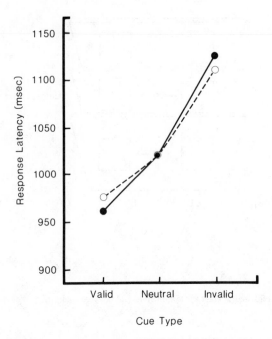

Figure 10.4 Average response latencies for within-field (solid line) and between-field (dashed line) trials for each spatial cue type. Data from commissurotomy patients JW and PS are averaged, with each given equal weight.

Interfield Performance Is Specific to the Cued Location

In order to determine whether attentional priming was specific to the cued location, we increased the number of cells in each field. In this study (see Holtzman, Sidtis, Volpe, Wilson & Gazzaniga, 1981, for a detailed description), the background display consisted of a 3 × 3 cell grid presented on each side of a central fixation stimulus (see Figure 10.5). As in the prior studies, on each trial the observer indicated with a manual response whether a digit appearing in one of the cells was odd or even. On within-field trials, the digit was always preceded by a spatial cue that appeared either in the cell in which the target appeared (valid cue); in a different cell in the same grid (invalid cue); or superimposed on the central fixation stimulus (neutral cue). In order to examine interfield performance, we modified our procedure: Rather than specifying the actual location of the target, the valid cue appeared, instead, in the homologous cell in the opposite grid. Analogously, the invalid cue appeared in a different relative position in the opposite grid. Thus for these between-field trials, the efficacy of the cue required visual information concerning specific spatial locations in both visual hemifields.

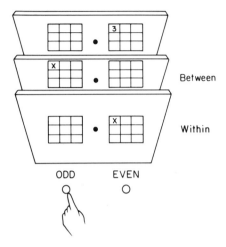

Figure 10.5 Example of valid-cue trial in within-field and between-field trials. For description of additional trials, see text.

The average of 544 trials collected from JW and PS are summarized in Figure 10.6. Approximately 11% of the trials were rejected from the analysis because of an incorrect response or a latency in excess of 2.5 seconds for JW or 2.0 seconds for PS. It can be seen that, on the average, response latencies were shortest when the observer knew where the target would appear (valid-cue trials), and longest when they expected it elsewhere (invalid-cue trials). This occurred on within-field trials in which the target and cue appeared in the same visual half-field and, thus, the efficacy of the spatial cue did not require perceptual access to both visual half-fields. However, similar results were also obtained for between-field trials, indicating that the spatial cue was effective even when the target subsequently appeared in the opposite hemifield.

Of particular interest is the detrimental effect on response latency of the invalid cue on between-field trials, which implies that when attention is directed across the midline, it is specific to the target's location and not simply directed in general to the contralateral visual half-field. If attention were directed diffusely, that is, if the opposite hemisphere were simply globally activated, then response latencies on valid-cue trials would not differ from those on invalid-cue trials. Our results are quite to the contrary: Performance on these two types of trials shows contrasting effects relative to the neutral cue trials. Thus, interhemispheric priming cannot be explained simply in terms of global activation, but must reflect a shift in attention across the midline to a specific spatial location.

The ability of commissurotomy patients to integrate the visual half-fields for the control of attention in this task was in dramatic contrast to their inability to perform explicit interfield visual comparisons. This was made clear when the

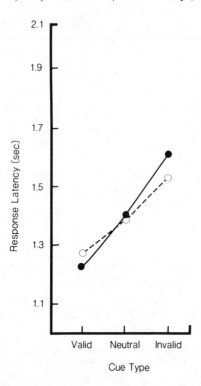

Figure 10.6 Average response latencies for within-field (solid line) and between-field (dashed line) trials for each spatial cue type. Data from commissurotomy patients PS and JW are averaged, with each given equal weight.

same stimuli were used in a task that required an explicit comparison of two spatial positions. In essence, we asked observers to compare the spatial location of the target and cue by responding "same," with the appropriate key press, if the target and cue fell in the same or homologous cells, and by responding "different" in all other conditions. On the whole, observers were accurate in their judgments under within-field conditions in which the target and cue fell in the same visual half-field (88% correct) but inaccurate under between-field conditions in which a comparison across the visual midline was required (60% correct). A further analysis of the error data revealed that observers were not utilizing a crude form of spatial information from both fields that may have facilitated performance in the priming task but that was not sufficiently precise for accurate interfield comparisons. Thus, bilateral visual information that was available for attentional control proved to be unavailable for explicit stimulus localization.

TABLE 10.1

Percentage of Correct Localizations of a Visual Target
with a Pointing Response by Commissurotomy Patients

Target location	Percentage correct	
	No eye movements	Eye movements
Within field	80	100
Between field	44	80

Attentional Control and Motor Control

Subsequently, we asked whether bilateral visual information is also available for motor responses to visual targets. Our pilot data regarding this question reveal that commissurotomy patients may have access to such information for oculomotor control, but that deficits in performance arise when visual information from the two fields must be integrated for the control of limb praxis.

In order to facilitate comparison between these observations and our priming studies, our experimental paradigm used in this context was very similar to that described in the preceding. The same two grids appeared on either side of a fixation stimulus; and, on each trial, an X appeared in one of the cells. The observer was required either to point to the cell in which the target appeared (within-field trials) or to point to the homologous cell in the opposite grid (between-field trials). For the first set of trials, the observer was required to maintain central fixation throughout each trial; on the second set, eye movements were allowed.

The percentage of trials in which the cued cell was accurately localized appear in Table 10.1, averaged for our two observers and collapsed across hand and visual half-field. Each value is based on approximately 20 trials for each observer.

It can be seen that these patients accurately localized the cued cell under conditions in which the target and cue fell in the same visual half-field and under conditions in which they fell in opposite fields and eye movements were allowed. They performed poorly, however, on those between-field trials in which central fixation was required. Although performance on these trials exceeded chance, these findings seem to imply that, at best, commissurotomy patients have only limited access to bilateral visual information for praxic control. Nevertheless, these results are in dramatic contrast to the availability of such information for the orienting of attention. The interesting question regarding these data is whether, when eye movements are allowed on between-field trials, the initial saccadic eye movement is accurate to the homologous cell in the opposite grid. If it is, this would imply that bilateral visual information for motor control under such circumstances is specific to the oculomotor system. This question is currently under investigation in our laboratory.

Finally, we ran an additional study in which the observers directed their manual responses within a metal reproduction of two lateralized 5 × 5 grids that appeared on the display screen. This 15- × 15-cm metal frame was placed in front of the subject and was thoroughly explored tactually and visually prior to testing. The patient was instructed to move his or her index finger to the location in the metal grid that corresponded to the location of the X that appeared on the screen. On each trial, the patient fixated the central dot and X flashed randomly in any one of 48 positions (24 possible locations in each grid on the display screen). The subjects began each trial with the index finger of either hand within the center cell of the metal grid. The grid and the tested hand were kept out of view, and the patient's forearm was fastened to the table to prevent proximal movement. Because control of the distal musculature involved in this task is strictly lateralized to the hemisphere contralateral to the responding hand (see Volpe, Sidtis, Holtzman, Wilson, & Gazzaniga, 1982), this procedure allowed us to assess the performance of each hemisphere when the target stimulus was presented to the ipsilateral or contralateral visual field.

A total of 124 trials were collected. Both observers showed significant impairments in performance in the ipsilateral condition: When the visual target appeared in the hemifield contralateral to the responding hand, PS and JW were accurate in their responses on 73% of the trials; when it appeared in the ipsilateral field, their performance fell to 25%. Analogous to the previous study, these results indicate that the hemispheres are severely impaired at directing a manual response based on visual information presented to the ipsilateral visual half-field.

Conclusions

In conclusion, our findings provide evidence that different kinds of visual information are used for attentional control and stimulus identification. When the connections between the hemispheres are severed, significant impairments in the perceptual integration of the visual hemifields results. Most likely, such integration depends on visual cortex because it is typically disrupted when callosal section or damage disconnects visual cortex (Gazzaniga & Freedman, 1973; Levine & Calvanio, 1980; Maspes, 1948; Siditis, Volpe, Holtzman, Wilson, & Gazzaniga, 1981; Sugishita, Iwata, Toyokura, Yoshioka, & Yamada, 1978) but not when the lesion is restricted to the anterior callosum, in which case occipital interconnections are spared (Gazzaniga, Risse, Springer, Clark, & Wilson,

1975; Geschwind & Kaplan, 1962; Gordon, Bogen, & Sperry, 1971; Sweet, 1941). Likewise, it would seem that manual responses to visual targets depend on visual cortex as well, because our findings indicate that such performance is also disrupted by callosal section. It remains to be determined whether, as in the case of patients with visual scotomas due to occipital lesions, interfield manual localization in commissurotomy patients would improve with prolonged practice.

In contrast, callosal section appears to have only minimal consequences on the control of selective attention. If, as the clinical data would suggest, the control of visual attention depends on parietal cortex, our data imply that a bilateral representation of the visual world within parietal cortex is preserved following cerebral disconnection. It is tempting to speculate that such information is provided directly through secondary visual pathways via the superior colliculus and pulvinar. Other explanations remain to be considered, however, including the potential for interhemispheric transfer via the anterior commissure, interactions between the occipital cortices via subcortical pathways, and the possible role of spatial memory in the control of orienting.

Reference Notes

1. Holtzman, J. D., and Sedgwick, H. A. *Higher order characteristics of the smooth pursuit system.* Paper presented at OMS-80, Pasadena, Calif., January 1980.
2. White, C. W., and Holtzman, J. D. *Eye movements, metacontrast, and visual masking: Retinotopic and spatiotopic theories.* Manuscript submitted for publication, 1980.

References

Barbur, J. L., Ruddock, K. H., & Waterfield, V. A. Human visual responses in the absence of geniculo-calcarine projection. *Brain,* 1980, *103,* 905–928.
Bridgeman, B., Lewis, S., Heit, G., & Nagle, M. Relation between cognitive and motor-oriented systems of visual position perception. *Journal of Experimental Psychology: Human Perception and Performance,* 1979, *5,* 692–700.
Cogan, D. G. Ophthalmic manifestations of bilateral non-occipital cerebral lesions. *British Journal of Ophthalmology,* 1965, *49,* 281–297.
Diamond, I. T., & Hall, W. C. Evolution of neocortex. *Science* 1969, *164,* 251–262.
Dichgans, J., Korner, F., & Voigt, K. Vergleichende Skalierung des efferenten Bewegungssehens beim Menschen: Linaere Funktionen mit verscheidener Ansteigssteirlheit. *Psychologische Forschung,* 1969, *32,* 277–295.
Ellenberg, L., & Sperry, R. W. Lateralized division of attention in the commissurotomized and intact brain. *Neuropsychologia,* 1980, *18,* 411–418.
Festinger, L., Sedgwick, H. A., & Holtzman, J. D. Visual perception during smooth pursuit eye movements. *Vision Research,* 1976, *16,* 1377–1386.

Gazzaniga, M. S. *The bisected brain.* New York: Appleton-Century-Crofts, 1970.

Gazzaniga, M. S., & Freedman, H. Observations on visual process after posterior callosal section. *Neurology, Minneapolis,* 1973, *23,* 1126–1130.

Gazzaniga, M. S., & Hillyard, S. A. Attention mechanisms following brain bisection. In S. Kornblum (Ed.), *Attention and performance IV.* New York: Academic Press, 1973, 221–238.

Gazzaniga, M. S., & LeDoux, J. E. *The integrated mind.* New York: Plenum, 1978.

Gazzaniga, M. S., Risse, G. L., Springer, S. P., Clark, E., & Wilson, D. H. Psychologic and neurologic consequences of partial and complete cerebral commissurotomy. *Neurology, Minneapolis,* 1975, *25,* 10–15.

Gazzaniga, M. S., Siditis, J. J., Volpe, B. T., Smylie, C. S., Holtzman, J. D., & Wilson, D. H. Evidence for para-callosal verbal transfer after callosal section. *Brain,* 1982, *105,* 53–63.

Gazzaniga, M. S., & Young, E. D. Effects of commissurotomy on the processing of increasing visual information. *Experimental Brain Research,* 1967, *3,* 368–371.

Geschwind, N., & Kaplan, E. A human cerebral disconnection syndrome. *Neurology, Minneapolis,* 1962, *12,* 675–685.

Gordon, H. W., Bogen, J. E., & Sperry, R. W. Absence of disconnexion syndrome in two patients with partial section of the neocommissures. *Brain,* 1971, *94,* 327–336.

Hallet, P. E., & Lightstone, A. D. Saccadic eye movements towards stimuli triggered during prior saccades. *Vision Research,* 1976, *16,* 99–106.

Hanson, R. M., & Skavinski. Accuracy of eye position information for motor control. *Vision Research,* 1976, *17,* 919–926.

Hecaen, H., & De Ajuriaguerra, J. Balint's syndrome (psychic paralysis of visual fixation) and its minor forms. *Brain,* 1954, *77,* 373–400.

Heywood, S., & Ratcliff, G. Long-term oculomotor consequences of unilateral colliculectomy in man. In G. Lennerstrand & P. Bach-Y-Rita (Eds.), *Symposium on basic mechanisms of ocular motility and their clinical implications.* New York: Oxford: University Press, 1975, 561–564.

Holmes, G. Disturbances of vision by cerebral lesions. *British Journal of Ophthalmology,* 1918, *2,* 253–384.

Holtzman, J. D., & Gazzaniga, M. S. Dual task interactions due exclusively to limits in processing resources. *Science,* 1982, *218,* 1325–1327.

Holtzman, J. D., Sedgwick, H. A., & Festinger, L. Interaction of perceptually monitored and unmonitored efferent commands for smooth pursuit eye movements. *Vision Research,* 1978, *18,* 1545–1555.

Holtzman, J. D., Sidtis, J. J., Volpe, B. T., Wilson, D. H., & Gazzaniga, M. S. Dissociation of spatial information for stimulus localization and the control of attention. *Brain,* 1981, *104,* 861–872.

Ingle, D. Two visual mechanisms underlying behavior of fish. *Psychologische Forschung,* 1967, *31,* 44–51.

Jonides, J. Towards a model of the mind's eye movement. *Canadian Journal of Psychology,* 1980, *34,* 103–112.

Kreuter, C., Kinsbourne, M., & Trevarthen, C. Are deconnected cerebral hemispheres independent channels? A preliminary study of the effect of unilateral loading on bilateral finger tapping. *Neuropsychologia,* 1972, *10,* 453–461.

Levine, D. M., & Calvanio, R. Visual discrimination after lesion of the posterior corpus callosum. *Neurology, Minneapolis,* 1980, *30,* 21–30.

Mack, A., & Herman, E. A new illusion: The underestimation of distance during pursuit eye movements. *Perception and Psychophysics,* 1972, *12,* 471–479.

Maspes, P. E. Le syndrome experimental chez l'homme de la section du splenium du corps calleux alexie visuelle pure hemianopsique. *Revue Neurologique,* 1948, *80,* 100–113.

Meienberg, O., Zangemeister, W. H., Rosenberg, M., Hoyt, W. F., & Stark, L. Saccadic eye movement strategies in patients with homonymous hemianopia. *Annals of Neurology*, 1981, *9*, 537–544.

Miller, J. M. Information used by the perceptual and oculomotor systems regarding the amplitude of saccadic and pursuit eye movements. *Vision Research*, 1980, *20*, 59–68.

Mohler, C. W., & Wurtz, R. H. Role of striate cortex and superior colliculus in visual guidance of saccadic eye movements in monkeys. *Journal of Neurophysiology*, 1977, *16*, 1–13.

Mountcastle, V. B. Brain mechanisms for directed attention. *Journal of the Royal Society of Medicine*, 1978, *71*, 14–28.

Oxbury, J. M., Campbell, D. C., & Oxbury, S. M. Unilateral spatial neglect and impairments of spatial analysis and visual perception. *Brain*, 1974, *97*, 551–564.

Perenin, M. T., & Jeannerod, M. Residual vision in cortically blind hemiphields. *Neuropsychologia*, 1975, *13*, 1–17.

Perenin, M. T., & Jeannerod, M. Visual function within the hemianopic field following early cerebral hemidecortication in man (PT. 1): Spatial localization. *Neuropsychologia*, 1978, *16*, 1–13.

Poppel, E., Held, R., & Frost, D. Residual visual function after brain wounds involving the central visual pathways in man. *Nature*, 1973, *243*, 295–296.

Posner, M. I. Orienting of attention. *Quarterly Journal of Experimental Psychology*, 1980, *32*, 3–25.

Posner, M. I., Snyder, C. R., and Davidson, B. J. Attention and the detection of signals. *Journal of Experimental Psychology: General*, 1980, *2*, 160–174.

Richards, W. Visual processing in scotomata. *Experimental Brain Research*, 1973, *17*, 333–347.

Riddoch, G. Dissociation of visual perceptions due to occipital injuries, with especial reference to appreciation of movement. *Brain*, 1917, *40*, 15–57.

Robinson, D. A. The oculomotor control system: A review. *Proceedings of the I.E.E.E.*, 1968, *56*, 1032–1049.

Robinson, D. L., Goldberg, M. E., & Stanton, G. B. Parietal association cortex in the primate: Sensory mechanisms and behavioral modulations. *Journal of Neurophysiology*, 1978, *41*, 910–932.

Schneider, G. E. Two visual systems. *Science*, 1969, *163*, 895–902.

Shaw, M. L., & Shaw, P. Optimal allocation of cognitive resources to spatial locations. *Journal of Experimental Psychology: Human Perception and Performance*, 1977, *3*, 201–211.

Sidtis, J. J., Volpe, B. T., Holtzman, J. D., Wilson, D. H., & Gazzaniga, M. S. Cognitive interaction after staged callosal section: Evidence for transfer of semantic activation. *Science*, 1981, *212*, 344–346.

Sprague, J. M. Interaction of cortex and superior colliculus in mediation of visually guided behavior. *Science*, 1966, *153*, 1544–1547.

Springer, S. P., & Gazzaniga, M. S. Dichotic testing of partial and complete split brain subjects. *Neuropsychologia*, 1975, *13*, 341–346.

Steinbach, M. J. Pursuing the perceptual rather than the retinal stimulus. *Vision Research*, 1976, *16*, 1371–1376.

Stoper, A. E. *Vision during pursuit movement: The role of oculomotor information.* Unpublished doctoral dissertation, Brandeis University, Waltham, Mass., 1967.

Sugishita, M., Iwata, M., Toyokura, Y., Yoshioka, M., & Yamada, R. Reading of ideagrams and phonograms in Japanese following partial commissurotomy. *Neuropsychologia*, 1978, *16*, 417–425.

Sweet, W. H. Seeping intracranial aneurysm simulating neoplasm. Syndrome of corpus callosum. *Archives of Neurology and Psychiatry, Chicago*, 1941, *45*, 86–104.

Teng, E. L., & Sperry, R. W. Interhemispheric rivalry during simultaneous bilateral task presentation in commissurotomized patients. *Cortex*, 1974, *19*, 111–120.

Teuber, H. L. Space perception and its disturbances after brain injury in man. *Neuropsychologia*, 1963, *1*, 47–57.

Torjussen, T. Visual processing in cortically blind hemifields. *Neuropsychologia*, 1978, *16*, 15–21.

Trevarthen, C. B. Two mechanisms of vision in primates. *Psychologische Forschung*, 1968, *31*, 299–337.

Trevarthen, C. B., & Sperry, R. W. Perceptual unity of the ambient visual field in human commissurotomy patients. *Brain*, 1973, *96*, 547–570.

Volpe, B. T., Sidtis, J. J., Holtzman, J. D., Wilson, D. H., & Gazzaniga, M. S. Cortical mechanisms involved in praxis: Observations following partial and complete section of the corpus callosum in man. *Neurology, Minneapolis*, 1982, *32*, 645–650.

Weinstein, E. A., & Friedland, R. P. (Eds.), *Hemi-inattention and hemisphere specialization*. New York: Raven, 1977.

Weiskrantz, L., Warrington, E. K., Sanders, M. D., and Marshall, J. Visual capacity in the hemianopic field following a restricted occipital ablation. *Brain*, 1974, *97*, 709–728.

Williams, D., & Gassel, M. M. Visual function in patients with homonymous hemianopia (Pt. 1): The visual fields. *Brain*, 1962, *85*, 175–250.

Wilson, D. H., Reeves, A., & Gazzaniga, M. Corpus callosotomy for control of intractable seizures. In J. A. Wadda & J. K. Penry (Eds.), *Advances in epileptology: The Xth international symposium*. New York: Raven, 1980, 205–213.

Wong, E. Unpublished doctoral dissertation, New School for Social Research, New York, 1981.

Wyatt, H. J., & Pola, J. The role of perceived motion in smooth pursuit eye movements. *Vision Research*, 1979, *19*, 613–618.

Zihl, J. 'Blindsight': Improvement of visually guided eye movements by systematic practice in patients with cerebral blindness. *Neuropsychologia*, 1980, *18*, 71–77.

Zihl, J., & von Cramon, D. The contribution of the 'second' visual system to directed visual attention in man. *Brain*, 1979, *102*, 835–856.

Zihl, J., & von Cramon, D. Restitution of visual field in patients with damage to the geniculostriate visual pathway. *Human Neurobiology*, 1982, *1*, 5–8.

11

Selective- and Sustained-Attention Tasks: Individual and Group Differences

D. R. Davies, D. M. Jones, and Ann Taylor

Introduction

Since the resurgence of interest in the topic of attention, which began in the late 1940s, several different paradigms utilizing a variety of psychological and physiological measures have been employed in the investigation of attentional processes. Researchers concerned with selective and sustained attention have tended to draw on a small range of task categories, somewhat wider in the case of selective attention than in that of sustained attention, and the performance of tasks within this range has been regarded as an index of the ability of subjects to focus, divide, or maintain their attention.

Individual differences in the performance of selective- and sustained-attention tasks are considerable; and, as Hoyer and Plude (1980) have observed, current information-processing models "leave room for differential psychologists to fill in the data on interindividual differences and intraindividual change" (p. 235). Whether or not the abilities involved in selecting relevant from irrelevant information and in maintaining attention over long periods of time are related to other abilities, such as general intelligence, or to characteristics such as sex, personality, and age is of practical interest to psychologists concerned with the development of selection and training procedures; and various measures of the ability to attend selectively have been employed with some success in predictive studies of driver and pilot performance (Gopher & Kahneman, 1971; Kahneman, Ben-Ishai, & Lotan, 1973; Mihal & Barrett, 1976). More fundamentally, individual differences in performance may be used as a "crucible" in nomothetic theory construction (Underwood, 1975); although, until fairly recently, theory construction in the areas of selective and sustained attention has taken little account of individual differences, perhaps because (for selective-attention tasks at least) there is a paucity of basic data concerning the range of individual variation in performance, the reliabilities of the tasks themselves, and the extent to which performance scores in different tasks intercorrelate. There are, however, some indications that individual differences in the performance of tasks involving attention are beginning to be employed for theoretical purposes (e.g., Lansman & Hunt, 1982; Parasuraman & Davies, 1977).

Selective-attention tasks can be broadly classified as involving either *focused* or *divided* attention (see Kahneman, 1973; Treisman, 1969, for classification schemes). The former require attention to be focused on one source or kind of information to the exclusion of others, for example, one of several competing sensory inputs or information channels, or one of several stimulus dimensions or attributes; whereas the latter require attention to be divided or shared between two or more sources or kinds of information, or two or more mental operations. Numerous tasks have been employed in studies of selective attention and only the principal results obtained with the tasks most frequently used in the investigation of individual and group differences are reviewed here. For the area of selective attention, the main task categories with which we are concerned in this chapter are the following:

1. Selective and dichotic listening
2. Central–incidental learning
3. Speeded classification and visual search
4. The Stroop test
5. Time-sharing

In contrast, our survey of individual and group differences in the performance of sustained-attention tasks is confined to vigilance tasks, which have been re-garded as providing "the fundamental paradigm for defining sustained attention as a behavioral category" (Jerison, 1977, p. 29). Such tasks require attention to be directed to one or more sources of information over long and generally unbroken periods of time for the purpose of detecting and responding to small changes in the information being presented (see Parasuraman, Chapter 6, this volume). These changes in the state of the display being monitored are known as *signals;* and usually, although not always, signals must be discriminated from a background of nonsignal events.

Selective Attention

Individual Differences

Selective and Dichotic Listening

In both selective and dichotic listening, two different auditory messages (con-tinuous prose, words, or digits) are simultaneously presented via headphones (one to each ear), with the rate of presentation being generally quite high (often between 150 and 200 items/min. In *selective-listening* tasks, the listener is instructed to attend to one message only and either to recall it later or to report the presence of "target" items immediately; in *dichotic-listening* tasks, the listener is required to attend to both messages, and again either to recall both (*dichotic memory*) or to detect target items in both (*dichotic monitoring*). Dichotic memory is exemplified by the so-called "split-span" procedure (Broadbent, 1954), involving rapid dichotic presentation of pairs of digits; in this task, subjects typically organize their report by ear of input, recalling as many items as possible from those presented to one ear (the first half-set) before reporting those presented to the other ear (the second half-set). For right-handed individuals in particular, the right ear is usually given priority in recall, a phenomenon known as the right-ear advantage (REA).

In attempts to ensure that attention is fully focused on the designated message in selective-listening tasks the *shadowing* technique has frequently been employed. In this technique, the listener is asked to repeat aloud each word in the message as soon as it has been presented; sometimes, while shadowing, the listener is additionally required to detect target items. The degree to which attention is focused can be assessed from the level of shadowing efficiency achieved and the amounts recalled from, or the proportions of target items detected in, the attended and unattended messages. Measures of shadowing efficiency include the number of words omitted or mispronounced, the shadowing latency (i.e., the time intervening between the pronunciation of each word in the shadowed message), and the number of intrusions from the unattended or secondary message. However, individual differences in shadowing ability are considerable (Lerner, 1975) and, as Underwood (1974) has pointed out, shadowing is not "a normal mode of transcription of information, and so the unpractised subject must first master this skill before any experiment can be attempted" (p. 368). Not surprisingly, as Underwood (1974) demonstrated, a highly skilled shadower can detect many more target items in both the attended and the unattended message than can relatively unpracticed subjects. It seems probable that in unpracticed subjects particularly, the requirement to shadow one of two auditory messages rather than merely to listen selectively to it consumes processing capacity that could otherwise be employed in extracting information from the two messages (e.g., Underwood & Moray, 1971). Furthermore, target items are likely to be masked by the shadowing voice. Because the reliability of measures of shadowing efficiency tends to be fairly low, and such measures do not seem to be significantly correlated with measures of selective attention obtained from speeded classification and central–incidental tasks (Pelham, 1979), there are some grounds for questioning the usefulness of the shadowing technique as a means of focusing the subject's attention, particularly in subjects who are unaccustomed to the procedure (Lewis, Honeck, & Fishbein, 1975).

Central–Incidental Learning

A visual task incorporating central and incidental task elements has been extensively employed in the investigation of selective attention in children (see Hagen & Hale, 1973, for a review). In the most widely used version of this task, subjects are shown a series of cards; on each card, there are two stimuli, an animal and a household object, one of which is placed at the top of the card and the other at the bottom. Subjects are instructed to direct their attention to one of the stimulus categories (animals or household objects) during the presentation of the picture arrays and are subsequently asked to recall the location of items in this category; the number of locations correctly recalled constitutes the central-task score. Subjects are also required to indicate the irrelevant stimulus with which items from the relevant stimulus category were paired; the number of correct pairings constitutes the incidental-task score. Changes in the degree to which attention can be focused on relevant items are inferred from the relation between central and incidental task scores: A high negative correlation between central and incidental task scores, provided that the former exceed the latter, is taken to indicate a high degree of attentional selectivity. Although the majority of studies employing the central–incidental-task paradigm have used visual tasks, some studies have used auditory tasks or have compared performance on both visual and auditory versions of the task (Anooshian & Prilop, 1980; Conroy & Weener, 1976; Hallahan, Kauffman & Ball, 1974; Pelham, 1979). Pelham (1979) reported the reliabilities of scores on both the auditory and visual tasks he used to be quite high, but the correlations with other measures of selective attention were, in general, very low; the median correlation, based on residualized-gain scores, was +0.08 in his sample of school children. Day (1978) pointed out that in central–incidental tasks, stimulus information is presented for "relatively long periods of time (at least 1 second and generally longer)," whereas tasks employed in studies of selective attention in adults "have required the rapid selection of task-relevant information from a perceptual field" (p. 2). These differences in task demands and information-processing requirements may account, at least in part, for the low and nonsignificant intercorrelations between central–incidental-task scores and other measures of selective attention.

Speeded Classification and Visual Search

In speeded classification tasks, subjects are typically required to sort cards— each of which bears a stimulus possessing one value on each of two dimensions, such as color, size, or shape—into two piles as quickly as possible. Usually, three experimental conditions, in which subjects sort the cards according to the presence or absence of the relevant dimensional value (e.g., A_1), are compared; and the performance measure is classification time. In the first condition, subjects sort on the basis of one dimension only; so that all cards possessing one value on that dimension (A_1) are placed in one pile, and all cards possessing the remaining value (A_2) are placed in the other, the value of the second dimension (B) being held constant. In the second condition, the values of A and B are correlated, so that cards bearing A_1B_1 are placed in one pile and cards bearing

A_2B_2 in the other. In the third condition, the values of A and B are orthogonal, each value on one dimension being paired equally often with each value on the other; cards bearing A_1B_1 and A_1B_2 are placed in one pile, and those bearing A_2B_1 and A_2B_2 in the other.

If attention can be completely focused on the relevant dimension, then the presence of irrelevant dimensions should have no effect on classification time; however, different effects of irrelevant dimensions have been observed depending on the combination of relevant and irrelevant dimensions involved. Several investigators (Garner, 1970, 1974; Lockhead, 1966; Shepard, 1964) have distinguished between combinations of dimensions that are integral, such as the hue and brightness of a single color chip, and combinations that are nonintegral or separable, such as the diameter of a circle and the angle of its radius, arguing that the perceived structure of these dimensional combinations is different and that, in consequence, selective attention only operates for separable, nonintegral dimensions.

In visual-search tasks, subjects scan visual displays for the presence of a target item or items, frequently letters, digits, or geometric forms. In general, search times are found to increase as the number of items in the target set increases (e.g., Holmes, Peper, Olsho & Raney, 1978). In the classic series of visual-search experiments conducted by Neisser and his associates (see Neisser, 1963), extensive practice was shown to abolish the effect of target-set size on search items, so that highly practiced subjects were eventually able to search for 10 target items as quickly as for only 1. This result may well be attributable to the use of nested target sets, in which the smaller target sets were selected from the largest target set employed (see Holmes, *et al.*, 1978). Practice does not seem to reduce the effect of processing load on search times either in visual-search tasks in which target sets are not nested (Gould & Carn, 1973; Kristofferson, Groen, & Kristofferson, 1973) or in Sternberg's (1966) well-known memory-search paradigm in which nested target sets are not used (Ross, 1970). But in a related series of experiments, Schneider and Shiffrin (1977; see also Schneider, Dumais, & Shiffrin, Chapter 1, this volume) found that extensive practice abolished both the effects of memory-set size and visual-array size in a memory-search–visual-search task. Schneider and Shiffrin compared the effects of practice on performance at two versions of the task, one in which stimulus-to-response mapping was consistent (target and distractor items being nonoverlapping), and the other in which it was varied (a target item on one trial could be a distractor item on the next). The effects of practice on search times in the consistently mapped (CM) versions of the task were explained in terms of the development of "automatic processing," which was considered to make minimal demands on attentional capacity. Once learned, target items could be detected "effortlessly" and become virtually impossible to ignore when used in other experiments (Shiffrin & Schneider, 1977) as distractor items. In the variously mapped (VM) condition of the task, however, in which there was no fixed set of target items, no learning could occur, and performance, which was considered to depend on "controlled processing," showed the usual effect of increases in processing load. The distinction between "automatic" processing on the one hand and "controlled" or "effortful" (Hasher & Zacks, 1979) processing on the other hand has been pursued in a number of studies of adult age differences, some of which are reviewed later.

The Stroop Test

There is no standard version of the color–word interference test generally named after J. R. Stroop, who introduced the technique to the American experimental literature in 1935 (Stroop, 1935b). Although there are many variations of the Stroop test, notably those involving tachistoscopic presentation and keypressing and card-sorting responses, the "traditional" Stroop procedure utilises three charts: a word chart, with color words printed in black; a color chart, with color patches; and a color–word chart with color words printed in incongruent ink colors (e.g., the word *red* printed in green ink). The subject's task is to read the color words on the word chart, to name the colors on the color chart, and to name the ink colors while ignoring the words on the color–word chart. It has consistently been found that word reading is faster than color naming; that is, the time taken to complete the word chart is less than that taken to complete the color chart. Although this finding is of considerable theoretical interest (see Fraisse, 1969), it is not our immediate concern here. The major finding of studies employing the Stroop test is that the color–word chart completion time is longer, frequently by as much as 50% to 100%, than the completion time for the color chart. This "interference" phenomenon, usually measured by subtracting the color chart score from the color–word score (CW − C) or by dividing the latter by the former (CW/C; Jensen, 1965), has been taken to indicate an individual's general "interference proneness" or, conversely, the individual's ability to focus attention on a relevant stimulus dimension (ink color) and to ignore an irrelevant one (word meaning).

The reliability of the Stroop test is generally good, particularly when repeated measures are taken to absorb practice effects, which are considerable for color–word chart times. Performance on the Stroop test has often been shown to correlate significantly with performance on the Gottschaldt Embedded Figures Test and sometimes with measures of perceptual–motor performance, learning, and memory (see, for example, Jensen, 1965; Jensen & Rohwer, 1966; Dyer, 1973). Its relation to other measures of distractibility, however, is uncertain, which has led some investigators to conclude that performance on the Stroop test may reflect a relatively specific type of interference that is essentially unrelated to any general selective-attention ability (see, for example, Thackray, Jones, & Touchstone, 1972). In particular, it has been argued that Stroop interference specifically reflects the dominance of word reading over color naming, and this interpretation is supported by the relative absence of a "reverse Stroop" effect when overt verbalization is the required response (e.g., Dyer, 1973; Martin, 1981). It is not surprising, therefore, that much of the work concerned with individual and group differences in Stroop performance has been developmental in nature and frequently has focused on the relation between Stroop-like performance and reading level (e.g., Ehri, 1976; Fournier, Mazzarella, Ricciardi, & Fingeret, 1975; Guttentag & Haith, 1978, 1979; Rosinski, 1977). Several of these studies have examined not color–word interference but picture–word interference, using such experimental material as a picture of a dog with the word *cat* superimposed on it. Although such tasks would seem analogous to the Stroop test, the analogy should not, perhaps, be taken for granted (e.g., Cammock & Cairns, 1979).

Time-sharing

Time-sharing must occur, to a greater or lesser extent, in situations in which two tasks are performed concurrently or two or more displays are monitored concurrently. In dual-task paradigms, one task is frequently designated as the primary task and the other as the secondary task. The tasks involved may also possess either many or few elements in common.

Several studies have examined whether a general time-sharing ability exists. Wickens, Mountford, and Schreiner (1981) have argued that in order to demonstrate the existence of such an ability, it is necessary to obtain high correlations between performance scores in qualitatively different dual-task combinations, and lower correlations between single- and dual-task performance and between the single-task performance scores in each of the qualitatively different task pairs. Sverko (Note 1) compared four different tasks performed singly and in each possible pair-wise combination. A principal-components analysis revealed only four factors corresponding to the task-specific factors and no additional general time-sharing component. In this study, however, subjects were relatively unpracticed; and for some task combinations, it was clear that subjects found it impossible to adhere to "equal-priority" instructions. These factors could have increased score variance and masked any general time-sharing ability. Wickens *et al.* (1981) required practiced subjects to perform singly and in dual-task combination four tasks: manual tracking, auditory running memory, digit classification, and visual line judgment. The degree of single-to-dual task performance decrement for each task differed significantly for different pairings; and factor analysis of single- and dual-task scores yielded only factors specific to task characteristics (for example, visual monitoring), with no evidence of a trans-situational time-sharing factor loaded exclusively on dual-task scores. Wickens *et al.* concluded that if there are time-sharing skills needed for complex-task performance, over and above those needed for the execution of single tasks, these are not general in nature. Jennings and Chiles (1977), for example, have produced factor-analytic evidence for a time-sharing factor that was specific to visual monitoring tasks of low signal frequency.

A series of studies by Hawkins and his colleagues (Hawkins, Church, & DeLemos, Note 2; Hawkins, Rodriguez, & Reicher, Note 3) also questions the assumption that time-sharing ability would take the form of a single, unitary trait. They argued that time-sharing could be governed by several specific independent subcapacities, each with its own structural limitations. Hawkins *et al.*, (Note 2) employed a task that required a speeded response to each of two stimuli in a psychological refractory-period paradigm. Interference between the two task elements was greatest either when the responses to the stimuli (manual versus vocal) or when stimuli (auditory versus visual) shared the same modality. Moreover demands on memory retrieval for each of the stimuli were mutually interfering, especially in the early stages of training. Evidence of the independence of each of these effects was reported by Hawkins *et al.*, (Note 3). It appears, therefore, that the evidence to support the notion of a general time-sharing ability is not particularly strong.

Age Differences

It seems clear that not only does a child's understanding of the nature of attentional skills and, in particular, of the conditions that facilitate the effective deployment of those skills become more accurate and more complete with age (Miller & Bigi, 1979; Yussen & Bird, 1979); but also the ability to attend selectively markedly improves as a child grows older. This conclusion is supported by the results of several studies of selective listening, speeded classification, central–incidental learning and Stroop performance in children, although, as discussed in the following, some difficulties of interpretation remain. Fewer studies have been conducted with elderly subjects, and their results are mixed; but there is some evidence to suggest that in old age the ability to attend selectively declines.

Selective and Dichotic Listening

The evidence from selective-listening studies suggests that the ability to focus attention on one of two competing auditory messages improves considerably between the ages of 5 and 14 years, as indicated either by measures of shadowing efficiency, by measures of retention of the content of the attended message, or by the number of intrusions from the unattended message (Anooshian & McCulloch, 1979; Doyle, 1973; Maccoby, 1967; Maccoby & Konrad, 1966, 1967; Pelham, 1979). It appears that in dichotic listening, retention for items in the attended message improves with age, whereas retention for items in the unattended message remains stable (Doyle, 1973); and a similar improvement with age has been found for detection of target words from the attended message but not for those from the unattended message (Geffen & Sexton, 1978). However, the precise age at which an improvement is manifest differs for different tasks. Doyle, for example, found that improvement on retention scores occurred between 8 and 14 years, and Geffen and Sexton found that improvement on detection scores occurred between 7 and 9 years. Doyle also found that for her 8-year-old group there was a nonsignificant positive correlation between the number of intrusions from the unattended message during shadowing and the number of words from the unattended message subsequently retained; for the 14-year-olds, on the other hand, there was a significant *negative* correlation between the number of intrusions and the number of words retained from the unattended message. Doyle concluded that "superior listening performance of older children is due not to a greater ability to filter out distracting material at an early stage of processing, but in large part due to an ability to inhibit intrusions from the distracting material during the selection task" (Doyle, 1973, p. 100). This conclusion was endorsed by Anooshian and McCulloch (1979), who found that differences in shadowing efficiency between second- and fifth-grade children could be abolished, or enhanced, by semantic properties of the unattended as well as of the attended message, and by the semantic "matching" of the two.

Geffen and Wale (1979) compared the performance of 7- and 9-year-olds in a digit-recall task in which the attended and to-be-recalled digits were defined by voice (male or female). Digit pairs were presented binaurally or dichotically at two different presentation rates; and in dichotic-presentation conditions, the specified voice switched between ears, the number of switches being varied systematically. Younger children recalled less efficiently in the dichotic-listening condition, and in the binaural condition when messages were presented at fast rates, than did the older children, and were more adversely affected by increases in presentation rate and frequency of switches between ears than were the older children. Geffen and Wale argued that these differences are attributable to developmental differences in the amount of processing capacity that is available to cope with increasing task demands.

Sexton and Geffen (1979) further compared the dichotic-monitoring performance of 7-, 11-, and 20-year-olds in two conditions: unequal division of attention, in which subjects were instructed to give priority to one ear but to report targets arriving at either ear, and focused attention, in which subjects were required to report only targets arriving at the designated ear. In both conditions, performance improved with age. Detection rate was superior in the focused-attention condition; but the difference was most marked in the case of 7-year-olds, less marked for 11-year-olds, and virtually nonexistent for 20-year-olds. Seven-year-olds thus seem able to some extent to employ a pure focusing attention strategy, but are less able to allocate attention unequally between two input channels. The ability to divide attention equally in dichotic-listening tasks also improves over the age range of 7–10 years, although at a slower rate than the ability to attend selectively (Geffen & Sexton, 1978). Sexton and Geffen (1979) also found that target-detection rate under divided attention conditions in a dichotic-monitoring task improved with age over the range of 7–11 years, but showed no further improvement over the range of 11–20 years, which is probably because of the faster event-presentation rate employed in testing the 20-year-old group.

In a study of adult age differences in focused attention Panek, Barrett, Sterns, and Alexander (1978) found that the performance of women aged between 57 and 72 years was significantly inferior to that of younger women on a dichotic-presentation task in which the attended message was designated by ear (see Mihal & Barrett, 1976). Ford, Hink, Hopkins, Roth, Pfefferbaum, and Kopell (1979) also reported an age-related deficit in a selective-listening task in which the performance measure was the number of targets (tones) correctly counted in sequence; however, as Ford et al. pointed out, it is unclear whether this deficit was due primarily to failures of attention or of memory. In a subsequent replication (Ford and Pfefferbaum, 1980) in which a button-pressing response had to be made whenever a target occurred, it was found that although both older and younger subjects were selectively attending to the relevant channel (as inferred from event-related potential (ERP) data), older subjects were less efficient at detecting targets, perhaps because they appeared to take longer to determine stimulus relevance (i.e., to decide whether a particular stimulus was or was not a target).

Other evidence concerning age differences in selective attention has been chiefly concerned with performance on the split-span task, the developmental aspects of which have been studied notably by Inglis and his associates (see Caird, 1966; Craik, 1977; Inglis, 1965; Inglis & Caird, 1963; Inglis & Sykes, 1967; Inglis & Tansey, 1967, for a review of these and related studies). The results of such studies can be briefly summarized as follows. First, as already noted, recall performance is generally better for the first half-set reported than for the second half-set. Second, the superiority of first half-set recall over second half-set recall diminishes with increasing age in children, at least over the age range of 5–10 years (Inglis & Sykes, 1967); but increases in the elderly from about the age of 60 onwards (e.g., Inglis, 1965), although when digit span is controlled for, differences between older and younger subjects are attenuated or abolished (Parkinson, Lindholm, & Urell, 1980). Third, all studies that have examined adult age differences report an age-related decrement for the second half-set recalled, although there is disagreement concerning whether or not such a decrement occurs for the first half-set.

Finally, some developmental studies have examined the REA in dichotic listening. In adults, focusing attention appears to attenuate or abolish the REA (Treisman & Geffen, 1968), and the ability to counteract the REA by focusing attention on the left ear seems to show a marked improvement between the ages of 6 and 8 years (Geffen, 1978). This finding may be complicated by the possibility that the REA itself increases with age (e.g., Bryden & Allard, 1978; Satz, Bakker, Teunissen, Goebel, & Van Der Vlught, 1975); on the other hand, some investigators have argued that the REA remains constant throughout childhood (e.g., Hiscock & Kinsbourne, 1980; Kinsbourne, 1975; Kinsbourne & Hiscock, 1977; Obrzut, Hynd, Obrzut, & Pirrozzolo, 1981), and an attempt to reconcile these opposing views in a "levels-of-processing" model has been made by Porter and Berlin (1975). With respect to adult age differences, Clark and Knowles (1973) found the REA to increase progressively with age between 15 and 74 years, but a subsequent replication incorporating rigorous audiological screening and objective adjustment for ear discrepancies in hearing (Borod & Goodglass, 1980) failed to confirm the finding for subjects ranging in age from 24 to 79 years.

Central–Incidental Tasks

Two main findings have emerged from studies employing visual central–incidental tasks in the investigation of age differences in selective attention. First, scores on the central task increase with age, at least up until early adulthood; whereas incidental-task scores either remain relatively stable or show a slower rate of increase up to the age of 12 and then decline thereafter, reaching near-chance levels in young adults (Conroy & Weener, 1976; Druker & Hagen, 1969; Hagen, 1967; Hagen, Meacham, & Mesibov, 1970; Maccoby & Hagen, 1965; Mergler et al., 1977; Wheeler & Dusek, 1973). A slight but significant reduction in both central and incidental task performance has been reported for adults in their late sixties and early seventies (Mergler et al., 1977). Broadly similar results have been obtained with auditory central–incidental tasks, at least with respect to age differences in children (Anooshian & Prilop, 1980; Conroy & Weener, 1976; Hallahan, et al., 1974; Pelham, 1979). The second main finding to emerge from studies employing the central–incidental-task paradigm is that the correlation between central- and incidental-task scores decreases with age; this correlation tends to be positive in younger children but negative in older ones, although in young adults it may be around zero and is slightly, but nonsignificantly, positive in the elderly. Hagen and Hale (1973) interpreted the results of studies employing the central–incidental paradigm with children as indicating "a developmental improvement in efficiency of attention deployment" (p. 136) and proposed a two-stage model of information processing, derived from that of Neisser (1967), to account for such results. During the first stage, relevant information is discriminated from irrelevant; and during the second, attention to relevant information has to be maintained while irrelevant information is ignored. Hagen and Hale suggested that the second stage of information processing was the more critical for successful performance in central–incidental tasks, and it is at this stage that developmental changes in selective attention become most apparent. This interpretation is supported by the results of studies that have manipulated the discriminability of central- and incidental-task elements. For example, when central features are made more readily distinguishable from incidental features, developmental trends in central–incidental performance remain essentially unaltered (Druker & Hagen, 1969; Sabo & Hagen, 1973), suggesting that the hypothetical first stage of information processing is not primarily responsible for developmental changes in selective attention. However, the discrimination and encoding stage may assume greater importance in task situations in which central and incidental features can be perceived as an integrated whole; and in such situations, central and incidental learning may both increase with age so that the progressive developmental discrepancy between them is attenuated (e.g., Anooshian & Prilop, 1980; Hale & Piper, 1973). Furthermore, labeling central stimuli, which presumably provides an efficient encoding strategy, facilitates central learning and reduces incidental learning; whereas merely pointing to central stimuli, which focuses attention on the relevant task feature without providing an encoding strategy, does not affect central learning, although it does reduce incidental learning (Dusek, 1978). If developmental differences in selective attention, as inferred from performance on central–incidental tasks, are mainly attributable to the attention-maintenance stage of information processing, then allowing subjects more time to observe the arrays containing central and incidental features should improve the performance of older children. In line with this expectation, Hale and Alderman (1978) found that although in 9-year-old children both central and incidental scores increased with the duration of exposure, in 12-year-old children there was a marked increase in central scores without any attendant change in incidental scores.

Both the central–incidental task itself and the attentional-selectivity interpretation of the results obtained with the central–incidental paradigm have been criticized on various grounds (Douglas & Peters, 1979; Lane, 1980; Miller & Weiss, 1981). For example, the central task requires recall of locations, whereas the incidental task requires recognition of associative pairings. It is possible, therefore, that a differential trend in central and incidental scores with age may reflect different rates of development of recall and recognition functions. Central-task learning is tested after each trial, but incidental-task learning is tested only after a block of trials; so that different retention intervals are employed for the two measures. Furthermore, as Lane (1980) has pointed out, possible changes in attention allocation are confounded with possible increases in total attentional capacity with age. Despite these criticisms, however, the central–incidental paradigm remains one of the principal sources of data on developmental trends in selective attention, and also provides a useful theoretical model within which these data may be interpreted.

Speeded Classification and Visual Search

Several studies have reported developmental changes in the performance of speeded classification and visual-search tasks. For example, Strutt, Anderson, and Well (1975) required subjects with average ages of 6, 9, 12, and 20 years to sort cards varying in one relevant and either 0, 1, or 2 irrelevant dimensions. They found that sorting times for 6-year-old children were significantly increased by the presence of irrelevant dimensions, and that two irrelevant dimensions produced significantly more 'interference' than did one; the same pattern of results was obtained, though less clearly, for older children but was absent in adults, who showed no interference effects. Strutt *et al.* concluded that speeded classification performance improves with age, older children and adults being more able to focus their attention on the relevant stimulus dimension. Von Wright and Nurmi (1979) confirmed this finding but found that it was abolished when subjects performed the task in 95-dB(A) white noise. Noise tended to reduce classification times for 6-year-olds, especially when irrelevant information was present; whereas noise tended to increase classification times for adults. However, although 6-year-olds worked more quickly in noise, they also made more errors; suggesting that noise may differentially affect the speed–accuracy trade-off (SATO) in children and adults. It has been argued that the developmental change in speeded classification performance in children reflects the growth, as perceptual learning proceeds, of "dimensional separability" (e.g., Shepp, 1978; Smith & Kemler, 1977); young children tend to integrate stimulus dimensions that older children are able to separate. Some dimensions are, in effect, integral for all perceivers (for example, brightness and saturation); whereas others, such as shape and color, are separable for adults and older children but may be viewed as integral by younger children. To test this hypothesis, Shepp and Swartz (1976) gave 6-year-old and 9-year-old children a task based on that used by Garner and Felfoldy (1970). Subjects were presented with drawings of houses in which the door color (hue or brightness) and the shape of the door window might be varied. In a single-dimension condition only one dimension, the basis for sorting, was varied; in a correlated condition, a second dimension also varied consistently with the first; and in an orthogonal condition, a second dimension was varied independently of the first. For integral dimensions (hue and brightness), both 6-year-olds and 9-year-olds showed interference (slower sorting times) in the orthogonal condition, as compared to the single-dimension condition, and 'facilitation' (faster sorting times) in the correlated condition, although facilitation only occurred when hue, rather than brightness, was the relevant dimension. For nonintegral dimensions (color and shape), however, there were no differences in sorting times among the three conditions for 9-year-olds, a similar result to that usually obtained with adult subjects. Six-year-olds, on the other hand, showed interference effects in the orthogonal condition and facilitation in the correlated. It thus appears that dimensions that are separable for older subjects may be nonseparable for younger children. However, Chapman (1981) conducted a similar experiment, using as stimuli cartoon faces in which the eyes might be open or closed and the mouth might be smiling or frowning. He found that although 6-year-olds, like the 6-year-olds in Shepp and Swartz's study, showed the patterns of interference and facilitation characteristic of integral dimensions; 9-year-old subjects also showed facilitation in a correlated condition, although no interference in an orthogonal condition. Chapman therefore argued that the developmental trend was not toward separability as such, but rather toward optional separability or flexibility of attention. Older subjects are able to treat separable dimensions either as integral or as separate, whichever is more advantageous for the task being performed.

Visual-search performance also improves with age in children (see Wickens, 1974, for a review of early studies); and because search times are significantly reduced in adults by the provision of various cues concerning target location (e.g., Williams, 1966), developmental trends in the effects of similar cues on selective attention in visual search have recently begun to be investigated (Day, 1978; Miller, 1978). Day (1978) required 7-, 9-, and 12-year-old children to search for a target letter in a 6×6 matrix of capital letters centered in forms differing in color and/or shape. The forms were either uniform, being all of the same color and shape, or varied in color only, shape only, or both color and shape. In addition, a shape cue, a color cue, or no cue at all was provided. Day found that search times decreased significantly with age but that the disruptive effects of background (form) variation on search performance were similar for all three age groups. Different developmental trends were obtained for different cue types: Color cues speeded search times and enhanced accuracy at all ages, although to a greater extent for older children; shape cues exerted no beneficial effect on search times for 7-year-olds and actually slowed the speed of search for 9- and 12-year-olds; and in no-cue searches, the selective attention of younger children was as efficient as that of older children. Thus, as Day observed, "depending upon the particular condition, attentional selectivity appeared to increase, decrease, or remain constant with age" (p. 15). In a comparable study, Miller (1978) found that color cues facilitated the speed of search in older children (mean age 11 years 8 months) and young adults (mean age 19 years) but not in younger children (mean age 7 years 4 months), whereas shape cues (in contrast to the findings of Day) had a smaller beneficial effect on the performance of the two older groups. Averaged overall search times, which decreased significantly with age, were also related to the mean number of visual fixations, which showed a similar age-related decrease. Developmental changes in children's visual-search performance thus appear to be situation dependent.

One of the first studies to examine adult age differences in the effects of irrelevant stimulation on speeded classification performance was conducted by Rabbitt (1965). Rabbitt required younger (age range 17–24 years) and older (age range 65–74 years) subjects to sort cards into two piles according to whether they bore the letter A or the letter B; each card bore in addition 0, 1, 4, or 8 irrelevant letters, and the relevant letter (A or B) might be in any of nine locations on the card. In a second condition the same subjects were required to sort cards into eight piles corresponding to relevant letters (A–H), again with 0, 1, 4, or 8 irrelevant letters accompanying the relevant one (the two conditions were in fact balanced for order of presentation across subjects). Rabbitt found that the effect on sorting time of an increase in the number of relevant letters was much the same for older and younger subjects. However, the sorting times of older subjects increased significantly more sharply than that of younger subjects with an increase in the number of irrelevant letters, particularly in the case of Condition 2 (in which eight relevant letters, rather than two, had to be sought). It should be noted that Rabbitt's task was concerned not with relevant and irrelevant stimulus dimensions but with relevant and irrelevant subsets of the same, in this case alphabetical, dimension; thus it is not directly comparable with the speeded classification tasks already quoted. Moreover, as Hoyer and Plude (1980) have noted, Rabbitt's task can be classified as a selective-search task, in which irrelevant stimuli have to be discriminated from relevant stimuli; such tasks may be contrasted with selective-filtering tasks, in which there is no discrimination required because the subject has merely to "ignore or filter out information that is irrelevant to task performance" (Hoyer and Plude, 1980, p. 233).

Selective filtering might be expected, like selective search, to provide support for the hypothesis, advanced by Layton (1975), that the aging process is accompanied by an increase in "perceptual noise" that reveals itself in several ways but most notably in the form of "a diminished ability to suppress irrelevant stimuli" (p. 881). However, Wright and Elias (1979) obtained no adult age differences in the effects of perceptual noise in a selective-filtering task requiring a simple toggle-switch response to a tachistoscopically presented target letter. Increased perceptual noise, defined as the addition of four irrelevant letters flanking the target, lengthened response latencies for younger (18–25 years) and older (60–82 years) subjects equally. Farkas and Hoyer (1980) investigated adult age differences in both selective search and selective filtering in a speeded classification task. Younger (18–30 years), middle-aged (37–58 years), and elderly (60–81 years) subjects sorted decks of cards on the basis of the orientation of a target figure, presented alone or with irrelevant figures that were similar to or different from the target figure in orientation. In their first "selective-search" experiment, the position of target figures varied from one card to the next; in their second "selective filtering" experiment, it remained constant.

Age differences were found in selective search under both same-irrelevant-information and different-irrelevant-information conditions, and in selective-filtering under the same-irrelevant-information conditions. In all cases, the slowing of classification times compared to the control (no irrelevant information) condition was greater for elderly than for middle-aged or younger subjects, who in fact showed no slowing at all in selective filtering. No age differences appeared, and indeed no slowing occurred, in selective filtering under the different-irrelevant-information condition. These results, taken together with those of Wright and Elias, suggest that there is no age-related deficit in the ability simply to ignore irrelevant information. Rather, age-related deficits occur when it is necessary to process irrelevant information because the discrimination between relevant and irrelevant items is too difficult to be effected solely by preattentive processes (Kahneman, 1973; Neisser, 1967).

In related experiments, involving tasks similar to that used by Schneider and Shiffrin (1977), adult age differences in automatic and in controlled or effortful processing have been investigated (Madden & Nebes, 1980; Plude & Hoyer, 1981). Madden and Nebes compared the effects of nine days of practice on the performance of a hybrid memory-search–visual-search task by young (age range 18–25 years) and older (age range 61–74 years) adults. Stimulus-to-response mapping was consistent and the display size was constant throughout their experiment; only the memory-set size was varied. Although Madden and Nebes found that increases in memory-set size slowed search times to a significantly greater extent for older subjects, the effects of practice (which reduced search times) were essentially the same for both age groups, indicating that the development of automatic processing proceeded at a similar rate for older and younger subjects. Plude and Hoyer (1981) compared the effects of consistent and varied stimulus-to-response mapping, and of increases in both display and target-set size on the visual-search times of young (age range 19.5–27.5 years) and elderly (age range 65.1–85.5 years) subjects over six 45-minute sessions. They found that increases in both display and target-set size significantly increased search times for both age groups; but that search times increased significantly with age in the VM condition at all levels of processing load, whereas in the CM condition, age differences were only found at the higher target-set size (four items). This result again suggests that the development of automatic processing can attenuate, if not eliminate, the effects of processing load on adult age differences in search times.

The Stroop Test

The most comprehensive study of age differences in Stroop performance has been that of Comalli, Wapner, and Werner (1962), who tested 235 individuals ranging in age from 7 to 80 years. Comalli *et al.* found that word-reading time, color-naming time, and interference (measured by $CW - C$ and CW/C) all declined with age from 7 years to adulthood, remained more or less stable over the adult years from 17 to 44, and increased somewhat for the oldest group tested (65–80 years). This increase seen in the oldest group was most marked for the color–word chart scores, and therefore for the interference scores (see Table 11.1). Other, less comprehensive, studies have generally confirmed Comalli *et al.*'s findings, with some additions and qualifications. For example, Wise, Sutton and Gibbons (1975) reported lower interference scores for young adults than for 7 to 10-year-old school children. Wise *et al.* employed a tachistoscopic presentation procedure rather than the "traditional" chart procedure, although because their "interference" measure was the difference in average response times to incongruent and congruent stimuli (e.g., the word *red* printed in red), the age-related decline they observed might have been due to the facilitating effect of congruence rather than, or in addition to, the interfering effect of incongruence. Rand, Wapner, Werner and McFarland (1963) analyzed different types of performance disruption in relation to age over the range of 6 to 18 years. They found that although most error types (e.g., naming the word instead of the color, omissions, insertions, and "contaminated" responses such as *gred, brue,* or *reen*) decreased linearly with age, one error category (the insertion of non-linguistic utterances such as *oh, um,* and *ah*) increased with age, and the frequency of inarticulate utterances (e.g., stutters, whispers, and mispronunciations) was higher for the youngest and oldest than for the intermediate age groups. Because the frequencies of many error types were low, the number of subjects relatively small, and the age range within each group undesirably large (at least for the youngest subjects—6–7.11 years), these findings merit replication and extension.

Comalli *et al.*'s (1962) finding that interference scores increase in the elderly has been confirmed by the results of several other studies (e.g., Comalli, 1965; Eisner, 1972; Schonfield & Trueman, Note 4), and increased interference in such subjects appears to be positively related to institutionalization (Comalli, Krus, & Wapner, 1965) and to the presence of organic brain syndrome (Bettner, Jarvik, & Blum, 1971). Increased interference with age in adult subjects, ranging in age from 20 to 75 years, has also been observed with both tachistoscopic presentation and card-sorting procedures (Taylor, Davies, & Marsh, Note 5).

There is little evidence relating to Stroop performance for children younger than 7 years for the obvious reason that reading ability is poorly established below this age. There are some tests, held to be analogous to the Stroop, that avoid this difficulty. Santostefano (1964, 1978) devised a Fruit Distraction Test in which the basic stimuli are line drawings of fruit appropriately or inappropriately colored. Cramer (1967) gave preschool children, aged 4 years 3 months to 5 years 10 months, a color–form test comprising a color-patch chart; a form chart bearing the four forms apple, tree, sun, and water; and a color–form chart in which the forms were incongruently colored. The children were required *either* to name the colors of the color-patch chart and then the colors of the color–form chart, *or* to name the forms of the form chart and then the forms of the color–form chart. Cramer found evidence of interference in both groups, the effect being greater for color naming than for form naming. However, as Cam-

TABLE 11.1

Mean Times (in Seconds) for Different Age Groups Engaged in Various Stroop Test Procedures[a]

Test procedure[c]	Age groups (years)[b]												
	7 (N = 24)	8 (N = 20)	9 (N = 20)	10 (N = 25)	11 (N = 29)	12 (N = 25)	13 (N = 29)	17–19 (N = 18)	25–34 (N = 14)	35–44 (N = 16)	65–80 (N = 15)
W	89.8	77.6	68.5	62.3	55.6	59.3	54.1	40.5	39.4	42.6	45.1
C	126.9	108.3	100.9	92.8	82.1	86.4	79.5	56.1	60.9	57.9	68.9
CW	264.7	208.3	191.4	184.3	160.8	157.9	147.6	103.0	106.2	109.9	165.1
CW − C	137.8	100.0	90.5	91.5	78.7	71.5	68.1	46.9	45.3	52.0	96.2

[a] After Comalli et al. (1962).
[b] N represents the number of subjects in each age group.
[c] Color–word reading (W), color naming (C), ink-color naming when a color word is printed in an incongruent ink color (CW), and Stroop interference score (CW − C).

mock and Cairns (1979) have reported for the Fruit Distraction Test, the correlation of such presumed analogs with the Stroop test itself may not be high.

Schiller (1966) included first-grade school children as well as second-, third-, fifth-, and eighth-grade students and college freshmen in a developmental study employing "classic" Stroop material as well as color–word stimuli of varying color association similar to the material used by Klein (1964). He found virtually no Stroop interference in the youngest children, but maximal interference for second- and third-graders, which declined with age thereafter. The critical condition for Stroop interference is probably that word reading should be faster than color naming; Schiller found that this was not so for his first-graders (although it did hold true for second-graders and onwards as well as for adults), and Ehri (1976) found that second-graders who took *longer* to read words than to name pictures did not show Stroop-like interference in a picture–word task. However, it then becomes a near paradox that interference should decline with increased age, which is accompanied by an increase in the relative dominance of word reading over color naming (Stroop, 1935a). Apparently the effect of practice at reading is first to increase and then to decrease interference; Ehri and Wilce (1979) have found that reading practice on 'distractor' words increased picture–word interference for children who were initially relatively unfamiliar with the words, but decreased it for children who were already familiar with the words prior to training. They suggested that as initially unfamiliar material becomes recognized more accurately, attention is no longer a prerequisite for processing, and hence interference from automatic processing increases; with further practice at recognition of familiar material, processing speed increases, and hence interference with concurrent tasks will decline. The other explanation that has been advanced for declining interference with age to adulthood has been in terms of developing perceptual and cognitive differentiation and hierarchical integration of function, with some regression in these characteristics with old age (Comalli *et al.*, 1962). Whatever explanation is found useful in describing developmental trends in interference between childhood and maturity, the nature (and extent) of increased interference proneness in old age and its similarities to or differences from the interference proneness of children remain open to interpretation.

Time-sharing

As noted above, the evidence for a general time-sharing ability in adults does not appear to be particularly strong, and comparatively few studies have investigated developmental trends in time-sharing skills. Because on most experimental tasks older children achieve higher performance scores than do younger children, baseline levels of performance need to be equated across age groups before conclusions can be drawn concerning possible developmental trends in dual-task performance. Different methods of equating baseline performance levels have been adopted in the three principal studies of the development of time-sharing (Lane, 1979; Lipps Birch, 1976, 1978). Lipps Birch (1976) compared the dual-task performance of 7-, 10-, and 13-year-old boys, using an auditory same–different matching task involving two levels of difficulty and a compensatory tracking task. The order in which task conditions were presented and the amount of practice in each condition were the same for each age group. Under single-task conditions, error rates declined significantly with age for both the matching and the tracking task, and the performance decrements for each task under dual-task conditions were converted from absolute to proportional change scores. Under equal-priority instructions, the time-sharing decrement for the tracking task reliably decreased with age; and for all age groups, tracking-task decrement scores were directly related to the difficulty of the auditory matching task. The results of this study thus suggest that there is a developmental improvement in time-sharing ability, but because the use of proportional change scores to equate age differences in baseline performance levels is indirect and may not be entirely satisfactory, Lipps Birch (1978) conducted a second experiment with the same matching and tracking tasks in which she equated the baseline performance levels of 8-year-old and 13-year-old children by giving differential amounts of practice. A second group of 8-year-old children, to whom extra practice was not given, served as a control group. In this experiment, it was found that although a developmental trend in time-sharing ability was obtained in comparisons involving the control group of 8-year-olds, no such trend was observed for the experimental group. Lipps Birch therefore concluded that performance under time-sharing conditions "is a function of single task baseline performance" (1978, p. 511). Although the differential practice method of equating performance levels has been questioned by Lane (1979), the results of Lane's own experiment, in which baseline differences in the performance of an auditory and a visual memory task by 7-year-old and 9-year-old children and by college students were controlled through the manipulation of task difficulty levels, also suggested the absence of any developmental trend in overall performance under dual-task conditions.

Yet Lane did find developmental changes in attention allocation when the payoff for correct responses on one of the memory tasks was increased, so that it became the primary task while the remaining memory task became the secondary task. The mean difference between the proportion of correct responses for the primary and secondary tasks reliably increased with age, being greatest for the college students and virtually nonexistent for the 7-year-olds. This result contrasts with that of Lipps Birch (1976), who found that when instructions designated one of two concurrently performed tasks as being more important, all age groups improved their performance on the primary task by a similar amount—except when the auditory matching task was the primary task, in which case the 7-year-old group showed the greatest improvement in performance. However, as Lane (1979) pointed out, this unexpected result could be due to the confounding of practice and instructional condition in the experimental design employed by Lipps Birch.

There is thus some evidence that the ability to allocate attention appropriately, in accordance with task and situational demands, improves from childhood to young adulthood; although there is little indication that any age-related improvement occurs in the overall level of dual-task performance, provided that baseline differences are adequately controlled. But it has frequently been observed that elderly individuals perform less well in dual-task situations than do young or middle-aged adults—not only when attention has to be divided between two or more sources of information, as in dichotic listening or multisource monitoring tasks (Maule & Sanford, 1980; Sanford & Maule, 1971, 1973), but also when it must be shared between two or more mental operations (Broadbent & Heron, 1962; Kirchner, 1958; Talland, 1962; Wright, 1981). It has been suggested that there is a reduction in processing capacity with increasing age, so that older individuals have fewer resources available with which to process incoming information (Craik, 1977) or to operate control processes in working memory (Wright, 1981). The performance of older people should thus begin to deteriorate at lower levels of task demand than those required to produce a decrement in the performance of young adults; furthermore, this result should obtain whether or not the task situation involves divided attention. To test this hypothesis, Wright manipulated memory load and the number of mental operations necessary for successful performance in two task situations, one being a dual-task condition and the other being a single task. The demands placed on processing capacity in the two situations could thus be assumed to be equivalent. Similar decrements with increases in task demands were observed for young (age range 18–22 years) and old adults (age range 63–75 years) in both situations although the performance decrement was greater and became apparent earlier (i.e., at lower levels of task demands) for older subjects. It is possible, therefore, that adult age differences in time-sharing situations only occur in conditions where there is competition for the same processing resources; and that when two tasks, or two mental operations, draw on different sources of processing capacity, the performance of older subjects is relatively unaffected. Further support for the view that time-sharing is not, in itself, disadvantageous for older individuals is provided in a pilot study also reported by Wright (1981) in which no age differences were found in a dual-task situation in which memory load was manipulated during the performance of a letter-matching task.

Intelligence, Sex, Personality, and Cognitive Style

Intelligence

A positive relation between intelligence and the ability to focus attention and resist distraction might be expected on a priori grounds, and there is some evidence that supports this expectation from studies of speeded classification and central–incidental task performance. Smith and Baron (1981), for example, obtained a significant positive correlation between intelligence, as measured by various tests (including Raven's Standard Progressive Matrices and The Scholastic Aptitude Test), and resistance to interference in a speeded classification task involving the sorting of angle stimuli. In two experiments, Hagen and Huntsman (1971) tested normal and retarded children ranging in chronological age from 4 years to 11 years 9 months and in mental age from 3 years 10 months to 9 years 3 months on a central–incidental task. In their first experiment, the sample of retardates was drawn from children living at home and attending either private nursery or public schools; whereas in the second, the sample was drawn from retardates who were institutionalized. When mental age was controlled, retardates were found to exhibit a selective-attention deficit in the second study but not in the first; retarded children in the second study obtained lower central but higher incidental scores than normal children of equivalent mental age. As far as the Stroop test is concerned, there appears to be a slight but negative relation between intelligence and Stroop interference (Jensen, 1965; Jensen & Rohwer, 1966); although the weakness of the relation may result in part from the restricted range of intelligence within the subject samples (often college students) tested. Studies of Stroop performance in mental retardates have found impaired performance, compared to that of normals, on all three charts, and comparatively greater impairment in the case of color–word scores (Silverstein & Franken, 1965; Vechi, 1972; Wolitzsky, Hofer, & Shapiro, 1972). Vechi (1972) reported significant negative correlations between intelligence and interference both for normal and for mentally retarded children; Wolitzsky et al. (1972) also found greater impairment in adult subjects with IQs between 50 and 59 than in subjects with IQs between 60 and 70, although Silverstein and Franken (1965) found no differences in performance between adolescent retardates with mental ages of 6 to 8 years and those with mental ages of 9 to 11 years. It is possible therefore that intelligence may be related to Stroop interference when a wide intelligence range is sampled (although not perhaps below an IQ of about 50) and when children rather than adults serve as subjects. Further, resistance to Stroop interference may be positively related to creativity (e.g., Golden, 1975).

Sex

Sex differences in the ability to focus attention in selective-listening tasks appear to be negligible or nonexistent among both children (Geffen, 1978; Geffen & Sexton, 1978; Geffen & Wale, 1979) and adults (Fairweather, 1976); and although there is some evidence from the Stroop test that women are superior to men in color–word chart performance (Golden, 1974; Peretti, 1969, 1971), this appears to be attributable to a general superiority in women for color naming (Jensen, 1965; Jensen & Rohwer, 1966; Ligon, 1932). No sex differences have been obtained in interference scores based on the difference between color–word chart and color chart performance (Golden, 1974). Sex differences may not, however, be entirely irrelevant to Stroop interference when considered in conjunction with personality variables; several studies of personality in relation to Stroop performance have employed only women as subjects or, alternatively, have found different patterns of relationship for women and for men (for example, Bush, 1975; Gardner, Holzman, Klein, Linton, & Spence, 1959).

Personality

Studies of personality and selective attention have mainly employed measures of extraversion such as the Maudsley Personality Inventory (MPI) or the Heron Sociability Scale. Eysenck and Eysenck (1979) reported evidence suggesting that introverts may be less efficient than extraverts in task situations requiring divided attention; and Jensen (1965) found a significant, although small, negative correlation between interference (CW − C) on the Stroop test and extraversion (measured by the MPI), but obtained no relation of interference with neuroticism. Similar findings were reported by Callaway (1959); and Davies (1967) found that introverts, so classified by their scores on the Heron Sociability Scale, produced significantly higher interference scores than did extraverts. However, Golden, Marsella, and Golden (1975b) obtained essentially negative results using the MPI and no clear relation between Stroop performance and scores on the Cattell 16PF test. The relationship of extraversion to measures of Stroop performance does not appear therefore to be particularly strong. Much the same conclusion may be drawn from investigations of the relation between selective attention and the field-independence dimension (Witkin, 1950; Witkin, Dyk, Faterson, Goodenough, and Karp, 1962). The degree of field dependence or independence is generally assessed by means of the rod-and-frame test (of which a portable version is available; Oltman, 1968), or the Gottschaldt Embedded Figures Test (of which a shortened form has been published by Jackson, 1956), or both. Gross, Moore, and Stern (1973) compared the performance of good, average, and poor field articulators, determined on the basis of combined field-articulation scores obtained from the portable rod-and-frame test and the short-form embedded figures test under the four conditions of selective listening employed by Treisman and Riley (1969). Although Treisman and Riley's findings were replicated, no differences were found in the selective-listening performance of the three field-articulation groups. Using the Stroop test, Bone and Eysenck (1972) found that field-dependent individuals tended to show more interference than did field-independent individuals; although this finding held only for the male subjects they tested. Hochman (1971) also obtained a positive relation between field dependence and Stroop interference for groups consisting of both men and women. Ray (1974), however, who also tested a mixed-sex group, obtained no relation between performance on the short form of the embedded figures test and Stroop performance except for interference scores obtained with nonsense symbol stimuli.

Cognitive Style

As far as the Stroop test is concerned, more encouraging results have come from those studies attempting to relate Stroop performance to aspects of "cognitive style." For example, Golden, Marsella, and Golden (1975a) reported that resistance to interference on the Stroop test was related to resistance to interference on other cognitive tasks, suggesting that this might define "a basic cognitive process." Klein (1954) related low interference proneness to flexible, rather than constricted, control; Gardner *et al.* (1959) claimed that for women it was associated with field independence; and Broverman (1960a, 1960b, 1964) held it to be characteristic of "strong automatizers," who are comparatively efficient in the performance of simple, repetitive tasks and who also appear to be interpersonally dominant, assertive, and reflective. However, the interrelations of these dimensions of cognitive style, and in particular the correlations of Stroop interference with other defining measures, are often unstable; and Gardner *et al.* (1959), like Bone and Eysenck (1972), found that different patterns of correlation obtained for men and for women. Stroop performance may well relate, at least to some extent, to more general dimensions of cognitive performance; but it is difficult to resist the conclusion of Golden *et al.* (1975b) that Stroop performance "is best understood in terms of specific cognitive processes . . . which have little implication for broader personality dimensions" (p. 602).

Sustained Attention

Performance in vigilance situations has traditionally been assessed in terms of (1) the *detection* or *hit rate,* that is, the proportion of signals correctly detected; (2) the *commission error* or *false-alarm rate,* that is, the number of occasions on which a signal is reported when none has, in fact, been presented; and (3) the *detection latency,* that is, the time taken to report the presence of a signal. In addition, decision-theory indexes and in particular the measures of detectability (d') and bias (β) derived from signal detection theory (SDT) have been employed to evaluate detection efficiency in vigilance tasks.

During the course of a vigil, which may last from about 30 minutes to 3 hours or more, detection rate typically declines and detection latency increases. This decline in detection efficiency is referred to as the vigilance decrement. When performance is evaluated in terms of SDT indexes, the vigilance decrement can be shown to be the result either of a criterion shift in the direction of greater stringency—so that the value of β increases, and fewer hits and false alarms are made—or of a progressive reduction in the observer's perceptual sensitivity—so that the value of d' declines, and the hit rate falls, whereas the false-alarm rate does not. Whether or not a sensitivity shift occurs appears to depend on the type of vigilance task being performed and reductions in perceptual sensitivity with time on task seem only to be found in task situations in which two conditions are satisfied: (1) signal and nonsignal events are presented for inspection at a high rate, around 24 events/min and above; and (2) signal detection requires a successive discrimination to be made, necessitating the comparison of successively presented stimulus configurations for identity or degree of similarity (see Davies, 1979; Parasuraman, 1979; Parasuraman & Davies, 1977).

There are thus several measures of performance in vigilance situations for which individual and group differences may be observed. In the following section, the degree to which the detection efficiency of the same individuals is consistent across successive time periods of the same testing session, across different testing sessions, and across different types of vigilance task is examined in an attempt to determine whether individual differences in vigilance performance are highly task specific, a view expressed by some investigators (e.g., Buckner & McGrath, 1963), or task-type specific, in the sense that such differences are closely linked to the ability requirements and information-processing demands imposed by different vigilance tasks.

Individual Differences in Vigilance: A Task Taxonomic Approach

Most vigilance tasks are either visual or auditory; although a few are vibrotactile or cutaneous, and in some studies, combined audio–visual presentations have been employed. Large individual differences in the performance of both auditory and visual vigilance tasks have been consistently reported, although for cutaneous and audio–visual tasks comparatively little evidence concerning individual differences is available. Detection efficiency, measured by the proportion of signals correctly detected, is generally quite consistent across time periods within the same task—whether visual or auditory (Baker, 1963; Buckner, 1963; Buckner, Harabedian, & McGrath, 1960, 1966; Mackworth, 1950)—and also across testing sessions with the same task (Buckner, *et al.,* 1960; Jenkins, 1958; Kennedy, 1971; Parasuraman, 1976; Sverko, 1968). Test–retest reliability coefficients for a variety of different vigilance tasks are thus usually fairly high. Significant correlations have also been reported between detection-efficiency measures obtained under "alerted conditions" prior to the main vigilance session and those obtained during the session itself (Benedetti & Loeb, 1972; Buckner *et al.,* 1966; Loeb & Binford, 1971).

In a number of studies conducted in the early 1960s correlations between measures of detection efficiency across tasks presented to different sensory modalities were found to be considerably lower than those obtained within or across sessions with the same task (e.g., Baker, 1963; Buckner *et al.,* 1960, 1966; Pope and McKechnie, Note 6). Such findings cast doubt on the existence of a common factor underlying vigilance performance and were interpreted as indicating that individual differences in detection efficiency were likely to be task specific (Buckner & McGrath, 1963). In several subsequent studies, attempts were made to determine those features of vigilance tasks contributing to inter and intramodal performance consistency. Among the task features that have been examined from this perspective are the degree to which the task is "coupled" to the observer, the difficulty of the discrimination required to detect signals, and the type of signal discrimination involved in the task, whether successive or simultaneous. One major difference between auditory and visual tasks is that the former are more tightly coupled to the observer's perceptual apparatus than are the latter (Elliott, 1960), and it might therefore be expected that higher correlations would be obtained for measures of detection efficiency between closely coupled visual tasks and auditory tasks than between loosely coupled visual tasks and auditory tasks. Although such an expectation is confirmed by the results of one study (Hatfield & Loeb, 1968), in other studies, it has been found that, if anything, intermodal correlations tend to be somewhat higher for loosely coupled than for closely coupled visual tasks (Hatfield & Soderquist, 1970; Loeb & Binford, 1971), and in any case, there are some inconsistencies between the intercorrelations obtained for different performance measures. It thus seems unlikely that the degree of task–observer coupling makes an important contribution to intermodal performance consistency in vigilance.

A number of studies have attempted to match the difficulty of the discrimination required to detect signals across tasks by equating group or individual values of signal detectability (d') prior to the main testing session through adjustments of such task parameters as signal intensity and duration. In the great majority of cases such manipulations produce significant intramodal and intermodal correlations for several measures of detection efficiency, including in addition to the proportion of correct detections, the false-alarm rate, d', and log β (e.g., Colquhoun, 1975; Loeb & Binford, 1971; Sverko, 1968; Tyler, Waag, & Halcomb, 1972).

The type of signal discrimination required to detect signals, as well as the difficulty of the discrimination involved, is an important determinant of performance consistency in sustained attention. In most studies of individual differences in vigilance performance, successive discrimination tasks have been employed in which, as noted earlier, a comparison must be made between successively presented signal and nonsignal events in terms of their identity or degree of similarity. Examples of widely used successive-discrimination vigilance tasks are those in which the observer is presented with a series of brief-duration light flashes and has to detect the occasional brighter, or dimmer, flash (e.g., Broadbent & Gregory, 1963b; Davies, Lang, & Shackleton, 1973; Hatfield & Loeb, 1968); or the observer is presented with a series of tones and has to detect the occasional louder, or shorter, tone (e.g., Deaton, Tobias, & Wilkinson, 1971; Hatfield & Soderquist, 1970). Successive-discrimination vigilance tasks may be contrasted with simultaneous-discrimination vigilance tasks in which the requirement is to identify a previously specified stimulus configuration that forms a part of a more complex sensory field. Examples of such tasks are those in which the requirement is to detect the presence of a disk of specified hue in a display of six simultaneously presented discs (e.g., Colquhoun, 1961, 1962) or the presence of a faint tone embedded in bursts of white noise (e.g., Hartley, Olsson, & Ingleby, Note 7).

Parasuraman and Davies (1977) obtained performance indexes from six pairs of vigilance tasks differing in presentation modality (visual or auditory) and in the type of discrimination required to detect signals (simultaneous or successive). They found that within task pairings in which neither the presentation modality nor the discrimination requirement was the same, correlations for both performance measures were low and nonsignificant; whereas when both task dimensions were compatible, the correlations observed were highly significant, varying between $+0.80$ and $+0.90$. The discrimination requirement also appeared to be a more important determinant of performance consistency than did presentation modality. These results, when considered in conjunction with the results from studies that have equated individual or group values of signal detectability, suggest that individual differences in vigilance are neither completely task specific nor mediated by a common vigilance factor. Instead, it appears that such differences are task-type specific, and that one of the major task characteristics determining performance consistency across tasks is the type of discrimination involved in signal detection.

Group Differences

In the development of possible selection tests for vigilance and monitoring tasks, researchers have used a variety of tests aimed at providing information about different psychological functions, in the hope that one of these would prove useful as a predictor of vigilance performance. In general, however, standard psychological tests of reasoning, memory span, and various aptitudes, both general and specific, have not been very successful in providing consistent and valid correlates of vigilance performance (Buckner et al., 1966); although in the most comprehensive study yet conducted, there was some indication that tests measuring clerical abilities might be useful predictors of within-session decrement scores (McGrath, Harabedian, & Buckner, 1960). However, this finding was not upheld in a subsequent cross-validation study (McGrath, 1963). Likewise, attempts to establish a relationship between monitoring performance and general intelligence have not been particularly fruitful, and a number of studies have failed to find differences between the vigilance performance of adults achieving relatively high and those of adults achieving relatively low scores on standard intelligence tests (Halcomb & Kirk, 1965; McGrath et al., 1960; Sipowicz & Baker, 1961; Ware, 1961). Incidental findings from several other experiments provide support for this result (Bakan, 1959; Colquhoun, 1959, 1962; Jenkins, 1958; Mackworth, 1950; Wilkinson, 1961), although one or two studies have found indications of a positive relationship between intelligence and vigilance performance (Cahoon, 1970; Kappauf & Powe, 1959). But, in general, the contribution of intelligence to the efficiency with which tasks requiring sustained attention are carried out seems to be slight; and, indeed, in one study, no differences between the detection scores of young mental deficients with a mean of IQ of 58.1 and those of normal intelligence groups were reported (Ware, Baker, & Sipowicz, 1962).

Similarly, little evidence has been advanced to support the view that sex accounts for a significant proportion of the variance in detection efficiency in vigilance (see Davies & Tune, 1970, for a review of early studies), and this conclusion is supported by the results of more recent studies conducted both with adults (Gale, Bull, Penfold, Coles, & Barraclough, 1972a; Parasuraman, 1976; Tolin & Fisher, 1974) and with children (Kirchner & Knopf, 1974; Sykes, Douglas, & Morganstern, 1973). However in most experiments, sex differences have been only of incidental interest to the experimenter, and sample sizes have been relatively small. The most comprehensive investigation of vigilance performance in which sex was the sole independent variable was carried out by Waag, Halcomb, and Tyler (1973), who tested 220 male and 220 female college students on a visual successive-discrimination task lasting for 1 hour. Although Waag et al., found that there was a significant difference in correct detection scores, with men detecting 10% more signals than women, and that men made significantly fewer false alarms during the first 20 minutes of the task, the magnitude of these effects was small. Sex accounted for only 4% of the variance in detection rate and for less than 10% of the variance in false alarms. Neither intelligence nor sex, therefore, appears to be a particularly important determinant of performance in sustained attention tasks, and in the remainder of this section the effects of age and personality are examined.

Age Differences in Vigilance Performance

In contrast to selective attention, age differences in sustained attention have been more extensively explored in adults and the elderly than in children, although several studies have compared the vigilance performance of children diagnosed as "learning disabled" (Dykman, Ackerman, Clements, & Peters, 1971) with that of children of "average" learning ability. Perhaps not surprisingly in view of the important part attention is presumed to play in learning (Friedrichs, Hertz, Moynahan, Simpson, Arnold, Christy, Cooper, & Stevenson, 1971; Trabasso & Bower, 1968), the results of these latter studies indicate that the detection efficiency of learning-disabled children is significantly poorer

TABLE 11.2

Mean Number and Range of Omission Errors Made by Boys and Girls
of Different Age Groups during the Performance
of a 40-Minute Auditory Vigilance Task[a]

Age (yrs.)	Boys			Girls		
	N^b	Errors	Range	N	Errors	Range
7	31	9.48	1–29	36	5.30	0–23
8	48	8.63	1–27	41	4.56	0–17
9	54	3.65	0–15	40	3.27	0–11
10	57	2.93	1–12	44	2.75	0–12
11	32	1.40	0–9	54	1.75	0–7
12	66	1.60	0–9	56	1.09	0–6
13	35	1.57	0–9	18	1.50	0–8

[a] From Gale and Lynn (1972).

[b] N represents the number of subjects in each age group.

than that of non-learning-disabled children (e.g., Anderson, Halcomb, & Doyle, 1973; Anderson, Halcomb, Gordon, & Oxolins, 1974; Douglas, 1972; Doyle, Anderson, & Halcomb, 1976).

The ability of children to sustain attention, as assessed by indexes of vigilance performance, appears to improve with age. In one of the most thorough investigations of the development of vigilance in children, Gale and Lynn (1972) administered a 40-minute auditory vigilance task, requiring the detection of an occasional digit in a series of letters, to groups of schoolchildren of average intelligence between the ages of 7 and 13.5 years, the total sample size being 612. Their results, with the scores of boys and girls presented separately, are shown in Table 11.2. Commission errors were apparently extremely rare and were not analyzed. As can be seen from Table 11.2, detection efficiency improved with age for both boys and girls up to 11 years, with a particularly marked improvement taking place between the ages of 8 and 9 years in boys. Girls detected significantly more signals than boys at ages 7, 8, and 12; but neither sex nor age differences in the extent of the vigilance decrement were obtained. Anderson et al., (1974) also reported an improvement in detection efficiency on a vigilance task for children aged 9 years and over compared to children between the ages of 6 and 8 years, and Sykes et al., (1973) obtained a significant correlation between age and detection rate on the Continuous Performance Test (a test originally developed to aid in the diagnosis of brain damage; Rosvold, Mirsky, Sarason, Bransome, & Beck, 1956) for children in the age range of 5–11 years.

Studies of adult age differences in vigilance suggest that detection efficiency tends to decrease with age, from about the late fifties onwards. The principal results obtained from 11 studies of age and vigilance are shown in Table 11.3,

TABLE 11.3

A Summary of the Principal Features of 11 Studies of Age and Vigilance[a]

Source	Task[b]	Task duration (min.)	Task type[c]	Composition of age groups — Mean age (yrs.)[d]	Age range (yrs.)	Mean difference[e]	Differential decrement
Canestrari (Note 8)							
Experiment 1	CPT	10	Sim (Signal: X or T) (A)	—	—	CD: Y > O FA: O > Y	—
Experiment 2	CPT	10	Succ. (Signal: A followed by X) (A)	—	—	CD: Y > O FA: NSD	—
Griew and Davies (1962)[f]							
Experiment 1	Bakan	40	Succ. (A)	—	Y (19–31), N = 20 M O (45–60), N = 20 M	CD: Y > O FA: NSD	—
Experiment 2	Audio–visual checking	40	Succ. (A)	—	Y (20–33), N = 20 M O (48–66), N = 20 M	CD: NSD FA: NSD	—
Experiment 3	Bakan	40	Succ. (A)	—	Y (18–31), N = 12 M O (44–61), N = 12 M	CD: NSD FA: NSD	No
York (1962)	Detection of double flash from background of single flashes	(?)	Succ. (V)	Y (c 30.0), N = 12 M; MA (c 50.0), N = 12 M; O (c 70.0), N = M;	—	CD: NSD	—
Davies and Griew (1963)	Bakan	75	Succ. (A)	—	Y (17–29), N = 15 M O (41–58), N = 15 M	CD: NSD FA: NSD	—
Surwillo and Quilter (1964)	Clock test	60	Succ. (V)	Y (43.7), N = 53 M O (71.0), N = 53 M	—	CD: Y > O DL: NSD	Yes O > Y
Neal and Pearson (1966)							
Experiment 1	Bakan	64	Succ. (A)	—	Y (21–30), N = 16 M and F O (39–62), N = 8 M	CD: NSD FA: NSD	
Experiment 2	Detection of increase in duration of 1000-Hz tone	60	Succ. (A)	—	Y (21–30), N = 16 M and F O (39–62), N = 8 M	CD: NSD FA: NSD	

Study	Task	Duration (min)	Task type[c]	Mean age (N)[d]	Age range[d]	Performance measures[e]	Age difference
Surwillo (1966)	Clock test	60	Succ. (V)	Y (36.4), O (74.3), N = 33 M, N = 33 M	Y (22–45), O (69–85)	—	Yes O > Y
Tune (1966a)	Detection of 3 consecutive digits from 10-digit sequence; sequences presented at 10-sec intervals	40	Succ. (A)	Y (36.9), O (60.6), N = 14, N = 14	—	CD: NSD FA: O > Y	—
Bicknell (1970)	Detection of a greater downward deflection of a dot of light in the second of a pair of downward light movements presented as one event	60	Sim. (V)	Y (21.0), MA (40.9), O (70.6), N = 10 M and F, N = 10 M and F, N = 10 M and F	Y (17–29); MA (30–53), O (60–85);	CD: NSD FA: O > MA and Y	Yes O and MA > Y Yes O > MA and Y
Harkins, Nowlin, Ramm & Schroeder (1974)[g]	Odd-even task	10.2	Succ. (V)	Y (21.3), O (67.6), N = 41 M and F, N = 105 M and F	—	CD: Y > O FA: O > Y DL: O > Y	Yes O > Y
Davies and Davies (1975)[h]	CPT[b]	20	Sim (Signal: A or X) (V)	—	Y (18–31), N = 20 M; O (65–72), N = 20 M;	CD: Y > O	No

[a] After Davies and Parasuraman (1982).

[b] Continuous Performance Test (CPT).

[c] Task types: Successive discrimination (Succ.), simultaneous discrimination (Sim.); auditory (A) and visual (V).

[d] Age groups: Young (Y); middle aged (MA), old (O); sex: male (M) and female (F); and N represents the number of subjects in each age group.

[e] Performance measures: Correct detection (CD), false alarms (FA), detection latency (DL), and no significant difference (NSD).

[f] In this study there was a difference in the response requirement between Experiments 1 and 3. In Experiment 1, subjects were instructed to write down the digits constituting each signal; in Experiment 3, they were asked to press a response button whenever they detected a signal.

[g] In this study, a middle-aged group of subjects was also tested.

[h] This study also investigated the effects of noise and time of day. Only the results for the quiet condition, pooled over times of day, are shown here.

from which it can be seen that when significant differences in performance have been reported, older individuals have consistently performed less well than younger individuals. In six of the experiments summarized in Table 11.3, the detection rate of older individuals is lower; in four, their false-alarm rate is higher; and in four, their detection efficiency declines at a faster rate with time at work. Age differences seem equally likely to occur in successive- and simultaneous-discrimination tasks, although there is a tendency for such differences to be found more frequently in visual tasks than in auditory ones; age differences in at least one performance measure were obtained in five out of six experiments in which a visual task was used, but in only four out of nine cases in which an auditory task was employed.

Adult age differences in vigilance performance have thus been reported fairly frequently, and the detection efficiency of individuals over the age of 60 tends to be poorer than that of individuals in younger age groups, especially for tasks in which the event-presentation rate is high (Davies, 1968; Talland, 1966; Thompson, Opton, & Cohen, 1963). Although decision theory measures have seldom been employed in studies of adult age differences in vigilance, there are some indications that the perceptual sensitivity of the observer may decline with age (Canestrari, Note 8, Experiment 2; Davies & Davies, 1975; Tune, 1966b), although any such reduction in sensitivity is likely to be fairly small and to occur quite gradually (Sheehan & Drury, 1971) unless brain damage is also present (see Davies & Parasuraman, 1982, for a review). Older people also seem to adopt more cautious response criteria in some signal detection and industrial inspection tasks (Craik, 1969; Davies & Sparrow, in press), but the scanty evidence from vigilance situations suggests that older individuals may sometimes adopt more risky criteria (Bicknell, 1970; Tune, 1966a). Although some reduction in perceptual sensitivity probably occurs with age, it is less clear what effect the aging process has on criterion placement in monitoring tasks. It is possible, however, that personality factors may exert some influence on age differences in criterion placement in vigilance. Tune (1966a), for example, found that older extraverts made over three times as many false alarms as did older introverts, although detection rates were about the same in both groups. Younger extraverts also made more false alarms than younger introverts, but the difference was much less marked.

Personality and Vigilance

The aspect of group differences that has been most thoroughly explored in relation to vigilance performance is undoubtedly personality, and the personality dimension that has received most attention is that of introversion–extraversion. The principal inspiration for studies of the relation between extraversion and detection efficiency comes from various theoretical speculations during the

1950s that suggested that introverts were better equipped for work on prolonged and monotonous tasks than were extraverts because of the former's higher cortical arousal and greater resistance to the establishment of inhibitory processes (Broadbent, 1958; Claridge, 1960; Eysenck, 1957). Despite some differences of emphasis among these theoretical positions, they were in agreement in predicting that extraverts should manifest a greater decrement in performance over time in vigilance tasks. The extent to which this prediction has been borne out can be seen in Table 11.4, which provides a summary of the main features of 13 studies comparing the detection efficiency of introverts and extraverts. As the table indicates, in the majority of studies differences have been reported between introverts and extraverts on some measure of vigilance performance; and when significant differences have been reported, introverts make more correct detections and fewer false alarms and exhibit less decrement. The only study in Table 11.4 to report no significant differences of any kind in the vigilance performance of introverts and extraverts is that of Gale, Bull, Penfold, Coles, & Barraclough (1972).

Of the studies summarized in Table 11.4, 10 provide data concerning a possible difference between introverts and extraverts in the magnitude of the vigilance decrement, but only 4 report that introverts exhibit a significantly smaller decrement than extraverts. As the table indicates, these studies differ from the remainder in two main ways: (1) Subjects were selected from the two extremes of the distribution of introversion–extraversion scores and (2) the type of task employed required a successive rather than a simultaneous distribution to be made in order for signals to be detected. Thus at first sight, the evidence for a differential decrement between introverts and extraverts is not, perhaps, as strong as might be expected on theoretical grounds. But, as noted earlier in this section, declines in detection efficiency can be associated either with a gradual reduction in perceptual sensitivity or with the adoption of a progressively more stringent response criterion with time on task. Reductions in perceptual sensitivity, as indexed by d' or a related measure, occur only when the vigilance task being performed possesses both a high event-presentation rate and a successive-discrimination requirement. Because it seems unlikely that sensitivity shifts can be abolished, or even greatly attenuated, through training (see Davies & Parasuraman, 1982), such shifts may be regarded as reflecting a more fundamental decline in perceptual efficiency than do criterion changes. If, therefore, there is a genuine difference between introverts and extraverts in the ability to sustain attention over relatively long periods of time, such a difference should be more readily observable in successive discrimination vigilance tasks with a high event-presentation rate. In the only relevant study (Hastrup, 1979), it was indeed found that extraverts exhibited a greater sensitivity decrement than did introverts, the difference being marginally significant. However this difference was observed only when the discrimination requirement was relatively easy. But because in

TABLE 11.4

A Summary of the Principal Features of 13 Studies of Temperament and Vigilance[a]

Source	Task[b]	Task duration (min.)	Task type[c]	Personality test[d]	Extreme groups[e]	Performance measure[f]	Mean difference	Differential decrement
Bakan (1959)	Bakan	80	Succ. (A)	HSS (Part 2)	No (M)	Hits	I > E (first two subperiods only)	No
Bakan, Belton, & Toth (1963)	Bakan[G] (only half the subjects)	48	Succ. (A)	MPI[N]	Yes (M + F)	Hits	NSD	Yes (I < E)
Davies and Hockey (1966)	Visual checking[G]	32	Succ. (V)	MPI[N]	Yes (F)	Hits	NSD	Yes (I < E)
						FAs	NSD	No
Hogan (1966)	CPT	10	Succ. (V)	MPI[N]	No (F)	Hits	Yes (I > E)	No
Tune (1966b)	Detection of 3 consecutive and different odd digits from a 10-digit sequence; sequences presented at 10-sec intervals	40	Succ. (A)	HSS (Part 2)	No (M + F)	Hits	NSC	NR
						FAs	Unsociability (introversion) significantly and negatively correlated with FAs	NR
						d'	NSC	NR
						β	Unsociability (introversion) significantly and positively correlated with β	NR
Carr (1969)	Detection of increase in duration of tone burst	40	Succ. (A)	EPI	Yes (F)	Hits	Yes (I > E)	Yes (I < E)
						FAs	Yes (I < E)	Yes (I < E)
						d'	Yes (I > E)	No
						β	Yes (I > E)	No
						DLs	Yes (I < E)	No

428

Study	Task	N	Task type	Test	Sex diff.	Measure	Result	
Davies, Hockey, & Taylor (1969)	Visual Bakan	40	Succ. (V)	MPI[N] and HSS (Part 2)	No (M + F)	Hits	NSD	No
						FAs	NSD	No
Krupski, Raskin, & Bakan (1971)	Bakan	48	Succ. (A)	EPI	No (M)	FAs	Extroversion significantly and positively correlated with FAs ($p < .10$)	NR
Gale, Bull, Penfold, Coles, & Barraclough (1972)	Bakan[G]	60	Succ. (A)	EPI[N]	No (M + F)	Hits	NSD	No
Keister and McLaughlin (1972)	Bakan	48	Succ. (A)	EPI[N]	Yes (M + F)	Hits	NSD	Yes (I < E)
Purohit (1972)	Detection of increase in intensity of light	40	Succ. (V)	NKT	Yes (M + F)	Hits	Yes (I > E)	NR
						FAs	I < E (significance level not reported)	NR
Harkins and Geen (1975)	Detection of unmodulated line on noisy CRT	42	Sim. (V)	EPI	Yes (F)	Hits	Yes (I > E)	No
						FAs	Yes (I < E)	No
						d'	Yes (I > E)	No
						$\log \beta$	Yes (I > E)	No
Gange, Geen, & Harkins (1979)	Detection of unmodulated line on noisy CRT	42	Sim. (V)	EPI	Yes (M)	Hits	Yes (I > E)	No
						FAs	NSD	No

[a] After Davies and Parasuraman (1982).

[b] Superscript G indicates that subjects were group tested; Continuous Performance Test (CPT) and cathode-ray tube (CRT).

[c] Task types: successive discrimination (Succ.); simultaneous discrimination (Sim.); auditory (A) and visual (V).

[d] Superscript N indicates that the study matched extroverts and introverts for neuroticism scores or reported no correlation between neuroticism and performance; Heron Sociability Scale (HSS). Eysenck Personality Inventory (EPI). Neymann–Kohlstad Test (NKT).

[e] Sex: male (M) and female (F); temperament: introvert (I) and extrovert (E).

[f] Performance measures: false alarms (FA), detection latency (DL), no significant correlation (NSC), no significant difference (NSD), and not reported (NR).

Hastrup's study subjects were classified as introverts and extraverts on the basis of the median extraversion scale score, this experiment merits replication using extreme groups.

Significant overall differences in detection rate between introverts and extraverts have been obtained in only about half the studies summarized in Table 11.4 that provide relevant data, although in each case the detection efficiency of introverts is greater. Introverts also appear to make fewer false alarms than do extraverts, and the few studies utilizing decision-theory analyses report that the perceptual sensitivity of introverts is superior to that of extraverts (Carr, 1969; Harkins & Geen, 1975). The fact that some studies report significant differences in the detection efficiency of introverts and extraverts whereas others do not may be due, at least in part, to procedural factors. There are, for instance, considerable differences between studies in the type of task employed and its relative difficulty, in the criterion cutoff scores adopted for the purpose of selecting introverted and extraverted groups, in the extent to which neuroticism (an additional measure provided by the Maudsley and Eysenck personality inventories) was controlled for, and with respect to whether the personality test used sampled only sociability scores (as in the case of Part 2 of the Heron inventory) or impulsivity scores as well (as in the case of the Eysenck Personality Inventory). There are some grounds for believing that impulsivity is a more important correlate of performance decrement in monotonous tasks than is sociability (e.g., Thackray, Jones, & Touchstone, 1974). However, as noted earlier, reliable differences between the vigilance performance of introverts and extraverts may only be found at the extremes of the distribution of extraversion scores and then only when the memory and time pressure demands characteristic of high event rate successive-discrimination tasks are present. The generally poorer performance of extraverts in vigilance situations may be a consequence of the greater boredom that extraverts apparently experience during monotonous work (see Davies, Shackleton, & Parasuraman, 1983, for a review), which may be attributable to greater "stimulus hunger" on the part of extraverts (Gale, 1969) coupled with the tendency to generate more vivid and more frequent visual imagery (Gale, Morris, Lucas, & Richardson, 1972; Morris & Gale, 1974), which is likely to result in attention being less completely and less consistently focused on task-relevant events. The probable outcome would be an overall reduction in the level of sensitivity, as has been shown in divided-attention experiments involving vigilance (Broadbent & Gregory, 1963a), and also, perhaps, a steeper decline in detection rate with time at work (Antrobus, Coleman, & Singer, 1967). Extraversion is related, albeit loosely, to two other personality measures, field dependence and autonomic lability. Extraverted subjects are more likely to be field dependent (Evans, 1966; Kennedy, 1977) and autonomically "stabile" (Coles, Gale, & Kline, 1971; Crider & Lunn, 1971; Lader & Wing, 1966; Mangan & O'Gorman, 1969). The field dependence–independence dimension was briefly described earlier in the chapter; the *autonomic lability dimension* refers to the frequency with which spontaneous electrodermal responses (EDRs) are emitted during rest or during stimulation (Lacey & Lacey, 1958), a measure that is inversely related to the speed with which the electrodermal orienting response habituates to a series of affectively neutral, above threshold, stimuli (e.g., Katkin & McCubbin, 1969). "Labile" individuals who produce a greater number of spontaneous EDRs, tend to exhibit a slower rate of EDR habituation than do stabile individuals; and there is a positive correlation between the number of spontaneous EDRs and the number of trials required to reach a criterion of habituation ranging, in different studies, from about $+0.50$ to $+0.75$. Crider and Lunn (1971) reviewed a number of studies of electrodermal lability and suggested that lability should be regarded as a dimension of personality measurable in terms of either the number of spontaneous EDRs or the rate of habituation of the orienting response (OR). These two measures were subsequently labeled *spontaneous* and *trial lability*, respectively (Sostek, 1978).

Very few studies have investigated the relationship of field dependence to detection efficiency in vigilance situations; and although there is some indication that the detection efficiency of field-independent subjects is superior to that of field-dependent subjects (Cahoon, 1970; Moore & Gross, 1973), it seems likely that performance differences between these two groups is affected by task type (Kennedy, 1977). On the other hand, several studies have examined the detection efficiency of stabile and labile subjects, so classified either by measures of spontaneous or trial lability or by some combination of the two (Coles *et al.,* 1971; Crider & Augenbraun, 1972; Hastrup, 1979; Parasuraman, 1975; Siddle, 1972; Sostek, 1976, 1978). All these studies employed auditory successive-discrimination tasks in which the event-presentation rate was relatively high. For every case in which a vigilance decrement was reported, stabile subjects showed a greater decline in detection efficiency with time; and in two experiments, those of Sostek (1978) and Hastrup (1979), they showed a greater decrement in perceptual sensitivity (d' or $P[A]$); although in Hastrup's study this finding was only obtained in the more difficult version of her task. In general, measures of trial lability seem to be more closely related to detection efficiency than do measures of spontaneous lability, and labile subjects tend to detect more signals and to make more false alarms than do stabile subjects. To some extent, therefore, the vigilance performance of labile and stabile subjects resembles that of introverts and extraverts; although, as indicated earlier, a reliable correlation between extraversion and autonomic lability has not been consistently observed.

Summary and Conclusions

The research reviewed thus far in this chapter provides a reasonably consistent, although incomplete, picture of individual and group differences in the performance of selective- and sustained-attention tasks. With respect to individual differences, there is little or no support for a general time-sharing ability or for a general vigilance ability; and the existence of a general selective-attention ability seems unlikely. Instead, a number of specific abilities, linked to specific task variables and information-processing demands, appear to be involved to varying degrees in the performance of all these tasks. In the case of vigilance tasks, for example, two critical determinants of intertask performance consistency are the modality to which information is presented and the type of discrimination required to detect target events, with the rate at which information is presented and the ratio of target to "background" events also being important variables. The nature of the information-processing demands imposed by a particular vigilance task is determined by the mix of critical variables that the task contains; some vigilance tasks impose heavier demands on working memory, some permit estimates of target probability to be more easily formulated, and so on. But although individual differences in vigilance performance are task-type specific, the translation of critical determinants of performance consistency into underlying specific abilities necessary for efficient vigilance performance must remain somewhat speculative in the absence of large-scale factor-analytic studies of monitoring behavior.

Whatever the specific abilities underlying vigilance performance may be, it seems probable that sustained and selective attention abilities are largely independent. One of the most widely used "cognitive" vigilance tasks is the Bakan task (Bakan, Note 9, 1959; Bakan & Manley, 1963; Bakan et al., 1963; Davies & Krkovic, 1965; Jones, Smith, & Broadbent, 1979), which consists of a series of digits presented at the rate of one per second from which subjects are required to detect certain specified three-digit sequences. This task was originally derived from Wittenborn's (1943) factor analysis of attention tests, in which Wittenborn found that picking out various sequences of numbers or letters was most heavily loaded on what he called an "attention" or "mental concentration" factor. Moray (1969) reported a correlational study in which performance on the Wittenborn digits and letters tests was examined in relation to shadowing efficiency (omission and commission errors) in a selective listening task. Although the correlation between performance on the digits and letters tests was found to be positive and significant, no other correlation proved to be reliable; and Moray concluded that the relation between the two kinds of attention was negligible. Despite the fact that Moray's study was a small-scale one and merits replication and extension, it reinforces the view expressed by many researchers that, in Kinchla's (1980) words, "attention should *not* be thought of as a single entity" (p. 214, emphasis in original). Kinchla suggested that three kinds of investigation bear on the issue of selectivity in information processing: the study of information trade-offs, in which selective listening tasks are included; the study of "perceptual intrusions," which principally involves the Stroop test; and the study of "attention switching," that is, of "situations which seem to involve a shift from processing information from one source to processing that from another" (p. 215). In a factor-analytic study of attention tasks, Sack and Rice (1974) obtained evidence for three factors labeled respectively *selectivity* (the ability to establish a focus of attention), *resistance to distraction* (the ability to maintain that focus for as long as is necessary), and *shifting* (the ability to relinquish one focus of attention and to establish a second). Various embedded figures tasks, used in the measurement of field articulation and dependence (discussed earlier in the chapter), were most closely associated with the selectivity factor; although as noted earlier, there appears to be no relation between field articulation and selective-listening performance (Gross *et al.*, 1973). A group version of the Stroop test loaded both on selectivity and shifting, and a cancellation task loaded both on the resistance to distraction and the shifting factors. Four other tasks (distracting contexts, arithmetic operations, triangles, and anagrams) loaded exclusively on either the shifting or the resistance to distraction factors.

There thus appear to be at least three distinct abilities involved in the performance of selective-attention tasks: selectivity, resistance to distraction, and switching or shifting. Following Bobrow and Norman (1975), Rabbitt (1979b) distinguished between two kinds of attentional selectivity: "passive data driven" attentional selectivity, which is illustrated, for example, by repetition effects in visual-search and choice-response tasks; and "active autonomous memory driven" attentional selectivity, which is involved in tasks in which subjects are "set" to detect targets possessing certain characteristics. Rabbitt observed that adult age differences are not found in data-driven attentional selectivity, whereas such differences are quite marked in memory-driven attentional selectivity, suggesting that "age decrements in selective attention may be related to failures in central control processes" (p. 93). Resistance to distraction can also be subdivided in terms of the kind of distraction involved, whether "task intrinsic," as in selective listening, speeded classification or the Stroop test; or "task extrinsic" as in the performance of a task in the presence of loud noise, in which considerable individual and group differences also exist (see Jones & Davies, 1983, for a review). The ability to shift or switch the focus of attention and to establish a new one has been shown to be a good predictor of accident rates among bus drivers (Kahneman, Ben-Ishai, & Lotan, 1973) and is of some practical importance. Identification of the abilities underlying performance in selective- and sustained-attention tasks is a preliminary to the development of an adequate task taxonomy, and, in turn, such a taxonomy may help to generate explanations for individual and group differences in task performance.

With respect to group differences, children show improvements with age in all the tasks surveyed in this chapter, although the age at which "adult" levels of performance are attained may differ from task to task. Older adults, over about the age of 60, show decrements compared to younger adults in all tasks except, according to one study, central–incidental tasks; and there is some uncertainty about an age-related decrement in time-sharing. Sex differences appear only to be found in the performance of vigilance tasks, and there is some evidence of a relationship between intelligence and performance in central–incidental and speeded classification tasks. Although the evidence relating to personality differences is not abundant, it seems clear that introverts are superior to extraverts in the performance of vigilance tasks, whereas it is likely that extraverts are superior to introverts both in time-sharing and in performance on the Stroop test. Such differences deserve further investigation.

Theories of attention can be divided into perhaps four interrelated categories: (1) structural theories, such as Broadbent's (1958) filter theory; (2) resource theories, such as Kahneman's undifferentiated capacity theory (Kahneman, 1973) and later approaches such as multiple-resource theory (see Wickens, Chapter 3, this volume); (3) state theories, such as unidimensional arousal theory, elaborations of this approach (Broadbent, 1971) and "variable state theory" (Hockey, Chapter 12, this volume); and (4) control theories (Rabbitt, 1979a, 1981). Although no theories have been developed specifically to deal with individual and group differences in the performance of selective- and sustained-attention tasks, some attempts have been made to use existing theories, particularly capacity and arousal theories, in addressing questions of individual and/or group differences. Thus versions of capacity theory have been used in the interpretation of both age-related performance improvements in children and age-related performance decrements in the elderly. Similarly, arousal theory has been employed to explain performance differences between introverts and extraverts.

Lansman and Hunt (1982) examined individual differences in secondary-task performance in dual-task situations in which one task is designated as primary and the other as secondary from a capacity-theory perspective. They argued that secondary-task performance provides a relatively direct measure of residual mental capacity and an indirect measure of the level of skill attained on the primary task; and they developed a paradigm designed to test the "easy-to-hard prediction," whereby secondary-task performance during an easy primary task should predict performance on a difficult version of the same primary task. The easy-to-hard prediction assumes that the performance of primary and secondary tasks is determined by the availability of a limited attentional resource for which both tasks compete, that spare mental capacity during the easy version of the primary task can be utilized in the performance of the more difficult version, and that the allocation of mental capacity to the primary and secondary tasks is both consistent and in accordance with the experimenter's instructions.

In a series of experiments, Lansman and Hunt (1982) tested the easy-to-hard prediction using a continuous paired-associate recall task and a spatial memory task requiring a same–different response as primary tasks; the secondary task in each case required either a manual or a vocal response to be made to simple visual or auditory probes. Clear support for the easy-to-hard prediction was obtained in the case of the paired-associate task but not in the case of the spatial memory task, a result attributed by Lansman and Hunt to the possibility that performance at the spatial memory task was less determined by resource availability than was performance on the paired-associate task. Therefore, only partial confirmation of a capacity-theory interpretation of individual differences in secondary-task performance was obtained in this study; and capacity theory also faces some difficulties in explaining age-related performance increments, as Chi (1976) has indicated in a review of memory development in children. It seems extremely improbable that explanations of age differences in performance will be of the same kind as are explanations of personality, sex, or intelligence differences; or even that explanations of age differences in performance in children will take the same form as explanations of age differences in performance in adulthood. The most successful theoretical accounts of individual and group differences are likely to be nonunitary in nature and to incorporate features from all the types of theory just outlined, but perhaps particularly from state and control theories.

Reference Notes

1. Sverko, B. Individual differences in time sharing performance. (Rep. No. TR ARL-77-4/ AFOSR-77-4). Urbana-Champaign: University of Illinois Aviation Research Laboratory, 1977.
2. Hawkins, H., Church, M. & DeLemos, S. Time-sharing is not a unitary ability. Eugene, Oregon: University of Oregon Center for Cognitive & Perceptual Research, ONR Technical Report No. 2, June, 1978.
3. Hawkins, H., Rodriguez, E. & Reicher, G. M. Is time-sharing a general ability? Eugene, Oregon: University of Oregon Center for Cognitive & Perceptual Research, ONR Technical Report, No. 3, June, 1979.
4. Schonfield, D. & Trueman, V. *Variations on the Stroop theme*. Paper read to a meeting of the Gerontological Society, Portland, Oregon, September 1974.
5. Taylor, A., Davies, D. R. & Marsh, G. R. *Adult age differences in two versions of the Stroop test*. Unpublished manuscript, University of Leicester, Leicester, 1983.
6. Pope, L. T. & McKechnie, D. F. *Correlation between visual and auditory vigilance performance*. (Tech. Rep. No. TR-63-57). US Air Force, Aerospace Medical Research Laboratory, Wright Patterson Air Force Base, 1963.
7. Hartley, L. R., Olsson, R. & Ingleby, J. D. *Visual assistance in an auditory vigilance task*. Unpublished Report, Medical Research Council Applied Psychology Unit, Cambridge, England, 1973.
8. Canestrari, R. E. *The effects of aging on vigilance performance*. Paper presented to a meeting of the Gerontological Society, Miami, Florida, December, 1962.
9. Bakan, P. *Preliminary tests of vigilance for verbal materials*. (Research Note No. 52–57): US Air Force Human Resources Research Center, Lackland Air Force Base, 1952.

References

Anderson, R. P., Halcomb, C. G., & Doyle, R. B. The measurement of attentional deficits. *Exceptional Children*, 1973, *39*, 534–539.

Anderson, R. P., Halcomb, C. G., Gordon, W., & Oxolins, D. A. Measurement of attention distractability in LD children. *Academic Therapy*, 1974, *9*, 261–266.

Anooshian, L. J., & McCulloch, R. A. Developmental changes in dichotic listening with categorized word lists. *Developmental Psychology*, 1979, *15*, 280–287.

Anooshian, L. J., & Prilop, L. Developmental trends for auditory selective attention: Dependence on central–incidental word relations. *Child Development*, 1980, *51*, 45–54.

Antrobus, J. S., Coleman, R., & Singer, J. L. Signal-detection performance by subjects differing in predisposition to day-dreaming. *Journal of Consulting Psychology*, 1967, *31*, 487–491.

Bakan, P. Extraversion–introversion and improvement in an auditory vigilance task. *British Journal of Psychology*, 1959, *50*, 325–332.

Bakan, P., Belton, J. A., & Toth, J. C. Extraversion–introversion and decrement in an auditory vigilance task. In D. N. Buckner & J. J. McGrath (Eds.), *Vigilance: A symposium*. New York: McGraw-Hill, 1963.

Bakan, P., & Manley R. Effect of visual deprivation on auditory vigilance. *British Journal of Psychology*, 1963, *54*, 115–119.

Baker, C. H. Consistency of performance in two visual vigilance tasks. In D. N. Buckner and J. J. McGrath (Eds.) *Vigilance: A symposium*. New York: McGraw-Hill, 1963.

Benedetti, L. H., & Loeb, M. A comparison of auditory monitoring performance in blind subjects with that of sighted subjects in light and dark. *Perception and Psychophysics*, 1972, *11*, 10–16.

Bettner, L. G., Jarvik, L. F., & Blum, J. E. Stroop color–word test, nonpsychotic organic brain syndrome, and chromosome loss in aged twins. *Journal of Gerontology*, 1971, *26*, 458–469.

Bicknell, A. *Aging, arousal and vigilance*. Unpublished doctoral thesis, Texas Tech University, Lubbock, 1970.

Bobrow, D. G., & Norman, D. A. Some principles of memory schemata. In D. G. Bobrow & A. M. Collins (Eds.), *Representation and understanding: Studies in cognitive science*. New York: Academic Press, 1975.

Bone, R. N., & Eysenck, H. J. Extraversion, field dependence and the Stroop test. *Perceptual and Motor Skills*, 1972, *34*, 873–874.

Borod, J. C., & Goodglass, H. Lateralization of linguistic and melodic processing with age. *Neuropsychologia*, 1980, *18*, 79–83.

Botwinick, J. *Aging and behaviour*. New York: Springer, 1978.

Broadbent, D. E. The role of auditory localization in attention and memory span. *Journal of Experimental Psychology*, 1954, *47*, 191–196.

Broadbent, D. E. *Perception and communication*. London: Pergamon, 1958.

Broadbent, D. E. *Decision and stress*. London: Academic Press, 1971.

Broadbent, D. E., & Gregory, M. Division of attention and the decision theory of signal detection. *Proceedings of the Royal Society (Series B)*, 1963a, *158*, 221–231.

Broadbent, D. E., & Gregory M. Vigilance considered as a statistical decision. *British Journal of Psychology*, 1963b, *54*, 309–323.

Broadbent, D. E., & Heron, A. Effects of a subsidiary task on performance involving immediate memory in younger and older men. *British Journal of Psychology*, 1962, *53*, 189–198.

Broverman, D. M. Cognitive style and intra-individual variation in abilities. *Journal of Personality*, 1960a, *28*, 291–295.

Broverman, D. M. Dimensions of cognitive style. *Journal of Personality*, 1960b, *28*, 169–185.

Broverman, D. M. Generality and behavioral correlates of cognitive styles. *Journal of Consulting Psychology*, 1964, *28*, 487–500.

Bryden, M. P., & Allard, F. Dichotic listening and the development of linguistic processes. In M. Kinsbourne (Ed.), *Asymmetrical function of the brain*. Cambridge: Cambridge University Press, 1978.

Buckner, D. N. An individual-difference approach to explaining vigilance performance. In D. N. Buckner & J. J. McGrath (Eds.), *Vigilance: A symposium*. New York: McGraw-Hill, 1963.

Buckner, D. N., Harabedian, A., & McGrath, J. J. *A study of individual differences in vigilance performance* (Tech. Rep. 2). Los Angeles: Human Factors Research Inc., 1960.

Buckner, D. N., Harabedian, A., & McGrath, J. J. Individual differences in vigilance performance. *Journal of Engineering Psychology*, 1966, *5*, 69–85.

Buckner, D. N., & McGrath, J. J. A comparison of performance on single and dual sensory mode vigilance tasks. In D. N. Buckner & J. J. McGrath (Eds.), *Vigilance: A symposium*. New York: McGraw-Hill, 1963.

Bush, M. Relationship between color–word test interference and MMPI indices of psychoticism and defensive rigidity in normal males and females. *Journal of Consulting and Clinical Psychology*, 1975, *43*, 926.

Caird, W. K. Aging and short-term memory. *Journal of Gerontology*, 1966, *21*, 295–299.

Cahoon, R. L. Vigilance performance under hypoxia. *Journal of Applied Psychology* 1970, *54*, 479–483.

Callaway, E. The influence of amobarbital (amylobarbitone) and methamphetamine on the focus of attention. *Journal of Mental Science*, 1959, *105*, 382–392.

Cammock, T., & Cairns, E. Concurrent validity of a children's version of the Stroop color–word test: The Fruit Distraction Test. *Perceptual and Motor Skills*, 1979, *49*, 611–616.

Carr, G. D. *Introversion–extraversion and vigilance performance*. Unpublished doctoral thesis. Tufts University, Boston, 1969.

Chapman, M. Dimensional separability or flexibility of attention? Age trends in perceiving configural stimuli. *Journal of Experimental Child Psychology*, 1981, *31*, 332–349.

Chi, M. T. H. Short-term memory limitations in children: Capacity or processing deficits? *Memory and Cognition*, 1976, *4*, 559–572.

Claridge, G. S. The excitation–inhibition balance in neurotics. In H. J. Eysenck (Ed.), *Experiments in personality* (Vol. 2). London: Routledge and Kegan Paul, 1960.

Clark, L., & Knowles, J. Age differences in dichotic listening performance. *Journal of Gerontology*, 1973, *28*, 173–178.

Coles, M. G. H., Gale, M. A., & Kline, P. Personality and habituation of the orienting reaction: Tonic and response measures of electrodermal activity. *Psychophysiology*, 1971, *8*, 54–63.

Colquhoun, W. P. The effect of a short rest pause on inspection efficiency. *Ergonomics*, 1959, *2*, 367–372.

Colquhoun, W. P. The effect of unwanted signals on performance in a vigilance task. *Ergonomics*, 1961, *4*, 41–52.

Colquhoun, W. P. Effects of a small dose of alcohol and certain other factors on the performance of a visual vigilance task. *Bulletin du C.E.R.P.*, 1962, *11*, 27–44. (In French, English summary.)

Colquhoun, W. P. Evaluation of auditory, visual and dual-mode displays for prolonged sonar monitoring in repeated sessions. *Human Factors*, 1975, *17*, 425–437.

Comalli, P. E., Jr. Cognitive functioning in a group of 80–90-year-old men. *Journal of Gerontology*, 1965, *20*, 14–17.

Comalli, P. E., Jr., Krus, D. M., & Wapner, S. Cognitive functioning in two groups of aged: One institutionalized, the other living in the community. *Journal of Gerontology*, 1965, *20*, 9–13.

Comalli, P. E., Jr., Wapner, S., & Werner, H. Interference effects of Stroop color–word test in childhood, adulthood and aging. *Journal of Genetic Psychology*, 1962, *100*, 47–53.

Conroy, R. L., & Weener, P. The development of visual and auditory selective attention using the central–incidental paradigm. *Journal of Experimental Child Psychology*, 1976, *22*, 400–407.

Craik, F. I. M. Applications of signal detection theory to studies of aging. In A. T. Welford & J. E. Birren (Eds.), *Decision making and age*. Basel: Karger, 1969.

Craik, F. I. M. Age differences in human memory. In J. E. Birren & K. W. Schale (Eds.), *Handbook of the psychology of aging*. New York: Van Nostrand-Reinhold, 1977.

Cramer, P. The Stroop effect in preschool aged children: A preliminary study. *Journal of Genetic Psychology*, 1967, *111*, 9–12.

Crider, A., & Augenbraun, C. B. Auditory vigilance correlates of electrodermal response habituation speed. *Psychophysiology*, 1975, *12*, 36–40.

Crider, A., & Lunn, R. Electrodermal lability as a personality dimension. *Journal of Experimental Research in Personality*, 1971, *5*, 145–150.

Davies, A. D. M. Temperament and narrowness of attention. *Perceptual and Motor Skills*, 1967, *24*(1), 42.

Davies, A. D. M., & Davies, D. R. The effects of noise and time of day upon age differences in performance at two checking tasks. *Ergonomics*, 1975, *18*, 321–336.

Davies, D. R. Age differences in paced inspection tasks. In G. A. Talland (Ed.), *Human Aging and Behavior*. New York: Academic Press, 1968.

Davies, D. R. Theories of vigilance and sustained attention. In M. A. Sinclair & J. N. Clare (Eds.), *Search and the human observer*. London: Taylor and Francis, 1979.

Davies, D. R., & Griew, S. A further note on the effect of aging on auditory vigilance performance: The effect of low signal frequency. *Journal of Gerontology*, 1963, *18*, 370–371.

Davies, D. R., & Hockey, G. R. J. The effects of noise and doubling the signal frequency on individual differences in visual vigilance performance. *British Journal of Psychology*, 1966, *57*, 381–389.

Davies, D. R., Hockey, G. R. J., & Taylor, A. Varied auditory stimulation, temperament differences and vigilance performance. *British Journal of Psychology*, 1969, *60*, 453–457.

Davies, D. R., & Krkovic, A. Skin conductance, alpha-activity, and vigilance. *American Journal of Psychology*, 1965, *78*, 304–306.

Davies, D. R., Lang, L., & Shackleton, V. J. The effects of music and task difficulty on performance at a visual vigilance task. *British Journal of Psychology*, 1973, *64*, 383–389.

Davies, D. R., & Parasuraman, R. *The psychology of vigilance*. London and New York: Academic Press, 1982.

Davies, D. R., Shackleton, V. J., & Parasuraman, R. Monotony and boredom. In G. R. J. Hockey (Ed.), *Stress and fatigue in human performance*. New York: Wiley, 1983.

Davies, D. R., & Sparrow, P. R. Age and work behavior. In N. R. Charness (Ed.), *Aging and human performance*. New York: Wiley (in press).

Davies, D. R., & Tune, G. S. *Human vigilance performance*. London: Staples, 1970.

Day, M. C. Visual search by children: The effect of background variation and the use of visual cues. *Journal of Experimental Child Psychology*, 1978, *25*, 1–10.

Deaton, M., Tobias, J. S., Wilkinson, R. T. The effects of sleep deprivation on signal detection parameters. *Quarterly Journal of Experimental Psychology*, 1971, *23*, 449–451.

Douglas, V. I. Stop, look and listen: The problems of sustained attention and impulse control in hyperactive and normal children. *Canadian Journal of Behavioral Science*, 1972, *4*, 259–282.

Douglas, V. I., & Peters, K. G. Toward a clearer definition of the attentional deficit of hyperactive children. In G. A. Hale & M. Lewis (Eds.), *Attention and cognitive development*. New York: Plenum, 1979.

Doyle, A. B. Listening to distraction: A developmental study of selective attention. *Journal of Experimental Child Psychology*, 1973, *15*, 100–115.

Doyle, R. B., Anderson, R. P., & Halcomb, C. G. Attention deficits and the effects of visual distraction. *Journal of Learning Disabilities*, 1976, *9*, 48–54.

Druker, J. F., & Hagen, J. W. Developmental trends in the processing of task relevant and task irrelevant information. *Child Development*, 1969, *40*, 371–382.

Dusek, J. B. The effect of labeling and pointing on children's selective attention. *Developmental Psychology*, 1978, *14*, 115–116.

Dyer, F. N. The Stroop phenomenon and its use in the study of perceptual, cognitive and response processes. *Memory and Cognition*, 1973, *1*, 106–120.

Dykman, R. A., Ackerman, P. T., Clements, S. D., & Peters, J. E. Specific learning disabilities: An attentional deficit syndrome. In H. R. Myklebust (Ed.), *Progress in Learning Disabilities* (Vol. 2). New York: Grune and Stratton, 1971.

Ehri, L. C. Do words really interfere in naming pictures. *Child Development*, 1976, *47*, 502–505.

Ehri, L. C., & Wilce, L. S. Does word training increase or decrease interference in a Stroop task? *Journal of Experimental Child Psychology*, 1979, *27*, 352–364.

Eisner, D. A. Life-span age differences in visual perception. *Perceptual and Motor Skills*, 1972, *34*, 857–858.

Elliott, E. Perception and alertness. *Ergonomics*, 1960, *3*, 357–369.

Evans, F. J. Field dependence and the Maudsley Personality Inventory. *Perceptual and Motor Skills*, 1967, *24*, 526.

Eysenck, H. J. *The dynamics of anxiety and hysteria*. New York: Praeger, 1957.

Eysenck, M. W., & Eysenck, M. C. Memory scanning, introversion–extraversion and levels of processing. *Journal of Research in Personality*, 1979, *13*, 305–315.

Fairweather, H. Sex differences in cognition. *Cognition*, 1976, *4*, 231–280.

Farkas, M. S., & Hoyer, W. J. Processing consequences of perceptual grouping in selective attention. *Journal of Gerontology*, 1980, *35*, 207–216.

Ford, J. M., Hink, R. F., Hopkins, W. F., Roth, W. T., Pfefferbaum, A., & Kopell, B. S. Age effects on event-related potentials in a selective attention task. *Journal of Gerontology*, 1979, *34*, 388–395.

Ford, J. M., & Pfefferbaum, A. The utility of brain potentials in determing age-related changes in central nervous system and cognitive functioning. In L. W. Poon (Ed.), *Aging in the 1980s*. Washington D.C.: American Psychological Association, 1980.

Fournier, P. A., Mazzarella, M. M., Ricciardi, M. M., & Fingeret, A. L. Reading level and locus of interference in the Stroop color–word task. *Perceptual and Motor Skills*, 1975, *41*, 239–242.

Fraisse, P. Why is naming longer than reading? *Acta Psychologica*, 1969, *30*, 96–103.

Friedrichs, A. G., Hertz, T. W., Moynahan, E. D., Simpson, W. E., Arnold, M. R., Christy, M. D., Cooper, C. R., & Stevenson, H. W. Interrelations among learning and performance tasks at the preschool level. *Developmental Psychology*, 1971, *4*, 164–172.

Gale, A. "Stimulus hunger": Individual differences in operant strategy in a button-pressing task. *Behaviour Research and Therapy*, 1969, *7*, 265–274.

Gale, A., Bull, R., Penfold, V., Coles, M., & Barraclough, R. Extraversion, time of day, vigilance performance and physiological arousal: Failure to replicate traditional findings. *Psychonomic Science*, 1972, *29*, 1–5.

Gale, A., & Lynn, R. A developmental study of attention. *British Journal of Educational Psychology*, 1972, *42*, 260–266.

Gale, A., Morris, P. E., Lucas, B., & Richardson, A. Types of imagery and imagery types: An EEG study. *British Journal of Psychology*, 1972, *63*, 523–531.

Gange, J. J., Geen, R. G., & Harkins, S. G. Autonomic differences between extraverts and introverts during vigilance. *Psychophysiology*, 1979, *16*, 392–397.

Gardner, R. W., Holzman, P. S., Klein, G. S., Linton, H. B., & Spence, D. P. Cognitive control: A study of individual consistencies in cognitive behavior. *Psychological Issues*, 1959, *1*, 1–185.

Garner, W. R. The stimulus in information processing. *American Psychologist*, 1970, *25*, 350–358.

Garner, W. R. *The processing of information and structure*. Potomac, Md.: Erlbaum, 1974.

Garner, W. R., & Felfoldy, G. L. Integrality of stimulus dimensions in various types of information processing. *Cognitive Psychology*, 1970, *1*, 225–241.

Geffen, G. The development of right ear advantage in dichotic listening with focussed attention. *Cortex*, 1978, *14*, 169–177.

Geffen, G., & Sexton, M. A. The development of auditory strategies of attention. *Developmental Psychology*, 1978, *14*, 11–17.

Geffen, G., & Wale, J. Development of selective listening and hemispheric asymmetry. *Developmental Psychology*, 1979, *15*, 138–146.

Golden, C. J. Sex differences in performance on the Stroop color and word test. *Perceptual Motor Skills*, 1974, *39*, 1067–1070.

Golden, C. J. The measurement of creativity by the Stroop color and word test. *Journal of Personality Assessment*, 1975, *39*, 502–506.

Golden, C. J. Identification of brain disorders by the Stroop color and word test. *Journal of Clinical Psychology*, 1976, *32*, 654–658.

Golden, C. J., Marsella, A. J., & Golden, E. E. Cognitive relationships of resistance to interference. *Journal of Consulting & Clinical Psychology*, 1975a, *43*, 432.

Golden, C. J., Marsella, A. J., & Golden, E. E. Personality correlates of the Stroop color and word test: More negative results. *Perceptual and Motor Skills*, 1975b, *41*, 599–602.

Gopher, D., & Kahneman, D. Individual differences in attention and the prediction of flight criteria. *Perceptual and Motor Skills*, 1971, *33*, 1335–1342.

Gould, J. D., & Carn, R. Visual search, complex backgrounds, mental counters, and eye movements. *Perception and Psychophysics*, 1973, *14*, 125–132.

Griew, S., & Davies, D. R. The effect of aging on auditory vigilance performance. *Journal of Gerontology*, 1962, *17*, 88–90.

Gross, S. J., Moore, S. F., & Stern, S. L. Subject–task interaction in selective attention research. *Perceptual and Motor Skills*, 1973, *36*, 259–262.

Guttentag, R. E., & Haith, M. M. Automatic processing as a function of age and reading ability. *Child Development*, 1978, *49*, 707–716.

Guttentag, R. E., & Haith, M. M. A developmental study of automatic word processing in a picture classification task. *Child Development*, 1979, *50*, 894–896.

Hagen, J. W. The effect of distraction on selective attention. *Child Development*, 1967, *38*, 685–694.

Hagen, J. W., & Hale, G. A. The development of attention in children. In: A. D. Pick (ed.) *Minnesota symposia on child psychology* (Vol. 7). Minneapolis: University of Minnesota Press, 1973.

Hagen, J. W., & Huntsman, N. J. Selective attention in mental retardation. *Developmental Psychology*, 1971, *5*, 151–160.

Hagen, J. W., Meacham, J. A., & Mesibov, G. Verbal labeling, rehearsal and short-term memory. *Cognitive Psychology*, 1970, *1*, 47–58.

Halcomb, C. G., & Kirk, R. E. Organismic variables as predictors of vigilance behavior. *Perceptual and Motor Skills*, 1965, *21*, 547–552.

Hale, G. A., & Alderman, L. B. Children's selective attention with variation in amount of stimulus exposure. *Journal of Experimental Psychology*, 1978, *26*, 320–327.

Hale, G. A., & Piper, R. A. Developmental trends in children's incidental learning: some critical stimulus differences. *Developmental Psychology*, 1973, *8*, 327–335.

Hallahan, D. P., Kauffman, J. M., & Ball, D. W. Developmental trends in recall of central and incidental auditory material. *Journal of Experimental Child Psychology*, 1974, *17*, 409–421.

Harkins, S. G., & Geen, R. G. Discriminability and criterion differences between extraverts and introverts during vigilance. *Journal of Research in Personality*, 1975, *9*, 335–340.

Harkins, S. W., Nowlin, J. B., Ramm, D., & Schroeder S. Effects of age, sex and time-on-watch on a brief continuous performance task. In: E. Palmore (Ed.), *Normal Aging, Vol. 2*. Durham, North Carolina: Duke University Press, 1974.

Hasher, L., & Zacks, R. T. Automatic and effortful processes in memory. *Journal of Experimental Psychology: General, 1979, 108,* 366–388.

Hastrup, J. L. Effects of electrodermal lability and introversion on vigilance decrement. *Psychophysiology,* 1979, *16,* 302–310.

Hatfield, J. L., & Loeb, M. Sense mode and coupling in a vigilance task. *Perception and Psychophysics,* 1968, *4,* 29–36.

Hatfield, J. L., & Soderquist, D. R. Coupling effects and performance in vigilance tasks. *Human Factors,* 1970, *12,* 351–359.

Hiscock M., & Kinsbourne M. Asymmetries of selective listening and attention switching in children. *Developmental Psychology,* 1980, *16,* 70–82.

Hochman, S. H. Field independence and Stroop color-word performance. *Perceptual & Motor Skills,* 1971, *33,* 782.

Hogan, M. J. Influence of motivation on reactive inhibition in extraversion-introversion. *Perceptual and Motor Skills,* 1966, *22,* 187–192.

Holmes, D. L., Peper, R., Olsho, L. W., & Raney, D. E. Searching for multiple targets simultaneously: is it really possible? *Perceptual & Motor Skills,* 1978, *46,* 227–234.

Hoyer, W. J., & Plude, D. J. Attentional and perceptual processes in the study of cognitive aging. In: L. W. Poon (Ed.) *Aging in the 1980s: Psychological issues.* Washington D.C.: American Psychological Association, 1980.

Inglis, J. Immediate memory, age and brain function. In A. T. Welford & J. E. Birren (Eds.) *Behavior, aging and the nervous system.* Springfield, Ill.: Thomas, 1965.

Inglis, J., & Caird, W. K. Age differences in successive responses to simultaneous stimulation. *Canadian Journal of Psychology,* 1963, *17,* 98–105.

Inglis, J., & Sykes, D. H. Some sources of variation in dichotic listening performance in children. *Journal of Experimental Child Psychology,* 1967, *5,* 480–488.

Inglis, J., & Tansey, C. L. Age differences and scoring differences in dichotic listening performance. *Journal of Psychology,* 1967, *66,* 325–332.

Jackson, D. N. A short form of Witkin's embedded figures test. *Journal of Abnormal and Social Psychology,* 1957, *53,* 254–255.

Jenkins, H. M. The effects of signal rate on performance in visual monitoring. *American Journal of Psychology,* 1958, *71,* 647–651.

Jennings, A. E., & Chiles, W. D. An investigation of time sharing ability as a factor in complex performance. *Human Factors,* 1977, *19,* 535–547.

Jensen, A. R. Scoring the Stroop test. *Acta Psychologica,* 1965, *24,* 398–408.

Jensen, A. R., & Rohwer, W. D., Jr. The Stroop color–word test: A review. *Acta Psychologica,* 1966, *25,* 36–93.

Jerison, H. J. Vigilance: Biology, psychology, theory and practice. In R. R. Mackie (Ed.), *Vigilance: Theory, operational performance and physiological correlates.* New York: Plenum, 1977.

Jones, D. M., & Davies, D. R. Individual and group differences in the response to noise. In D. M. Jones & A. J. Chapman (Eds.), *Noise and society.* New York: Wiley, 1983.

Jones, D. M., Smith, A. P., & Broadbent, D. E. Effects of moderate intensity noise on the Bakan vigilance task. *Journal of Applied Psychology,* 1979, *64,* 627–634.

Kahneman, D. *Attention and effort.* Englewood Cliffs, N.J.: Prentice-Hall, 1973.

Kahneman, D., Ben-Ishai, R., & Lotan, M. Relation of a test of attention to road accidents. *Journal of Applied Psychology,* 1973, *58,* 113–115.

Kappauf, W. E., & Powe, W. E. Performance decrement at an audio–visual checking task. *Journal of Experimental Psychology,* 1959, *57,* 49–56.

Katkin, E. S., & McCubbin, R. J. C. Habituation of the orienting response as a function of individual differences in anxiety and autonomic lability. *Journal of Abnormal Psychology,* 1969, *74,* 54–60.

Keister, M. E., & McLaughlin, R. J. Vigilance performance related to introversion–extraversion and caffeine. *Journal of Experimental Research in Personality,* 1972, *6,* 5–11.

Kennedy, R. S. Comparison of performance on visual and auditory vigilance tasks. *Human Factors,* 1971, *13,* 93–98.

Kennedy, R. S. The relationship between vigilance and eye movements induced by vestibular stimulation. In R. R. Mackie (Ed.), *Vigilance: Theory, operational performance and physiological correlates.* New York: Plenum, 1977.

Kinchla, R. A. The measurement of attention. In R. S. Nickerson (Ed.), *Attention and performance VIII.* Hillsdale, N.J.: Erlbaum, 1980.

Kinsbourne, M. The mechanism of hemispheric control of the lateral gradient of attention. In P. M. A. Rabbitt & S. Dornic (Eds.), *Attention and performance V.* London: Academic Press, 1975.

Kinsbourne, M., & Hiscock, M. Does cerebral dominance develop? In S. J. Segalowitz & F. A. Gruber (Eds.), *Language development and neurological theory.* New York: Academic Press, 1977.

Kirchner, G. L., & Knopf, I. J. Vigilance performance of second grade children as related to sex and achievement. *Child Development,* 1974, *45,* 490–495.

Kirchner, W. K. Age differences in short term retention of rapidly changing information. *Journal of Experimental Psychology,* 1958, *55,* 352–358.

Klein, G. S. Need and regulation. In M. R. Jones (Ed.), *Nebraska Symposium on Motivation* (Vol. 1). Lincoln: University of Nebraska Press, 1954.

Klein, G. S. Semantic power measured through the interference of words with color-naming. *American Journal of Psychology,* 1964, *77,* 576–588.

Kristofferson, M. W., Groen, M., & Kristofferson, A. B. When visual search functions look like item recognition functions. *Perception and Psychophysics,* 1973, *14,* 186–192.

Krupski, A., Raskin, D. C., & Bakan, P. Physiological and personality correlates of commission errors in an auditory vigilance task. *Psychophysiology,* 1971, *8,* 304–311.

Lacey, J. I., & Lacey, B. C. The relationship of resting autonomic activity to motor impulsivity. *Research Publications of the Association for Nervous and Mental Disease,* 1958, *36,* 144–209.

Lader, M. H., & Wing, L. *Physiological measures, sedative drugs and morbid anxiety.* Oxford: Oxford University Press, 1966.

Lane, D. M. Developmental changes in attention deployment skills. *Journal of Experimental Child Psychology,* 1979, *28,* 16–29.

Lane, D. M. Incidental learning and the development of selective attention. *Psychological Review,* 1980, *87,* 316–319.

Lansman, M., & Hunt, E. Individual differences in secondary task performance. *Memory and Cognition,* 1982, *10,* 10–24.

Layton, B. C. Perceptual noise and aging. *Psychological Bulletin,* 1975, *82,* 875–883.

Lerner, S. *A study of shadowing ability.* Unpublished doctoral thesis, The City University of New York, 1975.

Lewis, M., Honeck, R. P., & Fishbein, H. Does shadowing differentially unlock attention? *American Journal of Psychology,* 1975, *88,* 455–458.

Ligon, E. M. A genetic study of color naming and word reading. *American Journal of Psychology,* 1932, *44,* 103–121.

Lipps Birch, L. Age trends in children's time sharing performance. *Journal of Experimental Child Psychology,* 1976, *22,* 331–345.

Lipps Birch, L. Baseline differences, attention and age differences in time sharing performance. *Journal of Experimental Child Psychology,* 1978, *25,* 505–513.

Lockhead, G. R. Effects of dimensional redundancy on visual discrimination. *Journal of Experimental Psychology*, 1966, *72*, 95–104.

Loeb, M., & Binford, J. R. Modality, difficulty and coupling in vigilance behavior. *American Journal of Psychology*, 1971, *84*, 529–541.

Maccoby, E. E. Selective attention in children. In L. P. Lipsitt & C. C. Spiker (Eds.), *Advances in child development and behavior* (Vol. 3). New York: Academic Press, 1967.

Maccoby, E. E., & Hagen, J. W. The effects of distraction upon central and incidental recall: Developmental trends. *Journal of Experimental Child Psychology*, 1965, *2*, 280–289.

Maccoby, E. E., & Konrad, K. W. Age trends in selective listening. *Journal of Experimental Child Psychology*, 1966, *3*, 113–122.

Maccoby, E. E., & Konrad, K. W. The effect of preparatory set on selective listening. *Monographs of the Society for Research in Child Development*, 1967, *32*(Serial No. 112).

Mackworth, N. H. Researches on the measurement of human performance. *Medical research council special report* (No. 268). London: HMSO, 1950.

Madden, D. J., & Nebes, R. D. Aging and the development of automaticity in visual search. *Developmental Psychology*, 1980, *16*, 377–384.

Mangan, G. L., & O'Gorman, J. G. Initial amplitude and rate of habituation of orienting reaction in relation to extraversion and neuroticism. *Journal of Experimental Research in Personality*, 1969, *3*, 275–282.

Martin, M. Reverse Stroop effect with concurrent tasks. *Bulletin of the Psychonomic Society*, 1981, *17*, 8–9.

Maule, A. J., & Sanford, A. J. Adult age differences in multisource selection behaviour with partially predictable signals. *British Journal of Psychology*, 1980, *71*(1), 69–81.

McGrath, J. J. Cross-validation of some correlates of vigilance performance. In D. N. Buckner & J. J. McGrath (Eds.), *Vigilance: A symposium*. New York: McGraw-Hill, 1963.

McGrath, J. J., Harabedian, A., & Buckner, D. N. *Review and critique of the literature on vigilance performance* Los Angeles: (Tech. Rep. 1) Human Factors Research, Inc., 1960.

Mergler, N. L., Dusek, J. B., & Hoyer, W. J. Central/incidental recall and selective attention in young and elderly adults. *Experimental Aging Research*, 1977, *3*(1), 49–60.

Mihal, W. L., & Barrett, G. V. Individual differences in perceptual information processing and their relation to automobile accident involvement. *Journal of Applied Psychology*, 1976, *61*(2), 229–233.

Miller, L. K. Development of visual attention during visual search. *Developmental Psychology*, 1978, *14*, 439–440.

Miller, P. H., & Bigi, L. The development of children's understanding of attention. *Merrill-Palmer Quarterly*, 1979, *25*, 235–250.

Miller, P. H., & Weiss, M. G. Children's attention allocation, understanding of attention and performance on the incidental learning task. *Child Development*, 1981, *52*, 1183–1190.

Moore, S. F., & Gross, S. J. Influence of critical signal regularity, stimulus event matrix and cognitive style on vigilance performance. *Journal of Experimental Psychology*, 1973, *99*, 137–139.

Moray, N. *Attention: Selective processes in vision and hearing.* London: Hutchinson, 1969.

Morris, P. E., & Gale, A. A correlational study of variables related to imagery. *Perceptual and Motor Skills*, 1974, *38*, 659–665.

Neal, G. L., & Pearson, R. G. Comparative effects of age, sex and drugs upon two tasks of auditory vigilance. *Perceptual and Motor Skills*, 1966, *23*, 967–974.

Neisser, U. Decision time without reaction time: Experiments in visual scanning. *American Journal of Psychology*, 1963, *76*, 376–385.

Neisser, U. *Cognitive psychology.* New York: Appleton-Century-Crofts, 1967.

Obrzut, J. E., Hynd, G. W., Obrzut, A., & Pirrozzolo, F. J. Effect of directed attention on cerebral asymmetries in normal and learning-disabled children. *Developmental Psychology*, 1981, *17*, 118–125.

Oltman, P. K. A portable rod-and-frame apparatus. *Perceptual and Motor Skills*, 1968, *26*, 503–506.

Panek, P. E., Barrett, G. V., Sterns, H. L., & Alexander, R. A. Age differences in perceptual style, selective attention and perceptual–motor reaction time. *Experimental Aging Research*, 1978, *4*, 377–387.

Parasuraman, R. Response bias and physiological reactivity. *Journal of Psychology*, 1975, *91*, 309–313.

Parasuraman, R. Consistency of individual differences in human vigilance performance: An abilities classification analysis. *Journal of Applied Psychology*, 1976, *61*, 486–493.

Parasuraman, R. Memory load and event rate control sensitivity decrements in sustained attention. *Science*, 1979, *205*, 924–927.

Parasuraman, R., & Davies, D. R. A taxonomic analysis of vigilance performance. In R. R. Mackie (Ed.), *Vigilance: Theory, operational performance and physiological correlates*. New York: Plenum, 1977.

Parkinson, S. R., Lindholm, J. M., & Urell, T. Aging, dichotic memory and digit span. *Journal of Gerontology*, 1980, *35*, 87–95.

Pelham, W. E. Selective attention deficits in poor readers? Dichotic listening, speeded classification, and auditory and visual central and incidental learning tasks. *Child Development*, 1979, *50*, 1050–1061.

Peretti, P. Cross-sex and cross-educational level performance in a color word interference task. *Psychonomic Science*, 1969, *16*, 321–323.

Peretti, P. Effects of non-competitive, competitive instructions and sex on performance in a color–word interference task. *Journal of Psychology*, 1971, *79*, 67–70.

Plude, D. J., & Hoyer, W. J. Adult age differences in visual search as a function of stimulus mapping and processing load. *Journal of Gerontology*, 1981, *36*, 598–604.

Porter, R. J., Jr., & Berlin, C. I. On interpreting developmental changes in the dichotic right-ear advantage. *Brain and Language*, 1975, *2*, 186–200.

Posner, M. I., & Snyder, C. R. R. Attention and cognitive control. In R. L. Solso (Ed.), *Information processing and cognition: The Loyola Symposium*. Hillsdale, N.J.: Erlbaum, 1975.

Purohit, A. K. Personality types and signal detection. *Indian Journal of Psychology*, 1972, *47*, 161–165.

Rabbitt, P. M. A. An age decrement in the ability to ignore irrelevant information. *Journal of Gerontology*, 1965, *20*, 233–238.

Rabbitt, P. M. A. Current paradigms and models in human information processing. In V. Hamilton & D. M. Warburton (Eds.), *Human stress and cognition: An information processing approach*. New York: Wiley, 1979a.

Rabbitt, P. M. A. Some experiments and a model for changes in attentional selectivity with old age. In F. Hoffmeister & C. Muller (Eds.), *Brain function in old age*. Berlin: Springer-Verlag, 1979b.

Rabbitt, P. M. A. Cognitive psychology needs models for changes in performance with old age. In J. Long & A. D. Baddeley (Eds.), *Attention and performance IX*. Hillsdale, N.J.: Erlbaum, 1981.

Rand, G., Wapner, S., Werner, H., & McFarland, J. H. Age differences in performance on the Stroop color–word test. *Journal of Personality*, 1963. *31*, 534–558.

Ray, C. Some components of color–word interference and their relationship with field dependence. *Acta Psychologica*, 1974, *38*, 323–330.

Rosinski, R. R. Picture–word interference is semantically based. *Child Development*, 1977, *48*, 643–647.

Ross, J. Extended practice with a single-character classification task. *Perception and Psychophysics*, 1970, *8*, 276–278.

Rosvold, H. E., Mirsky, A. F., Sarason, I., Bransome, E. D., & Beck, L. N. A continuous performance test of brain damage. *Journal of Consulting Psychology*, 1956, *20*, 343–350.

Sabo, R. A., & Hagen, J. W. Color cues and rehearsal in short-term memory. *Child Development*, 1973, *44*, 77–82.

Sack, S. A., & Rice, C. E. Selectivity, resistance to distraction and shifting as three attentional factors. *Psychological Reports*, 1974, *34*, 1003–1012.

Sanford, A. J., & Maule, A. J. Age and the distribution of observing responses. *Psychonomic Science*, 1971, *23*, 419–420.

Sanford, A. J., & Maule, A. J. The allocation of attention in multisource monitoring behaviour: Adult age differences. *Perception*, 1973, *2*(1), 91–100.

Santostefano, S. Cognitive controls and exceptional states in children. *Journal of Clinical Psychology*, 1964, *20*, 213–218.

Santostefano, S. *A biodevelopmental approach to clinical child psychology: Cognitive controls and cognitive control therapy*. New York: Wiley, 1978.

Satz, P., Bakker, D. J., Teunissen, J., Goebel, R., & Van Der Vlugt, H. Developmental parameters of the ear asymmetry: A multivariate approach. *Brain and Language*, 1975, *2*, 123–130.

Schiller, P. H. Developmental study of color–word interference. *Journal of Experimental Psychology*, 1966, *72*, 105–108.

Schneider, W., & Shiffrin, R. M. Controlled and automatic information processing (Pt. 1): Detection, search and attention. *Psychological Review*, 1977, *84*, 1–66.

Sexton, M. A., and Geffen, G. Development of three strategies of attention in dichotic monitoring. *Developmental Psychology*, 1979, *15*, 299–310.

Sheehan, J. J., & Drury, C. G. The analysis of industrial inspection. *Applied Ergonomics*, 1971, *2*, 74–78.

Shepard, R. N. Attention and the metric structure of the stimulus space. *Journal of Mathematical Psychology*, 1964, *1*, 54–87.

Shepp, B. E. From perceived similarity to dimensional structure: A new hypothesis about perceptual development. In E. Rosch, & B. B. Lloyd (Eds.), *Cognition and categorization*. Hillsdale, N.J.: Erlbaum, 1978.

Shepp, B. E., & Swartz, K. B. Selective attention and the processing of integral and non-integral dimensions: A developmental study. *Journal of Experimental Child Psychology*, 1976, *22*, 73–85.

Shiffrin, R. M., & Schneider, W. Controlled and automatic human information processing (Pt. 2): Perceptual learning, automatic attending, and a general theory. *Psychological Review*, 1977, *84*, 127–190.

Siddle, D. A. T. Vigilance decrement and speed of habituation of the G.S.R. component of the orienting response. *British Journal of Psychology*, 1972, *63*, 191–194.

Silverstein, A., & Franken. R. E. Performance of the mentally retarded on the Stroop color–word test. *Perceptual and Motor Skills*, 1965, *21*, 618.

Sipowicz, R. R., & Baker, R. A. Effects of intelligence on vigilance: A replication. *Perceptual and Motor Skills*, 1961, *13*, 398.

Smith, J. D., & Baron, J. Individual differences in the classification of stimuli by dimensions. *Journal of Experimental Psychology: Human Perception and Performance*. 1981, *7*, 1132–1145.

Smith, L. B., & Kemler, D. G. Levels of experienced dimensionality in children and adults. *Cognitive Psychology*, 1977, *10*, 502–532.

Sostek, A. J. *Vigilance performance as a function of autonomic lability and differential payoffs*. Unpublished doctoral thesis, State University of New York, Buffalo, 1976.

Sostek, A. J. Effects of electrodermal lability and payoff instructions on vigilance performance. *Psychophysiology*, 1978, *15*, 561–568.

Sternberg, S. High-speed scanning in human memory. *Science*, 1966, *153*, 652–654.

Stroop, J. R. The basis of Ligon's theory. *American Journal of Psychology*, 1935a, *47*, 499–504.

Stroop, J. R. Studies of interference in serial verbal reactions. *Journal of Experimental Psychology*, 1935b, *18*, 643–662.

Strutt, G. F., Anderson, D. R., & Well, A. D. A developmental study of the effects of irrelevant information on speeded classification. *Journal of Experimental Child Psychology*, 1975, *20*, 127–135.

Surwillo, W. W. The relation of autonomic activity to age differences in vigilance. *Journal of Gerontology*, 1966, *21*, 257–260.

Surwillo, W. W., & Quilter, R. E. Vigilance, age and response time. *American Journal of Psychology*, 1964, *77*, 614–620.

Sverko, B. Intermodal correlations in vigilance performance. In *Proceedings of the 16th International Congress of Applied Psychology*. Amsterdam: Swets and Zeitlinger, 1968.

Sykes, D. H., Douglas, V. I., & Morgenstern, G. Sustained attention in hyperactive children. *Journal of Child Psychology and Child Psychiatry*, 1973, *14*, 213–221.

Talland, G. A. The effect of age on speed of simple manual skill. *Journal of Genetic Psychology*, 1962, *100*, 69–76.

Talland, G. A. Visual signal detection as a function of age, input rate and signal frequency. *Journal of Psychology*, 1966, *63*, 105–115.

Thackray, R. I., Jones, K. N., & Touchstone, R. M. The color–word interference test and its relation to performance impairment under auditory distraction. *Psychonomic Science*, 1972, *28*, 225–227.

Thackray, R. I., Jones, K. N., & Touchstone, R. M. Personality and physiological correlates of performance decrement on a monotonous task requiring sustained attention. *British Journal of Psychology*, 1974, *65*, 351–358.

Thompson, L. W., Opton, E. M., & Cohen, L. D. Effects of age, presentation speed, and sensory modality on performance of a 'vigilance' task. *Journal of Gerontology*, 1963, *18*, 366–369.

Tolin, P., & Fisher, P. G. Sex differences and effects of irrelevant auditory stimulation on performance of visual task. *Perceptual and Motor Skills*, 1974, *39*, 1255–1262.

Trabasso, T., & Bower, G. H. *Attention in learning*. New York: Wiley, 1968.

Treisman, A. Strategies and models of selective attention. *Psychological Review*, 1969, *76*, 282–299.

Treisman, A., & Geffen, G. Selective attention and cerebral dominance in perceiving and responding to speech messages. *Quarterly Journal of Experimental Psychology*, 1968, *19*, 1–17.

Treisman, A., & Riley, J. G. A. Is selective attention selective perception or selective response? A further test. *Journal of Experimental Psychology*, 1969, *79*, 27–34.

Tune, G. S. Age differences in errors of commission. *British Journal of Psychology*, 1966a, *57*, 391–392.

Tune, G. S. Errors of commission as a function of age and temperament in a type of vigilance task. *Quarterly Journal of Experimental Psychology*, 1966b, *18*, 358–361.

Tyler, D. M., Waag, W., & Halcomb, C. G. Monitoring performance across sense modes: An individual differences approach. *Human Factors*, 1972, *14*, 539–549.

Underwood, B. J. Individual differences as a crucible in theory construction. *American Psychologist*, 1975, *30*, 128–134.

Underwood, G. Moray vs. the rest: The effects of extended shadowing practice. *Quarterly Journal of Experimental Psychology*, 1974, *26*, 368–372.

Underwood, G., & Moray, N. Shadowing and monitoring for selective attention. *Quarterly Journal of Experimental Psychology*, 1971, *23*, 284–295.

Vechi, Y. Cognitive interference and intelligence: Re-examination of the measures of SCWT. *Japanese Journal of Educational Psychology*, 1972, *20*, 92–100.

Von Wright, J., & Nurmi, L. Effects of white noise and irrelevant information on speeded classification: A developmental study. *Acta Psychologica*, 1979, *43*, 157–166.

Waag, W. L., Halcomb, C. G., & Tyler, D. M. Sex differences in monitoring performance. *Journal of Applied Psychology*, 1973, *58*, 272–274.

Ware, J. R. Effects of intelligence on signal detection in visual and auditory monitoring. *Perceptual and Motor Skills*, 1961, *13*, 99–102.

Ware, J. R., Baker, R. A., & Sipowicz, R. R. Performance of simple mental deficients on a simple vigilance task. *American Journal of Mental Deficiency*, 1962, *66*, 647–650.

Wheeler, R. J., & Dusek, J. B. The effects of attentional and cognitive factors on children's incidental learning. *Child Development*, 1973, *44*, 253–258.

Wickens, C. D. Temporal limits on human information processing: A developmental study. *Psychological Bulletin*, 1974, *81*, 739–755.

Wickens, C. D., Mountford, S. J., & Schreiner, W. Multiple resources, task-hemispheric integrity, and individual differences in time-sharing. *Human Factors*, 1981, *23*, 211–229.

Wilkinson, R. T. Comparison of paced, unpaced, irregular and continuous displays in watchkeeping. *Ergonomics*, 1961, *4*, 259–267.

Williams, L. G. The effect of target specification on objects fixated during visual search. *Perception and Psychophysics*, 1966, *1*, 315–318.

Wise, L. A., Sutton, J. A., & Gibbons, P. D. Decrement in Stroop interference time with age. *Perceptual and Motor Skills*, 1975, *41*, 149–150.

Witkin, H. A. Individual differences in ease of perception of embedded figures. *Journal of Personality*, 1950, *19*, 1–15.

Witkin, H. A., Dyk, R. B., Faterson, H. F., Goodenough, D. R., & Karp, S. A. *Psychological differentiation: Studies of development.* New York: Wiley, 1962.

Wittenborn, J. R. Factorial equations for tests of attention. *Psychometrika*, 1943, *8*, 19–35.

Wolitzky, D. L., Hofer, R., & Shapiro, R. Cognitive controls and mental retardation. *Journal of Abnormal Psychology*, 1972, *79*, 296–302.

Wright, L. L., & Elias, J. W. Age differences in the effects of perceptual noise. *Journal of Gerontology*, 1979, *34*, 704–708.

Wright, R. E. Aging, divided attention, and processing capacity. *Journal of Gerontology*, 1981, *36*, 605–614.

York, C. M. Behavioral efficiency in a monitoring task as a function of signal rate and observer age. *Perceptual and Motor Skills*, 1962, *15*, 404.

Yussen, S. R., & Bird, J. E. The development of metacognitive awareness in memory, communication and attention. *Journal of Experimental Psychology*, 1979, *28*, 300–313.

12

Varieties of Attentional State: The Effects of Environment

Robert Hockey

Introduction

This chapter examines the ways in which changes in state brought about by environmental factors are manifested in terms of human performance. Although I shall be primarily concerned with attention as a central process involved in the control and execution of performance, I shall also have something to say about other features of behavior, notably those involving short-term memory (STM) and response processes in speeded decision-making tasks. In no sense can this chapter be considered a review of the literature on this topic; instead, certain areas are considered in depth in order to illustrate the nature of the problem more clearly. The chapter has two objectives: (1) to demonstrate the limits of applicability of the general arousal theory for the understanding of performance changes under stress; and (2) to outline an alternative approach to the study of environmental effects, based on the mapping of qualitative patterns of performance change and to illustrate the application of this approach to available data.

It is now relatively easy to demonstrate effects of, for example, noise or sleeplessness on performance. Yet this was not always so. Numerous early studies failed to find anything other than transient reductions in work rate resulting from the imposition of quite severe distractions such as buzzers, horns, and fire gongs (Morgan, 1917; Ford, 1929). The first convincing effects of noise under laboratory conditions were not reported until the early 1950s (see Broadbent, 1957a), whereas the effects of a whole night's loss of sleep on task performance were difficult to detect consistently until the late 1950s (Wilkinson, 1964). Even then, only certain kinds of tasks (so-called "sensitive" tasks) could be relied on to reveal these impairments of efficiency. Broadbent (1957a) argued that noise produced brief interruptions in the intake of task events and so would only produce decrements on tasks such as vigilance and serial reaction, which are characterized by sustained attention or a high rate of information flow. Studies conducted since 1970, however, have shown effects with tasks lasting only a few minutes or in which information intake is a minor component (e.g., retrieval from long-term memory [LTM]).

What is the explanation for these changes? First, it is clear that part of the reason concerns an improvement in design and instrumentation, as well as the use of more sophisticated analytic procedures. In addition, however, it is apparent that the kinds of experiment that are carried out reflect views prevailing at the time on the nature of the processes underlying overt behavior. The improvements in methodology during the 1950s owe much to the insight of Bartlett, Craik, Broadbent, and others that the system was, to a certain extent, self-regulating and could compensate for momentary reductions in efficiency by an increase in the rate of responding. Such behavior would effectively mask all but the most subtle effects of noise or sleeplessness in the short term until the regulatory process itself became inefficient through fatigue. This remains an important idea in theories of stress effects (e.g., Broadbent, 1971). The more recent tendency to find effects on other kinds of tasks is related to the shift of interest during the 1970s away from sustained attention and continuous work towards the study of situations having a more clearly defined cognitive basis, such as those requiring considerable use of the working-memory system. These studies will not be reviewed here, except indirectly (see, for example, "States of Attention and Cognition"). More interesting for the present purposes is the apparent trade-off between speeded processing and working memory that may be observed in many cases (Hamilton, Hockey, Rejman, 1977). This trade-off can be seen as a first approximation to the more general position that I present in this chapter. When the patterns of performance associated with different changes of state are considered the speed–memory trade-off is not always found; and the pattern is, in any case, modified by the consideration of other kinds of behavioral change. The more general rule is that stressors change the pattern of efficiency, not the level.

The chapter begins by seriously examining the arousal (or activation) concept as it has been used in its areas of greatest success, that of sustained attention and speeded decision making. Although arousal appears to offer valuable insights into the nature of the organismic state underlying controlled performance, its explanatory value is, in fact, illusory. It achieves its success by masking those very issues that are central to the understanding of the problem: Is there a general state of arousal, rather than a number of related states? Why should overarousal lead to reduced efficiency? What are the primary dimensions of task difficulty? What is the functional role of state changes in the detailed patterning of behavior? The following section considers the use of the concept of arousal in the interpretation of data from studies of sequential reaction and points out some of the more obvious difficulties of the theory. The third section describes how various models of attention have tried to use the data obtained in studies of environmental effects, whether they directly address the concept of arousal or not. Also examined in this section are the problems raised, by both theoretical and methodological considerations, for arousal theory in general and for the Yerkes–Dodson law in particular. The fourth section describes an alternative approach to the study of environmental influences. This involves the qualitative analysis of performance changes across a representative sample of task situations, and is illustrated by an analysis of the effects of loud noise. Lastly in the fifth section some of the broader aspects of the theoretical framework that underlies the state-analysis approach are discussed, together with some particular features of the framework that relate to performance change under stress.

Environmental Stress and Sustained Attention

As is noted earlier, it is not possible within the confines of the present chapter to provide a detailed review of research in this field. Poulton (1970) provides a useful coverage across a very wide area, and more analytic reviews are provided by Broadbent (1971), Eysenck (1982), and Hockey (1983). It will be useful, however, to review briefly some of the main findings in the areas of vigilance and serial reaction because the current use of arousal theory in performance is largely based on these findings.

Much of the work discussed in this chapter was carried out at the Medical Research Council's Applied Psychology Unit, in Cambridge, England, largely between 1950 and 1970. The particular value of this work, which forms the basis for our knowledge about the effects of different environments on attention, lies in the fact that a small number of performance tests was used throughout this period to provide a test-bench for assessing the effects of different stressors. Although these tasks had a practical origin, they were designed to take into account the kinds of changes expected from theories of performance; this represented a considerable advance over the rather arbitrary nature of most tests used in pre–World War II research. The kinds of tests used in the Cambridge experiments involved vigilance (monitoring), serial reaction, and pursuit tracking; all requiring continuous performance over a period of 30 minutes or more. As mentioned previously, it is now clear that environmental effects can be found with briefer tasks involving memory, search and decision making. I shall not deal with this research directly, except to refer to changes in the patterning of performance. Reviews of this material can be found in Broadbent (1981), Eysenck (1982), and Hockey (1979, 1983).

Vigilance

The vigilance situation has proved itself over the past 30 years to be sensitive to a wide range of environmental influences (see Davies & Parasuraman, 1982). Mackworth's (1950) original studies showed that the decrement in detection rate with time on task was increased by working in high ambient temperatures, and could be reduced by the administration of the stimulant drug amphetamine, or more simply, by arranging for a telephone call to be made to the operator during the watch. The general observations that decrements occur as a result of continued work of the same kind and that the effects of stressors tend to be more pronounced once the decrement has developed characterize much of the sustained-attention research discussed in this section.

Vigilance tasks have since been shown to be sensitive to effects of a wide range of environmental conditions, including sleep loss (Hamilton, Wilkinson, & Edwards, 1972; Wilkinson, 1959, 1964; Williams, Lubin, & Goodnow, 1959), variations in ambient temperature (Pepler, Note 1; Ramsey, 1983), circadian rhythms (Blake, 1967; Colquhoun, 1971), and both stimulant and depressant drugs (Colquhoun, 1962; Wesnes & Warburton, 1983). Colquhoun (1962) found that the impairment produced by alcohol was greatly aggravated by the presence of either meclozine or hyoscine, both used to counteract the effects of travel sickness. The effects of noise appear to be more complex. In general, impairment is more usual when subjects are asked to monitor displays that have a number of separate sources of information or that present events at a high rate (Broadbent, 1971; Hockey, 1970). Noise may enhance detection performance on the type of vigilance display in which a single source must be monitored and the rate of information flow is low. As will be further discussed in a subsequent section, these observations provide some support for the view that noise increases attentional selectivity because a narrowing of attention is more likely to impair tasks requiring a flexible attentional strategy. A similar point has been made by Jerison (1959) to account for noise impairing performance only on a multiple-source display.

Relatively few stress studies have used signal detection methods of analysis. Broadbent and Gregory (1965) found evidence of impairment with noise only at low criteria settings (those associated with high false-alarm rates), rather than any clear shift in the sensitivity parameter, d'. This suggests a change in strategy with noise rather than any effect on true detection efficiency. Relatively clear changes in sensitivity have been found with some stressors. Sleep deprivation, for example, whether total or partial, has been found to produce a lowering of d' (Hamilton et al., 1972; Wilkinson, 1968), whereas amphetamines appear to genuinely enhance detection efficiency (Mackworth, 1965). The effects of heat and time of day are less clear. Poulton and Edwards (1974) found evidence for a reduction in d' with increases in ambient temperature, whereas Wilkinson, Fox, Goldsmith, Hampton, and Lewis (1964) observed an improvement in sensitivity using a technique for maintaining body temperature at a high level. Colquhoun and Goldman (1972), also using the raised-body-temperature method, found increases in both detections and false-alarm rate, suggesting a general relaxation of the response criterion rather than a change in d'. These are few studies that report signal detection parameters for time of day, although there is considerable evidence for an enhancement in detection rate over the waking day and very little change in false-alarm rate (Colquhoun, 1971)—suggesting a real increase in sensitivity. Craig, Wilkinson, and Colquhoun (1981) have reexamined the data from a number of studies, however, and found little evidence for any change in sensitivity. Instead, they conclude that the data support the interpretation of a general relaxation of the response criterion over the day.

Taken together the findings on vigilance must be seen as rather disappointing. The simplicity of the original assumption that some fundamental change in sustained attention is reflected in the proportion of signals detected has had to be abandoned. Yet, the new signal detection methodology has not, as might have been expected, provided an unequivocal basis for separating effects of processing efficiency from those of decision strategies. This issue is discussed further by Parasuraman (Chapter 6, this volume). Part of the problem is almost certainly that environmental effects are multidimensional. It cannot be assumed that they will always be reflected in a particular measure of behavioral efficiency, or that any kind of vigilance task will be affected in the same way. In particular, as Davies and Parasuraman (1982) have pointed out, vigilance tasks often include a significant memory component, which, as is discussed later, may have dramatic consequences for the form that environmental effects take. Certainly, it is not possible to conclude from the work on vigilance that sustained attention is impaired by working in unusual environments. Apart from the effects of quite considerable changes, such as total sleep deprivation (Wilkinson, 1968) or hypoxia (Cahoon, 1970), clear evidence of impairment is rather rare.

Serial Responding

The second type of situation studied in the Cambridge work involved continuous serial reaction, using the task known as the "five-choice serial-reaction task" (Leonard, 1959). This required subjects to make sequential responses to whichever of five lights came on by tapping a metal disk with a stylus. The task was normally used in its self-paced version so that both rate of work and accuracy could be measured. In addition, pronounced "gaps" in the response sequence (delays of more than 1.5 seconds) were used as an index of breakdowns in skilled performance; (a similar measure had been shown by Bills (1931) to be sensitive to fatigue brought about by prolonged serial responding even in the absence of errors).

Environmental Effects

Typically, as with vigilance tasks, any effects of environmental conditions are more likely to be observed toward the end of the work period (usually about 30

TABLE 12.1

Changes in Performance on the Five-Choice Serial Reaction Task for Different Environmental
Conditions[a]

Environment	Typical manipulation	Work rate	Gaps	Errors	Sources[b]
Prolonged work	No breaks for 20–30 minutes	−	+	+	1–10
Sleep loss	One night without sleep	−	+	+	4–10
Noise	90–100 db steady broad-band	0	0	+	1, 3, 5, 9
Heat	Effective temperature 39°C	0	+	+	6
Alcohol	0.21/0.42 g/kg (peak blood alcohol level about 0.04%)	0	0	+	3, 10
Hyoscine	0.7 mg 1-hyoscine	−	+	0	4
Time of day	Testing at 0800, 1030, 1300, 1530, 2100	+	−	0	2
Incentive	Augmented feedback and competition	+	−	−	8–10

[a] For each performance measure, an increase (+) or decrease (−) refers to the typical effect where more than one study is cited; no effect is indicated by 0.

[b] Sources: 1, Broadbent (1953); 2, Blake (1967, 1971); 3, Colquhoun and Edwards (1975); 4, Colquhoun and Wilkinson (Note 3); 5, Corcoran (1962); 6, Pepler (1959); 7, Wilkinson (1959); 8, Wilkinson (1961); 9, Wilkinson (1963); 10, Wilkinson and Colquhoun (1968).

minutes into the period) than soon after the beginning. One exception appears to be that of heat, which often impairs performance even at the beginning of the work period. Table 12.1 summarizes the results of the major studies of stress on the five-choice task. A number of different patterns of performance change may be seen in Table 12.1. Prolonged performance reduces the rate of work and increases both kinds of inefficient response, errors and gaps. Noise increases errors (primarily), whereas sleep loss affects both speed and gaps. These may, of course, be related, because a reduction in the overall rate of work is logically likely to give rise to a greater number of long response times. Similarly, although the absolute number of errors may not be increased in the sleeplessness state, the proportion of all responses that are errors may be larger (Wilkinson, 1963). Heat and alcohol, like noise, also have their main effect on errors, whereas the depressant drug, hyoscine, produces a pattern more like that of sleep loss. Incentive generally improves performance in all respects. The details of these results have been dealt with at length in a number of previous reviews (Broadbent, 1971; Hockey, 1979; Poulton, 1970). At first glance, the results seem to fall into three groups: (1) slowing (with or without a loss of accuracy) with prolonged work, sleeplessness, and hyoscine; (2) loss of accuracy with no loss of speed with noise, heat, and alcohol; and (3) overall improvement with incentive and later times of day. In fact, a further distinction may be necessary to accommodate the observed interactions with time on task (or prolonged work). Whereas the effects of noise, loss of sleep, incentives, time of day, and drugs clearly increase over time, those associated with heat apparently do not. They are present at the start of the work period and remain approximately at the same level (Pepler, 1959). A further difficulty in attempting to understand the differences between environmental conditions is the fact that comparisons cannot meaningfully be made between particular values of, for example, sleep loss and alcohol level in terms of the severity of stress produced. The particular pattern of performance change may well depend on the *degree* of stress produced as well as the *kind* of stressor.

Combination of Environments

A different approach to the problem has been to examine the nature of the performance changes found when environmental conditions are applied in combination, rather than singly. It has been assumed that conditions affecting the same function will give rise to interactive rather than to additive effects. For example, part of the effect of each stress on its own may be absorbed by the built-in spare capacity (''safety margin'') of the system; any inefficiency observed, particularly during the early part of the task when the subject is still fresh, may therefore be rather slight. If two stressors affect the same process, however, the effect of adding the second would be considerably greater once the spare capacity had been taken up by the first; the system is less resistant to the effect of stress. If the two conditions affected different processes, the effects of combining them would simply be the sum of the changes produced by exceeding the safety margins of the two separate processes.

This line of argument produces a kind of model of stress effects on performance, resting on the implicit assumption that all stressors lower efficiency by depleting a nonspecific resource such as attentional capacity. A number of studies have used the five-choice task to examine the effects of various combinations of environments. A summary of the results of these studies is presented in Table 12.2, which shows which combinations yield interactions and which additive (A) effects. I have also indicated whether interactions are negative ($-$) or positive ($+$). Interactions that are less than additive suggest that there is a ceiling to the effect or that the two stressors are, to some extent, antagonistic. Supradditive effects would be expected on the basis of the general depletion model described in the preceding discussion.

It is clear that the evidence from these experiments offers little support for the general depletion view. When one stressor is added to another, the result is normally either a summation of effects or a negative interaction. In fact, the only clear indication of a positive interaction comes from Colquhoun's (1962) vigilance study, mentioned previously, where the effects of alcohol are markedly potentiated by the presence of meclozine or hyoscine. Such an effect is only

TABLE 12.2

Combinations of Two Environmental Stressors on Performance of the Five-Choice Serial Reaction Task

Environment	Sleep loss				Noise				Incentive			
	Work rate	Gaps	Errors	Source[a]	Work rate	Gaps	Errors	Source	Work rate	Gaps	Errors	Source
Alcohol	Additive[b]	Additive[b]	Negative	7	Additive	Negative[c]	Negative	1	Negative	Negative	Additive	1
Incentive	Additive	Negative	Negative	5	Additive	Negative	—	6	—	—	—	—
Noise[d]	Negative	Negative	Additive	3	—	—	—	—	—	—	—	—
Hyoscine	Additive	Additive	Additive	2	—	—	—	—	—	—	—	—
Heat	Additive	Additive	Additive	4	—	—	—	—	—	—	—	—

[a] Sources: 1, Colquhoun and Edwards (1975); 2, Colquhoun and Wilkinson (Note 3); 3, Corcoran (1962); 4, Pepler (1959); 5, Wilkinson (1961); 6, Wilkinson (1963); 7, Wilkinson and Colquhoun (1968).

[b] When subjects were divided into groups having high or low blood alcohol levels, both work rate and gaps showed a negative interaction with high BA but a positive interaction with low BA. The reliability of these interactions is suspect however.

[c] Gaps could not be analyzed because of an apparatus fault.

[d] The results of two separate studies are shown for the noise–sleep loss combination.

observed with the five-choice task for combinations of environmental stressors with prolonged work. This suggests that fatigue may be an important factor in the lowering of resistance to the effects of stress. There is little evidence to support the view, however, that all stressors affect the same general resource in the same way. Generally speaking, although the effect of one stressor depends on what other conditions are present, the form of these interactions requires a more complex interpretation of the nature of environmental effects.

The Arousal Theory of Environmental Effects

Broadbent (1963) and other theorists (Corcoran, 1962; Wilkinson, 1963) interpreted the findings from the studies mentioned in the preceding section on the five-choice task in relation to converging evidence from studies of tracking, vigilance, and other continuous work tasks as providing firm evidence for the general applicability of the arousal theory, which gained popularity during the late 1950s. Roughly stated, the theory assumed that the level of behavioral efficiency is, to a large extent, limited by the general level of activation (or arousal) of the physiological systems underlying behavior (Duffy, 1957, 1962, 1972). This is determined by both endogenous and exogenous fluctuations in the degree of stimulation present in these systems. Arousal level is a hypothetical construct representing an overall (nonspecific) index of the degree of stimulation of the system as a whole. Although this concept, as used by Duffy in particular, has a much broader scope than that considered in this chapter, its application to the interpretation of stress effects can be thought of as involving two principal assumptions. The first is that there is a curvilinear (inverted-U) relationship between arousal level and performance, such that any task is performed best at some intermediate level of arousal. This can be considered the "weak" form of arousal–performance theory, the *inverted-U hypothesis*. A stronger, and fuller model is provided by the second principal assumption, the *Yerkes–Dodson law*. This proposes that the optimum level of arousal is inversely related to the degree of difficulty of a task, such that more difficult tasks will be impaired at arousal levels lower than those found to produce impairment in easier tasks.

The Yerkes–Dodson law derives originally from a study by Yerkes and Dodson (1908) that illustrated such a relationship between shock intensity and difficulty of discrimination in mice. It has mistakenly been considered a central feature of arousal theory, yet it is not referred to by any of the main arousal theorists (e.g., Duffy, 1957, 1962; Hebb, 1955; Malmo, 1959). The relevance of the result for arousal theory appears to have been pointed out by Easterbrook (1959) and it has since become a major idea in explaining changes in performance under conditions thought to alter arousal level.

How well does the theory of arousal account for the effects of environmental conditions on sustained attention? In responding to this question, the application

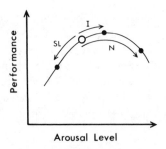

Figure 12.1 The assumed effects of (SL) sleep loss, (N) noise, and (I) incentive on arousal and performance, in terms of measurements along a single arousal dimension. The baseline (control) condition (open circle) is assumed to lie just below the optimal arousal level. Performance may be impaired by either a reduction in arousal with sleep loss or an excess of arousal under noise. Incentive increases arousal to a level that is almost optimal for the task. Combinations of two stressors are assumed to give rise to performance levels appropriate for additive effects on arousal level. (Based on the arguments of Broadbent, 1963, 1971; Corcoran, 1962; Wilkinson, 1963.)

of the theory to the results summarized in Tables 12.1 and 12.2 as well as some of the theory's limitations are considered.

Evidence for the Inverted-U Relation

First, the data show that the deleterious effects of sleep deprivation are counteracted by noise, which itself impairs performance in subjects who have slept normally. Second, incentive (in the form of augmented feedback about performance) effectively counteracts the effects of sleep loss. Finally, when incentives are present, performance in noise is worse rather than better as might be naively supposed. Thus, whatever the process may be by which sleep loss impairs efficiency, it is different from (and, indeed, opposite to) that for noise and for incentive. Yet, noise and incentive generally exert opposing effects on performance. The conclusion that emerged from attempts to come to terms with these challenging findings was that performance was related to the underlying change in state by a curvilinear rather than a monotonic function, as in Figure 12.1. Impairment could thus result from either too little arousal (as in the case of sleep loss) or too much (as in that of noise). Incentives must be assumed to produce "just the right amount," because performance is nearly always optimal under these conditions. It should be noted that Willett (1964) did find impairment on the five-choice task under the very high incentives associated with real-life motivation. Subjects were told that selection for a highly valued training scheme depended on their performance on the task. This result reinforces the general arousal type of explanation; of course, incentives can result in hyperarousal under some circumstances. As far as it goes, the simple arousal model works well. It handles the complex set of data adequately and offers a plausible physiological basis for stress effects in performance via changes in brain-stem activation (Lindsley, 1960). Before looking at this claim in a more general context, some of the problems in the data that such a view overlooks are considered.

Inconsistencies and Conceptual Problems

Although the patterns of stress combinations appear to fit the arousal theory, a number of detailed problems remain.

1. The direction of the effects of different environmental variables is rather inconsistent. First, all the effects represented in Figure 12.1, as well as the interactions between them, increase with time spent at the task. This is the case whether the overall effect on performance is positive or negative and whether the stressor is assumed to produce an increase or a decrease in arousal level. This is not the pattern of results that would be expected if the impairment with prolonged work alone was due to lowered arousal. Clearly, although the greater impairment with sleep loss is consistent with this interpretation, one would expect *reduced* impairment from the two arousers incentive and noise. Only the former does this; whereas noise, which effectively counteracts the effects of sleeplessness, typically increases the impairment with time at work. Second, interpretations of effects on arousal often seem to be determined by the data. For example, Wilkinson and Colquhoun (1968) found that incentive increased the impairment obtained with a small dose of alcohol and so claimed (as they had to) that alcohol is arousing in small doses, though it is still considered depressing in larger ones (Colquhoun, 1962). In a later study (Colquhoun & Edwards, 1975), both high and low doses of alcohol were found to reduce the effect of noise, with the high level having its expected greater effect. Here, alcohol is interpreted as simply being dearousing. The force of the explanation is clearly devalued by such circularity in interpretation.

2. The effects of incentive on performance under sleep deprivation are not merely to reduce the level of impairment; they are to abolish it completely (Wilkinson, 1961). Is this the kind of effect to be expected of an underlying process which loses x units of arousal and gains y units? The assumed drop in arousal (with sleep loss) is, in fact, apparently considerably greater than the rise produced by incentives; but the resultant level of arousal from the two conditions (inferred from performance level) is about the same as that for the combination of incentives with normal sleep. Furthermore, noise (assumed to result in overarousal) produces much less of an apparent rise in arousal level under sleep loss than when combined with incentive (Wilkinson, 1963). Again, there are major inconsistencies here in what constitutes adequate evidence for the arousal view.

3. The form that the interaction takes has little consistency across the different dependent variables used. Corcoran (1962) found that the combinations of sleep loss and noise produced interactions both in output and gaps but not in errors. Wilkinson (1963), on the other hand, reported only additive effects of sleep loss and noise for gaps and output, with the interaction effect emerging in the errors measure. With noise and incentives (Wilkinson, 1963), the effect again appears in the gaps index, with the effect on output and errors being nonsignificant (Wilkinson used a one-directional test in making comparisons of the effects of incentive at the two noise levels). Nowhere is there any attempt to provide any rationale for expecting the interaction to be found in a particular performance measure. With three indexes of performance change to pick from, the results are therefore less impressive than they appear at first sight.

Despite all these problems it must nevertheless be admitted that the pattern of findings overall is one that restricts the kind of theory of stress effects that can be held. Certainly, the evidence does not support the naive idea that each stress merely depletes some general performance resource, or that additional stressors

Type	Direction of the separate effects of A and B on (a) Performance	(b) Arousal	Typical performance data	Explanation in terms of the inverted-u model	Predicted pattern of combination of stressors
1a	same (+)	same (+)	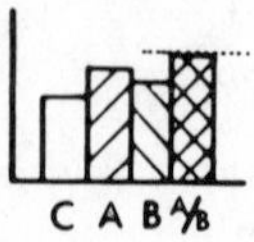C A B A/B	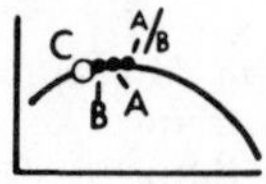C A/B B A	additive or -ve
1b	same (−)	same (+)	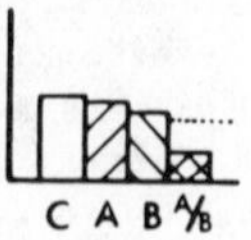C A B A/B	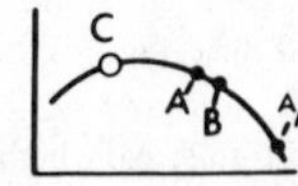C A B A/B	+ve
1c	same (−)	same (−)	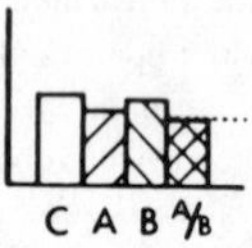C A B A/B	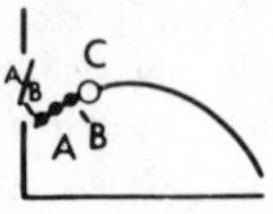A/B C A B	additive
2	same (−)	opposite	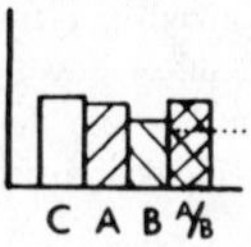C A B A/B	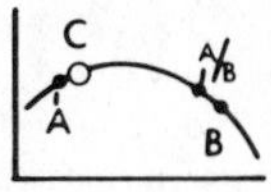C A/B A B	− ve (disordinal)
3	opposite	same (+)	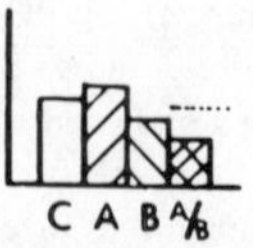C A B A/B	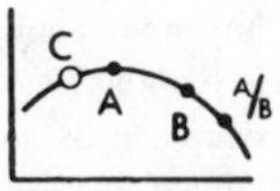C A B A/B	+ve
4	opposite	opposite	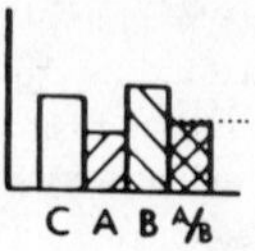C A B A/B	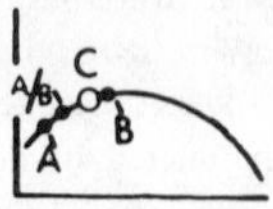A/B C B A	additive

Figure 12.2 The relation between changes in arousal and changes in performance for combinations of stressors. With Type 1, the two stressors have the same effect on performance (increase or decrease) and the same effect, on arousal: (1a) both increase; (1b) performance is decreased and arousal increased; (1c) both decrease. With Type 2, the two stressors have the same effect on performance (decrease) but opposite effects on arousal. With Type 3, the two stressors have opposite effects on performance, but the same effect on arousal (increase). With Type 4, the effects are opposite for both performance and arousal.

For the typical performance data, the control condition is indicated by C, and the two stressors by A and B. The level of their combined effect (A/B) may be compared with that resulting from a take advantage of lowered resistance following the first. Furthermore, they suggest both (1) that different stressors may affect particular performance characteristics in opposite ways, yet not combine antagonistically (as in the case of incentives and noise); and also (2) that two stressors may produce apparently similar performance effects, yet not combine synergistically (noise and sleep loss). The arousal theory clearly provides a framework for these kinds of observations because it embodies the principle of a curvilinear relationship between the degree of change in state and the quality of performance. The evidence concerning these assumptions is discussed in the following section. However, a final point concerning the simple arousal explanation of the stress effects observed on the five-choice task should be made. The inverted-U function has never been used as anything other than a convenient graphical metaphor, much as a Gaussian bell-shaped curve is used to provide a model for assumptions about the distribution of observations of performance measures. Unlike the latter, however, it is rarely tested; nor is it even used to generate testable predictions about data. When it is known what effect on arousal level is produced by various environmental changes, more precise predictions should be able to be made regarding *how* they will combine. Figure 12.2 illustrates four different situations resulting from combinations of stress effects and corresponding arousal level changes.

From this it may be seen that almost any kind of outcome is possible from a combination of two stressors. This is true even for the three examples of Type 1, in which the two variables affect both performance and arousal level in the same direction. These predictions can however, only be made when the effects of the two variables on arousal level can be specified independently of performance. For example, in 1b, if it is known that, say, anxiety and noise both impair performance and that they both increase arousal, it can be predicted that a clear positive interaction will result when they are combined. Similarly, in Type 2, if sleep loss and noise both impair performance, and it is known that they affect arousal in opposite directions; a negative interaction would be predicted. Such outcomes would then provide strong evidence of the nature of the underlying relationship between arousal and performance. Although there is evidence consistent with both these patterns, I have avoided providing examples of combinations in Figure 12.2. This is because the effects of stress variables on arousal level have only rarely been tested directly. As a counter-example, consider Type 4, which might be taken to represent the combination of sleep loss and incentive.

---

summation of the separate effects (dashed line). In the inverted-U model of the data, the control condition, C, is assumed to be below the optimal level (open circle). The assumed effects of A, B, and A/B are shown in relation to this (darkened circles). The final column indicates the type of combination expected from the assumed arousal model of the data ($-$ve, negative interaction; $+$ve, positive interaction.)

Sleep loss and incentive have opposite effects on performance and (supposedly) opposing influences on arousal level. As I have indicated, this might be expected to result in something close to an additive combination (as long as performance is suboptimal without incentive). Instead, as Wilkinson's (1961) data show, the result is a very marked negative interaction: The effect of sleep loss is effectively absent in the presence of incentive. I am not suggesting that Figure 12.2 helps to resolve the interpretive problems of the inverted-U hypothesis. Rather, it indicates the futility of attempting to test this hypothesis without first trying to establish a satisfactory method for (independently) testing how different independent variables affect arousal level. If this is done it becomes possible to make predictions about stress combinations that are within quite narrow limits. The explanatory value of the theory is minimal without such a step.

For the reasons I have mentioned in the preceding section, as well as others considered in the next section, the simple arousal model is clearly inadequate for the data to which it has been applied. Yet it is still used widely, often as a convenient adjunct to models of attention or memory. Theorists should be aware that the arousal model, in the usual form it takes, makes almost no unambiguous predictions about performance change; and the few that can be made often turn out to be generally inconsistent with the data.

Evaluation of Arousal Theory in Attention and Performance

The previous section has illustrated the scope of the arousal concept in accounting for effects of environmental changes on sustained-attention tasks. It is clear that there are certain findings not easily encompassed by the general theory. Before considering these difficulties more formally and looking more closely at the assumptions underlying the Yerkes–Dodson law, it may be helpful to consider briefly both formal and informal attempts to link arousal concepts with theories of attention.

Models of Attention

Structural Theories

During the 1960s, Broadbent's filter theory occupied a central role in theorizing about effects of stress, though there have been no specific attempts to relate these arguments to those of arousal theory. Broadbent (1957a, 1958) interpreted the effects of noise (as well as those of prolonged work and other distracting stimuli) in terms of disruption of the filtering process. These external environmental events were seen as distracting because they effectively captured the selective process, preventing the continuous intake of task information. One of the arguments rested on the demonstration that the kind of noise (loud and high pitched) that most readily disrupted continuous visual serial reaction-time performance actually resulted in the fastest reaction time when it was presented as the signal for response (Broadbent, 1957b). It affected performance not because of some general inhibitory effect of noise on the system, but because it was an effective "attention-getter." In fact, the two effects may be quite unrelated, particularly when the first involves continuous noise and the second short bursts. There are reasonable grounds for supposing that noise bursts do indeed capture selective attention (Fisher, 1972), particularly when their timing cannot be predicted. Such a view has great difficulty, however, in accounting for facilitatory effects of noise, such as those found when subjects are sleepy, or in explaining the detrimental effects of nondistracting stressors, such as sleeplessness or drugs. Broadbent makes these points in a full and clear analysis of the development of his thinking; the interested reader is referred to Broadbent (1971, pp. 400–437).

In the two-level model referred to in the following, under the heading "Control Theories" (Broadbent, 1971), arousal is considered as a nonspecific state affecting the efficiency of the mechanism responsible for the execution of well-learned responses, though its locus of action is not specified. Elsewhere, Broadbent makes a case for arousal having its effect on input selection (filtering) and, through this, affecting later components in the system such as those associated with STM and decision making (Broadbent, 1978). The primary role of the upper level control process is to regulate the behavior of the system according to task demands, and so prevent changes in arousal from affecting the quality of performance.

Capacity Theories

Capacity theories have emphasized the amount of information processing that the system is capable of, rather than the arrangements of components involved in processing. This kind of attention model has always seemed more suitable as a vehicle for arousal theory because both capacity and arousal refer to rather general properties of the system. The most influential attempt to incorporate arousal into capacity theory was that put forward by Kahneman (1973) in his book *Attention and Effort*. Kahneman argued that capacity is a variable commodity that is related to the current level of arousal. It may be allocated to different activities on the basis of an evaluation of current and long-term priorities, and may be increased in accordance with task demands by the expenditure of effort. This active mobilization of resources results in the various manifestations of arousal observed in the activation of the sympathetic nervous system (SNS) or endocrine function (Frankenhaeuser, 1975; Mandler, 1979)—

Cannon's (1932) "fight or flight" reaction. This involves increased respiration, heart rate, sweat secretion, and pupil dilation; constriction of peripheral blood vessels (and rise in blood pressure); increased discharge of adrenalin and nor-adrenalin; and other detailed changes. Kahneman uses the construct of effort as the direct antecedent of both changes in capacity and increases in arousal level. There seems to be no direct evidence for the implied link between capacity and arousal, although it is difficult to know what would constitute a satisfactory test of this hypothesis. The most important feature of Kahneman's model is the direct link between arousal and the *patterning* of behavior. As is discussed later, this proves to be the most obvious feature of performance change under stress. The idea that changes in environmental stimulation can act (via the internal state) to alter the relative efficiency of different processes is one which has important consequences for theories of stress.

Control Theories

Rabbitt (1979, 1981) has argued that models of performance have been gener-ally ill equipped to handle change, whether brought about by stress, aging, or extended practice. This is largely because these models contain no process capa-ble of modifying behavior in the light of feedback, so that they are precisely driven by inputs to carry out the same operations in the same way. One class of theories that does allow for change is that which includes a control process to guide the flow of information through the system. Broadbent (1971), for exam-ple, found it necessary to provide such a mechanism to supervise the changes in efficiency of habitual responses brought about by arousal. This would require an upper control process, responsible for the preservation of current task priorities, recent information, and the like; whereas nonspecific changes in stimulation would exert their effects via a lower control process, responsible for the execu-tion of overlearned responses and operating according to the inverted-U rule. Because the control of the system is ultimately the responsibility of the upper process, effects of arousal only become apparent when this mechanism is im-paired by fatigue or prolonged work. The upper mechanism was also regarded by Broadbent as the locus of the effects of alcohol, time of day, and temperament. A model of this complexity (at least) is demanded by the data discussed earlier in this chapter and successfully solves most of the problems found in applying the inverted-U model to the results of sustained-attention tasks. It would seem more consistent to include incentive in the group of variables that affect the upper process, in view of its dramatic effects on sleep-deprived subjects; though this would offer new problems concerning its combination with noise. The two-level model proposed by Broadbent retains the central ideas of arousal theory; the upper level merely provides a mechanism for the control of the effects of arousal on performance. This kind of model can only be justified if arousal can be shown to be a *general* process in relation to different stressors and different performance characteristics, a view that is questioned here. Although Teichner (1968) did not specifically propose a control mechanism such as Broadbent's, he suggested that effects of internal and external environmental changes are modified by attention, which promotes compensatory and regulatory activity to maintain appropriate criteria for system parameters. In Hamilton *et al.'s* model (1977) the locus of control is not restricted to an "upper" system, but can shift between upper and lower components of the system according to the current state of internal and external demands. Thus, top–down control is relinquished whenever highly compatible input–output operations are required, and executive decisions are used to shift from an automatic to a controlled (e.g., prepared) state.

Although all these models consider the ways in which environmental effects are mediated by attention, they vary in the assumptions they make about the underlying nature of these effects. The major question still to be dealt with in this chapter is How can we best conceive of the changes resulting from exposure to environmental stress? Broadbent has considered the general arousal theory to provide a useful approximation of the main effects of stress, as has Kahneman; and Teichner (1968), despite a discussion of the differences in the physiological response to different environmental conditions, also assumed the general stress reaction to be the primary consequence of environmental changes. A more recent approach (Hamilton *et al.,* 1977; Hockey, 1979; Hockey & Hamilton, 1983) has been to consider qualitative changes associated with different types of stressors. This view is expressed more fully in the fourth section of this chapter.

Difficulties of Arousal Theory

It is puzzling that arousal theory has not readily been incorporated into mainstream attention theory, because its popularity is widespread. At the same time, the interpretation of the effects of environmental variables in terms of arousal is comparatively recent. Even Broadbent's (1971) discussion of stress effects could not provide a convincing argument for considering the effects of arousal as being on filtering rather than on pigeonholing, though the available evidence pointed that way. It will be useful to consider the nature of the arousal concept and misunderstandings that may arise from its application.

Modern Origins of Arousal Theory

The conception of arousal as a nonspecific and widespread brain process having important implications for psychological theory (Hebb, 1955; Malmo, 1959) may be seen as an attempt to provide a theoretical basis for Hull's (1943) notion of the generalized drive state, resulting from the summation of individual drives. This concept was implicit in the earlier theorizing of Freeman, Courts, and Duffy (see Duffy, 1962) and emphasized the energetic or intensive aspects of attention. Malmo and Hebb found a firm basis for the arousal concept in work on the electroencephalogram (EEG) and reticular formation (see Lindsley, 1960) and suggested the generality of the inverted-U relation. Since that time, it has become clear that the arousal (or activation) system cannot be considered in any sense unitary (Routtenberg, 1966) or nonspecific (Pribram & McGuinness, 1975). Furthermore, Lacey (1967) has shown that dissociation can be found at all levels between different aspects of arousal; between EEG and behavioral arousal, between different autonomic components of arousal, and even within the same autonomic response (heart rate) under different task demands. The clear anatomical and physiological bases of arousal theory can no longer be assumed.

Methodological Arguments

Experimental psychologists have tended to use arousal as if it were a kind of *volume* control, turning up the level of all responses or possible activities equally. Some traditional theorists (Broen & Storms, 1961) have demonstrated that such an assumption can nevertheless give rise to selective effects in overt behavior (by virtue of Hull–Spence rules governing competition between dominant and subdominant responses) and to the inverted-U (through the postulation of a ceiling of response strength). It is increasingly apparent that arousal effects are selective in a direct way, not merely by default; some activities may be impaired, whereas others are actually facilitated. This kind of evidence is discussed more fully later in the chapter, but it clearly suggests a process more akin to *tuning*. Easterbrook's (1959) hypothesis describes the effects of arousal in terms of a shift in the range of stimuli taken in, according to consistent rules of admission concerning their relevance to task demands; this must require a tuning explanation—a realignment of system resources.

A different kind of argument has been put forward by Näätänen (1975). He suggests that many of the claimed demonstrations of *over*arousal are the result not of a quantitative increase in some nonspecific process having a curvilinear relation to efficiency, but of the occurrence of a quite separate set of competing task demands. Attention may become withdrawn from the task as a direct result of the difficulty of meeting the demands of the procedures used to produce the high levels of stress. In the case of induced muscle tension this may be brought about by the requirement to hold a near-maximum force. Näätänen shows that when activation is increased through exercise, and performance tests are given *afterwards,* the curvilinear relationship between heart rate and reaction time is abolished. Similarly, anxiety induced by threat of shock or social pressure may impair performance not by virtue of its high arousal properties, but because of distraction through worry (Eysenck, 1982; Wine, 1971). The same may be claimed for the effects of any extreme environmental factor, such as those of noise, heat, cold, and dangerous environments. The impairment in performance on the five-choice serial reaction task with high incentives observed by Willett (1964) may also fit into this category. Because subjects in this condition regarded good performance as a requirement for admission to a much-prized apprenticeship scheme, it is likely that they were not just motivated but actually anxious during the test. As Näätänen suggests, it is this change in the pattern of the underlying state that produces impairment, rather than merely too much of the state.

Näätänen argues that activation should be considered not in terms of the level of some general process but as a qualitative patterning of bodily state. Effectiveness of performance is then determined by the relationship between this patterning of activation and that required by the current set of task demands. This view, which is very close to that of Hamilton *et al.* (1977), again emphasizes the selective tuning function of arousal. As I have stated previously in another publication (Hockey, 1979), it is not necessary to assume that decrements in performance are *never* the direct consequence of increases in some environmental condition. A decrement in any particular psychological function in a particular activation state may be expected as a direct result of shifts in the balance of available resources. This argument is discussed in more detail in the following section.

Easterbrook's (1959) version of the inverted-U hypothesis, one of the two components of the Yerkes–Dodson law, has already been discussed. Easterbrook went beyond the "commonsense" explanations offered by providing some sort of answer to the question about what arousal does. In his terms, arousal progressively reduces the range of environmental cues taken in; in Hockey's (1970), it increases the selectivity of attention; and in Teichner's (1968), it reduces the bandwidth of attention. In all cases, the inverted-U is explained by a biphasic change in the effects of information selection on task behavior: (1) increased task orientation through more selective sampling of environmental information; and (2) interruption of relevant input information through excessive selectivity. Furthermore, this formulation provides a plausible basis for the optimality component of the Yerkes–Dodson law. Simpler tasks (involving a more restricted range of cues) would be able to withstand greater increases in selectivity before reaching the point of inflection than would more complex tasks.

Easterbrook's analysis has received considerable support from studies of narrowing of attention (Broadbent, 1971; Hockey, 1970; Kahneman, 1973; Teichner, 1968), but it is not as satisfactory as it may seem. Is the ubiquitous increase in selectivity with high arousal *the* explanation for changes in mental function with stress? Apparently not, because other changes can readily be demonstrated (for example, those in memory function or SATO). It may of course be argued that all such changes are different manifestations of the same fundamental effect on the system, as suggested on several occasions by Hamilton and Hockey (e.g., Hamilton *et al.*, 1977; Hockey, 1979). If this is the case, however, then one would expect different stressors to change performance in the same kinds of ways. Yet, there are cases of attentional selectivity being affected similarly by, say, noise and incentives, both biasing performance toward primary-task efficiency; whereas immediate memory may be affected differently (Eysenck, 1982). Perhaps other possible cognitive changes with stress should be considered. If arousal may not easily be defined in terms of the level of some general function, but rather as a qualitative pattern, then different stressors may produce different patterns of cognitive change. As I shall show later, this appears to be the case.

A second problem for the Yerkes–Dodson law (and Easterbrook's version of it) is the way in which difficulty (or complexity) is handled. How does one know whether one task requires a broader range of cue utilization than another? One usually has some intuitive understanding of difficulty, but what must be considered seriously is the question of what characteristics of a task contribute to such a classification. Certainly, a broad attentional strategy (as opposed to a narrow one) can be assumed to be required by tasks having more sources of information to monitor or more information-reduction requirements in decision-making, but what about other characteristics? Working-memory load is a particularly potent source of interference in dual-task situations (Baddeley & Hitch, 1974) and appears to have its effect on central planning operations rather than at any particular structural locus (Logan, 1979). It can result in a marked shift in the phase of the circadian rhythm for visual search (Folkard, Knauth, Monk, & Rutenfrantz, 1976), and reverse the effects of noise on letter-transformation speed (Hamilton et al., 1977). Difficulty may also depend on features such as the number or order of different processing resources demanded by a task, or more simply, the extent to which central control strategies are needed to maintain effective activity (as discussed, for example, by Schneider, Dumais, & Shiffrin, Chapter 1, this volume). In fact, of course, there is very little known about what it is that makes something difficult. Instead of passively accepting the Yerkes–Dodson law as a convenient commonsense notion to squeeze our results into, it seems preferable to dispense with the Yerkes–Dodson law, inverted-U hypothesis, and optimum arousal frameworks altogether. They may well have more than a grain of truth in them, but they now seem very unlikely to help us understand the relation between attention and bodily states, escept in a limited, quite superficial way.

States of Attention and Cognition

I now turn to an alternative methodology and theoretical framework for considering effects of environment on performance. Hamilton et al., (1977) and Hockey and Hamilton (1983) have referred to this as a *state analysis,* following the approach of Prechtl (1974) in describing patterns of behavior in young infants. Following this terminology, a *state* is defined here as a multidimensional pattern of changes in critical behavioral indicators. On another level, however, the term *stress state* refers to the underlying pattern of physiological changes produced by that stressor, and *cognitive* (or *resource*) *state* refers to the underlying pattern of operating efficiency of the major performance resources. The central feature in our approach is the compilation of fairly detailed patterns of cognitive change in different environments or stress states (loosely referred to as *maps*), and a comparison of these with one another in order to look for evidence of groups of similar states or of differences between conditions. The use of a number of indicators of cognitive change, rather than one or two as is usual, allows observation of subtle differences in the patterns of effect. In illustrating the application of this method to analysis of the effects of stressors, I will focus on a particular stressor—loud, continuous, broad-band noise. Noise is used as an example for two reasons: (1) It has been studied more systematically than most other stressors from the point of view of theories of performance, and (2) our (Hamilton *et al.,* 1977) approach has been developed around the observation of performance in this state.

A Sketchmap of the Noise State

Performance under loud noise may be seen to be the result of a number of separate changes in the components of performance, rather than a single decrease in attentional efficiency. Hockey (1970) showed that the principle of increased selectivity with high arousal could be successfully applied to the effects of noise, as well as to those of other stressors, in order to account for the apparent discrepancies in the literature between studies that demonstrated impairment in vigilance performance and those that did not. A change in selectivity is not one that can be directly mapped onto a dimension of efficiency. It is a qualitative change, the implications of which for the efficiency of the person's behavior must be made in the light of the demand characteristics of particular tasks. If noise makes people more selective, they will certainly tend to be less efficient, in general, on more complex tasks, in as much as these can be said to require a flexible attentional strategy or a more broad-band analysis of task information. The change is one of *style,* however, and not competence; on other tasks the same change will facilitate the job the person has to do. In other components of performance, however, a genuine change in the efficiency of the process may be found with noise. Our analysis of the overall pattern of effects associated with a stressor considers both the strategic and structural changes in cognition. Instead of asking how good attention or cognitive efficiency are *in general,* however we concern ourselves with asking What is it like (in this state or that)?

In addition to the changes in selectivity, which have been well documented (see Broadbent, 1971; Hockey, 1970, 1979), a number of other changes can be identified. These are discussed in some detail in papers by Hamilton *et al.* (1977) and Hockey and Hamilton (1983), and so are discussed only briefly here. It is clear that there are marked effects on *memory* function, although the underlying basis for these effects have proved difficult to deduce (Broadbent, 1981). It seems quite likely that noise reduces the real efficiency of working memory. Many measures of STM function are reduced by noise, and multicomponent tasks are more likely to suffer under noise when they include a heavy working-memory requirement (Hamilton *et al.*, 1977). On the other hand, the recall of *very* recent information (the last few items in a running-memory task) can be facilitated by noise (Hamilton *et al.*, 1977). Strategic changes are clearly involved, then, in addition to any underlying shift in system parameters. A related feature of this is the tendency for the recall of order information to be relatively better in noise (Hamilton *et al.*, 1977; Wilding & Mohindra, 1980).

Tasks that require rapid continuous output (serial reaction time, cancellation, classification) almost always exhibit SATO patterns (Rabbitt, 1981). Noise appears to shift the balance of this trade-off in the direction of increased errors. In some cases, there are clear indications of increased speed with noise (e.g., Blake, 1971; Davies & Davies, 1975), most studies show increased errors, and some studies show both effects (Blake, 1971). The direction overall, in terms of changes in the speed–accuracy balance, is, however, fairly consistent for this type of task situation. It should be made quite clear that these changes in speed and accuracy are *implied* by the data, but may be due to other factors. Such conclusions would only be warranted if the distribution of reaction times remained the same. A shift in the distribution may require a different kind of interpretation (e.g., in terms of reduced skill in monitoring average response speed; Rabbitt, 1981). Such analyses of reaction-time data have not been carried out, though they will undoubtedly clarify the nature of this change. I would argue that some kind of strategic change (speed at the expense of accuracy) underlies the effects of noise in such situations, though reduced monitoring of feedback from the response production system may also be involved.

A summary of the component features of the noise state is as follows:

1. An increase in the selectivity of attention
2. A decrease in the use of working memory
3. A tendency for increased speed at the expense of a loss of accuracy.

In addition, we (Hamilton *et al.*, 1977; Hockey & Hamilton, 1983) can add the following:

4. A decrease in subjective uncertainty (in signal detection and recall)

It is possible to integrate these different observed features of the noise state into a composite map, as Broadbent (1978) has done. I can do no better than to reproduce his scenario here, with a few comments of my own added:

[through greater selectivity] a more aroused person will select information from a smaller area of the environment. He will therefore pick up less fragmentary and doubtful information outside that area. Consequently he will rarely give qualified and doubtful judgments about, say, visual signals seen in peripheral attention; but will give confident assertions and denials. This will be good for performance so long as the centre of attention is on the task; early in the work session this will be true most of the time. Any shift away from the task later on, may give rise to missed signals, or inefficiencies in continuous performance. (Broadbent, 1978, p. 1063)

I would add that because he or she is ignoring some aspects of the task, the subject will work quickly and also make more errors. Because sampling of the environment is constricted and processing of inputs rapid, storage of old information is kept to a minimum: He or she takes in less and holds onto it for briefer periods. This enables the subject to maintain a fast selective strategy, while making him or her less sensitive to changes in the spatial or temporal structure of task information.

Notice two things. First, Broadbent talks not of noise but of the aroused person. Second, these changes have been described as if they all follow from some single fundamental change in cognitive state; the separate effects are but different aspects of the same basic change. Both of these assumptions may be correct, but I believe that the evidence is insufficient for either and probably contradictory to the first. There is a more complete (though still woefully inadequate) picture of the noise state than for any other state (even anxiety). As will become clear in the following analysis, this picture is indeed fairly consistent for noise and anxiety; but it is different in small but important ways for other aroused states. Whether these changes all reflect a single central process is unclear; but because most of the possible patterns of performance can be observed, it is difficult to consider any one of the changes just mentioned (e.g., selectivity) as primary.

Indicators of System State

In order to provide descriptions of cognitive states, it is necessary to decide on a suitable set of state variables that can be used to represent the changes produced by environmental factors. There is no generally agreed on taxonomy of mental function, though several guidelines may be adopted to provide these indicators. There appear to be two distinct types of changes in performance; those associated with fundamental shifts in system parameters (changes in capacity, rate of processing, and so on), and those arising from the adoption of strategies (SATO and decision criteria, for example). I shall refer to these as *structural variables* and *strategic variables,* respectively. There is good evidence that both kinds of effects occur in task behavior under stress.

A fuller discussion of the arguments in favor of different indicators is given by Hockey and Hamilton (1983). Based on the literature of stress studies, the following measures of performance change may be distinguished.

Selectivity

In general terms, *selectivity* refers to a shift in task set. Behavior becomes more oriented towards task priorities, *high selectivity*, or less controlled by these features, *low selectivity*. This kind of change has sometimes been referred to as a narrowing of attention (or broadening) and may be considered a strategic shift in system operating characteristics.

Speed and Accuracy

In tasks requiring rapid responding, performance may be defined in terms of both speed and accuracy. A particular environmental change may result in an increase (or decrease) in speed with or without a corresponding change in accuracy. A complementary change (e.g., increased speed and decreased accuracy) is interpreted as a strategic shift in behavioral parameters, whereas a change in the same direction (e.g., increase in both speed and accuracy) is interpreted as a shift in the true efficiency (information-processing rate) of the system.

Working Memory

Although information on the use of working memory is rather complex, it is possible to infer changes in the capacity of the system to store information for brief periods—either from performance in STM tasks or from the effects of working-memory demands during other mental tasks. (*Capacity* is here used to refer to the apparent storage space available to the system, rather than to a particular view of memory structure.)

Alertness

This is not strictly a change in performance, but an indication of the generally accepted effect of environmental factors on the intensive aspects of attention— usually referred to as the *arousal level*. I shall use this as a convenient criterion measure of state in considering states of high arousal (increased alertness) on the one hand, and those of low arousal (decreased alertness) on the other. Unfortunately it has not been possible to include other measures, such as LTM, decision strategies, sensitivity, either because of difficulties of interpretation or because of a shortage of suitable evidence. It seems certain that their inclusion would only serve to buttress the arguments presented here, however, because such data can only increase the number of states that may be differentiated.

The Patterning of Environmental Effects

The results of a rather crude analysis of the effects of environmental conditions on performance are illustrated in Table 12.3. This gives a summary of the changes observed in each of the state indicators just outlined.

TABLE 12.3

Changes in Various Performance Indicators of System Function Resulting from Different Stressors[a]

	General alertness	Attentional selectivity	Fast responding		STM capacity	Sources[b]
			Speed	Accuracy		
Anxiety	+	+	0	−	−	4
Noise	+	+	0	−	−	2, 3, 4, 6
Amphetamine	+	+	+	−	?	(?)
Nicotine	+	+	+	+ ?	−	8
Incentive	+	+	+	+	+	2, 4
Time of day (p.m.)	+	?	+	−	−	1, 2, 4, 5
Heat	+ ?	+	0	−	0	3, 7
Alcohol	−	+ ?	−	−	−	2, 8
Tranquilizers	−	−	−	−	−	2, 8
Sleeplessness	−	−	−	−	0	2, 4, 6
Prolonged work	−	+ ?	−	−	0	2, 4, 6
Time of day (a.m.)	−	?	−	+	+	1, 2, 4, 5

[a] Changes observed: indicator generally shows an increase in the particular condition (+), generally shows a decrease (−), no change (0), and lack of clear data or conflicting evidence (?).

[b] Sources: 1, Blake (1967, 1971); 2, Broadbent (1971); 3, Broadbent (1981); 4, Eysenck (1982); 5, Folkard (1983); 6, Hamilton et al. (1977); 7, Ramsey (1983); and 8, Wesnes and Warburton (1983).

Two major conclusions can be drawn from this pattern of results. First, it should be noted that the traditional major breakdown into high and low arousal states does provide a broad basis for grouping the various effects. High arousal states appear to belong to a family as do those characterized by low arousal. Second, it can be seen however, that within-family differences are quite marked, suggesting that more influences are at work than the single one of arousal level. In short, a number of different high-arousal and low-arousal states can be distinguished according to the particular combination of changes typically observed in the various indicator variables. These are summarized graphically in Figure 12.3, which indicates each of the changes as an increase or decrease in the length of a bar, which represents the normal effective range of this system parameter. The resulting pattern can be interpreted as a graphical representation of the state profile.

The data presented in Table 12.3 represent the general pattern of stress effects, though there are exceptions for almost all the cells in the table. The main purpose of the analysis is to illustrate the kind of data that a theory of stress and arousal ought to be able to explain and to present conclusions from the most widely used environmental manipulations. It will be observed that I have included morning and afternoon as two separate conditions, although these are of course defined only with respect to each other, because they are often contrasted in ways that are similar to discussions of effects of environmental stressors (e.g., Revelle,

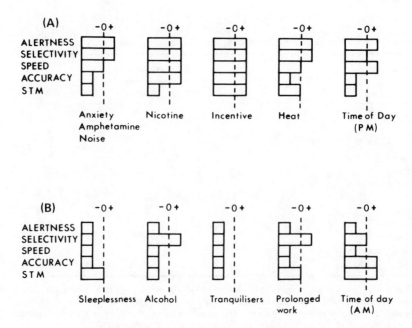

Figure 12.3 Performance profiles for different activation states: (A) "high"-arousal states and (b) "low"-arousal states. The length of the bar corresponds to the relative change in each indicator, with respect to a modal (nonstressed) state (vertical dashed line). For time of day changes, AM and PM are shown as complementary patterns.

Humphreys, Simon, & Gilliand, 1980). In addition, they serve to define the range of natural changes in the baseline state, which has implications for all other patterns. Within the limitations of these observations, I have grouped the patterns together for the typical high-arousal set (noise, anxiety, amphetamine), but left others, for the moment, as separate states.

The main limitation of this analysis is the difficulty of finding studies in which performance function is sufficiently specified for our purposes. The details are justified in a full review of stress patterns (Hockey & Hamilton, note 4), though a few comments are appropriate in view of the distinctions I have made:

1. There is no direct evidence for an increase in selectivity with time of day, although later times of day would be expected to be similar to noise, incentives and stimulant drugs in this respect. At the present time, however, there are very few studies that are relevant to this question. Selectivity may be increased in states thought to be characterized by low arousal, such as those produced by alcohol or prolonged work. Teichner (1968) has argued that such an effect might be an adaptive response to any stressful environment and provides evidence of this with respect to sleep loss. Hockey (1970) in fact found a short-lived effect of increased selectivity under sleeplessness, though this was reversed later in the 40-minute session. What is clear, in general, is that high arousal is neither a sufficient nor a necessary condition for increased selectivity.

2. A SATO appears to occur for high-arousal conditions, with speed being preserved or increased at the expense of accuracy. Incentives generally improve both speed and accuracy (as in the case of the five-choice task discussed in an earlier section, except when very high levels of incentive are used (Eysenck, 1982); as I have suggested, these situations probably involve an additional anxiety component. Nicotine generally increases speed without a loss of accuracy (Wesnes & Warburton, 1983), though more data are again needed to confirm the generality of this result.

3. Immediate memory is worse in high arousal states, though incentive normally enhances STM performance (Eysenck, 1982). It also seems poor under conditions of low arousal produced by alcohol and minor tranquilizers. Wesnes and Warburton (1983) have suggested that this may be due to the impairment of selective attention during the presentation of material, though it may also represent a genuine impairment in memory function (Hockey, McLean, & Hamilton, 1981).

Summary of State Changes

Our analysis provides evidence of eight or nine states, though it is clear that this number is somewhat arbitrary. It is dependent on the number of indicator variables used, the weight placed on differences in each, and so on. It is also dependent on a fuller understanding of the functional properties of the system. Greater use of detailed system specifications is likely to produce as many states as there are environmental variables, whereas a proper understanding of the relations between resources and functions may reduce the number to three or four. The major implication of this analysis is that premature classification of results simply to make data fit the general theory of arousal should be avoided. Instead, the practice of letting the data speak for themselves should be adopted. This can only be done by looking at a wide range of performance characteristics for each individual stressor. This has previously been referred to as a *broad-band* methodology (Hockey, 1979; Hockey & Hamilton, 1983). The data should at least allow detection of differences in the patterning of effects where such differences exist.

Adaptive Resource Management

The view of performance changes under stress that I have put forward here derives from a more general approach to the understanding of the organization and control of mental function that we have developed from our work over the past 10 years or so (Hamilton *et al.*, 1977; Hockey *et al.*, 1981; Hockey & Hamilton, 1983). Although we have not yet developed these ideas into a formal theory, it seems useful to outline the central assumptions and conceptions of this view in the context of stress effects.

Resource States

Our view of the system is one which may loosely be related to the multiple-resources type of model (see Wickens, Chapter 3, this volume). It is assumed that there are a number of functionally separable processing facilities (special purpose resources) in addition to a general purpose executive process. Specific resources are limited in processing capacity by either rate or space limitations, though the principal limitation on efficient performance is usually the limited capacity of the executive process. This system is responsible for the active direction of control between resources, for compiling temporary sequences of processes required for particular task demands, and for shifting the overall bias in processing from one pattern of resource availability to another in response to long-term priorities and current environmental influences on the resource state. The *resource state* is defined as the pattern of the functional levels of the various resources at a particular time. Executive control is not required for operations that can proceed automatically, such as those involving highly compatible input–output mappings, or those that require the use of resources that are currently active.

The Acquisition and Maintenance of States

Internal or external environmental changes are assumed to alter the resource state by changing the pattern of availability of resources. This makes some kinds of cognitive operation easier to execute, and others harder; whereas some will not be significantly affected. Without effective executive control, these changes would be readily observed in performance patterns because they would reflect the underlying strengths and weaknesses of the various components of the system under these conditions. The executive is used, however, to override these changes in conditions in which the resulting state is unsuitable for current infor-mation-processing requirements. In the absence of environmental changes, its function is the same—to acquire and to maintain the appropriate balance of resource availability for current requirements. A particular environmental change will impair performance only to the extent that it results in a resource state that is poorly correlated with that required for optimal efficiency. The further the dis-tance between required and current state, the greater will be the difficulty in overcoming the discrepancy and maintaining the control needed.

This suggests that environmental effects will be more likely to be observed when the executive process becomes less effective (with fatigue or prolonged work, for example), which is typically what happens. It is also true that effects may be seen on more complex cognitive tasks without prolonged exposure. This would be interpreted in terms of the greater complexity of the executive control needed for these tasks, compared, for example, to the relatively simple demands of sustained attention. Any effects of stress may be more difficult to overcome in cognitive tasks because of the need to shift the pattern of cognitive operations very rapidly. Hamilton *et al.* (1977) suggested that controlled shifts of state may be achieved by the execution of internal orienting, in order to promote desired behavior patterns.

Throughout this chapter little has been said about individual differences, mainly to avoid unnecessary complication of already difficult issues. However, it should be said in this context that the state concept can also be applied to this problem. Any individual may be characterized by a general pattern of resource availability; that is, he or she may be said to have a typical cognitive state corresponding to his or her more public personality characteristics. This is a baseline, or modal, state for the individual. It may even be said that the signal that could be averaged from fluctuations in this state over a long period would represent that individual's *unstressed state*. Thus, one individual may have a modal pattern much like that produced generally by sleeplessness and so would not be unduly stressed by sleep loss, whereas another whose modal state is like that produced by high anxiety would regard sleep loss as stressful. I should make it clear here that stress will only result if there is a requirement to counteract it. If sleep is allowed in the example just mentioned, neither individual should have any problem. If individual differences can be described in the same terms as can patterns of performance changes under stress, it would be possible to make some very specific predictions about individual differences in environmental effects.

Effort, Task Demands, and Costs

Shifts in state produced by environmental changes do not, then, impose any strict limitations on performance capabilities. Rather, as I have said in the preceding, they push the system into a different baseline state. Whenever this state is unsuitable for current activity, it is necessary to attain or maintain the appropriate balance of function by means of executive effort. Hamilton and Hockey (1974) showed that such a shift (between states of acceptance and rejection of auditory events) was markedly time limited and associated with reduced detection of secondary-task probes. Kahneman (1973) has shown that such effort can be measured in the dilation of the pupil and other autonomic indexes under some circumstances and is related directly to the information-processing demands of the task. According to Pribram and McGuinness (1975) effort is involved whenever "the situation demands the regulation of arousal and activation to produce a change in information processing competency" (p. 135). *Arousal* is defined more specifically here as the physiological effects of input, whereas *activation* refers to the preparation of response mechanisms. Effort is interpreted as an active process of coordination and control of system state, in much the same way as it is in our framework. The pattern of competency (the cognitive state in our terms) is altered by the inhibition of arousal in favor of activation (vigilant readiness), the promotion of arousal processes (external orienting), and so on. Pribram and McGuinness locate the effort process in hippocampal circuits on the basis of animal work. It seems to me that the subtlety of behavioral detail required to separate effects of coordinating effort from those of a more general arousal process of the type discussed here are beyond the reach of studies of animal attention, so that the validity of this three-stage system must be questioned. On the other hand, it is clear that anatomical and physiological data are capable of providing a basis for the central role of effort in the regulation of state.

Certainly, such a control mechanism has been found essential in attempts by Broadbent (1977), Reason (Chapter 14, this volume), and Shallice (1978) to model complex activity. Environmental stressors impose restrictions on the processing capabilities of the system. It is true that these may be overcome in the short term surprisingly well (Kahneman, 1970), and that changes rarely appear until the individual is fatigued, unless the cognitive demands are very high; it is also true that considerable costs may be associated with such attempted control. Sleep-deprived subjects who maintain normal levels of performance may show marked increases in muscle tension (Wilkinson, 1962), or a more general pattern of sympathetic activation when punished painfully for poor performance (Malmo & Surwillo, 1960). Lundberg (1982) has shown that individuals may cope with having to perform calculations in noise either by increasing effort (and catecholamine output) in order to maintain normal levels of performance, or by accepting a lower level of performance (with no corresponding change in catecholamines). The physiological patterns associated with performance under adverse environmental conditions may be better considered not as the direct effect of increased arousal level, but in terms of the attempts made by the individual to maintain a particular prestress state by resisting the change. Pribram and McGuinness (1975) argue that much of the difficulty in interpreting results of psychophysiological studies of performance may be attributable to the failure to consider this active role of effort. In the present theory, effort is always required when an individual tries to carry out a task optimally, both to promote the best combination of resources and to maintain them in a suitable program for the duration of the task.

Environmental effects on the state of the system can thus be considered in terms of a particular pattern of changes in processing capabilities. This is rarely likely to be optimal for the execution of familiar tasks because these optimal patterns will normally have been learned under a variety of conditions and will be represented to some extent by the averaged modal state. Effort will thus normally be required to produce the appropriate state for the task. One would expect coping with noise, for example, to be more of a problem with tasks that place heavy demands on memory than in situations in which selective monitoring or speeded responses are required in the absence of a high memory load. Noise may be thought of as producing state changes that are more suitable for the latter kind of operation because of some commonality in the physiological states resulting from noise on the one hand and from these kinds of performance tasks on the other. One would further expect physiological costs to be more clearly correlated with the efficiency of performance in the high-memory-load task, in which an effortful shift of state is required. A more traditional arousal theory would associate the general impairment here with overarousal, so that individuals exhibiting the greatest physiological activity should be the most overaroused, and so should perform most poorly.

Although coping with environmental changes will normally require effort, which is limited and costly, so that a pattern of decrement will emerge eventually; it is nevertheless the case that for any state change, whether it is produced by noise, sleeplessness, old age, or drugs, there may well be some set of task demands that is consonant with it. In this case, little or no effort will be required to maintain the appropriate state, and no decrements will be observed. The many examples of counter-intuitive effects of stressors in the literature provide ample support for this prediction.

Reference Notes

1. Pepler, R. D. *The effects of climatic factors on the performance of skilled tasks by young European men living in the tropics* (Pt. 4): *A task of prolonged visual vigilance* Applied Psychology Unit (Rep. No. 156/53). Cambridge, England: 1953.
2. Leonard, J. H. *Five-choice serial reaction apparatus* Council Applied Psychology Unit, (Rep. No. 326/59). Cambridge, England: Medical Research, 1959.
3. Colquhoun, W. P., & Wilkinson, R. T. *Interaction of l-hyoscine with sleep deprivation.* Unpublished manuscript, available from author, Medical Research Council, Perception and Cognitive Performance Unit, University of Sussex.
4. Hockey, G. R. J., & Hamilton, P. *The analysis of changes in performance patterning* Article in preparation, 1983.

References

Baddeley, A. D., & Hitch, G. J. Working memory. In G. H. Bower (Ed.), *The psychology of learning and motivation* (Vol. 8). New York: Academic Press, 1974.

Bills, A. G. Blocking: A new principle in mental fatigue. *American Journal of Psychology,* 1931, *9,* 349–350.

Blake, M. J. F. Time of day effects on performance in a range of tasks. *Psychonomic Science,* 1967, *9,* 349–350.

Blake, M. J. F. Temperament and time of day. In W. P. Colquhoun (Ed.), *Biological rhythms and human behaviour.* London: Academic Press, 1971.

Broadbent, D. E. Noise, paced performance and vigilance tasks. *British Journal of Psychology,* 1953, *44,* 295–303.

Broadbent, D. E. Effects of noise on behavior. In C. M. Harris (Ed.), *Handbook of noise control*, New York: McGraw-Hill, 1957.

Broadbent, D. E. Effects of noises of high and low frequency on behavior. *Ergonomics*, 1957, *1*, 21–29.

Broadbent, D. E. *Perception and communication*. London: Pergamon, 1958.

Broadbent, D. E. Differences and interactions between stressors. *Quarterly Journal of Experimental Psychology*, 1963, *15*, 205–211.

Broadbent, D. E. *Decision and stress*. London: Academic Press, 1971.

Broadbent, D. E. Levels, hierarchies and the locus of control. *Quarterly Journal of Experimental Psychology*, 1977, *29*, 181–201.

Broadbent, D. E. The current state of noise research: Reply to Poulton. *Psychological Bulletin*, 1978, *85*, 1052–1067.

Broadbent, D. E. The effects of moderate levels of noise on human performance. In J. V. Tobias & E. D. Schubert (Eds.), *Hearing: Research and theory*. New York: Academic Press, 1981.

Broadbent, D. E., & Gregory, M. Effects of noise and signal rate upon vigilance analysed by decision theory. *Human Factors*, 1965, *7*, 155–162.

Broen, W. E., & Storms, L. H. A reaction-potential ceiling and response decrements in complex situations. *Psychological Review*, 1961, *68*, 405–415.

Cahoon, R. I. Vigilance performance under hypoxia. *Journal of Applied Psychology*, 1970, *54*, 479–483.

Cannon, W. B. *Wisdom of the Body*. New York: Norton, 1932.

Colquhoun, W. P. Effects of hyoscine and meclozine on vigilance and short-term memory. *British Journal of Industrial Medicine*, 1962, *19*, 287–296.

Colquhoun, W. P. Circadian variation in mental efficiency. In W. P. Colquhourn (Ed.), *Biological rhythms and human behaviour*. London: Academic Press, 1971.

Colquhoun, W. P., & Edwards R. S. Interaction of noise with alcohol on a task of sustained attention. *Ergonomics*, 1975, *18*, 81–87.

Colquhoun, W. P., & Goldman, R. F. Vigilance under induced hyperthermia. *Ergonomics*, 1972, *15*, 621–632.

Corcoran, D. W. J. Noise and loss of sleep. *Quarterly Journal of Experimental Psychology*, 1962, *14*, 178–182.

Craig, A., Wilkinson, R. T., & Colquhoun, W. P. Diurnal variation in vigilance efficiency. *Ergonomics*, 1981, *24*, 641–651.

Davies, A. D. M., & Davies, D. R. The effects of noise and time of day upon age differences in performance at two checking tasks. *Ergonomics*, 1975, *18*, 333–336.

Davies, D. R., & Parasuraman, R. *The psychology of vigilance*. London: Academic Press, 1982.

Duffy, E. The psychological significance of the concept of "arousal" or "activation." *Psychological Review*, 1957, *64*, 265–275.

Duffy, E. *Activation and behavior*. Wiley: New York, 1962.

Duffy, E. Activation. In N. S. Greenfield & R. A. Sternbach (Eds.), *Handbook of psychophysiology*. New York: Holt, 1972.

Easterbrook, J. A. The effect of emotion on cue utilisation and the organisation of behavior. *Psychological Review*, 1959, *66*, 183–201.

Eysenck, M. W. *Attention and arousal: Cognition and performance*. Heidelberg: Springer-Verlag, 1982.

Fisher, S. A. A distraction effect of noise bursts. *Perception*, 1972, *1*, 223–236.

Folkard, S. Diurnal variation. In G. R. J. Hockey (Ed.), *Stress and fatigue in human performance*. New York: Wiley, 1983.

Folkard, S., Knauth, P., Monk, T. H., & Rutenfrantz, J. The effect of memory load upon the circadian variation in performance efficiency under a rapidly-rotating shift system. *Ergonomics*, 1976, *19*, 479–488.

Ford, A. Attention–automatisation: An investigation of the transitional nature of mind. *American Journal of Psychology*, 1929, *41*, 1–32.

Frankenhauser, M. Experimental approaches to the study of catecholamines and emotion. In L. Levi (Ed.), *Emotions: Their parameters and measurement*. New York: Raven, 1975.

Hamilton, P. & Hockey, G. R. J. Active selection of items to be remembered: The role of timing. *Cognitive Psychology*, 1974, *6*, 61–83.

Hamilton, P., Hockey, G. R. J., & Rejman, M. The place of the concept of activation in human processing theory: An integrative approach. In S. Dornic (Ed.), *Attention and performance VI*. New York: Academic Press, 1977.

Hamilton, P., Wilkinson, R. T., & Edwards, R. S. A study of four days partial sleep deprivation. In W. P. Colquhoun (Ed.), *Aspects of human efficiency*. London: English Universities Press, 1972.

Hebb, D. R. Drives and the C.N.S. (conceptual nervous system). *Psychological Review*, 1955, *62*, 243–254.

Hockey, G. R. J. Effect of loud noise on attentional selectivity. *Quarterly Journal of Experimental Psychology*, 1970, *22*, 28–36.

Hockey, G. R. J. Stress and the cognitive components of skilled performance. In V. Hamilton, & P. M. Warburton (Eds.), *Human stress and cognition: An information-processing approach*. New York: Wiley, 1979.

Hockey, G. R. J. (Ed.) *Stress and fatigue in human performance*. New York: Wiley, 1983.

Hockey, G. R. J., & Hamilton, P. The cognitive patterning of stress states. In G. R. J. Hockey (Ed.), *Stress and fatigue in human performance*. New York: Wiley, 1983.

Hockey, G. R. J., McLean, A., & Hamilton, P. State changes and the temporal patterning of component resources. In J. Long, & A. D. Baddeley (Eds.), *Attention and performance IX*. Hillsdale, N.J.: Erlbaum, 1981.

Hull, C. L. 1943. *Principles of behavior*. New York: Appleton-Century, Crofts, 1943.

Jerison, H. J. Effects of noise on human performance. *Journal of Applied Psychology*, 1959. *43*, 96–101.

Kahneman, D. Remarks on attentional control. In A. F. Sanders, *Attention and performance III*. Amsterdam: North-Holland, 1970.

Kahneman, D. *Attention and effort*. Englewood-Cliffs, N.J.: Prentice-Hall, 1973.

Lacey, J. J. Somatic response patterning and stress. In M. H. Appley & R. Trumbull (Eds.), *Psychological stress*. New York: Appleton-Century-Crofts, 1967.

Lindsley, D. B. Attention, consciousness, sleep and wakefulness. In J. Field & W. H. Magoun (Eds.), *Handbook of physiology* (Sect. 1): *Neurophysiology* (Vol. 3). Washington, D.C.: American Physiological Society, 1960.

Logan, G. D. On the use of concurrent memory load to measure attention and automaticity. *Journal of Experimental Psychology: Human Perception and Performance*, 1979, *5*, 189–207.

Lundberg, U. Psychophysiological aspects of performance and adjustment to stress. In H. W. Krohne, & L. Laux (Eds.), *Achievement, stress and anxiety*. Washington, D.C.: Hemisphere, 1982.

Mackworth, J. F. The effects of amphetamine on the detectability of signals in a vigilance task. *Canadian Journal of Psychology*, 1965, *19*, 104–109.

Mackworth, N. H. *Researches on the measurement of human performance*. (MRC Special Report Series No. 268). London: HMSO, 1950.

Malmo, R. B. Activation: A neuropsychological dimension. *Psychological Review*, 1959, *66*, 357–386.

Malmo, R. B., & Surwillo, W. W. Sleep deprivation: Changes in performance and physiological indicants of activation. *Psychological Monographs*, 1960, *74*, No. 15, Whole No. 502.

Mandler, G. Thought processes, consciousness and stress. In V. Hamilton & D. M. Warburton (Eds.), *Human stress and cognition: An information processing approach*. New York: Wiley, 1979.

Morgan, J. J. B. The effect of sound distraction upon memory. *American Journal of Psychology,* 1917, *28,* 191–208.

Näätänen, R. The inverted-U relationship between activation and performance: A critical review. In P. M. A. Rabbitt & S. Dornic (Eds.), *Attention and performance V.* New York: Academic Press, 1975.

Pepler, R. D. Warmth and lack of sleep: Accuracy or activity reduced? *Journal of Cognitive and Physiological Psychology,* 1959, *52,* 446–450.

Poulton, E. C. *Environment and human efficiency.* Springfield, Ill.: Charles C. Thomas, 1970.

Poulton, E. C., & Edwards, R. S. Interactions and range effects in experiments on pain of stresses: Mild heat and low-frequency noise. *Journal of Experimental Psychology,* 1974, *102,* 621–626.

Prechtl, H. The behavioral stress of the new-born infant (a review). *Brain Research,* 1974, *76,* 185–212.

Pribram, K. H., & McGuinness, D. Arousal, activation and effort in the control of attention. *Psychological Review,* 1975, *82,* 116–149.

Rabbitt, P. M. A. Current paradigms and models in human information processing. In V. Hamilton & D. M. Warburton (Eds.), *Human Stress and Cognition: An information processing approach.* New York: Wiley, 1979.

Rabbitt, P. M. A. Sequential reactions. In D. H. Holding (Ed.), *Human skills,* New York: Wiley, 1981.

Ramsey, J. D. Heat and cold. In G. R. J. Hockey (Ed.), *Stress and fatigue in human performance.* New York: Wiley, 1983.

Revelle, W., Humphreys, M. S., Simon, L., & Gilliland, K. The interaction effect of personality, time of day and caffeine: A test of the arousal model. *Journal of Experimental Psychology: General,* 1980, *109,* 1–31.

Routtenberg, A. The two arousal hypotheses: Reticular formation and limbic system. *Psychological Review,* 1966, *75,* 51–80.

Shallice, T. The dominant action system: An information-processing approach to consciousness. In K. S. Pope & J. L. Singer (Eds.), *The stream of consciousness,* New York: Plenum, 1978.

Teichner, W. H. Interaction of behavioural and physiological stress reactions. *Psychological review,* 1968, *75,* 271–291.

Wesnes, K., & Warburton, D. M. Stress and drugs. In G. R. J. Hockey (Ed.), *Stress and fatigue in human performance.* New York: Wiley, 1983.

Wilding, J., & Mohindra, N. Effects of sub-vocal supression, articulating aloud and noise on sequence recall. *British Journal of Psychology,* 1980, *71,* 247–262.

Wilkinson, R. T. Rest pauses in a task affected by lack of sleep. *Ergonomics,* 1959, *2,* 373–380.

Wilkinson, R. T. Interaction of lack of sleep with knowledge of results, repeated testing and individual differences. *Journal of Experimental Psychology,* 1961, *6,* 263–271.

Wilkinson, R. T. Muscle tension during mental work under sleep deprivation. *Journal of Experimental Psychology,* 1962, *64,* 565–571.

Wilkinson, R. T. Interaction of noise with knowledge of results and sleep deprivation. *Journal of Experimental Psychology,* 1963, *66,* 332–337.

Wilkinson, R. T. Effects of up to 60 hours sleep deprivation in different types of work. *Ergonomics,* 1964, *7,* 175–186.

Wilkinson, R. T. Sleep deprivation: Performance tests for partial and selection sleep deprivation. In L. A. Abt & B. F. Reiss (Eds.). *Progress in clinical psychology* (Vol. 7). New York: Grune and Stratton, 1968.

Wilkinson, R. T., & Colquhoun, W. P. Interaction of alcohol with incentive and with sleep deprivation. *Journal of Experimental Psychology,* 1968, *76,* 623–629.

Wilkinson, R. T., Fox, R. H., Goldsmith, R., Hampton, I. F. G., & Lewis, H. E. Psychological and physiological responses to raised body temperature. *Journal of Applied Psychology,* 1964, *19,* 287–291.

Willett, R. A. Experimentally induced drive and performance on a five-choice serial reaction task. In H. J. Eysenck (Ed.), *Experiments in human motivation*. London: Pergamon, 1964.

Williams, H. L., Lubin, A., & Goodnow, J. J. Impaired performance with acute sleep loss. *Psychological Monographs*, 1959, *73*, (Whole No. 484).

Wine, J. Test anxiety and direction of attention. *Psychological Bulletin*, 1971, *76*, 92–104.

Yerkes, R. M., & Dodson, J. D. The relation of strength of stimulus to rapidity of habit formation. *Journal of Comparative and Neurological Psychology*, 1908. *18*, 459–482.

13

Attention to Dynamic Visual Displays in Man–Machine Systems

Neville Moray

Introduction

Auditory attention theory has been built on generalizations from data. The Filter Theory arose from Broadbent's attempt to account for a large amount of data that was available by the late 1950s, in particular the results of the so-called "split-span" memory experiment (Broadbent, 1954). The later developments by Treisman (1967), Moray (1967), Norman (1968), Deutsch and Deutsch (1963), Schneider and Shiffrin (1977), and others, are all theories that start from data. Except for attention to pure tones, discussed in this volume by Swets, there are no analytical models of auditory attention. Furthermore, auditory research began with a series of experiments almost all of which required the listener to process language (Broadbent, 1958; Moray, 1969); and as a result, theories of auditory attention were forced to become involved with very difficult problems such as pattern perception, semantics, and high-level cognitive processes. On the other hand, all models of visual attention that are discussed in this chapter are analytical. They start by considering some optimal way in which an information-processing task might be carried out, and proceed to predict what the human operator should do if he or she were such an optimal processer.

The visual tasks to which I shall refer in this chapter do not include linguistic or linguistic-related information. There are semantic characteristics to the tasks, characteristics that are often very important and indeed central to the tasks; but analysis of these tasks does not require linguistically based models. Hence in a very obvious sense, they are less complicated models. In another sense they are extremely powerful, especially in that they are designed for real-time, dynamic, often continuous multivariate and multichannel inputs and for interaction between the viewer and the task. Most of the tasks are a far cry from the discrete trial, statistically independent experimental paradigms characteristic of auditory attention research. In visual monitoring, the simplest typical paradigm is the

485

following. An operator watches a meter that has a scale across which a pointer is moving to and fro. The process driving the meter requires the operator to intervene occasionally. When should the operator look at the meter?

Notice two things about the paradigm. First, even though there is only one source of information, there is still an attentional problem. Second, the concern is not with how attention is paid (whether there is an early or late filter, whether analyzers are selected, whether there are several processers that operate in parallel), but with when attention is paid. The concern here is with tactics and strategies of attention (Moray, 1978), not with hypothetical explanatory mechanisms.

One reason this is a sensible way to approach dynamic visual attention is that there is little doubt that a Broadbentian Filter is involved in visual attention. Owing to the need for foveal vision if acute vision is required, the eyes must be pointed in an appropriate direction to scan or sample a source of information. There is no switch more effective than turning the head 180°. Hence, the primary question is to find the optimal tactics for a single-channel sampler to sample sources of information. A second assumption is that it is undesirable to keep attention constantly on a task even if it is the only task. It is assumed that there is a cost of some kind associated with observing. Later in the chapter, this concept is discussed in more detail. For now, it is enough to note that although paid subjects may be prepared to keep their eyes glued to a single fluctuating dial for long periods without looking anywhere else even if nothing appears to be happening, more rational creatures feel that they have better things to do with their time.

The statistical structure of real systems is such that the need for strategies of attention is quite clear. To illustrate this laboratory and industrial tasks are contrasted. The former tend to be simple; very seldom do they have more than three or four variables. They are carried out with well-defined discrete trials, between which the subjects of the experiments know that nothing will happen and can afford to rest. The statistical structure of most tasks is such that events are independent of each other, and several variables interact rather little. Payoffs associated with action are either so rigidly defined that if a subject carries out the task in an unusual way, his or her data are rejected; or are so ill defined that it is up to the subject to induce the payoff structure from the behavior of the experimenter. Above all, the tasks are statistically stationary. They do not change with time; time is not an important independent variable; and if time is noted at all, usually it is a dependent measure.

By contrast industrial tasks are dynamic. The property that interests the human controller is the fact that the state of the system changes over time. There are marked correlations and causal dependencies among variables, and there are often very large payoffs associated with the various actions open to the operator. The number of state variables needed to describe the operation of the system can be extremely large, and a desired outcome may be achieved in many equally acceptable ways.

Sources of Uncertainty

The operator's task in industrial systems is to know the system and to respond in whatever way the state of the system requires. The operator is concerned at all times to reduce uncertainty about the system state. It is for that purpose that tactical and strategic decisions have to be made about where to direct attention from moment to moment.

The causes of uncertainty can be divided into two classes: exogenous and endogenous. *Exogenous* uncertainty arises from the dynamics of the system. Temperatures and pressures fluctuate, either deterministically or in the face of disturbances, which themselves may be deterministic or stochastic. The quality of the product fluctuates as the quality of the raw feedstock changes. Windshear disturbs the flight path of the aircraft. Mechanisms wear out. For these and other reasons the operator cannot predict the future state of the system for an indefinite period even if he or she knows the current values of all the state variables; they must be sampled from time to time.

Endogenous sources of uncertainty include forgetting, misreading instruments, failure to make observations, failure to weight evidence correctly, and the whole range of psychological factors that are known to render less accurate with the passing of time a human's ability to keep track of information that he or she has initially acquired. Even given well-designed instruments that give accurate information about all state variables, and even if the initial observations are accurate, the operator will, at some time in the future, not have an accurate memory of what was observed, and hence be unable to be sure of the state of the system. Hence the operator will again have to pay attention to a state variable that he or she examined at some time in the past.

The human operator must therefore decide:

1. Which instrument needs examination.
2. At what moment to examine it.
3. How long to examine it.
4. How to combine the information with other information the operator possesses.
5. Whether the new observation is reliable, or whether the operator would do better to rely on his or her partly forgotten earlier knowledge.
6. What action to take, if any.
7. How the new information that he or she acquires is to be used to make further decisions as described in this list.

In some sense or other, attention plays a role in all of these decisions. But for the rest of this chapter, the main concern is with items 1, 2, 3, and 7.

Measures of Visual Sampling Behavior

There are four main measures used in the analysis of visual sampling behavior: fixation frequency, fixation duration, fixation interval (or sampling or scanning interval), and the transition-probability matrix. The last measure, sometimes called *link values,* represents the probabilities describing where the eye will go next, given the place on which it currently is fixating. (Throughout this chapter I shall use *fixate, look at,* and *sample* as synonyms. All workers in this field are well aware that there have been occasions recorded when a person has fixated a signal or display and failed to acquire the information from that source. These are, however, rare.) Sampling may on occasion not be observable, as in the case of two samples taken without an intervening eye movement. But this can be allowed for in the statistical analysis, and is discussed by Senders, Elkind, Grignetti, and Smallwood (Note 1). To a first approximation, it may be said that *fixation frequency* is a measure of the rate at which a source generates *information* and of that information's *importance; fixation duration* is a measure of the difficulty of extracting information from the source and of the desired extraction accuracy; *fixation timing* is a measure of the dynamics of the source and of the properties of the memory of the observer; and *transition probabilities* are a measure of the properties of the internal model that the operator has of the statistical structure in time and space of the system.

Theories and Models

I now consider a number of theories and models of visual sampling behavior. Throughout this chapter, I will use the words *sampling* or *scheduling* to mean the act of redirecting attention from one source to another, or to one source at different times. I shall use the phrase *data acquisition* to mean the action of acquiring information from the source that is being sampled. This is, by and large, in agreement with most usage in the literature, except for Allen, Clement, and Jex (Note 2), who used the word *scanning* to refer to the act of paying attention, and *sampling* to mean what I shall call data acquisition.

Senders's Model

Senders *et al.* (Note 1) were the first to propose a formal model for visual sampling, which suggested that the human operator may be regarded as a classical Shannon communication channel (Shannon & Weaver, 1949). The signal, as in most of the work in this area, was defined as time-varying, limited-bandwidth white noise with a cutoff frequency W Hz, the frequency components of which have random phase, and the amplitude of which is distributed as a Gaussian (0, 1) probability distribution.

Shannon proved that to extract all the information in such a waveform, it is necessary and sufficient to sample it $2W$ times per second if the aim is to reconstruct the signal. It follows from this that samples should be taken at $1/2W$ second intervals by an optimal sampler. Intuitively this makes sense. The signal, being band limited, cannot change amplitude at more than a limited rate. Hence, the amplitude that is observed when a sample is taken will be a good estimate of the amplitude for a short time into the future, and a poorer and poorer estimate as time passes. Hence it is not necessary to observe it at very short intervals, let alone continuously, but it is necessary to sample it again at some time later. Clearly if one waits long enough, the best estimate of the then value of the amplitude will simply be the mean of the distribution. This interval should be related to bandwidth; the more rapidly the signal varies, the more quickly will it become impossible to predict its current value on the basis of a past observation. In fact, for Gaussian band-limited noise, the quality of future prediction based on an observation is related to the autocorrelation function of the signal. The time at which the autocorrelation function first reaches 0 is $1/2W$ seconds, the so-called *Nyquist interval.*

A problem of attention distribution arises even for a single source, because an optimal processor should take samples only at intervals $1/2W$ seconds apart; and the rest of time, attention would be available for any other purpose. Thus if Senders' assumption that man is indeed a Shannon channel holds, one would expect someone monitoring a single source to pay attention to it only at discrete intervals if their task were to reconstruct the signal, their memory were perfect, and their internal computations were completely accurate.

It is not assumed here or elsewhere that the observer knows what calculations he or she is performing. Indeed one only would expect to see performance in accord with the predictions of the models that will be discussed after prolonged practice, when the observer has constructed in his or her head an accurate internal model of the statistics of the observed processes. The experiments that best fit the predictions of the models are those in which the participants have practiced for prolonged periods in industrial tasks, perhaps years in the case of pilots, and at least for tens of hours in laboratory studies. Those experiments in which the operators perform at less than the predicted optimum are often characterized by relatively little practice. In any model in which there are statistics to be learned or discovered, one would not expect optimal performance unless enough exposure was given to the sources for the statistics to be learned. Attempts to repeat the experiments discussed here will not be successful without something on the order of 10 hours practice per participant. The bandwidths used in these experiments are always less than 1.0 Hz, and frequently far lower. (Readers should also note that in many papers, frequencies are expressed not in Hz, but in

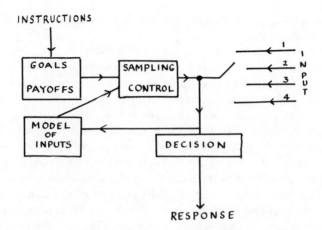

Figure 13.1 Senders's (1964) model of visual sampling behavior.

radians per second.) Such bandwiths are characteristic of lifelike tasks, and the upper limit of the tracking by manual control is around 1 Hz.

In some of the experiments to be described, mixtures of sine waves rather than true band-limited white noise were used for analytical convenience. For many purposes, this makes no difference. But from at least one piece of evidence discussed here, although the two may appear indistinguishable for humans, they are not exactly equivalent. Operators find it subjectively harder to deal with broadband noise than with mixed sine waves.

Senders's (Note 1) model then would predict periodic sampling of a single source at intervals proportional to the bandwidth of the signal. If several sources of equal importance were to be monitored, and their bandwidths differed; each would be sampled at a rate proportional to its bandwidth:

$$f_i(t) = 2w_i$$

where t is the sampling interval for the ith instrument and W its bandwidth (see Figure 13.1).

Contrary to what most secondary sources say, Senders *et al.* (Note 1) did not claim that periodic sampling would be seen in practice. Senders noted that in most practical tasks the observer is not trying to reconstruct the signal, but is monitoring it to make sure that it does not exceed some specified limit. Hence the basic periodicity is likely to be modified if, for example, an observation shows that the signal is currently a long way from the limit compared with an observation that shows that it is close to the limit. Furthermore for very low bandwidths, the $1/2W$ may be so long that there will be significant forgetting between Nyquist moments, and hence extra samples may be taken. Hence, as Senders *et al.* (Note 1) pointed out, there will be a distribution of sampling intervals associated with a particular source if the task is to monitor for extreme values, and if it is the mean of the distribution that one would expect to approximate to $1/2W$. Sampling frequency will, however, be a monotonic increasing function of bandwidth even if it is not exactly equal to $2W$. Sampling is to be measured by eye movements because the existence of clear vision only at the fovea requires sources of information to be fixated. Senders *et al.* (Note 1) also predicted the durations of fixations from a further application of Shannon's work. If a continuous Gaussian time function is sampled, the amount of information per sample is undefined unless the required precision of the observation is specified. If the function has rms amplitude A, and an rms error of E is acceptable, then the information per observation is

$$\overline{H}_i = \log_2\frac{A_i^2}{E_i^2} \text{ bits.}$$

Extending the experimental work on discrete information processing of Hick (1952) and Hyman (1953), Senders (1964) proposed that the fixation duration would be proportional to the information content of the sample:

$$\overline{D}_i = K \log_2\frac{A_i}{E_i} + C,$$

where C is a constant associated with eye-movement time and the shortest possible fixation time.

Finally Senders (1964) proposed to model the transition probabilities, or link values that describe the order in which the eyes moved from one instrument to the next, as a zero-order Markov process. Given data on relative frequencies, the probability that an instrument i will be fixated as the relative frequency with which it is fixated can be identified. The simplest possible rule for where the eye goes next, given that it is currently on instrument i, is that instrument j is chosen randomly from among instruments in accordance with the probability of fixations. The eye behaves as if it has dipped into an urn filled with instruments, each present in proportion to the frequency with which, over a long run, they are fixated. To put it another way, the next thing the observer looks at is not dependent on what he or she is now looking at, but on the long-term probabilistic distribution of his or her eye movements. Sampling is not causally determined; it is stochastically determined.

A most important assumption of this model is that the task involves signal reconstruction—the ability to copy the input. It is more common in real settings, such as aircraft cockpits and power stations, to watch instruments to see whether or not their readings exceed some danger limit. In this case, reconstruction is not required, and intuition suggests that the sampling rule will not be Shannon's, but will be related to how close the observed value of the signal is to the limit. The observer who looks at the signal and sees that it is currently close to the limit may be expected to look at it again sooner, on the average, than if he or she looked at it and found it at, say, its mean. Senders *et al.* (Note 1) examined several other models to deal with this situation.

The first model assumes that the observer will make an observation of one of the sources and will sample it again when, given the value of the prior observation, the probability of the limit being exceeded is at maximum. In their model, the interval can be shown to be a function of the size of the limit, L, and the amplitude of the observation, Y, both expressed in units of the standard deviation of the forcing function, σ, that is driving the observed process:

$$p(\rho, Y) = 0.5\left[1 - \Phi\left(\frac{L - \rho Y}{\sigma(1 - \rho^2)^{\frac{1}{2}}}\right)\right] \, ,$$

where Φ is the normal probability integral, and $p(\rho, Y)$ is the probability that the limit L will be exceeded at the time when the autocorrelation function has reached ρ given that the observation had magnitude Y. The autocorrelation function of the forcing function ρ becomes zero at the Nyquist instant, which is $1/2W$ seconds after the observation for a bandwidth of W Hz. At that point in time, the observation is useless for predicting the value of the function. If the observation shows that the current value is greater than the limit, the operator will observe it again immediately (the autocorrelation function is only 1.0 for zero delay); if the observation is at the mean, the operator will wait until the autocorrelation has fallen to zero (the Nyquist interval); and otherwise, the operator will wait until the autocorrelation function has fallen to a value of Y/L. Table 13.1, reproduced from Senders *et al.* (Note 1) gives some values of L and ρ. Note that the equivalent in time to these autocorrelation values can be recovered by multiplying the value of ρ by $1/2W$.

In the second model, the next sample is taken not when the probability of the limit being exceeded is at maximum, but when the probability exceeds some arbitrary threshold that the observer has adopted. The main difference is that ρ is larger, especially for large values of L.

Finally, a still more complex model was proposed. Rather than having a fixed permissible error as in Senders's *et al.* (Note 1) model, it might be assumed that when the signal is near its mean, a large error is acceptable in estimating its value; but as it comes closer and closer to the limit, greater and greater precision is required. For example, it might be assumed that if E is the permissable rms tolerance as in the first model, then $E^2 = K(L - Y)^2$, all measurements being in σ. It can be shown that this is equivalent to changing the Nyquist interval as the observation comes closer to the boundary beyond which the process must not go.

Notice that all of the four models predict a change of sampling with bandwidth. The main difference between the first model and the latter three is that the

TABLE 13.1

Values of the Autocorrelation Function (ρ) and the
Size of Limit L in the Visual Sampling Experiment
of Senders et al. (Note 1)

L (in units of $s.d.$)	ρ (Autocorrelation value)
0.1	0.48
0.2	0.46
0.5	0.41
1.0	0.28
2.0	0.20
5.0	0.08

first assumes that the task is to reconstruct the signal, whereas the latter three assume that the task is to notice when a signal exceeds limits. Notice also that all assume that there is no difference in the importance of the sources of information. The detection of a signal exceeding the limit is equally important in all cases. In all the four models, it is simply the physical properties of the sources and the displays that are responsible for the sampling strategies observed. No ''understanding'' of the ''meaning'' of the signals is required.

By way of contrast, next examined are models that claim that the main determinant of sampling strategy is the payoff structure as seen by the observer.

Kvålseth's Model

For both monitoring behavior and closed-loop control, Kvålseth (1979) proposed a model based on decision theory and used the expected value of the sampling behavior as the criterion for when to sample. ''An optimal process monitor uses a sampling strategy that maximises the expected value (worth or utility) at any point in time'' (Kvålseth, 1979, p. 672). The costs for the operator are the costs of making an observation and the cost of allowing the process to exceed limits, $\pm L$. In this respect, the model is similar to the later models of Senders et al.'s (Note 1).

Kvålseth's model includes the following variables: $\theta_{i1}(t + \tau)$: $X_i(t + \tau)$ exceeds limits $\pm L$; $\theta_{i2}(t + \tau)$: $X_i(t + \tau)$ is within limits $\pm L$; $a_{i1}(t + \tau)$: sample X_{in} at $n = t + \tau$; $a_{i2}(t + \tau)$: do not sample X_{in} at $n = t + \tau$; $v_{ijk}(t + \tau)$ is the value (worth or utility) of $a_{ij}(t + \tau)$ and $\theta_{ik}(t + \tau)$ for $j, k = 1, 2$ and $i = 1, 2, \ldots, I$. The expected value of sampling at moment $(t + \tau)$ is

$$EV_{ij}(t + \tau) = \sum_{k=1}^{2} V_{ijk}(t + \tau)p\left[\frac{\theta_{ik}(t + \tau)}{D_{it}}\right],$$

where D_{it} is the datum available to the observer at t, which includes any information carried forward from the past about the state of the process. The appropriate strategy for the operator is then to choose the action that maximizes EV.

Most workers in this field use forcing functions that are Gaussian voltages or sums of sinusoids to drive instruments with analog displays. Kvålseth instead programmed a digital computer to print numbers; and the limit L is a numerical value, not a pointer position. The new number is calculated from a first-order autoregressive process (ARP) of the form $X(n) = aX(n - 1) + Z(n)$, where $Z(n)$ is a Gaussian $(0, \sigma)$ process and a determines the strength of the autocorrelation function. In these experiments, therefore, both time and the signal are discrete. Kvålseth claims, correctly, that such tasks are quite widespread in industry, although whether the first-order ARP is a good model for real-world processes is doubtful. It is also possible that this fairly drastic change in methodology could make it hard to compare Kvålseth's results with those obtained with more traditional displays.

In an earlier paper, Kvålseth (1978) proposed a model based on information theory that is much closer in spirit to that of Senders *et al.* (Note 1). Again using a first-order ARP, he obtained information measure as a function of the number of intervals since the last observation. The information in an observation at time $(n + k)$ is $\overline{H}(X_n + k) = 0.5 \log_2 2\pi e \sigma^2$, where σ^2 is the variance of the Gaussian forcing function. The information in that observation, given a previous observation at time (n), is

$$\overline{H}\left(\frac{X_{n+k}}{X_n}\right) = E\left[-\log_2 f\left(\frac{X_{n+k}}{X_n}\right) \right],$$

where f is the conditional probability function and E the expectation operator. From this it can be shown that the information gain from an observation at time $(n + k)$ is

$$I\,(X_{n+k}|X_n) = -0.5 \log_2(1 - \rho^2(k) + 0.5 \log_2 e \left|\frac{X_n^2}{\sigma^2} - 1\right| \rho^2(k),$$

where ρ is dependent on the ARP parameters, and k is the number of intervals since time n. The redundancy of the information at the time of sampling is

$$R(k) = -\frac{1}{\log_2 2\pi e \sigma^2} \log_2(1 - \rho^2(k))$$

Using the task as in the later study (1979), but with only the monitoring mode, Kvålseth (1978) investigated the effects of exceeding the limit L, the value of a, the ARP parameter, and the value of L. He concluded that (1) samples were taken when the entropy of the observation had reached between 83 and 100% of its asymptotic value; (2) the entropy at sampling rose with the variance of the observed process; (3) the cost of exceeding L had little effect; and (4) samples were collected when about 75% of the information from the previous sample had been lost. He also pointed out that the model assumed that there was no forgetting in the intersample interval and suggested that this was an unrealistic assumption, so that the real loss of information was higher than his calculations indicated. It is interesting to note, in view of work on radar operators discussed in the following, that Kvålseth's time interval was measured in units of 2 seconds. From this data, this means that entropy would reach 90% of its value after 15–20 seconds. As discussed in the following, this is about the time that severe forgetting sets in for radarlike patterns viewed by experienced operators.

Sheridan's Model

Sheridan, like Kvålseth, concentrates on solving the sampling problem in terms of the value of the outcome to the operator rather than in terms merely of the statistics of the physical process being controlled. But unlike Kvålseth, Sheridan is concerned with keeping the payoff structure for the task more closely coupled to the physical properties of the forcing function (Sheridan, 1970). He discusses the single-channel question: How often should a single function of time be sampled in order to optimize some goal, even when there is no other competing task? The goal here is to maximize net gain for the operator. Let us assume that there is, for any state of the observed process, some action that the operator could take in order to control the process and thus be rewarded for his or her action. A simple paradigm would be to think in terms of compensatory tracking, of which the aim is to keep the error signal at zero, but the task can be defined in any way that requires the operator to sample the system output. Assume the forcing function is a limited bandwidth Gaussian time function, with mean and standard deviation $(0, \sigma)$. How often should the operator sample and exercise control (if required)? If the operator is well practiced and knows the statistics of the observed process, then he or she also knows that if the controls are left alone, the expected value of the process over a long period will be its mean, and the expected variance of the output will be the variance of the process. But clearly the operator can do better than that. To never sample it is to wait too long. On the other hand, because the process is band limited, it need not be sampled again immediately after a sample has been taken, because it has an autocorrelation function that will not go to zero for a time equal to the Nyquist interval. During this period, the knowledge gained at the last observation will slowly become of less value for predicting the current state of the process as the expected value decays toward the mean of the process and the variance of the expected value grows from zero at the moment the observation was made toward the variance of the process. Because continuous sampling is too frequent and no sampling is too seldom, there must be an intermediate value that is optimal.

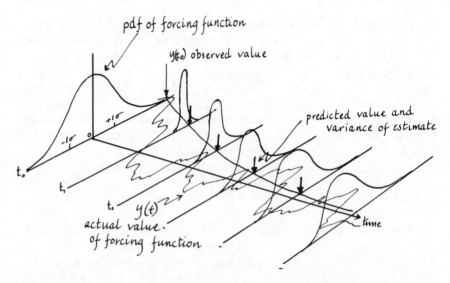

Figure 13.2 Model of the effect of time on the value of observation $y(t_o)$ of a continuous process driven by a forcing function $y(t)$ (pdf, probability density function; σ, standard deviation).

Sheridan assumes that the value of the last observation can be represented by the decay of the autocorrelation function, or some monotonic function thereof. Assume now that there is a cost associated with each observation. The average cost per unit time will be lower the less frequently an observation is made. For a short interval, the average cost per unit time will be large; for a long interval, it will be small. If we can take the difference between the average cost at each instant and the current value of the last observation, then it is true for a variety of (but not all) functions describing the way in which the average cost and value vary with time that the difference between them will be nonmonotonic and will have a maximum value at some moment prior to the Nyquist interval. That moment represents the greatest net expected value and defines the moment at which the sample should be taken. Sheridan gives a quantitative formalization of the problem and provides some examples of normative behavior, using Howard's information value theory to develop the model (Howard, 1966).

In Figure 13.2, an observation, assumed accurate, is made at time t_o. As time passes, the best estimate of the current value of the function returns to the mean at a rate related to the bandwidth, and the uncertainty of the estimate grows from zero at time t to the variance of the forcing function. Hence the observation becomes less valuable. If the cost of an observation is C, the average cost is $C/(t + \tau)$, where τ is the time since the observation was made. Hence the relation between the cost and the value gives the sampling instant as shown in Figure 13.3.

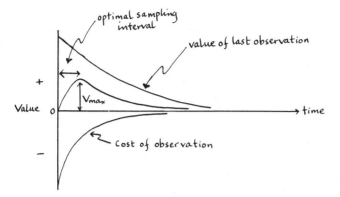

Figure 13.3 Sheridan's model of the relation between the cost of observation and the value of the last observation of a continuous process.

Gai and Curry's and Moray's Models

Sheridan's model defines the cost of observations in terms of monetary payoffs. But it is possible to generalize the idea of cost for a multitask situation, and in so doing to draw attention to a complication that is not apparent from those discussions that have concentrated on sampling a single channel, nor in effect from those that have used several instruments, because of the bandwidths used and the nature of the signals. Moray (1981) argued that Sheridan's model could be extended by seeing costs not as monetary, but rather as the cost of the undesirable outcome, monetary or otherwise. Thus the cost of making an observation on instrument i of a set of instruments I_a, I_b, . . . , I_m would be the monetary cost of the observation plus the probability that while observing I_i, one of the other instruments would exceed its permissable limit. This suggestion that cost is related to the probability of failing on some other task while observing the chosen task had been made earlier by Carbonell, in a treatment that is discussed in the following and that has, perhaps, the best claim to be the "canonical" model so far (Carbonell, 1966). Carbonell, however, omits one idea that has been developed by Gai and Curry (1976) and Moray (1981). There is good evidence from behavioral research that humans can often be modeled as sequential decision makers. Senders *et al.* (Note 1), as discussed earlier, suggested that the duration of the fixation would be a function simply of the information content of the source being sampled. But consider in more detail the multichannel case. The observer chooses an instrument and begins to sample it. As time passes, he or she accumulates information from the (noisy) observation, a process that can be modeled in terms, for example, of Wald's (1947) sequential decision model. But before enough evidence has accumulated for the operator to reach a decision that satisfies his or her a priori criteria, the operator's internal model suggests that it is time to sample one of the other sources because the probability that it is exceeding a limit is high or because his or her uncertainty about its value has grown intolerable. The operator is then faced with a conflict between what Moray (1981) calls the *scheduling algorithm* and the *data acquisition algorithm*. Either the operator must cut short observation of the display and make a decision on what he or she considers insufficient evidence; or delay sampling, even though he or she knows there is a high risk that another instrument is beyond the limits. Providing that the bandwidths and power of the observed processes are such that the sampling intervals are long compared with the time taken to reach a decision, there will be no conflict; and this has been the case in most studies.

But as the number of instruments grows and the bandwidths become high, conflict will occur; and for large numbers of displays, it may be that this speed–accuracy trade-off (SATO) problem will come to dominate sampling. Gai and Curry have successfully applied the idea of the human as a sequential decision maker to the problem of detecting a plant failure (Gai & Curry, 1976), but to date no experiments have been carried out on the speed–accuracy approach to multiinstrument sampling. It would seem that where present, suboptimal performance would arise because of shortened data-acquisition intervals leading to poor decisions; and sampling intervals would become longer than optimal if the operator opted for good data acquisition, so that the cases of instruments exceeding limits would go more frequently unnoticed or be detected with an increasing latency.

Moray's Model

It is perhaps worth including one case of a model rather more in the spirit that is common in psychological work on auditory attention. It may strike the reader that so far not one author of a major model is primarily a psychologist. All are, at least in the first instance, engineers. It may not be entirely coincidence that the only data-based model to be mentioned is by the only psychologist—the present writer.

Moray, Richards, and Low (1980), and Moray, Neil, and Brophy (1982) have modeled the eye movements of fighter controllers while they directed live and simulated interceptions on radars. The radar plot is very different from the other kinds of displays mentioned in this chapter. It is certainly dynamic, but its power spectrum is peculiar. At any point on the screen, there is a sudden change in the information about every 10 seconds, due to the rotation of the radar aerial; and the region in which the change is occurring sweeps round the screen at the rate, therefore, of about 0.1 Hz. Furthermore, the rate of change of the display at the moment the scan passes over a region of the screen is a function of the speed of the aircraft from which echoes are returning, the range of the radar, and so on. For displays using raw radar, the echo then fades, and is refreshed and slightly changed 10 seconds later. But apart from this fading of the trace, there is no change in the echo until the antenna has completed its sweep. In a sense then, one fixation every 10 seconds on each "important" echo is all that is required. Moray *et al.* (1980), however, measured the rate at which the fighter controllers forgot the location of the echos after seeing them, using paper and pencil tests of simulated radar echos, and found that the uncertainty of the location of the echos increased as the $\frac{3}{2}$ power of the time since the "echo" was seen. They suggested that the controller had a threshold of uncertainty; and when his or her forgetting drove his or her uncertainty above that threshold, he or she would take another sample. In addition, they proposed a mechanism that interacted with forgetting to estimate the likelihood that two aircraft were "dangerously" close, and derived an expression that called for the sampling of such aircraft. In this respect, their model is similar to the third model proposed by Senders and his co-workers (Note 1). Providing that the two aircraft are widely separated, the sampling interval is determined by the forgetting threshold, which is set in the light of the subjective importance of the aircraft.

In this model therefore, the main emphasis is not on the bandwidth of the display (which in this kind of display is extremely low), but on endogenous uncertainty due to forgetting—a source of uncertainty that has been mentioned by most of the workers cited, but not investigated. The duration of the fixation was derived from empirical measures of eye movements, which—when combined with the sampling intervals derived from the model—enabled Moray *et al.* (1980, 1982) to derive transition probabilities, proportion of times spent on different features of the radar, and the mean first-passage times for examining different aspects of the display.

Carbonell's Model

Shortly after the publication of Senders's *et al.* (Note 1) pioneering work, Carbonell (1966) proposed a model that has many of the characteristics scattered through the other models examined thus far, and that is probably the best point of departure for future developments. He noted that (at the time he was writing) it was comparatively rare for operators merely to check the level of a signal without doing anything about it if it were found to be out of bounds. Normally, some control action would be called for to make the process return to the desired set point or to null the error. Furthermore, he suggested that in the real world, if an instrument is found to have exceeded a set limit, it is unlikely to return to the mean of the forcing function with the passage of time. He proposed that a suitable model for the observed process was not a zero-mean Gaussian signal, but a mixture of Gaussian noise and a deterministic signal that would force continued divergence in the absence of action. He also suggested that the relative importance of the different instruments would not usually be equal. He saw the overall situation as a closed-loop multichannel queuing problem in which m instruments queued for service.

If $C(t)$ is the total cost of not looking at any instrument at all, C the cost associated with instrument i exceeding its limit, and $p(t)$ the probability that instrument i will exceed its limit L at instant t; then the probabilities and costs are related by

$$C(t) = \sum_{i=1}^{m} \frac{C_i p_i(t)}{1 - p_i(t)},$$

and the cost of looking at a particular instrument j at time t will be $C^*(t) = C(t) - C_j p_j(t)$. The strategy is then to choose that instrument at time t, which makes C^* a minimum, and hence $C_i p_i(t)$ a maximum.

Carbonell attempted to derive the optimal strategy using queuing theory; but because the equations proved rather intractable analytically, he simulated the model. The simulation showed that as the variance of the instruments increased, the sampling behavior became increasingly aperiodic. The "pilot" (that is, the output of the model) showed quite variable behavior in different phases of flight; and in particular whenever the threshold of risk was exceeded and action was required, the "pilot" continued to fixate the relevant instrument until its value had returned to within the prescribed limits.

This is interesting in relation to the well-known fact that under stress, human operators frequently "lock up" on some instrument or subset of instruments and fail to share their attention (see, for example, Moray, 1981). Carbonell's model, then, incorporates bandwidth, limits, differential costs, differential probabilities of exceeding limits, interinstrument correlation, and queuing theory in a very powerful model. Senders and Posner (1976) have succeeded in generalizing the queuing theory approach and solving the equations analytically.

Control Theory

The model that is most firmly based on closed-loop control rather than on monitoring is due to Allen *et al.* (Note 2). Starting from the well-known McRuer quasi-linear manual control model, they ask what effect sampling would have on closed-loop performance. The theory is a frequency-domain theory unlike the time-domain theories examined in the preceding. To quote from their paper:

> It is assumed that the pilot's learning process has been stabilized so that the scanning behaviour is stable (in the statistical sense). Sampling a given display is assumed to be

"almost periodic" with appreciable statistical fluctuations which randomize the data. The model then treats the average properties of this scanning during typical task intervals. Although sampling effects on loop closures and scanning statistics are well represented this way, it is not possible to account for the particular order in which the displays are scanned. This assumption should improve as the number of instruments and control axes increases, thereby tending to randomize the scanning. The detailed high frequency effects of the scanning, sampling and reconstruction are circulated around the closed loop system, giving rise to a broadband "sampling" remnant. This is modelled as an injected noise at the pilot's input (that is, "observation noise") . . . The resulting model for scanning, sampling and reconstruction comprises: 1) a quasi-linear, random-input "perceptual describing function" which multiplies the human operator's continuous describing function, and 2) a broadband sampling remnant, n, which adds to the basic remnant, and is described as a spectrum of wide band observation noise injected at the pilot's perceptual input (pp. 16–17).

For those who are not familiar with the classical control theory models of the human operator that have been successfully used for the solution of practical problems of man–machine design since the early 1960s, largely ignored by psychologists, the following is a rather general summary of the model. When there are several instruments to be attended, as in flying an aircraft under manual rather than automatic control, it is not possible to look at them all continuously. Therefore, the pilot samples them from time to time, trying to reconstruct the missing information from each source. If the pilot tries to do this between samples so as to decide what control he or she should exercise over the system, he or she will add noise due to his or her incorrect actions; and because the system is a closed-loop feedback system, that noise will circulate around the loop. This noise will alter the power spectrum of the control task, and the model predicts what the effect of this sampling induced noise will be.

Although not apparent from the passage just quoted, Allen *et al.* also considered the extent to which peripheral, that is parafoveal, vision will be used in scanning, the layout of instruments, and so on. The aim is to relate the extent to which the human operator can continue to be a successful stable controller despite the limits of his or her information due to scanning. Allen *et al.* draw heavily on the earlier literature on pilot eye movements and, indeed, provide an excellent and useful summary of some little-known work. Note that the kind of predictions that this model makes are rather distantly related, when taken at face value, to the other models. The important distinction is that this model is intimately connected with closed-loop manual control, unlike any of those discussed so far, which are primarily concerned with open-loop monitoring.

A model of monitoring devised by van de Graaf and Wewerinke (Note 3) is based on optimal, rather than classical, Control Theory. The reader unfamiliar with optimal control and estimation theory is recommended to see the special edition of the journal *Human Factors* (Applications of Control Theory, 1977), which contains several tutorials. Van de Graaf and Wewerinke assume that the observer keeps a running statistical estimate of the mean and variance of each of the monitored variables. This is updated by the "Kalman filter" of optimal estimation theory. The observer compares the current value observed with that expected on the assumption that the process has still the mean and the variance that is expected based on the past history of the observations. After each observation, a likelihood-ratio test is performed on the data to see whether it is more probable that the mean is still at its normal value or that the parameters of the observed process have changed. Using this model, van de Graaf and Wewerinke predict the transition probabilities, fixation durations, latency of error detections, and proportion of time spent looking at each variable. The model is close to that devised by Gai and Curry (1976), which was mentioned earlier.

Empirical Results and Evaluation of Theories

In order to validate most of the models discussed here, it is necessary to obtain eye-movement records. This is a task that even today is beset with formidable technical problems. However, several sources of data do exist, although none are readily accessible. Moreover, even when the records are available, either on film or on videotape, analysis is extremely time-consuming. By far the largest set of data on eye movements that has ever been recorded is the monumental effort made by Fitts, Milton, and Jones to analyze the eye movements of pilots flying real aircraft during the late 1940s. A summary of the work appeared in the *Aeronautical Engineering Review* (Fitts, Jones, & Milton, 1950), but the original reports are filed as U.S. Air Force research reports (Fitts, Jones, & Milton, Note 4; Jones, Milton, & Fitts, Note 5, Note 6; Milton, Jones, & Fitts, Note 7, Note 8; Milton, McIntosh, & Cole, Note 9). These workers analyzed in all more than 75,000 frames of cine film taken in the cockpit during experimental flights. These data provide a firm base for certain assertions about the patterns of visual attention, although the fact that only the eyes, and not the readings on the instruments, were recorded makes the data unsuitable for testing some of the models. Senders (Note 10) also has a data bank of photographic records of pilots while flying. Moray has videotapes of several hours of radar operator eye movements, but these are only accessible through the United Kingdom Ministry of Defence. In addition, there are numerous pieces of research in which relatively small amounts of data have been recorded. This chapter does not attempt to review them all. The reader's best hope of obtaining data relevant to his or her interest is to contact the authors directly. The concern here is only with data that have been analyzed for the purpose of testing the models that have been described in this chapter. The considerable body of work on eye movements in automobile drivers, for example, is not discussed despite the fact that in a more thorough review it should certainly be examined.

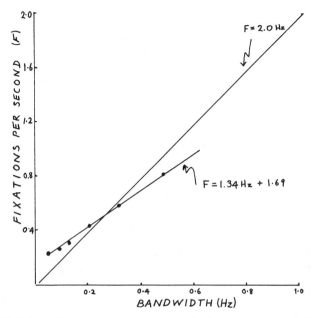

Figure 13.4 Relationship between the number of eye fixations per second made of a source and the bandwidth of the forcing function driving the source. The $F = 2.0$ Hz line shows the predicted relationship for an optimal (Shannon) sampler that observes a source with bandwidth W Hz every $1/2W$ seconds. (Data from Senders, 1964.)

Of the four models developed by Senders *et al.*, only one, namely the first, has been tested directly. Senders compared the predictions of the model with the data obtained by Fitts and his co-workers, as well as with data obtained in a laboratory study and with some pilot eye-movement data obtained by himself. The re-analysis of the Fitts data revealed that Senders's approach to the calculation of transition probabilities among instruments on the basis of the relative frequency of fixation was very successful (Senders, 1966). Indeed, it is the present writer's experience that this feature of the model can readily be demonstrated on the basis of half an hour's data from unpracticed subjects in a psychology practical class. The rest of his predictions could not be tested on Fitts's data because it requires the fixations to be related to the statistical structure of the displays, and the latter were not recorded. Senders therefore, set up a task so that he could collect data in a laboratory setting, in which students monitored 6 instruments against their exceeding specified limits. Subjects received more than 10 hours practice, and their behavior was stable.

Typical results from this study are shown in Figure 13.4. Although the eye fixations are a monotonic and indeed linear function of signal bandwidth as predicted, the slope is incorrect. The particular departure from the exact prediction based on the sampling theorem is of a kind that is almost, if not quite, universally found. High-bandwidth sources are sampled less frequently than they should be, and low bandwidths more frequently than they should be. A plausible account of this discrepancy was proposed by Senders *et al.* (Note 1) and now can be developed further. They pointed out that the undersampling of high frequencies could be explained if the observers were reading the rate of change of the instrument as well as its absolute value when they fixated it. Fogel (1955) has shown that if the first derivative (rate) of a function is known as well as its momentary value, then samples need be taken only half as often as the Shannon sampling theorem states. If, then, some rate information is available from the high-frequency signals, the undersampling would only be apparent, not real, because the rate information would compensate for the infrequent sampling. Turning to the oversampling of the low-frequency signals, Senders's *et al.* (Note 1), on the average, observers, seem to begin to oversample when the bandwidth of the display falls below about 0.02 Hz. The lowest bandwidth he used was 0.03 Hz. The average value of the zero–bandwidth intercept for the three experiments Senders's *et al.* reported is 0.14 fixations per second. Changing rate to time, oversampling begins when the Nyquist interval is about 10 seconds, and the interval at which the observer would sample a DC (0 Hz) signal would be about once every $1/0.14 = 7.14$ seconds. Is the latter value the time when intolerable forgetting occurs? It will be recalled that in one of Kvålseth's experiments (1979), he found that sampling occurred when the entropy of the observer's information had risen to between 85 and 100% of its maximum value; and that, given the timing of his presentation of new material, this corresponds to an interval of about 9–12 seconds. Furthermore, Moray *et al.* (1980) estimated that severe forgetting began to set in at around 12 seconds. Taking all these data together, it is plausible to infer that somewhere around 10 seconds, forgetting is sufficient—almost regardless of the task—for endogenous uncertainty to rise to a point at which the observer feels compelled to sample a source again.

Because in his experiment the signal power and the required accuracy were equal for all the sources, Senders's *et al.* (Note 1) model predicts that the fixation duration should be equal for all the sources; and this was the case. Finally, Senders *et al.* (Note 1) found an effect of intersignal correlation in the direction predicted, but the effect was rather slight. Observers seemed to sample a signal that was a mixture of random noises with bandwidths of 0.12 Hz and 0.20 Hz as if it were a source of the former bandwidth. On balance then, Senders's *et al.* (Note 1) model, within its limitations and within the limitations of the experimental situation, fares rather well. The reader should, however, be warned that there are a number of important but subtle effects discussed in detail in the original report that merit close study. But the model is justly regarded as the "un-sampler" from which are descended all the other models and as playing an important and profound role in the development of attentional theory.

Carbonell's (1966) initial "validation" was, as already mentioned, in the form of a simulation rather than a measurement compared with human data. However in subsequent investigation (Carbonell, Ward, & Senders, 1966), the model was compared with pilot eye-movement data, and predicted well.

The approaches of Moray (1982) and Gai and Curry (1976) have not been investigated directly; although, as mentioned, the use of sequential decision making as a model for the human observer's data aquisition is well established, the existence of the SATO is accepted, and Gai and Curry (1976) have successfully applied sequential decision making to the detection of plant failures by human operators.

Moray (1981) predicted that correlations among sources would mean that under normal conditions the scanning patterns will be affected by the relationships in such a way that only one of a group of closely coupled instruments would be examined. This prediction was not supported by Senders's data, although there seems to be evidence of it in the data from Fitts's group *et al.* (1950); and in industry, Iosif (1969) reports data that seem to show the effect. It may be that perceived causality rather than mere correlation is required. The converse, seen in Carbonell's (1966) simulation, and suggested by Moray (1982), that under stress the operator may "lock up" or show "cognitive tunnel vision" is well established. Moray's empirical model successfully predicted the mean first-passage times and proportion of time spent attending to echos on the radar displays and also showed the "lock up" effect as aircraft approached one another closely, as the probability threshold model or variable Nyquist model of Senders's group (Note 1) would predict.

Kvålseth (1979) tested his decision-theory model by presenting a number series to his observers, and giving them the option of choosing to see or not to see each number in the series. To see the number, they had to pay 1 Kroner; whereas failure to report that the process was beyond L cost 20 Kroner in one condition and 10 Kroner in another. In the control condition, the operator could type in a number representing his or her control action; and it was then added into the system through a first-order plant. The ARP parameter a was set at 0.9, L was set to 13 or 16, and the process standard deviation was set to 10.0. (That is, L was set at 1.3 or 1.6 times the standard deviation of the process.) The results do not support his model. Changing the limits from 13 to 16 had no significant effect on the output of the operator's behavior but considerable effect on the normative behavior of the model. The ratio of costs of observation to cost of exceeding limits had a strong effect on the model but no effect on the operators, and there was a significant difference between the model and Kvålseth's operators on almost all measures. There was, however, a significant correlation between individual operator behavior and that of the model, ranging from 0.45 to 0.9 on the sampling interval measure. When the operators had to control the system as well as observe it, they did no better than if they had exercised no control at all, produced oscillation, and made far too many control actions. There was no correlation between the behavior of the model and that of the operators. In both the monitoring and the control modes of operation, the sampling interval decreased (samples were taken more often) when the observation was near L.

Kvålseth's (1979) model does not appear, on the basis of these data, particularly promising. But in fairness, several comments must be made. First, although Kvålseth says that several practice runs were given to all operators, it is clear from the work quoted earlier, and from the study of Ostry, Moray, and Marks (1976) that several hours of practice are required to stabilize performance. Moreover, this is especially likely to be true when complicated interactions of accuracy and payoff are required; because it is when actions become automatic, rather than consciously thought out, that optimal behavior is seen. Second, the kind of display used by Kvålseth (1979) is one that is unusual in sampling research and is likely to be very difficult for an observer to handle. There is no analog display and no rate information. All that is seen is a single numerical value at each sample taken. Moreover, in the control situation, control was digital. It is as if the operator were required to nominate verbally the position to which he or she wished his or her joystick to be put rather than moving it. Perforce, the "effective joystick" was not moved continuously, but placed at discrete positions at aperiodic discrete movements of time. Although one can see the logic of Kvålseth's model, little is known about the kind of behavior one is likely to see from the human operator in this kind of task; and intuitively one feels that the task was probably much harder for the operators than an equivalent analogical display–control system would have been. It is hard enough tracking a display with continuous control; here the operator is asked to inject impulses of varying magnitude at varying intervals into an integrator and is expected to be able to be aware of the outcome of this when mixed with an ARP function with added noise. It is quite possible that repeating the work with more conventional display–control relations and with much more highly practiced operators would have led to a better prediction. It should be noticed that the findings that more observations were taken when an observation was near the limit L is what was predicted from the variable Nyquist model of Senders *et al.* (Note 1).

Rouse (Note 11) attempted to validate Sheridan's (1970) model and found that, in general, his (Rouse's) operators were suboptimal. Rouse asked the operators to predict the output of the second-order filter forced by white noise, with a cost for observation. Sheridan and Rouse (1971) summarize their conclusions as follows:

> None of the subjects were able to score as low as the optimal (although training helped). This was due to their inability or unwillingness to pick appropriate sampling or prediction periods and to predict optimally. Inappropriate shift of T is attributable to two sources. First, inability on the part of subjects to predict over longer periods of time without sampling may have caused them to choose shorter sampling periods over which they felt

their skills more closely resembled optimal. Second, the subjects were unwilling to take the chance of a larger error that might arise from a longer sampling period even though this also gave them a very small time averaged sampling cost and thus a chance at a very high reward. This tendency is termed risk aversion and is evidenced by the subjects comments that were collected. Inability to predict optimally resulted from various sources. The subject's internal model of the input process may have been erroneous. Subjects may have not realized what prediction strategy would minimize the specific value function. In particular, some of the subjects did not know that predicting the estimated mean of the signal distribution was the optimal strategy and consequently, they attempted to make their y's look like the x's. This strategy is disastrous if the subject guesses the wrong direction after sampling. Subject's comments also indicated that they may need more than the last two points to predict the next point. In effect, this amounts to their assuming a higher order filter than actually existed. (That is, having an incorrect model of the process) (p. 86).

In addition, Rouse found that the subjects failed to predict that the process would return to the mean as quickly as it did, having a tendency to extrapolate linearly rather than exponentially. This passage has been quoted at length because within it are sources of suboptimality that one can be fairly sure are present in many studies. Whenever observers are expected to respond to the statistical structure of a time-varying process, to subjective probabilities, or to complex payoff matrices embedded in the task, many hours of practice will be required to ensure that they have acquired adequate internalized representations of such task parameters. In general, no experiment can be considered a valid test of one of these models unless the participants have had at least 5 hours of practice on the task, and 10 hours of practice is safer. When the participant becomes used to the task, he or she approaches constrained optimality. Prior to that point, what one is seeing is the desperate struggle of a limited capacity, fallible, conscious cognitive decision maker struggling with a task to which he or she is ill fitted.

The closed-loop control model of Allen *et al.* (Note 2) fares rather well, although as pointed out, its applicability is rather different from some of the other models. They summarized the questions in which they were interested as follows: (1) Do different pilots adopt the same average scanning sample (i.e., data acquisition) and reconstruction strategy? (2) Are the sampling intervals distributed about some mean value? (3) Is the sampling frequency high enough to justify a describing function representation? (4) Does the form of the describing function equation fit the equation that they propose? (5) Is the sampling remnant broadband? (6) To what extent does reconstruction take place between fixations? The report of their results is a very detailed and instructive document that requires close reading and cannot be covered adequately here given the scope of this chapter. However, the answer to the first five questions was broadly "yes." The first is important as showing the generality of their results. The intervals were randomly distributed but were not well fitted by a simple Poisson distribution. The range of values was restricted to between 0.4 and 0.8 seconds and was sharply cut off at the lower end. These values agree with other data. Questions 3,

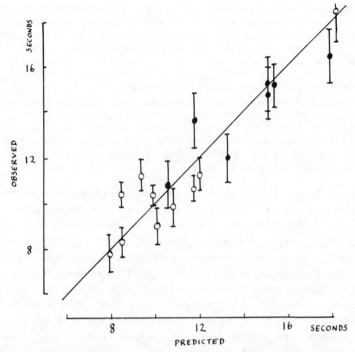

Figure 13.5 Observed and predicted detection latencies (with standard deviations) for abnormal readings for frequent (open circles) and rare (closed circles) faults on four meters. (From van der Graaf and Wewerinke, Note 3.)

4, and 5 relate to the way in which the describing function approach can be extended to apply to multiaxis tasks with visually sampled data channels, and the result shows that the model holds up well. Only Question 6 received a qualified "no." But a close analysis, particularly when a difficult secondary task was added to the main task, suggested that the reason was that reconstruction was unnecessary when the main task was performed in isolation. When the side task imposed a heavier load, there was reconstruction used in the side task, rather than the main task.

We are justified in concluding that Allen *et al.*'s model is rather successful for predicting and analysing closed-loop behavior. Their report deserves close and detailed scrutiny. They point out some interesting features of the collective eye-movement data that are now available if one collates all the studies. For example, it seems rather rare to find eye movements at rates higher than about two per second, at least in tracking tasks. (There is only one report that suggests that very much higher rates around four per second, may be seen in industrial inspectors doing fault detection in products. Note that in that case, the nature of the target may be well defined, and there is no statistical uncertainty of the kind that is seen in the tasks discussed in this chapter.) Moreover, there may be a tendency for longer fixations to occur in the multiples of the base time, although this is less well established. Very few fixations of duration longer than about 1.25 seconds are seen. These generalizations may not be of great significance for understanding, say, the neural control of eye movements because there is little doubt that experimental conditions could be set up in the laboratory to show other values. But from the viewpoint of the designers of user–machine systems, they are of great practical worth.

Finally, van de Graaf and Wewerinke's model also fares well. They asked their observers to view four displays. Displays 1 and 2 were driven by independent band-limited white noise sources. Displays 3 and 4 were respectively correlated with Displays 1 and 2. They were able to predict fixation duration, sampling intervals, and transition probabilities. Some of the results are shown in Figure 13.5. This experiment and the theory underlying it are related sources that were examined frequently together. It appears that the observers were using the redundant information to check their estimates of the state variables. But as in Senders's (1964) experiment, the bandwidths were so low that the observers were not overloaded; and the possibility remains that in a situation of overload, the observer will sacrifice redundant sources (Iosif, 1969).

Discussion and Conclusions

This chapter has been but a brief introduction to a very detailed body of work that is largely unknown to psychologists due to its relative inaccessibility. The large number of models is at first aesthetically unsatisfactory, but they are noteworthy for the fact that all except one are analytical. That is, they are strongly based in theory and prescribe normative optimal behavior against which human behavior can be evaluated. Moreover, in a sense, they are not all that different. Although they emphasize different aspects of the various tasks, they share a number of similar assumptions; and it is worth summarizing them. First, they are all concerned with the strategic and tactical direction of attention, not with its mechanisms. Second, they all implicitly concentrate on tasks that are either actual "real-world" tasks, or are analogs thereof. Third, the tasks are dynamic and stochastic. Fourth, the emphasis on a few highly practiced operators is of vital importance; no serious test of models of real-world behavior can be made on subjects paid a few dollars for quasi-compulsory attendance in a Psychology 100 course. The reason is, that absolutely central to all of the models and theories is the notion that the human operator embodies in all serious tasks, an "internal model" of the task, the process, and his or her own ability.

Putting together the explicit features and the implicit emphases of all the models discussed, it seems that the canonical model will contain the following features. The statistical properties of the sources to be sampled produce uncertainty that the operator wishes to reduce. If he or she is doing a checking task in which limits on a process are involved, his or her attention will be a function of the magnitude of the limit relative to the excursions of the process. The operator's decisions as to when to sample will be determined by the dynamics of the observed processes, by the costs and payoffs associated with the different instruments, and by the probability matrices relating the value of the different intervals. Correlation and causal links among instruments will affect the pattern of scanning; and the signal-to-noise ratio and the importance of the information will determine the duration of the fixation, although a single fixation will seldom exceed 1 second. The dynamics of forgetting will play an important role. If the task involves closed-loop control, then the existing models will need to be coupled to the models of open-loop sampling.

This research has the potential for aiding design engineers in coping with the immensely complex systems now prevalent in process control. As the systems grow in complexity and the sizes of crew decrease, it is already not uncommon to find a single operator monitoring several hundred or more displays and controls. If the human is really limited to two eye movements per second, how can such systems be optimized for the user? How should the information be displayed? Knowledge of "real-life" settings apart from aerospace is not well founded. In process control, the bandwidth of systems tends to be so low that even in manual control, the operator treats the system as a series of discrete problems. The time taken to become skilled and to learn the nature of the process and the requisite control actions may be of the order of months or years, and the problems of the tactical direction of attention are quite unlike the laboratory or aerospace problems. One must assume that there is massive forgetting of much of the information between glances, and perhaps the greatest problem is simply that of ensuring that all variables get sampled sooner or later, however seldom. Rasmussen and Rouse (1981) have suggested that several modes of information processing may exist and distinguish between information as signals, signs, and symbols. If the observer treats the sampled information as a signal, the appropriate behavior is to respond as a closed-loop servomechanism and null the error. If the information is treated as a sign, the appropriate behavior is to search for a pattern that it represents and the appropriate rule to follow. If the information is treated as a symbol the operator uses knowledge-based behavior in a problem-solving mode as a means of updating his or her understanding of the system and its relation to his or her goals. Vigilance is not so much then a problem of detecting signals as of detecting the need for different modes of behavior and the appropriate types of knowledge to use.

Rasmussen and Rouse (1981) speak of the problem of "cognitive coupling":

Only if the information obtained from samples is appropriate to the type of control required will efficient control be possible. Hence in real industrial systems, attention may appear to be directed to instruments, but may actually be directed to highly abstract relationships between sources and data. For obvious reasons, little work has so far been done in this area. It is expensive, time-consuming, and fraught with practical difficulties. Some of the classic papers are to be found in Edwards and Lees (1974). Of particular interest are those by Crossman, extending Senders's (1964) work to industrial settings and anticipating Kvålseth's (1979) use of information theory, and Bainbridge's analysis of the strategies used by experienced process controllers. More research work can be found in Rasmussen and Rouse (1981).

It is a pity that because the work in this chapter has mainly appeared in engineering journals or contract reports, it has gone largely unnoticed by psychologists. It is, to this writer, a most exciting body of work that shows steady evolution. Starting with the very simple assumptions of Senders (1964), which were nonetheless able to make some strong predictions, more complex models have appeared. But despite their complexity, they are all rigorously formulated and make clear and testable predictions in their turn. They form a formidible body of theory about attention, and, moreover, one that is not merely applicable but one that has been, and is being, used in applied settings and in designing safer and more efficient systems for humans to use. As user–machine systems become increasingly complex, operator and population safety is coming increasingly to depend on human factors in systems design. There is a vital need to achieve strong theory in the field of attention, for in supervisory control, it becomes of increasing importance. Mankind does physically, less and less. But that does not mean that the information-processing demands on people are lessened; and as systems are built that have hundreds or thousands of displayed variables, in large aircraft and in nuclear and conventional power situations, attentional theory will come to be, in the next few years, at the heart of the design process.

Reference Notes

1. Senders, J. W., Elkind, J. I., Grignetti, M. C., & Smallwood, R. *An investigation of the visual sampling behavior of human observers.* (National Aeronautics and Space Administration Rep. 76. CR-434). National Aeronautics Space Administration, 1964.

2. Allen, R. W., Clement, W. F., & Jex, H. R. *Research on display scanning, sampling, and reconstruction using separate main and secondary tracking tasks* (National Aeronautics and Space Administration Rep. No. CR-1569). National Aeronautics and Space Administration, July 1970.

3. van de Graaf, R. C., & Wewerinke, P. H. *Experimental and theoretical analysis of human monitoring and decision making behavior in failure detection tasks.* (Rep. No. NLR MP 81032 U)., Netherlands: National Aerospace Laboratory, 1981.

4. Fitts, P. M., Jones, R. E., & Milton, J. L. *Eye fixations of aircraft pilots* (Pt. 3): *Frequency, duration, and sequence fixation When flying Air Force ground controlled approach system (GCA)* (U.S. Air Force Tech. Rep., No. 5967). Dayton: Wright–Patterson Air Force Base, 1949.

5. Jones, R. E., Milton, J. L., & Fitts, P. M. *Eye fixation of aircraft pilots* (Pt. 1): *A review of prior eye movement studies and a description of a technique for recording the frequency, duration and sequence of eye movements during instrument flight* (U.S. Air Force Tech. Rep. No. 5837). Dayton: Wright–Patterson Air Force Base, 1949.

6. Jones, R. E., Milton, J. L., & Fitts, P. M. *Eye fixations of aircraft pilots* (Pt. 4): *Frequency, duration and sequence of fixations during routine instrument flight* U.S. Air Force Tech. Rep. No. 5975). Dayton: Wright–Patterson Air Force Base, 1950.

7. Milton, J. L., Jones, R. E., & Fitts, P. M. *Eye fixations of aircraft pilots* (Pt. 2): *Frequency, duration, and sequence of fixations when flying the USAF instrument low approach system (ILAS)* (U.S. Air Force Tech. Rep. No. 5839). Dayton: Wright–Patterson Air force Base, 1949.

8. Milton, J. L., Jones, R. E., & Fitts, P. M. *Eye fixations of aircraft pilots* (Pt. 5): *Frequency, duration, and sequence of fixations when flying selected maneuvers during instrument and visual flight conditions* (U.S. Air Force Tech. Rep. No. 6018). Dayton: Wright–Patterson Air Force Base, 1950.

9. Milton, J. L., McIntosh, B. B., & Cole, E. L. *Fixations during day and night GCA approaches using an experimental instrument panel arrangement* (U.S. Air Force Tech. Rep. No. 6709). Dayton: Wright–Patterson Air Force Base, 1952.

10. Senders, J. W. Personal communication, 1982.

11. Rouse, W. B. *Cognitive sources of suboptimal human prediction* (Engineering Projects Laboratory Rep. DSR 70283-19). Cambridge: Massachussetts Institute of Technology, 1972.

References

Applications of control theory in human factors. Special Issue, *Human Factors*, 1977, *19*, 313–413.

Broadbent, D. E. The role of auditory localization and attention in memory span. *Journal of Experimental Psychology*, 1954, *47*, 191–196.

Broadbent, D. E. *Perception and communication*. London: Pergamon, 1958.

Carbonell, J. A queueing model of many-instrument sampling. *IEEE Transactions on Human Factors in Electronics* 1966. *HFE-7*, 157–164.

Carbonell, J., Ward, J., & Senders, J. W. A queueing model of visual sampling: Experimental validation. *IEEE Transactions on Man–Machine Systems*, 1966, *MMS-9*, 82–87.

Deutsch, J. A. & Deutsch, D. Attention: Some theoretical considerations. *Psychological Review*, 1963, *70*, 80–90.

Edwards, E., & Lees, F. *The human operator in process control*. London: Taylor and Francis, 1974.

Fitts, P. M., Jones, R. E., & Milton, J. L. Eye movements of aircraft pilots during instrument landing approaches. *Aeronautical Engineering Review*, 1950, *9*, 1–5.

Fogel, L. A note on the sampling theorem. *Transactions of professional group on information theory, IRE*, 1956.

Gai, E. G., & Curry, R. E. A model of the human observer in failure detection tasks. *IEEE Transactions on Systems, Man and Cybernetics* 1976, *SMC-6*, 85–95.

Hick, W. E. On the rate of gain of information. *Quarterly Journal of Experimental Psychology*, 1950, *4*, 11–26.

Howard, R. A. Information value theory. *IEEE Transactions on Systems Science and Cybernetics,* 1966, *SSC-2,* 22–26.

Hyman, R. Stimulus information as a determinant of reaction time. *Journal of Experimental Psychology,* 1953, *45,* 188–195.

Iosif, G. Influence de la correlation fonctionelle sur parametres technologiques. *Revue roumanienne science sociales-psychologie,* 1969, *13,* 105–110.

Kvålseth, T. O. Human information processing in visual sampling. *Ergonomics,* 1978, *21,* 439–454.

Kvålseth, T. O. A decision theoretic model of the sampling behavior of the human process monitor: Experimental evaluation. *Human Factors,* 1979, *21,* 671–686.

Moray, N. Where is attention limited? A survey and a model. *Acta Psychologica,* 1967, *27,* 84–92.

Moray, N. *Attention: Selective process in vision and hearing.* London: Hutchinson, 1969.

Moray, N. The strategic control of information processing. In G. Underwood (Ed.), *Strategies of information processing,* New York: Academic Press, 1978, 301–328.

Moray, N. The role of attention in the detection of errors and the diagnosis of failures in man–machine systems. In J. Rasmussen & W. B. Rouse (Eds.), *Human detection and diagnosis of system failures.* New York: Plenum, 1981, 185–198.

Moray, N., Neil, G., & Brophy, C. *The behavior and selection of fighter controllers.* London: Ministry of Defence Report, 1982.

Moray, N. Richards, M., & Low, J. *The behavior of fighter controllers.* London: Ministry of Defence Report, 1980.

Norman, D. Toward a theory of memory and attention. *Psychological Review,* 1968, *75,* 522–536.

Ostry, D., Moray, N., & Marks, J. Attention, practice and semantic targets. *Journal of Experimental Psychology: Human Perception and Performance,* 1976, *2,* 326–336.

Rasmussen, J., & Rouse, W. B. *Human detection and diagnosis of system failures.* New York: Plenum, 1981.

Schneider, W. & Shiffrin, R. M. Controlled and automatic human information processing: I. Detection, search, and attention. *Psychological Review,* 1977, *84,* 1–66.

Senders, J. W. The human operator as a monitor and controller of multidegree of freedom systems. *IEEE Transactions on Human Factors in Electronics,* 1964, *HFE-5,* 1–6.

Senders, J. W. A re-analysis of pilot eye movement data. *IEEE Transactions on Human Factors in Electronics,* 1966, *HFE-7,* 2–4.

Senders, J. W., & Posner, M. J. M. A queuing model of monitoring and supervisory behavior. In T. Sheridan & G. Johannsen (Eds.), *Monitoring behavior and supervisory control.* New York: Plenum, 1976, 245–260.

Shannon, C., & Weaver, W. *The mathematical theory of communication.* Urbana: University of Illinois Press, 1949.

Sheridan, T. B. On how often the supervisor should sample. *IEEE Transactions on Systems Science and Cybernetics,* 1970, *SSC-6,* 140–145.

Sheridan, T. B. & Rouse, W. B. Supervisory sampling and control: Sources of suboptimality in a prediction task. *Proceedings of the 7th NASA Annual Conference on Manual Control,* 1971.

Treisman, A. M. Selective attention in man. *British Medical Bulletin,* 1967, *20,* 12–16.

Wald, E. *Sequential analysis.* New York: Wiley, 1947.

14

Lapses of Attention in Everyday Life[1]

James Reason

Introduction

Although preachers traditionally take their texts from the scriptures, contemporary psychologists—particularly those with an interest in the cognitive processes of everyday life—have come increasingly to rely on the writings of William James. It is not just that he gave elegant expression to a wide range of cognitive experiences, though this is reason enough, but also that he addressed himself to the immediate, ordinary, and recognizable aspects of mental life. This stands in marked contrast to the relentless pursuit of the recondite and the counter-intuitive that characterized, in the name of behavioral science, much of psychology in the years that followed him. Nor did James shrink from stating the obvious when he found it among the commonplace. It is one such statement of the obvious that serves as the text for this chapter: "Habit diminishes the conscious attention with which our acts are performed" (James, 1890, p. 114). That this is a self-evident truth does not alter the fact that understanding how automatization comes about still remains one of the central problems of psychology. The aim of this chapter is to explore a small aspect of this problem: the relationship between attention and skilled performance; or, more precisely, the interaction between the control of highly routinized activities and the deployment of attention necessary to ensure their successful outcome.

Habit and Attention

Habit and attention are words that have more or less equal currency in everyday language, but the mental processes they denote are far from comparable in their conceptual clarity. Whereas the notion of *habit* is something one can hold fast in the mind, something that is as solid and predictable as "the enormous flywheel of society" in James's metaphor, the concept of attention is a flickering wraith by comparison. *Attention,* James wrote, "is the taking possession by the

[1]This work was supported by research grant number HR 6290/1 from the Social Science Research Council.

515

mind, in clear and vivid form, of one out of what seem several simultaneously possible objects or trains of thought. Focalization, concentration, of consciousness are of its essence. It implies withdrawal from some things in order to deal more effectively with others" (James, 1890, pp. 403–404). This expresses well enough our common understanding of the term, emphasizing as it does the role of attention as the gatekeeper to consciousness; but what James omitted to mention, at least in this passage, is the extraordinarily labile nature of attentional focus, which varies continually both in its direction and in its breadth. Elsewhere, James (1908) commented on the reciprocity that exists between attention and interest. Novel and exciting objects capture one's attention involuntarily, but those less naturally engrossing demand an effort of will to bring attention to bear on them. And one of the most conspicuous features of this voluntary mode of attention is that it cannot be sustained. "When we are studying an uninteresting subject, if our mind tends to wander, we have to bring back our attention every now and then by using distinct pulses of effort, which revivify the topic for a moment, the mind then running on for a certain number of seconds or minutes with spontaneous interest, until again some intercurrent idea captures it and takes it off" (James, 1908, p. 101). It is this continual switching of attention and particularly its occasional misdirection that constitutes the main concern of this chapter because it is this feature that appears to have the most relevance for an understanding of the control of automatized behavior.

Both habit and attention clearly have leading parts to play in the guidance of action. Both serve one's purpose in varying degrees depending on the level of skill that has been attained. In a novel task, one needs to pay close and labored attention to the consequences of one's actions in order to achieve one's ends. In the jargon of the skills theorists, one needs to function in a *feedback* mode of control. But with increasing practice, one shifts more and more to a *feedforward* mode in which preformed motor programs (Keele, 1973; Stelmach, 1976), schemata (Schmidt, 1976), action systems (Shallice, 1972, 1979), or action schemas (Norman, 1980, 1981) determine the course of action with only limited reference to conscious attention. Indeed, when a sufficient degree of proficiency has been achieved, too much attentional involvement can actually disrupt the smooth flow of motor output, as when a skilled typist or pianist is directed to concentrate on the movements of individual fingers.

All of this is common knowledge; but what is not is the extent to which attentional mechanisms are still needed for the guidance of highly practiced activities. Introspection can reveal little because it is in the nature of skilled performance that moment-to-moment control, and hence detailed awareness of what one is doing and how one is doing it, lies mostly beyond the reach of consciousness. This is the realm that James (1890) described as the "fringe of consciousness" or what Polanyi (1958) has called "tacit knowledge," something that involves a nonfocal or subsidiary awareness. But there is at least one, largely neglected, class of everyday events that can yield important clues as to the role of attention in the guidance of routinized behavior, namely the "slips of action" that seemingly arise from the misdirection of focal attention.

If one's actions deviate from one's intentions due to some kind of attentional failure, then it seems reasonable to argue by default that a greater degree of attentional involvement was necessary on these occasions in the action sequence to ensure the desired outcome. A similar point was made by Jastrow in 1905: "It is a peculiar type of straying of the process from the intended path that directs attention to it and makes one aware of a momentary lapse in the relation of issue and purpose; such lapses not only disclose the nature of the ordinary well-adjusted relations, but offer an interesting means of determining what otherwise would be but vaguely recognised" (Jastrow, 1905, pp. 481–482). The remainder of this chapter is devoted to a consideration of the nature and circumstances of these "actions not as planned," and the light they can throw on the function of attentional processes in skilled or habitual behavior.

Everyday Slips and Lapses

Those who have stepped into their baths still wearing some garment, or struggled to open a friend's front door with their own latch key, or switched on the light as they left the room in the daytime, or attempted to pour a second kettle of water into a pot of freshly made tea, or turned off the television set when they meant to extinguish the gas fire, or said "Thank you" to a stamp machine, will recognize the species. Our daily lifes are strewn with such trifling and usually inconsequential blunders—what Freud (1901, 1922) called "the refuse of the phenomenal world," or, in a more daunting phrase, "the psychopathology of everyday life."

One of the factors that makes these lapses worthy of close study is that they are *not* bizarre or random events, determined exclusively by the idiosyncracies of those who commit them, or by the place and period in which they occur. Rather, they follow a clearly discernible pattern that is largely independent of their perpetrator or the surrounding circumstances. Two quotations will serve to demonstrate the timelessness of these "absent-minded" errors. The first comes from the French essayist, Jean de La Bruyère. Writing in the seventeenth century, he described the antics of one of his contemporaries. the Comte de Brancas, thus:

> [He] comes downstairs, opens the door to go out and shuts it again; he perceives that his nightcap is still on, and examining himself a little more carefully, discovers that only one side of his face is shaved, that his sword is on his right side, that his stockings are hanging about his heels, and his shirt out of his breeches. . . .
>
> In his walks about town he thinks that he has lost his way, puts himself into a fret, and asks of passers-by where he is; they tell him the name of his own street, he at once enters his own house but hastily runs out again, fancying himself mistaken. . . .

> He plays at backgammon and asks for something to drink; it is his turn to play, and
> having the dice-box in one hand and the glass in the other, being very thirsty, he gulps
> down the dice, and almost the box as well, throwing the liquor on the board and half
> drowning his antagonist. (Pritchard, 1953, pp. 363–366)

Consider also the following charming account of a slip of action contributed to the *Spectator* in 1711 by an English journalist and man-about-town, Mr. Budgell:

> My Friend Will Honeycomb is one of the Sort of Men who are very often absent in
> Conversation, and what the French call *a reveur* and *a distrait*. A little before our Club-
> time last Night we were walking together in Somerset Garden, where Will picked up a
> small Pebble of so odd a make, that he said he would present it to a Friend of his. After we
> had walked some time, I made a full stop with my Face towards the West, which Will
> knowing to be my usual method of asking . what's o'Clock, in an Afternoon, immediately
> pulled out his Watch and told me we had seven Minutes good. We took a turn or two more
> when, to my great Surprize, I saw him squirr [fling] away his Watch a considerable way
> into the Thames, and with great Sedateness in his Looks put up the Pebble, he had before
> found, in his Fob. As I have naturally an Aversion to much Speaking, and do not love to be
> the Messenger of ill News, especially when it comes too late to be useful, I left him to be
> convinced of his Mistake in due time, and continued my Walk. (Bond, 1965, pp. 329–330)

Note the similarity between this incident and that in which the Comte de Brancas attempted to swallow the dice instead of his drink. In both cases, the actions were appropriate, but the objects to which they were directed had become reversed. Such errors bear a close resemblance to the spoonerisms that occur in speech; as, for example, saying "queer old dean" instead of "dear old queen," or "you kissed my mystery lectures" for "you missed my history lectures." Slips such as these, involving complete or, more commonly, partial reversals, occur often in action as well as in speech, as is discussed later in this chapter.

Although slips of action rather than slips of the tongue are the principal concern of this chapter, it is worth noting that although psycholinguists have been assiduously recording, analyzing and making useful theoretical inferences from speech and writing errors for nearly a century (Fromkin, 1973, 1979), their nonverbal counterparts have been largely ignored until the 1970s. The causes of this neglect are many and complex (see Reason, 1979); but there were some notable exceptions to this rule, possibly the best known being Freud's (1901, 1922) minute observations of his own and other people's "erroneously carried out actions," or what he termed *parapraxes*. These too have been considered in some detail elsewhere (Reason, 1979). Of more relevance to the present issue was the interest taken in these slips by William James at Harvard and his younger contemporary at the University of Wisconsin, Joseph Jastrow.

James and Jastrow

For James, the key to understanding slips of action lay in the cognitive mechanisms that enable one to carry out well-practiced tasks with only a minimal degree of conscious involvement. A brief quotation from his chapter on "Habit" will best convey the flavor of his argument:

> Not only is it the right thing at the right time that we involuntarily do, but the wrong thing also, if it be an habitual thing. Who is there that has never wound up his watch on taking off his waistcoat in the daytime, or taken his latch-key out on arriving at the doorstep of a friend? Very absent-minded persons on going to their bedroom to dress for dinner have been known to take off one garment after another and finally get into bed, merely because that was the habitual issue of the first few movements when performed at a later hour . . . We all of us have a definite routine manner of performing certain daily offices. . . . Our lower centres know the order of these movements, and show their knowledge by their "surprise" if the objects are altered so as to oblige the movement to be made in a different way. But our higher thought-centres know hardly anything about the matter. (James, 1890, p. 115).

For James, therefore, these unintended actions arise out of the mechanism governing the running off of more or less invariant sequences of behavior. "In action grown habitual, what instigates each new muscular contraction to take place in its appointed order is not a thought or a perception, but the sensation occasioned by the muscular contraction just finished" (James, 1890, p. 115). This view of action slips is appealing because it acknowledges the two most salient features of these errors: that their occurrence is a part of highly practiced and routinized activities; and also that the erroneous actions themselves take the form of intact segments of automatized behavior, albeit unsuited for the prevailing intention.

Implicit in this view is the idea that some kind of attentional intervention is necessary to prevent actions forever running along frequently and recently trodden pathways. Jastrow (1905) makes this explicit with an equine analogy. "As to the conditions favoring such lapses, they are so familiar as to make it sufficient to recall that they occur in moments of weakened or too dispersed attention. It is because the reins are too freely relaxed, or are relaxed at an inopportune moment, that our habits take the bit between the teeth, and, it may be, lead us where we had no intention of wandering" (Jastrow, 1905, p. 482). And, in reviewing his corpus of some 300 lapses of consciousness contributed by students at the University of Wisconsin, he commented, "This collection of illustrations thus suggests upon what various occasions, with what different tempos, the mind freed of its normal guidance continues to trot with the accustomed gait, stopping, like the horse that draws the milk-cart, at the proper points of call without the direction of the driver (who for the moment may be asleep)" (Jastrow, 1905, p. 501).

Both James and Jastrow present a hierarchical picture of action control that, in its broad essentials at least, is perfectly compatible with contemporary computer metaphors (see Stelmach, 1976). In the modern idiom, one might say that repeated performance of a task permits the central processor to delegate control to largely automatic subroutines, the sequencing and timing of which are governed by superordinate executive programs, or plans. But the penalty one pays for this necessary downgrading of the locus of control is the degree of autonomy attained by these subroutines. This allows them, on occasions when the central processor is engaged elsewhere, to divert action along unintended pathways. And it also follows that these errant pathways are likely to be more familiar than the intended ones. In other words, slips of action, as has been demonstrated for many verbal slips (Timpanaro, 1976) are likely to take the form of banalizations, or what Chapman and Chapman (1973) have termed *strong associate substitutions.*

Slips of Action: Circumstances and Frequency of Occurrence

This section is concerned with presenting new data bearing on a number of basic questions relating to the production of slips of action. Under what circumstances do they occur? What form do the erroneous actions take? Are they associated with particular times of the day? How frequently do they occur during the normal course of everyday life?

For none of these questions was it thought possible to seek answers through direct observation. As both James and Jastrow have indicated, slips frequently occur as the result of misdirected or diminished attention, and such attentional states would seem to be especially vulnerable to any intrusive mode of investigation. Moreover, although inferences can be made about people's intentions from their behavior, the fact remains that only the person in question has firsthand knowledge of the plans governing his or her actions, and only he or she can claim directly to recognize a departure of action from intention. Inevitably, considerable reliance must be placed on self-reports in order to obtain data about slips of action. In view of the largely unpredictable and ephemeral nature of these lapses, some form of diary keeping seemed the most appropriate way to approach the question of the conditions under which they occur.

Before considering the findings of these diary studies, it is worth making some cautionary remarks about this technique. In addition to the more obvious problems of diary keeping (Oppenheim, 1966), our experience suggests that there are at least three kinds of bias peculiar to the reporting of action slips:

1. *Volunteer bias:* Individuals who undertake to keep a diary often do so on the assumption that they are unduly prone to absent-minded behavior.
2. *Selection bias:* It must be assumed that not all the slips of action committed by the respondent during the diary-keeping period will get recorded. Some slips will pass unnoticed, others will be regarded as too fleeting or trivial to be of interest, yet others will be forgotten before they are written down. Only the more noteworthy, amusing, or memorable slips are likely to find their way into the diary.
3. *Recording bias:* Less information will be recorded in the diary than was available to the diarist

at the time of making the slip. Moreover, what goes into the diary report may well be influenced by the diarist's personal theory as to why the error occurred. This seems especially true of whatever additional information the diarist chooses to give concerning the circumstances of the error.

These difficulties clearly set limits on the kind of inferences that can be drawn from diary studies. Not only would it be unwise to use diary material to obtain estimates of action slip incidence in the general population, but also the selection and recording biases suggest that these data cannot even be taken as representative samples of the diarist's own error behavior over the recording period. So what are diary studies good for?

It is believed they serve a useful function as wide-gauge trawl nets, picking up the more salient slips of action. If the trawls are extensive enough, it is reasonable to expect to catch a qualitatively representative sample of action slips as a whole, even if the quantities of any particular type of slip cannot be taken as reflecting their presence in the error population at large.

The Extended-Diary Study

In a preliminary diary study (Reason, 1979), the diarists were asked to note whenever their actions deviated from intention, and to record the data and time of the slip, what they had intended to do, what they actually did, and the circumstances prevailing at the time. The second study, discussed here, involved a more elaborate—extended—diary form in which, as well as providing the basic details of each error, subjects were also required to answer a standard set of questions in regard to every slip recorded. These questions were divided into five sections relating to the nature of the intended actions, the nature of the erroneous actions, the relationship between the intended actions and any wrong actions that were recognizable as belonging to some other activity, the mental and physical state at the time of the slip, and the prevailing environmental conditions.

The extended-diary study was primarily designed to test a number of hypotheses emerging both from the preliminary diary study and from the observations of James and Jastrow. The most important of these was the notion that the performance of a highly automatized task in relatively predictable and familiar surroundings liberates the central processor from moment-to-moment control. As a consequence, focal attention tends to be "captured" by some pressing but parallel mental activity or by some unrelated external event so that, on occasion, it fails to switch back to the task in hand at some "critical decision point." This permits the guidance of action to fall by default under the control of some "strong" habit. In addition, the extended-diary was constructed to yield raw data suitable for cluster analysis; namely, N entities (slips) each with seven-point ordinal scale values on p variables (the answers to the questions discussed above).

Sixty-three undergraduates used the diaries to provide a record of their slips of action over a continuous period of 7 days. They were instructed to note down what happened whenever they became aware that their actions had deviated from their intentions, no matter how trivial these lapses might appear. They were asked to record these details and to answer the standard questions as soon as possible after the occurrence of the slip. This study yielded a total of 192 slips, with an average of 3 per person.

The data presented in Figure 14.1a show very clearly that the activities that produced these slips were recently and frequently executed, and were perceived as being carried out in a largely automatic way. Figure 14.1b indicates that in 77 of the 192 slips (40%), a relationship between the erroneous actions and some other activity, not intended on this occasion, was very clearly recognizable. This other activity was recently and frequently engaged in, and the data summarized in Figure 14.1c reveal that it was seen as sharing similar locations, movements, and objects with the intended actions on the occasion the error was committed. Similarity of timing and purpose, however, was less clearly evident. In the case of purpose, the scale ratings were bimodally distributed with 35.1% giving ratings below and 57.1% above the midpoint of the scale. Inspection of Figure 14.1d and e reveal that slips were associated with either internal preoccupation or with some external distraction. Only 24% of the errors were assigned scale values greater than 4 for both preoccupation and distraction, indicating that for three quarters of the recorded errors, it was either preoccupation or distraction that was perceived as being the most influential factor. Figure 14.1b also shows that worry, one's emotional state, and feeling unwell or pressed for time were generally regarded as unimportant in contributing to the slip. Responses to the fatigue question, on the other hand, were fairly evenly distributed along the scale. Finally, Figure 14.1e makes it evident that slips occurred in highly familiar circumstances, but that potentially bothersome factors such as noise, cold, heat, and illumination were not regarded as contributing in any significant fashion to the making of the slip.

Taken as a whole, these findings indicate a high degree of homogeneity in the nature of the error-producing activities and in the mental and physical conditions associated with the occurrence of the slips netted in this study. The data provide clear support for the notion that slips of action occur during the execution of highly familiar tasks requiring little in the way of close attention. In those cases where the erroneous actions were identified as more properly belonging to some "other activity," it seems evident that they took the form of "strong-habit" intrusions or strong-associate substitutions. The remaining 60% of the errors involved omissions, repetitions, and the use of wrong objects.

These data provided little basis for classifying the slips, other than the distinction just made between intrusion errors and others. But even here the conditions of occurrence were remarkably similar. This conclusion was further supported by the results of three hierarchical clustering procedures: Ward's error sums of

			1	2	3	4	5	6	7	
(A)	1.	Hardly ever	0.5*	1.6	2.1	3.1	8.3	14.6	69.8	Very often
	2.	Not for a long time	0*	1.5	4.2	3.7	10.4	17.7	62.5	Very recently
	3.	Required constant attention	1.0*	0.5	3.1	9.9	17.7	26.0	41.8	Very automatic
(B)	1.	Only just recognizable	1.3*	0	5.2	6.5	5.2	13.0	68.8	Very clearly recognizable
	2.	Hardly at all	0*	1.3	3.9	1.3	13.0	22.1	58.4	Very often
	3.	Not for a long time	1.3*	1.3	1.2	5.2	9.1	24.7	57.1	Very recently
(C)		Locations	6.5*	3.9	5.2	2.6	7.8	7.8	66.2	
		Movements	10.4	5.2	2.6	5.2	3.9	15.6	57.1	
		Objects	15.6	7.8	2.6	5.2	1.3	16.9	50.7	
		Timing	16.9	10.4	1.3	11.7	5.2	10.4	44.2	
		Purpose	23.4	7.8	3.9	7.8	10.4	7.8	38.9	
(D)		Preoccupied	6.4*	10.1	9.5	12.6	20.1	27.0	14.3	
		Upset or worried	52.9	21.9	6.9	5.8	7.9	3.7	1.1	
		Emotional or excited	42.3	22.2	5.3	10.1	11.1	5.8	3.2	
		Tired or sleepy	15.3	20.1	9.5	16.4	15.9	13.8	9.0	
		Unwell	50.0	22.9	6.4	5.8	9.6	3.7	1.6	
		Rushed	30.7	16.4	8.5	7.4	13.8	16.4	6.8	
(E)	1.	Not at all	1.1*	0	2.6	1.6	3.1	11.5	80.1	Very familiar
	2.	Not at all	48.2*	26.7	7.3	8.9	3.1	4.7	1.1	Very bothersome
	3.	Not at all	2.6*	10.0	15.2	6.7	7.9	20.9	36.7	Very distracted

Figure 14.1 Results of extended diary study (scale value range, 1–7; asterisk (*) indicates a percentage error associated with the scale values). In (A) responses to questions regarding the nature of the intended actions are shown ($N = 192$ errors): (1) How often have you successfully carried out actions identical or very similar to those you intended on this occasion? (2) How recently did you successfully perform actions identical or very similar to those you intended on this occasion? (3) To what extent were the intended actions ones that would normally be carried out in an automatic way without demanding close attention? In (B), responses to questions regarding the nature of the erroneous actions are shown ($N = 77$ errors): (1) Were the wrong actions on this occasion recognizable as being appropriate to some other task or activity? To which 40% of the subjects responded *yes* and 60% *no*. Subjects who responded *yes* were asked, To what extent were these wrong actions recognizable as belonging to this other activity? (Responses are recorded on Scale 1.) (2) How often do you engage in this other activity? (3) How recently have you engaged in this other activity? In (C), responses regarding the similarity in locations, movements, objects, timing, and purpose between intended actions and some other activity not intended on this occasion are shown (scale values—1, not at all similar and 7, very similar; ($N = 77$ errors). In (D), responses regarding the subjects' mental and physical state at the time of the slip are shown (scale values—1, not at all and 7, feeling very preoccupied, upset or worried, emotional or excited, tired or sleepy, unwell, or rushed, N = 192 errors). In (E), responses regarding the circumstances prevailing at the time of the slip are shown (N = 192 errors): (1) How familiar to you were the surroundings in which the slip occurred? (2) How bothersome were your surroundings at the time that the slip was made (e.g., too noisy, cold, hot, bright, dark)? (3) To what extent did something other than your own thoughts distract your attention?

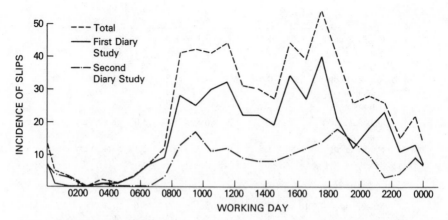

Figure 14.2 Hourly distribution of reported slips of action throughout the day. Slips are shown for two diary studies (see text), both separately and together.

squares, average linkage, and medians. All three algorithms gave a picture of a central core of slips with outliers at various distances from the centroid, rather than of disjoint clusters.

Distribution of Slips over Hours of the Day

In both the initial and the extended-diary studies, subjects were asked to record the time at which the slip occurred. To determine whether there were any discernible temporal patterns in the occurrence of slips of action, the distributions over hours of the day were plotted for each study, both separately and together (433 slips from the initial study and 192 from the extended-diary study). The resulting histograms, broken down into hourly periods, are shown in Figure 14.2.

Both groups of diarists revealed a similar temporal pattern of slips, with a rapid increase in their occurrence during the early hours of the waking day, a decline between noon and 3.00 p.m., and a clear tendency to "peak" somewhere between 5:00 and 7:00 in the evening. Chi-squared values computed for the total sample ($N = 625$) were all highly significant ($p < .001$), regardless of whether they encompassed the whole 24-hour cycle, the working day (9 a.m.–5 p.m.) or the waking day (8 a.m.–12 p.m.). The variations that existed between these two samples could reasonably be accounted for by their differences in lifestyle. The initial diary study utilized a much more heterogeneous group, both in age and occupation, than did the extended-diary study in which subjects were all undergraduates aged between 18 and 25 years. Thus, the somewhat earlier "peak" for the initial study sample could be explained, in part at least, by the

Figure 14.3 Comparison of hourly distributions of slips for males (dashed line) and females (solid line). ($N = 625$ slips.)

fact that many of the diarists were involved in preparing meals between 5:00 and 6:00 in the evening.

A comparison of the hourly distributions for males and females is shown in Figure 14.3. It can be seen that there were no marked differences in the temporal patterns of slips committed by the two sexes.

These hourly distributions suggest, obviously enough, that errors are associated with periods of maximum activity. There is also a hint that slips are most likely to occur during transitions between home and work; that is, when people are either preparing to depart for work, or immediately on their return home. In general, these distributions appear to reflect the influence of situational factors rather than what is known about diurnal variations in efficiency.

The Relative Frequencies of Error Types

In this section, the concern is with estimates of the relative frequency with which different kinds of slips and lapses occur during the course of everyday life. To obtain these estimates an error-proneness questionnaire (EPQ) was constructed that comprised 30 items. Each item took the form of a general statement of a particular type of error; and for 26 of the items, this statement was followed by 3 instances. For example the question How often do you make mistakes in which you omit something because you have switched to some other activity prematurely? was followed by the following 3 instances:

1. "I was just about to step into the bath when I discovered I still had my socks on."
2. "While running water into a bucket from the kitchen tap, I put the lid back on before turning off the tap."
3. "I walked out of the shop without waiting for my change."

TABLE 14.1

Relative Frequencies of Error Types as Shown by Error-Proneness Questionnaire Data[a]

		Response (percentage of sample)[b]					
Rank	Error type	More than daily	Daily	More than weekly	Weekly	More than monthly	Monthly
1	Attending but not taking in	20.0	21.2	18.8*	10.6	14.1	9.4
2	Forgetting plan item	4.7	11.8	14.1	27.1*	20.0	8.2
3	Blocked on name	5.9	8.2	18.8	17.6*	23.5	10.6
4	Forgetting intention (to do something)	3.5	4.7	27.1	17.6*	22.4	12.9
5	Forgetting intention (to say something)	3.5	8.2	22.4	11.8	27.1*	12.9
6	Should-be-doing-something feeling	3.5	8.2	17.6	18.8	9.4*	20.0
7	Action different from intention	2.4	2.4	17.1	11.8	25.6*	17.6
8	Recall blank on known fact	2.4	11.0	8.5	17.1	14.6*	15.9
9	Executing necessary actions	2.4	8.2	14.1	15.3	15.3*	12.9
10	Time-gap experience	2.4	4.7	15.3	20.0	14.1*	10.6
11	Omission after interruption	0	4.7	5.9	10.6	23.5	21.2*
12	Forget to consult reminder	0	1.2	14.1	18.8	10.6	16.5*
13	Losing place in sequence	1.2	1.2	9.4	5.9	24.7	17.6*
14	Searching for carried object	1.2	0	8.2	3.5	18.8	24.7*
15	Carrying object after disposal time	1.2	0	8.2	10.6	8.2	21.1*
16	Omission of step from sequence	0	0	7.1	9.4	11.8	11.8
17	Right actions but objects reversed	0	1.2	5.9	5.9	8.2	23.5
18	Premature exit from sequence	1.2	0	2.4	9.4	14.1	21.4
19	Familiar but unintended actions	0	0	2.4	5.9	22.4	28.2
20	Wrong receptacle	0	0	3.5	9.4	14.1	14.1
21	Familiar action in changed conditions	0	0	1.2	7.1	12.9	22.4
22	Note need for change but continue	0	0	8.3	4.8	10.7	17.9
23	Revert to abandoned plan	0	1.2	4.8	2.4	10.7	15.5
24	No recollection of previous action	1.2	0	3.7	7.2	9.8	17.1

TABLE 14.1 (*Continued*)

		Response (percentage of sample)[b]					
Rank	Error type	More than daily	Daily	More than weekly	Weekly	More than monthly	Monthly
25	Picked up wrong object	0	0	´7.1	4.8	7.1	8.3
26	Repetition of action	0	3.5	0	2.4	3.5	8.2
27	Intrusion from some other activity	0	3.5	0	2.4	3.5	8.2
28	Right action but wrong object	0	1.2	3.5	2.4	5.9	7.1
29	Action reversal	0	0	2.4	2.4	2.4	12.9
30	Wrong remembrance of place	0	0	1.2	1.2	5.9	7.1

[a] Number of subjects sampled was 85.
[b] Asterisk (*) indicates mean category.

The respondents were required to indicate how often they made that particular kind of mistake by selecting one of eleven possible response categories: (1) never; (2) about once in my life; (3) more than once in my life, but less than once a year; (4) about once a year; (5) more than once a year, but less than once a month; (6) about once a month; (7) more than once a month, but less than once a week; (8) about once a week; (9) more than once a week, but less than once a day; (10) about once a day; (11) more than once a day.

The EPQ was made up of two classes of items: action slips and nonaction slips. Eighteen of the items involved a clear deviation of action from intention, and seemed, on the face of it, to implicate some form of control or attentional failure. The remaining 12, the nonaction slips, could for the most part be described as lapses of memory, involving failures of encoding, storage, or retrieval.

The EPQ was administered to 85 undergraduate and postgraduate psychology students. The data relating to the relative frequency of these 30 error types is summarized in Table 14.1. The items are listed in the order of their mean frequency of perceived occurrence.

It can be seen from Table 14.1 that there was a clear tendency for nonaction or memory slips to be assessed as occurring more frequently than slips of action. Table 14.2 compares the numbers of action and nonaction items falling above and below the frequency median ($\chi^2 = 6.81$, $df = 2$, $p < .01$).

Factor analysis of these data also discriminated reasonably well between the action and nonaction slips. Figure 14.4 shows the unrotated loadings for the two-factor solution. It can be seen that all the items have moderately high loadings on the general factor (Factor I); but (with some minor degree of overlap) the nonac-

TABLE 14.2

Comparison of the Numbers of Action and Nonaction Error-Proneness
Questionnaire Items Falling Above and Below the Frequency Median

Relation to median for EPQ	Action items	Nonaction items
Above	5	10
Below	13	2

tion items tend to have positive loadings on Factor II, whereas the action slips
have negative loadings on Factor II. Figure 14.5 shows the same data after
Varimax rotation with Kaiser normalization. Here Factor I would appear to be
one of attentional failure, and Factor II to be memory failure. The four items
loading most highly on each of these factors are listed in Table 14.3.

The results of this factor analysis indicate, in general, that those people who
regard themselves as liable to mental lapses perceive this disposition to be
present for all types of error, and the converse. However, relatedness *within* the
separate sets of action and nonaction slips is greater than *between* these two
groups. In other words, perceived liability to commit certain kinds of, say, action
slips is a better predictor of one's tendency to perform other kinds of deviant
actions than it is of one's proneness to nonaction lapses, and vice versa. Though,
as can be seen from Figures 14.4 and 14.5, these differences are minimal or
nonexistent for a number of intermediate items. Those items most poorly discriminated by the factor analysis tended to be ones that involved both action and

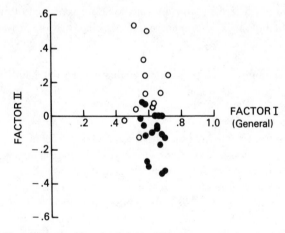

Figure 14.4 Nonrotated two-factor loadings for EPQ (error proneness questionnaire) items. ○,
nonaction items; ●, action items.

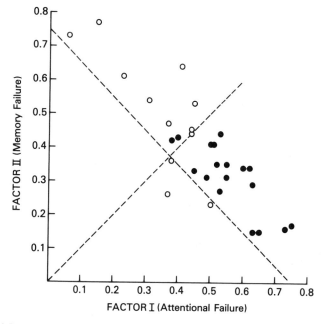

Figure 14.5 Rotated two-factor loadings for EPQ items. ○, nonaction items; ●, action items.

TABLE 14.3

The Four Items Loading Highest on Factors I and II (Rotated)

Item	Factor loadings	
	I	II
Note need for change but continue with familiar actions	.750	.177
Omission after unexpected interruption	.739	.165
Reverse direction of actions	.655	.145
Still carrying something that should have been disposed of earlier	.638	.158
Apparently attending but not taking in	.146	.766
Cannot immediately recall a name	.065	.733
Forget to carry out planned action	.406	.645
Forget intention to say something	.234	.612

nonaction components, for example, How often do you write down a reminder to yourself to do something and then forget to consult it so that you fail to carry out the intended activity?

Classifying Slips of Action

From Aristotle onwards, many attempts have been made to classify the varieties of human error. These taxonomies are too numerous to consider here, though limited reviews may be found elsewhere (Meister, 1971; Singleton, 1972; Swain & Guttman, 1980). However, if one examines those taxonomies concerned primarily with the intraindividual origins of error, it is possible to penetrate beyond the idiosyncracies of terminology to distinguish at least three levels of analysis in the classificatory process.

At the most superficial level, mistakes may be classified according to some easily observable feature of the erroneous behavior. At this purely behavioral level, are such categories as omission, insertion, substitution, and reversal. Other classifications are predicated on assumptions about the cognitive mechanisms involved in the production of errors. Since the mid-1970s, these conceptual taxonomies have usually been expressed in terms of the information-processing stage at which some failure was presumed to have occurred. Taxonomies of this kind, concerned specifically with the slips and lapses of everyday life, have been constructed by Norman (1980, 1981) and by the present author (Reason, 1976, 1977, 1979).

At a third and more fundamental level, are errors assigned to classes according to which of a number of underlying biases or determining tendencies they are thought to reveal. A seventeenth century example was Bacon's (1960) list of "the idols and false notions which are now in possession of the human understanding" (p. 47). According to Bacon, there are a number of omnipresent warps in human judgment and reasoning that exists because the mind acts like a "false mirror, which, receiving rays irregularly, distorts and discolours the nature of things by mingling its own nature with it" (p. 48). Contemporary echoes of Bacon's classification can be found in the work of Tversky and Kahneman, who since the early 1970s have demonstrated that when people are required to assess the probability of an uncertain event or the value of an uncertain quantity, they rely on a limited number of heuristic principles that work well enough for the most part but occasionally lead to severe and systematic errors (Tversky & Kahneman, 1974; Nisbett & Ross, 1980).

Because the main purpose for studying slips of action is to gain insights into the underlying cognitive mechanisms, an error classification based on a conceptual rather than a behavioral level of analysis would clearly be the more useful. But earlier attempts at constructing such a taxonomy have revealed at least two major difficulties. First, it is rarely possible to make confident inferences about the specific nature of the mediating cognitive failure on the basis of the brief error descriptions supplied by subjects. The available evidence is hardly ever sufficient to allow the assignment of a particular slip to a unique conceptual category, although one may be fairly certain that one of a limited number of "error mechanisms" is implicated. The second difficulty is that such taxonomies almost invariably end up by mixing both the behavioral and conceptual levels of analysis (Reason, 1979).

One way to avoid these problems is to accept at the outset that the error descriptions that constitute our primary data are only sufficient to allow some form of behavioral classification. Even if, as is most likely, such behavioral categories are far from homogeneous with respect to their underlying cognitive mechanisms, they have the advantage of reducing the error corpus to a limited number of generally agreed classes. Having achieved this first stage of data reduction without going beyond the constraints imposed by evidence, it is then possible to relate these behavioral categories to a range of possible cognitive mechanisms that must, necessarily, be embodied in some model of the control of human action.

A Behavioral Taxonomy

Examination of the 625 slips of action netted in the two diary studies suggested that a large proportion of them could be assigned to one of four behavioral categories of error:

1. Repetition: Some actions in the intended sequence are repeated unnecessarily.
2. Wrong object(s): The intended actions were made, but in relation to the wrong object(s).
3. Intrusion: Unintended actions (other than those associated with repetitions or wrong object(s)) become incorporated into the sequence at some point.
4. Omission: Intended actions (other than those arising from repetitions, wrong objects, or intrusions) were left out of the sequence.

Strictly speaking, all deviations of action from intention involve an omission in that they constitute failure to carry out a particular action at the time specified by the plan. Hence, all slips are omissions to some extent. Similarly, all repetitions and wrong objects involve intrusions in the sense that they both contribute additional unintended features to the planned sequence. These distinctions become important when people other than the investigator attempt to classify slips of action according to these predetermined categories. Such a study is reported below.

A Classificatory Study

In order to determine the extent of agreement between different "judges" when they are required to allocate slips of action to these four behavioral classes, an inventory was constructed containing 100 error statements, expressed in the first person, selected from the two diary studies. The subjects were instructed as follows:

> The only information you will have in assigning slips to categories will be brief descriptions of the errors provided by the individuals who committed them. The categories are all defined in simple behavioral terms. You will not be asked nor expected to speculate about the underlying causes of the mistakes. You merely have to decide which of the available categories best fits the described circumstances of the error. If you feel that the slip fits none of these categories, or you are not sure which one is appropriate, then you will have an opportunity to indicate this in the inventory.

The classification procedure for each slip involved making a series of yes–no decisions in a standard order. This order was the same as that shown in the previous section. In other words, the judges were required to decide whether or not the slip involved a repetition, then whether it was a wrong-object error, then whether it was an intrusion, and then whether it was an omission. If they answered no to all four, they were asked to consider whether the slip failed to fit into any of these categories. If they responded negatively, they were then asked if they were unsure which of the above categories best fitted the slip in question. If they still answered no, they were directed to repeat the decision process again. Fifty psychologists (researchers, academics, postgraduates and third-year undergraduates) acted as subjects.

For 86 of the 100 items, more than 50% of the sample selected the same category; and for 56 of the items, more than 80% of the sample were agreed on this allocation. But for 16 items, no clear majority decision was obtained (50% or less assignment to the most popular category). Further analysis indicated that confusions occurred most frequently between intrusions and wrong objects, largely arising from the subjects' uncertainty as to what constituted an object. In the item, for example, "I meant to phone my parents but rang an old friend instead," 50% of the sample judged this to involve wrong objects, whereas 42% assigned it to the intrusion category. However, no confusions were found between repetitions, wrong objects, and omissions.

The results of this study suggested that, for these fairly sophisticated subjects at least, the four behavioral categories were adequate to classify the majority of slips. Only 12 of the 100 items were allocated at any point to the "None of these" category, and there were no "unsure" responses. Furthermore, with the exception of the intrusion–wrong-object confusions, most items were assigned to categories with an acceptable level of agreement between judges.

Theoretical Considerations

A Heuristic Model of Action

In order to proceed beyond the behavioral level of analysis, it is necessary, as indicated earlier, to have at least some rudimentary model of the underlying

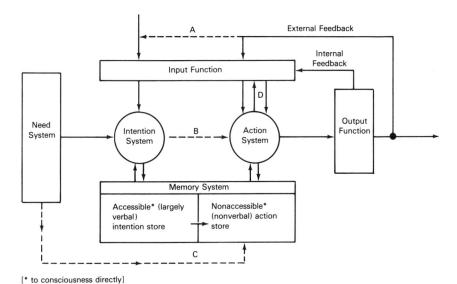

Figure 14.6 A model of human action.

mechanisms governing human action. The model to be presented here is, in most essentials, similar to that described previously (Reason, 1977). However, two important modifications have been made. First, some account is taken of the motivational springs of human action in the addition of a "need system." Second, greater significance is given to the "memory system"; in particular, the action schemata held in the nonverbal section of this system are assigned a far more active role in their potential for gaining control of the motor output. This latter modification is owed directly to Norman's (1980, 1981) theoretical statements regarding the origins of mental slips. The basic components of this revised action model are shown in Figure 14.6.

The *intention system* is the chief executive within the hierarchy of action control. It operates in close conjunction with the accessible (to consciousness) or predominantly verbal portion of the memory system to organize plans of future action, to monitor and guide ongoing activity, and to review past actions. Intentions may be prompted by external events (via the input function), or by internal states (via the need system). To a large extent, the moment-to-moment activity of the intention system is reflected in the current contents of consciousness and is a function of the breadth and direction of attentional focus that switches continually between present, past, and future events. It is this attentional component that imposes the limits that are evident in the capacity of the intention system.

The manipulanda of plannning are usually short verbal tags ("Must buy some carrots," "I want a cup of tea," and so on) that invariably encompass a large number of automatized action schemata. The fine details of these schemata are, for the most part, beyond the reach of verbal expression and are held as intact action sequences—or more exactly, as instructions for action sequences—within the nonaccessible or largely nonverbal portion of the memory system. The current concerns of the intention system, particularly planned actions, are held in store (something akin to working memory) when attention is claimed elsewhere.

For those activities that through their frequency and recency of use have become largely preprogrammed, the detailed control of the effector organs (the *output function*) is achieved by the *action system,* which is simply the action schema that is currently governing the motor output. It is presumed that only one action schema at a time usually has control of any particular part of the musculature.

Following Norman (1980, 1981), it is proposed that the action schemata held in the nonverbal portion of the memory system vary considerably at any one point in time in their level of activation, or their likelihood of becoming the action system. This level of activation is determined by many factors: the current activities of the intention and need systems, external events, the recency and frequency of use, and the state of activation in related schemata (for example, the intention to make tea and the process of filling and boiling the kettle is likely to increase the level of activation in other "beverage schemata").

A critical feature of the model is the extent to which the intention system is involved in closed-loop (CL) control of ongoing activity. When carrying out an unfamiliar task, or when making spot checks on the progress of a largely routinized activity, the intention system may gain direct control of the output function through the closure of the two shunts shown in Figure 14.6 as the dotted lines labeled A and B. But during the execution of familiar tasks; these shunts remain open for much of the time, indicating that the activity is being open-loop (OL) with respect to the intention system. During these periods of OL control, the intention system occupies itself with matters other than the immediate control of the present behavior. These "other matters" have been labeled elsewhere as *parallel mental activity* (see Reason, 1979).

It can also be seen from Figure 14.6 that the need system has the possibility of gaining control of the action system through the dotted channel C. This feature has been added to take account of the so-called "Freudian slip" in which the control of action is achieved without the intervention of consciousness; indeed, the resulting word or action may be directly contrary to the current plan formulated by the intention system. Such a channel also allows for the motivational "priming" of action schemata (Lashley, 1951; Reason, 1979).

A further dotted channel in Figure 14.6, D, is included to accommodate the fact that during the execution of highly automatized tasks, not only the motor output but also the perceptual input associated with this activity will be largely preprogrammed to the extent that it is very predictable. Under these circumstances, it is more economical of effort to degrade the "settings" of the input function's recognition schemata so they will accept relatively crude approxima-tions of the various classes of stimuli expected at different points in the action sequence. The implications of this coarsening of the perceptual matching pro-cesses for the occurrence of discrimination failures has been discussed elsewhere (Reason, 1979), and is considered again at a later point in this chapter.

Relating Behavioral Error Types to Conceptual Categories of Failure

Do observable similarities in the behavioral characteristics of a group of action slips give any grounds for the supposition that they share a common failure location within the model of action? Does the available evidence suggest that all omissions arise from similar underlying causes, and likewise for intrusions, repetitions, and wrong-object errors. The answer would appear to be in the negative.

Consider the following descriptions of omissions given as items in the classi-ficatory study described earlier. In all cases, there was better than 80% agree-ment among the judges as to their most appropriate behavioral class.

1. "I intended to take my pills, get my coat and go out. I put my coat on and left forgetting to take my medicine."
2. "I bought something and started to leave the shop without waiting for my change."
3. "I got into bed with my slippers on."
4. "I wrote out a cheque and put the cheque book back into my bag without tearing the cheque out."
5. "I intended to put the key in the lock and open the door. I put the key in but did not turn it and tried unsuccessfully to open the door."

In the case of Slip 1, there are at least two possible interpretations for the slip: either the plan item "take my pills" was insufficiently processed by the intention system and its associated store, and so was lost; or this intention remained intact, but was preempted by the more familiar routine of putting on a coat and leaving the house. In other words, this slip may have constituted a "strong-habit" exclusion, probably associated with preoccupation or momentary distraction. Slips 2 and 3 both appear to be instances of *premature exit;* that is, when the actor proceeds to the next stage of his or her planned sequence without having completed some necessary prior phase. Slips 4 and 5, on the other hand, seem more typical of *place-losing* errors in which the intention system makes a cursory spot check on progress of a largely automatic activity and comes up with the wrong answer: In both cases, this answer was that the activity was further along than it actually was. Another possibility, particularly in the case of the key-turning error, is that some unrecorded external event occurred that, though not directly attended to, was "counted in" as part of the door-opening sequence in lieu of the key-turning.

For the moment, however, it does not matter which of these alternatives is the most likely, nor even whether these speculations represent the only possible hypotheses; what is relevant here is that although these omission errors have common behavioral features, they are clearly far from homogeneous with regard to their underlying mechanisms. And the same is also true for intrusions, wrong objects, and, to a lesser extent, repetitions. In short, there is no simple and direct mapping of these behavioral error types onto categories of cognitive failure within the action model. Rather, the available evidence indicates that members of the same behavioral class of error are mediated by quite different cognitive failures, and that members of different behavioral classes may share common etiologies.

Possible Categories of Cognitive Failure

Consideration of the action model suggests that four loosely defined and overlapping categories of cognitive failure can be identified. These are listed in the following.

Control Mode Failures

Control-mode failures are errors that arise as the result of being in the wrong control mode with respect to the demands of the task in hand. In terms of the model displayed in Figure 14.6, this relates to whether Shunts A and B are open or closed. Two kinds of inappropriate control mode are possible: being OL at a time when a high-level decision is required of the intention system—for which the consequence is usually a strong-habit intrusion, that is, the most familiar path of action is followed rather than the intended one; or going CL during the execution of a highly automated sequence of actions for which intervention by the intention system is both unnecessary and undesirable. This possibility was referred to earlier in the case of the key-turning omission in which the intention system may have sought to establish the point reached in the sequence and arrived at the wrong answer. Other examples are considered later.

Intention System (and Associated Store) Failures

Here it must be stressed that although the intention system is depicted as a separate entity in the action model, its functions are so closely bound to the consciously accessible portion of the memory system as to be inseparable from it. Failures of this subsystem are primarily those concerned with the formation of plans and with the storage and retrieval of plan-related information. Again, these are considered in further detail at a later point.

Action System (and Associated Store) Failures

These failures involve the unintended triggering of action schemata. At least three ways in which this may occur are suggested by the corpus of action slips: the blending of elements from two currently active schemata, the unintended activation of schemata by external contextual cues, and "program counter" failures. Examples of each are provided later.

Input Function Failures

If one allocates to the input function the task of stimulus recognition, particularly for cases in which this has become largely routinized through the repeated execution of some activity in highly predictable surroundings; then it is possible to associate at least two classes of error with failures of this subsystem. One is *misdiscrimination,* in which actions are carried out in relation to wrong objects that can be similar in appearance, function, or location to the intended objects. The other is the phenomenon of *local unawareness,* a condition in which, possibly through preoccupation or distraction, the person's attention to his or her immediate surroundings and particularly to his or her own body is diminished. Examples of this are continuing to carry something one has intended to dispose of earlier or searching for something that one is actually carrying.

Varieties of Cognitive Failure

The principal rationale for collecting and analyzing slips of action is the belief that regularities in the occurrence of these usually inconsequential everyday errors will yield valuable insights into the cognitive mechanisms responsible for the initiation and guidance of action, particularly skilled or habitual action. But it is clear from the previous discussion that at this stage there are insufficient data to determine uniquely the causes of any particular slip. The evidence derived from the analysis of a large number of slips allows the formulation of only speculative inferences about the cognitive mechanisms involved in their production. Such inferences can be made most easily from a recurrent error form which, although it may vary in its precise circumstances and behavioral characteristics, seems to implicate some specific cognitive process. But this is a comparatively rare occurrence. More usually, a number of cognitive functions could conceivably be involved, and there is not sufficient information to favor one of them over the rest. In general, therefore, the best that can be hoped for from this kind of investigation is the formulation of a set of hypotheses about the possible varieties of cognitive failure. To evaluate these hypotheses, it would be necessary to proceed to a more experimental mode of study by setting up the conditions believed to be sufficient to create a particular kind of error, and then studying the relationship between variations in the provocative conditions and the likelihood of eliciting this error.

But this is looking beyond the present state of progress. All that is legitimate at present is to summarize the various possible hypotheses. The list of hypotheses so far formulated is set out in the following, and is subdivided into the four possible classes of cognitive failure described in the previous section. It should be emphasized, however, that this list only includes those hypotheses that at the present stage of analysis seem the most probable. Further analysis is likely to produce additional hypotheses as well as the modification or rejection of existing ones.

Control-Mode Failure

Double-Capture Slips

Double-capture slips are so-named because they appear to involve two distinct, though causally related, kinds of capture. First, the intention system (or focal attention) is captured either by some internal preoccupation (parallel mental activity) or by some unexpected external event at a time when a higher-order intervention is necessary to set action along the intended pathway. As a consequence, the control of action is usurped by the strongest (i.e., the most frequently and/or recently used) motor program leading onwards from that particular point in the action sequence. In other words, the action system is "captured" by a strong habit.

Of all the slips that one can reasonably attribute to attentional failure, double-capture slips are the most common. Indeed, relatively few slips of action do not reveal some evidence of strong habit intrusion. These errors are so apparently lawful that one can formulate strong hypotheses as to when they will occur and what form they will take. Thus one can predict that they will occur when the open-loop mode of control coincides with a critical decision point or node in the instructional sequence beyond which the "strengths" of the connecting motor programs are markedly different, and when the current intention is to take some route other than that most recently and frequently traveled in those particular circumstances. When this occurs, one can also predict that the slip will involve the unintended activation of the strongest motor program (see also Reason, 1979).

These slips can take a wide variety of forms. Examples of some of the commonest variants are listed in the following:

1. "I had decided to cut down my sugar consumption and wanted to have my cornflakes without it. However, I sprinkled sugar on my cereal just as I had always done."

2. "We now have two fridges in our kitchen and yesterday we moved our food from one to the other. This morning I repeatedly opened the fridge that we used to have our food in."
3. "On starting a letter to a friend I headed the paper with my previous home address instead of my new address."
4. "I intended to stop on the way to work to buy some shoes, but woke up to find that I had driven right past."
5. "I brought the milk in to make myself a cup of tea. I had put the cup out previously. But instead of putting the milk into the cup, I put the bottle in the fridge."
6. "I meant to get my car out, but as I passed through the back porch on my way to the garage I stopped to put on my wellington boots and gardening jacket as if to work in the garden."
7. "I have two mirrors on my dressing table. One I use for making up and brushing my hair, the other for inserting and removing my contact lenses. On this occasion, I intended to brush my hair, but sat down in front of the wrong mirror, and removed my contact lenses instead."
8. "I went up to my bedroom to change into something more comfortable for the evening, and the next thing I knew I was getting into my pyjama trousers."
9. "I meant to take off only my shoes but took my socks off as well."
10. "I was making shortbread and decided to double the amounts shown in the recipe. I doubled the first ingredient—butter—and then failed to double anything else."
11. "I decided to make pancakes for tea. Then I remembered we didn't have any lemons, so I decided not to bother. Five minutes later, I started getting together the ingredients for pancakes having completely forgotten my change of mind."
12. "I was putting cutlery away in the drawer when my wife asked me to leave it out as she wanted to use it. I heard her, agreed, and yet continued to put the cutlery away."

Examples 1–3 are clearly very similar. They all involve a change of routine that, presumably as the result of attentional capture, leads to an old-habit intrusion. Examples 4 and 5 also show clear signs of strong-habit capture during a moment of inattention; but in these instances, the double-capture leads to an exclusion rather than an intrusion. Here then are five slips that apparently share a very similar etiology; but in three of them, the outcome is an intrusion error, whereas in the other two, it is an omission. This underlines the point made earlier about the lack of any direct relationship between the behavioral characteristics of the error and its underlying mechanics.

Examples 6 and 7 are instances of *branching errors* in which some initial common pathway leads to different outcomes, whereby attention is captured at the branch point so that the wrong route is followed. Examples 8 and 9 are conceptually very similar except that they involve overshooting a stop rule that is not regularly imposed. Compare these with William James's example (1890): "Very absent-minded persons in going to their bedroom to dress for dinner have been known to take off one garment after another and finally to get into bed, *merely because that was the habitual issue of the first few movements when performed at a later hour*" (p. 115; emphasis added).

Examples 10–12 share the failure to attend to the need for change at the critical moment. In errors 10 and 11, this results in a reversion to some earlier plan; whereas in 12, it results in the continuation of an habitual set of actions. This last example is particularly interesting because it reveals something about the actor's attentional state. He clearly heard and remembered his wife's request, but failed to act on it. Leaving aside the possibility that this was some unconsciously motivated act of marital war, it suggests that the wife's request was attended to and recorded by the fringes of consciousness while the husband's focal attention was directed elsewhere. Such peripheral attentional states seem to be implicated in a wide variety of errors as is discussed later.

In all of the examples discussed so far, it seems reasonable to assume that the factor contributing most to the strength of the emergent but unwanted action sequence was its frequency of prior employment. However, some experiences of my own suggest that there are occasions, albeit fairly infrequent ones, in which the recency factor is dominant, even to the extent of overriding frequency considerations. Two personal examples should help to make the point clearer.

> "I had recently acquired a dictating machine and was busy getting the hang of writing letters on it. To gain some confidence with the machine, I would write the letters in note form and then record them. In reading them onto the tape, I was very scrupulous about including such things as 'comma,' 'colon,' 'semicolon,' and the like. After I had been using the machine for a few days, I gave a lecture in which I read out a passage from a book. It was only after I had read a sentence or two that I realised—to my acute embarrassment—that I was also reading out all the punctuation as if dictating into the recorder."
>
> "I pulled up outside a friend's house in a quiet residential street and parked the car facing the wrong way for the traffic flow (i.e., on the right-hand side of the street). On leaving the house with the friend, I drove off on the wrong side of the road without noticing the fact. Indeed, I wondered why the vehicle coming towards us was driving on the wrong side. Then I realised what I was doing and pulled in to the kerb—as if to park in front of another house. Two things seem to have contributed to this slip. The first was that I was attending very closely to what was being said to me, and the second was that I had just returned from driving in France—where I became accustomed for eight days or so to having the driver's side nearest the kerb."

The interesting thing about both of these examples is that the recency effect ran directly contrary to well-established skills: reading aloud and driving on the left-hand side of the road. It appears as if, in certain circumstances, the effort to modify an existing routine for another purpose leaves powerful residues for some while after the change of procedure is no longer appropriate.

Place-Losing and Place-Mistaking Errors

How slips can arise from the failure of focal attention to switch to the task at hand at the appropriate moment has just been discussed. When this happens, the reins of action are likely to be snatched by some strong habit. What is less intuitively obvious, however, is that errors can also be produced by exactly the opposite process; that is, focal attention being directed to some ongoing routine activity at a time when control is best left to the action system. Anyone who has concentrated too closely on what his or her feet were doing when running down the stairs two at a time will know how disruptive too much attention paid to a largely automatic activity can be. But more subtle errors arise when the intention system makes a cursory check on the progress of some routine task at an inappropriate moment.

Activities such as tea making are particularly prone to these kinds of error. This is a task of the test–wait–test–exit variety (Harris & Wilkins, 1982) in which a sequence of largely automatic actions needs to be carried out in the right order, and in which there are periods of relative inactivity—while the kettle boils and the teapot brews. Furthermore, it is also a procedure in which a quick visual check on one's progress does not always yield the right answer. Consider the case in which one interrupts a parallel mental activity to ask oneself where one has got to. Low-level checks such as these can produce at least two kinds of wrong answers. Either one concludes that one is further along than one really is, and, as a consequence, omits some necessary step such as putting the tea into the pot or switching on the kettle. Or, one concludes that one is not as far along as one really is, and then repeats an action already done such as setting the kettle to boil for a second time when the pot has already been filled with freshly made tea. The interesting thing about these omissions and repetitions is that if these closed-loop checks on progress had not been made, the automatic tea-making action schema would probably have carried on without error.

In most tasks, a quick look at what one is doing will supply adequate information with which to judge progress. But on some occasions, this visual evidence is lacking and one draws a complete blank, as in the following examples:

> "I was spooning tea into the teapot, and I realised I had no idea of how many spoonfuls I'd put in."
>
> "In the shower this morning, I 'came to' to find that I didn't know whether or not I had washed my hair. It was wet and there was no easy way of telling. I could have washed it and all the soap suds could have disappeared down the plug. I certainly had no recollection of anything except my preceding thoughts."
>
> "I didn't know whether I had put water into the kettle. I had to lift the lid to check."

Another kind of slip that could arise as the result of an inadequate or inappropriate check on progress by the intention system is that in which the direction of an automatic action sequence is reversed, as in the following examples:

> "I intended to take off my shoes and put on my slippers. I took my shoes off and then noticed that a coat had fallen off the hanger. I hung the coat up and then instead of putting on my slippers, I put my shoes back on again."
>
> "I ladled soup into the soup bowl, and then started to ladle it back into the pan again."
>
> "I got the correct fare out of my purse to give to the bus conductor. A few moments later I put the money back into the purse before the conductor had come to collect it."

With these reversal slips, it is difficult to establish precisely whether they are due to inappropriate checking, or to inattention in a bidirectional sequence in which, on that occasion, the strength of the reversed path was greater than that of the intended one. In other words, they could also be caused by a form of double-capture error.

Intention System Failures

Detached Intentions

Some slips suggest that after an intention has been formed, the active component of the intention, the "verb" as it were, becomes *detached* from its proper setting and is subsequently misapplied to something other than that intended. Possible explanations are that either the intention system framed the intention incompletely, perhaps because the focus of attention was claimed elsewhere; or that the intention was formulated correctly, but was subsequently not processed to a sufficient level to allow it to be retained until the moment of its execution. Another possibility is that some of these errors arise from a combination of the presence of stored intents to carry out a particular action plus contextual triggering from another object to which the same kind of action is appropriate. For example, in the case in which a person switches off the gas fire instead of the television, it could be that the switching-off-the-gas-fire schema is jointly activated by the switch-off component of the original intention and the sight of the gas fire. Such an error could also occur as the result of misordering the going-to-bed routine; though this is less likely to be noted as an error because the turning off of both the gas fire and the television are likely to be part of the intended procedure and would in any case occur within a relatively short time of one another.

Some examples of possible detached intentions are given in the following:

> "I intended to place my hairbrush in its usual place by the bookcase. I put my boy-friend's lighter there instead."
> "I had an appointment at the dentist's, but went to the doctor's instead."
> "I intended to close the window as it was cold. I closed the cupboard instead."

Of course, the distinction between a presumed detached intention and a perceptually based confusion of objects is a fine one to draw. But the accumulated error data appear to justify the retention of the detachment possibility, at least for the present.

Lost Intentions

Whereas detached intentions indicate some partial failure of the intention system and its associated store, *lost intentions* suggest a more complete breakdown at one or more of the stages involved in the formulation, encoding, storage, or retrieval of a plan of action. Lost intentions appear as two distinct kinds of lapses.

One familiar variant manifests itself as a *retrieval* failure: the what-am-I-doing-here? experience. In the course of doing something like walking into a room or a shop, or opening a drawer or cupboard, one suddenly becomes aware that one cannot recall the purpose of this activity. Some actual examples are the following:

> "I went upstairs to the bedroom and stopped—not remembering what I had gone there for."
>
> "I opened the fridge and stood there looking at its contents, unable to remember what it was I wanted."
>
> "I stopped halfway down the stairs. I couldn't remember what I was going for."

In these instances, the most salient feature is the subjective experience of not knowing what one should be doing next. In another type of lost intention; this experience is absent, presumably because no attempt is made to interrogate the purpose of one's actions. Instead, one is deflected from one's intention by a series of small side steps, usually of the strong-associate kind. It is only later that one realizes that one's original intention has not been fulfilled, for example:

> "I went into my room intending to fetch a book. I took off my rings, looked in the mirror and came out again—without the book."
>
> "I went to the bathroom to clean my teeth. When I got there I picked up a towel and walked out again, without brushing my teeth."
>
> "I meant to get my wallet from the bedroom. Instead, I wound the bedside clock and came down again without the wallet."
>
> "I intended to go to the cupboard under the stairs to turn off the immersion heater. I dried my hands to turn off the switch, but went into the larder instead. Then I wandered into the living room, looked at the table, wandered back and then suddenly remembered my original intention."

Personal experience suggests that these multiple side steps occur when one is abstracted by some pressing mental concern, or when one is freewheeling in a state of diminished or weakened intention—a condition not dissimilar to that described by Luria (1973) for patients with frontal lobe damage. The outcome in both cases is similar: One's actions become captured by strong habits appropriate to the physical context. The failure here is not so much one of conscious retrieval, as one of the intention system to revive and activate the stored intention at the right time. The intention is not forgotten as such, because one often becomes aware of it soon afterwards.

Conceptually, very little distinction can be made between this sidestepping form of lost intention and the double-capture slips described in relation to control-mode failures. However, there does seem to be some value in juxtaposing these two kinds of lost intentions, if only to draw attention to the fact that the difference between them lies mainly in the manner in which the actor becomes aware of the lapse.

Action System Failures

Blends and Behavioral Spoonerisms

Although the action system—the "driving seat" of the effector organs—is presumed to be occupied by only one action schema at a time, certain slips suggest that two currently active schemata have dismembered themselves in the struggle to gain control, and that the elements of these two schemata have become blended in some incongruous way. But as with verbal blends, these combinations appear to obey the syntactical rules of action. The following are two examples:

> "During a morning in which there had been several knocks on my office door, the phone rang. I picked up the receiver and bellowed "Come in" at it."
>
> "I had just finished talking on the phone when my secretary ushered in some visitors. I got up from behind the desk and walked to greet them with my hand outstretched saying "Smith speaking"."

A very similar kind of error is the behavioral spoonerism in which the correct actions are carried out, but the objects for which they were intended become reversed. Some examples were given earlier in the chapter, and some more contemporary ones are set out in the following:

> "In a hurried effort to finish the housework and have a bath, I put the plants meant for the lounge in the bedroom and my underwear in the window in the lounge."
>
> "I unwrapped a sweet, put the paper in my mouth and threw the sweet into the waste-paper basket."
>
> "I threw my glasses in the bin and kept some dirty tissues I was holding in my other hand."

An important feature of these errors is the clue they offer as to the units of action. Of particular interest is the temporal proximity of the reversed objects within the intended action sequence. As compared to verbal spoonerisms, in which the reversed elements are usually separated by milliseconds only, an action sequence is often extended over a much longer time scale; and it is presumably for this reason that partial reversals are more common in action than are complete spoonerisms. It would require an unusually sustained bout of preoccupation or distraction to divert attention for a sufficiently long enough time not to catch the reversal before its symmetry is complete.

External Activation of Action Schemata

Some errors are best understood in terms of the environmental context in which they occur, rather than the prevailing intentional state. Norman (1981) has argued that action schemata may be activated by the presence of schema-related contextual cues as well as by specific intentions. The following errors appear to support these ideas:

> "As I approached the turnstile on my way out of the library, I pulled out my wallet as if to pay—although I knew no money was required."
>
> "Walking up the front path to my friend's house, I pulled out my own front door key and was just about to place it in the lock when I realised my mistake."

In both of these cases, the actions were appropriate not to the actual circumstances, but to ones that were contextually very similar. And, in both, the erroneous actions were highly routinized. These observations suggest a direct connection between the input function and the action system store that bypasses the intention system.

Program Counter Failures

A basic requirement for the Action System is a process, analogous to a program counter, that keeps track of the point reached in the instructional sequence. Logically, this process could fail in one of two ways. It could count some extraneous event as part of the intended sequence, giving rise to an omission error. Or it could fail to count a correct action, thus giving rise to a repetition error.

The error corpus provides a number of examples that could fit the former possibility. They are all characterized by an omission error associated with some unexpected event or interruption.

> "I picked up my coat to go out when the phone rang. I answered it and then went out of the front door without my coat."
>
> "The kettle was just about to boil when I noticed the tea caddy was empty. I fetched a fresh packet of tea from the cupboard and filled the caddy. Then I poured the water into the teapot and only when I came to pour it into the cup did I notice I hadn't put any tea in the pot."
>
> "I walked to my bookcase to find the dictionary. In the process of taking it off the shelf, other books fell onto the floor. I put them all back, together with the dictionary, and went back to my desk not having looked up the word I wanted."

Examples of the second kind, the repetition errors, are harder to find, partly because these lapses are comparatively rare anyway, and partly because when they occur it is hard to distinguish the possibility of a program failure from that of inappropriate monitoring. However, the corpus contains one rather curious example that might have arisen from the failure to "count off" a particular action, or in this case repeated actions. "I intended to put 2 spoonfuls of sugar into my coffee but put in seven or eight instead."

This error bears some resemblance to the motor perseverations reported by Luria (1966) in patients suffering from deep lesions in the premotor areas of the brain. Particularly conspicuous in these patients were the frequent repetitions of circular movements in drawing or writing.

Input Function Failures

Perceptual Confusions

The nature of a fairly common class of errors suggests that they occur because the recognition schemata accept for the intended object something that looks like it, or is in a similar location, or does the same kind of job. As suggested earlier, this may well arise because, in a highly routinized set of actions, it is not necessary to invest the same amount of attention in the matching process. It is likely that recognition schemata, as well as action schemata, become automatized, and as a consequence accept rough approximations to the expected class of stimuli. This coarsening or degradation of the acceptance criteria is in keeping with the principle of economy of effort, and its associated liberation of conscious capacity, that underlies the control of practiced action in general. The following are some examples:

> "I intended to pick up the deodorant, but picked up the air freshener instead."
> "I intended to pick up the milk bottle but actually reached out for the orange squash bottle."
> "I meant to open a tin of Kit-E-Kat, but opened a tin of rice pudding instead."

Another common form of these errors involves pouring or placing something into a receptacle for which it was not intended.

> "I put the coffee jar into the fridge instead of the cupboard."
> "I put a piece of dried toast on the cat's dish instead of in the bin."
> "I began to pour tea into the sugar bowl instead of the cups."

Local Unawareness

One of the obvious consequences of preoccupation, abstraction, or distraction is a reduction of the conscious attention given not only to particular key actions, but also to one's bodily state in general. An extreme form of this *local unawareness* was displayed by Archimedes who "was so absorbed in geometrical meditation that he was first made aware of the storming of Syracuse by his own death wound" (Hamilton, quoted by James, 1890). However, in lesser mortals this lack of attention tends to take more mundane forms. Two of the commonest instances in the corpus involve continuing to carry objects that should have been disposed of earlier, and looking for something that one is actually carrying or wearing.

> "I left the bedroom carrying yesterday's underwear which I had intended to dispose of in a container in the bathroom before going downstairs for breakfast. However, on this occasion, I reached the kitchen before realising I was still carrying the cast-off clothes."
> "After having a quick cup of coffee in the Staff Room, I went to the sink and washed the cup but, instead of putting it in the cupboard where it belongs, I kept it in my hand and walked back to the classroom with it."
> "I went looking for my glasses. Then I realised I had them on."
> "I took out my pen and continued to search for it in my case."

Conclusions

To summarize the story so far: It has been argued that slips of action can provide valuable information about the role of conscious attention in the guidance of highly routinized or habitual activities by indicating retrospectively those points at which the attentional mechanism was inappropriately deployed. Evidence has been presented to show that these slips occur under relatively uniform conditions: during the execution of some automatized task in a familiar setting in which attention has been claimed by some internal preoccupation or by some external distraction. Errors seem to happen either because attention was not switched back to the task in hand at a critical decision point, thus allowing the control of action to be snatched by some strong motor program normally associated with that juncture, or because attention is directed to the ongoing routine activity at a time when it would have been better to leave the guidance of action to the "automatic pilot." In the former case, the errors take the form of strong-habit intrusions or exclusions; and in the latter, omissions and repetitions.

It has also been demonstrated that slips of action can be readily classified into four behavioral categories—repetitions, wrong objects, intrusions, and omissions—on the basis of the error statements provided by the subjects. However, as the subsequent theoretical analysis has attempted to show, it is clear that behavioral categories derived from natural history studies are far from homogeneous with regard to the underlying information-processing stages at which failure is presumed to be located.

The conceptual analysis of these slips was predicated on a model of action consisting of a number of information-handling functions linked by communication channels and feedback loops so as to mimic certain aspects of human skilled performance. Examination of the error corpus suggests that explanations of slips and lapses could be organized around four theoretical mechanisms: control-mode failures, intention system failures, action system failures, and input function failures. These possible categories of failure were best regarded as overlapping "sets" rather than as hard and fast distinctions.

Associated with each of these failure types is a series of hypotheses relating to specific classes of error. It has been stressed that neither the evidence nor the theoretical assumptions are sufficient to permit the unique determination of the causes of any one error. Rather, the accumulation of distinct classes of error allow the formulation of tentative inferences about the nature of the underlying cognitive processes. The relationship between these various levels of argument is summarized diagrammatically in Figure 14.7.

In Figure 14.7, an attempt has been made to convey what one can and cannot conclude on the basis of naturalistic error data. As indicated in the preceding, one can predict with some confidence the circumstances under which these lapses occur. One can also state what behavioral forms these errors are likely to take. But, on moving to a more thoretical mode of classification, one cannot assume any direct mapping of behavioral classes on the underlying error-producing mechanisms. A particular behavioral error form could arise from a variety of possible cognitive failures, and different behavioral categories of action slips could be due to the same type of failure.

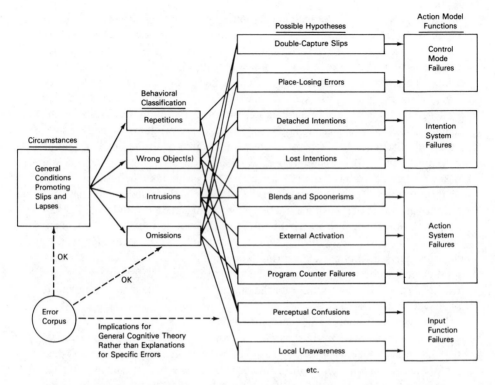

Figure 14.7 Diagrammatic summary of "the state of the art" regarding the etiology of lapses of attention.

   In conclusion, it is useful to emphasize the distinction between this kind of error research and that engaged in by applied psychologists. The task of the latter is to prevent error; but when some catastrophic lapse does occur, the human factors specialist asks what knowledge of cognitive processes can reveal about the origins of this particular disaster. In this case, however, both the question and the procedure are reversed: What has been examined here is a large number of inconsequential errors, and the question asked has been what can these errors reveal about the underlying cognitive mechanisms.

Acknowledgments

I would like to thank Lala Mycielska and Alan Fish for their great help in the collection and analysis of the data, and for their valuable comments on draft versions of this chapter. I am also considerably indebted to Professor Alan Forbes, Victoria University of Wellington, New Zealand, whose enthusiasm for the project and statistical wisdom proved invaluable during his sabbatical with us.

References

Bacon, F. *The new organon and related writings,* F. H. Anderson, (Ed.). Indianapolis: Bobbs-Merrill, 1960.

Bond, D. F. *The spectator* (Vol. 1). Oxford: Clarendon, 1965.

Chapman, L. B., & Chapman, J. P. *Disordered thought in schizophrenia.* Englewood Cliffs, N.J.: Prentice-Hall, 1973.

Freud, S. *The psychopathology of everyday life.* Harmondsworth, England: Penguin, 1901.

Freud, S. *Introductory lectures on psychoanalysis.* London: Allen & Unwin, 1922.

Fromkin, V. *Speech errors as linguistic evidence.* The Hague: Mouton, 1973.

Fromkin, V. *Errors of linguistic performance: Slips of the tongue, ear, pen and hands.* New York: Academic Press, 1979.

Harris, J. E., & Wilkins, A. Remembering to do things: A theoretical framework and illustrative experiment. *Human Learning,* 1982, *1,* 123–136.

James, W. *The principles of psychology.* New York: Holt, 1890.

James, W. *Talks to teachers on Psychology: and to students on some of Life's Ideals.* London: Longmans, Green & Co. (1908)

Jastrow, J. The lapses of consciousness. *The Popular Science Monthly,* 1905, *67,* 481–502.

Keele, S. W. *Attention and human performance.* Pacific Palisades, Calif.: Goodyear, 1973.

Lashley, K. S. The problem of serial order in behaviour. In L. A. Jeffress (Ed.), *Cerebral mechanisms in behaviour.* New York: Wiley, 1951.

Luria, A. R. *Human brain and psychological processes.* New York: Harper & Row, 1966.

Luria, A. R. *The working brain.* Harmondsworth, England: Penguin, 1973.

Meister, D. *Human factors: Theory and practice.* New York: Wiley, 1971.

Nisbett, R., & Ross, L. *Human influence: Strategies and shortcomings of social judgement.* Englewood Cliffs, N.J.: Prentice-Hall, 1980.

Norman, D. A. Post-Freudian slips. *Psychology Today,* 1980, *13,* 42–50.

Norman, D. A. Categorization of action slips. *Psychological Review,* 1981, *88,* 1–15.

Oppenheim, A. N. *Questionnaire design and attitude measurement.* London: Heinemann, 1966.

Polanyi, M. *Personal knowledge.* London: Routledge & Kegan Paul, 1958.

Pritchard, F. H. *The world's best essays: From confucius to mencken.* London: MacMillan, 1953.

Reason, J. T. Absent minds. *New Society,* 1976, 4 November, 244–245.

Reason, J. T. Skill and error in everyday life. In M. Howe (Ed.), *Adult learning.* London: Wiley, 1977.

Reason, J. T. Actions not as planned: The price of automatization. In G. Underwood & R. Stevens (Eds.), *Aspects of consciousness* (Vol. 1). London: Academic Press, 1979.

Schmidt, R. A. The schema as a solution to some persistent problems in motor learning theory. In G. E. Stelmach (Ed.), *Motor control: Issues and trends* New York: Academic Press, 1976.

Shallice, T. Dual functions of consciousness. *Psychological Review,* 1972, *79,* 383–393.

Shallice, T. The dominant action system: An information-processing approach to consciousness. In J. L. Singer & K. Pope, (Ed.), *The Stream of Consciousness.* New York: Plenum, 1979.

Singleton, W. T. *Theoretical approaches to human error. Ergonomics,* 1973, *16,* 727–737.

Stelmach, G. E. *Motor control: Issues and trends.* New York: Academic Press, 1976.

Swain, A. D., & Guttmann, H. E. *Handbook of human reliability analysis with emphasis on nuclear power plant applications.* Albuquerque, N.M.: Sandia Laboratories, 1980.

Timpanaro, S. *The Freudian slip.* London: New Left Books, 1976.

Tversky, A., & Kahneman, D. Judgment under uncertainty: Heuristics and biases. *Science,* 1974, *185,* 1124–1131.

Index

A

Activation, *see* Arousal
Age, *see* Individual differences
Alertness, 244–246, 434, 472
Arousal, 250–254, 340, 348–350, 466, 467
  effects of stressors on, 253, 254, 348–350
  inverted-U hypothesis, 457–462, 466, 467
  psychophysiological measures of, 252, 253
  and sustained attention, 250–254
  theory, difficulties of, 465–468
  theory of stress, 457–467
  Yerkes–Dodson Law, 457, 467
Attention
  analytical models of, 485–513
  and automatic processing, 1–27, 29–61
  blackboard model of, 54–57
  control theories of, 464, 465
  effects of environmental stressors on,
    449–483
  and effort, 11–18, 463, 464, 477, 478
  following commissural section, 375–394
  and habit, 515–517
  individual differences in, 395–447
  and information accumulation, 244–248
  lapses of, 515–545
  and long-term memory (LTM), 39, 40, 54
  mathematical models of, 183–242, 485–513
  neural model of, 294–297
  and object selection, 51, 52
  optimization theory of, 125–171, 176
  preattentive processing, 275, 276, 297
  and reading, 48–53
  research paradigms in, 3–18, 30–32,
    114–125, 396
  and signal detection, 103–181, 183–242,
    243–271
  switching, 86, 87, 198, 199
  temporal distribution of, 248–250
  and visual form perception, 211–221
  and visual search, 273–291
Attention operating characteristic, 111–116,
134, 155, 166, *see also* Performance operating characteristic (POC)
Attentional field, 108, 120–122, 347, 348
Attentional resources, 67–70, 72–75, 103,
  112, 138, 139, 166–171, 264–266, 476
  allocation of, 70, 72–75, 84, 85, 89, 90,
    264–266
  measurement of, 67–70
  multiple, 78–88, 93–95, 168–171
  stages of, 64, 80–82
  strategies of allocation of, 88–90
Automatic processing, 1–27, 29–61, 73–75,
  89, 399, 400, 417, 418, 515–520
  and cognitive style, 418
  criteria for, 42–46
  experimental tests of, 41–53
  functions and limitations of, 21–23
  and semantic processing, 35–39
  and slips of action, 537–548
  and subliminal perception, 38, 39, 56
  and sustained attention, 15, 264, 265
  versus controlled processing, 1–3, 89
Autonomic lability, 430, 431
Autonomic responses, functions of, 340

B

β, *see* Signal detection theory
Blindsight, 338, 376–379
Brain damage and attention, 375–394
Brain mechanisms of attention, 293–321

C

Capacity, *see* Attentional resources
Catastrophe theory, 164
Channels, aggregation of information over,
204–211
Cocktail party effect, 31
Cognitive failure, 535–546, *see also* Errors
Cognitive style, *see* Individual differences
Commissural section, 378, 379
Concurrent and compound tasks, 114–125

ACADEMIC PRESS
SERIES IN COGNITION AND PERCEPTION

SERIES EDITORS:
Edward C. Carterette
Morton P. Friedman
Department of Psychology
University of California, Los Angeles
Los Angeles, California

Stephen K. Reed: *Psychological Processes in Pattern Recognition*

Earl B. Hunt: *Artificial Intelligence*

James P. Egan: *Signal Detection Theory and ROC Analysis*

Martin F. Kaplan and Steven Schwartz (Eds.): *Human Judgment and Decision Processes*

Myron L. Braunstein: *Depth Perception Through Motion*

R. Plomp: *Aspects of Tone Sensation*

Martin F. Kaplan and Steven Schwartz (Eds.): *Human Judgment and Decision Processes in Applied Settings*

Bikkar S. Randhawa and William E. Coffman: *Visual Learning, Thinking, and Communication*

Robert B. Welch: *Perceptual Modification: Adapting to Altered Sensory Environments*

Lawrence E. Marks: *The Unity of the Senses: Interrelations among the Modalities*

Michele A. Wittig and Anne C. Petersen (Eds.): *Sex-Related Differences in Cognitive Functioning: Developmental Issues*

Douglas Vickers: *Decision Processes in Visual Perception*

Margaret A. Hagen (Ed.): *The Perception of Pictures, Vol. 1: Alberti's Window: The Projective Model of Pictorial Information, Vol. 2 Dürer's Devices: Beyond the Projective Model of Pictures*

J. B. Deregowski: *Illusions, Patterns and Pictures: A Cross-Cultural Perspective*

Graham Davies, Hadyn Ellis and John Shepherd (Eds.): *Perceiving and Remembering Faces*

Hubert Dolezal: *Living in a World Transformed: Perceptual and Performatory Adaptation to Visual Distortion*

Gerald H. Jacobs: *Comparative Color Vision*